THE
CONTEMPORARY
READER

THE CONTEMPORARY READER

FOURTH EDITION

Edited by
GARY GOSHGARIAN
Northeastern University

HarperCollins *College Publishers*

Acquisitions Editor: Patricia Rossi
Project Editor: Brigitte Pelner
Assistant Art Director: Dorothy Bungert
Text Design Adaptation and
  Cover Design/Illustration: Molly Heron
Photo Researcher: Carol Parden
Production Administrator: Kathleen Donnelly
Compositor: ComCom Division of Haddon Craftsmen, Inc.
Printer and Binder: R. R. Donnelley & Sons Company
Cover Printer: The Lehigh Press, Inc.

The Contemporary Reader, Fourth Edition

Library of Congress Cataloging-in-Publication Data

The Contemporary reader / edited by Gary Goshgarian.—4th ed.
    p.   cm.
  ISBN: 0-673-52221-0 (Student Edition)
  ISBN: 0-673-52222-9 (Instructor Edition)
    1. College readers.   2. English language—Rhetoric.
  I. Goshgarian, Gary.
  PE1417.C6523   1993
  808'.0427—dc20   92-18333
                                                CIP

93 94 95 9 8 7 6 5 4 3 2

This book is dedicated to my sons,
Nathan and David

▼ CONTENTS

the family? The decline of Western Civilization? Don't blame
TV, says this network reporter.

10 CONTEMPORARY ISSUES: PROS AND CONS   382

12 SPORTS   **463**

14 ON DEATH AND DYING

"If I had to design an ecosystem in which creatures had to live off each other and in which dying was an indispensable part of living, I could not think of a better way to manage."

This famous Swiss-American psychiatrist contrasts the way people of older cultures dealt with death with the way Americans confront death today.

"I was trying to bargain with AIDS: If I wrote about it, maybe I wouldn't get it. . . . But AIDS didn't keep its part of the bargain."

America's most famous baby doctor reflects on the end of a life—his own.

▼RHETORICAL TABLE OF CONTENTS

NARRATION: Telling a Story

DESCRIPTION: Using Your Senses

ILLUSTRATION: Explaining with Examples

PROCESS ANALYSIS: Step-by-Step Explanation of How Something Operates

COMPARISON AND CONTRAST:
Examining Similarities and Differences

DIVISION AND CLASSIFICATION: Sorting
Things Out

DEFINITION: Determining the Nature and Limits of Something

CAUSE AND EFFECT: Telling Why

PERSUASION AND ARGUMENT:
Appealing to Reason and Emotions

HUMOR AND SATIRE: Making Us Laugh
While We Think

▼ PREFACE

The Contemporary Reader is a collection of essays chosen to challenge today's college students—essays on subjects they can relate to, essays that talk about the times and culture of which they are part. And, of course, essays that inspire thought, stimulate class discussion, and serve as writing models.

By its very nature a book on contemporary matters must be kept up to date. Therefore, for the fourth edition I have made some major changes, several at the suggestions of instructors and students who used the third edition. These changes include:

New topics and new essays. Naturally, material that was dated or that was no longer useful to students and instructors has been dropped. In fact, of the 95 selections, 70 are new to this edition. Many new topics have been added to the already broad spectrum covered in past editions, for example, multiculturalism, minority experiences, college-age children and divorce, women and the military, safe sex, consumerism, the homeless, male culture, date rape, Madonna, women and the workout revolution, horror movies, sex in advertising, violence against women, abortion, free speech, and college course work, to name a few.

New chapters. Two new chapters have been added. Race and Class (Chapter 5) reflects the growing multiculturalism in our country and contains nine pieces written by African-American, Hispanic, Asian, and Native American authors.

The other new chapter, Education (Chapter 13), contains six essays that assess some of the major concerns about the way we educate our young from kindergarten through college.

Increased number of women writers. Women composed 43 of the 95 selections in this edition.

Increased number of minority writers. People of several ethnic minorities composed 24 of the 95 selections in this edition.

Improved apparatus. Almost all of the apparatus in the book has been updated with great effort to create penetrating and stimulating assignments. This book is not just a collection of interesting thoughts on contemporary experience. The selections offer varied but solid assistance to composition students trying to develop their own writing abilities. First, each section has an introduction outlining the rationale behind the selections and giving a brief overview of it. Second, each selection is preceded by a headnote containing thematic and biographic information as well as clues to writing techniques and strategies. Third, each piece is followed by a series of review questions covering both thoughts and themes (Topical Considerations) and compositional features (Rhetorical Considerations)—questions designed to help students think analytically about the content and form of the essays. Additionally, some writing assignments are included to suggest how students might relate the essays to other selections and to their own experience. There is also a Rhetorical Table of Contents grouping the essays according to particular writing strategies.

ABOUT THE ESSAYS

Diversity

The fourth edition still reflects the wide range of student interests: television, movies, music, advertising, the media, crime, sports, the natural world, abortion, dating, sexual roles, the latest fads, jogging, gun control, weight control, drug control, capital punishment, teenage pregnancy, religious conversion, death and dying, and more.

This edition also contains the writings of some of the finest journalists and authors of our time. Writers as diverse as the subjects: Maya Angelou, Jonathan Kozol, Martin Luther King, Jr., Robert Fulghum, Elisabeth Kübler-Ross, and Ishmael Reed, as well as familiar humorists such as Dave Barry, P. J. O'Rourke, and Diane White.

Many of the authors are well-known columnists and novelists: Ellen Goodman, Diane White, Jeff Greenfield, Gwynne Dyer, Anna Quindlen, Andrew Ward, Robert B. Parker, and Garrison Keillor. There are also pieces by students and nonprofessional writers.

Assorted writing styles and techniques are represented in this collection. There are examples of the "basic" essay, as well as editorials, satirical narratives, letters, parodies, journal entries, parables, news reports, descriptive narratives, pointed arguments, commercial ads, and more. They vary in length from 500 words to 2000—a range most writing assignments fall within.

Debates

Essays on controversial topics are a special feature of *The Contemporary Reader*. As in the first three editions, many contemporary issues are examined from opposing points of view. Most of the fourteen sections contain a debate. They might be indirect as in Chapter 7, Television, where Jeff Greenfield's article "Don't Blame TV" argues against some of the preceding viewpoints on the dangers of television. Sometimes the arguments meet head on, as do Edward Koch's and David Bruck's opposing views on capital punishment (in Chapter 10, Contemporary Issues).

Debates can be found in nonissue sections as well, such as in Chapter 8, Advertising. Here some barbed attacks on TV commercials challenge a cogent defense of familiar ads by professional advertiser Charles O'Neill.

Humor

There is no reason why the writing experience should not be fun, nor is there any reason why writing models cannot be entertaining. As you will discover, many of the selections are quite funny while having something to say. Nearly every section contains some humorous pieces. Even Chapter 13, Education, contains Pulitzer Prize winning humorist Dave Barry's hilarious defense, "Can America Be No. 1 in Math? You Bet Your Noogie."

Advertisements

Because of the strong response to the magazine ads in this book's section on advertising, we have included a new sampling of recently run ads with specific questions to help students closely analyze how advertising works on us—and to spark some lively class discussions.

ACKNOWLEDGMENTS

Many people behind the scenes are at the very least deserving of acknowledgment and gratitude. It would be impossible to thank all of them, but there are some for whose help I am particularly grateful. First, I would like to thank all the instructors and students who used the first three editions of *The Contemporary Reader*. Their continued support has made possible this latest edition. Also, I would like to thank those instructors who spent hours answering lengthy questionnaires on the effectiveness of the essays and who supplied careful reviews and suggestions. They are W. Dale Brown, Calvin College; Kathleen Shine Cain, Merrimack College; Jo A. Chern, University of Wisconsin at Green Bay; Noel Comeree, Columbia Basin College; Gay Davidson, University of Wisconsin at Madison; Anita Gandolfo, West Virginia University; Ann Matthews, Princeton University; Robert Mayberry, University of Nevada at Las Vegas; Michael Slaughter, Illinois Central College; Robert Spiegel, Central Connecticut College; and John Taylor, South Dakota State University.

Special thanks go to Professors Robert Schwegler of the University of Rhode Island, David Vinopal of Paul Smith's College, Ann Taylor and Richard Elia of Salem State College, and Mary Lee Donahue of Glassboro State College; I also thank my colleagues Guy Rotella, Kathy Howlett, Kathleen Kelly, Janet Carr, Ken Capobianco, and Timothy Donovan for their suggestions of new material, as well as Stuart Peterfreund for his support.

Thanks also to Pamela Farrell, Catherine McCarron, Laurie Nardone, and E. Kim Stone who assisted me in putting together the apparatus for this text.

Very special thanks to the people of HarperCollins, especially my editor, Patricia Rossi; her former assistant, David Munger; development editor Linda Buchanan Allen; and sales representative Kelly Bell.

Finally, to my wife Kathleen for her keen insight, her many hours of assistance, and her encouragement, once again—my loving appreciation.

Gary Goshgarian

1 ▼ PERSONAL DISCOVERIES

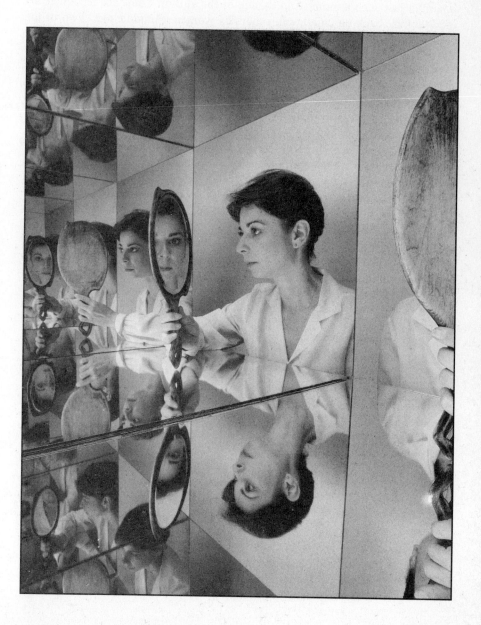

Self-discovery, the ancient philosophers tell us, is the greatest virtue. The high premium, of course, implies the difficulty of attainment. For some, self-discovery constantly evades. For others, it brings pain. For others still, the experience is enlightening. In some measure we all come to know ourselves as we move from childhood to old age. More often than not, discovery arises from a particular experience. Whether big or small, accidental or sought, good or bad—it is a moment that forever marks our souls. Nearly every essay in this chapter describes just such a moment in the life of the author. Some are recounted by men looking back on childhood, others by women in middle age. Two of the authors are white, four are black, one is Hispanic, and another is Native American. But universal is the experience, for it declares to us who we are in the world.

The first three essays explore childhood experiences that marked turning points for the authors. In his narrative, "Think About It," Frank Conroy tells of encounters with individuals very different from himself—subway shoeshine men, black jazz-club musicians, and a Supreme Court justice. But, as he says, years pass before he fully comprehends the meaning of those encounters. The next two essays look back to grade school experiences that ignited personal and racial consciousness for the authors. In "Shame," Dick Gregory describes a profoundly painful moment in second grade when a teacher's comment suddenly defines his place in the classroom and the world outside. For Maya Angelou and her classmates, eighth-grade graduation promised to be "the hush-hush magic time" of their young lives. But as described in "Graduation," ugly racial insensitivity during the ceremony turned the young black woman's expectations into bitter pain and anger. Then an epiphany turns the moment into a triumphant celebration of the proud heritage out of which she was born.

A manifestation of a different sort is the motivation behind Langston Hughes's brief narrative, "Salvation." In this flashback to a church revival meeting in his childhood, Hughes poignantly illustrates how he failed to live up to adult-world demands to be saved.

Self-discovery does not always burst in key moments. Sometimes intense soul-searching is required as we see in the next two pieces. In "Angry," Julianne Malveaux faces up to the rage in her breast. While she sees herself in the tradition of black women "raising hell" over discrimination, poverty, and war, she confesses that being angry all the time is counterproductive. In an honest self-analysis, the author tells how she learned to swallow some rage and pick her battles. The battle for Linda Bird Francke is clearly stated in the title of her essay, "The Ambivalence of Abortion." In a powerful piece of introspection, the author explains how her mind and heart tore at each other when faced with an unwanted pregnancy.

The final essays illustrate how the act of writing can lead to self-discovery. In "Ordinary Spirit," Joy Harjo says that in poetry she creates unexpected adventures while tapping into the heritage of her French and Cherokee blood. And in "Out of the Frying Pan," Puerto Rican-born Rosario Ferré describes how in short fiction she remakes herself and the world with a vengeance.

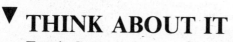

▼ THINK ABOUT IT

Frank Conroy

How many times have you experienced something you did not fully understand until months if not years later? We all have. It is a personal discovery fundamental to growing up. We begin with Frank Conroy's reflection on three very different experiences he had as a young man—experiences that exposed him to unknown levels of society and opened him to a truth about life: that education doesn't end until life does. Frank Conroy is director of the Iowa Writer's Workshop and author of *Stop-Time* and *Midair*. His stories and essays have appeared in *The New Yorker, Esquire, Harper's,* and *GQ*. He has worked as a jazz pianist and has often written about American music. This article first appeared in *Harper's Magazine* in 1988.

When I was sixteen I worked selling hot dogs at a stand in the Fourteenth Street subway station in New York City, one level above the trains and one below the street, where the crowds continually flowed back and forth. I worked with three Puerto Rican men who could not speak English. I had no Spanish, and although we understood each other well with regard to the tasks at hand, sensing and adjusting to each other's body movements in the extremely confined space in which we operated, I felt isolated with no one to talk to. On my break I came out from behind the counter and passed the time with two old black men who ran a shoeshine stand in a dark corner of the corridor. It was a poor location, half hidden by columns, and they didn't have much business. I would sit with my back against the wall while they stood or moved around their ancient elevated stand, talking to each other or to me, but always staring into the distance as they did so. **1**

As the weeks went by I realized that they never looked at anything in their immediate vicinity—not at me or their stand or anybody who might come within ten or fifteen feet. They did not look at approaching customers once they were inside the perimeter. Save for the instant it took to discern the color of the shoes, they did not even look at what they were doing while they worked, but rubbed in polish, brushed, and buffed by feel while looking over their shoulders, into the distance, as if awaiting the arrival of an important person. Of course there wasn't all that much distance in the underground station, but their behavior was so focused and consistent they seemed somehow to transcend the physical. A powerful mood was created, and I came almost to believe that these men could see through walls, through girders, and around corners to whatever hyperspace it was where whoever it was they were waiting and watching for would finally emerge. Their scattered talk was hip, elliptical, and hinted at mysteries beyond my white boy's ken, but it was the staring off, the long, steady staring off, that had me hypnotized. I left for a better job, with handshakes from both of them, without understanding what I had seen. **2**

3   Perhaps ten years later, after playing jazz with black musicians in various Harlem clubs, hanging out uptown with a few young artists and intellectuals, I began to learn from them something of the extraordinarily varied and complex riffs and rituals embraced by different people to help themselves get through life in the ghetto. Fantasy of all kinds—from playful to dangerous—was in the very air of Harlem. It was the spice of uptown life.

4   Only then did I understand the two shoeshine men. They were trapped in a demeaning situation in a dark corner in an underground corridor in a filthy subway system. Their continuous staring off was a kind of statement, a kind of dance. Our bodies are here, went the statement, but our souls are receiving nourishment from distant sources only we can see. They were powerful magic dancers, sorcerers almost, and thirty-five years later I can still feel the pressure of their spell.

5   The light bulb may appear over your head, is what I'm saying, but it may be a while before it actually goes on. Early in my attempts to learn jazz piano, I used to listen to recordings of a fine player named Red Garland, whose music I admired. I couldn't quite figure out what he was doing with his left hand, however; the chords eluded me. I went uptown to an obscure club where he was playing with his trio, caught him on his break, and simply asked him. "Sixths," he said cheerfully. And then he went away.

6   I didn't know what to make of it. The basic jazz chord is the seventh, which comes in various configurations, but it is what it is. I was a self-taught pianist, pretty shaky on theory and harmony, and when he said sixths I kept trying to fit the information into what I already knew, and it didn't fit. But it stuck in my mind—a tantalizing mystery.

7   A couple of years later, when I began playing with a bass player, I discovered more or less by accident that if the bass played the root and I played a sixth based on the fifth note of the scale, a very interesting chord involving both instruments emerged. Ordinarily, I suppose I would have skipped over the matter and not paid much attention, but I remembered Garland's remark and so I stopped and spent a week or two working out the voicings, and greatly strengthened my foundations as a player. I had remembered what I hadn't understood, you might say, until my life caught up with the information and the light bulb went on.

8   I remember another, more complicated example from my sophomore year at a small liberal-arts college outside Philadelphia. I seemed never to be able to get up in time for breakfast in the dining hall. I would get coffee and a doughnut in the Coop instead—a basement area with about a dozen small tables where students could get something to eat at odd hours. Several mornings in a row I noticed a strange man sitting by himself with a cup of coffee. He was in his sixties, perhaps, and sat straight in his chair with very little extraneous movement. I guessed he was some sort of distinguished visitor to the college who had decided to put in some time at a student hangout. But no one ever sat with him. One morning I approached his table and asked if I could join him.

9   "Certainly," he said. "Please do." He had perhaps the clearest eyes I had

ever seen, like blue ice, and to be held in their steady gaze was not, at first, an entirely comfortable experience. His eyes gave nothing away about himself while at the same time creating in me the eerie impression that he was looking directly into my soul. He asked a few quick questions, as if to put me at my ease, and we fell into conversation. He was William O. Douglas from the Supreme Court, and when he saw how startled I was he said, "Call me Bill. Now tell me what you're studying and why you get up so late in the morning." Thus began a series of talks that stretched over many weeks. The fact that I was an ignorant sophomore with literary pretensions who knew nothing about the law didn't seem to bother him. We talked about everything from Shakespeare to the possibility of life on other planets. One day I mentioned that I was going to have dinner with Judge Learned Hand. I explained that Hand was my girlfriend's grandfather. Douglas nodded, but I could tell he was surprised at the coincidence of my knowing the chief judge of the most important court in the country save the Supreme Court itself. After fifty years on the bench Judge Hand had become a famous man, both in and out of legal circles—a living legend, to his own dismay. "Tell him hello and give him my best regards," Douglas said.

Learned Hand, in his eighties, was a short, barrel-chested man with a large, square head, huge, thick, bristling eyebrows, and soft brown eyes. He radiated energy and would sometimes bark out remarks or questions in the living room as if he were in court. His humor was sharp, but often leavened with a touch of self-mockery. When something caught his funny bone he would burst out with explosive laughter—the laughter of a man who enjoyed laughing. He had a large repertoire of dramatic expressions involving the use of his eyebrows—very useful, he told me conspiratorially, when looking down on things from behind the bench. (The court stenographer could not record the movement of his eyebrows.) When I told him I'd been talking to William O. Douglas, they first shot up in exaggerated surprise, and then lowered and moved forward in a glower.

"*Justice* William O. Douglas, young man," he admonished. "Justice Douglas, if you please." About the Supreme Court in general, Hand insisted on a tone of profound respect. Little did I know that in private correspondence he had referred to the Court as "The Blessed Saints, Cherubim and Seraphim," "The Jolly Boys," "The Nine Tin Jesuses," "The Nine Blameless Ethiopians," and my particular favorite, "The Nine Blessed Chalices of the Sacred Effluvium."

Hand was badly stooped and had a lot of pain in his lower back. Martinis helped, but his strict Yankee wife approved of only one before dinner. It was my job to make the second and somehow slip it to him. If the pain was particularly acute he would get out of his chair and lie flat on the rug, still talking, and finish his point without missing a beat. He flattered me by asking for my impression of Justice Douglas, instructed me to convey his warmest regards, and then began talking about the Dennis case, which he described as a particularly tricky and difficult case involving the prosecution of eleven leaders of the Communist party. He had just started in on the First Amendment and free speech when we were called in to dinner.

William O. Douglas loved the outdoors with a passion, and we fell into the habit of having coffee in the Coop and then strolling under the trees down toward the duck pond. About the Dennis case, he said something to this effect: "Eleven Communists arrested by the government. Up to no good, said the government; dangerous people, violent overthrow, etc. First Amendment, said the defense, freedom of speech, etc." Douglas stopped walking. "Clear and present danger."

14   "What?" I asked. He often talked in a telegraphic manner, and one was expected to keep up with him. It was sometimes like listening to a man thinking out loud.

15   "Clear and present danger," he said. "That was the issue. Did they constitute a clear and present danger? I don't think so. I think everybody took the language pretty far in Dennis." He began walking, striding along quickly. Again, one was expected to keep up with him. "The FBI was all over them. Phones tapped, constant surveillance. How could it be clear and present danger with the FBI watching every move they made? That's a ginkgo," he said suddenly, pointing at a tree. "A beauty. You don't see those every day. Ask Hand about clear and present danger."

16   I was in fact reluctant to do so. Douglas's argument seemed to me to be crushing—the last word, really—and I didn't want to embarrass Judge Hand. But back in the living room, on the second martini, the old man asked about Douglas. I sort of scratched my nose and recapitulated the conversation by the ginkgo tree.

17   "What?" Hand shouted. "Speak up, sir, for heaven's sake."

18   "He said the FBI was watching them all the time so there couldn't be a clear and present danger," I blurted out, blushing as I said it.

19   A terrible silence filled the room. Hand's eyebrows writhed on his face like two huge caterpillars. He leaned forward in the wing chair, his face settling, finally, into a grim expression. "I am astonished," he said softly, his eyes holding mine, "at Justice Douglas's newfound faith in the Federal Bureau of Investigation." His big, granite head moved even closer to mine, until I could smell the martini. "I had understood him to consider it a politically corrupt, incompetent organization, directed by a power-crazed lunatic." I realized I had been holding my breath throughout all of this, and as I relaxed, I saw the faintest trace of a smile cross Hand's face. Things are sometimes more complicated than they first appear, his smile seemed to say. The old man leaned back. "The proximity of the danger is something to think about. Ask him about that. See what he says."

20   I chewed the matter over as I returned to campus. Hand had pointed out some of Douglas's language about the FBI from other sources that seemed to bear out his point. I thought about the words "clear and present danger," and the fact that if you looked at them closely they might not be as simple as they had first appeared. What degree of danger? Did the word "present" allude to the proximity of the danger, or just the fact that the danger was there at all—that it wasn't an anticipated danger? Were there other hidden factors these great men were weighing of which I was unaware?

21   But Douglas was gone, back to Washington. (The writer in me is tempted

to create a scene here—to invent one for dramatic purposes—but of course I can't do that.) My brief time as a messenger boy was over, and I felt a certain frustration, as if, with a few more exchanges, the matter of *Dennis* v. *United States* might have been resolved to my satisfaction. They'd left me high and dry. But, of course, it is precisely because the matter did not resolve that has caused me to think about it, off and on, all these years. "The Constitution," Hand used to say to me flatly, "is a piece of paper. The Bill of Rights is a piece of paper." It was many years before I understood what he meant. Documents alone do not keep democracy alive, nor maintain the state of law. There is no particular safety in them. Living men and women, generation after generation, must continually remake democracy and the law, and that involves an ongoing state of tension between the past and the present which will never completely resolve.

Education doesn't end until life ends, because you never know when you're going to understand something you hadn't understood before. For me, the magic dance of the shoeshine men was the kind of experience in which understanding came with a kind of click, a resolving kind of click. The same with the experience at the piano. What happened with Justice Douglas and Judge Hand was different, and makes the point that understanding does not always mean resolution. Indeed, in our intellectual lives, our creative lives, it is perhaps those problems that will never resolve that rightly claim the lion's share of our energies. The physical body exists in a constant state of tension as it maintains homeostasis, and so too does the active mind embrace the tension of never being certain, never being absolutely sure, never being done, as it engages the world. That is our special fate, our inexpressibly valuable condition. **22**

▼ TOPICAL CONSIDERATIONS

1. In "Think About It," Conroy has chosen three periods in his life in which he has come to some understanding. How did these experiences help him to understand things he hadn't understood before? At your age, what diverse life experiences have you had that have led you to understand something you hadn't understood before?
2. Compare the eyes and vision of the shoeshine men to that of Justice William O. Douglas. What are the differences? Does race or class have anything to do with their differing gazes? How does eye contact affect your relationship with a person?
3. Explain how Conroy's "light bulb" theory worked to make him really understand the concept of "sixths." When has your life had to catch up "with the information" until "the light bulb went on" (paragraph 7)?
4. Of Douglas and Hand Conroy asks, "Were there other hidden factors these great men were weighing of which I was unaware?" (paragraph 20). Aside from telling the reader that these two men

were prominent U.S. judges, how does Conroy convey their greatness? Have you ever encountered someone whom you consider
"great"? If so, what traits constitute that person's greatness?

5. In the final paragraph, Conroy concludes that "understanding does
not always mean resolution." To what specifically is he referring?
How does Conroy come to some level of understanding? Describe
an event for which you have grasped an understanding, but are not
aware of the resolution.

6. In paragraph 2, Conroy writes about the shoeshine men, "their
scattered talk was hip, elliptical, and hinted at mysteries beyond my
white boy's ken." What does *elliptical* speech mean? What does the
ability to communicate with scattered and elliptical talk say about
the two men's relationship? Is there anyone with whom you have
such a communication? If so, try to describe how it works.

7. Looking back on your life, did Frank Conroy make you "think
about it" a little more? Did you learn something from this essay? If
so, what exactly? Or, did he tell you something you already knew?
Explain your answer.

▼ RHETORICAL CONSIDERATIONS

1. Consider the series of prepositional phrases in the following statement from paragraph 4: "They were trapped in a demeaning situation in a dark corner in an underground corridor in a filthy subway
system." How does the series help project the plight of the shoeshine men? Does it make you feel trapped like the men? Describe
the progression of the objects of the prepositions—"situation,"
"corner," "corridor," "subway system."

2. As a reader and writer, how do you feel about Conroy's statement,
"(The writer in me is tempted to create a scene here—to invent one
for dramatic purposes—but of course I can't do that)" (paragraph
21)? Would the essay have been better if Conroy had created a
fictional ending? Does Conroy owe his readers the absolute truth?
As a writer, do you feel that essays should only contain true elements?

3. Conroy calls himself the "messenger" who facilitates the dialogue
between Judge Hand and Justice Douglas. In the exchange between
the two men, explain how Conroy shifts from Hand's response to
that of Douglas. Are the shifts too abrupt? Do the shifts seem more
like scene changes in a film or play?

4. Consider the essay's conclusion. According to Conroy, what is "our
special fate, our inexpressibly valuable condition"? Does the conclusion follow logically from the rest of the essay? Does it serve as
a resolution by rounding off matters?

▼ WRITING ASSIGNMENTS

1. Conroy writes, "Education doesn't end until life ends, because you never know when you're going to understand something you hadn't understood before." Write a paper in which you list three things that you only understood some time after they had been introduced to you. Like Conroy, specifically quote the people involved and try to describe each scene.

2. Conroy describes himself in paragraph 9 as an "ignorant sophomore with literary pretensions who knew nothing about the law," who talked with Justice Douglas "about everything from Shakespeare to the possibility of life on other planets." Would you consider Conroy a typical college student? Although he was a college student many years ago, are his interests and feelings still relevant? Write a paper in which you address these questions and determine whether college students are at the age in which they are most ready to come to understandings about complex things?

▼ SHAME
Dick Gregory

Dick Gregory is a well-known satirist, whose humor cuts below the surface of comedy. As a stand-up comic, he was a regular on a variety of television shows during the 1960s and 1970s. He continues to be active in the Civil Rights Movement. Additionally, Gregory has become a noted nutritionist, devoting his efforts to helping people suffering from obesity. The essay below is a sensitive narrative of a childhood experience that taught Gregory the meaning of shame. The selection comes from Gregory's 1964 autobiography, *nigger*.

I never learned hate at home, or shame. I had to go to school for that. I was about seven years old when I got my first big lesson. I was in love with a little girl named Helene Tucker, a light-complexioned little girl with pigtails and nice manners. She was always clean and she was smart in school. I think I went to school then mostly to look at her. I brushed my hair and even got me a little old handkerchief. It was a lady's handkerchief, but I didn't want Helene to see me wipe my nose on my hand. The pipes were frozen again, there was no water in the house, but I washed my socks and shirt every night. I'd get a pot, and go over to Mister Ben's grocery store, and stick my pot down into his soda machine. Scoop out some chopped ice. By evening the ice melted to water for washing. I got sick a lot that winter because the fire would go out at night before the clothes were dry. In the morning I'd put them on, wet or dry, because they were the only clothes I had.

2   Everybody's got a Helene Tucker, a symbol of everything you want. I loved her for her goodness, her cleanness, her popularity. She'd walk down my street and my brothers and sisters would yell, "Here comes Helene," and I'd rub my tennis sneakers on the back of my pants and wish my hair wasn't so nappy and the white folks' shirt fit me better. I'd run out on the street. If I knew my place and didn't come too close, she'd wink at me and say hello. That was a good feeling. Sometimes I'd follow her all the way home, and shovel the snow off her walk and try to make friends with her Momma and her aunts. I'd drop money on her stoop late at night on my way back from shining shoes in the taverns. And she had a Daddy, and he had a good job. He was a paper hanger.

3   I guess I would have gotten over Helene by summertime, but something happened in that classroom that made her face hang in front of me for the next twenty-two years. When I played the drums in high school it was for Helene and when I broke track records in college it was for Helene and when I started standing behind microphones and heard applause I wished Helene could hear it, too. It wasn't until I was twenty-nine years old and married and making money that I finally got her out of my system. Helene was sitting in that classroom when I learned to be ashamed of myself.

4   It was on a Thursday. I was sitting in the back of the room, in a seat with a chalk circle drawn around it. The idiot's seat, the troublemaker's seat.

5   The teacher thought I was stupid. Couldn't spell, couldn't read, couldn't do arithmetic. Just stupid. Teachers were never interested in finding out that you couldn't concentrate because you were so hungry, because you hadn't had any breakfast. All you could think about was noontime, would it ever come? Maybe you could sneak into the cloakroom and steal a bite of some kid's lunch out of a coat pocket. A bite of something. Paste. You can't really make a meal of paste, or put it on bread for a sandwich, but sometimes I'd scoop a few spoonfuls out of the paste jar in the back of the room. Pregnant people get strange tastes. I was pregnant with poverty. Pregnant with dirt and pregnant with smells that made people turn away, pregnant with cold and pregnant with shoes that were never bought for me, pregnant with five other people in my bed and no Daddy in the next room, and pregnant with hunger. Paste doesn't taste too bad when you're hungry.

6   The teacher thought I was a troublemaker. All she saw from the front of the room was a little black boy who squirmed in his idiot's seat and made noises and poked the kids around him. I guess she couldn't see a kid who made noises because he wanted someone to know he was there.

7   It was on a Thursday, the day before the Negro payday. The eagle always flew on Friday. The teacher was asking each student how much his father would give to the Community Chest. On Friday night, each kid would get the money from his father, and on Monday he would bring it to the school. I decided I was going to buy me a Daddy right then. I had money in my pocket from shining

shoes and selling papers, and whatever Helene Tucker pledged for her Daddy I was going to top it. And I'd hand the money right in. I wasn't going to wait until Monday to buy me a Daddy.

I was shaking, scared to death. The teacher opened her book and started **8** calling out names alphabetically.

"Helene Tucker?" **9**

"My daddy said he'd give two dollars and fifty cents." **10**

"That's very nice, Helene. Very, very nice indeed." **11**

That made me feel pretty good. It wouldn't take too much to top that. I had **12** almost three dollars in dimes and quarters in my pocket. I stuck my hand in my pocket and held onto the money, waiting for her to call my name. But the teacher closed her book after she called everybody else in the class.

I stood up and raised my hand. **13**

"What is it now?" **14**

"You forgot me." **15**

She turned toward the blackboard. "I don't have time to be playing with **16** you, Richard."

"My Daddy said he'd . . ." **17**

"Sit down, Richard, you're disturbing the class." **18**

"My Daddy said he'd give . . . fifteen dollars." **19**

She turned around and looked mad. "We are collecting this money for you **20** and your kind, Richard Gregory. If your Daddy can give fifteen dollars you have no business being on relief."

"I got it right now, I got it right now, my Daddy gave it to me to turn in **21** today, my Daddy said . . ."

"And furthermore," she said, looking right at me, her nostrils getting big **22** and her lips getting thin and her eyes opening wide, "we know you don't have a Daddy."

Helene Tucker turned around, her eyes full of tears. She felt sorry for me. **23** Then I couldn't see her too well because I was crying, too.

"Sit down, Richard." **24**

And I always thought the teacher kind of liked me. She always picked me **25** to wash the blackboard on Friday, after school. That was a big thrill, it made me feel important. If I didn't wash it, come Monday the school might not function right.

"Where are you going, Richard?" **26**

I walked out of school that day, and for a long time I didn't go back very **27** often. There was shame there.

Now there was shame everywhere. It seemed like the whole world had been **28** inside that classroom, everyone had heard what the teacher had said, everyone had turned around and felt sorry for me. There was shame in going to the Worthy Boys Annual Christmas Dinner for you and your kind, because everybody knew what a worthy boy was. Why couldn't they just call it the Boys Annual Dinner; why'd they have to give it a name? There was shame in wearing the brown and orange and white plaid mackinaw the welfare gave to three thousand boys. Why'd it have to be the same for everybody so when you walked down the street the people could see you were on relief? It was a nice warm mackinaw and it had a hood, and my Momma beat me and called me a little rat when she found out I stuffed it in the bottom of a pail full of garbage way over on Cottage Street. There was shame in running over to Mister Ben's at the end of the day and asking for his rotten peaches, there was shame in asking Mrs. Simmons for a spoonful of sugar, there was shame in running out to meet the relief truck. I hated that truck, full of food for you and your kind. I ran into the house and hid when it came. And then I started to sneak through alleys, to take the long way home so the people going into White's Eat Shop wouldn't see me. Yeah, the whole world heard the teacher that day, we all know you don't have a Daddy.

▼ TOPICAL CONSIDERATIONS

1. Gregory tried so hard to impress Helene Tucker that he often got sick from wearing wet clothes that couldn't dry because the fire had gone out in the night. When you were growing up, was there any one person for whom you went to such extremes to impress? What did you do? What was he or she like? Do you know any adults who would go (or have gone) to such extremes?

2. Helene Tucker seems to have been a success symbol for Gregory when he was a child. He comments: "Everybody's got a Helene Tucker, a symbol of everything you want" (paragraph 2). What does Gregory's description of Helene tell you about what success meant to him? What influenced his view? Describe a person who represents success to you. What influences have shaped this view?

3. What do you think of the way Gregory handled himself in school the day the teacher embarrassed him? Would you have responded in the same way? Was his refusal to go to school after this incident the only way he could deal with his shame? What would have been your answer?

4. Is shame caused by outward circumstances or by what an individual has done himself? Which should it be? What does shame mean to Gregory? What does it mean to you?

5. Why did the memory of Helene Tucker's presence the day he was shamed in class motivate Gregory to excel as a teenager? Do you think this is a useful motivational device? What other incentives can be effective?

6. Gregory remarks that he wasn't able to get Helene Tucker out of his system for twenty-two years. Why was he finally able to forget her? Do you think that if he were confronted with the same kind of experience now, he would respond in the same way? Why? Is there anything about Gregory's experience that you can relate to your own life?

7. How sensitive was the teacher? How else might she have responded to Gregory?
8. Do you think most welfare recipients are like Gregory and do not want to be on welfare? Give reasons for your answer.

▼ RHETORICAL CONSIDERATIONS

1. Where does Gregory state his thesis? Is this the best place for it? Explain.
2. What adjectives does Gregory use in his description of Helene Tucker in the first paragraph? Does he use too many? Not enough? Are they essential to the development of his thesis? Why or why not?
3. What is the primary rhetorical pattern Gregory uses in this essay? Are others used as well? Cite sample passages.
4. Does Gregory *tell* or *show* his reader how he feels about Helene Tucker? What rhetorical patterns does he use to accomplish this?
5. What can you say about Gregory's conclusion? Does it tie in with his thesis? Is it an effective ending? Why or why not?

▼ WRITING ASSIGNMENTS

1. Have you ever had an experience that caused you to feel shame? Write an essay describing the incident. Include concrete details, illustrations, and dialogue (as Gregory does) that will show your reader exactly what happened.
2. What does success mean to you? In an essay, analyze your own answer to this question. Discuss the influences that have shaped your view.
3. Write an essay describing someone you idealize and would like to impress. Narrate some of the things you would do or have done to gain this person's esteem.

▼ GRADUATION

Maya Angelou

One of the most important events in a young person's life is graduation day. This selection, a vivid recollection of one such day and the events leading up to it, is by the famous black author, Maya Angelou. Born Marguerita Johnson in 1928, Angelou survived some terrible childhood experiences—a broken home, being raped at the age of eight, becoming an unwed mother at sixteen. As an adult, she involved herself in theatre, television, and journalism. She also served as a coordinator of Martin Luther King's Southern Christian Leadership Conference. She is perhaps best known for her autobiographical books, including *I Know Why the Caged Bird Sings* (1970), from which this piece was taken, and *The Heart of a Woman* (1981), a memoir.

1   The children in Stamps trembled visibly with anticipation. Some adults were excited too, but to be certain the whole young population had come down with graduation epidemic. Large classes were graduating from both the grammar school and the high school. Even those who were years removed from their own day of glorious release were anxious to help with preparations as a kind of dry run. The junior students who were moving into the vacating classes' chairs were tradition-bound to show their talents for leadership and management. They strutted through the school and around the campus exerting pressure on the lower grades. Their authority was so new that occasionally if they pressed a little too hard it had to be overlooked. After all, next term was coming, and it never hurt a sixth grader to have a play sister in the eighth grade, or a tenth-year student to be able to call a twelfth grader Bubba. So all was endured in a spirit of shared understanding. But the graduating classes themselves were the nobility. Like travelers with exotic destinations on their minds, the graduates were remarkably forgetful. They came to school without their books, or tablets, or even pencils. Volunteers fell over themselves to secure replacements for the missing equipment. When accepted, the willing workers might or might not be thanked, and it was of no importance to the pregraduation rites. Even teachers were respectful of the now quiet and aging seniors, and tended to speak to them, if not as equals, as beings only slightly lower than themselves. After tests were returned and grades given, the student body, which acted like an extended family, knew who did well, who excelled, and what piteous ones had failed.

2   Unlike the white high school, Lafayette County Training School distinguished itself by having neither lawn, nor hedges, nor tennis court, nor climbing ivy. Its two buildings (main classrooms, the grade school and home economics) were set on a dirt hill with no fence to limit either its boundaries or those of

bordering farms. There was a large expanse to the left of the school which was used alternately as a baseball diamond or a basketball court. Rusty hoops on the swaying poles represented the permanent recreational equipment, although bats and balls could be borrowed from the P.E. teacher if the borrower was qualified and if the diamond wasn't occupied.

Over this rocky area relieved by a few shady tall persimmon trees the **3** graduating class walked. The girls often held hands and no longer bothered to speak to the lower students. There was a sadness about them, as if this old world was not their home and they were bound for higher ground. The boys, on the other hand, had become more friendly, more outgoing. A decided change from the closed attitude they projected while studying for finals. Now they seemed not ready to give up the old school, the familiar paths and classrooms. Only a small percentage would be continuing on to college—one of the South's A & M (agricultural and mechanical) schools, which trained Negro youths to be carpenters, farmers, handymen, masons, maids, cooks, and baby nurses. Their future rode heavily on their shoulders, and blinded them to the collective joy that had pervaded the lives of the boys and girls in the grammar school graduating class.

Parents who could afford it had ordered new shoes and ready-made clothes **4** for themselves from Sears and Roebuck or Montgomery Ward. They also engaged the best seamstresses to make the floating graduating dresses and to cut down second-hand pants which would be pressed to a military slickness for the important event.

Oh, it was important, all right. Whitefolks would attend the ceremony, and **5** two or three would speak of God and home, and the Southern way of life, and Mrs. Parsons, the principal's wife, would play the graduation march while the lower-grade graduates paraded down the aisles and took their seats below the platform. The high school seniors would wait in empty classrooms to make their dramatic entrance.

In the Store I was the person of the moment. The birthday girl. The center. **6** Bailey* had graduated the year before, although to do so he had had to forfeit all pleasures to make up for his time lost in Baton Rouge.

My class was wearing butter-yellow piqué dresses, and Momma launched **7** out on mine. She smocked the yoke into tiny crisscrossing puckers, then shirred the rest of the bodice. Her dark fingers ducked in and out of the lemony cloth as she embroidered raised daisies around the hem. Before she considered herself finished she had added a crocheted cuff on the puff sleeves, and a pointy crocheted collar.

I was going to be lovely. A walking model of all the various styles of fine **8** hand sewing and it didn't worry me that I was only twelve years old and merely graduating from the eighth grade. Besides, many teachers in Arkansas Negro schools had only that diploma and were licensed to impart wisdom.

The days had become longer and more noticeable. The faded beige of **9**

* Angelou's brother.—Ed.

former times had been replaced with strong and sure colors. I began to see my classmates' clothes, their skin tones, and the dust that waved off pussy willows. Clouds that lazed across the sky were objects of great concern to me. Their shiftier shapes might have held a message that in my new happiness and with a little bit of time I'd soon decipher. During that period I looked at the arch of heaven so religiously my neck kept a steady ache. I had taken to smiling more often, and my jaws hurt from the unaccustomed activity. Between the two physical sore spots, I suppose I could have been uncomfortable, but that was not the case. As a member of the winning team (the graduating class of 1940) I had outdistanced unpleasant sensations by miles. I was headed for the freedom of open fields.

10 Youth and social approval allied themselves with me and we trammeled memories of slights and insults. The wind of our swift passage remodeled my features. Lost tears were pounded to mud and then to dust. Years of withdrawal were brushed aside and left behind, as hanging ropes of parasitic moss.

11 My work alone had awarded me a top place and I was going to be one of the first called in the graduating ceremonies. On the classroom blackboard, as well as on the bulletin board in the auditorium, there were blue stars and white stars and red stars. No absences, no tardinesses, and my academic work was among the best of the year. I could say the preamble to the Constitution even faster than Bailey. We timed ourselves often: "WethepeopleoftheUnited-Statesinordertoformamoreperfectunion . . ." I had memorized the Presidents of the United States from Washington to Roosevelt in chronological as well as alphabetical order.

12 My hair pleased me too. Gradually the black mass had lengthened and thickened, so that it kept at last to its braided pattern, and I didn't have to yank my scalp off when I tried to comb it.

13 Louise and I had rehearsed the exercises until we tired out ourselves. Henry Reed was class valedictorian. He was a small, very black boy with hooded eyes, a long, broad nose and an oddly shaped head. I had admired him for years because each term he and I vied for the best grades in our class. Most often he bested me, but instead of being disappointed I was pleased that we shared top places between us. Like many Southern Black children, he lived with his grandmother, who was as strict as Momma and as kind as she knew how to be. He was courteous, respectful, and soft-spoken to elders, but on the playground he chose to play the roughest games. I admired him. Anyone, I reckoned, sufficiently afraid or sufficiently dull could be polite. But to be able to operate at a top level with both adults and children was admirable.

14 His valedictory speech was entitled "To Be or Not to Be." The rigid tenth-grade teacher had helped him to write it. He'd been working on the dramatic stresses for months.

15 The weeks until graduation were filled with heady activities. A group of small children were to be presented in a play about buttercups and daisies and bunny rabbits. They could be heard throughout the building practicing their hops and their little songs that sounded like silver bells. The older girls (non-

graduates, of course) were assigned the task of making refreshments for the night's festivities. A tangy scent of ginger, cinnamon, nutmeg, and chocolate wafted around the home economics building as the budding cooks made samples for themselves and their teachers.

In every corner of the workshop, axes and saws split fresh timber as the **16** woodshop boys made sets and stage scenery. Only the graduates were left out of the general bustle. We were free to sit in the library at the back of the building or look in quite detachedly, naturally, on the measures being taken for our event.

Even the minister preached on graduation the Sunday before. His subject **17** was, "Let your light so shine that men will see your good works and praise your Father, Who is in Heaven." Although the sermon was purported to be addressed to us, he used the occasion to speak to backsliders, gamblers, and general ne'er-do-wells. But since he had called our names at the beginning of the service we were mollified.

Among Negroes the tradition was to give presents to children going only **18** from one grade to another. How much more important this was when the person was graduating at the top of the class. Uncle Willie and Momma had sent away for a Mickey Mouse watch like Bailey's. Louise gave me four embroidered handkerchiefs. (I gave her three crocheted doilies.) Mrs. Sneed, the minister's wife, made me an underskirt to wear for graduation, and nearly every customer gave me a nickel or maybe even a dime with the instruction "Keep on moving to higher ground," or some such encouragement.

Amazingly the great day finally dawned and I was out of bed before I knew **19** it. I threw open the back door to see it more clearly, but Momma said, "Sister, come away from that door and put your robe on."

I hoped the memory of that morning would never leave me. Sunlight was **20** itself still young, and the day had none of the insistence maturity would bring it in a few hours. In my robe and barefoot in the backyard, under cover of going to see about my new beans, I gave myself up to the gentle warmth and thanked God that no matter what evil I had done in my life He had allowed me to live to see this day. Somewhere in my fatalism I had expected to die, accidentally, and never have the chance to walk up the stairs in the auditorium and gracefully receive my hard-earned diploma. Out of God's merciful bosom I had won reprieve.

Bailey came out in his robe and gave me a box wrapped in Christmas paper. **21** He said he had saved his money for months to pay for it. It felt like a box of chocolates, but I knew Bailey wouldn't save money to buy candy when we had all we could want under our noses.

He was as proud of the gift as I. It was a soft-lather-bound copy of a **22** collection of poems by Edgar Allan Poe, or, as Bailey and I called him, "Eap." I turned to "Annabel Lee" and we walked up and down the garden rows, the cool dirt between our toes, reciting the beautifully sad lines.

Momma made a Sunday breakfast although it was only Friday. After we **23** finished the blessing, I opened my eyes to find the watch on my plate. It was a dream of a day. Everything went smoothly and to my credit. I didn't have to be reminded or scolded for anything. Near evening I was too jittery to attend to chores, so Bailey volunteered to do all before his bath.

24 Days before, we had made a sign for the Store and as we turned out the lights Momma hung the cardboard over the doorknob. It read clearly: CLOSED. GRADUATION.

25 My dress fitted perfectly and everyone said that I looked like a sunbeam in it. On the hill, going toward the school, Bailey walked behind with Uncle Willie, who muttered, "Go on, Ju." He wanted him to walk ahead with us because it embarrassed him to have to walk so slowly. Bailey said he'd let the ladies walk together, and the men would bring up the rear. We all laughed, nicely.

26 Little children dashed by out of the dark like fireflies. Their crepepaper dresses and butterfly wings were not made for running and we heard more than one rip, dryly, and the regretful "uh uh" that followed.

27 The school blazed without gaiety. The windows seemed cold and unfriendly from the lower hill. A sense of ill-fated timing crept over me, and if Momma hadn't reached for my hand I would have drifted back to Bailey and Uncle Willie, and possibly beyond. She made a few slow jokes about my feet getting cold, and tugged me along to the now-strange building.

28 Around the front steps, assurance came back. There were my fellow "greats," the graduating class. Hair brushed back, legs oiled, new dresses and pressed pleats, fresh pocket handkerchiefs and little handbags, all homesewn. Oh, we were up to snuff, all right. I joined my comrades and didn't even see my family go in to find seats in the crowded auditorium.

29 The school band struck up a march and all classes filed in as had been rehearsed. We stood in front of our seats, as assigned, and on a signal from the choir director, we sat. No sooner had this been accomplished than the band started to play the national anthem. We rose again and sang the song, after which we recited the pledge of allegiance. We remained standing for a brief minute before the choir director and the principal signaled to us, rather desperately I thought, to take our seats. The command was so unusual that our carefully rehearsed and smooth-running machine was thrown off. For a full minute we fumbled for our chairs and bumped into each other awkwardly. Habits change or solidify under pressure, so in our state of nervous tension we had been ready to follow our usual assembly pattern: the American National Anthem, then the pledge of allegiance, then the song every Black person I knew called the Negro National Anthem. All done in the same key, with the same passion and most often standing on the same foot.

30 Finding my seat at last, I was overcome with a presentiment of worse things to come. Something unrehearsed, unplanned, was going to happen, and we were going to be made to look bad. I distinctly remember being explicit in the choice of pronoun. It was "we," the graduating class, the unit, that concerned me then.

31 The principal welcomed "parents and friends" and asked the Baptist minister to lead us in prayer. His invocation was brief and punchy, and for a second I thought we were getting back on the high road to right action. When the

principal came back to the dais, however, his voice had changed. Sounds always affected me profoundly and the principal's voice was one of my favorites. During assembly it melted and lowed weakly into the audience. It had not been in my plan to listen to him, but my curiosity was piqued and I straightened up to give him my attention.

He was talking about Booker T. Washington, our "late great leader," who said we can be as close as the fingers on the hand, etc. . . . Then he said a few vague things about friendship and the frienship of kindly people to those less fortunate than themselves. With that his voice nearly faded, thin, away. Like a river diminishing to a stream and then to a trickle. But he cleared his throat and said, "Our speaker tonight, who is also our friend, came from Texarkana to deliver the commencement address, but due to the irregularity of the train schedule, he's going to, as they say, 'speak and run.' " He said that we understood and wanted the man to know that we were most grateful for the time he was able to give us and then something about how we were willing always to adjust to another's program, and without more ado—"I give you Mr. Edward Donleavy." **32**

Not one but two white men came through the door offstage. The shorter one walked to the speaker's platform, and the tall one moved over to the center seat and sat down. But that was our principal's seat, and already occupied. The dislodged gentleman bounced around for a long breath or two before the Baptist minister gave him his chair, then with more dignity than the situation deserved, the minister walked off the stage. **33**

Donleavy looked at the audience once (on reflection, I'm sure that he wanted only to reassure himself that we were really there), adjusted his glasses, and began to read from a sheaf of papers. **34**

He was glad "to be here and to see the work going on just as it was in the other schools." **35**

At the first "Amen" from the audience I willed the offender to immediate death by choking on the word. But Amens and Yes, sir's began to fall around the room like rain through a ragged umbrella. **36**

He told us of the wonderful changes we children in Stamps had in store. The Central School (naturally, the white school was Central) had already been granted improvements that would be in use in the fall. A well-known artist was coming from Little Rock to teach art to them. They were going to have the newest microscopes and chemistry equipment for their laboratory. Mr. Donleavy didn't leave us long in the dark over who made these improvements available to Central High. Nor were we to be ignored in the general betterment scheme he had in mind. **37**

He said that he had pointed out to people at a very high level that one of the first-line football tacklers at Arkansas Agricultural and Mechanical College had graduated from good old Lafayette County Training School. Here fewer Amen's were heard. Those few that did break through lay dully in the air with the heaviness of habit. **38**

He went on to praise us. He went on to say how he had bragged that "one **39** of the best basketball players at Fish sank his first ball right here at Lafayette County Training School."

40   The white kids were going to have a chance to become Galileos and Madame Curies and Edisons and Gauguins, and our boys (the girls weren't even in on it) would try to be Jesse Owenses and Joe Louises.

41   Owens and the Brown Bomber were great heroes in our world, but what school official in the white-goddom of Little Rock had the right to decide that those two men must be our only heroes? Who decided that for Henry Reed to become a scientist he had to work like George Washington Carver, as a bootblack, to buy a lousy microscope? Bailey was obviously always going to be too small to be an athlete, so which concrete angel glued to what county seat had decided that if my brother wanted to become a lawyer he had to first pay penance for his skin by picking cotton and hoeing corn and studying correspondence books at night for twenty years?

42   The man's dead words fell like bricks around the auditorium and too many settled in my belly. Constrained by hard-learned manners I couldn't look behind me, but to my left and right the proud graduating class of 1940 had dropped their heads. Every girl in my row had found something new to do with her handkerchief. Some folded the tiny squares into love knots, some into triangles, but most were wadding them, then pressing them flat on their yellow laps.

43   On the dais, the ancient tragedy was being replayed. Professor Parsons sat, a sculptor's reject, rigid. His large, heavy body seemed devoid of will or willingness, and his eyes said he was no longer with us. The other teachers examined the flag (which was draped stage right) or their notes, or the windows which opened on our now-famous playing diamond.

44   Graduation, the hush-hush magic time of frills and gifts and congratulations and diplomas, was finished for me before my name was called. The accomplishment was nothing. The meticulous maps, drawn in three colors of ink, learning and spelling decasyllabic words, memorizing the whole of *The Rape of Lucrece*—it was nothing. Donleavy had exposed us.

45   We were maid and farmers, handymen and washerwomen, and anything higher that we aspired to was farcical and presumptuous. Then I wished that Gabriel Prosser and Nat Turner had killed all whitefolks in their beds and that Abraham Lincoln had been assassinated before the signing of the Emancipation Proclamation, and that Harriet Tubman had been killed by that blow on her head and Christopher Columbus had drowned in the *Santa Maria.*

46   It was awful to be Negro and have no control over my life. It was brutal to be young and already trained to sit quietly and listen to charges brought against my color with no chance of defense. We should all be dead. I thought I should like to see us all dead, one on top of the other. A pyramid of flesh with the whitefolks on the bottom, as the broad base, then the Indians with their silly tomahawks and teepees and wigwams and treaties, the Negroes with their mops and recipes and cotton sacks and spirituals sticking out of their mouths. The Dutch children should all stumble in their wooden shoes and break their necks.

The French should choke to death on the Louisiana Purchase (1803) while silkworms ate all the Chinese with their stupid pigtails. As a species, we were an abomination. All of us.

Donleavy was running for election, and assured our parents that if he won we could count on having the only colored paved playing field in that part of Arkansas. Also—he never looked up to acknowledge the grunts of acceptance—also, we were bound to get some new equipment for the home economics building and the workshop.

He finished, and since there was no need to give any more than the most perfunctory thank-you's, he nodded to the men on the stage, and the tall white man who was never introduced joined him at the door. They left with the attitude that now they were off to something really important. (The graduation ceremonies at Lafayette County Training School had been a mere preliminary.)

The ugliness they left was palpable. An uninvited guest who wouldn't leave. The choir was summoned and sang a modern arrangement of "Onward, Christian Soldiers," with new words pertaining to graduates seeking their place in the world. But it didn't work. Elouise, the daughter of the Baptist minister, recited "Invictus," and I could have cried at the impertinence of "I am the master of my fate, I am the captain of my soul."

My name had lost its ring of familiarity and I had to be nudged to go and receive my diploma. All my preparations had fled. I neither marched up to the stage like a conquering Amazon, nor did I look in the audience for Bailey's nod of approval. Marguerite Johnson, I heard the name again, my honors were read, there were noises in the audience of appreciation, and I took my place on the stage as rehearsed.

I thought about colors I hated: ecru, puce, lavender, beige, and black.

There was shuffling and rustling around me, then Henry Reed was giving his valedictory address, "To Be or Not to Be." Hadn't he heard the whitefolks? We couldn't *be,* so the question was a waste of time. Henry's voice came out clear and strong. I feared to look at him. Hadn't he got the message? There was no "nobler in the mind" for Negroes because the world didn't think we had minds, and they let us know it. "Outrageous fortune"? Now, that was a joke. When the ceremony was over I had to tell Henry Reed some things. That is, if I still cared. Not "rub," Henry, "erase." "Ah, there's the erase." Us.

Henry had been a good student in elocution. His voice rose on tides of promise and fell on waves of warnings. The English teacher had helped him to create a sermon winging through Hamlet's soliloquy. To be a man, a doer, a builder, a leader, or to be a tool, an unfunny joke, a crusher of funky toadstools. I marveled that Henry could go through with the speech as if we had a choice.

I had been listening and silently rebutting each sentence with my eyes closed; then there was a hush, which in an audience warns that something unplanned is happening. I looked up and saw Henry Reed, the conservative, the proper, the A student, turn his back to the audience and turn to us (the proud graduating class of 1940) and sing, nearly speaking,

> Lift ev'ry voice and sing
> Till earth and heaven ring
> Ring with the harmonies of Liberty . . .

It was the poem written by James Weldon Johnson. It was the music composed by J. Rosamond Johnson. It was the Negro National Anthem. Out of habit we were singing it.

55   Our mothers and fathers stood in the dark hall and joined the hymn of encouragement. A kindergarten teacher led the small children onto the stage and the buttercups and daisies and bunny rabbits marked time and tried to follow:

> Stoney the road we trod
> Bitter the chastening rod
> Felt in the days when hope, unborn, had died.
> Yet with a steady beat
> Have not our weary feet
> Come to the place for which our fathers sighed?

56   Every child I knew had learned that song with his ABC's and along with "Jesus Loves Me This I Know." But I personally had never heard it before. Never heard the words, despite the thousands of times I had sung them. Never thought they had anything to do with me.

57   On the other hand, the words of Patrick Henry had made such an impression on me that I had been able to stretch myself tall and trembling and say, "I know not what course others may take, but as for me, give me liberty or give me death."

58   And now I heard, really for the first time:

> We have come over a way that with tears has been watered,
> We have come, treading our path through the blood of the slaughtered.

59   While echoes of the song shivered in the air, Henry Reed bowed his head, said "Thank you," and returned to his place in the line. The tears that slipped down many faces were not wiped away in shame.

60   We were on top again. As always, again. We survived. The depths had been icy and dark, but now a bright sun spoke to our souls. I was no longer simply a member of the proud graduating class of 1940; I was a proud member of the wonderful, beautiful Negro race.

61   Oh, Black known and unknown poets, how often have your auctioned pains sustained us? Who will compute the lonely nights made less lonely by your songs, or the empty pots made less tragic by your tales?

62   If we were a people much given to revealing secrets, we might raise monuments and sacrifice to the memories of our poets, but slavery cured us of that weakness. It may be enough, however, to have it said that we survive in exact relationship to the dedication of our poets (include preachers, musicians, and blues singers).

▼ TOPICAL CONSIDERATIONS

1. What signs does Angelou give that reveal graduation to be an important occasion for the children in Stamps? Why do you think it was so important, not only to the children and parents but also to the community?

2. Is there any particular reason why the principal should allude to Booker T. Washington just prior to Mr. Donleavy's speech? How does the audience's response to his speech reflect the black leader's own feelings about how blacks should act toward white people?

3. Angelou appears to have been particularly sensitive to what was happening during the graduation ceremony. What first prompted her to suspect that something was amiss? How does the atmosphere change as Mr. Donleavy's speech progresses? What specifically does he say to cause the change?

4. What does Angelou resent most about Donleavy's remarks? Are his assumptions about the future aspirations of the Lafayette County Training School graduates justified? What clues do we have about the quality of education at Angelou's school that might suggest otherwise? Note Angelou's frequent historical and literary allusions.

5. The Negro National Anthem was not sung at the usual place in the program. Why does its postponement turn out to be a blessing? What effect does it have on Angelou?

6. If Dick Gregory had been attending Angelou's graduation as an adult, he no doubt would have been singing as loudly as the next person. Why? How might graduation have been different if he had been the guest speaker instead of Mr. Donleavy? What might Gregory have said?

7. How is this graduation a "commencement" for Angelou?

▼ RHETORICAL CONSIDERATIONS

1. Look closely at Angelou's first paragraph. What specific word choices does she use to suggest how important graduation is for children and teachers? How do these words contribute to the development of the essay?

2. How would you describe Angelou's point of view? Does she exaggerate the importance of this event? Or do you think her account is fairly accurate? How might the narrative have been different if told by Bailey (Angelou's older brother)? By the minister? By Mr. Donleavy?

3. In paragraph 36, Angelou remarks that "Amens and Yes, sir's began to fall around the room like rain through a ragged umbrella."

What does this suggest about the atmosphere in the room during Mr. Donleavy's speech? What other figurative language does Angelou use?

4. Writers strive to make their material interesting by using specific, concrete details. How successful is Angelou in doing this? Cite specific examples to prove your point.

▼ WRITING ASSIGNMENTS

1. If Maya Angelou were asked to be a guest speaker at Lafayette County Training School today, what do you think she would say? Write her speech. Imitate her frequent allusions to important historical events and literary works.

2. In an essay, describe the graduation ceremonies at Lafayette County Training School from the minister's point of view, from Bailey's, and from Mr. Donleavy's.

3. Write an essay about your own graduation. Describe how you, your classmates, the school, and the community prepared for the event. Use figurative language and other vivid word pictures to recreate the atmosphere of the graduation hall during the ceremony.

4. Maya Angelou concludes, "It may be enough, however, to have it said that we survive in exact relationship to the dedication of our poets (include preachers, musicians, and blues singers)." Write a research paper in which you compare the influence of black poets (include preachers, musicians, and blues singers) from one earlier period (e.g., the Harlem Renaissance or the Charlie Parker days or the Martin Luther King era) to black poets of the 1990s.

▼ SALVATION
Langston Hughes

Langston Hughes (1902–1967) was a remarkably prolific and celebrated writer. In addition to his autobiography, *The Big Sea* (1940), Hughes published seventeen books of poetry, two novels, seven short story collections, and twenty-six plays. He also wrote a column for the *New York Post*. Much of his life was devoted to the promotion of black art, music, and history. In the essay below, Hughes looks back to a dramatic event that took place when he was twelve—an event that would forever leave its mark on him. The essay, taken from his autobiography, is a fine example of how a writer's control of language and detail can recreate the point of view of a child.

1 I was saved from sin when I was going on thirteen. But not really saved. It happened like this. There was a big revival at my Auntie Reed's church. Every night for weeks there had been much preaching, singing, praying, and shouting, and some very hardened sinners had been brought to Christ, and the membership of the church had grown by leaps and bounds. Then just before the revival ended, they held a special meeting for children, "to bring the young lambs to the fold." My aunt spoke of it for days ahead. That night I was escorted to the front row and placed on the mourners' bench with all the other young sinners, who had not yet been brought to Jesus.

2 My aunt told me that when you were saved you saw a light, and something happened to you inside! And Jesus came into your life! And God was with you from then on! She said you could see and hear and feel Jesus in your soul. I believed her. I have heard a great many old people say the same thing and it seemed to me they ought to know. So I sat there calmly in the hot, crowded church, waiting for Jesus to come to me.

3 The preacher preached a wonderful rhythmical sermon, all moans and shouts and lonely cries and dire pictures of hell, and then he sang a song about the ninety and nine safe in the fold, but one little lamb was left out in the cold. Then he said: "Won't you come? Won't you come to Jesus? Young lambs, won't you come?" And he held out his arms to all us young sinners there on the mourners' bench. And the little girls cried. And some of them jumped up and went to Jesus right away. But most of us just sat there.

4 A great many old people came and knelt around us and prayed, old women with jet-black faces and braided hair, old men with work-gnarled hands. And the church sang a song about the lower lights are burning, some poor sinners to be saved. And the whole building rocked with prayer and song.

5 Still I kept waiting to *see* Jesus.

6 Finally all the young people had gone to the altar and were saved, but one

boy and me. He was a rounder's son named Westley. Westley and I were surrounded by sisters and deacons praying. It was very hot in the church, and getting late now. Finally Westley said to me in a whisper: "God damn! I'm tired o'sitting here. Let's get up and be saved." So he got up and was saved.

7   Then I was left all alone on the mourners' bench. My aunt came and knelt at my knees and cried, while prayers and songs swirled all around me in the little church. The whole congregation prayed for me alone, in a mighty wail of moans and voices. And I kept waiting serenely for Jesus, waiting, waiting—but he didn't come. I wanted to see him, but nothing happened to me. Nothing! I wanted something to happen to me, but nothing happened.

8   I heard the songs and the minister saying: "Why don't you come? My dear child, why don't you come to Jesus? Jesus is waiting for you. He wants you. Why don't you come? Sister Reed, what is this child's name?"

9   "Langston," my aunt sobbed.

10   "Langston, why don't you come? Why don't you come and be saved? Oh, Lamb of God! Why don't you come?"

11   Now it was really getting late. I began to be ashamed of myself, holding everything up so long. I began to wonder what God thought about Westley, who certainly hadn't seen Jesus either, but who was now sitting proudly on the platform, swinging his knickerbockered legs and grinning down at me, surrounded by deacons and old women on their knees praying. God had not struck Westley dead for taking his name in vain or for lying in the temple. So I decided that maybe to save further trouble, I'd better lie, too, and say that Jesus had come, and get up and be saved.

12   So I got up.

13   Suddenly the whole room broke into a sea of shouting, as they saw me rise. Waves of rejoicing swept the place. Women leaped in the air. My aunt threw her arms around me. The minister took me by the hand and led me to the platform.

14   When things quieted down, in a hushed silence, punctuated by a few ecstatic "Amens," all the new young lambs were blessed in the name of God. Then joyous singing filled the room.

15   That night, for the last time in my life but one—for I was a big boy twelve years old—I cried. I cried, in bed alone, and couldn't stop. I buried my head under the quilts, but my aunt heard me. She woke up and told my uncle I was crying because the Holy Ghost had come into my life, and because I had seen Jesus. But I was really crying because I couldn't bear to tell her that I had lied, that I had deceived everybody in the church, that I hadn't seen Jesus, and that now I didn't believe there was a Jesus any more, since he didn't come to help me.

▼ TOPICAL CONSIDERATIONS

1. Why does Hughes say in the first sentence that he was "saved from sin" then, in the second sentence, "But not really saved"?

2. Young Hughes does not get up until the very end. What finally moves him to rise up and be saved? How do his motives compare or contrast with those of Westley's?

3. What reasons does Hughes offer for his crying at the end? How does it compare with his aunt's explanation? What has young Hughes learned from his experience?

4. If you were Hughes's aunt or uncle and were aware of his plight, how might you have comforted young Langston? What words of consolation or explanation would you have offered him?

5. How does Hughes's experience underscore the problems inherent in some people's expectations of religion?

▼ RHETORICAL CONSIDERATIONS

1. Hughes chose to recreate the scene of his actual "salvation" like a short story, rather than simply tell what happened in an expository format. Why do you think he chose this format? How effective do you think his efforts were to recapture the episode?

2. Comment on how effective Hughes was in recreating the scene in the church. Consider his use of descriptive details.

3. Hughes recalls the story of his "salvation" as an adult. How does Hughes's language help create a twelve-year-old's point of view? Find passages where the adult author's attitude toward the experience comes through. How would you describe that attitude?

▼ WRITING ASSIGNMENTS

1. Have you ever had a religious experience? If so, try to describe the circumstances and the experience as best you can.

2. Have you ever been compelled by group pressure to do something you didn't believe in? If so, describe the experience.

3. Write a paper in which you explore your own religious beliefs. Do you believe in a supreme being and find evidence of such in the natural world? Do you not believe in a supreme being? In either case, state the reasons behind your stand.

▼ ANGRY

Julianne Malveaux

Julianne Malveaux is angry and proud of it. "I don't mind raising hell. I thrive on it," she says. In the essay below, the author takes a close look at her anger—where it comes from and where it is focused. As a black woman, she relates her fire to a long tradition of hell-raising, of outrage against the social and political injustices of the world. But she admits to sometimes flying off the handle on issues far less global than race, war, and welfare—such as a friend not keeping a date. With admirable candidness, she tells what hard reflection has taught her: to "fine-tune" her anger, and to pick her battles. A lesson for us all. Julianne Malveaux is an economist and a contributing editor to *Essence* magazine where this article first appeared in May 1989.

1   I don't mind raising hell. I thrive on it. I think of hell-raising as a useful endeavor. Of course, everybody doesn't have a stomach for raising hell. It requires you to get angry, to go out on a limb, to scream and shout, to shake trees and boggle minds, to move people from a comfort zone to a place where they are willing to consider change. In order to raise hell you've got to be an angry person. And that I am. Angry. Angry and proud. Upon hearing myself described by a white feminist as "one of those hostile Black women," I beamed with pleasure because she got exactly what I was putting out: an anger and assertiveness that would not allow her simplest remark—on women, feminism or anything else—to go unchallenged. Her description gave me even more pleasure when I remembered that critics once described James Baldwin as an "angry Black man." If I can walk in company like that, I told myself, that's good company to keep.

2   Anger, writes author Carol Tavris, is a sign of something amiss, something wrong. In her book *Anger: The Misunderstood Emotion,* Tavris writes of women and anger, of targeted anger and of anger used as a tool or weapon. She concludes that anger is okay, but urges women to look carefully at their anger and understand where it comes from and where it is focused.

3   Her book is one of a series of books that examines this intense emotion. In the days of "do your own thing," people were encouraged to shout, scream and get angry to express their feelings. This kind of self-expression was said to be healthy, preferable to holding it in and letting feelings fester. Then other experts began studying anger and raising questions about its unharnessed use. Letting it all out, some said, hurt feelings, left residual resentments and created hostility.

4   I agree with Tavris: Anger is a sign of something gone wrong. Every hell-raiser knows that. What alert Black woman living in this racist society doesn't have a right to be angry? Walk down any city street and see strong and

healthy Black men out of work. Who doesn't feel a burst of anger? Flip through the pages of our federal budget and look at the tax dollars spent on MX missiles and B-1 bombers, not food or books. Isn't that cause for anger? Think about Michael Griffith chased to his death by white men in Howard Beach. Anger. The U.S. Supreme Court trying, again, to snatch our hard-won civil rights by challenging affirmative-action set-asides by asking for "proof" of discrimination in the recent *Richmond* vs. *Croson* ruling. Anger. Or what about the thousands of Black women who crave marriage and families and the forces that conspire to keep them from having them? Anger. And that Bill Moyers special "The Vanishing Family: Crisis in Black America," and the arrogance implicit in his wishful thinking? Anger. Or workfare programs, some of which look like a new kind of slavery, being implemented in city after city? Anger—a reaction to something very wrong.

But there are a lot of wrongs in this unjust world, and as I get older and 5 wiser I consider the advice of people who say "Pick your battles." I can't raise hell all the time; if I did, I'd be a raving, raging fool. So I step back from time to time and ask myself these questions: Why this anger? What does it mean? What do I want to do about it? Reflecting on my anger lets me fine-tune it, revise it, enjoy it, use it as a powerful, motivating tool.

My anger has fueled many a protest, been part of many a movement. My 6 crisp letters, composed in the middle of the night, have caused many an institution to consider change. I got angry about San Francisco's investment in companies doing business in South Africa and wrote a successful initiative to remove pension funds from such businesses. I got angry that Robert H. Bork could be nominated to the Supreme Court, and so prepared dozens of letters for colleagues to send protesting that choice. Thousands of angry people like me, from all over the country, stopped that appointment. I was angry about the Feminization of Power campaign because it excluded the interests of women of color; I wrote an article that was printed in newspapers across the country. I got angry about a woman being denied her food stamps, so I helped her get them back.

Black women have a hell-raising tradition. Many of us share the social 7 anger that I feel, and lots of us do things about it—organize for change, write letters to editors, make phone calls or march in protests. Often our anger is triggered by racism or sexism, but many of us choose to "take no stuff" in our personal lives as well: We speak up when things go wrong instead of swallowing our words to keep the peace. But "take no stuff" women often get labeled "bitches," "hostile" or "Sapphires," and people who are turned off by rage or raised voices parody our legitimate anger as extreme. Many women, not wanting to be "Sapphires," shy away from anger as something unfeminine.

But who defined anger as unfeminine? We can trace Black women's angry, 8 hell-raising responses through the centuries. Angry Harriet Tubman responded to something wrong by leading hundreds of slaves through the Underground Railroad. Angry Sojourner Truth raised her voice and asked "And ain't I a woman?" Angry Ida B. Wells documented lynchings and agitated for change. Angry women from Delta Sigma Theta sorority marched down Pennsylvania

Avenue in 1919 in support of women's suffrage. Angry Mary McLeod Bethune founded the National Council of Negro Women. Angry Rosa Parks said she wouldn't move to the back of the bus. Anger is not a dirty word; it is a justified and understandable response.

9   I'd be less than honest if I described my anger solely as the social kind. Sometimes my angry antennae settle on issues far less global than war and peace, race and rage, welfare and workfare. Yet my personal response to things gone wrong is often as strong as my political one: A friend fails to repay a loan as promised, and I respond with crushing and chilling anger. A man I am seeing fails to show up for a date, and I chew him up and spit him out with stinging words. A neighbor blocks my garage, preventing me from backing my car out; I call her everything but a child of God with wings. I am told that these displays of anger are inappropriate for the incidents that occur. Part of me agrees, but another part of me says I am just drawing lines around my personal rights the same way I do around my political and civil rights.

10   Perhaps I could learn to "lighten up" from time to time, but I respond angrily to people who say they want social change but are unwilling to change the way they treat others. Often at the cost of harmony, I bristle vocally at contradictions. I find it infuriating that a man who works for a civil-rights organization will not pay his child support. That a woman working for an equal-rights–advocacy group will pay her household help less than minimum wage and claim it's economics. That a group of Black women will gather to talk about aging and dignity but not treat other sisters in their community with respect.

11   The minutiae, the little stuff that seems too petty to get angry about, is often an indicator of something bigger. The man who always asks a woman to pour coffee at a meeting can be ignored or he can be called on it, even though he may say it was "unintentional" and do it again. (Of course, "unintentional" discrimination is the kind that has resulted in fewer than 3 percent of all middle managers having Black faces.) And then there are those liberal white people who say they are on "our side" with issues, but behave as if Jim Crow is alive and well. For example, an aide to a progressive congressman who clearly has her head in the right place on issues, but tells me she can't be bothered with the Black press (too small) and makes a point of confusing two Black women who write for the same paper (a mistake, or shades of a racist past?). Or that modern-day Miss Ann who goes to the head of a book line at a "peace and justice" rally because *she* is in a hurry.

12   There is not much one can do about minutiae except point them out and risk being called disruptive, belligerent, hostile, difficult and angry. I'll admit a fourth of that, the angry part. I get angry that you have to go along to get along (if Black people always went along, we'd probably still be picking cotton). Angry enough to distance myself from friends who say I overreact, mind other people's business and take a "hard line" with "good people" who have just made one or two mistakes.

13   Sometimes I joke that I am so angry that I get up in the morning fighting,

but the ability to "pick my battles" is coming to me slowly. I'm learning to cover my trigger points so the gun doesn't always go off. The lesson hit home one Saturday when I sat in a restaurant with friends eating a long, leisurely lunch. Despite the fact that the place wasn't crowded, our waitress kept trying to hustle us out, plopping down the check just as we were asking for another pot of tea and walking by asking "Anything else?" every two minutes. I was shocked, then angered, when I heard her complain loudly that she wished "those Black women" would hurry up and leave. My first inclination was to ask for her supervisor. My second was to picket the place. But my friends sipped their tea with such serenity that I understood that we made our point as much by sitting there as by making an angry scene. I shrugged off my cloak of anger, slipped it around the back of my chair and turned inward, asking myself a series of questions.

Do we angry people have to carry our cloak everywhere? Does our anger prevent us from enjoying our lives? Are we people who must be watched askance because our friends and colleagues don't know what will set us off? When does our anger serve us and when does it do us wrong? When is it "acceptable" and when does it go too far? When should we let our anger go so we can keep our balance? **14**

The way we women show our anger is as personal and unique as everything else about us. Some women wear anger like a special hat, later packing it back into tissue paper until another occasion arises. Others wear it like a stole, shrugging it off only occasionally when the weather makes it oppressive. Some feel anger, then hide it, like money under a mattress or a lace camisole beneath a severely tailored suit. Others exult in their anger like frisky ducks splashing the water for all it's worth. But we should understand that anger, neither bad nor unfeminine, is part of our legacy. It can be shouted or screamed, or even whispered or swallowed, but it is part of us. And when we stop feeling there is something wrong with our society, we will have divorced ourselves from our heritage. **15**

The third cup of tea my friends and I sipped that Saturday was as delicious as the first; it blended with our kinship and my insights to make me feel content. I was glad that we sat at our table until we were ready to go, glad I didn't shatter our tranquility with a lecture to management. We departed in our own sweet time, leaving a small tip and a handwritten note that said, "The tip would have been larger if the service had been better." And we laughed on our way out, not so much at the incident as at the good time we had. **16**

These reflections about anger don't have a resolution; anger never ends for a hell-raiser. As quickly as I learn to probe my anger, I learn to appreciate it. But as I read and think about my hell-raising ways and about the lives of other angry people I have begun to place my anger in some perspective—it doesn't define me, but it is a very essential part of who I am. And so when people ask me what I do, I tell them that I "write, talk and raise hell." In light of my history, I can't suppress the pleasure I feel when I'm described as a "strong and angry" Black woman. **17**

▼ TOPICAL CONSIDERATIONS

1. What specific incidents recollected in Frank Conroy's essay would make Julianne Malveaux angry? How about in Dick Gregory's essay? What do they have in common? Do you think Malveaux's anger would be justified in the examples you chose? Explain.

2. In the opening paragraph, Malveaux is pleased to hear a white feminist call her "one of those hostile Black women." Does she make clear how she has offended the other woman? Why exactly is she pleased? Do you think she has placed race above gender? Consider this issue in your life. Do you feel that your race or your gender more strongly defines who you are as a person? What gets you angry?

3. According to "Angry," what successful initiatives had Malveaux launched as a result of her anger? Have you ever channelled your anger to right a wrong? If so, explain.

4. In the essay how does Malveaux prove that "Black women have a hell-raising tradition"? Malveaux's historical examples end with Rosa Parks. Are there any angry black women in politics, the media, the literary world, or the entertainment world who show that black women of the nineties have continued their hell-raising tradition?

5. Do you think Malveaux is justified in settling her "angry antennae" on personal situations? Consider paragraph 9 and her defense that "another part of me says I am just drawing lines around my personal rights the same way I do around my political and civil rights." Is your political self the same as your personal or social self? Or do you switch on different selves in different situations?

6. What are the paradoxes Malveaux points out in paragraph 10? What causes these contradictions, and do you think she is right not to "lighten up" with respect to this situation? Do you know many people who embody these contradictions, who say one thing and do another? What about yourself?

7. In the first essay in this chapter, "Think About It," Frank Conroy writes, "Education doesn't end until life ends, because you never know when you're going to understand something you hadn't understood before" (paragraph 22). What is Malveaux still learning about? What understanding has she come to and where is she still looking for answers?

▼ RHETORICAL CONSIDERATIONS

1. Look at the similes Malveaux uses to describe anger in paragraph 15. How does she use metaphorical language to show that anger is "neither bad nor unfeminine"?

2. Malveaux begins her essay, "I don't mind raising hell. I thrive on it." How does the tone of the essay prove or disprove the opening statements?

3. In Malveaux's essay several phrases appear in quotation marks. What do phrases such as "Pick your battles" (paragraph 5), "bitches," "hostile," "Sapphires" (paragraph 7), "unintentional" (paragraph 11), "our side" (paragraph 11), and take a "hard line" with "good people" (paragraph 12) have to do with fitting into a predominantly white America?

4. Is the series of questions Malveaux asks in paragraph 14 rhetorical or are they answered in the context of the essay?

▼ WRITING ASSIGNMENTS

1. Malveaux writes that anger "doesn't define me, but it is a very essential part of who I am" (paragraph 17). Write an essay that explores a trait—such as anger, sensitivity, your sense of humor, and so on—that is an essential part of who you are. How has it affected your life? What positive initiatives have been made because of it?

2. Malveaux in paragraph 5 mulls over the advice: "Pick your battles." And she names some of her most difficult battles (paragraph 6). Consider some of your own battles in life. Write an essay that explores the battles you had to pick in. As Malveaux has done, try to get at the roots of these battles.

3. When Malveaux ate a "long, leisurely lunch with friends," she learned that displaying anger wasn't the only way to make a point. Write an essay in which your friends helped you to see a problem and its solution from a different perspective. Re-create the scene and reveal how you came to an understanding.

▼ THE AMBIVALENCE OF ABORTION

Linda Bird Francke

Abortion is one of the most controversial issues in our society. At the heart of all the moral, political, legal, and religious debates is the very definition of life itself. Does it begin at conception, or not? Does a fetus have human status and rights, or not? Science and the courts have not yet resolved these questions, and the issue is further complicated by the demands for a woman's right not to give birth to unwanted children. The author of the piece below powerfully dramatizes this fundamental conflict—a conflict between heart and mind. Francke tells how her strong prochoice convictions suddenly came into question with her own conscience, when faced with her own unwanted pregnancy. Francke, who is a journalist and biographer, collaborated with Rosalynn Carter on *First Lady from Plains* (1984) and with Geraldine Ferraro on her autobiography, *Ferraro* (1986). Her latest collaboration is a work on Madame Jihan Sidat. Francke is also the author of *Growing up Divorced: Children of the Eighties* (1983). This article first appeared in *The New York Times* in 1976.

1　We were sitting in a bar on Lexington Avenue when I told my husband I was pregnant. It is not a memory I like to dwell on. Instead of the champagne and hope which had heralded the impending births of the first, second and third child, the news of this one was greeted with shocked silence and Scotch. "Jesus," my husband kept saying to himself, stirring the ice cubes around and around, "Oh, Jesus."

2　Oh, how we tried to rationalize it that night as the starting time for the movie came and went. My husband talked about his plans for a career change in the next year, to stem the staleness that fourteen years with the same investment-banking firm had brought him. A new baby would preclude that option.

3　The timing wasn't right for me either. Having juggled pregnancies and child care with what freelance jobs I could fit in between feedings, I had just taken on a full-time job. A new baby would put me right back in the nursery just when our youngest child was finally school áge. It was time for *us,* we tried to rationalize. There just wasn't room in our lives now for another baby. We both agreed. And agreed. And agreed.

4　How very considerate they are at the Women's Services, known formally as the Center for Reproductive and Sexual Health. Yes, indeed, I could have an abortion that very Saturday morning and be out in time to drive to the country that afternoon. Bring a first morning urine specimen, a sanitary belt and napkins, a money order or $125 cash—and a friend.

5　My friend turned out to be my husband, standing awkwardly and ill at ease as men always do in places that are exclusively for women, as I checked in at nine A.M. Other men hovered around just as anxiously, knowing they had to be there, wishing they weren't. No one spoke to each other. When I would be cycled out of there four hours later, the same men would be slumped in their same seats, locked downcast in their cells of embarrassment.

The Saturday morning women's group was more dispirited than the men in the waiting room. There were around fifteen of us, a mixture of races, ages and backgrounds. Three didn't speak English at all and a fourth, a pregnant Puerto Rican girl around eighteen, translated for them.   **6**

There were six black women and a hodgepodge of whites, among them a T-shirted teenager who kept leaving the room to throw up and a puzzled middle-aged woman from Queens with three grown children.   **7**

"What form of birth control were you using?" the volunteer asked each one of us. The answer was inevitably "none." She then went on to describe the various forms of birth control available at the clinic, and offered them to each of us.   **8**

The youngest Puerto Rican girl was asked through the interpreter which she'd like to use: the loop, diaphragm, or pill. She shook her head "no" three times. "You don't want to come back here again, do you?" the volunteer pressed. The girl's head was so low her chin rested on her breastbone. *"Sí,"* she whispered.   **9**

We had been there two hours by that time, filling out endless forms, giving blood and urine, receiving lectures. But unlike any other group of women I've been in, we didn't talk. Our common denominator, the one which usually floods across language and economic barriers into familiarity, today was one of shame. We were losing life that day, not giving it.   **10**

The group kept getting cut back to smaller, more workable units, and finally I was put in a small waiting room with just two other women. We changed into paper bathrobes and paper slippers, and we rustled whenever we moved. One of the women in my room was shivering and an aide brought her a blanket.   **11**

"What's the matter?" the aide asked her. "I'm scared," the woman said. "How much will it hurt?" The aide smiled. "Oh, nothing worse than a couple of bad cramps," she said. "This afternoon you'll be dancing a jig."   **12**

I began to panic. Suddenly the rhetoric, the abortion marches I'd walked in, the telegrams sent to Albany to counteract the Friends of the Fetus, the Zero Population Growth buttons I'd worn, peeled away, and I was all alone with my microscopic baby. There were just the two of us there, and soon, because it was more convenient for me and my husband, there would be one again.   **13**

How could it be that I, who am so neurotic about life that I step over bugs rather than on them, who spend hours planting flowers and vegetables in the spring even though we rent out the house and never see them, who make sure the children are vaccinated and inoculated and filled with vitamin C, could so arbitrarily decide that this life shouldn't be?   **14**

"It's not a life," my husband had argued, more to convince himself than me. "It's a bunch of cells smaller than my fingernail."   **15**

16   But any woman who has had children knows that certain feeling in her taut, swollen breasts, and the slight but constant ache in her uterus that signals the arrival of a life. Though I would march myself into blisters for a woman's right to exercise the option of motherhood, I discovered there in the waiting room that I was not the modern woman I thought I was.

17   When my name was called, my body felt so heavy the nurse had to help me into the examining room. I waited for my husband to burst through the door and yell "stop," but of course he didn't. I concentrated on three black spots in the acoustic ceiling until they grew in size to the shape of saucers, while the doctor swabbed my insides with antiseptic.

18   "You're going to feel a burning sensation now," he said, injecting Novocain into the neck of the womb. The pain was swift and severe, and I twisted to get away from him. He was hurting my baby, I reasoned, and the black saucers quivered in the air. "Stop," I cried. "Please stop." He shook his head, busy with his equipment. "It's too late to stop now," he said. "It'll just take a few more seconds."

19   What good sports we women are. And how obedient. Physically the pain passed even before the hum of the machine signaled that the vacuuming of my uterus was completed, my baby sucked up like ashes after a cocktail party. Ten minutes start to finish. And I was back on the arm of the nurse.

20   There were twelve beds in the recovery room. Each one had a gaily flowered draw sheet and a soft green or blue thermal blanket. It was all very feminine. Lying on these beds for an hour or more were the shocked victims of their sex, their full wombs now stripped clean, their futures less encumbered.

21   It was very quiet in that room. The only voice was that of the nurse, locating the new women who had just come in so she could monitor their blood pressure, and checking out the recovered women who were free to leave.

22   Juice was being passed about, and I found myself sipping a Dixie cup of Hawaiian Punch. An older woman with tightly curled bleached hair was just getting up from the next bed. "That was no goddamn snap," she said, resting before putting on her miniskirt and high white boots. Other women came and went, some walking out as dazed as they had entered, others with a bounce that signaled they were going right back to Bloomingdale's.

23   Finally then, it was time for me to leave. I checked out, making an appointment to return in two weeks for an IUD insertion. My husband was slumped in the waiting room, clutching a single yellow rose wrapped in a wet paper towel and stuffed into a Baggie.

24   We didn't talk the whole way home, but just held hands very tightly. At home there were more yellow roses and a tray in bed for me and the children's curiosity to divert.

25   It had certainly been a successful operation. I didn't bleed at all for two days just as they had predicted, and then I bled only moderately for another four days. Within a week my breasts had subsided and the tenderness vanished, and my body felt mine again instead of the eggshell it becomes when it's protecting someone else.

My husband and I are back to planning our summer vacation and his career switch. **26**

And it certainly does make more sense not to be having a baby right now—we say that to each other all the time. But I have this ghost now. A very little ghost that only appears when I'm seeing something beautiful, like the full moon on the ocean last weekend. And the baby waves at me. And I wave at the baby. "Of course, we have room," I cry to the ghost. "Of course, we do." **27**

▼ TOPICAL CONSIDERATIONS

1. What are the reasons the author and her husband do not want another child?
2. How does Francke describe the state of the men in the waiting room of the abortion clinic? What feelings do they seem to share?
3. According to Francke, what "common denominator" links the women at the clinic?
4. In paragraph 13, Francke says she suddenly panicked. Why did she?
5. What had been Francke's political stand on the abortion issue before her visit to the clinic? Do you think she has had a change of heart since? Explain your reasons for your answer.
6. In paragraph 16, Francke admits that she "was not the modern woman" she had thought she was. What does she mean by this statement? Why the term "modern woman"?
7. In paragraph 17, Francke says that she waited for her husband to burst through the door of the operating room and yell "stop." What does this say about what was going on in Francke's mind? What does it say about her own strength of will? Do you think this is another confession that she is not the "modern woman" she thought she was but, rather, one who hopes to be rescued from a bad situation by a man? Or is this a momentary fantasy that goes beyond sex roles?
8. Francke says that the physical pain of the operation was "swift and severe." But the mental pain, though also severe, is not so swift in passing. What evidence is there in the essay that Francke's mental anguish persisted after the operation?

▼ RHETORICAL CONSIDERATIONS

1. What does *ambivalence* mean? How does the author demonstrate ambivalence in the first paragraph? Where in the essay does she actually discuss her ambivalence rather than simply dramatize it?
2. Explain the rhetorical effect of the repetition in paragraph 3: "We

both agreed. And agreed. And agreed." Where else do you find such repetition? Explain its effect, too.

3. This is a highly emotional and moving essay. Does the author convey her emotional trauma by becoming overly emotional or sentimental in the piece? If you think so, cite examples. If you think not, how does she avoid being sentimental?

4. What is the effect of telling us that the Women's Services is formally known as the Center for Reproductive and Sexual Health? What does the name difference suggest about the clinic's self-perception? About the clinic's relationship to the community?

5. Discuss the matter-of-fact tone of paragraph 4. How is Francke's own emotional anxiety sustained by the seemingly neutral tone? Is her tone ironic? Explain your answers.

6. Francke says that the women at the abortion clinic were a mixture of ages, races, and social strata. How would you describe Francke's attitude toward these other women? What is her feeling toward the youngest girl?

7. At the end of paragraph 12, the aide with a smile tells one scared woman, "This afternoon you'll be dancing a jig." What is the effect of the observation of the aide's manner and words? How does it contrast with what is going on inside the author?

8. Discuss the effect of the first two lines of paragraph 19: "What good sports we women are. And how obedient."

9. Why would Francke mention the seemingly minor detail of her husband "clutching a single yellow rose wrapped in a wet paper towel and stuffed into a Baggie" (paragraph 23)? Does this detail have a higher, symbolic function in the essay?

10. Throughout the essay, Francke writes in the past tense. Why did she switch to the present tense in the last two paragraphs? To what effect?

▼ WRITING ASSIGNMENTS

1. Abortion is one of our society's most controversial issues, because what is being debated hinges on the definition of life itself—whether life begins at conception or at birth. Write an essay stating your own feelings about when life begins and about the abortion issue. In your essay, also discuss whether modern science has helped or complicated the problem of determining when life occurs.

2. Write a political speech defending a woman's right to have a legal abortion.

3. Write a political speech against the legalization of abortion.

4. Linda Bird Francke's essay is about her ambivalence on a particularly sensitive social issue. Write a paper in which you face your

own ambivalence about some social issue. Like Francke, consider both sides and explain your ambivalence. You might want to consider some of the other social issues talked about in this book—capital punishment, legalization of drugs, gun control, etc.

5. None of the women at Francke's abortion clinic had used any birth control measures. Write an essay in which you argue for or against compulsory sex education programs in elementary schools. In your essay, be sure to state your stand clearly and give your reasons behind it.

6. Francke's essay is a powerful piece, not just because the issue is highly controversial but because she was caught up in an emotional tug-of-war between strong political convictions and an intense personal experience. If you have ever been caught up in such a conflict between ideals and real experience, write a first-person account describing it, and explore any ambivalence or change of heart you might have experienced as a result. (If you have been a victim of a crime, for example, you might want to consider your attitudes toward criminals and punishment before and after the event.)

▼ ORDINARY SPIRIT

Joy Harjo

Joy Harjo is a poet with a Creek, Cherokee, and French heritage. As a young woman she says that she discovered in writing a form of adventure—one that connected her to the worlds of her mixed blood. In the essay below, Ms. Harjo talks about her experience of writing and the personal discoveries made in the process of crafting some poems. Joy Harjo is a professor of creative writing at the University of New Mexico. She is author of several books of poetry including *What Drove Me to This* (1980), *She Had Some Horses* (1983), and her award-winning *In Mad Love and War* (1991). This essay originally appeared in *I Tell You Now* (1987), a collection of autobiographical essays by Native American writers edited by Brian Swann and Arnold Krupat.

I was born in Tulsa, Oklahoma, on May 9, 1951, after a long hard labor that occurred sporadically for over a week. My mother didn't know it was labor because I wasn't due until mid-July. I also surprised her because I was a single birth; she had been told to possibly expect twins. The birth was hard on both of us. I was kept alive on a machine for the first few days of my life until I made a decision to live. When I looked around I saw my mother, only nineteen, of mixed Cherokee and French blood, who had already worked hard for her short life. And my father, a few years older, a tall, good-looking Creek man who was then working as a mechanic for American Airlines. I don't think I was ever what they expected, but I am grateful that they made my life possible and honor them for it.

2   I was the first of four children who were born evenly spaced over the next eight years or so. And much later had my own children, Phil and Rainy Dawn. We are descended from a long line of tribal speakers and leaders from my father's side. Menawa, who led the Red Stick War against Andrew Jackson, is our great-great (and possibly another great) grandfather. I don't know much about the family on my mother's side except there were many rebels and other characters. They are all part of who I am, the root from which I write, even though I may not always name them.

3   I began writing around the time I was twenty-two years old. I am now thirty-four and feel that after all this time I am just beginning to learn to write. I am only now beginning to comprehend what poetry is, and what it can mean. Each time I write I am in a different and wild place, and travel toward something I do not know the name of. Each poem is a jumping-off edge and I am not safe, but I take more risks and understand better now how to take them. They do not always work, but when they do it is worth it. I could not live without writing and/or thinking about it. In fact, I don't have to think about it; it's there, some word, concept always being born or, just as easily, dying.

4   I walk in and out of many worlds. I used to see being born of this mixed-blood/mixed-vision a curse, and hated myself for it. It was too confusing and destructive when I saw the world through that focus. The only message I got was not belonging anywhere, not to any side. I have since decided that being familiar with more than one world, more than one vision, is a blessing, and know that I make my own choices. I also know that it is only an illusion that any of the worlds are separate.

5   It is around midnight. I often write at this time in my workroom near the front of an old Victorian-style house near downtown Denver. Tonight a thick snow has muffled the sounds of traffic. The world is quiet except for the sound of this typewriter humming, the sometimes dash of metallic keys, and the deep breathing of my dog who is asleep nearby. And then, in the middle of working, the world gives way and I see the old, old Creek one who comes in here and watches over me. He tries to make sense of this world in which his granddaughter has come to live. And often teases me about my occupation of putting words on paper.

6   I tell him that it is writing these words down, and entering the world through the structure they make, that has allowed me to see him more clearly, and to speak. And he answers that maybe his prayers, songs, and his belief in them has allowed him to create me.

7   We both laugh, and continue our work through many seasons.

8   This summer, during one of those sultry summer evenings when the air

hums with a chorus of insects and there's the sound of children playing in the street, I sat, writing. Not actually writing but staring into that space above the typewriter where vision telescopes. I began remembering the way the world was before speech in childhood. A time when I was totally conscious of sound, and conscious of being in a world in which the webbed connections between us all were translucent yet apparent. I remember what it felt like to live within that space, where every live thing had a voice, and each voice/sound an aurora of color. It was sometime during that reminiscence that I began this poem:

SUMMER NIGHT

The moon is nearly full,
                 the humid air sweet like melon.
Flowers that have cupped the sun all day
                        dream of iridescent wings
under the long dark sleep.
                  Children's invisible voices call out
in the glimmering moonlight.
                  Their parents play wornout records
of the *cumbia.* Behind the screendoor
                  their soft laughter swells
into the rhythm of a smooth guitar.
                  I watch the world shimmer
inside this globe of a summer night,
                  listen to the wobble of her
spin and dive. It happens all the time, waiting for you
                        to come home.
There is an ache that begins
                  in the sound of an old blues song.
It becomes a house where all the lights have gone out
                     but one.
And it burns and burns
                  until there is only the blue smoke of dawn
and everyone is sleeping in someone's arms
                  even the flowers
even the sound of a thousand silences.
                  And the arms of night
in the arms of day.
              Everyone except me.
But then the smell of damp honeysuckle twisted on the vine.
And the turn of the shoulder
                  of the ordinary spirit who keeps watch
over this ordinary street.
              And there you are, the secret

of your own flower of light
blooming in the miraculous dark.
(from *Furious Light,* Watershed Foundation cassette, 1986)

9   For years I have wanted to capture that ache of a summer night. This summer in Denver was especially humid, reminded me of Oklahoma. I wanted that feel, in the poem, of a thick, sweet air. And I wanted the voices I remembered, my parents' talking and scratchy, faint music of the radio. In the poem it is my neighbors I hear, and their old records of the *cumbia.* I also wanted to sustain a blues mood, pay homage to the blues because I love the blues. There was the sound of a sensuous tenor saxophone beneath the whole poem. I also added the part of everyone being in someone else's arms, "everyone except me," for the blues effect.

10   But I did not want to leave the poem there, in the center of the ache; I wanted to resolve it. I looked out the front door into the night and caught a glimpse of someone standing near the streetlight, a protecting spirit who was keeping watch over the street. I could have made that up, but I believe it is true. And I knew the spirit belonged in the poem and, because the spirit lives in the poem, too, helps turn the poem around to a place of tender realization. Hence, "And there you are, the secret/of your own flower of light/blooming in the miraculous dark."

11   When I first began writing, poetry was simply a way for me to speak. I was amazed that I could write anything down and have it come out a little more than coherently. Over the years the process has grown more complicated, more intricate, and the world within the poem more immense. In another recent poem the process is especially important:

TRANSFORMATIONS

This poem is a letter to tell you that I
have smelled the hatred you have tried
to find me with; you would like to destroy me.
Bone splintered in the eye of one you choose
to name your enemy won't make it better for you
to see. It could take a thousand years if you name it
that way, but then, to see after all that time, never
could anything be so clear. Memory has many forms.
When I think of early winter I think of a blackbird
laughing in the frozen air; guards a piece of light. I
saw the whole world caught in that sound. The sun
stopped for a moment because of tough belief. I don't
know what that has to do with what I am trying to tell you
except that I know you can turn a poem into something
else. This poem could be a bear treading the far northern
tundra, smelling the air for sweet alive meat. Or a piece
of seaweed stumbling in the sea. Or a blackbird, laughing.

What I mean is that hatred can be turned into something
else, if you have the right words, the right meanings
buried in that tender place in your heart where
the most precious animals live. Down the street
an ambulance has come to rescue an old man who is slowly
losing his life. Not many can see that he is already
becoming the backyard tree he has tendered for years,
before he moves on. He is not sad, but compassionate
for the fears moving around him.
That's what I mean to tell you. On the other side
of the place you live stands a dark woman.
She has been trying to talk to you for years.
You have called the same name in the middle of a nightmare,
from the center of miracles. She is beautiful.
This is your hatred back. She loves you.

When I began writing the poem, I knew I wanted an actual transformation **12** to be enacted within it. I began with someone's hatred, which was a tangible thing, and wanted to turn it into love by the end of the poem. I was also interested in the process of becoming. I tried to include several states of becoming. The "process of the poem" becoming was one. I entered the poem very consciously with lines such as, "I don't know what that has to do with what I am trying to tell you," and "What I mean is. . . ." I also consciously switched tenses partly for that reason, and others. I often change tense within a poem and do so knowing what I am doing. It isn't by accident that it happens. Time doesn't realistically work in a linear fashion.

Within the poem is also the process of the "hater" becoming one who is **13** loved, and who ultimately loves. The "I" is also involved in the process.

Earlier in the day an ambulance came into the neighborhood to pick up an **14** elderly neighbor who had suffered a stroke and was near death. It was a major event. All who witnessed it walked carefully through the rest of the day. I was still thinking of him when I wrote the poem and knew that somehow he, too, belonged in the poem, for he was also part of the transformation.

I was not sure how the poem would end when I began writing it, but looking **15** back I realize the ending must have originated in one of two places. One was a story I heard from a woman who during times of deep emotional troubles would be visited by a woman who looked just like her. She herself would never see her, but anyone passing by her room while she was asleep would see this imaginary woman, standing next to her bed. I always considered the "imaginary" woman as her other self, the denied self who wanted back in.

And I was reminded, too, of the woman who had followed me around at **16** an all-night party in Santa Fe a few years before. We had all drifted around the house, talking, dancing, filled with music and whatever else we had tasted. She finally caught up with me around dawn and told me that she was sorry she was white, and then told me that she believed white people had no souls. I was shocked and sad. And I saw her soul, starved but thinly beautiful, knocking hard on the wall of cocaine and self-hatred she was hiding behind.

17   So the poem becomes a way of speaking to her.

18   It is now very late and I will let someone else take over this story. Maybe the cricket who likes to come in here and sing and who probably knows a better way to write a poem than me.

19   It is not the last song, but to name anything that, only means that I would continue to be amazed at the creation of any new music.

▼ TOPICAL CONSIDERATIONS

1. For Harjo, how is writing like taking a risk? What is unsafe about it? When you are writing, do you feel as if you are taking a risk, accepting a challenge, completing a duty, or embarking on an unknown adventure? What possibilities does writing hold for you? Explain your answers.

2. How has writing empowered Harjo? Trace what writing meant for her in her first days as a writer to its role in her present life. Aside from your own academic experience, is writing a part of your personal life or personal discovery? Can you see writing becoming a part of your future?

3. Harjo writes, "I began remembering the way the world was before speech in childhood" (paragraph 8). Consider Harjo's early memories. How does Harjo's life "before speech" enhance her poetry? What is your earliest memory? Is it a preverbal, sensory perception? Is it possible to have such early vivid memories, or is Harjo simply taking poetic license?

4. What details does Harjo give about her family? How is her family important to her writing? Do you believe that your family and heritage will seep into your writing whether on a conscious or subconscious level?

5. In the essay, Harjo explains the inspiration and meaning behind two poems: "Summer Night" and "Transformations." Do you as a student of literature find Harjo's explanations helpful to your understanding the poem, or do they interfere with your own interpretation of it? After a poet explains her poem, does the reader have the right to offer an alternative meaning? Explain your answer.

6. Harjo's essay is entitled "Ordinary Spirit." In the development of Harjo's spirit, did she ever feel any of the shame Dick Gregory experiences in his essay? If so, how did she recover?

7. In her discussion of the poem "Transformations," Harjo talks about the process of writing a poem. What does she say about this process? What expectations does she have when starting out? What, if anything, did you gain from her explanation of this process?

▼ RHETORICAL CONSIDERATIONS

1. In paragraph 12 what is the meaning of "Time doesn't realistically work in a linear fashion"? How does Harjo reveal this in her prose and in her poetry?

2. Harjo's essay mentions the birth of a child, of a poem, and of a writer. How does the birth/labor imagery in the first paragraph serve as a thematic metaphor for the essay? Cite some passages and try to explain how they work together metaphorically.

3. Harjo's essay revolves around interconnectedness. Examine some of the images in her poem "Summer Night" and show how they appeal to the different senses and how they interconnect.

4. What part of the essay was the most interesting to you? What part was the least interesting? Can you explain the differences between the two?

▼ WRITING ASSIGNMENTS

1. Harjo writes about the birth of herself as a person and as a writer. Write an essay that explains her two births and compare it to your birth as a writer.

2. Harjo writes in "Transformations," "Memory has many forms." Harjo chooses her poetry as one form of memory. Her poetry is filled with memories of smells, tastes, people, sounds, and sights. Write an essay, or a poem, that deals with several connected memories. Capture as many of the senses that you remember from your past.

▼ OUT OF THE FRYING PAN

Rosario Ferré

In the preceding essay, Joy Harjo describes how through poetry she discovers herself while she makes connections to the worlds of her Native
American blood. In the essay below, the daughter of a former governor of
Puerto Rico, Rosario Ferré, explains how through fiction she creates an
all-new identity for herself and "a more compassionate tolerable world."
Recalling the experience of writing her first published story, "La muñeca
menor" ("The Youngest Doll"), she explains how she tried but failed to
make of it a large sociopolitical statement in the style of her literary
mentors, Virginia Woolf and Simone de Beauvoir. Her failure contains a
lesson about the creative process: Do not try to tackle themes beyond you,
your writing will shape itself. Rosario Ferré is the author of several
volumes of short stories, poems, essays, and children's stories as well as
two novels *Maldito Amor* ("Damned Love," 1986) and *Sweet Diamond Dust*
(1988). Ms. Ferré currently teaches literature at Johns Hopkins University.
This essay originally began as a talk to several Latin American literary
conferences and was later translated and published in 1988 for *Lives on
the Line: The Testimony of Contemporary Latin American Authors*, edited
by Doris Meyer.

1   Throughout time, women narrators have written for many reasons: Emily
Brontë wrote to prove the revolutionary nature of passion; Virginia Woolf
wrote to exorcise her terror of madness and death; Joan Didion writes to
discover what and how she thinks; Clarice Lispector discovered in her writing
a reason to love and be loved. In my case, writing is simultaneously a constructive and a destructive urge, a possibility for growth and change. I write to build
myself word by word, to banish my terror of silence; I write as a speaking,
human mask. With respect to words, I have much for which to be grateful.
Words have allowed me to forge for myself a unique identity, one that owes its
existence only to my efforts. For this reason, I place more trust in the words I
use than perhaps I ever did in my natural mother. When all else fails, when life
becomes an absurd theater, I know words are there, ready to return my confidence to me. This need to reconstruct which moves me to write is closely tied
to my need for love. I write so as to reinvent myself, to convince myself that
what I love will endure.

2   But my urge to write is also destructive, an attempt to annihilate myself and
the world. Words are infinitely wise and, like all mothers, they know when to
destroy what is worn out or corrupt so that life may be rebuilt on new foundations. To the degree that I take part in the corruption of the world, I turn my
instrument against myself. I write because I am poorly adjusted to reality;
because the deep disillusionment within me has given rise to a need to re-create

life, to replace it with a more compassionate, tolerable reality. I carry within me a utopian person, a utopian world.

This destructive urge that moves me to write is tied to my need for hate, my need for vengeance. I write so as to avenge myself against reality and against myself; I write to give permanence to what hurts me and to what tempts me. I believe that deep wounds and harsh insults might someday release within me all the creative forces available to human expression, a belief that implies, after all, that I love the word passionately.

Now I would like to address these constructive and destructive forces with relation to my work. The day I finally sat down at my typewriter to write my first story, I knew from experience how hard it was for a woman to obtain her own room with a lock on the door, as well as those metaphorical five hundred pounds a year that assure her independence. I had gotten divorced and had suffered many changes because of love, or because of what I had then thought was love: the renouncing of my own intellectual and spiritual space for the sake of the relationship with the one I loved. What made me turn against myself was the determination to become the perfect wife. I wanted to be as they were telling me I should be, so I had ceased to exist; I had renounced my soul's private obligations. It has always seemed to me that living intensely was the most important of these obligations. I did not like the protected existence I had led until then in the sanctuary of my home, free from all danger but also from any responsibilities. I wanted to live, to enjoy firsthand knowledge, art, adventure, danger, without waiting for someone else to tell me about them. In fact, what I wanted was to dispel my fear of death. We all fear death, but I had a special terror of it, the terror of those who have not lived. Life tears us apart, making us become partners to its pleasures and terrors, yet in the end it consoles us; it teaches us to accept death as a necessary and natural end. But to see myself forced to face death without having known life—without passing through its apprenticeship—seemed to me unforgivable cruelty. I would tell myself that that was why children who die without having lived, without having to account for their own acts, all went to Limbo. I was convinced that Heaven was for the good, and Hell for the evil, for those men who had arduously earned either salvation or damnation. But in Limbo there were only women and children, unaware of how we had gotten there.

The day of my debut as a writer, I sat at my typewriter for a long time, mulling over these thoughts. Inevitably, writing my first story meant taking my first step toward Heaven or Hell, and that made me vacillate between a state of euphoria and a state of depression. It was as if I were about to be born, peering timidly through the doors of Limbo. If my voice rings false or my will fails me, I said to myself, all my sacrifices will have been in vain. I will have foolishly given up the protection that despite its disadvantages, at least allowed me to be a good wife and mother, and I will have justly fallen from the frying pan into the fire.

In those days, Virginia Woolf and Simone de Beauvoir were my mentors; I wanted them to show me how to write well, or at least how not to write poorly.

I would read everything they had written like a person who takes several spoonfuls of a health potion nightly before retiring. The potion would prevent death from a host of plagues and ills that had killed off the majority of women writers before them, as well as some of their contemporaries. I must admit that those readings didn't do much to strengthen my as yet newborn and fragile identity as a writer. My hand's instinctive reflex was still to hold the frying pan patiently over the fire—not to blandish my pen aggressively through the flames—and Simone and Virginia, while recognizing the achievements that women writers had attained up to that time, criticized them quite severely. Simone was of the opinion that women too frequently insisted on themes traditionally considered feminine, the preoccupation with love, for example, or the denunciation of training and customs that had irreparably limited their existence. Justifiable though these themes were, to reduce oneself to them meant that the capacity for freedom had not been adequately internalized. "Art, literature, and philosophy," Simone would say to me, "are attempts to base the world on a new human freedom, the freedom of the individual creator, and to achieve this goal a woman must, above all, assume the status of a being who already has freedom."

7   In her opinion, a woman should be constructive in her literature, not of interior realities, but of exterior realities, principally of those of a historical and social nature. For Simone, the intuitive capacity, the contact with irrational forces, the capacity for emotion, were all important talents, but they were also of secondary importance. "The functioning of the world, the order of political and social events which determine the course of our lives, are in the hands of those who make their decisions in the light of knowledge and reason," Simone would say to me, "and not in the light of intuition and emotion," and it was with those themes that women should henceforth occupy themselves in their literature.

8   Virginia Woolf, for her part, was obsessed with the need for an objectivity and distance which, she thought, had seldom been found in the writings of women. Of the writers of the past, Virginia excluded only Jane Austen and Emily Brontë, because only they had managed to write, like Shakespeare, "with a mind incandescent, unimpeded." "It is deadly for a writer to think about his or her gender," Virginia would say to me, and "it is deadly for a woman to register a complaint, however mild, to advocate a cause, however justifiably"—deadly then, to speak consciously as a woman. In Virginia's opinion, the books of a woman writer who doesn't free herself from rage will contain distortions, deviations. She will write with anger instead of with sensitivity. She will speak of herself, instead of about her characters. At war with her fate, how can she avoid dying young, frustrated, always at odds with the world? Clearly, for Virginia, women's literature should never be destructive or irate, but rather harmonious and translucid as was her own.

9   I had, then, chosen my subject—nothing less than the world—as well as my style—nothing less than an absolutely neutral and serene language, which could let the truth of the material emerge, exactly as Simone and Virginia had advised.

Now I had only to find my starting point, that most personal window, from among the thousands that Henry James says fiction possesses, through which I would gain access to my theme, the window to my story. I thought it best to select a historical anecdote, perhaps something related to how our Puerto Rican bourgeois culture changed from an agrarian one based on sugar cane and ruled by a rural oligarchy to an urban or industrial one ruled by a new professional class, an anecdote that would convey how this change brought about a shift in values at the turn of the century—the abandonment of the land and the replacement of a patriarchal code of behavior, based on exploitation but also on certain ethical principles and on Christian charity, with a new utilitarian code that came to us from the United States.

A story centered on this series of events seemed excellent to me in every way. **10** There was no possibility whatever that I might be accused of useless constructions or destructions; there was nothing further from the boring feminine conflicts than that kind of plot. With the context of my plot finally chosen, I raised my hands to the typewriter, ready to begin writing. Under my fingers, ready to leap to the fore, trembled the twenty-six letters of the Latin alphabet, like the chords of a powerful instrument. An hour passed, two, then three, without a single idea crossing the frighteningly limpid horizon of my mind. There was so much information, so many writable events in that moment of our historical becoming, that I had not the faintest idea where to begin. Everything seemed worthy, not just of the clumsy and amateurish story I might write, but of a dozen novels yet to be written.

I decided to be patient and not to despair, to spend the whole night keeping **11** vigil if necessary. Maturity is everything, I told myself, and this was, after all, my first story. If I concentrated hard enough, I would at last find the starting point of my story. It was dawn and a purple light washed over my study windows. Surrounded by full ashtrays and abandoned cups of cold coffee, I fell into a deep sleep, draped over my typewriter's silent keyboard.

Fortunately, I have since learned that the setbacks we must face don't **12** matter, for life keeps right on living us. That night's defeat, after all, had nothing to do with my love for short stories. If I couldn't write stories I could at least listen to them, and in daily life I have always been an avid listener of stories. Verbal tales, the ones people tell me in the street, are the ones that always interest me the most, and I marvel at the fact that those who tell them tend to be unaware that what they are telling me is a story. Something like this took place a few days later, when I was invited to lunch at my aunt's house.

Sitting at the head of the table, dropping a slow spoonful of honey into her **13** tea, my aunt began to tell a story while I listened. It had taken place at a sugarcane plantation some distance away, at the beginning of the century, she said, and its heroine was a distant cousin of hers who made dolls filled with honey. The strange woman had been the victim of her husband, a ne'er-do-well and a drunkard who had wasted away her fortune, kicked her out of the house, and taken up with another woman. My aunt's family, out of respect for the customs of the time, had offered her room and board, despite the fact that by that time the cane plantation on which they lived was on the verge of ruin. To reciprocate for their generosity she had dedicated herself to making honey-filled dolls for the girls in the family.

14   Soon after her arrival at the plantation, my aunt's cousin, who was still young and beautiful, had developed a strange ailment: her right leg began to swell with no apparent cause, and her relatives sent for the doctor from the nearby town so he could examine her. The doctor, an unscrupulous young man recently graduated from a university in the United States, made the young woman fall in love with him, then falsely diagnosed her ailment as being incurable. Applying plasters like a quack, he condemned her to live like an invalid in an armchair while he dispassionately relieved her of the little money the unfortunate woman had managed to save from her marriage. The doctor's behavior seemed reprehensible to me, of course, but what moved me most about the story were not his despicable acts but the absolute resignation with which, in the name of love, that woman had let herself be exploited for twenty years.

15   I am not going to repeat here the rest of the story my aunt told me that afternoon because it appears in "La muñeca menor," my first story. True, I didn't tell it with the words my aunt used, nor did I repeat her naive praises to a world fortunately gone by, a world in which day-laborers in the cane fields died of malnutrition while the daughters of plantation owners played with honey-filled dolls. But the story I listened to, in its broad outlines, fulfilled the requirements I had imposed on myself: it dealt with the ruin of one social class and its replacement by another, with the metamorphosis of a value system based on the concept of family into one based on profit and personal gain, a value system implanted among us by strangers from the United States.

16   The flame was lit. That very afternoon I locked myself in my study and didn't stop until the spark that danced before my eyes stopped right at the heart of what I wanted to say. With my story finished, I leaned back in my chair to read the whole thing, sure of having written a story with an objective theme, a story absolutely free of feminine conflicts, a story with transcendence. Then I realized that all my care had been in vain. That strange relative, victim of a love that subjected her twice to exploitation by her loved one, had appropriated my story; she reigned over it like a tragic, implacable vestal. My theme, while framed in the historical and sociopolitical context I had outlined, was still love, complaint, and—oh! I had to admit it—even vengeance. The image of that woman, hovering for years on end at the edge of the cane field with her broken heart, had touched me deeply. It was she who had finally opened the window for me, the window that had been so hermetically sealed, the window to my story.

17   I had betrayed Simone, writing once again about the interior reality of women; and I had betrayed Virginia, letting myself get carried away by my anger, by the fury the story produced in me. I confess that I was on the verge of throwing my story into the trash so as to rid myself of the evidence that, in the opinion of my mentors, identified me with all the women writers past and present who had tragically wasted themselves. Luckily I didn't do it; I kept it in

a desk drawer to await better times, to await a day when I would perhaps arrive at a better understanding of myself.

Ten years have passed since I wrote "La muñeca menor," and I have written **18** many stories since then; I think now I can objectively analyze the lessons I learned that day with more maturity. I feel less guilt toward Simone and Virginia because I have discovered that, when one tries to write a story (or a poem or novel), stopping to listen to advice, even from those masters whom one most admires, almost always has negative consequences. Today I know from experience that it is no use to write by setting out beforehand to construct exterior realities or to deal with universal and objective themes if one doesn't first create one's own interior reality. It is no use to try to write in a neutral, harmonious, distant way if one doesn't first have the courage to destroy one's own interior reality. When writing about her characters, a writer is always writing about herself, or about possible versions of herself because, as with all human beings, no virtue or vice is alien to her.

By identifying with the strange relative from "La muñeca menor" I had **19** made possible both processes. On the one hand I had reconstructed, in her misfortune, my own amorous misfortune; and on the other hand, by realizing where her weaknesses and failings were—her passivity, her acceptance, her terrifying resignation—I had destroyed her in my name. Although I may also have saved her. In subsequent stories, my heroines have managed to be braver, freer, more energetic and positive, perhaps because they were born from the ashes of "La muñeca menor." Her betrayal was, in any case, what brought about my fall from the frying pan into the fire of literature.

▼ TOPICAL CONSIDERATIONS

1. For Rosario Ferré, how is writing "simultaneously a constructive and a destructive urge" (paragraph 1)? In your own writing, do you feel these contradictory urges? When have you been able to "reinvent yourself" or "re-create life" (or reality) through your writing?

2. Ten years after completing "La muñeca menor" what does Ferré consider to be integral to the craft? What has she learned since her early days as a writer? How did that affect her relationship with Simone de Beauvoir and Virginia Woolf? At this stage in your writing, do you closely identify with the philosophy of any professional writers? If so, who are they? Explain why you admire them so?

3. According to Ferré, why are women's lives more like children's than men's? Do you feel that in our society only men can earn salvation or damnation?

4. Reread Joy Harjo's "Ordinary Spirit" earlier in this chapter. How vital is writing to both Ferré and Harjo? Does Harjo, like Ferré, write about "interior realities"? What form of self-discovery does

each gain through writing? Look back on your writing career. How has a school assignment, a childhood diary, a daily journal, or a letter to a friend helped you tap your "interior realities" to reach self-discovery?

5. What practical tips can the budding writer gain from Ferré's struggle to become a writer? If you were to write the next Great American Novel, what advice would you take from Ferré?

6. In her essay "Angry," Julianne Malveaux writes that anger "doesn't define me, but is a very essential part of who I am" (paragraph 17). Where in "Out of the Frying Pan" does the reader know that anger is "a very essential part" of who Ferré is, too?

▼ RHETORICAL CONSIDERATIONS

1. How do the length and words in the last sentence in paragraph 9 reflect its meaning in the essay? Is Ferré betraying her own writing style? Is she being true to herself in her choice of topic? Have you ever found yourself writing this way for a difficult school assignment?

2. In the final paragraph, Ferré writes that her characters in other short stories were "braver, freer, more energetic and positive, perhaps because they were born out of the ashes of "La muñeca menor." Being born out of the ashes is an allusion to the mythological Phoenix. Research the symbol of the Phoenix and explain how it relates to the conclusion and to paragraphs 1 and 2.

3. In paragraph 4 Ferré writes, "I knew from experience how hard it was for a woman to obtain her own room with a lock on the door, as well as those metaphorical five hundred pounds a year that assure her independence." This statement is an allusion to Virginia Woolf's famous essay, "A Room Of One's Own," in which she details what is needed for a woman to be a writer. If you didn't know the source of the allusion, does this statement still have any meaning in the essay? Do you think allusions such as this one are effective rhetorical devices for personal essays?

4. Ferré concludes, "Her betrayal was, in any case, what brought about my fall from the frying pan into the fire of literature." What is the "frying pan"? What is the "fire"? How does Ferré's use of the "frying pan into the fire" expression differ from its usual connotation?

▼ WRITING ASSIGNMENTS

1. Simone de Beauvoir and Virginia Woolf had significant impact on Ferré's writing. Consider your own aspirations. Who has influenced

you greatly? Write a paper that explains your admiration for this person and the extent to which his or her philosophy has affected you.

2. Ferré admits that "verbal tales" interest her the most (paragraph 12). Have a relative or friend tell you some tales. Retell, in writing, the story that most impresses you. Put yourself in the place of your characters and try to capture their emotions. After you have written the story, review it objectively for "interior and exterior realities."

3. In paragraph 8, Ferré quotes Virginia Woolf: "It is deadly for a writer to think about his or her gender." Consider Ferré, Julianne Malveaux, and at least one other writer in this chapter. Is gender an integral part of their writing? Would each essay be more powerful if gender was absent from the text on both a literal and subconscious level? Include yourself in this analysis. Do you think of gender when you write, or do you follow Woolf's advice? Write a paper that frames this argument.

4. Ferré's essay deals with the writing process—a process that she finds "constructive and destructive," "a possibility for growth and change." Try to write about your own writing process. How difficult is the process? Can you "reinvent" yourself or create new realities through writing? Or do you write as an observer objectively recording your present self and reality?

2 ▼ FAMILY MATTERS

Our first relationships and, perhaps, our most important are those with the people in our family—our mothers and fathers, siblings, grandparents, and others. It is in the family context where we develop as people and social beings, where we become who and what we are, and where we learn about love. Each of the essays in this chapter will explore some aspect of family identity and love.

The opening piece by Mary Ann Kuharski, "A Family Affair," is occasioned by a large annual family gathering. But in the warm reminiscence the author reflects on the forces of reality that are redefining and reshaping the modern American family.

"In Search of Our Mothers' Gardens" is Alice Walker's homage to her own mother as well as to the generation of nameless black women whose spirit of creativity managed to survive centuries of misery and degradation. The next essay, "My Grandmother, the Bag Lady," is Patsy Neal's tribute to her grandmother. It is also a poignant and loving portrait of an elderly woman who has lost so much of her world and her memory of it.

In "The Aquarium and the Globe" we learn a little of what it was like growing up with two of the most famous anthropologists of the twentieth century for parents—Margaret Mead and Gregory Bateson. Under her parents' guidance, Mary Catherine Bateson tells how childhood interludes with nature led her to profound appreciation of our biosphere.

"Homosexuality: One Family's Affair" is a report of how a family dealt with the announcement that the oldest son was gay. Broken dreams of the parents gave way to anger while the son struggled with loneliness and guilt. And, yet, the story is ultimately a celebration of the power of family love and acceptance.

Randall Williams was born in poverty and raised in its humiliation. Nonetheless, in "Daddy Tucked the Blanket," the author recalls his parents' love—a devotion so intense that it transcended the jagged edge of destitution.

The family is the most basic of society's institutions. It is also the most vulnerable. With the soaring divorce rate, the very structure of the family is being reshaped. The final piece examines divorce and its fallout. However, as she suggests in the title, "Older Children and Divorce," author Barbara Cain approaches the subject from a slant not often taken: the effects of family breakup on college-age children.

▼ A LOVE OF FAMILY AFFAIRS

Mary Ann Delmonico Kuharski

What follows is an evocative description of the family reunion—that ritual coming-together of generations separated by distance and time. The author of this piece gives testimony to the power of the family unit to endow one with a sense of identity, of belonging and acceptance. At the same time she bemoans the mobile and acquisitive among us, too busy to make time to come home. This piece first appeared in *Newsweek* magazine in 1989. Kuharski is a freelance writer who makes her home in Minneapolis, Minnesota.

1   I recently drove my folks to Hudson, Wis. (once known as Little Italy), where more than 200 relatives gathered to celebrate a distant member's 80th birthday. During the drive from Minneapolis, Mom spoke of her high blood pressure, stiff joints and arthritic knees. Dad relived the "last time we went to Hudson," reciting the names of those loved ones who have since died, and reminding us at intervals that it's "tough to get old."

2   When we drove into the parking lot the small-town VFW hall was bursting with music, dancing and a crowd of hand-waving, cheek-pinching Italian mamas and papas.

3   As I watched my folks talk to cousins, nieces, nephews, aunts and uncles, it seemed as if troubles appeared manageable, sorrow bearable, and age took a leap backward. Ten minutes after our arrival, Mom and Dad were joking with relatives about bygone days and shared moments of joy. The warm eyes, gladdened hearts and fond embraces easily erased the added wrinkles and padded waistlines. My mother, a transplanted German from Oelwein, Iowa, blended with Dad's Italian kin as if serving pasta and canning hot peppers was her native birthright. The only giveaway was her name and red hair.

4   "Wilma, you never seem to age. You barely have a wrinkle and you're just as pretty as ever."

5   "Aw Luigi, you old flirt, you always say such nice things. You know I'm getting old . . .," my Mom, who is in her mid-70s, laughingly retorted, looking more youthful and lighthearted as she spoke. A reunion is an invitation to let nostalgia take over, to leave behind the workaday world of stress, the impersonal universe of high-tech pressures.

6   Large family gatherings bring back the sweet and not-so-sweet memories that remind us of who we were and why we were and why we are—those innocent childhoods and perhaps not-so-innocent adolescent antics. It's a time to remember, reminisce, recall and relive.

7   Family members are the people you don't have to work to impress. You can be yourself. There's no test to pass, no fee to belong. You have a right to be included simply because you are.

In family life, there's little room for superficiality, not to say phoniness, **8** arrogance or a "better than thou" attitude. So who's going to be impressed? These are the people who know you best; you're related and they knew you when.

On another side of the family, my husband's brother-in-law travels from **9** Washington state to North Dakota every other year for what has become a family reunion of more than 250 relatives. It's a party he refuses to miss.

My friend Anne goes home to Detroit each Christmas to be with her **10** Serbian relatives. When her mother, the matriarch of the clan, died during the year, they still came together. "She was our reason for going home," Anne said. "Yet now more than before we want to get together, so we don't lose touch."

But it is a demographic fact that America is experiencing the most mobile **11** "disconnected" generation ever. Henry, an acquaintance of ours, is a case in point. He uprooted his wife and children from Minnesota, friends and familiarity for one reason: the promise of more money (read comfort level) in Oklahoma. So it was goodbye hometown. Goodbye Grandma and Grandpa, brothers and sisters. Goodbye friends, neighbors and family ties. And hello Oklahoma and hello money. Only Henry will be able to measure if the profit is worth the loss.

Homestead and heritage: Today children often work and raise their children **12** far from the grandparents whose lives may have to revolve around some antiseptic retirement community. Even holidays that were once exclusively reserved for family are now used by some as mini-vacation opportunities, with little regard for the traditions, custom or kin left behind. We may be nearing an era when Disneyland, Epcot Center and Sea World take precedence over Grandma and Grandpa.

And yet paradoxically, this mobile age has brought with it a fixation on **13** roots and bonds, even if in fleeting, small doses. More and more, we read and hear about giant family reunions when individuals, who bear little more than a last name in common, will eagerly fly across the continent just to be one of the tribe. They'll sleep in cabins, tents, trailers and spare rooms, all for the luxury of congregating with others who claim kinship and mutual ancestry. Not much time for in-depth interaction, mind you—just a few days off for fun and nostalgia. We have the highly mobile strivers who reject family homestead and heritage for adventure and the unknown, and seem to hunger for the very bonds and ties they so easily broke. A reunion, wedding, birthday, anniversary—or, yes, even a funeral can for a brief moment restore the sense of identity and bearings lost when family ties are broken. Perhaps it is not until the ties are broken that many people realize just how much they meant.

In the end, the kids of this generation may be the most deprived of all. Few **14** have experienced the thrill of a big family celebration or know, except in a formal and planned setting, their great Uncle Joe, Aunt Betty and, for that matter, even Grandma and Grandpa.

With today's attitude toward unwanted children and abortion talked of as **15** a choice, I've come to realize that I'm one of the most fortunate of individuals to so freely celebrate the gift of the large Italian family in which I was raised, with all its interwoven roots, shared heritage and sibling ties. After all, I was adopted and have no real bloodlines with anyone in my immediate world. Adopted and twice loved, as the saying goes; once by a mother who selflessly gave me life and a future, and again by a family that taught me how to love and gave me roots and a sense of belonging—as if there'd been a gaping void without me.

▼ TOPICAL CONSIDERATIONS

1. The author says she associates "pasta and canning hot peppers" (paragraph 3) with her Italian background. Are there certain foods that you associate with your family background? Are there special dishes associated with annual gatherings or holidays or special events? If so, describe the foods you associate with such a gathering and tell of their connection with your family.
2. The author says, "Family members are the people you don't have to work to impress" (paragraph 7). Do you agree or disagree with this statement? Explain your answer.
3. What is the paradox in America's being a mobile society? How can it be both beneficial and harmful to the family? Is this mobility the real problem?
4. Kuharski believes, "In the end, the kids of this generation may be the most deprived of all" (paragraph 14). Do you agree? Have you attended a family gathering? If so, describe it. If you have not attended a family affair, do you wish you had? Are you perhaps one of the people the author thinks has been deprived? Explain your response.
5. The author describes the lives of the elderly who have little contact with their children and grandchildren. How does she characterize their lives? Do you agree with her point of view? Why or why not?
6. Why does the author think she is particularly fortunate because of her Italian heritage? Explain your answer.

▼ RHETORICAL CONSIDERATIONS

1. The tone at the beginning is somewhat melancholy when Kuharski describes her parents as old. What clues does she give to the elderly state of her parents? Give specific words or phrases.
2. Paragraph 2 sets the change in tone with "music, dancing and a crowd of hand-waving, cheek-pinching Italian mammas and papas." In paragraph 3 after the family arrives at the VFH hall, how does the description of her parents change? Give examples.
3. The author, in paragraphs 4 and 5, captures some dialogue between

her mother and a relative. Does this dialogue help reinforce the point she makes in the paragraphs before and after? As a reader, do you think the use of dialogue is effective in this essay?

4. In paragraph 11, the author moves from personal experience to more general observations about American families today. Does she lose the reader in this shift of perspective? Or is it a good transition to what follows? Explain.

5. In the last paragraph, the author surprises the reader with a twist. Are we prepared for her revelation about her own background? Do you think this ending is appropriate? Why or why not?

▼ WRITING ASSIGNMENTS

1. Describe a family gathering to a friend. Use as many details as possible to make the experience come alive for the reader. Be sure to explain any ethnic details of food, entertainment or actions that your reader may not know about.

2. Write a letter to the author that voices your opinion of family affairs. You may tell her you hate them, try to avoid them, or wish you had them. Be as honest with her as she has been with you.

3. What do you think of "antiseptic retirement communities"? Discuss the advantages and disadvantages of such communities for older citizens who are the older generation in our families.

▼ IN SEARCH OF OUR MOTHERS' GARDENS

Alice Walker

Alice Walker is an eminent writer who has chronicled the black experience in novels such as *The Color Purple* (1982)—winner of both the Pulitzer Prize and the American Book Award—and *The Temple of My Familiar* (1989). She has written collections of poems, short stories, and essays including *Living by the Word: Selected Writings (1973–1987)* (1988). In the piece below, Ms. Walker seeks to understand how the creativity of black women has survived despite centuries of degradation and misery. With some bitterness she reflects on the shunted lives of black women who never had the freedom or license to be the poets, novelists, and artists they might have been. Yet Walker credits these countless unknown with nurturing and passing on the creative spirit. This discovery is made when Walker remembers her own mother's garden and recognizes it as the place where she cultivated the seed of creativity—her legacy to her daughter.

I described her own nature and temperament. Told how they needed a larger life for their expression. . . . I pointed out that in lieu of proper channels, her emotions had overflowed into paths that dissipated them. I talked, beautifully I thought, about an art that would be born, an art that would open the way for women the likes of her. I asked her to hope, and build up an inner life against the coming of that day. . . . I sang, with a strange quiver in my voice, a promise song.

Jean Toomer, "Avey,"
CANE

1 The poet speaking to a prostitute who falls asleep while he's talking—

2 When the poet Jean Toomer walked through the South in the early twenties, he discovered a curious thing: black women whose spirituality was so intense, so deep, so *unconscious,* that they were themselves unaware of the richness they held. They stumbled blindly through their lives: creatures so abused and mutilated in body, so dimmed and confused by pain, that they considered themselves unworthy even of hope. In the selfless abstractions their bodies became to the men who used them, they became more than "sexual objects," more even than mere women: they became "Saints." Instead of being perceived as whole persons, their bodies became shrines: what was thought to be their minds became temples suitable for worship. These crazy Saints stared out at the world, wildly, like lunatics—or quietly, like suicides; and the "God" that was in their gaze was as mute as a great stone.

3 Who were these Saints? These crazy, loony, pitiful women?

Some of them, without a doubt, were our mothers and grandmothers.   **4**

In the still heat of the post-Reconstruction South, this is how they seemed   **5**
to Jean Toomer: exquisite butterflies trapped in an evil honey, toiling away their
lives in an era, a century, that did not acknowledge them, except as "the *mule*
of the world." They dreamed dreams that no one knew—not even themselves,
in any coherent fashion—and saw visions no one could understand. They wandered or sat about the countryside crooning lullabies to ghosts, and drawing the
mother of Christ in charcoal on courthouse walls.

They forced their minds to desert their bodies and their striving spirits   **6**
sought to rise, like frail whirlwinds from the hard red clay. And when those frail
whirlwinds fell, in scattered particles, upon the ground, no one mourned. Instead, men lit candles to celebrate the emptiness that remained, as people do
who enter a beautiful but vacant space to resurrect a God.

Our mothers and grandmothers, some of them: moving to music not yet   **7**
written. And they waited.

They waited for a day when the unknown thing that was in them would be   **8**
made known; but guessed, somehow in their darkness, that on the day of their
revelation they would be long dead. Therefore to Toomer they walked, and even
ran, in slow motion. For they were going nowhere immediate, and the future
was not yet within their grasp. And men took our mothers and grandmothers,
"but got no pleasure from it." So complex was their passion and their calm.

To Toomer, they lay vacant and fallow as autumn fields, with harvest time   **9**
never in sight: and he saw them enter loveless marriages, without joy; and
become prostitutes, without resistance; and become mothers of children, without fulfillment.

For these grandmothers and mothers of ours were not Saints, but artists;   **10**
driven to a numb and bleeding madness by the springs of creativity in them for
which there was no release. They were Creators, who lived lives of spiritual
waste, because they were so rich in spirituality—which is the basis of Art—that
the strain of enduring their unused and unwanted talent drove them insane.
Throwing away this spirituality was their pathetic attempt to lighten the soul to
a weight their work-worn, sexually abused bodies could bear.

What did it mean for a black woman to be an artist in our grandmothers'   **11**
time? In our great-grandmothers' day? It is a question with an answer cruel
enough to stop the blood.

Did you have a genius of a great-great-grandmother who died under some   **12**
ignorant and depraved white overseer's lash? Or was she required to bake
biscuits for a lazy backwater tramp, when she cried out in her soul to paint
watercolors of sunsets, or the rain falling on the green and peaceful pasture-
lands? Or was her body broken and forced to bear children (who were more
often than not sold away from her)—eight, ten, fifteen, twenty children—when
her one joy was the thought of modeling heroic figures of rebellion, in stone or
clay?

How was the creativity of the black woman kept alive, year after year and   **13**
century after century, when for most of the years black people have been in

America, it was a punishable crime for a black person to read or write? And the freedom to paint, to sculpt, to expand the mind with action did not exist. Consider, if you can bear to imagine it, what might have been the result if singing, too, had been forbidden by law. Listen to the voices of Bessie Smith, Billie Holiday, Nina Simone, Roberta Flack, and Aretha Franklin, among others, and imagine those voices muzzled for life. Then you may begin to comprehend the lives of our "crazy," "Sainted" mothers and grandmothers. The agony of the lives of women who might have been Poets, Novelists, Essayists, and Short-Story Writers (over a period of centuries), who died with their real gifts stifled within them.

14   And, if this were the end of the story, we would have cause to cry out in my paraphrase of Okot p'Bitek's great poem:

> O, my clanswomen
> Let us all cry together!
> Come,
> Let us mourn the death of our mother,
> The death of a Queen
> The ash that was produced
> By a great fire!
> O, this homestead is utterly dead
> Close the gates
> With *lacari* thorns,
> For our mother
> The creator of the Stool is lost!
> And all the young women
> Have perished in the wilderness!

15   But this is not the end of the story, for all the young women—our mothers and grandmothers, *ourselves*—have not perished in the wilderness. And if we ask ourselves why, and search for and find the answer, we will know beyond all efforts to erase it from our minds, just exactly who, and of what, we black American women are.

16   One example, perhaps the most pathetic, most misunderstood one, can provide a backdrop for our mothers' work: Phillis Wheatley, a slave in the 1700s.

17   Virginia Woolf, in her book *A Room of One's Own,* wrote that in order for a woman to write fiction she must have two things, certainly: a room of her own (with key and lock) and enough money to support herself.

18   What then are we to make of Phillis Wheatley, a slave, who owned not even herself? This sickly, frail black girl who required a servant of her own at times—her health was so precarious—and who, had she been white, would have been easily considered the intellectual superior of all the women and most of the men in the society of her day.

19   Virginia Woolf wrote further, speaking of course not of our Phillis, that "any woman born with a great gift in the sixteenth century [insert "eighteenth

century," insert "black woman," insert "born or made a slave"] would certainly have gone crazed, shot herself, or ended her days in some lonely cottage outside the village, half witch, half wizard [insert "Saint"], feared and mocked at. For it needs little skill and psychology to be sure that a highly gifted girl who had tried to use her gift for poetry would have been so thwarted and hindered by contrary instincts [add "chains, guns, the lash, the ownership of one's body by someone else, submission to an alien religion"], that she must have lost her health and sanity to a certainty."

The key words, as they relate to Phillis, are "contrary instincts." For when   **20** we read the poetry of Phillis Wheatley—as when we read the novels of Nella Larsen or the oddly false-sounding autobiography of that freest of all black women writers, Zora Hurston—evidence of "contrary instincts" is everywhere. Her loyalties were completely divided, as was, without question, her mind.

But how could this be otherwise? Captured at seven, a slave of wealthy,   **21** doting whites who instilled in her the "savagery" of the Africa they "rescued" her from . . . one wonders if she was even able to remember her homeland as she had known it, or as it really was.

Yet, because she did try to use her gift for poetry in a world that made her   **22** a slave, she was "so thwarted and hindered by . . . contrary instincts, that she . . . lost her health. . . ." In the last years of her brief life, burdened not only with the need to express her gift but also with a penniless, friendless "freedom" and several small children for whom she was forced to do strenuous work to feed, she lost her health, certainly. Suffering from malnutrition and neglect and who knows what mental agonies, Phillis Wheatley died.

So torn by "contrary instincts" was black, kidnapped, enslaved Phillis that   **23** her description of "the Goddess"—as she poetically called the Liberty she did not have—is ironically, cruelly humorous. And, in fact, has held Phillis up to ridicule for more than a century. It is usually read prior to hanging Phillis's memory as that of a fool. She wrote:

> The Goddess comes, she moves divinely fair,
> Olive and laurel binds her *golden* hair.
> Wherever shines this native of the skies,
> Unnumber'd charms and recent graces rise. [My italics]

It is obvious that Phillis, the slave, combed the "Goddess's" hair every   **24** morning; prior, perhaps, to bringing in the milk, or fixing her mistress's lunch. She took her imagery from the one thing she saw elevated above all others.

With the benefit of hindsight we ask, "How could she?"   **25**

But at last, Phillis, we understand. No more snickering when your stiff,   **26** struggling, ambivalent lines are forced on us. We know now that you were not an idiot or a traitor; only a sickly little black girl, snatched from your home and country and made a slave; a woman who still struggled to sing the song that was your gift, although in a land of barbarians who praised you for your bewildered tongue. It is not so much what you sang, as that you kept alive, in so many of our ancestors, *the notion of song*.

27   Black women are called, in the folklore that so aptly identifies one's status in society, "the *mule* of the world," because we have been handed the burdens that everyone else—*everyone* else—refused to carry. We have also been called "Matriarchs," "Superwomen," and "Mean and Evil Bitches." Not to mention "Castraters" and "Sapphire's Mama." When we have pleaded for understanding, our character has been distorted; when we have asked for simple caring, we have been handed empty inspirational appellations, then stuck in the farthest corner. When we have asked for love, we have been given children. In short, even our plainer gifts, our labors of fidelity and love, have been knocked down our throats. To be an artist and a black woman, even today, lowers our status in many respects, rather than raises it: and yet, artists we will be.

28   Therefore we must fearlessly pull out of ourselves and look at and identify with our lives the living creativity some of our great-grandmothers were not allowed to know. I stress *some* of them because it is well known that the majority of our great-grandmothers knew, even without "knowing" it, the reality of their spirituality, even if they didn't recognize it beyond what happened in the singing at church—and they never had any intention of giving it up.

29   How they did it—those millions of black women who were not Phillis Wheatley, or Lucy Terry or Frances Harper or Zora Hurston or Nella Larsen or Bessie Smith; or Elizabeth Catlett, or Katherine Dunham, either—brings me to the title of this essay, "In Search of Our Mothers' Gardens," which is a personal account that is yet shared, in its theme and its meaning, by all of us. I found, while thinking about the far-reaching world of the creative black woman, that often the truest answer to a question that really matters can be found very close.

30   In the late 1920s my mother ran away from home to marry my father. Marriage, if not running away, was expected of seventeen-year-old girls. By the time she was twenty, she had two children and was pregnant with a third. Five children later, I was born. And this is how I came to know my mother: she seemed a large, soft, loving-eyed woman who was rarely impatient in our home. Her quick, violent temper was on view only a few times a year, when she battled with the white landlord who had the misfortune to suggest to her that her children did not need to go to school.

31   She made all the clothes we wore, even my brothers' overalls. She made all the towels and sheets we used. She spent the summers canning vegetables and fruits. She spent the winter evenings making quilts enough to cover all our beds.

32   During the "working" day, she labored beside—not behind—my father in the fields. Her day began before sunup, and did not end until late at night. There was never a moment for her to sit down, undisturbed, to unravel her own private thoughts; never a time free from interruption—by work or the noisy inquiries of her many children. And yet, it is to my mother—and all our mothers who were not famous—that I went in search of the secret of what has fed that muzzled and often mutilated, but vibrant, creative spirit that the black woman has inherited, and that pops out in wild and unlikely places to this day.

33   But when, you will ask, did my overworked mother have time to know or care about feeding the creative spirit?

The answer is so simple that many of us have spent years discovering it. We **34** have constantly looked high, when we should have looked high—and low.

For example: in the Smithsonian Institution in Washington, D.C., there **35** hangs a quilt unlike any other in the world. In fanciful, inspired, and yet simple and identifiable figures, it portrays the story of the Crucifixion. It is considered rare, beyond price. Though it follows no known pattern of quilt-making, and though it is made of bits and pieces of worthless rags, it is obviously the work of a person of powerful imagination and deep spiritual feeling. Below this quilt I saw a note that says it was made by "an anonymous Black woman in Alabama, a hundred years ago."

If we could locate this "anonymous" black woman from Alabama, she **36** would turn out to be one of our grandmothers—an artist who left her mark in the only materials she could afford, and in the only medium her position in society allowed her to use.

As Virginia Woolf wrote further, in *A Room of One's Own:* **37**

> Yet genius of a sort must have existed among women as it must have existed among the working class. [Change this to "slaves" and "the wives and daughters of sharecroppers."] Now and again an Emily Brontë or a Robert Burns [change this to "a Zora Hurston or a Richard Wright"] blazes out and proves its presence. But certainly it never got itself on to paper. When, however, one reads of a witch being ducked, of a woman possessed by devils [or "Sainthood"], of a wise woman selling herbs [our root workers], or even a very remarkable man who had a mother, then I think we are on the track of a lost novelist, a suppressed poet, of some mute and inglorious Jane Austen. . . . Indeed, I would venture to guess that Anon, who wrote so many poems without signing them, was often a woman. . . .

And so our mothers and grandmothers have, more often than not anony- **38** mously, handed on the creative spark, the seed of the flower they themselves never hoped to see: or like a sealed letter they could not plainly read.

And so it is, certainly, with my own mother. Unlike "Ma" Rainey's songs, **39** which retained their creator's name even while blasting forth from Bessie Smith's mouth, no song or poem will bear my mother's name. Yet so many of the stories that I write, that we all write, are my mother's stories. Only recently did I fully realize this: that through years of listening to my mother's stories of her life, I have absorbed not only the stories themselves, but something of the manner in which she spoke, something of the urgency that involves the knowl- edge that her stories—like her life—must be recorded. It is probably for this reason that so much of what I have written is about characters whose counter- parts in real life are so much older than I am.

But the telling of these stories, which came from my mother's lips as **40** naturally as breathing, was not the only way my mother showed herself as an artist. For stories, too, were subject to being distracted, to dying without conclu- sion. Dinners must be started, and cotton must be gathered before the big rains.

The artist that was and is my mother showed itself to me only after many years. This is what I finally noticed:

41   Like Mem, a character in *The Third Life of Grange Copeland,* my mother adorned with flowers whatever shabby house we were forced to live in. And not just your typical straggly country stand of zinnias, either. She planted ambitious gardens—and still does—with over fifty different varieties of plants that bloom profusely from early March until late November. Before she left home for the fields, she watered her flowers, chopped up the grass, and laid out new beds. When she returned from the fields she might divide clumps of bulbs, dig a cold pit, uproot and replant roses, or prune branches from her taller bushes or trees—until night came and it was too dark to see.

42   Whatever she planted grew as if by magic, and her fame as a grower of flowers spread over three counties. Because of her creativity with her flowers, even my memories of poverty are seen through a screen of blooms—sunflowers, petunias, roses, dahlias, forsythia, spirea, delphiniums, verbena . . . and on and on.

43   And I remember people coming to my mother's yard to be given cuttings from her flowers; I hear again the praise showered on her because whatever rocky soil she landed on, she turned into a garden. A garden so brilliant with colors, so original in its design, so magnificent with life and creativity, that to this day people drive by our house in Georgia—perfect strangers and imperfect strangers—and ask to stand or walk among my mother's art.

44   I notice that it is only when my mother is working in her flowers that she is radiant, almost to the point of being invisible—except as Creator: hand and eye. She is involved in work her soul must have. Ordering the universe in the image of her personal conception of Beauty.

45   Her face, as she prepares the Art that is her gift, is a legacy of respect she leaves to me, for all that illuminates and cherishes life. She has handed down respect for the possibilities—and the will to grasp them.

46   For her, so hindered and intruded upon in so many ways, being an artist has still been a daily part of her life. This ability to hold on, even in very simple ways, is work black women have done for a very long time.

47   This poem is not enough, but it is something, for the woman who literally covered the holes in our walls with sunflowers:

> They were women then
> My mama's generation
> Husky of voice—Stout of
> Step
> With fists as well as
> Hands
> How they battered down
> Doors
> And ironed
> Starched white
> Shirts

How they led
Armies
Headragged Generals
Across mined
Fields
Booby-trapped
Kitchens
To discover books
Desks
A place for us
How they knew what we
Must know
Without knowing a page
Of it
Themselves.

Guided by my heritage of a love of beauty and a respect for strength—in search of my mother's garden, I found my own. 48

And perhaps in Africa over two hundred years ago, there was just such a mother; perhaps she painted vivid and daring decorations in oranges and yellows and greens on the walls of her hut; perhaps she sang—in a voice like Roberta Flack's—*sweetly* over the compounds of her village; perhaps she wove the most stunning mats or told the most ingenious stories of all the village storytellers. Perhaps she was herself a poet—though only her daughter's name is signed to the poems that we know. 49

Perhaps Phillis Wheatley's mother was also an artist. 50

Perhaps in more than Phillis Wheatley's biological life is her mother's signature made clear. 51

▼ TOPICAL CONSIDERATIONS

1. Alice Walker speaks of women who were what poet Jean Toomer called "Saints." Who were these women and why were they referred to as "Saints"?
2. Then Walker refutes Toomer's epithet and calls the black women of the past "Creators," "Artists." In what ways were they "Creators"? "Artists"?
3. Explain how black American women like Phillis Wheatley managed to use their creativity under such adverse conditions.
4. What is the meaning of the title and why does the author say she uses it?
5. In what ways did the author's mother hand "on the creative spark, the seed of the flower they themselves never hoped to see" (paragraph 38)?
6. What does the author mean when she says, "Guided by my heritage

of a love of beauty and a respect for strength—in search of my mother's garden, I found my own" (paragraph 48)?

▼ RHETORICAL CONSIDERATIONS

1. Walker uses strong emotional language to depict the way in which black women were abused. She also uses lyrical language, describing these women as "exquisite butterflies trapped in an evil honey" (paragraph 5). Select an example of Walker's emotional language and explain why it is or is not effective.
2. Walker begins the essay with a quotation from *Cane* by Jean Toomer. Do you think the passage sets the tone for the essay? Do you think this excerpt by a black male is effective?
3. The author takes editorial license when she uses Virginia Woolf's *A Room of One's Own*. Do you think her editorial insertions in Woolf's quotation are effective? What points do these insertions make?
4. Walker next uses a quotation from Phillis Wheatley's poem describing the "Goddess," Freedom. Relate this example to the use of the Woolf quotation. Is there any irony there?
5. In paragraph 27, the author puts herself into the essay when she says, "we have been handed the burdens that everyone else—*everyone* else—refused to carry." This paragraph shows the strong feelings Walker herself has toward the way she and other black women have been treated. Explain the change in tone from this paragraph to the next one.
6. Toward the end of the essay Walker returns to Woolf and again uses editorial insertions. For what purpose does she use them this time?

▼ WRITING ASSIGNMENTS

1. Select a parent or grandparent to describe. Was there a special talent or creativity that person possessed? Write an essay in search of your relative's "garden" and see where it leads you.
2. Consider the roles of race and gender in this essay. If you feel that any of your relatives had their creativity stifled because of their ethnic background or gender, describe the experience in an essay.
3. Write a letter to Alice Walker telling her what language, emotions, or points in her essay moved you in a positive or negive way. Try to be as specific as possible.
4. Interview a relative or an older friend. Ask them to describe a talent that they would have liked to cultivate if their lives had been differ-

ent. If they did cultivate a talent, have them describe it. Present the information you have gathered in an essay called "[Name]'s Garden."

5. Consider the legacy you will leave your children or grandchildren. Write an essay from the point of view of your child or grandchild, describing your "garden."

▼ MY GRANDMOTHER, THE BAG LADY
Patsy Neal

What follows is a touching portrait of an elderly woman, the author's grandmother, whose world has shrunken away to the contents of a paper bag. Not one of the pathetic homeless who roam big-city streets, this "bag lady" lives comfortably in a nursing home with around-the-clock attendants and a family who cares and visits her regularly. Yet she shares with the homeless the loss of possessions, place, and independence. Neal is Wellness Coordinator at Memorial Mission Hospital in Asheville, North Carolina. This article first appeared in the "My Turn" column in *Newsweek* in 1985.

Almost all of us have seen pictures of old, homeless ladies, moving about the streets of big cities with everything they own stuffed into a bag or a paper sack.   1

My grandmother is 89 years old, and a few weeks ago I realized with a jolt that she, too, had become one of them. Before I go any further, I had best explain that I did not see my grandmother's picture on TV. I discovered her plight during a face-to-face visit at my mother's house—in a beautiful, comfortable, safe, middle-class environment with good china on the table and turkey and chicken on the stove.   2

My grandmother's condition saddened me beyond words, for an 89-year-old should not have to carry around everything she owns in a bag. It's enough to be 89, without the added burden of packing the last fragments of your existence into a space big enough to accommodate only the minutest of treasures.   3

Becoming a bag lady was not something that happened to her overnight. My grandmother has been in a nursing home these last several years; at first going back to her own home for short visits, then less frequently as she became older and less mobile.   4

No matter how short these visits were, her greatest pleasure came from   5 walking slowly around her home, touching every item lovingly and spending hours browsing through drawers and closets. Then, I did not understand her need to search out all her belongings.

6   As she spent longer days and months at the nursing home, I could not help noticing other things. She began to hide her possessions under the mattress, in her closet, under the cushion of her chair, in every conceivable, reachable space. And she began to think that people were "stealing" from her.

7   **Unsteady:** When a walker became necessary, my mother took the time to make a bag that could be attached to it, so that my grandmother could carry things around while keeping her hands on the walker. I had not paid much attention to this bag until we went to the nursing home to take her home with us for our traditional Christmas Eve sharing of gifts.

8   As we left, my grandmother took her long, unsteady walk down the hallway, balancing herself with her walker, laboriously moving it ahead, one step at a time, until finally we were at the car outside. Once she was safely seated, I picked up her walker to put it in the back. I could barely lift it. Then I noticed that the bag attached to it was bulging. Something clicked, but it still wasn't complete enough to grasp.

9   At home in my mother's house, I was asked to get some photographs from my grandmother's purse. Lifting her pocketbook, I was surprised again at the weight and bulk. I watched as my mother pulled out an alarm clock, a flashlight, a small radio, thread, needles, pieces of sewing, a book and other items that seemed to have no reason for being in a pocketbook.

10   I looked at my grandmother, sitting bent over in her chair, rummaging through the bag on the walker, slowly pulling out one item and then another, and lovingly putting it back. I looked down at her purse with all its disconnected contents and remembered her visits to her home, rummaging through drawers and through closets.

11   "Oh, Lord," I thought with sudden insight. "That walker and that purse are her home now."

12   I began to understand that over the years my grandmother's space for living had diminished like melting butter—from endless fields and miles of freedom as a child and young mother to, with age, the constrictions of a house, then a small room in a nursing home and finally to the tightly clutched handbag and the bag on her walker.

13   When the family sent her to a nursing home, it was the toughest decision it had ever had to make. We all thought she would be secure there; we would no longer have to worry about whether she had taken her medicine, or left her stove on, or was alone at night.

14   But we hadn't fully understood her needs. Security for my grandmother was not in the warm room at the nursing home, with 24-hour attendants to keep her safe and well fed, nor in the family who visited and took her to visit in their homes. In her mind her security was tied to those things she could call her own—and over the years those possessions had dwindled away like sand dropping through an hourglass: first her car, sold when her eyes became bad and she

couldn't drive; then some furnishings she didn't really need. Later it was the dogs she had trouble taking care of. And finally it would be her home when it became evident that she could never leave the nursing home again. But as her space and mobility dwindled, so did her control over her life.

Dignity: I looked at my grandmother again, sitting so alone before me, hair   15
totally gray, limbs and joints swollen by arthritis, at the hearing aid that could no longer help her hear, and the glasses too thick but so inadequate in helping her to see . . . and yet there was such dignity about her. A dignity I could not understand.

The next day, after my grandmother had been taken back to the nursing   16
home and my mother was picking up in her room, she found a small scrap of paper my grandmother had scribbled these words on:

"It is 1:30 tonight and I had to get up and go to the bathroom. I cannot go   17
back to sleep. But I looked in on Margaret and she is sleeping *so* good, and Patsy is sleeping too."

With that note, I finally understood, and my 89-year-old bag-lady grand-   18
mother changed from an almost helpless invalid to a courageous, caring individ-ual still very much in control of her environment.

What intense loneliness she must have felt as she scribbled that small note   19
on that small piece of paper with the small bag on her walker and her small purse next to her. Yet she chose to experience it alone rather than wake either of us from much-needed sleep. Out of her own great need, she chose to meet our needs.

As I held that tiny note, and cried inside, I wondered if she dreamed of   20
younger years and more treasured possessions and a bigger world when she went back to sleep that night. I certainly hoped so.

▼ TOPICAL CONSIDERATIONS

1. Describe how Neal's 89-year-old grandmother became a bag lady.
2. The grandmother's family sent her to a nursing home to provide security. How did the family's definition of security differ from the grandmother's? How, paradoxically, did the nursing home erode the woman's sense of security?
3. What does the grandmother's note reveal to the author?
4. Although she is feeble and infirm, control is still a major issue for Neal's grandmother. In what ways does she manifest control over her life?

▼ RHETORICAL CONSIDERATIONS

1. How does the labeling of a grandmother as a bag lady capture the reader's attention?

2. What similes does the author use to describe the gradual diminishing of her grandmother's world and possessions? Are they effective? Are they original? Try to supply some of your own, if you can.
3. Did you find the concluding paragraph of the essay sentimental, that is, a deliberate ploy of the author to evoke emotion from the reader?

▼ WRITING ASSIGNMENTS

1. In this essay, seemingly minor events give great insight into the grandmother's character. Write a brief character sketch, in which a seemingly insignificant event (or events) lends insight into the character of someone you know.
2. Write a portrait of someone in your neighborhood, community, or school, who for whatever reasons, does not seem to adjust. Use specific details about the person's behavior and dialogue to capture the individual.

▼ THE AQUARIUM AND THE GLOBE

Mary Catherine Bateson

Mary Catherine Bateson's parents were both renowned anthropologists. Margaret Mead authored *Coming of Age in Samoa* (1928), *Growing up in New Guinea* (1930), and *Male and Female* (1949). Her father wrote several books including Steps to an *Ecology of Mind* (1972) and *Mind and Nature* (1979). In her memoir, *With a Daughter's Eye* (1985), from which this piece is taken, Ms. Bateson remembers growing up with her famous parents. The times described at their New Hampshire retreat exploring blankets of moss, creating worlds in sand, and tending an aquarium seem to blend magic and instruction, to blur education and enchantment. As she explains, these childhood experiences ultimately led her to an appreciation for the interconnectedness of life on our planet. Mary Catherine Bateson is the Clarence Robinson Professor of Anthropology at George Mason University in Fairfax, Virginia. She has written extensively on anthropological and linguistic topics. She is also the author of *Our Own Metaphor* (1987), coauthor of *Thinking AIDS* (1989), and coauthor with her father of *Angels Fear: Towards an Epistemology of the Sacred* (1988). Additionally, in 1990 she published *Composing a Life*.

My parents, Gregory Bateson and Margaret Mead, were scientists and teachers, **1** not only in the wider community in which they worked and published, each becoming famous in different ways and touching many lives, but in the domestic circles of family and friendship as well. For them, the intimate was projected on the widest screen, even as knowledge from far places was worked into the decisions of everyday life. The minds of both sought patterns of completeness, wholes, and so they thought of worlds entire, whether these worlds were minute images of microscopic life within a drop of water or the planet wreathed in cloud.

They thought of worlds and drew me into them. There were worlds to be **2** built and worlds to be imagined, worlds to be held and cherished in two hands and worlds of abstract argument, in spherical tautology. The small primitive societies in which each did ethnographic work were worlds of one kind, complete communities to be described and understood, but along with these there was the challenge to construct and be responsible for the wholeness of family, a world for a child to grow in, a biosphere to protect, the possibility of the bright sphere shattered. Growing up was a passage from the microcosm, a motion through concentric metaphors. Even in the smallest of shared spaces, a camera or a notebook stood for a possible opening up to the macrocosm.

A child moves out through concentric worlds even with her first steps, but **3** whether these worlds are encountered as wholes or as fragments and whether they provide an entry to other spheres of imagination and experience depend on how they are presented, how attention is gradually shaped and the cosmos gradually unfolded.

4   In Holderness, New Hampshire, where we spent many summers, a long field runs down toward the lake. At the bottom, just short of the strip of woods that shields the shore, there lies a broad patch of spring moss, like a bright green eiderdown spread out under the trees. This was a place my mother had picked to be alone with me in counterpoint to the large household in which we stayed. We used to wander there for an hour or so, especially in the early morning. Sometimes we found spiderwebs stretched flat above the moss between protruding grass stems, with dewdrops still shining on them. These she showed to me as fairy tablecloths, the damask spun by tiny fingers, with crystal goblets and silver plates still spread out, for the feckless fairies went off to sleep at dawn without cleaning up. Then she showed me red-tipped lichens as small as a pinhead—fairy roses—and searching along the ground we found their serving bowls, the bases of acorns.

5   My great-grandmother had taught my mother how to identify and draw all the plants of her Pennsylvania childhood, but for me the flowers had only colloquial names and were lenses of fantasy: Indian paintbrush, black-eyed Susan, milkweed, Jack-in-the-pulpit. "I know," she sang, "where the fringed gentians grow."

6   My father had the English habit of latinizing in the woods or in the garden. The intricacies he showed me between the grass stems were of another sort, perhaps a beetle or a moth living out quite different dramas. When I look at the field with his eyes, I see it as a series of complex symmetries and relationships, in which the position of the spiderweb above the moss hints at the pathways of foraging insects. The petals of daisies can be used to count—"He loves me, he loves me not"—because they are not true petals but flowerets—otherwise their number would be set in the precise morphology of the flowering plants.

7   "Once upon a time," my mother would narrate as the sun moved higher in the sky, "in the kingdom between the grass stems, there lived a king and a queen who had three daughters. The eldest was tall and golden-haired and laughing, the second was bold and raven-haired. But the youngest was gray-eyed and gentle, walking apart and dreaming." The story varies but the pattern remains the same, woven from the grass of the meadow and the fears and longings of generations. For this king and queen lived in no anarchic world, but in a world of rhythm and just symmetries. Their labors, quests, and loves grew out of each other with the same elegance that connects the parts of a flowering plant and its cycles of growth. At their court, as at the fairies' banquets, crystal goblets and courtly etiquette reflected a social order. Prince and princess find one another in a world of due peril and challenge and happiness ever after. The flower is pollinated, seed is formed, scattered, and germinated. Look! The silk in the milkweed pods is what the fairies use to stuff their mattresses. Blow on the dandelion down to make a wish, anticipating the wind. Pause in the middle of

fantasy to see the natural world as fragile and precious, threatened as well as caressed by human dreaming.

Worlds can be found by a child and an adult bending down and looking together under the grass stems or at the skittering crabs in a tidal pool. They can be spun from the stuff of fantasy and tradition. And they can be handled and changed, created in little from all sorts of materials. On a coffee table in the center of our living room, which often held toys and projects of mine, I constructed a series of worlds on trays. One of these was meant to depict a natural landscape, built up from rocks and soil, with colored sand and tinted straw-flowers set into it. Another was inspired by a book my father had read to me in which a child constructs a city with cups, dishes, and utensils from the kitchen and then visits it in his dreams. My mother, in that same period, was fascinated by the World Test of Margaret Lowenfield, an English child analyst. This projective test consists of a tray of moist sand and a vast array of miniatures: people and animals, trees and houses and vehicles. In using the test, one molds the soil and handles the objects, arranging and changing them, and then weaves narratives within the world one has created, so that the creation of a microcosm becomes the expression of an inner, psychic world, a world that embodies pain and perplexity as well as symmetry. **8**

The other kind of world that I constructed as a child was represented by a series of aquaria set up with my father. An aquarium is bounded, like a city or a landscape built on a tray, but the discipline that goes into building it is different, for it is alive. In the fantasy world, the discipline is primarily aesthetic; here is the forest and here the open valley; here the dragon lurks and here the river runs. In any aquarium it is necessary to balance the needs of living creatures and their relationships with each other, the cycles of growth and respiration and decay. Here among the thicker water plants, newly spawned swordtails shelter lest they be devoured. The snails that move sedately on the grass control the algae, and on the sandy bottom catfish prowl continually, scavenging the pollution of living that never occurs in fairy tales. **9**

It is not easy to give a child a sense of the integrity of the biosphere. Even today there seem to be few who see themselves as living within and responsible to a single interconnected whole. As a very small child, asked what I wanted for Christmas, I am supposed to have answered that I wanted the world, and my parents gave me a globe. I do not know now whether I found the hollow painted sphere a very satisfactory present. I remember it standing at one end of the long living room for years, next to the aquarium, and yet I am sure that none of us in those days saw the two as metaphors, each of the other, a metaphor that we now can easily make through the mediating symbolism of the picture of the earth as seen from space. **10**

Through my mother's writing echoes the question "What kind of world can we *build* for our children?" She thought in terms of building. She set out to create a community for me to grow up in, she threw herself wholeheartedly into the planning and governance of my elementary school, and she built and sustained a network of relationships around herself, at once the shelter in which I **11** rested and the matrix of her work and thought. Not so my father, for the most complex actual worlds I knew him to set out to build have been aquaria and conferences, temporary constellations of people who learn to think in counterpoint to each other, moving toward a unity of mental process. He was less free than my mother to build and imagine, but I remember him for creating moments of attention when the patterned wonder of some wild place or human interaction became visible.

▼ TOPICAL CONSIDERATIONS

1. Mary Catherine Bateson's parents were famous, yet she remembers them as something far more than that. In what ways were they "scientists and teachers"? How did her parents relate the worlds they studied to her world?
2. Does the author present a flattering portrait of her parents and of her early family life? Explain your answer.
3. Can you recall a special time with a parent or relative when you were younger? Read again paragraph 4 to reflect on the special time and place that the author shared with her mother. Describe a special time and/or place in which you learned something from a parent, relative, or special friend.
4. The author speaks of the worlds she constructed as a child. Describe those worlds. Did you create any "worlds" as a child? Describe any worlds you created.
5. Explain the differences between building a series of worlds on trays and building a series of worlds in aquaria.

▼ RHETORICAL CONSIDERATIONS

1. Do you like Bateson's title? Do you think it is appropriate? How does it relate to her childhood experience?
2. In paragraph 10, Bateson says the globe and aquarium are metaphors "each of the other." How can each represent the other? Explain what you think the author means.
3. The author uses the word *symmetry* several times in the essay. She has a real sense of balance from her parents. Do you think the essay itself is symmetrical? Explain your answer.
4. Bateson uses words like spherical tautology, ethnographic, biosphere, and morphology in this essay. Are you surprised that they are used in an essay describing her childhood memories of her parents? Do you think these words are part of her everyday vocabulary? Why?
5. In the first three paragraphs, the author leads the reader into her

experiences in Holderness, New Hampshire. She talks of the time she spent alone with her mother in paragraphs 4, 5, and 7. What do you think is the function of paragraph 6? Does paragraph 8 lead the reader into paragraph 9 when the author begins speaking again of her experiences with her father?

6. Both Bateson and Mary Ann Delmonico Kuharski use first person point of view. How do they describe their experiences? How do these authors involve the readers?

▼ WRITING ASSIGNMENTS

1. Write a letter to the author comparing the way you learned about nature from your parents or guardians to her upbringing. Use specific details to support your views.

2. Describe how, as a parent, you would raise your child to understand the world and the people in it. Would you put as much emphasis on nature as the author's parents did?

3. As a review for the school paper, summarize this essay giving its strengths and weaknesses. Consider that your audience is other college students.

4. Describe Margaret Mead and Gregory Bateson. Base your responses on their relationship with their daughter.

5. Bateson uses imagery that is rather poetic in this essay. Select a few phrases from the essay and create a poem using some of these phrases.

▼ HOMOSEXUALITY: ONE FAMILY'S AFFAIR

Michael Reese and Pamela Abramson

> The Chronisters lived an ideal American life until their son, Kelly, told them he was gay. It was a moment of dashed expectations for Joan and Paul. That moment was soon followed by anger and anguish, but they gradually began to accept their only son's homosexuality. The report below is the story of the Chronister family's struggle to accept and understand. It is also Kelly's story, the sharing of his pained loneliness and guilt, his depression and fears, and his courage. Thoughtfully and sensitively written, this essay served as a cover story for *Newsweek* in January 1986.

1   It was the hardest question she'd ever had to ask. "Are you gay?" Joan Chronister finally blurted out to her son, Kelly, who was fidgeting at the other end of the sofa. When he begrudgingly, almost bitterly, replied yes, Joan immediately felt her tears and disgust dissolve into detachment. After 22 years of nursing him through mumps and measles, tending his cuts and bruises and applauding his football feats and straight-A report cards, Joan suddenly saw her son as a stranger. *He's my child,* she thought as he walked out the door. *And I don't even know him.*

2   That afternoon Joan sat and sobbed, unsure whether she was crying for Kelly or the family's dashed expectations. He had been named after K. O. Kelly, Brenda Starr's rough-and-tough comic-strip boyfriend, because his father wanted him to be "tough as hell." But expectations die hard, and if Paul Chronister was disappointed that Kelly hadn't always been his idea of tough, it was nothing compared with the betrayal he felt when he learned that his son was homosexual. It was, he says bitterly, like "the son I knew had died, and a new one was born." Four years have passed, and the Chronisters are still trying to cope with that jarring midlife adjustment. It's been both an individual and a family struggle—and has coincided with the nation's heightened awareness of homosexuality because of the AIDS health crisis. What the Chronisters have learned is that there is no easy way for an American family to confront homosexuality. Joan has taped a saying to her refrigerator door to remind herself of that. "Be into acceptance," it says. "Not understanding."

3   The Chronisters' entire notion of homosexuality had been shaped by stereotypes: effeminate men with limp wrists. But Kelly wasn't like that. His preppy good looks, athletic prowess and All-America demeanor never foretold that today, at 26, he would be living with his lover, Randy Ponce, in a fashionable brownstone in a gay enclave of northwestern Portland, Ore. It's just 15 miles south of his parents' tidy ranch house in Vancouver, Wash., but it might as well be a foreign country. Though Joan was raised in a tolerant rural Canadian

family and Paul broke early from his own Pentecostal upbringing, they have remained conservative in their social values—clinging to tenets that took them from being penniless newlyweds to life as owners of three successful pizza franchises in Washington state.

Paul was proud of his own aggressive instincts in business but thought them lacking in his son. "If we could just get him to be a little meaner," Paul would say, "he could go as far as he wanted to go." That wasn't Kelly. He could be competitive, playing a hard game of street hockey or starring as first-string tackle on his high-school football team. But he was always hardest on himself, a perfectionist who still remembers a B in seventh-grade science as a crushing defeat. Even at home Kelly was almost *too* good, always eager to fix dinners and do the laundry. "Odd that a teen-age boy wants to help his mom," Joan remembers thinking. Both she and Paul came to regard Kelly's perfectionism as his greatest fault. "Everyone is looking for the perfect kid," sighs Paul. "Then you have one and you wish they'd be a little bit ornery." **4**

ON THE FRINGE

Kelly saw his perfectionism as a way of hiding from himself and from others. By always being the teacher's pet, by being a hustler in football practice and by being the fringe member of many social groups but the leader of none, Kelly managed to mask his insecurities. Despite his achievements, he had long felt himself an outsider, separate from his peers. He remembers vague sexual feelings as early as the age of seven, when he would linger in the boys' showers after swimming lessons. When his feelings blossomed in his early teens, Kelly had no point of reference and no one he felt comfortable talking to. The only person he even suspected might be gay was a coach whom all the other boys laughed at when they caught him eyeing them in the showers. And though Kelly knew he was only looking for guys when he peeked at his father's girlie magazines, it confused him when he once saw a pornographic picture of a man putting on nylons. "That isn't me," he thought. **5**

It was easier for Kelly to know what he wasn't. He wasn't comfortable when his football buddies told faggot jokes; he knew he might betray himself by not laughing, so he even told a few himself. He wasn't able to join in their postgame drinking and picking-up-girls sprees: he was afraid that if he got drunk the truth might slip out. Most of all, he wasn't interested in girls. He came up with lame excuses for those bold enough to ask him out. When that failed, he made up an imaginary girlfriend who lived out of town and to whom he loudly professed he would always remain loyal. **6**

At home, Kelly's cover-ups were just as elaborate. He refused to ask his parents to buy him a coat and tie for his senior yearbook photo session because he was afraid they would expect him to wear the new clothes to a dance or on a date. Then, when his father inevitably asked why he wasn't going to the senior prom, Kelly could shrug and say he had nothing to wear. The ruse seemed to **7** work. His parents never suspected that their son might be homosexual. That was something entirely beyond their realm of experience; Kelly, they assured each other, was simply shy and would "come out of his shell" in college. But Kelly knew all along that he was postponing the crisis. He saw college as his only escape.

8　　After a few months at Eastern Washington University near Spokane, Kelly began to feel despair. There was no one on campus he even remotely thought might be gay. Then one fall day Kelly found himself on the athletic field staring at another student; the young man returned Kelly's stare, came over and struck up a conversation. That night Kelly agonized over the overture: *Maybe he's gay. Maybe it'll finally happen.* But Kelly still wasn't sure, even when they met again the next day on the athletic field and exchanged an awkward touch. Finally, a few weeks later, they moved into a private music room, where Kelly listened for hours while his friend played the piano. There Kelly had his first sexual experience with another man.

9　　It left him scared, happy but even more confused than before. "What's going to happen to me? What kind of a life will I have?" he kept asking himself between encounters with his friend that continued sporadically for the next four years. "Why do I feel this way?" There were few places to turn for answers. At that time the gay community at Eastern Washington was virtually invisible. There was not—as there is now—a Gay Students' Union nor places that openly offered counseling to gay students. His sexual contact throughout college was restricted to that single relationship. Kelly channeled his energy into his business studies and long, lonely bicycle rides along the wheat fields near campus. He sometimes rode a hundred miles a day, as if just by pedaling hard enough and fast enough he could push away his feelings.

10　　Knowing what he now knew about himself, Kelly couldn't face long family visits or summers working for his father at the pizza parlor. Instead, he moved from the dorms into an apartment of his own, immersed himself in classes and timidly continued his sexual education. He went to the campus bookstore, furtively browsing through gay psychology texts he was too afraid to buy. Through the mail he ordered a "gay guide" of Spokane but couldn't work up the nerve to go into the three gay bars that were listed. Finally, one Thanksgiving, he imploded. After fixing himself Cornish game hen, mashed potatoes, gravy and pumpkin pie, he went for a long walk in the snow. *I know what I am,* he thought, *but why me? Why was I dealt this?* He began to cry. *I'm alone,* he sobbed, *and it's because I'm gay that I'm alone.*

11　　Kelly's fear of rejection meant he could share his secret with no one, especially not his family. When his parents called and teased him about girls, he always responded with a curt "Leave me alone." That's just Kelly's way, they told themselves, glad that at least he seemed to be doing well in school. And when he graduated with high honors in business management, they proudly drove the six hours to Spokane thinking their son's future was made—that surely a wife and grandchildren would soon follow. But Paul never made it to the ceremonies. After suffering chest pains, he was rushed by air ambulance back to Portland for open-heart surgery. Kelly, who had made no firm post-graduate plans, suddenly found himself back in Vancouver watching TV and helping to run the pizza parlors.

He could stand it only for so long. Soon he was back on his bicycle—speeding across the river to Portland, a gay-bar guide tucked in his back pocket. Still too scared to go inside, Kelly usually ended up alone in some shopping-mall restaurant, drinking coffee. That's where he met David, whom Kelly, despite his apprehension, accompanied to his first gay bar, The Rafters. It was not at all what he had imagined. Instead of being dark and ominous, it was bright and friendly; instead of aging drag queens and tough guys in leather, the bar was filled with good-looking young men dancing and having a good time. *They're just average Joes!* Kelly thought. *Guys just like me.* **12**

Kelly didn't feel that way about David, who was loud, flamboyant and sissified in his dress—not at all the sort Kelly wanted his parents to meet. Or did he? To this day, Kelly isn't sure whether he wasn't trying to make a statement the one time he brought David home—or whether he really wanted to slip him out before Joan, eager to meet the first friend Kelly had brought home in years, confronted them at the front door. Joan took one look and went pale. "Oh, my God," she said to Paul after they had left. "That boy with Kelly is queer." **13**

A SECRET SEARCH

She tried to make sense of it. She looked back on Kelly's mood swings, his long, unexplained bike rides into Portland and his almost giddy excitement about going to a Halloween party; that wasn't like Kelly, especially staying out all night with the excuse he'd had too much to drink. But Joan needed proof. Shaking with guilt and apprehension, she steamed open a letter and searched through his dresser drawers, where she found a scrap of paper. Written on it was the title of a book: "Young, Gay and Proud." "He's queer! He's queer!" she screamed, running hysterically into the arms of her husband, who held her and tried to tell her it was going to be OK. **14**

When Joan confronted Kelly the next day, Paul decided to get "the hell out of the house." Unable to face Kelly or more of Joan's tears, Paul beat a hasty overnight retreat to one of his pizza parlors; he felt he needed to be alone with his anger, sadness and confusion. He tried not to place blame, but the thoughts came anyway: "Jesus, Joan was more domineering than I was." He felt anger toward Kelly: "He can't cope with the ladies. He's taking the easy way out." He wondered whether they should send him to a psychiatrist: "You have a flat tire, you fix it." Finally, alone in a motel room, Paul broke down and cried, an uncharacteristic release for a man who always held everything inside. But it didn't help: that night Paul suffered a mild heart attack. **15**

With Paul sick and uneager to talk about Kelly, Joan had no one to share her own quandary. Finally she looked in the Yellow Pages under "H" for homosexuals and then under "G," where she found a listing for a gay-crisis hot **16** line. She was trembling when she picked up the phone, and her voice cracked when she first heard herself say the words out loud: "My son is gay." The hot line put her in touch with another mother, who listened to Joan's story and promised to send her a pamphlet about a support group for friends and parents of gay people. She invited Joan to a Gay Men's Chorus Christmas performance. Joan, accompanied by Kelly's older sister, Rhonda, was overwhelmed to see hundreds of gay men, so many of them just like Kelly. She asked them questions: "Where do you work?" "Where do you live?" "Do your parents accept you?" But most of all she kept asking, "Are you happy?"

ICY STARES

17 Joan realized she'd been closed off from Kelly's world, and she wanted to make up for lost time. But she had to do it on her own. Paul was in retreat, refusing to talk about it or even to acknowledge Kelly when he came home to pick up some of his possessions; he had moved in with a man in Portland. Kelly continued to keep his mother at arm's length; their phone calls and visits consisted of monosyllables and icy stares. Finally, while Paul slumped silently in his chair in the family room, Joan attended a monthly support-group meeting. It took her months to choke out the words: "I'm Joan Chronister and I have a gay son."

18 She listened and learned, quickly realizing that Kelly was not going to change and that no one was to blame. She started manning the hot line and joining excursions to Portland's gay bars. She talked with all kinds of people—from drag queens and lesbians to other parents of gays—and if she couldn't completely understand, at least she was beginning to accept. One June day she attended Portland's Gay Pride Day parade. As she watched the curious crowd go by, Joan noticed a lone man holding a sign, "Parents and Friends of Lesbians and Gay Men." Overcome with emotion, she stepped out into the street and joined him.

19 Paul never marched or went to a support-group meeting. Instead, he stayed at home and hoped time would work its wonders. For a while he thought Kelly might come home lisping and limp-wristed; when he didn't, Paul breathed a sigh of relief and decided it was enough to accept what he'd accepted that first night in his motel room: that as much as he hated Kelly's homosexuality, he could never close the door on his only son. He still doesn't want to know what Kelly's gay life and friends are like, or to imagine what he does inside his bedroom. Joan's transformation into self-proclaimed gay-rights activist sometimes creates a strain. "I don't want to hash it over all the time," says Paul. "But she has the need, an exceptional need."

STABLE RELATIONSHIP

20 It's also hard on Kelly, who is still trying to find a comfortable way to express his sexuality. He's come a long way since he and a boyfriend showed up at Rhonda's wedding wearing identical blazers and pink shirts. Now Kelly tried to

make a softer statement by inviting his parents to dinner and letting his relationship with Randy speak for itself. They met more than two years ago through a mutual friend; they found they shared a distaste for the bar scene and a desire for a stable relationship. Since then they've exchanged identical gold rings, furnished a home together and worked side by side at a suburban Portland video store; with their joint savings account, they now plan to go back to college and maybe start a business. And if Paul still can't bring himself to refer to Randy as his son's "lover," Kelly understands. He knows by the way his father teases and firmly shakes Randy's hand that Paul is, in his own way, making an effort to accept them both.

It is problematic whether the fractures Kelly's homosexuality have opened   21
in the Chronister family will ever completely heal. Paul continues to struggle with his inner anguish and could not bring himself to accompany his wife to the Portland Gay Pride Day parade, where she spoke last June ("My name is Joan Chronister and I'm proud my child is homosexual"). Joan for her part blames her husband for not being more understanding. Both are trying to reach some sort of common ground between themselves.

And for Kelly there remains detachment from his parents and uncertainty   22
about the future. He was all of 10 when the gay-rights movement was born with the 1969 Stonewall Inn riot. And though he has never been inside a bathhouse or slipped into the boozy world of obsessive sex, he knows that AIDS—not cries of liberation—is the historical force shaping his generation of gay men. He hears evangelists call the epidemic divine retribution for crimes against nature and he fears the political backlash that might come. But he has no illusions about changing society—or changing himself. Says Kelly, "It's part of my being."

▼ TOPICAL CONSIDERATIONS

1. How was Kelly's "perfectionism . . . a way of hiding from himself and from others"?
2. When did Kelly first realize that he was gay? How did he deal with that realization?
3. How did Kelly cover up his homosexuality at home?
4. The article says that Kelly anticipated college life "as his only escape" from his crisis. What escape, if any, did campus life afford him?
5. How did Kelly announce to his parents that he was gay?
6. How did Kelly's parents blame themselves for his being gay?
7. How have Joan and Paul Chronister adjusted to Kelly's homosexuality?

▼ RHETORICAL CONSIDERATIONS

1. Where exactly do the authors give their thesis statement?
2. As the title suggests, the article looks at the struggle of the entire

family. Did the authors give equal time to the struggles of each of the three Chronisters?

3. From the tone of the essay, did you feel that the authors were judgmental of any of the Chronisters? If so, explain where.
4. Consider the audience for which this article was written. Would you say that it was addressed to the "enlightened" reader, one who would accept and understand the issues of a gay man coming out? Or would you say the reader addressed is someone who might experience extreme discomfort at the discovery of a gay family member?

▼ WRITING ASSIGNMENTS

1. What are your own feelings regarding homosexuality? Are you tolerant toward gays, or not? Write a paper in which you explore what prejudices you have against gays, if any. You might even talk about how this article affected your attitude toward gays, if it did.
2. How would your parents react if you told them that you were gay? Do you think the news would have an impact like that on Joan and Paul Chronister in the article? Write a paper in which you speculate on how your parents might react to your announcement.

▼ DADDY TUCKED THE BLANKET
Randall Williams

> In this autobiographical account of a young man who grew up in poverty, Randall Williams illustrates the physical and emotional conditions of growing up poor. He also shows how the environment of poverty—the deprivation and humiliation—can destroy a family. Williams is a journalist living in Alabama. This article first appeared in *The New York Times* in 1975.

1   About the time I turned 16, my folks began to wonder why I didn't stay home any more. I always had an excuse for them, but what I didn't say was that I had found my freedom and I was getting out.

2   I went through four years of high school in semirural Alabama and became active in clubs and sports; I made a lot of friends and became a regular guy, if you know what I mean. But one thing was irregular about me: I managed those four years without ever having a friend visit at my house.

I was ashamed of where I lived. I had been ashamed for as long as I had been conscious of class. **3**

We had a big family. There were several of us sleeping in one room, but that's not so bad if you get along, and we always did. As you get older, though, it gets worse. **4**

Being poor is a humiliating experience for a young person trying hard to be accepted. Even now—several years removed—it is hard to talk about. And I resent the weakness of these words to make you feel what it was really like. **5**

We lived in a lot of old houses. We moved a lot because we were always looking for something just a little better than what we had. You have to understand that my folks worked harder than most people. My mother was always at home, but for her that was a full-time job—and no fun, either. But my father worked his head off from the time I can remember in construction and shops. It was hard, physical work. **6**

I tell you this to show that we weren't shiftless. No matter how much money Daddy made, we never made much progress up the social ladder. I got out thanks to a college scholarship and because I was a little more articulate than the average. **7**

I have seen my Daddy wrap copper wire through the soles of his boots to keep them together in the wintertime. He couldn't buy new boots because he had used the money for food and shoes for us. We lived like hell, but we went to school well-clothed and with a full stomach. **8**

It really is hell to live in a house that was in bad shape 10 years before you moved in. And a big family puts a lot of wear and tear on a new house, too, so you can imagine how one goes downhill if it is teetering when you move in. But we lived in houses that were sweltering in summer and freezing in winter. I woke up every morning for a year and a half with plaster on my face where it had fallen out of the ceiling during the night. **9**

This wasn't during the Depression; this was in the late 60's and early 70's. **10**

When we boys got old enough to learn trades in school, we would try to fix up the old houses we lived in. But have you ever tried to paint a wall that crumbled when the roller went across it? And bright paint emphasized the holes in the wall. You end up more frustrated than when you began, especially when you know that at best you might come up with only enough money to improve one of the six rooms in the house. And we might move out soon after, anyway. **11**

The same goes for keeping a house like that clean. If you have a house full of kids and the house is deteriorating, you'll never keep it clean. Daddy used to yell at Mama about that, but she couldn't do anything. I think Daddy knew it inside, but he had to have an outlet for his rage somewhere, and at least yelling isn't as bad as hitting, which they never did to each other. **12**

But you have a kitchen which has no counter space and no hot water, and you will have dirty dishes stacked up. That sounds like an excuse, but try it. You'll go mad from the sheer sense of futility. It's the same thing in a house with no closets. You can't keep clothes clean and rooms in order if they have to be stacked up with things. **13**

14   Living in a bad house is generally worse on girls. For one thing, they traditionally help their mother with the housework. We boys could get outside and work in the field or cut wood or even play ball and forget about living conditions. The sky was still pretty.

15   But the girls got the pressure, and as they got older it became worse. Would they accept dates knowing they had to "receive" the young man in a dirty hallway with broken windows, peeling wallpaper and a cracked ceiling? You have to live it to understand it, but it creates a shame which drives the soul of a young person inward.

16   I'm thankful none of us ever blamed our parents for this, because it would have crippled our relationships. As it worked out, only the relationship between our parents was damaged. And I think the harshness which they expressed to each other was just an outlet to get rid of their anger at the trap their lives were in. It ruined their marriage because they had no one to yell at but each other. I knew other families where the kids got the abuse, but we were too much loved for that.

17   Once I was about 16 and Mama and Daddy had had a particularly violent argument about the washing machine, which had broken down. Daddy was on the back porch—that's where the only water faucet was—trying to fix it and Mama had a washtub out there washing school clothes for the next day and they were screaming at each other.

18   Later that night everyone was in bed and I heard Daddy get up from the couch where he was reading. I looked out from my bed across the hall into their room. He was standing right over Mama and she was already asleep. He pulled the blanket up and tucked it around her shoulders and just stood there and tears were dropping off his cheeks and I thought I could faintly hear them splashing against the linoleum rug.

19   Now they're divorced.

20   I had courses in college where housing was discussed, but the sociologists never put enough emphasis on the impact living in substandard housing has on a person's psyche. Especially children's.

21   Small children have a hard time understanding poverty. They want the same things children from more affluent families have. They want the same things they see advertised on television, and they don't understand why they can't have them.

22   Other children can be incredibly cruel. I was in elementary school in Georgia—and this is interesting because it is the only thing I remember about that particular school—when I was about eight or nine.

23   After Christmas vacation had ended, my teacher made each student describe all his or her Christmas presents. I became more and more uncomfortable as the privilege passed around the room toward me. Other children were reciting the names of the dolls they had been given, the kinds of bicycles and the grandeur of their games and toys. Some had lists which seemed to go on and on for hours.

24   It took me only a few seconds to tell the class that I had gotten for

Christmas a belt and a pair of gloves. And then I was laughed at—because I cried—by a roomful of children and a teacher. I never forgave them, and that night I made my mother cry when I told her about it.

In retrospect, I am grateful for that moment, but I remember wanting to die at the time.   **25**

▼ TOPICAL CONSIDERATIONS

1. Why, after he had turned 16, did Williams not stay home any more?
2. What were some of the conditions of the houses Williams and his family lived in? Why was it so hard to keep those houses neat and clean?
3. How does he characterize his parents? Why, according to the author, did the Williams family never make much "progress up the social ladder"?
4. According to Williams, what was the main reason his parents' marriage fell apart?
5. How do you interpret the last sentence in the essay? Why would Williams be "grateful for that moment"?

▼ RHETORICAL CONSIDERATIONS

1. Where exactly does Williams make his thesis statement?
2. How does the author illustrate the impoverished conditions of his family life?
3. How does Williams illustrate how poverty helped ruin his parents' marriage?
4. Cite some descriptive details Williams employs. Do you think he could have used more?
5. The author's style of writing is quite direct and simple. How is this style created? Consider his sentence length and structure, his vocabulary and expressions, and the length of most of his paragraphs.
6. Why do you think Williams chose the title he did for this essay? Where in the essay does it have particular meaning?
7. Did you find this essay sentimental in places? If so, where? Did you think there were places where Williams consciously avoided being overly emotional or sentimental?

▼ WRITING ASSIGNMENTS

1. We have all seen evidence of poverty; many of us have lived in poverty. Write an essay in which you show through specific illustra-

tions poverty as you have experienced or seen it in your neighbor-hood or city or state, or some place you have visited.

2. Williams talks about how poverty adversely affected his parents. Write an essay in which you describe through illustration how certain conditions affected your parents' relationship. You might choose to talk about how the economic status of your family af-fected them. Or you might focus on sickness in the family, educa-tion, religion, love, children, and so on.

3. Williams selects from his past a few key instances that characterize the relationship between his mother and father. Write an essay in which you recall a few telling moments that help characterize the relationship between your parents.

▼ OLDER CHILDREN AND DIVORCE

Barbara S. Cain

Most studies examining the effect of divorce focus on young children living at home. Unfortunately, the impact of midlife divorce on college-age chil-dren has been a neglected topic. Barbara S. Cain, the author of this article and a clinical supervisor at the Psychological Clinic at the University of Michigan, narrows this gap in research and, at the same time, dispels the myth that older children are less vulnerable to the trauma of divorce. Having interviewed fifty college students between the ages of 18 and 20, Cain discovered recurrent themes and reactions to divorce. In the follow-ing essay, which originally appeared in the *New York Times* Magazine in February 1990, these interviews come to life as students recall the shock, disbelief, and profound sense of loss they experienced when their parents announced their separation. While shedding new light on the fallout of divorce for the older child, this piece is also compelling reading for anyone touched by family breakup.

1 They were more sanguine about Laura. She was, after all, in college and on the far side of growing up. They said she had loosened her tether to the family and was no longer hostage to the twists of their fate. They allowed that she would be shaken for a time by their divorce, but insisted that before long she would find her balance and regain her stride. Her younger brothers, on the other hand, were a constant source of nagging concern. At home and in the eye of the storm, they were in closer range and at higher risk. But Laura, they said, was less vulnerable. Not to worry, Laura would be fine.

So go the prevailing attitudes toward college-age children of a midlife **2** divorce. Moreover, these assumptions appear to be shared by social scientists and cultural tribunes who have rigorously investigated the impact of divorce on younger children but have, nevertheless, overlooked the plight of a college-age population, even though statistics show increased incidence of divorce during midlife, thereby involving greater numbers of young adult offspring.

In an effort to narrow this gap in the literature, a study was launched in **3** 1984 at the University of California at San Diego and the University of Michigan at Ann Arbor—in which 50 college students between the ages of 18 and 26 were interviewed by this writer, who reported the findings in the journal *Psychiatry* in May 1989. There were obvious differences among the students, their families and each individual divorce process, but recurrent themes and threads of discourse wove themselves within and across the interviews with striking regularity.

Perhaps most consistent among them were the students' initial reactions to **4** news of their parents' divorce. All but three in the study recalled an immediate state of shock followed by a lingering sense of disbelief. Even those who grew up amid a turbulent marriage were incredulous when a separation was announced.

"I shouldn't have been surprised," a 20-year-old woman reflected. "I used **5** to hear them argue night after night. I used to hear Mom cry and Dad take off in the car. I used to lie awake until he came back, but he always did come back, so I just assumed they would carry on like that for the rest of their lives."

Others who had observed their parents slowly disengage solaced themselves **6** with the belief that though a marriage of more than two decades might inevitably lose its luster it would not necessarily lose its life. "Sure, I noticed them drift apart," a 21-year-old woman remarked. "But then I surveyed the marriages in our neighborhood, and nobody was exactly hearing violins, so I relaxed and told myself that Mom and Dad were like every other couple who had spent half their lives in one relationship."

An unexpected finding was that more than half the youngsters surveyed had **7** glorified the marriage preceding its breach, claiming theirs was "the all-American family," their parents were "the ideal couple"—and "the envy of everyone they knew."

"I mean I wasn't exactly naïve about divorce," a 19-year-old woman explained. "Half my friends grew up with a single parent, but my Mom and Dad **8** were considered Mr. and Mrs. Perfect Couple. So when they split up, all our friends were just as freaked out as I was."

When the veil of denial began to lift and reality took hold, these young **9** adults experienced a profound sense of loss. They felt bereft of the family of childhood, the one in the photo album, the one whose members shared the same history, the same humor, the same address. Many described in graphic detail the wrenching pain when the family house was sold, when the furniture was divided and delivered to two separate addresses, neither of which "would ever be home."

10   "Nothing really sank in," explained a 20-year-old man, "until I watched the movers denude the house I lived in for most of my life. And then I sat on the bare floor and stared at the marks on the wall which outlined the places where our furniture used to be. And I cried until I couldn't see those borders anymore." Clearly the dismantling of the family house symbolized in stark relief the final dismantling of the family itself.

11   As each parent began living with new partners, the young adults surveyed said that they felt estranged from the resented interloper and displaced by the new mate's younger (often live-in) children. Others felt virtually evicted from the parents' new homes, which simply could not accommodate two sets of children during overlapping visits.

12   "When neither Mom nor Dad had room for me during spring break," a 19-year-old man recalled, "it finally hit me that I no longer had a home to go back to and, like it or not, I'd better get my act together because it was, 'Welcome to the adult world, kid, you're now completely on your own.'"

13   Because the divorce represented the first sobering crisis in their young adult lives, many in the study believed it marked the end of an era of trust and ushered in a new apprehension about life's unforeseen calamities. They reported an unprecedented preoccupation with death, disease and crippling disabilities. They became self-described cynics, and began scanning relationships for subterfuge. "I used to believe what people said," a 22-year-old woman recalled. "I used to trust my roommates. I used to trust my boyfriends, and now I know I also used to be certifiably 'judgment impaired.'"

14   Striking among this age group was the way in which harsh moral opprobrium became the conduit through which anger toward parents was expressed. Pejoratives like irresponsible, self-indulgent and hypocritical punctuated the interviews.

15   "You accept as an article of faith that your parents will stay together until they die," explained a thoughtful 20-year-old woman, "and then they pull the rug out from under you and you want to scream out" and ask, "How can you break the very rules you yourselves wrote?"

16   Many described being gripped by an unforgiving fury toward parents who they felt had deprived them of a home, a family and that inseparable parental pair they assumed would always be there, together, at birthdays, holidays and vacations at home. Furthermore, they viewed these losses to have been preventable, hence they deeply resented learning of the decision when it was a fait accompli. And they upbraided their parents for excluding them from a process they might have otherwise reversed.

17   "Why didn't they tell me they were having trouble?" one young woman asked in barely muted exasperation. "If I had known, I would have helped them find a marriage counselor. If they were unhappy then why didn't they do something about it? My dad spent more time fixing his car than he ever did his marriage."

18   Most in the study blamed the parent who initiated the break and relentlessly hectored that parent for explanations. "Every day I'd ask my mother 'Why,'"

one young woman recalled, "and no answer ever made sense. They all sounded so feeble, and so absolutely wrong."

The young adults surveyed were most staggered by the apparent moral reversals in their parents' behavior. In stunned disbelief, a 20-year-old woman discovered her "buttoned up, Bible-carrying" mother in bed with a man two years older than her son. Another student witnessed his ambitious, seemingly conscience-ridden father walk away from his family and his lucrative law firm for destinations unknown. As though looking through lenses badly out of focus, many gazed upon parents they no longer recognized and struggled over which image was false, which authentic. **19**

"Was the old Mom just hiding under the real one that was coming out now?" a 21-year-old man wondered. "Was that tender, loving person all a lie? Was I just not seeing what I didn't want to see? And if that's true, then how am I supposed to trust what I think I see now?" **20**

Upon observing their mothers' unbridled sexuality, several young women withdrew from romantic relationships, retreated to solitary study, became abstemious and, in Anna Freud's words, declared war on the pursuit of pleasure. **21**

In sharp contrast, others plunged into hedonism, flaunting their indulgences, daring their parents to forbid activity that mirrored their own. A 20-year-old woman launched a series of sexual liaisons with older married men. A 19-year-old moved in with a graduate student after knowing him for 10 days. And a 22-year-old male dropped out of school to deal in drugs. **22**

In response to their parents' apparent moral inversion, a small subgroup temporarily took refuge in a protective nihilism, reasoning that illusions that never form are illusions that never shatter. "Since their breakup I don't pin my hopes on anything anymore," a disenchanted young man declared. "And I no longer have a secret dream. What will be will be. Since I can't change any of that, why even try and why even care?" **23**

At variance with the familiar loyalty conflict observed in younger children of divorce, most young adults considered one parent worthy of blame, the other worthy of compassion. Several openly stated they were sorely tempted to sever ties permanently with the parent who initiated the break. And when asked, "What would you advise someone your age whose parents were divorcing?" many answered, "Do not write one parent off totally, even though you might be tempted to at the time of the split." **24**

Several said they feigned an affectionate tie to the rejected parent simply because of financial need. "Between you and me," a spunky 19-year-old man confessed, "I can't wait till I'm self-supporting, so then I won't have to humor my father with a phony song and dance every time my tuition is due." And a number reported that their overt condemnation of their father cost them a long-enjoyed relationship with paternal grandparents as battle lines between "his" and "her" side of the family were drawn. **25**

Despite their censoriousness and ascriptions of blame, these young adults staunchly insisted that each parent honor their attempted neutrality. "I refused to let my Mom put down my Dad," one 23-year-old man declared emphatically, **26** "and I artfully dodged every invitation to spy on one and report to the other."

27   Remarks such as these suggest that, whatever else, these college-age young-sters are better able than younger children to remove themselves from the internecine warfare and resist colluding with the parent "spurned" in excoriat-ing the parent blamed.

28   In sharp contrast to younger children of divorce who frequently hold them-selves responsible for the separation, the young adults surveyed did not reveal even the slightest traces of guilt or blame. Though most were certain they had not caused their parents' divorce, several lamented having failed to prevent it. A 19-year-old woman believed that had she managed her mother's domestic chores more effectively, her mother would not have ended her marriage in favor of her career. And a 21-year-old woman chided herself for not noticing her parents' estrangement: "Sometimes I still wonder if I had paid more attention to *them,* maybe we would all still be *us.*"

29   And because each youngster in the study was living away from home at the time of the separation, many believed that their parents had literally "stayed together for the sake of the children." Indeed, several parents did not disabuse their children of this notion. When a 20-year-old man accused his father of being foolishly headstrong in abruptly ending his 25-year marriage, his father in-formed him that he had wanted to end his marriage for more than 20 years but had waited until his son was grown and gone.

30   Three in the study proudly announced that they were responsible for their parents' separations and celebrated the fact that they urged upon their mothers a much overdue separation from chronically abusive alcoholic fathers. "Do I feel responsible for my parents splitting? You bet I do," one 24-year-old man trumpeted. "And my only regret is not pushing for it sooner."

31   With few exceptions, the young adults surveyed described an unremitting concern for their single parents, particularly the one who opposed the break. They dropped courses, cut classes, extended weekends away from school in an effort to bolster the spirit of the parent at home. "I flew home so often," one young man mused, "I was awarded three free tickets in less than one year."

32   In striking role reversals, these youngsters disavowed their own wish for support and ministered to their parents instead. They nurtured mothers who cried in their arms, they discouraged fathers from reckless decisions, they vari-ously counseled, succored, reassured and advised. And many reported they were unable to resume the natural rhythms of their lives until their parents were clearly back on track.

33   "I was nervous most of the time I wasn't with my Mom," a 20-year-old man explained. ". . . I called her constantly and went home as often as I could. . . . Deep down, I was worried she'd take her own life or accidentally smash the car as she was thinking about Dad or money or being too old and too fat to start over again."

34   These young adults also assumed the role of proxies. "After the split, I felt I was wearing a thousand hats," a 19-year-old woman recalled. "In one day I could be a college student, my mother's therapist, my dad's escort and my brother's mother. Small wonder I was a little ditzy that year."

After their parents had parted, some of those surveyed recalled allowing **35**
themselves to return to a recently relinquished parent-child relationship in
which they "tolerated" parental overprotection from the "spurned" partner.
They no longer balked at queries about eating habits and dating behavior. "If
Mom's happier treating me like a kid, I'm willing to be that for her," a 20-year-
old man admitted. "She just lost her husband, the least I can do is let her have
her kid." Others described a quasi-symbiotic relationship with one or the other
parent in which both parent and child were by turns both host and parasite.

Though many felt compelled to rescue their parents, several baldly stated **36**
that they deeply resented the "hysterical calls in the middle of the night," the
incessant ruminations about "the same old stuff." It is noteworthy, however,
that those who were enraged by parental pleas and demands felt, nonetheless,
obliged to leave school at times and comfort the beleaguered parent at home.
As a young woman stated succinctly, "If I stayed at school, I was worried about
my Mom; if I went home I was worried about me."

Perhaps the most uniform finding in this study was the radically altered **37**
attitudes toward love and marriage held by many following their parents' divorce.

When a young woman's parents separated soon after their 20th anniver- **38**
sary, she created her own theory of marriage: "People marry in order to have
children, and parenthood is what holds a marriage together. When children are
grown and gone, marriage no longer has a reason for being and couples will then
drift apart and the marriage will slowly die. If couples stay together even after
their last child leaves home, then they are truly in love and they are the lucky
few."

Several categorically forswore marriage, vowing to spare themselves and **39**
their unborn children the pain and dislocation they had recently endured. Others allowed for a long-term live-in relationship but pledged to forestall indefinitely a legally binding commitment. A disenchanted young man spoke for
many: "Since their divorce, I'm gun-shy about love and spastic about marriage.
To me, getting married is like walking over a minefield, you know it's going to
explode . . . you just don't know when!"

Those who were already involved in longstanding romances felt their par- **40**
ents' divorce cast a long shadow on their own relationship. As a 20-year-old
woman explained: "You become super alert to everything your boyfriend does.
You suddenly notice his wandering eye as you walk together across campus.
You start resenting it when he yawns or fidgets or looks at his watch while
you're talking. And you spend a whole lot of time holding your breath braced
for the moment when he hits you with, 'I mean I really like you, but I really need
more space.' "

Some young women withdrew from boyfriends they suddenly suspected as **41**
being unfaithful, indifferent or increasingly remote. Others demanded prema-
ture commitments or promises thereof. And many abruptly aborted solid relationships in an effort to actively master what they believed they might otherwise
helplessly endure.

With rare exception, most in the study feared they were destined to repeat **42** their parents' mistakes, a concern frequently reinforced by the parents themselves. "You're attracted to the same kind of charming Don Juan who did me in," one mother admonished. "Beware of the womanizer just like your father or you'll be dumped in your 40's, just like me." Many of the youngsters deeply resented these apocalyptic, cautionary tales. Others felt burdened by having to wrestle with the ghosts of their parents' past. "Most people meet, fall in love and marry," a 21-year-old lamented, "but I have to find someone who convinces my mother he's not my father and then he has to fit the job description of a saint."

43   Whereas most felt fated to repeat their parents' past, many were determined to avoid the perils their parents did not. Many pledged never to let feelings fester until "they explode in everybody's face." They planned a "playmate relationship" in order to avoid the pallor of their parents' middle years. In an effort to revise their parents' history, some feared they would submit a potential partner to such dissecting scrutiny no mortal would qualify, and marriage would be forever postponed.

44   Nevertheless, when asked at the close of their interviews, "Where do you see yourself 10 years from now?" many of those who earlier had denounced marriage stated unhesitatingly that they would in all probability "be married with kids and a house of my own."

45   Not every divorce was emotionally wrenching. It was least disruptive when the parents' decision was mutual and their initial rancor was relatively short-lived. Youngsters fared best when their attachment to each parent was honored by the other, when their quest for neutrality was respected and when their relationship with each parent remained virtually unmarred. Few were so fortunate, however.

46   Friendship and religion were great comforts for many, but the majority said that soul-baring marathons with siblings clearly offered the greatest amount of comfort with the least amount of shame.

47   "I couldn't have made it without my sister," one college junior recalled. "Talking to friends was like going public, but with my sister it was safe, it was private, and a lifeline for us both."

48   Whether or not the profound sense of loss, the disillusionment, the revised attitudes toward love and marriage remain an enduring legacy of parental divorce for college-age youngsters, only future studies can determine. It should be noted, however, that most of these youngsters unsuccessfully disguised a deep and abiding wish to marry, to have children and to recapture the family of childhood—the one in the picture frame, animated, intertwined and inseparable.

▼ TOPICAL CONSIDERATIONS

1. Why does the author think this study was necessary? Do you agree with the author's concern for college-age children of divorce? Why or why not?

2. The study indicates that many respondents expected their parents

to drift apart. Do you think that most college-age students expect their parents to drift apart after twenty years of marriage? Why or why not?

3. The author mentions the shock by college students at the apparent "moral reversals in their parents' behavior" (paragraph 19). She goes on to describe the students' reactions to this behavior. What three responses were most common? What would be your reaction? Explain your answer.

4. The author discovered two important contrasts to younger children of divorce. Describe one difference and explain why you think that difference showed up in the study.

5. In the report, the author describes how many young adults indicated that they ministered to their parents and neglected their own concerns. Would you respond in the same way if one or both of your parents needed your help to get "back on track" (paragraph 32)?

▼ RHETORICAL CONSIDERATIONS

1. What is the function of the opening paragraph? How does it prepare the reader for the second paragraph?

2. Interspersed throughout this essay are words like "moral opprobrium," "pejorative," "fait accompli," "abstemious," "internecine," and "excoriating." Do you think such words fit the tone and style of this essay? Did the language prevent you from focusing on the report? If you found any unfamiliar words, did you look them up in the dictionary? Did the language enhance the essay? Explain using an example.

3. In paragraph 9 the author mentions "the family of childhood." This phrase is repeated at the end of the essay. Why does the author repeat it?

4. Cain uses quotations from interviews with college-age children of divorce in this essay. She mixes these quotations with the results of the report. Is this strategy effective or not? Why?

5. The author reports the feelings of young adults when their family house was sold. She says, "The dismantling of the house symbolized in stark relief the final dismantling of the family itself." Explain the ways in which the family house itself represents the family itself.

▼ WRITING ASSIGNMENTS

1. Imagine that you write an advice column for colleagues in the school paper. Respond to a letter from a fellow student who wants to know how to deal with his parents' divorce.

2. Imagine that it is 20 years from now. Report on whether the profound sense of loss, disillusionment, and "revised attitudes toward love and marriage remain an enduring legacy of parental divorce for college-age youngsters" (paragraph 48).

3. As a college-age child of divorce, write a letter to Barbara S. Cain in which you tell her why you agree or disagree with the results of her study.

4. Did your parents divorce? If so, write a personal account of how the divorce affected you.

5. Do you know parents who have divorced? If so, how would they respond to this essay? You may write a response as if you are the divorced parents of a college-age student.

3 ▼ CHANGING TIMES

Ours is a fast-forward age. An era of dizzying social and cultural change. Caught up in the whirl, we can barely stand back to examine what we've made of ourselves. Yet when we do, we may not like what we see. The essays in this chapter take a hard look at contemporary American society in flux—at its values and its costs.

The overview piece is a provocative letter by a college student to his parents' generation. In "The Terrible Twenties," Daniel Smith-Rowsey complains that the future of today's 20-year-olds is bleak. The past generation has consumed too much and given too little. What chance, he asks, do young people have in a society that prefers pop culture to education, whose selfishness and mall-culture indulgence has reduced "us all to 12-year-olds who want everything now."

Surviving in today's society is also the topic of "On Kids and Slasher Movies." Here, Michael Ventura speculates on young people's attraction to Hollywood psycho-killers. His concern is not that slasher movies may lead to violence. Rather he wonders if we've created a world where kids need heavy doses of horror to deal with everyday life.

The popular media also project a culture obsessed with sexuality. Racy television sitcoms, fleshy commercials, and soft-porn MTV videos bear the message that sex and fun are what adolescence is all about. As for movies: Happiness is a full sexual calendar. No wonder today's young people are sexually more active than past generations. What disturbs physician Robert C. Noble in "There Is No Safe Sex" is no moral issue. It is AIDS.

The next two pieces examine all-American progress—or, more precisely, the myth of progress. "What Price Consumption?" by Alan Durning is a sobering assessment of our consumer culture. Since the 1920s technological advances, rising capital, and cheaper goods have conspired to make America the world's most affluent and most acquisitive society. But the pursuit of unlimited consumption is pushing the world beyond its ability to sustain itself. The next essay brings the future of American commerce down to the local gas station. And the title of Andrew Ward's essay just about says it all: "They Also Wait Who Stand and Serve Themselves." In humorous detail, the author describes how in the name of progress a giant oil company turned Sal's Gas into a slick and efficient Self-Serv Machine.

During the rush-to-riches 1980s much of America looked up and saw only endless blue sky. As never before, the good life was upon us. As never before, our culture defined itself in terms of what we owned. Yet, while Wall Street and Main Street enjoyed a feeding frenzy, others went hungry in body and spirit. The penalties for the imbalance are the focus of the next two essays. Jonathan Kozol's "The New Untouchables" reports on the most vulnerable victims of poverty—poor children who receive little at home and less from public education. In "A Child of Crack," Michele Norris offers a graphic picture of a 6-year-old boy growing up in a crack house apartment in the shadow of the nation's Capitol.

But our future need not be all gloom and doom. We end this chapter on a note of hope. As Charles R. Larson suggests in "The Value of Volunteering," we as a nation have the wealth, technology, and people to attack the problems of our time—to do something about poverty, illiteracy, homelessness, disease, and a decaying infrastructure. What we need, says Larson, is the spirit of the Peace Corps to turn the country around.

▼ THE TERRIBLE TWENTIES
Daniel Smith-Rowsey

Like most of you reading this essay, Daniel Smith-Rowsey is from the "twentysomething" generation. And like most of you, he was brought up in a culture of MTV, Nintendo, latchkey freedom, cellular phones, BMWs, and sprawling malls. But as adulthood weighs in on him, he questions the values and resources he and his indulged generation inherited from their parents. "You never taught us to be smart—you only taught us to be young." With skyrocketing costs and unemployment and a college degree that no longer guarantees a good job, he wonders if today's twentysome-things have the wherewithall to survive a future rushing down on them. At the time he wrote this article, Smith-Rowsey was a senior majoring in politics and film-making at the University of California, Santa Cruz. This article first appeared in *Newsweek* in June 1991.

Sometimes I wonder what it would be like to have been 20, my age, in the '60s. Back when you could grow up, count on a career and maybe think about buying a house. When one person could expect to be the wage earner for a household.   1

In the space of one generation those dreams have died. The cost of living has skyrocketed, unemployment has gone up, going to college doesn't guarantee you can get a good job. And no one seems to care. Maybe it's because the only people my age you older people have heard from are those who *do* make a lot of money: investment bankers, athletes, musicians, actors. But more and more of us twentysomethings are underachievers who loaf around the house until well past our college years.   2

This is an open letter to the baby boomers from the *next* generation. I think it's time we did a little hitting back. Aside from the wealthy, none of you ever told your children, "Someday this will all be yours," and you're the first middle class to fail that way. Did you think we wouldn't care? Thanks a lot. But the real danger lies in the way we've been taught to deal with failure: gloss over and pretend the problem doesn't exist. It's evidence you never taught us to be smart—you only taught us to be young.   3

4   We are the stupidest generation in American history, we 20-year-olds. You already know that. We really do get lower SAT scores than our parents. Our knowledge of geography is pathetic, as is our ability with foreign languages and even basic math. We don't read books like you did. We care only about image. We love fads. Talk to college professors, and they'll tell you they don't get intelligent responses like they used to, when you were in school. We're perfectly mush-headed.

5   You did this to us. You prized your youth so much you made sure ours would be carefree. It's not that you didn't love us; you loved us so much you pushed us to follow your idea of what you were—or would like to have been— instead of teaching us to be responsible. After legitimizing youthful rebellion you never let us have our own innocence—perhaps because Vietnam and Watergate shattered yours. That's why we're already mature enough to understand and worry about racism, the environment, abortion, the homeless, nuclear policy. But we also were fed on the video culture you created to idealize your own irresponsible days of youth. Your slim-and-trim MTV bimbos, fleshy beer commercials and racy TV shows presented adolescence as a time only for fun and sex. Why should we be expected to work at learning anything?

6   Not that we're not smart—in some ways. We're street smart, David Letterman clever, whizzes at Nintendo. We can name more beers than presidents. Pop culture is, to us, more attractive than education.

7   I really don't think we can do this dance much longer. Not a single industrialized country has survived since 1945 without a major re-evaluation of its identity except ours. That's what you thought you were doing in the '60s, but soon you gave way to chasing the dreams of the Donald Trump–Michael Milken get-rich-quick ethos—and all you had left for us was a bankrupt economy. The latchkey lifestyle you gave us in the name of your own "freedom" has made us a generation with missing parents and broken homes. And what about the gays and blacks and Hispanics and Asians and women who you pretended to care so much about, and then forgot? It's not that I'm angry at you for selling out to the system. It's that there won't be a system. It's that there won't be a system for *me* to sell out to, if I want to. The money isn't there anymore because you spent it all.

8   To be honest, I can't blame you for all that's happened. The pre-eminence of new technologies and the turn toward cutthroat capitalism over the past two decades would have happened with or without the peculiarities of your generation. If I had been born in the '50s, I too would have been angry at racism and the war in Vietnam. But that's not the same thing as allowing the system to unravel out of my own greed. Don't say you didn't start the fire of selfishness and indulgence, building it up until every need or desire was immediately appeased. Cable TV, BMWs, cellular phones, the whole mall culture has reduced us all to 12-year-olds who want everything *now*. I'm not in love with everything your parents did, but at least they gave you a chance. As Billy Joel said, "Every child had a pretty good shot to get at least as far as their old man

got." For most of us, all we've been left with are the erotic fantasies, aggressive tendencies and evanescent funds of youth. Pretty soon we won't have youth *or* money, and that's when we may get a little angry.

Or maybe we won't. Perhaps you really have created a nation of mush-heads who will always prefer style over substance, conservative politics and reading lessons. If that's so, the culture can survive, as it seems to be doing with the bright smile of optimism breaking through the clouds of decaying American institutions. And then you really will be the last modern smart generation because our kids will be even dumber, poorer and more violent than us. You guys will be like the old mule at the end of Orwell's "Animal Farm," thinking about how great things used to be when you were kids. You will differ from your own parents in that you will have missed your chance to change the world and robbed us of the skills and money to do it ourselves. If there's any part of you left that still loves us enough to help us, we could really use it. And it's not just your last chance. It's our only one.

▼ TOPICAL CONSIDERATIONS

1. In paragraph 8, Smith-Rowsey writes, "For most of us, all we've been left with are the erotic fantasies, aggressive tendencies and evanescent funds of youth." In the context of the essay, how does he substantiate this claim? As a member of the "twentysomething" generation, do you agree with this claim?

2. In paragraph 4, the author says, "We are the stupidest generation in American history, we 20-year-olds." On what does he base his assessment? Does his claim offend you? On what points do you agree or disagree with him?

3. In paragraph 6, Smith-Rowsey states, "Pop culture is, to us, more attractive than education." Is Smith-Rowsey indicting 1990s youth or explaining a universal experience felt by 20-year-olds for generations? Do you find pop culture more attractive than education? Has your parents' generation influenced your preference?

4. According to Smith-Rowsey in paragraph 7, how have the Civil Rights and Equal Rights movements survived? How does the author feel about social causes? Do you believe that youth today are apathetic to social causes or that there has been a resurgence in political activism?

5. How does the essay prove or disprove the Billy Joel line, "Every child had a pretty good shot to get at least as far as their old man got"? Considering America today, do you think you can achieve what your parents did?

6. According to Smith-Rowsey, what products and technological advancements has the younger generation gained from the older gen-

eration? Are all of Smith-Rowsey's examples negative? What products and advancements from his parents' generation can you think of to present a more balanced picture?

▼ RHETORICAL CONSIDERATIONS

1. This essay is written as an open letter. To whom is the letter addressed? How are first person and second person used in the essay? Do you as a reader feel part of Smith-Rowsey's "twentysomethings"?
2. In paragraph 7 what does the word "latchkey" connote? What other allusions or terms in the essay are products of 1980s and 1990s culture? What do these products say about American culture? Add your own list of 1990s vocabulary words that reveal contemporary American philosophy.
3. Does Smith-Rowsey's lead grab you? Why or why not? As a member of the twentysomethings, have you wondered about the same things he has?
4. Characterize the tone of the essay. Do you think it captures the attitude of your generation? Would you have written the essay from a different approach?

▼ WRITING ASSIGNMENTS

1. Billy Joel is part of the older generation whose creed was, "Every child had a pretty good shot to get at least as far as their old man got." Consider songwriters and singers of your generation. Write a paper that explains the 1990s creed using lyrics from at least three different songs.
2. Smith-Rowsey writes (paragraph 9), "And then you really will be the last modern smart generation because our kids will be even dumber, poorer and more violent than us." Write a paper that shows how we can turn future generations around and begin to create a smarter, more peaceful society. Consider our current technological, environmental, and global-political knowledge.
3. Do you think Smith-Rowsey has fairly characterized your generation and that of your parents? If not, write a rebuttal to him. In it, try to render a more positive portrayal of the twentysomething generation and the influences that have molded it.

▼ ON KIDS AND SLASHER MOVIES

Michael Ventura

One day Michael Ventura spotted a 10-year-old boy buying a Halloween costume in Woolworth's. The package consisted of a lifelike rubber meat cleaver and the faceless mask from one of the many horror movies. What got to him was not so much the maniac-killer getup as the boy's eagerness to make believe. In the narrative below, the author wonders what the little scene says about us and the world we have made for our kids. Michael Ventura is a freelance writer living in Los Angeles. This article first appeared in the *L.A. Weekly* in November 1989.

1   It's a simple thing, really. I shouldn't take it so seriously, I realize that. For it was only a child, a boy of about 10, buying a toy. For Halloween. This was the toy:

2   A sinister white mask and a quite convincing little rubber meat cleaver. Packaged together in cellophane. It's the "costume" of a maniac killer from one of the slasher movies. The boy wants to play at being a faceless, unstoppable murderer of innocent people (mostly women). At this moment, in this Woolworth's, that's this boy's idea of fun.

3   Understand that I didn't stand there and decide intellectually that this simple and small event is, when all is said and done, the worst thing I've seen. My body decided. My intestines, my knees, my chest. It was only later that I tried to think about it.

4   This boy's eagerness to "play" maniac killer is an event worse than the Bomb, worse even than Auschwitz. Reduced to its simplest terms, the bomb is a fetish, an object of worship—like other objects of worship before it, it is used as an excuse for arranging the world in a certain fashion, allocating resources, assigning powers. It is insane, but in many ways it is an extension of familiar, even honored, insanities. As for the Nazi camps: The people being murdered knew, as they were being murdered, *that* they were being murdered; the murderers knew they were murdering; and, when the world finally knew, the camps became the measure of ultimate human evil. A crime to scar us all, and our descendants, forever.

5   There is nothing so clear in the Woolworth's scene. The boy is certainly not committing a crime. The toy's merchandisers are within their rights. To legislate against them would be to endanger most of our freedoms. The mother buying the toy is perhaps making a mistake, perhaps not. Without knowing the boy, and knowing him well, who's to be certain that it isn't better for him to engage in, rather than repress, such play? The mother did not put the desire for the toy in him. Three thousand years of Judeo-Christian culture did that. Nor has the

mother the power to take that desire from him. Nobody has that power. If he can want the toy at all, then it almost doesn't matter whether the toy exists or not. Doesn't the boy's need for such play exist with or without the toy?

6   Nor would I be too quick to blame the boy's desire on television and slasher films. The Nazis who crewed the camps and the scientists who built the bomb did not need television and slasher films to school them in horror. In fact, the worst atrocities from the pharaohs to Vietnam were committed quite ably before the first slasher film was made. Keeping your child away from TV may make *you* feel better, but can any child be protected from the total weight of Western history?

7   In a world shorn of order, stripped of traditions, molting every decade, every year, a dancing, varicolored snake of a century—pointless violence is evident everywhere, on every level. Professional soldiers are statistically safer than urban women; senseless destruction is visited on trees and on the ozone and on every species of life. No one feels safe anywhere. This has become the very meaning of the 20th century.

8   So I am in a Woolworth's one day and I feel a sort of final horror as I watch a boy buy a psycho-killer toy so that he can pretend he's an unstoppable maniacal murderer. What is so horrible is that this boy is doing this instinctively, for his very survival. In order to live, in order not to go mad, this boy is acclimating himself to the idea of the killer-maniac, because killer-maniac energy is so present in his world. He's trying to inoculate himself through play, as all children have, everywhere, in every era. He thus lets a little bit of the energy into him—that's how inoculations work. Too little, and he is too afraid of the world—it's too terrifying to feel powerless amid the maniacal that's taken for granted around him; to feel any power at all he needs a bit of it inside him. But if he takes in too much, he could be swamped.

9   How horrible that he is forced to such a choice. You'd think it would be enough to stop the world in its tracks. And what can we do for him? Struggle for a different world, yes, but that won't change what's already happened to him. What can we do for that boy except be on his side, stand by his choice, and pray for the play of his struggling soul?

▼ TOPICAL CONSIDERATIONS

1. According to the author, what does the boy's choice of costume say about today's society? In light of your own costume choices as a kid, what do you think has gone into the child's choice? Does he really long for the power of a maniacal killer, or is he simply following a fad?

2. According to the author, what is attractive about "being a faceless, unstoppable murderer of innocent people (mostly women)" (paragraph 2)? Do you agree with Ventura's theory, or do you think his assessment of the contemporary world is unfair?

3. According to Ventura, is there a direct connection between slasher movies and kids' violence? What is your opinion of slasher movies? Do you think young people are too hooked on them? Do you think they have any socially redeeming values? Do you think they are damaging to young viewers? Could movie violence inspire violence in children? Explain your answer.

4. Ventura says in paragraph 3 that his "body decided" that the boy's purchase was "the worst thing" he had seen some time before his mind caught up. How does that distinction make his reaction seem more significant? Can you recall ever feeling horror before you thought about it?

5. Explain Ventura's assertion in paragraph 4 that the bomb is "used as an excuse for arranging the world in a certain fashion." What alternatives to the bomb do we have for rearranging the world? What or who do you think will determine the arrangement of the world in the next century?

6. How would Smith-Rowsey react to this essay? What would he think was the source for a child's wanting to be an "unstoppable murderer"?

▼ RHETORICAL CONSIDERATIONS

1. How well does the essay's title forecast Ventura's discussion and his moral stand?

2. Look up the definition of *fetish*. Explain the metaphor of the bomb as a fetish object in paragraph 4. Which definition of *fetish* is most applicable?

3. In the last paragraph Ventura appeals to the reader. What does he expect from the reader? Is this strategy effective? How are you affected by the essay? Does it call you to action against the "pointless violence" that is everywhere?

4. In paragraph 7, how is the twentieth century like a snake? Do you agree with this comparison? Choose an animal and develop a metaphor that describes your own lifetime.

5. What does Ventura mean in paragraph 5 by "Three thousand years of Judeo-Christian culture did that"? How is this statement ironic?

▼ WRITING ASSIGNMENTS

1. Do you think that particularly gruesome, violent, or offensive Halloween costumes should be banned from the market? Are there limits of propriety? Write a paper in which you explore these ques-

tions, taking into account the First Amendment rights to freedom of expression.

2. Ventura writes in paragraph 6, "Keeping your child away from TV may make *you* feel better, but can any child be protected from the total weight of Western history?" Does this statement negate the cause of parents against violence on TV? Can children be spared the violence of our world? Should they, and to what age? Write a paper in which you explore these questions.

3. Who are the usual victims in slasher films? What do they have in common? How are their death's portrayed? Select some slasher movies you have seen, then write a paper in which you explore these questions and how such films relate to young adults. What moral messages do the movies project?

▼ THERE IS NO SAFE SEX
Robert C. Noble

The title of this essay is a dead giveaway, so to speak. It is a blunt warning about sexual casualness, carelessness and just plain ignorance about the scourge of our times—AIDS, which has so far claimed 130,000 lives in the U.S. And it is aimed at today's generation of sexually active youth. While some communities grapple with the moral ins and out of providing condoms to high-school students, Robert C. Noble, an AIDS doctor, says that the real issue is death. Noble is a professor of medicine at the University of Kentucky College of Medicine, Lexington, Kentucky. His essay first appeared in *Newsweek* in April 1991.

1 The other night on the evening news, there was a piece about condoms. Someone wanted to provide free condoms to high-school students. A perky, fresh-faced teenage girl interviewed said everyone her age was having sex, so what was the big deal about giving out condoms? Her principal replied that giving out condoms set a bad example. Then two experts commented. One was a lady who sat very straight in her chair, white hair in a tight perm, and, in a prudish voice, declared that condoms didn't work very well; teenagers shouldn't be having sex anyway. The other expert, a young, attractive woman, said that since teenagers were sexually active, they shouldn't be denied the protection that condoms afforded. I found myself agreeing with the prude.

2 What do I know about all this? I'm an infectious-diseases physician and an AIDS doctor to the poor. Passing out condoms to teenagers is like issuing them squirt guns for a four-alarm blaze. Condoms just don't hack it. We should stop kidding ourselves.

3 I'm taking care of a 21-year-old boy with AIDS. He could have been the

model for Donatello's David, androgynous, deep blue eyes, long blond hair, as sweet and gentle as he can be. His mom's in shock. He called her the other day and gave her two messages. I'm gay. I've got AIDS. His lover looks like a fellow you'd see in Sunday school; he works in a bank. He's had sex with only one person, my patient (*his* second partner), and they've been together for more than a year. These fellows aren't dummies. They read newspapers. You think condoms would have saved them?

Smart people don't wear condoms. I read a study about the sexual habits of college women. In 1975, 12 percent of college women used condoms when they had sexual intercourse. In 1989, the percentage had risen to only 41 percent. Why don't college women and their partners use condoms? They know about herpes. They know about genital warts and cervical cancer. All the public-health messages of the past 15 years have been sent, and only 41 percent of the college women use condoms. Maybe your brain has to be working to use one. In the heat of passion, the brain shuts down. You have to use a condom every time. *Every time.* That's hard to do. **4**

I can't say I'm comforted reading a government pamphlet called "Condoms and Sexually Transmitted Diseases Especially AIDS." "Condoms are not 100 percent safe," it says, "but if used properly will reduce the risk of sexually transmitted diseases, including AIDS." *Reduce* the risk of a disease that is 100 percent fatal! That's all that's available between us and death? How much do condoms reduce the risk? They don't say. So much for Safe Sex. Safe Sex was a dumb idea anyway. I've noticed that the catchword now is "Safer Sex." So much for truth in advertising. Other nuggets of advice: "If you know your partner is infected, the best rule is to avoid intercourse (including oral sex). If you do decide to have sex with an infected partner, you should *always* be sure a condom is used from start to finish, every time." Seems reasonable, but is it really helpful? Most folks don't know when their partner is infected. It's not as if their nose is purple. Lots of men and women with herpes and wart-virus infections are having sex right now lying their heads off to their sexual partners—that is, to those who ask. At our place we are taking care of a guy with AIDS who is back visiting the bars and having sex. "Well, did your partner use a condom?" I ask. "Did you tell him that you're infected with the virus?" "Oh, no, Dr. Noble," he replies, "it would have broken the mood." You bet it would have broken the mood. It's not only the mood that gets broken. "Condoms may be more likely to break during anal intercourse than during other types of sex . . ." Condoms also break in heterosexual sex; one study shows a 4 percent breakage rate. "Government testing can *not* guarantee that condoms will always prevent the spread of sexually transmitted diseases." That's what the pamphlet says. Condoms are all we've got. **5**

Nobody these days lobbies for abstinence, virginity or single lifetime sexual partners. That would be boring. *Abstinence and sexual intercourse with one mutually faithful uninfected partner are the only totally effective prevention strategies.* That's from another recently published government report. **6**

Media messages: What am I going to tell my daughters? I'm going to tell **7**

them that condoms give a false sense of security and that having sex is dangerous. *Reducing* the risk is not the same as *eliminating* the risk. My message will
fly in the face of all other media messages they receive. In the movie "The Tall
Guy," a nurse goes to bed with the "Guy" character on their first date, boasting
that she likes to get the sex thing out of the way at the beginning of the
relationship. His roommate is a nymphomaniac who is always in bed with one
or more men. This was supposed to be cute. "Pretty Woman" says you can find
happiness with a prostitute. Who are the people that write this stuff? Have the
'80s passed and everyone forgotten sexually transmitted diseases? Syphilis is on
the rise. Gonorrhea is harder to treat and increasing among black teenagers and
adults. Ectopic pregnancies and infertility from sexually transmitted diseases are
mounting every year. Giving condoms to high-school kids isn't going to reverse
all this.

8   That prim little old lady on TV had it right. Unmarried people shouldn't be
having sex. Few people have the courage to say this publicly. In the context of
our culture, they sound like cranks. Doctors can't fix most of the things you can
catch out there. There's no cure for AIDS. There's no cure for herpes or genital
warts. Gonorrhea and chlamydial infection can ruin your chances of ever getting pregnant and can harm your baby if you do. That afternoon in the motel
may leave you with an infection that you'll have to explain to your spouse. Your
doctor can't cover up for you. Your spouse's lawyer may sue him if he tries.
There is no safe sex. Condoms aren't going to make a dent in the sexual
epidemics that we are facing. If the condom breaks, you may die.

▼ TOPICAL CONSIDERATIONS

1. According to Noble, what is the one form of "safe sex" in the
   1990s? Do you agree? What kind of sexual freedom and experimentation are open to people today? Has your generation grown sexually conservative because of current knowledge of AIDS?
2. According to Noble, how does the public view abstinence from
   sexual intercourse and/or monogamous relationships? Do you
   agree? Do you think more statements such as Noble's will affect
   public opinion? Would you speak out on Noble's behalf? Explain.
3. What does Noble say about the effectiveness of condoms as protection against AIDS? Who ignores these facts and for what reasons?
   Are any of these facts news to you? Are you or your friends among
   those who ignore the facts? Will this essay change your attitude?
   Will it change your sexual behavior?
4. How is AIDS portrayed in the public service media compared to
   entertainment media (film and TV)? Have you noticed any change
   in the image of sex in the media over the last five years? Do you feel
   that television, the film industry, and advertising have any responsibility to hype the seriousness of the disease and advocate abstinence
   or monogamy?

5. The first paragraph discusses condom distribution in high schools. According to the essay, what are the issues surrounding condom distribution? Was this an issue at your high school? Do you believe schools should make condoms available to students?

6. How would this essay fit into both Michael Ventura's and Daniel Smith-Rowsey's view of contemporary American society? How does your view of present day society compare to theirs? Have you experienced positive aspects of society that neither author mentions?

▼ RHETORICAL CONSIDERATIONS

1. In paragraph 2 of Michael Ventura's essay, he writes, "The boy wants to play at being a faceless, unstoppable murderer of innocent people." Explain how the image of the "faceless, unstoppable murderer" can serve as a metaphor for the AIDS epidemic.

2. Discuss the description of the two "experts" in the first paragraph. How do their physical descriptions fit their opinions? What purpose do these descriptions serve? Do they cause you to agree with one over the other?

3. In paragraph 3, Noble describes the 21-year-old as looking like "Donatello's David" and his lover as a man who "looks like a fellow you'd see in Sunday school; he works in a bank." How do these descriptions appeal to the reader? Would the author have achieved the same result if he had not described them?

4. Consider the words and phrases in italics throughout the essay. What do they add to the piece? Explain the possible reasons behind their placement within the text. How do the italics work to influence the reader?

5. Analyze the impact of the essay's final line: "If the condom breaks, you may die." Would this statement influence a reader's view of casual sexuality? Or do so on the issue of condom distribution in high schools? What feelings do you leave the essay with?

▼ WRITING ASSIGNMENTS

1. Earlier, Michael Ventura mentions slasher movies in his essay; Noble cites "Pretty Woman" here. Many horror films and romances are centered around sex. With some recent movies in mind, write a paper in which you discuss the degree to which Hollywood is being responsible to its audiences regarding its messages about sex in this age of AIDS.

2. Has this essay changed your attitude about the dangers of AIDS or about the risks of condom use? If so, write a paper in which you

discuss how Noble's warnings have affected your thinking and, perhaps, your behavior. If not, explain your reasoning.

3. What are your views on the distribution of condoms to high-school students? Write a paper in which you explore the issue from both a moral and medical point of view.

4. In the fall of 1991, Earvin "Magic" Johnson of the Los Angeles Lakers made the startling announcement that he was retiring from basketball because he had contracted the AIDS virus. Six months later former tennis star Arthur Ashe announced that he had AIDS. Write a paper in which you attempt to evaluate the impact of Johnson's and Ashe's announcements on people's awareness of the disease—your own and your friends included. In your paper try to assess the importance of celebrity in educating young people about the disease.

▼ WHAT PRICE CONSUMPTION?
Alan Durning

America is the most affluent society on earth. America is also the most consumptive society on earth. In fact, consumption is the central dynamo driving the American way of life and forging its social values. But like our wealth, our consumption is grossly out of line with that of the rest of the world. In the essay below, Alan Durning, a senior researcher at World-watch Institute in Washington, D.C., takes a detailed look at how we have made overconsumption our way of life. In comparison to other cultures, he comes to some chilling conclusions about what we are doing to ourselves and the earth. Durning is the author of three Worldwatch Papers that focus on the relationship between economic inequalities and environmental degradation. This article first appeared in *Technology Review* in 1991.

1   Early in the age of affluence that followed World War II, an American retailing analyst named Victor Lebow proclaimed, "Our enormously productive economy . . . demands that we make consumption our way of life, that we convert the buying and use of goods into rituals, that we seek our spiritual satisfaction, our ego satisfaction, in consumption. . . . We need things consumed, burned up, worn out, replaced, and discarded at an ever increasing rate."

2   Americans responded to Lebow's call, and much of the world has followed. Consumption has become a central pillar of life in industrial nations and is even embedded in social values. The Japanese speak of the "new three sacred treasures": color television, air conditioning, and the automobile.

The affluent lifestyle born in the United States is emulated by those who can **3** afford it around the world. And many can: the average person is four and a half times richer than were his or her great-grandparents at the turn of the century. But the wealth is unevenly spread. One billion live in unprecedented luxury, 1 billion in destitution. American children have more pocket money—$230 a year—than the half-billion poorest people.

Overconsumption by the fortunate is an environmental problem un- **4** matched in severity by anything except perhaps population growth. Their surging exploitation of resources threatens to exhaust or unalterably disfigure forests, soils, water, air, and climate.

High consumption may be a mixed blessing in human terms, too. Time- **5** honored values—integrity, good work, friendship, family, community—have often been sacrificed in the rush to riches. Thus, many in the industrial lands have a sense that the world of plenty is hollow—that they have been fruitlessly attempting to satisfy essentially social, psychological, and spiritual needs with things.

Of course, the opposite of overconsumption—poverty—is no solution to **6** either environmental or human problems. We are left to wonder how much is enough. What level of consumption can the earth support? When does having more cease to add appreciably to human satisfaction?

Answering these questions definitively is impossible, but for each of us in **7** the consuming class, asking is essential. Unless we see that more is not always better, our appetites will overwhelm efforts to forestall ecological decline.

THE CONSUMING SOCIETY

The headlong advance of technology, rising earnings, and cheaper material **8** goods have lifted overall consumption to levels never dreamed of a century ago. The trend is visible in statistics for almost any indicator. Since mid-century, the per capita global intake of copper, energy, meat, steel, and wood has approximately doubled; car ownership and cement consumption have quadrupled; plastic use has quintupled; aluminum consumption has grown sevenfold; and air travel has multiplied 32 times.

In the United States, the world's premier consuming society, the average **9** person owns twice as many cars, drives two and a half times as far, uses 21 times as much plastic, and travels 25 times as far by air as did a person in 1950. Air conditioning spread from 15 percent of households in 1960 to 64 percent in 1987, and color televisions from 1 to 93 percent.

Not since the '20s was conspicuous consumption so lauded as in the '80s. **10** During that decade, microwave ovens and videocassette records found their way into almost two-thirds of American homes. Between 1978 and 1987, sales of Jaguar automobiles increased eightfold, and the average age of first-time buyers of fur coats fell from 50 to 26. The select club of U.S. millionaires more than doubled to 1.5 million over the decade.

11   Japan and Western Europe display parallel trends. Per person, the Japanese consume more than four times as much aluminum, almost five times as much energy, and 25 times as much steel as they did in 1950. They also own four times as many cars and eat nearly twice as much meat. Ironically, in 1990 a *reja bumu* (leisure boom) and concern for nature combined to create two new status symbols: English four-wheel-drive Range Rovers and cabins made of American logs.

12   As in Japan, West European consumption is only a notch below that in the United States. France, the former West Germany, and the United Kingdom have almost doubled their per capita use of steel, more than doubled the intake of cement and aluminum, and tripled paper consumption since mid-century. Just in the first half of the '80s, per capita consumption of frozen prepared meals rose more than 30 percent in every West European country except Finland; in Switzerland, the jump was 180 percent.

13   In Eastern Europe, the collapse of socialist governments unleashed a tidal wave of consumer demand that had gone unsatisfied in ossified state-controlled economies. A young man in a Budapest bar captured his country's mood when he told a Western reporter, "People in the West think that we in Hungary don't know how they live. Well, we do know how they live, and we want to live like that, too." Those living in the former East Germany bought 200,000 used Western cars in the first half of 1990 alone.

14   The late '80s saw some poor societies begin the transition to consuming ways. In China, a sudden surge in spending shows up in data from the State Statistical Bureau: between 1982 and 1987, color TVs spread from 1 percent to 35 percent of urban homes, the share with washing machines quadrupled from 16 to 67 percent, and refrigerators grew in prevalence from 1 percent to 20 percent of homes.

15   In India, an emerging middle class of perhaps 100 million members, a liberalized consumer market, and the introduction of buying on credit have led to explosive growth in sales of everything from cars to frozen dinners. The *Wall Street Journal* gloats, "The traditional conservative Indian who believes in modesty and savings is gradually giving way to a new generation that thinks as freely as it spends."

16   Few would begrudge anyone the simple advantages of cold food storage or mechanized clothes washing. The point is that non-Western nations are emulating the high-consumption lifestyle—and that long before all the world can achieve the American dream, the planet will be laid waste.

17   For one thing, supporting the lifestyle of the world's 1 billion meat eaters, car drivers, and throwaway consumers requires resources from far away. A Dutch person's food, wood, natural fibers, and other products of the soil exploit five times as much land outside the country as inside—much of it in the Third World. Industrial nations account for about two-thirds of global use of steel, more than two-thirds of aluminum, copper, lead, nickel, tin, and zinc, and three-fourths of energy.

18   Even 1 billion profligate consumers is too much for the earth. Those in the

wealthiest fifth of humanity have built more than 99 percent of the world's nuclear warheads. Their appetite for wood is a driving force behind destruction of tropical rainforests. Over the past century, their economies have pumped out two-thirds of the greenhouse gases that threaten the earth's climate, and each year their energy use releases perhaps three-fourths of the sulfur and nitrogen oxides that cause acid rain.

19 Beyond environmental costs, some perplexing findings throw doubt on the wisdom of consumption as a personal and national goal: rich societies have had little success in turning consumption into fulfillment. Whatever Americans are buying, it doesn't seem to be enough. Regular surveys by the national Opinion Research Center of the University of Chicago reveal, for example, that no more Americans report they are very happy now than in 1957. The share has fluctuated around one-third since then, despite a doubling of per capita spending on personal consumption.

20 The world's people have consumed as many goods and services since 1950 as all previous generations together. Since 1940, Americans have used up as much of the earth's mineral resources as did everyone before them combined. If such high consumption fails to provide personal fulfillment, perhaps environmental concerns can help us redefine our goals.

IN SEARCH OF SUFFICIENCY

21 In simplified terms, an economy's total burden on the ecological systems that undergird it depends on three factors: the size of the population, average consumption, and the technology—from clotheslines to satellite communications—the economy uses to provide goods and services.

22 Changing agricultural patterns, transportation, urban design, energy use, and the like could radically reduce the damage wrought by consuming societies, while allowing those at the bottom of the economic ladder to rise without causing egregious harm. Thus, efficient technology partly explains why, for each unit of energy used, Japan produces three times as much worth of goods and services as the Soviet Union. Norwegians use half as much paper and cardboard apiece as their neighbors in Sweden, though they are equals in literacy and richer in monetary terms.

23 But while technological change holds extraordinary potential, it is ultimately limited by the compulsion to consume. Eventually, reduced material wants will need to complement technological change. Physicist José Goldemberg of the University of São Paulo and an international team of researchers carefully studied the potential of renewable energy and greater efficiency to cut fossil fuel consumption. The entire world, they found, *could* have the quality of life Western Europe now enjoys—modest but comfortable homes, refrigerated food, ready access to public transit, and limited auto use. However, the study implicitly concludes, the world could *not* live American-style, with larger homes, more numerous gadgets, and auto-centered transportation.

24   Some guidance on what the American lifestyle means for the earth emerges from global patterns for three ecologically important types of consumption—transportation, diet, and use of raw materials.

25   About 1 billion people travel mostly on foot, many of them never going 50 miles from their birthplaces. The lack of transportation options severely hinders their ability to get jobs, attend school, or bring complaints before the government. Meanwhile, the massive middle class of the world, some 3 billion people, travels by bus and bicycle.

26   The automobile class is relatively small: only 8 percent of humans, about 400 million people. Their vehicles are directly responsible for an estimated 13 percent of carbon-dioxide emissions from fossil fuels, along with air pollution, acid rain, and a quarter-million traffic fatalities a year.

27   The automobile makes itself indispensable: cities sprawl, public transit atrophies, shopping centers multiply, workplaces scatter. As suburbs spread, families start to need a car for each driver. One-fifth of American households own three or more vehicles. Working Americans spend nine hours a week behind the wheel, and 90 percent of new cars are air-conditioned, doubling the contribution to climate change.

28   The auto industry's great marketing achievement has been to turn its machines into cultural icons. As French philosopher Roland Barthes writes, "Cars today are almost the exact equivalent of the great Gothic cathedrals . . . the supreme creation of an era, conceived with passion by unknown artists, and consumed in image if not in usage by a whole population which appropriates them as . . . purely magical object[s]."

29   A select group within the auto class also takes the overwhelming majority of air trips. Four million Americans account for 41 percent of domestic trips. Each mile traveled by air uses more energy than one traveled by car, so jet-setters consume six-and-a-half times as much energy for transportation as do others in the car class.

30   The food consumption ladder also has three rungs. At the bottom, 630 million people are unable to provide themselves with a healthy diet, estimates the World Bank. On the next rung, 3.4 billion grain eaters get enough calories and plenty of plant-based protein, giving this global middle class the healthiest basic diet.

31   The top of the ladder is populated by the meat eaters, who obtain close to 40 percent of their calories from fat. These 1.25 billion people eat three times as much fat per person as the remaining 4 billion, mostly because they eat so much red meat. The meat class pays a price in high death rates from the diseases of affluence—heart disease, strokes, and certain cancers.

32   The earth also pays for the high-fat diet. Indirectly, the meat-eating quarter of humanity consumes nearly 40 percent of the world's grain, since grain fattens the livestock they eat. Meat production is behind a substantial share of the environmental stresses induced by agriculture, from soil erosion to overpumping of underground water. In the extreme case of American beef, it takes 5 kilograms of grain and the energy of 2 liters of gasoline to produce 1 kilogram of steak.

The affluent diet also rings up an ecological bill through its heavy depen- **33** dence on transportation. North Europeans eat lettuce trucked from Greece and decorate their tables with Kenyan flowers. Japanese eat turkey from the United States and ostrich from Australia. One-fourth of the grapes eaten in the United States are Chilean, and the typical mouthful of American food travels over 1,000 miles from farm to table. This far-flung system is only partly a product of the economics of agriculture. It is also a result of massive government subsidies for irrigation, farm policies and health standards that favor large producers, and a highway system that transfers tax burdens from truckers to other highway users.

Processing and packaging add further costs to the way the affluent eat. **34** Even seemingly simple foods consume a surprising amount of energy: ounce for ounce, getting canned corn to a consumer takes 10 times the energy of fresh corn in season. To be sure, canned and frozen vegetables make a healthy diet easy even in winter. Of more concern are microwave-ready instant meals. Loaded with disposable pans and multilayer packaging, their resource needs are orders of magnitude larger than preparing the same dishes at home from scratch.

Global beverage consumption reveals a similar pattern. The 1.75 billion **35** people at the bottom have no option but to drink water that is often contaminated with human, animal, and chemical waste. Those in the next group, nearly 2 billion people, get more than 80 percent of their liquid refreshment from clean water, with the remainder coming from beverages such as tea, coffee, and, for children, milk. At the quantities consumed, these beverages pose few environmental problems; they are packaged minimally and transport energy needs are low. In the top class once again are the billion people in industrial countries who imbibe soft drinks, bottled water, and other prepared beverages packaged in single-use containers and transported long distances. Ironically, where tap water is purest and most accessible, its use is declining. Americans drink more soda than water.

The same consumption pattern emerges with raw materials. About 1 billion **36** rural people subsist on local biomass. Most of what they use each day—about a half-kilogram of grain, 1 kilogram of fuelwood, and fodder for their animals— could be provided by renewable resources. Unfortunately, landlessness and population growth often push people into fragile, unproductive ecosystems, and their minimal needs are not always met. These materially destitute billion are part of a larger group lacking many benefits provided by modest use of non-renewables—particularly durable things like radios, refrigerators, water pipes, quality tools, and carts with ball bearings and light wheels. More than 2 billion people live in countries where per capita consumption of steel, the most basic modern material, is under 50 kilograms a year.

At the top of the heap is the throwaway class. A typical inhabitant of the **37** industrialized fourth of the world uses 15 times as much paper, 10 times as much steel, and 12 times as much fuel as a Third World inhabitant. The extreme case is again the United States, where each day the average person consumes most of his or her own weight in terms of raw material flowing into the economy—18 kilograms of petroleum and coal, 13 kilograms of other minerals, 12 kilograms of agricultural products, and 9 kilograms of forest products.

38   In the throwaway economy, packaging becomes an end in itself, disposables proliferate, and durability suffers. Four percent of U.S. per capita expenditures on consumer goods go for packaging—$225 a year. Each year, Americans toss away 180 million razors, enough paper and plastic plates and cups to feed the world six picnics, and enough aluminum cans to make 6,000 DC-10s. Likewise, the Japanese dispose of 30 million single-roll cameras each year, and the British dump 2.5 billion diapers.

39   Where disposability and planned obsolescence fail to accelerate the trip from cash register to junk heap, fashion sometimes succeeds. Most clothing goes out of style long before it wears out. Kevin Ventrudo, chief financial officer of L.A. Gear, whose sales multiplied 50 times over in four years, told the *Washington Post,* "If you talk about shoe performance, you only need one or two pairs. If you're talking fashion, you're talking endless pairs of shoes."

40   In transportation, diet, and raw material use, as consumption rises so does waste—both of resources and of health. Bicycles and public transit are cheaper, more efficient, and healthier transportation than cars. A diet founded on the basics of grains and water is gentle to the earth and the body. And a lifestyle that fully uses raw materials for durable goods is ecologically sound while providing many modern comforts.

41   Yet few who can afford high consumption opt to live simply. What prompts us to consume so much?

THE CULTIVATION OF NEEDS

42   "The avarice of mankind is insatiable," wrote Aristotle, providing one obvious answer to why people never seem satisfied with what they have. A century before Christ, the Roman philosopher Lucretius wrote, "We have lost our taste for acorns. So [too] we have abandoned those couches littered with herbage and heaped with leaves. So the wearing of wild beasts' skins has gone out of fashion. . . . Skins yesterday, purple and gold today—such are the baubles that embitter human life with resentment." Nearly 2,000 years later, Leo Tolstoy echoed Lucretius: "Seek among men, from beggar to millionaire, one who is contented with his lot, and you will not find one such in a thousand."

43   Some would say that what distinguishes modern consuming habits from those of interest to Lucretius and Tolstoy is simply that we are richer than our ancestors. There is a great deal of truth in that view, but there is also reason to believe that certain forces encourage modern people to act on their consumptive desires as never before.

44   In the anonymous mass societies of advanced industrial nations, daily interactions with the economy lack the face-to-face character prevailing in local communities. Traditional virtues like integrity, honesty, and skill are too hard to measure to serve as yardsticks of social worth. By default, they are sup-

planted by a simple, single indicator—money. As a Wall Street banker put it bluntly to the *New York Times,* "Net worth equals self-worth."

The satisfaction derived from money does not come from simply having it. **45** It comes from having more of it than others do, and from having more this year than last. Thus, the bulk of survey data reveals that the upper classes in any society are more satisfied with their lives than the lower classes are—but no more so than the upper classes of much poorer countries.

More striking, the main determinants of happiness are unrelated to con- **46** sumption: prominent among them are satisfaction with family life, followed by satisfying work, leisure, and friendships. Yet when alternative measures of success are unavailable, the human need for respect is acted out through consumption. Buying proves self-esteem—"I'm worth it," chants one ad slogan.

Beyond social pressures, the affluent live enveloped in pro-consumption **47** advertising. One analyst estimates that the typical American is exposed to 50 to 100 ads each morning before 9:00 A.M. In their weekly 22-hour diet of television, American teenagers are typically exposed to 3 to 4 hours of ads a week, or at least 100,000 ads between birth and high school graduation.

Marketers have found ever more ways to push their products. Advertise- **48** ments are broadcast by over 10,000 U.S. television and radio stations, towed behind airplanes, plastered on billboards, and bounced from satellites. They are piped into classrooms and doctors' offices, woven into the plots of films, mounted in bathroom stalls, and played back between rings on public phones in the Kansas City airport. The Viskase company of Chicago offers to print edible slogans on hot dogs, and Eggverts International uses a similar technique to advertise on eggs in Israel.

Advertising has been one of the fastest-growing industries during the past **49** half-century. In the United States, ad expenditures rose from $198 per capita in 1950 to $498 in 1989. Global advertising expenditures rose from an estimated $39 billion in 1950 to $237 billion in 1988, and per person advertising expenditures grew from $15 to $46. In developing countries, the increases are astonishing. Ad billings in India jumped fivefold in the '80s.

Mall design itself encourages acquisitive impulses, many critics believe, but **50** perhaps more important, suburban malls and commercial strips suck commerce away from downtown and neighborhood merchants. Shopping by public transit or on foot becomes difficult, auto traffic increases, and sprawl accelerates. In the end, town squares and city streets are robbed of their vitality.

Particularly in the United States, shopping seems to have become a primary **51** cultural activity. Some 93 percent of American teenage girls surveyed in 1987 deemed shopping their favorite pastime. That year, the 32,563 shopping centers in the country surpassed high schools in number. Shopping centers now garner 55 percent of U.S. retail sales, compared with 16 percent in France and 4 percent in Spain.

But even in Europe, shopping centers are proliferating. Britain's one-stop **52** superstores doubled to about 500 in the '80s. Italy recently relaxed controls on mall development, leading to predictions that its shopping centers will multiply from 35 to 100 in five years. Spain's 90-odd centers are expected to triple in number by 1992.

53 Countless government policies also promote high consumption and worsen its ecological impact. Urban and transport planning favor private motorized vehicles to the exclusion of cleaner modes. Most governments in both North and South America subsidize beef production on a massive scale. Land-use and materials policies in most of the world undervalue renewable resources and underprice raw materials extracted from public domains.

54 More fundamentally, national economic goals are built on the assumption that more is better. For example, national statistics refer to people more frequently as consumers than as citizens. Economic policy, because it is based on a system of accounting that ignores the depletion and pollution of natural resources, views as healthy growth what is often feverish and debilitating overconsumption.

55 Finally, the sweeping advance of the mass market into realms once dominated by families and local enterprises has made consumption far more wasteful. In the past, a recycling ethos was built upon a materials economy that valued things and embodied that value in institutions. Not long ago—and to this day in nonindustrial regions—ragpickers, junkyard dealers, scrap collectors, and dairy deliverers kept used materials and containers flowing back into the economy.

56 Today, flush with cash but pressed for time, households opt for the questionable "conveniences" of prepared foods, miracle cleaners, and disposable everythings. While saving time, this costs the earth dearly and changes the household from the primary economic unit to a passive, consuming entity.

57 Like the household, the community economy has atrophied under the blind force of a money economy. Shopping malls, superhighways, and strips have replaced corner stores, local restaurants, and neighborhood theaters—the very things that help create a sense of common identity and community. Traditional vegetable stands and fish shops in Japan are giving way to supermarkets and convenience stores. Along the way, Styrofoam and plastic film have replaced newspaper as fish wrap. Even in France, with its legendary passion for fresh foods, the microwave and *grande surface* (shopping mall) are edging out bakeries, dairies, and farmers' markets

58 The search for status in massive and anonymous societies, omnipresent advertising, a shopping culture that edges out alternatives, government biases favoring consumption, and the spread of the commercial market into private life all nurture acquisitive desires. Can we, as individuals and as citizens, confront these forces?

A CULTURE OF PERMANENCE

59 When Moses came down from Mount Sinai he could count the rules of ethical behavior on his hands. In our complex global economy, in which the simple act

of turning on an air conditioner sends greenhouse gases into the atmosphere, the rules for ecological living run into the hundreds. Even so, the basic value of a sustainable society, the ecological equivalent of the Golden Rule, is simple: each generation should meet its needs without jeopardizing the prospects of future generations.

Lacking in consumer society is practical knowledge of what it means to live by that principle. Environmental ethics will arrive when most people think first of the pollution a large car causes, not the status it conveys. In a fragile biosphere, humanity's fate may depend on whether we can cultivate deeper sources of fulfillment, founded on an ethic of limiting consumption and finding nonmaterial enrichment.   **60**

For individuals, the decision to live a life of sufficiency—to answer the question "How much is enough?"—is to begin a highly personal process. The goal is to put consumption in its proper place among the many sources of personal fulfillment, and to find ways of living within the means of the earth. One inspiration in this quest is the body of human wisdom. All the sages, from Buddha to Muhammad, denounced materialism. "What shall it profit a man," the Bible asks, "if he shall gain the whole world and lose his own soul?" As Arnold Toynbee observed, "Religious founders all said with one voice that if we made material wealth our paramount aim, this would lead to disaster."   **61**

People often find that simpler living offers its own rewards. Many people find a sense of purpose in working to foster a just, sustainable world. Others describe the way simpler technologies add unexpected qualities to life. Some come to feel, for example, that clotheslines, window shades, and bicycles have a utilitarian elegance that clothes dryers, air conditioners, and automobiles lack. These modest devices are silent, manual, climate-friendly, easily repaired, and inexpensive. Vicki Robin, president of the Seattle-based New Road Map Foundation, which offers courses on getting off the more-is-better treadmill, notices that those who succeed in her program always have "a sense of purpose larger than their own needs, wants, and desires."   **62**

Still, shifting emphasis from material to nonmaterial satisfaction is no mean feat: it means trying both to curb personal appetites and to resist the external forces encouraging consumption. As Davidson College historian David Shi chronicles, the call for a simpler life has been perennial in North America, from the Puritans to the back-to-the-landers of the 1970s. None of these movements gained many adherents.   **63**

But while it would be naive to believe that entire populations will suddenly experience a moral awakening, renouncing greed, envy, and avarice, what can be hoped for is a gradual weakening of the consumerist ethos. The challenge is to bring environmental matters under cultural controls. The goal of creating a sustainable culture—a culture of permanence—is a task that will occupy several generations.   **64**

Personal restraint will do little if not wedded to bold political steps against the forces promoting consumption. In addition to the oft-repeated agenda of environmental reforms, action is needed to restrain the excesses of advertising,   **65** curb the shopping culture, abolish policies that push consumption, and revitalize household and community economies as human-scale alternatives to the high-consumption lifestyle.

66   The advertising industry is a formidable foe, but it is already vulnerable when it pushes products dangerous to human health. Tobacco ads are or soon will be banished from television throughout the West, and alcohol ads are under attack as never before. In 1990, Congress wisely hemmed in TV commercials aimed at children, and the European Community's standards after 1992 will put strict limits on some types of TV ads.

67   At the grassroots level, the Vancouver-based Media Foundation has set out to turn television to anticonsuming ends. Their "High on the Hog" campaign shows an animated pig frolicking on a map of North America as a narrator intones: "Five percent of the people in the world consume one-thrid of the planet's resources. . . . Those people are us." The Media Foundation is on target: in a culture of permanence, commercial television will need a fundamental reorientation.

68   Some countries have resisted the advancing shopping culture (though only rarely is the motive to oppose consumerism itself). England and Wales have restricted Sunday trading for 400 years, and labor groups beat back a recent proposal to lift those limits. Similarly, protected green belts around British cities have slowed the development of malls. German stores must close most evenings at 6:00 and have limited weekend hours as well. Most Japanese still shop in neighborhood lanes that are closed to traffic during certain hours to become *hokoosha tengoku*—"pedestrian heavens."

69   Direct incentives for overconsumption are also essential targets. If prices reflected something close to the environmental cost of production, through revised subsidies and tax systems, the market would guide consumers toward less damaging consumption. Disposables and packaging would rise in price, and local unprocessed food would cost less.

70   Ultimately, efforts to revitalize household and community economies may prove decisive in the attempt to create a culture less prone to consumption. At a personal level, commitment to nonmaterial fulfillment requires reinforcement from family, friends, and neighbors. At a political level, strong local institutions, may be the only counterweight to the colossus of vested interests that benefit from profligate consumption.

71   Despite the ominous scale of the challenge, many more people could be ready to begin saying "enough" than prevailing opinion suggests. After all, much of what we consume is wasted or unwanted. How much of the packaging in trash would we rather never see? How many of the unsolicited sales pitches in the post are nothing but junk? How much newspaper advertising would we not gladly see left out? How many miles of driving would we not give up if livable neighborhoods were closer to work, a variety of merchants closer to home, streets safe to walk, and public transit faster? How much of the rural land being built up into housing developments, industrial parks, and commercial strips could be left alone if we planned land use better inside city limits?

In the final analysis, we might be happier with less. Accepting and living by **72** sufficiency rather than excess offers a return to the human cultural home: to the ancient order of family, community, good work, and good life; to a reverence for skilled handiwork; to a true materialism that cares *for* things, not just *about* them.

For the lucky, a human life encompasses perhaps a hundred trips around **73** the sun. Regardless of religion, the sense of fulfillment received on that journey has to do with the timeless virtues of discipline, hope, allegiance to principle, and character. Consumption has little part in the play that inspires the young or the bonds of love and friendship that nourish adults. The things that make life worth living, that give depth and bounty to human existence, are infinitely sustainable.

▼ TOPICAL CONSIDERATIONS

1. In paragraph 2, Durning writes, "Consumption has become a central pillar of life in industrialized nations and is even embedded in social values." How does Durning variously support this claim in the essay?

2. Do you think of yourself as someone caught up with consummerism? If so, how are your personal and social values embedded in consumption? Can you answer "how much is enough" in your own life?

3. What are some of the most surprising facts in the essay? How has the essay changed the way you view the world and America's place in it?

4. What are the three kinds of consumption that distinguish the American lifestyle from that of the rest of the world? Do you see yourself as one of these consumers? Do you see yourself changing your consumer behavior as a result of reading this essay?

5. How would Smith-Rowsey respond to Durning's point that: each generation should meet its needs without jeopardizing future generations? Consider your generation: Do you think this is possible in present day society?

6. Is the loss of Communism and the turn to a free market economy by East Germany, Poland, and the former Soviet Union proof that a consumer-based society is best? Does the essay support this assumption?

7. What do you suppose Durning wants you to get from his essay?

8. How does the essay categorize the world food situation? How have the media, journalism, and pop culture informed you of the world food situation and of the plight of other countries? Were you aware of such imbalances in the world regarding food and consumption?

▼ RHETORICAL CONSIDERATIONS

1. Analyze Roland Barthes's analogy in paragraph 28 relating cars to Gothic cathedrals. Who are the "unknown artists"? What does it mean to appropriate something as a "purely magical object"?
2. Comment on the relevance of the Aristotle, Lucretius and Tolstoy quotes in paragraph 42. Are they still relevant today? Write your own saying using 1990s language and philosophy.
3. The essay is filled with statistics. Do you believe this makes the essay more or less convincing? Would you have enjoyed the essay more with fewer statistics? Why or why not?
4. Comment on the essay's concluding paragraph. What is its tone? Does it clash with the body of the essay?

▼ WRITING ASSIGNMENTS

1. Durning writes in paragraph 61 that "to answer the question 'How much is enough?' is to begin a highly personal process." Write a paper in which you analyze "how much is enough" for yourself. Consider your socioeconomic background, and also consider "how much is enough" for people of different backgrounds when shaping your answer. In your paper address both the Biblical quote and the Arnold Toynbee quote.
2. Ventura writes in "On Kids and Slasher Movies" (paragraph 7), "In a world shorn of order, stripped of traditions, molting every decade, every year . . . pointless violence is evident everywhere, on every level." Write a paper in which you explore the relationship between consumerism and violence. (Consider the Nike controversy of 1990 in which inner-city youths were supposedly murdering each other for sneakers.)
3. According to Durning, how has consumption affected the notion of "community"? Write a paper that shows the effect of consumption on the community. Consider your own community and that of your parents and grandparents.
4. Does this essay make you feel hopeless about the future? Do you think the current worldwide trend in consumerism can be reversed? Can an individual still make a difference? Explore the questions in an essay.
5. How is morality related to consumption? What is the moral fiber of America in the 1990s according to Durning, Noble, Smith-Rowsey and Ventura? Do you see any chance for a stronger morality to emerge? Draw from these authors and write an essay in which you advance your own route to moral recovery for America.

▼ THEY ALSO WAIT WHO STAND AND SERVE THEMSELVES

Andrew Ward

One of the most familiar institutions in modern America is the corner gas station. Like the corner grocery store and movie house, however, it is rapidly being replaced by the slick, efficient, and impersonal. Andrew Ward, contributing editor to the *Atlantic Monthly* and the author of *Bits and Pieces* (1980), *The Blood Seed* (1985), and *A Cry of Absence* (1988) describes in vivid, humorous detail his local gas station and what, in the name of progress, happens to it—and by extension to the quality of American life. This article first appeared in the *Atlantic Monthly* in 1979.

Anyone interested in the future of American commerce should take a drive sometime to my neighborhood gas station. Not that it is or ever was much of a place to visit. Even when I first moved here, five years ago, it was shabby and forlorn: not at all like the garden spots they used to feature in the commercials, where trim, manicured men with cultivated voices tipped their visors at your window and asked what they could do for you. 1

Sal, the owner, was a stocky man who wore undersized, popped-button shirts, sagging trousers, and oil-spattered work shoes with broken laces. "Gas stinks" was his motto, and every gallon he pumped into his customers' cars seemed to take something out of him. "Pumping gas is for morons," he liked to say, leaning indelibly against my rear window and watching the digits fly on the pump register. "One of these days I'm gonna dump this place on a Puerto Rican, move to Florida, and get into something nice, like hero sandwiches." 2

He had a nameless, walleyed assistant who wore a studded denim jacket and, with his rag and squeegee, left a milky film on my windshield as my tank was filling. There was a fume-crazed, patchy German shepherd, which Sal kept chained to the air pump, and if you followed Sal into his cluttered, overheated office next to the service bays, you ran a gantlet of hangers-on, many of them Sal's brothers and nephews, who spent their time debating the merits of the driving directions he gave the bewildered travelers who turned into his station for help. 3

"I don't know," one of them would say, pulling a bag of potato chips off the snack rack, "I think I would have put 'em onto 91, gotten 'em off at Willow, and then—bango!—straight through to Hamden." 4

Sal guarded the rest room key jealously and handed it out with reluctance, as if something in your request had betrayed some dismal aberration. The rest room was accessible only through a little closet littered with tires, fan belts, and cases of oil cans. Inside, the bulb was busted and there were never any towels, so you had to dry your hands on toilet paper—if Sal wasn't out of toilet paper, too. 5

6   The soda machine never worked for anyone except Sal, who, when complaints were lodged, would give it a contemptuous kick as he trudged by, dislodging warm cans of grape soda which, when their pop-tops were flipped, gave off a fine purple spray. There was, besides the snack rack in the office, a machine that dispensed peanuts on behalf of the Sons of Garibaldi. The metal shelves along the cinderblock wall were sparsely stocked with cans of cooling system cleaner, windshield de-icer, antifreeze, and boxed head lamps and oil filters. Over the battered yellow wiper case, below the Coca Cola clock, and half hidden by a calendar from a janitorial supply concern, hung a little brass plaque from the oil company, awarded in recognition of Salvatore A. Castallano's ten-year business association.

7   I wish for the sake of nostalgia that I could say Sal was a craftsman, but I can't. I'm not even sure he was an honest man. I suspect that when business was slow he may have cheated me, but I never knew for sure because I don't know anything about cars. If I brought my Volvo in because it was behaving strangely, I knew that as far as Sal was concerned it could never be a simple matter of tightening a bolt or re-attaching a hose. "Jesus," he'd wearily exclaim after a look under the hood. "Mr. Ward, we got problems." I usually let it go at that and simply asked him when he thought he could have it repaired, because if I pressed him for details he would get all worked up. "Look, if you don't want to take my word for it, you can go someplace else. I mean, it's a free country, you know? You got spalding on your caps, which means your dexadrometer isn't charging, and pretty soon you're gonna have hairlines in your flushing drums. You get hairlines in your flushing drums and you might as well forget it. You're driving junk."

8   I don't know what Sal's relationship was with the oil company. I suppose it was pretty distant. He was never what they call a "participating dealer." He never gave away steak knives or NFL tumblers or stuffed animals with his fill-ups, and never got around to taping company posters on his windows. The map rack was always empty, and the company emblem, which was supposed to rotate thirty feet above the station, had broken down long before I first laid eyes on it, and had frozen at an angle that made it hard to read from the highway.

9   If, outside of television, there was ever such a thing as an oil company service station inspector, he must have been appalled by the grudging service, the mad dog, the sepulchral john. When there was supposed to have been an oil shortage a few years ago, Sal's was one of the first stations to run out of gas. And several months ago, during the holiday season, the company squeezed him out for good.

10   I don't know whether Sal is now happily sprinkling olive oil over salami subs somewhere along the Sun Belt. I only know that one bleak January afternoon I turned into his station to find him gone. At first, as I idled by the no-lead pump, I thought the station had been shut down completely. Plywood had been nailed over the service bays, Sal's name had been painted out above the office door, and all that was left of his dog was a length of chain dangling from the air-pump's vacant mast.

But when I got out of the car I spotted someone sitting in the office with his **11** boots up on the counter, and at last caught sight of the "Self-Service Only" signs posted by the pumps. Now, I've always striven for a degree of self-sufficiency. I fix my own leaky faucets and I never let the bellboy carry my bags. But I discovered as I squinted at the instructional sticker by the nozzle that there are limits to my desire for independence. Perhaps it was the bewilderment with which I approach anything having to do with the internal combustion engine; perhaps it was my conviction that fossil fuels are hazardous; perhaps it was the expectation of service, the sense of helplessness, that twenty years of oil company advertising had engendered, but I didn't want to pump my own gas.

A mongrel rain began to fall upon the oil-slicked tarmac as I followed the **12** directions spelled out next to the nozzle. But somehow I got them wrong. When I pulled the trigger on the nozzle, no gas gushed into my fuel tank, no digits flew on the gauge.

"Hey, buddy," a voice sounded out of a bell-shaped speaker overhead. **13** "Flick the switch."

I turned toward the office and saw someone with Wild Bill Hickok hair **14** leaning over a microphone.

"Right. Thanks," I answered, and turned to find the switch. There wasn't **15** one. There was a bolt that looked a little like a switch, but it wouldn't flick.

"The switch," the voice crackled in the rain. "Flick the switch." **16**

I waved back as if I'd finally understood, but I still couldn't figure out what **17** he was talking about. In desperation, I stuck the nozzle back into my fuel tank and pulled the trigger. Nothing.

In the office I could see that the man was now angrily pulling on a slicker. **18** "What the hell's the matter with you?" he asked, storming by me. "All you gotta do is flick the switch."

"I couldn't find the switch," I told him. **19**

"Well, what do you call this?" he wanted to know, pointing to a little lever **20** near the pump register.

"A lever," I told him. **21**

"Christ," he muttered, flicking the little lever. The digits on the register **22** suddenly formed neat rows of zeros. "All right, it's set. Now you can serve yourself," the long-haired man said, ducking back to the office.

As the gas gushed into my fuel tank and the fumes rose to my nostrils, I **23** thought for a moment about my last visit to Sal's. It hadn't been any picnic: Sal claimed to have found something wrong with my punting brackets, the German shepherd snapped at my heels as I walked by, and nobody had change for my ten. But the transaction had dimension to it: I picked up some tips about color antennas, entered into the geographical debate in the office, and bought a can of windshield wiper solvent (to fill the gap in my change). Sal's station had been a dime a dozen, but it occurred to me, as the nozzle began to balk and shudder in my hand, that gas stations of its kind were going the way of the village smithy and the corner grocer.

I got a glob of grease on my glove as I hung the nozzle back on the pump, **24** and it took more than a minute to satisfy myself that I had replaced the gas cap properly. I tried to whip up a feeling of accomplishment as I headed for the office, but I could not forget Sal's dictum: Pumping gas is for morons.

25   The door to the office was locked, but a sign directed me to a stainless steel teller's drawer which had been installed in the plate glass of the front window. I stood waiting for a while with my money in hand, but the long-haired man sat inside with his back to me, so at last I reached up and hesitantly knocked on the glass with my glove.

26   The man didn't hear me or had decided, in retaliation for our semantic disagreement, to ignore me for a while. I reached up to knock again, but noticed that my glove had left a greasy smear on the window. Ever my mother's son, I reflexively reached into my pocket for my handkerchief and was about to wipe the grease away when it hit me: at last the oil industry had me where it wanted me—standing in the rain and washing its windshield.

▼ TOPICAL CONSIDERATIONS

1. In this short piece, Ward gives us a clear sense of Sal's gas station and the men associated with it. Cite some examples of succinct descriptions. How typical of gas stations is Sal's place? Does familiarity with gas stations help us visualize the place?

2. A writer's attitude toward his subject is determined not just by what he says about it but by the details he selects to describe it. What would you say Ward's attitude is toward Sal and his station? What select details reflect that attitude?

3. How does Ward feel toward what replaces Sal's station? How does Ward convey that attitude (or attitudes)?

4. In paragraph 7, Ward brings up the topic of nostalgia. How does this essay transcend a simple nostalgic reflection on a neighborhood gas station? In other words, what is Ward talking about on a higher level?

5. In paragraph 23, the author says that, even though his last visit to Sal's "hadn't been any picnic . . . the transaction had dimension to it." What does Ward mean by this statement? How did the transaction with the man with the "Wild Bill Hickok hair" lack dimension?

6. How does the scene in the last paragraph dramatize Ward's major complaint in this essay?

▼ RHETORICAL CONSIDERATIONS

1. Cite examples of descriptions in this essay that typify gas stations we know. Do any descriptions here strike you as unique to Sal's place?

2. Cite descriptions that help create humor. Does our familiarity with gas stations help carry the humor?
3. What is the effect of Sal's award of recognition coming where it does in paragraph 6?
4. Diagnosing the problems with Ward's Volvo, Sal says "You got spalding on your caps, . . . your dexadrometer isn't charging, and pretty soon you're gonna have hairlines in your flushing drums" (paragraph 7). Are these real car problems, or is Sal trying to pull a fast one on Ward? Is this the author's way of admitting his ignorance of auto repair talk?
5. Why does Ward call the rain "mongrel" in paragraph 12? What does the word connote, and how does it characterize the rain?
6. This essay contains several examples of irony. Cite some and describe how the irony works and its effects.

▼ WRITING ASSIGNMENTS

1. Good writing uses details and specifics. Inferior writing is just the opposite; it lacks sharp details and is riddled with vague generalities. Paragraph 6 is a good example of Ward's use of sharp details and specifics. First make note of them all, and then rewrite the paragraph, substituting vague generalities for the details and specifics.
2. Write an essay in which you describe how some familiar and traditional element of American society is "going the way of the village smithy and the corner grocer." You might consider the plight of the corner grocer, the proprietor of a general store, the family doctor who once made house calls, a human bank teller.
3. Write an essay in which you describe an experience you've had with depersonalizing institutions.
4. Take the opposite stand from that in Assignment 3—that is, write an essay arguing that you prefer the added efficiency of the modern supermarket, for example, to the personal touch of the corner grocer. You might discuss the virtues of the computerized, twenty-four-hour bank teller versus a human one, or an automatic highway toll gate versus a human toll collector.

▼ THE NEW UNTOUCHABLES
Jonathan Kozol

While most of America may be caught up in its own consumption, 33 million other Americans live in poverty. And 13 million of those poor are children. The disparities in wealth in this country—the greatest since figures were recorded—translates into the financing of education. As Jonathan Kozol reports, "Low-income children, who receive the least at home, receive the least from public education." What is the future of children who today are poorly housed, poorly fed, and poorly educated? What is the future of American society that today looks the other way? As Kozol warns in this profile of America's youngest outcasts, the way we treat our children says a lot about our arrogance toward the future. Jonathan Kozol is the author of the National Book Award–winning *Death At An Early Age* (1967), *Illiterate America* (1985), *Rachel and Her Children: Homeless Families in America,* which received the Robert F. Kennedy Book Award for 1989, and, *Savage Inequalities* (1991).

1   On an average morning in Chicago, about 5,700 children in 190 classrooms come to school only to find they have no teacher. Victimized by endemic funding shortages, the system can't afford sufficient substitutes to take the place of missing teachers. "We've been in this typing class a whole semester," says a 15-year-old at Du Sable High, "and they still can't find us a teacher."

2   In a class of 39 children at Chicago's Goudy Elementary School, an adult is screaming at a child: "Keisha, look at me . . . Look me in the eye!" Keisha is fighting with a classmate. Over what? It turns out: over a crayon, said The Chicago Tribune in 1988. Last January the underfunded school began rationing supplies.

3   The odds these black kids in Chicago face are only slightly worse than those faced by low-income children all over America. Children like these will be the parents of the year 2000. Many of them will be unable to earn a living and fulfill the obligations of adults; they will see their families disintegrate, their children lost to drugs and destitution. When we later condemn them for "parental failings," as we inevitably will do, we may be forced to stop and remember how we also failed them in the first years of their lives.

4   It is a commonplace that a society reveals its reverence or contempt for history by the respect or disregard that it displays for older people. The way we treat our children tells us something of the future we envision. The willingness of the nation to relegate so many of these poorly housed and poorly fed and poorly educated children to the role of outcasts in a rich society is going to come back to haunt us.

5   With nearly 30 percent of high-school students dropping out before they

graduate—60 percent in segregated high schools—it is not surprising that illiteracy figures have continued to grow worse. The much publicized volunteer literacy movement promoted for the last six years by Barbara Bush serves only 200,000 of the nation's estimated 30 million functional illiterates. Meanwhile, the gulf in income between rich and poor American families is wider than at any time since figures were recorded, starting in the 1940s. The richest 20 percent received 44 percent of national family income; the poorest 20 percent got only 4.6 percent. More than 5 million of the poorest group are children.

Disparities in wealth play out in financing of schools. Low-income children, **6** who receive the least at home, receive the least from public education. New Trier High School, for example, serving children from such affluent suburbs as Winnetka, Ill., pays its better teachers 50 percent above the highest paid teachers at Du Sable, by no means the worst school in Chicago. The public schools in affluent Great Neck and White Plains, N.Y., spend twice as much per pupil as the schools that serve the children of the Bronx.

Infant-mortality figures, classic indices of health in most societies, have also **7** worsened for poor children and especially for nonwhite children. The gap between white and black mortality in children continues to widen, reaching a 47-year high in 1987 (the most recent year for which data are available). Black children are more than twice as likely to die in infancy as whites—nine times as likely to be neurologically impaired. One possible consequence: black children are three times as likely as whites to be identified as mentally retarded by their public schools.

Federal programs initiated in the 1960s to assist low-income children, **8** though far from universally successful, made solid gains in preschool education (Head Start), compensatory reading (Chapter I) and precollege preparation (Upward Bound), while sharply cutting the rates of infant death and child malnutrition. Limited funding, however, narrowed the scope of all these efforts. Head Start, for example, never has reached more than one of five low-income children between its start-up in the '60s and today.

Rather than expand these programs, President Reagan kept them frozen or **9** else cut them to the bone. Living stipends paid to welfare families with children dropped to 35 percent (adjusted for inflation) below the 1970 level. Nearly half a million families lost all welfare payments. A million people were cut from food stamps. Two million kids were dropped from school-lunch programs. The WIC program (Women, Infants, Children), which provides emergency nutrition supplements to low-income infants, young children and pregnant women, was another target of Reagan administration cuts, but Congress successfully fought them off. Despite their efforts, the WIC budget is woefully inadequate, and has never been able to provide services to even half of the children and women who meet the eligibility requirements.

Federal housing funds were also slashed during these years. As these cut- **10** backs took their tolls, homeless children were seen begging in the streets of major cities for the first time since the Great Depression. A fivefold increase in homeless children was seen in Washington, D.C., in 1986 alone. By 1987 nearly half the occupants of homeless shelters in New York City were children. The average homeless child was only 6 years old.

11   The lives of homeless children tell us much of the disregard that society has shown for vulnerable people. Many of these kids grow up surrounded by infectious illnesses no longer seen in most developed nations. Whooping cough and tuberculosis, once regarded as archaic illnesses, are now familiar in the shelters. Shocking numbers of these children have not been inoculated and for this reason cannot go to school. Those who do are likely to be two years behind grade level.

12   Many get to class so tired and hungry that they cannot concentrate. Others are ashamed to go to school because of shunning by their peers. Classmates label them "the hotel children" and don't want to sit beside them. Even their teachers sometimes keep their distance. The children look diseased and dirty. Many times they are. Often unable to bathe, they bring the smell of destitution with them into school. There *is* a smell of destitution, I may add. It is the smell of sweat and filth and urine. Like many journalists, I often find myself ashamed to be resisting the affection of a tiny child whose entire being seems to emanate pathology.

13   So, in a terrifying sense, these children have become American untouchables. Far from demonstrating more compassion, administration leaders have resorted to a stylized severity in speaking of poor children. Children denied the opportunity for Head Start, sometimes health care, housing, even certified schoolteachers, have nonetheless been told by William J. Bennett, preaching from his bully pulpit as U.S. secretary of Education under Reagan, that they would be held henceforth to "higher standards." Their parents—themselves too frequently the products of dysfunctional and underfunded urban schools—have nonetheless been lectured on their "lack of values." Efforts begun more than 10 years ago to equalize school funding between districts have been put on the back burner and are now replaced by strident exhortations to the poor to summon "higher motivation" and, no matter how debilitated by disease or hunger, to "stand tall." Celebrities are hired to sell children on the wisdom of not dropping out of school. The White House tells them they should "just say no" to the temptations of the streets. But hope cannot be marketed as easily as blue jeans. Certain realities—race and class and caste—are there and they remain.

14   What is the consequence of tougher rhetoric and more severe demands? Higher standards, in the absence of authentic educative opportunities in early years, function as a punitive attack on those who have been cheated since their infancy. Effectively, we now ask more of those to whom we now give less. Earlier testing for schoolchildren is prescribed. Those who fail are penalized by being held back from promotion and by being slotted into lower tracks where they cannot impede the progress of more privileged children. Those who disrupt classroom discipline are not placed in smaller classes with more patient teachers; instead, at a certain point, they are expelled—even if this means expulsion of a

quarter of all pupils in the school. The pedagogic hero of the Reagan White House was Joe Clark—a principal who roamed the hallways of his segregated high school in New Jersey with a bullhorn and a bat and managed to raise reading scores by throwing out his low-achieving pupils.

In order to justify its abdication, the federal government has called for **15** private business to assist the underfunded urban schools. While business leaders have responded with some money, they have also brought a very special set of values and priorities. The primary concern of business is the future productivity of citizens. Education is regarded as capital investment. The child is seen as raw material that needs a certain processing before it is of value. The question posed, therefore, is how much money it is worth investing in a certain child to obtain a certain economic gain. Educators, eager to win corporate support, tell business leaders what they want to hear. "We must start thinking of students as workers," says the head of the American Federation of Teachers, Albert Shanker.

The notion of kids as workers raises an unprecedented question. Is future **16** productivity the only rationale for their existence? A lot of the things that make existence wonderful are locked out of the lives of children seen primarily as future clerical assistants or as possible recruits to office pools at IBM. The other consequence of "productivity" thinking is an increased willingness to make predictions about children, based almost entirely on their social status. Those whose present station seems to promise most are given most. Those whose origins are least auspicious are provided with stripped-down education. IQ testing of low-income babies has been recently proposed in order to identify those who are particularly intelligent and to accord them greater educational advantages, although this means that other babies will be stigmatized by their exclusion.

A heightened discrimination in the use of language points to a dual vision: we **17** speak of the need to "train" the poor, but "educate" the children of the middle class and rich. References to "different learning styles" and the need to "target" different children with "appropriate" curricula are now becoming fashionable ways of justifying stratified approaches. Early tracking is one grim result. A virtual retreat from any efforts at desegregation is another: if children of different social classes need "appropriate" and "different" offerings, it is more efficient and sensible to teach them separately.

A century ago, Lord Acton spoke thus of the United States: "In a country **18** where there is no distinction of class a child is not born to the station of its parents, but with an indefinite claim to all the prizes that can be won by thought and labor. It is in conformity with the theory of equality . . . to give as near as possible to every youth an equal start in life." Americans, he said, "are unwilling that any should be deprived in childhood of the means of competition."

That this tradition has been utterly betrayed in recent years is now self- **19** evident. The sense of fairness, however, runs deep in the thinking of Americans. Though frequently eclipsed, it is a theme that stubbornly recurs. A quarter century ago, it took disruptions in the streets to force Americans to question the unfairness of de jure segregation. Today it is not law but economics that condemns the children of the very poor to the implacable inheritance of a diminished destiny. "No matter what they do," says the superintendent of Chicago's public schools, "their lot has been determined."

20 Between the dream and the reality there falls the shadow of the ghetto school, the ghetto hospital, the homeless shelter. Appeals to the pocketbook have done no good. Black leaders have begun to contemplate the need for massive protests by poor people. Middle-class students, viscerally shocked by the hard edge of poverty they see in city streets, may be disposed to join them. The price may be another decade of societal disruption. The reward may be the possibility that we can enter the next century not as two nations, vividly unequal, but as the truly democratic nation we profess to be and have the power to become. Whether enough people think this outcome worth the price, however, is by no means clear.

▼ TOPICAL CONSIDERATIONS

1. Before reading this essay, were you aware of the extent and plight of our nation's poor? Has your own experience put you in touch with "the untouchables?" Explain your answer.

2. According to Kozol, how were the nation's poor children affected by the Reagan administration? What evidence does he present? What is your reaction to these findings? How does it affect your view of the poor? Ronald Reagan? The Reagan administration? Jonathan Kozol?

3. Kozol writes in paragraph 13, "Certain realities—race and class and caste—are there and they remain." What does Kozol suggest by this? Do you agree with this statement?

4. Paragraph 14 begins, "What is the consequence of tougher rhetoric and more severe demands?" What is the "tougher rhetoric," and who is enforcing it?

5. How have public schools been affected by the fact that "the gulf in income between rich and poor American families is wider than at anytime since figures were recorded" (paragraph 5)?

6. How would you evaluate your own secondary education—excellent, good, fair or poor? Explain your answer. Had you ever felt handicapped because of lack of funds? If so, how could your education have been improved?

7. How does teachers' "rationing supplies" illustrate Alan Durning's theories on American consumption?

8. Consider Lord Acton's nineteenth-century commentary on the American way of life in paragraph 18. Has twentieth-century America proven or disproven Acton's assumptions?

9. In his essay, "The Terrible Twenties," Daniel Smith-Rowsey also talks about the suffering of a new generation during the Reagan era. Do you see any overlapping of his complaints and the suffering of "the new untouchables" described by Kozol? What about in the appeals of the authors for solutions?

10. What measures does Kozol offer to heal the "new untouchables" in America? Do these sound like reasonable steps to you? ones that might work? What suggestions can you offer?

▼ RHETORICAL CONSIDERATIONS

1. Jonathan Kozol has spent many years researching and writing about the poor in America. Does this experience show in the essay? Why do you suppose he wrote the piece from a third-person point of view? Explain the effect of his lapse into the first person in paragraph 12.

2. Who is Joe Clark and what does he represent? What image does his name generate? How does Kozol use the Joe Clark reference?

3. Paragraph 17 begins, "A heightened discrimination in the use of language points to a dual vision." Explain this statement. Can language be a form of discrimination?

4. Analyze the conclusion. Kozol speaks of the American "dream," "reality," and the "shadow" bridging the two. Do you think the wording makes for an effective conclusion?

5. Consider the title "The New Untouchables." Did you find it provocative? Catchy? How well does it fit what is discussed in the essay. Who might be "the old untouchables"?

▼ WRITING ASSIGNMENTS

1. In his 1988 inaugural speech, President Bush said "1,000 points of light" would help curb homelessness, the "war on drugs," crime, and poverty. Would you say that the government has backed away from social problems too much? Have private individuals kept their part of the bargain? Who is morally responsible to correct such problems? Write an essay that addresses these questions.

2. Kozol writes in paragraph 20, "Between the dream and the reality, there falls the shadow of the ghetto school, the ghetto hospital, the homeless shelter." Consider your knowledge of the American dream as it appears in American Literature—The Great Gatsby, Death of a Salesman, the Horatio Alger stories, and so on. Write an essay that examines just what the American dream in the 1990s

is. You might consider in your discussion Alan Durning's essay or any others in this chapter.

3. Consider the American family and the essays in this chapter. From what you have observed and read here, would you say that the American family is still the stable nucleus of our nation? Or is it falling apart? Write a paper in which you address these questions.

4. You have been invited to be the keynote speaker at your high school alma mater. You have been asked to respond to Kozol's statement in paragraph 19: "Today it is not law but economics that condemns the children of the very poor to the implacable inheritance of a diminished destiny." Gear your speech to high-school seniors and their parents.

▼ A CHILD OF CRACK
Michele L. Norris

As Jonathan Kozol just explained, the children of poverty are the most maligned and most deprived subclass in America. They are also the most vulnerable to the violence that plagues inner-city neighborhoods. The essay below is a dramatic and disturbing portrait of 6-year old Dooney Waters who was raised in an inner-city apartment where his mother conducted a steady trade in crack cocaine. Sadly, the destructive impact of drugs and drug money illustrated here is a story played out in the daily lives of thousands of children throughout the country. "A Child of Crack" is an excerpt from the 1989 *Washington Post* series on Dooney Waters by reporter Michele L. Norris—a series that won Ms. Norris several awards for journalism.

1 Dooney Waters, a thickset six-year-old missing two front teeth, sat hunched over a notebook, drawing a family portrait.

2 First he sketched a stick-figure woman smoking a pipe twice her size. A coil of smoke rose from the pipe, which held a white square he called a "rock." Above that, he drew a picture of himself, another stick figure with tears falling from its face.

3 "Drugs have wrecked my mother," Dooney said as he doodled. "Drugs have wrecked a lot of mothers and fathers and children and babies. If I don't be careful, drugs are going to wreck me too."

4 His was a graphic rendering of the life of a child growing up in what police and social workers have identified as a crack house, an apartment in Washington Heights, a federally subsidized complex in Landover, Maryland, where people congregated to buy and use drugs. Dooney's life was punctuated by days

when he hid behind his bed to eat sandwiches sent by teachers who knew he would get nothing else. Nights when Dooney wet his bed because people were "yelling and doing drugs and stuff." And weeks in which he barely saw his thirty-two-year-old mother, who spent most of her time searching for drugs.

Addie Lorraine Waters, who described herself as a "slave to cocaine," said she let drug dealers use her apartment in exchange for the steady support of her habit. The arrangement turned Dooney's home into a modern-day opium den where pipes, spoons, and needles were in supply like ketchup and mustard at a fast-food restaurant. . . .   **5**

Addie's apartment was on Capital View Drive, site of more than a dozen slayings last year. Yet, the locks were removed from the front door to allow an unyielding tide of addicts and dealers to flow in and out. Children, particularly toddlers, often peered inside to ask: "Is my mommy here?"   **6**

While he was living in the crack house, Dooney was burned when a woman tossed boiling water at his mother's face in a drug dispute, and his right palm was singed when his thirteen-year-old half brother handed him a soft drink can that had been used to heat crack cocaine on the stove.   **7**

Teachers say that Dooney often begged to be taken to their homes, once asking if he could stay overnight in his classroom. "I'll sleep on the floor," Dooney told an instructor in Greenbelt Center Elementary School's after-school counseling and tutorial program. "Please don't make me go home. I don't want to go back there."   **8**

Dooney was painfully shy or exhaustively outgoing, depending largely on whether he was at home or in school—the one place where he could relax. In class, he played practical jokes on friends and passed out kisses and hugs to teachers. But his mood darkened when he boarded a bus for home.   **9**

The violence that surrounded Dooney at home was, in most cases, a by-product of the bustling drug trade. Washington Heights was host to one of the largest open-air drug markets in Prince George's County, Maryland, until a series of police raids last winter drove the problem indoors.   **10**

On Saturday, April 29, Dooney was sitting in the living room near his mother when a fifteen-year-old drug dealer burst in and tossed a pan of boiling water, a weapon that anybody with a stove could afford. Dooney, his mother, and two neighbors recalled that the dealer then plopped down on a sofa and watched as Dooney's weeping mother soothed the burns on her shoulder and neck. Dooney also was at home when another adolescent enforcer leaned through an open window on Sunday, May 14 and pitched a blend of bleach and boiling water in the face of nineteen-year-old Clifford E. Bernard, a regular in the apartment, for ignoring a $150 debt.   **11**

"People around here don't play when you owe them money," said Sherry Brown, twenty-five, a friend of Addie Waters who frequented the apartment. Brown said she smokes crack every day and has given birth to two crack-addicted babies in the past three years. "These young boys around here will burn you in a minute if you so much as look at them the wrong way," she said. "I'm telling you sure as I'm sitting here, crack has made people crazy."   **12**

Almost everyone was welcome at "Addie's place." Her patrons included   **13** some unlikely characters, but as one said, "Addie don't turn nobody away." Not the fifteen-year-old who in May burned her furniture and clothing inten- tionally with a miniature blow torch. Not even the twenty-one-year-old man who "accidentally" shot her thirteen-year-old son, Frank Russell West, five inches above the heart last Dec. 16. Police ascribed the shooting to a "drug deal gone bad."

14   Dooney was sleeping when Russell, shot in the left shoulder, stumbled back into the apartment. Dooney will not talk about the night his half brother was shot except to say, "Russell was shot 'cause of drugs."

15   Waters did not press charges against Edward "June" Powell, the man police charged with shooting Russell. Powell, whose trial has been continued because he did not have an attorney, is out on bail. "He didn't mean to do it," said Waters, who referred to Powell as a close friend of the family. "It was an accident. He meant to kill someone else." . . .

16   Dooney's mother and others who congregated in her apartment were bound by a common desperation for drugs. The majority, in their late twenties or early thirties, described themselves as "recreational" drug users until they tried the highly addictive crack. Many said they had swapped welfare checks, food stamps, furniture, and sexual favors to support their craving for crack. They had lost jobs, spouses, homes, and self-respect. Nearly all were in danger of losing children, too.

17   The Prince George's County Department of Social Services was investigat- ing charges of parental neglect against many of the people who frequented Waters's apartment. But they rarely took the county's investigations seriously. Some would joke about timid caseworkers who were too "yellow" to visit Washington Heights or would pass around letters in which officials threatened to remove children from their custody. The problem, as in Dooney's case, was that the county's threats lacked teeth. Caseworkers were usually so overloaded that they rarely had time to bring cases to court, even after they had cor- roborated charges of abuse and neglect.

18   Prince George's County police said they knew about Waters's operation but never found enough drugs in the apartment to charge her or others. "The problem is that drugs don't last long up there," said Officer Alex Bailey, who patrols the Washington Heights neighborhood. "They use them up as soon as they arrive."

19   Such explanations seemed lost on Dooney.

20   "Everybody knows about the drugs at my house," he said with a matter-of- fact tone not common to a first-grader. "The police know, too, but they don't do nothing about it. Don't nobody do nothing about it," he said.

21   Police did raid Dooney's apartment on Saturday, May 13, after they were called there by a neighbor who complained about noise. "They were looking for the drugs," Dooney said two days later, as his eyes grew full of tears. "They took all the clothes out of my mother's closets. They threw it all on my mother. They called my mother names."

Dooney also said he was afraid of the police, and when asked why, he **22** inquired, "How do you spell the word 'shoot'?" Supplied with a notebook and pen, he wrote the word slowly in large, shaky letters and then repeatedly punched the pen into the paper to form a circle of black marks. Pausing a minute, he drew a person holding a pipe, a smiling face atop a body with a circle in her belly. "That's my mother," Dooney said, pointing to the figure's face. He moved his finger toward the circle. "And that's a bullet hole."

Around the apartment, Dooney was constantly on guard, watchful for signs **23** of a ruckus or a raid. "Don't stand too close," he told a visitor standing near the front door, warning that the lockless door was often kicked open.

Since kindergarten, Dooney has pulled himself out of bed almost every **24** school morning without the help of adults or alarm clocks, said his mother, who boasted about his independence. Asked how he got himself up in the morning, Dooney tapped a finger to his foreheard and said, "My brain wakes me up. I get up when it gets light outside."

Dooney rarely bathed or brushed his hair before he went to school while he **25** was living with his mother. The bathroom was inoperable during the period that a *Washington Post* reporter and photographer regularly visited. The toilet overflowed with human waste. Stagnant water stood in the bathtub. There was no soap, no shampoo, no toilet paper or toothpaste.

When Dooney did wash, he used a yellow dishpan that doubled as a **26** washtub for rinsing out his clothes. Without a working toilet in the apartment, Dooney went across the hall when he needed to use the bathroom. If he couldn't wait, or if the neighbors weren't home, Dooney went outside in the bushes or urinated in the bathtub. He reasoned that this was the root of his bed-wetting. "I didn't want to get up to go to the bathroom, and now I pee in my bed every night," he said. . . .

Dooney's mother moved to Washington Heights in 1977, a time when the **27** complex advertised "luxury apartments." During Dooney's preschool years, Waters says, the complex was "a nice, clean place full of working class folks." Even then, marijuana, speed, powder cocaine, and other drugs circulated through the community.

But the introduction of crack swept in a new era. Nothing before it had **28** spawned so rapid and so wrenching an addiction.

Not all Washington Heights residents are involved in the drug trade. Many **29** families take pains to shield themselves and their children from drugs and violence. But the vast numbers that started using crack tell similar tales about addictions that rapidly exceeded their incomes.

Three years ago, Dooney's father worked as an electrician's apprentice. His **30** mother was a typist for the Prince George's County Board of Education and took night courses in interior design at a nearby community college.

"We had two incomes, two kids, all the things that you dream about in a **31** marriage," Waters said. "There was always food in the refrigerator and money in the bank. We did drugs then, but only at night and on weekends."

32   Dooney's parents were introduced to crack shortly after their separation, and their drug use became less recreational. Dooney's father said he became a small-time drug dealer to support his crack habit and spent six months in jail in 1988 for selling drugs. Dooney's mother said she traded away most of the family belongings—and all of her sons' toys—to buy drugs.

33   Waters, who has no criminal record, said she lost her job with the Armed Forces Benefit and Relief Association in the District of Columbia a few months after she was hired last year because she kept falling asleep on the job after smoking crack all night. With an abundance of time and a circle of drug-addicted neighbors, Waters's occasional crack use became an insatiable ache. She said she began selling crack to support her mounting habit by buying one large rock, smoking some, and selling the rest at a profit. By her account, the addiction quickly outgrew her drug-dealing income, and she began to let people smoke or sell drugs in her apartment on the condition that they shared their bounty with her.

34   At that point, Dooney's apartment became a crack house. "All of a sudden, they just set up shop," his mother said. "I told people never to keep more than $100 worth in my house. Smoking is one thing but for the police to walk up in your house and have people selling, that's two charges."

35   The children's lives declined in step with their parents. Dooney's thirteen-year-old half brother dropped out of the seventh grade last fall and has been arrested six times in two years on charges ranging from jumping trains to stealing cars.

36   Both of Waters's sons begged her to seek help. In the last three years, addiction had whittled her body from a size 16 to a size 5. Her eyes were sunken, underlined by tufts of purplish skin. Her complexion, which she said was once "the envy" of her three sisters, was lifeless, almost like vinyl.

37   Pictures in a blue photo album she kept in her living room show a more attractive Addie L. Waters—a buxom woman with radiant eyes, bright red lipstick, and a voluminous hairdo. Dooney paged through the photo album one afternoon and said, "My mother used to be pretty."

38   Dooney comes from a family with a legacy of addiction. His mother said she bought her first bag of drugs, a $5 sack of marijuana, from her alcoholic father in the late seventies. Dooney's father said he started smoking marijuana in high school and moved on to using PCP, speed, and powder cocaine.

39   Dooney's father says he smoked his first hit of crack about two years ago, when a girlfriend encouraged him to try the drug. Dooney's mother also tried crack for the first time with a lover, a boyfriend who said it "was the best high around."

40   When she first started smoking crack, Waters said, she would lock herself in the bathroom to hide from her two sons. The charade didn't last long. One evening Russell threw open the bathroom door and discovered his mother with a plastic pipe in her mouth.

41   "I tried to hide it and he saw me," says Waters, who went on to describe how Russell, then in the fifth grade, slapped her several times and flushed the

drugs down the toilet. "By him seeing me, it really affected me," Waters says. "I left it alone for about an hour."

Eventually she says, Russell's reactions became less extreme, and he got involved with the drug trade himself by selling soap chips on the street to unsuspecting buyers. 42

In early interviews, Waters called herself a good parent, a claim her two sons disputed. During the two months a reporter and photographer visited the apartment, Waters never checked Dooney's homework after school and in interviews couldn't remember his teachers' names. 43

Over time, Waters backed away from her earlier descriptions of herself. "I can't be the kind of mother I should be when I'm smoking crack," she said. "If I could do it all over again I would not do drugs." 44

Waters will take the blame for Russell, but she maintained that it would not be her fault if Dooney started using or selling drugs. 45

"If he does, it won't be because of me," Waters said. "I learned with Russell so I tell [Dooney] not to smoke or sell drugs. It's my fault that I'm doing it but I think [Dooney] knows better. I tell him all the time that he don't want to live like me." 46

Waters said that Dooney had seen her smoke crack "hundreds" of times. "He would always tell me, 'Mommy, say no to drugs' and I would say, 'Okay, baby.' " She eventually stopped trying to hide her crack habit from Dooney. 47

Crack became such a part of Dooney's life that he could list the steps for cooking it before he could tie his shoelaces. Perhaps that's why he sometimes scoffed at school programs designed to teach pupils to "just say no" to drugs. 48

"The Drug Avengers ain't real," he said, referring to an educational cartoon in which a band of superheroes prevents children from buying and using drugs. "They couldn't stop my mother from doing drugs." 49

"You have to ask yourself, 'What am I telling a child when I say to him that drugs are bad and yet everyone he knows is using drugs regularly?' " says John Van Schoonhoven, principal of Greenbelt Center. "It worries me that perhaps we aren't reaching these children and teaching them that they don't have to get involved with drugs, even though almost everyone they know already has." . . . 50

To help Dooney and others like him, teachers are being called on increasingly to attend to physical and emotional needs that are ignored in the pupils' homes. 51

"You do more parenting than teaching nowadays," says Wendy Geagan, an instructional aide who tutors children with learning problems at Greenbelt Center. "It's all so different now. We have always had to help children with their problems, but these kids want to be held. They want to be mothered. They need affection. They need their emotions soothed." . . . 52

Dooney's teachers began to suspect that his mother had a drug problem shortly after he entered kindergarten. 53

"It was rather sudden," said Janet Pelkey, Dooney's kindergarten teacher. 54

"He wasn't bathed. He became very angry and started striking out. He started gobbling down food whenever he got it, even candy and snacks in the classroom. It was obvious that something was going on at home."

55   School officials said they could not reach Dooney's mother by phone and no one answered the door during several home visits. The school-community link is difficult to maintain for many pupils from Washington Heights because they are bused to the school for desegregation purposes. Many families in Washington Heights do not own cars, making it difficult to visit a school that took three bus transfers to reach. Conversely, teachers say they are afraid to visit Washington Heights, particularly during the winter, when daylight is scarce. So teachers had little or no contact with the parents of pupils with the most turbulent home lives.

56   Concerned about his emotional problems, Dooney's kindergarten teacher placed him in the "transitional first grade," a class for students with academic problems that set them a few steps behind other children their age.

57   Dooney's condition worsened when he entered first grade last September, teachers said. He was given to fits of screaming and crying and came to school wearing torn and filthy clothes. "It was almost like he was shellshocked when he came to school . . . ," Field said. "He is such a sad little boy. He walks around with his head down and he's always sucking his little thumb."

58   "When I discovered what he was going through at home, I thought, 'My goodness, it's amazing that he even gets to school,' " Field said.

59   His mood swung like a pendulum. "Sometimes he comes in and he is just starving for affection," said Susan Bennett, an instructional assistant. "He clings to his teacher like he is afraid to let go. . . . Or sometimes when he comes to school he is angry. You brush by him and he is ready to attack."

60   Dooney entered first grade lacking several basic skills children normally master before leaving kindergarten. Teachers say he had a difficult time distinguishing among colors and could not count past ten. But Dooney's academic skills improved in classes that provided special equipment and individual tutoring. By the end of the year, his test scores put him in line with others his age, though he still had trouble tying his shoes and telling time.

61   Acting on the advice of teachers, the Prince George's County Department of Child Protective Services investigated Dooney's mother in April 1988.

62   "Based on the provided investigative information, the allegations of neglect have been indicated," child protective services worker Conchita A. Woods wrote in a letter to Waters dated April 24, 1989, a year after the investigation began. But a caseworker said that it would be "months, maybe even years" before they could seek to remove Dooney from his mother's custody.

63   Russell Brown, the investigator, said he had about twenty cases on his desk just like Waters's.

64   "We have a lot of cases that are much worse than that," Brown said. "There's probably not a whole lot I can do" for Dooney. Brown said that he does not have time to go through the arduous process of taking a child from a parent unless there is imminent danger.

"It's up to you guys to help this little boy because we just don't have the manpower to do it," Brown told Dooney's teachers over lunch on April 27. . . . **65**

At the principal's urging, Prince George's school and government officials created a pilot after-school program that offers tutoring, counseling, and drug education for students at Greenbelt Center. Equally important, it shields them from neighborhood violence for a few extra hours. Although its primary function is to help children with drug-related trauma, the program also provides academic enrichment and free day care for other students. From 3:00 to 6:30 P.M., children get help with homework, counseling, playtime, and a snack—the last meal of the day for many of them. **66**

School officials around the country say such programs may be the vanguard of school reform as more children enter schools with a crush of physical and emotional problems that detract from standard academic work. **67**

"It's become apparent that schools cannot do all that they are supposed to be doing in a six-hour day," says Nancy Kochuk, a spokeswoman for the National Education Association. "The schools are basically set up as an industrial model. It's like a factory line. That doesn't seem to serve our society very well anymore when we are dealing with children with such intense and overwhelming problems." . . . **68**

Last spring Dooney said he hated drugs and what they have done to his life. Yet he seemed to view the drug trade as an inevitable calling in the way that some children look at the steel mills and coal mines in which their forebears worked. **69**

Asked if he would sell or use drugs when he grows up, Dooney shook his head violently and wrinkled his nose in disgust. But the expression faded, and Dooney looked at the floor: "I don't want to sell drugs, but I will probably have to." **70**

▼ TOPICAL CONSIDERATIONS

1. Describe Addie and Dooney Waters's apartment. How is it a perversion of the typical middle-class American home? How do you think growing up in such conditions would have affected your intellectual and moral development?
2. What specific instances of violence has Dooney already witnessed? What is particularly shocking about the nature of these experiences? Has this essay exposed a kind of violence you never imagined existed? If so, has this exposure changed your attitudes at all?
3. Use Dooney Waters as a case study for Kozol's essay. How is Dooney a "new untouchable"? Think of your early childhood. Were there any students who came into school filthy and hungry? Were they regarded as "untouchables"?
4. Explain the bureaucratic problems exposed in paragraph 17 when

Norris introduces Prince George's County Department of Social Services. Do the problems described occur in your community? If so, is there a need for national change with respect to social services departments?

5. What is the socioeconomic history of the Washington Heights apartment complex? How had it changed so drastically? Are you aware of similar apartment complexes that have suffered such ruin? Do you think cities should cease funding for housing projects in high-risk areas?

6. According to Dooney Waters and Jonathan Kozol, how effective is the "Just Say No" to drugs campaign? Do you agree or disagree with their assessment? Has the program been effective in your community? Do you believe the campaign is geared toward people of all classes?

7. Explain the role of public schools and their teachers in Dooney Waters's case. Public school systems today receive much criticism and little praise. If you attended public school, how did the system treat you?

▼ RHETORICAL CONSIDERATIONS

1. Explain the analogy in paragraph 5: "The arrangement turned Dooney's home into a modern-day opium den where pipes, spoons, and needles were in supply like ketchup and mustard at a fast-food restaurant." How apt and effective is the comparison?

2. To what degree is the essay journalistically responsible? Did Norris thoroughly research her subject, or do you find gaps in her evidence?

3. Analyze the power of the introduction. How exactly does Norris capture your interest? Explain the contradictions and ironies.

4. Consider Dooney's language. Where does his speech belie his 6 years of age? Use specific examples. How does Dooney's speech compare to that of a 6-year-old white child from a two-parent middle-class family that cares about education?

5. Comment on the conclusion of the essay. Is it effective? Did it move you? Use evidence from the essay to determine whether the ending is logical, consistent or contrived.

▼ WRITING ASSIGNMENTS

1. Assume the perspective of a child psychologist. Write a paper that explains Dooney's behavior, appearance, and belief that he will one day sell drugs. Determine what has caused his pain. Decide whether

or not he can escape the crack world. Consider issues of race and class.

2. Explore the implications of the essay's title, "A Child of Crack." How is Dooney a child of crack? And how are Sherry Brown's children (paragraph 12) also crack babies? Using the other essays in this chapter, show how children are the victims of society's decay.

3. What antidrug measures are being taken in your community? Which seem the most effective? Write a paper in which you discuss the kinds of measures you would take. Consider federal and local government, school systems, parents, civic leaders, the law, and private citizens.

▼ THE VALUE OF VOLUNTEERING
Charles R. Larson

Poverty, violence, misery, and disease. As we have read, these are the byproducts of the imbalance of power in America. But instead of simply hoping for the best, there is something we can do. In the essay below, Charles R. Larson suggests how a whole civic culture can be developed along the line of the Peace Corps which for 30 years has raised the quality of life in so many third world countries. We know how to eliminate illiteracy, to put people to work, to provide better health care, to educate the young, to clean up the environment. We have the wealth and the technological know-how. What we need to turn America around, Larson says, is simply people who care. The author is a professor of literature at American University. This article first appeared in *Newsweek* in July 1991.

The Peace Corps is 30 years old this summer. The 130,000 people who volun- 1
teered over the past three decades may have made little dent on American foreign policy. But they have left a mark on individual communities around the world—entire nations, even—that is irreversible. Just to mention two examples, the improved educational standards and increased literacy rates in countries as disparate as Nigeria and Micronesia are due in large part to the work of diligent volunteers during the '60s and '70s.

If the Peace Corps never became a powerful force or an international model 2
for politically acceptable aid (neither of which it was intended to be), that's due to the individual volunteers themselves, not the program itself. Each volunteer goes through a process of awakening to the possibilities of self-awareness. Few

volunteers I know would disagree: they were the real beneficiaries of this people-to-people experiment, not the countries that hosted them.

3   My own particulars were not that extraordinary. When I joined in 1962, at 24, there were fewer than a thousand volunteers. Why did I join? I feared I would be drafted and end up in Vietnam. When told I was assigned to Nigeria, I had to check a map to learn where the country was. I had no burning sense of altruism, or commitment to the objectives (improved education) for my host country. My most evident quality was that I knew little about myself and even less about others. I was a blank sheet of paper at a moment of crucial self-discovery.

4   It was a transforming experience. I saw ways of life I would never have seen had I remained within the comfortable domain of my provincial Midwestern upbringing. For the first time, I learned to think of someone besides myself, to consider that there is no single way of observing a problem or answering a troubling question. I discovered that without the mutual tolerance and respect of other peoples' cultures, there is no possibility for harmony in our world.

5   I'm convinced that what I learned overseas as a Peace Corps volunteer was fairly typical. Yes, there were others who had difficult assignments, but few will deny that their gains were greater than their losses. Would they do it again? You bet, on a moment's notice, as some already have and others plan to do once lives now immersed in families and careers have taken another turn.

6   Our nation needs the lessons of the Peace Corps today. We talk about the economic morass our country has fallen into, but our moral muddle is much more disturbing. We are a nation of factions, with hardly any two groups agreeing about anything. We have forgotten how to share or how to be understanding of the bottom 20 percent of the population we have largely written out of our lives. Poverty, declining health standards, illiteracy, a deteriorating infrastructure, a general intolerance of anyone different from ourselves—all cry out for serious measures. Yet we are afraid to render even a quick fix for fear of stepping on someone's toes.

7   We need to get people back together, working with and listening to one another. We need to do this with our young people, at a time when careers haven't been fully launched and when they will still pay attention to another opinion, welcome a differing view. President Kennedy set up the Peace Corps quickly, through executive order, knowing that endless debate would kill the idea by slow suffocation. We need the same kind of forceful action now if we want to change where this country is headed.

8   **Gifted educators:** We need a two-year national-service plan for every young American—no exemptions, period. That includes the rich and the poor, the educated and the uneducated, even the handicapped. We need to convince each and every individual that there is something that he or she can contribute, that work has value, that an enormous effort will be needed to help turn our nation around.

9   Most of all, we need teachers—but not only those with university degrees. There are plenty of gifted educators who have never stood in front of a class-

room. They can help with literacy programs or teach English to our rising number of immigrants. Others can teach job skills—the value of using one's hands—which include anything from auto mechanics to computer programming. We need health-care workers, nurses' aides—skilled and unskilled—providing care for the elderly and the young. We need preschool centers run by welfare mothers, sharing their frustrations and their joys, but doing something to connect with other people. We need highway and road crews of young men and women, restoring our transportation system before it collapses under the weight of inattention and the lack of funds. We need all of these and more to demonstrate once again that people can make a difference, both individually and collectively.

We've had the Teachers Corps, and VISTA, and other movements that   **10** were short-lived. They came at difficult times (the war in Vietnam, the war on poverty) but were little more than precursors of our current urgency. In this present do-nothing era, when our elected leaders refuse to address the troubling issues of our time, it is necessary for people to assume that sense of action, to give to the nation so that it can give back to us what has been forgotten: tolerance and responsibility. Besides a cure for our moral poverty, we might even help the economy. Or at least learn that every individual has something to offer.

▼ TOPICAL CONSIDERATIONS

1. How would Larson respond to Kozol's claim that someday our indifference to the nation's poor, underfed and poorly educated will come back to haunt us?
2. What do you think of Larson's domestic Peace Corps plan? Do you agree that it should be mandatory? Considering all the societal problems you've read about in this chapter, would you volunteer for such a two-year national service? Explain your answer.
3. Larson claims that "our moral muddle" is "much more disturbing" than the economic polarization in our country. Do you agree? Which do you think is more to blame for our country's problems? Would any other authors in this chapter agree with Larson?
4. According to Larson what has the Peace Corps achieved in the world? From what you know of the Peace Corps, do you agree with Larson that it "never became a powerful force or an international model for politically acceptable aid" (paragraph 2)?
5. Larson writes in paragraph 3 that he "was a blank sheet of paper at a moment of crucial self-discovery." How did this state enhance his Peace Corps experience? When have you had a moment of self-discovery? Did it require open-mindedness? Are you, as a college student, ready for self-discovery?
6. Do you agree that not all teachers have to be university-educated?

Have you ever met a truly gifted teacher who had no degree and "never stood in a classroom"? If so, describe that person. When have you been called upon to be a teacher? What skills did it require you to use? How was it a challenge?

▼ RHETORICAL CONSIDERATIONS

1. Larson shifts his point of view from first-person singular to first-person plural. Who is included in the "we"? Do you feel part of his appeal?
2. Nine sentences begin with "We need." Is this repetition an effective rhetorical device? Rewrite six of these sentences and determine if your rewrite is more effective.
3. How would you describe the tone of Larson's writing? How does his tone fit or not fit his appeal here?
4. Analyze the effectiveness of the conclusion. Would it encourage you to take action?

▼ WRITING ASSIGNMENTS

1. Design a two-year human services program that would reach out to people like Dooney Waters. Write a proposal to submit to Charles Larson that outlines the philosophy and goals of your program.
2. You have been asked to speak in Washington D.C. at the Thirtieth Anniversary of the Peace Corps Celebration. The subject of your talk is achieving tolerance for others through self-discovery. Write a ten minute speech.
3. Interview a Peace Corps volunteer. Find out if his or her experience was "the toughest job [he or she] ever loved." Write a paper that investigates the value of volunteering. Is volunteering predominantly done for self-satisfaction?

4 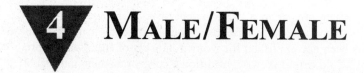 MALE/FEMALE

The feminist movement was reborn, some twenty-five years ago, out of the recognition that women lacked the access to power enjoyed by men. Over the decades much has been accomplished for women in areas of equal pay, reproductive rights, and child care. Likewise, traditional roles of women and men at home, in the workplace, and in society have been challenged and, to a great extent, altered. The essays in this chapter explore the struggles and triumphs of both women and men who in the last decade of the twentieth century continue to redefine who they are.

Our opening piece, "Masculine/Feminine," is the lament of Prudence Mackintosh who went out of her way to raise her sons in a nonviolent, nonsexist environment. In her home toy guns were replaced by dolls, dads and moms did dishes, and it was okay for boys to cry. Despite all her efforts at consciousness raising, the forces of culture and nature, alas, conspired to demonstrate that boys will be boys.

Because of the feminist movement, today's young women are free to make active choices instead of forced accommodations. From medical schools to welding unions, many of the old barriers are down. But what worries Anna Quindlen in "Feminist" is that 1990s women are taking for granted the hard-won victories of the past. She warns that unless today's women become more politically active, old walls and stereotypes may reemerge.

To Kay Ebeling the feminist movement has backfired on women. In "The Failure of Feminism" she complains that a woman "can't live the true feminist life unless she denies her child-bearing biology." Linking the movement to unrealistic demands and expectations, Ebeling condemns feminism for creating a caste of overworked women abandoned by men free to live the good life.

In the next piece, "Requiem for a Soldier," Linda Bird Francke tells of a final gender barrier that appears to be breaking down: women in the military. But instead of applauding the growing equality of roles, Francke tries to sort out her feelings about the equality of the grave.

The next essay exposes what the author sees as a "violent backlash against feminism"—a dark and punishing conspiracy to keep women from power. In the "The Beauty Myth," Naomi Wolf contends that our male-dominated mass culture has put such a premium on female beauty that it has created in women a cult of self-contempt, physical obsession, and terror.

Over the last few years interest in men's issues has mushroomed as reflected in the next three essays. In "Men as Success Objects" psychologist Warren Farrell examines the roots of men's anxiety about themselves. Just as women in our culture are unfairly valued for their beauty, men, he argues, are valued for their wallets—even by successful women.

Finally, Sam Allis examines "postfeminist males" confused and angry over the limited roles they can choose from today compared to the new options women have won. Is macho outdated? Is the "sensitive" male the solution? Will beating tom-toms at wilderness retreats make men feel more like men? Can the "Daddy Track" be part of corporate life? In "What Do Men Really Want?" Allis paints a turbulent picture of 1990s men desperately seeking manhood.

▼ MASCULINE/FEMININE

Prudence Mackintosh

Prudence Mackintosh, a freelance writer, is the author of a very funny book, *Thundering Sneakers* (1981) from which this essay was taken. She is also the mother of three boys, whom she intended to raise free of sex-role differences and cultural stereotyping. She gave them dolls to play with rather than guns and taught them that mom and dad shared household chores. As she has sadly learned, however, there is "more to this sex-role learning than the home environment can handle," including powerful forces of culture and, perhaps, nature.

1 I had every intention to raise liberated, nonviolent sons whose aggressive tendencies would be mollified by a sensitivity and compassion that psychologists claim were denied their father's generation.

2 I did not buy guns or war toys (although Grandmother did). My boys even had a secondhand baby doll until the garage sale last summer. I did buy Marlo Thomas' *Free to Be You and Me* record, a collection of nonsexist songs, stories, and poems, and I told them time and time again that it was okay to cry and be scared sometimes. I overruled their father and insisted that first grade was much too early for organized competitive soccer leagues. They know that moms *and dads* do dishes and diapers. And although they use it primarily for the convenient bathroom between the alley and the sandpile, my boys know that the storeroom is now mother's office. In such an environment, surely they would grow up free of sex-role stereotypes. At the very least wouldn't they pick up their own socks?

3 My friends with daughters were even more zealous. They named their daughters strong, cool unisex names like Blakeney, Brett, Brook, Lindsay, and Blair, names that lent themselves to corporate letterheads, not Tupperware party invitations. These moms looked on Barbie with disdain and bought trucks and science kits. They shunned frilly dresses for overalls. They subscribed to Feminist Press and read stories called "My Mother the Mail Carrier" instead of "Sleeping Beauty." At the swimming pool one afternoon, I watched a particularly fervent young mother, ironically clad in a string bikini, encourage her daughter. "You're so strong, Blake! Kick hard, so you'll be the strongest kid in this pool." When my boys splashed water in Blakeney's eyes and she ran whimpering to her mother, this mom exhorted, "You go back in that pool and shake your fist like this and say, 'You do that again and I'll bust your lights out.' " A new generation of little girls, assertive and ambitious, taking a backseat to no one?

4 It's a little early to assess the results of our efforts, but when my seven-year-old son, Jack, comes home singing—to the tune of *"Frère jacques"*—"Farrah

Fawcett, Farrah Fawcett, I love you" and five minutes later asks Drew, his five-year-old brother, if he'd like his nose to be a blood fountain, either we're backsliding or there's more to this sex-role learning than the home environment can handle.

5   I'm hearing similar laments from mothers of daughters. "She used to tell everyone that she was going to grow up to be a lawyer just like Daddy," said one, "but she's hedging on that ambition ever since she learned that no one wears a blue fairy tutu in the courtroom." Another mother with two sons, a daughter, and a very successful career notes that, with no special encouragement, only her daughter keeps her room neat and loves to set the table and ceremoniously seat her parents. At a Little League game during the summer, fearful that this same young daughter might be absorbing the stereotype "boys play while girls watch," her parents readily assured her that she too could participate when she was eight years old. "Oh," she exclaimed with obvious delight, "I didn't know they had cheerleaders."

6   How does it happen? I have my own theories, but decided to do a little reading to see if any of the "experts" agreed with me. I was also curious to find out what remedies they recommended. The books I read propose that sex roles are culturally induced. In simplistic terms, rid the schools, their friends, and the television of sexism, and your daughters will dump their dolls and head straight for the boardroom while your sons contemplate nursing careers. *Undoing Sex Stereotypes* by Marcia Guttentag and Helen Bray is an interesting study of efforts to overcome sexism in the classroom. After reading it, I visited my son's very traditional school and found it guilty of unabashedly perpetrating the myths that feminists abhor. Remember separate water fountains? And how, even if the line was shorter, no boy would be caught dead drinking from the girls' fountain and vice versa? That still happens. "You wouldn't want me to get cooties, would you, Mom?" my son says, defending the practice. What did I expect in a school where the principal still addresses his faculty, who range in age from 23 to 75, as "girls"?

7   Nevertheless, having been a schoolteacher myself, I am skeptical of neatly programmed nonsexist curriculum packets like Guttentag and Bray's. But if you can wade through the jargon ("people of the opposite sex hereafter referred to as POTOS"), some of the observations and exercises are certainly thought-provoking and revealing. In one exercise fifth-grade students were asked to list adjectives appropriate to describe women. The struggle some of the children had in shifting their attitudes about traditional male roles is illustrated in this paragraph written by a fifth-grade girl who was asked to write a story about a man using the adjectives she had listed to describe women:

Once there was a boy who all his life was very *gentle*. He never hit anyone or started a fight and when some of his friends were not feeling well, he was *loving* and *kind* to them. When he got older he never changed. People started not liking him because he was *weak, petite,* and he wasn't like any of the other men—not strong or tough. Most of his life he sat alone thinking about why no one liked him. Then one day he went out and tried to act like the other men. He joined a baseball team, but he was no good, he always got out. Then he decided to join the hockey team. He couldn't play good. He kept on breaking all the rules. So he quit the team and joined the soccer team. These men were *understanding* to him. He was really good at soccer, and was the best on the team. That year they won the championship and the rest of his life he was happy.*

After reading this paragraph it occurred to me that this little girl's self-esteem and subsequent role in life would be enhanced by a teacher who spent less time on "nonsexist intervention projects" and more time on writing skills. But that, of course, is not what the study was meant to reveal. **8**

The junior high curriculum suggested by *Undoing Sex Stereotypes* has some laudable consciousness-raising goals. For example, in teaching units called "Women's Roles in American History" and "The Socialization of Women and the Image of Women in the Media" teenagers are encouraged to critically examine television commercials, soap operas, and comic books. But am I a traitor to the cause if I object when the authors in another unit use *Romeo and Juliet* as a study of the status of women? Something is rotten in Verona when we have to consider Juliet's career possibilities and her problems with self-actualization. The conclusions of this project were lost on me; I quit reading when the author began to talk about ninth-graders who were "cognitively at a formal operational level." I don't even know what my "external sociopsychological situation" is. However, I think I did understand some of the conclusions reached by the kids: **9**

> "Girls are smart."
> "If a woman ran a forklift where my father works, there would be a walkout."
> "Men cannot be pom-pom girls."

Eminently more readable, considering that both authors are educators of educators, is *How to Raise Independent and Professionally Successful Daughters,* by Drs. Rita and Kenneth Dunn. The underlying and, I think, questionable assumption in this book is that little boys have been reared correctly all along. Without direct parental intervention, according to the Dunns, daughters tend to absorb and reflect society's values. The Dunns paint a dark picture indeed for the parents who fail to channel their daughters toward professional success. The woman who remains at home with children while her husband is involved in the "real world" with an "absorbing and demanding day-to-day commitment that brings him into contact with new ideas, jobs, and people (attractive self-actualized females)" is sure to experience lowered IQ, according to the Dunns. They go on to predict the husband's inevitable affair and the subsequent divorce, **10**

* From *Undoing Sex Stereotypes* by Marcia Guttentag and Helen Bray © 1976 McGraw-Hill, Inc. Used with permission of McGraw-Hill Book Co.

which leaves the wife emotionally depressed and probably financially dependent on her parents.

11 Now I'm all for women developing competency and self-reliance, but the Dunns' glorification of the professional is excessive. Anyone who has worked longer than a year knows that eventually any job loses most of its glamour. And the world is no less "real" at home. For that matter, mothers at home may be more "real" than bankers or lawyers. How is a corporate tax problem more real than my counseling with the maid whose boyfriend shot her in the leg? How can reading a balance sheet compare with comforting a five-year-old who holds his limp cat and wants to know why we have to lose the things we love? And on the contrary, it is my husband, the professional, who complains of lowered IQ. Though we wooed to Faulkner, my former ace English major turned trial lawyer now has time for only an occasional *Falconer* or Peter Benchley thriller. Certainly there is value in raising daughters to be financially self-supporting, but there is not much wisdom in teaching a daughter that she must achieve professional success or her marriage probably won't last.

12 In a chapter called "What to Do from Birth to Two," the authors instruct parents to introduce dolls only if they represent adult figures or groups of figures. "Try not to give her her own 'baby.' A baby doll is acceptable only for dramatizing the familiar episodes she has actually experienced, like a visit to the doctor." If some unthinking person should give your daughter a baby doll, and she likes it, the Dunns recommend that you permit her to keep it without exhibiting any negative feelings, "but do not lapse into cuddling it or encouraging her to do so. Treat it as any other object and direct attention to other more beneficial toys." I wonder if the Dunns read an article by Anne Roiphe called "Can You have Everything and Still Want Babies?" which appeared in *Vogue* a couple of years ago. Ms. Roiphe was deploring the extremes to which our liberation has brought us. "It is nice to have beautiful feet, it may be desirable to have small feet, but it is painful and abusive to bind feet. It is also a good thing for women to have independence, freedom and choice, movement, and opportunity; but I'm not so sure that the current push against mothering will not be another kind of binding of the soul. . . . As women we have thought so little of ourselves that when the troops came to liberate us we rushed into the streets leaving our most valuable attributes behind as if they belonged to the enemy."

13 The Dunns' book is thorough, taking parents step-by-step through the elementary years and on to high school. Had I been raising daughters, however, I think I would have flunked out in the chapter "What to Do from Age Two to Five." In discussing development of vocabulary, the Doctors Dunn prohibit the use of nonsensical words for bodily functions. I'm sorry, Doctors, but I've experimented with this precise terminology and discovered that the child who yells "I have to defecate, Mom" across four grocery aisles is likely to be left in the store. A family without a few poo-poo jokes is no family at all.

14 These educators don't help me much in my efforts to liberate my sons. And although I think little girls are getting a better deal with better athletic training

and broader options, I believe we're kidding ourselves if we think we can raise our sons and daughters alike. Certain inborn traits seem to be immune to parental and cultural tampering. How can I explain why a little girl baby sits on a quilt in the park thoughtfully examining a blade of grass, while my baby William uproots grass by handfuls and eats it? Why does a mother of very bright and active daughters confide that until she went camping with another family of boys, she feared that my sons had a hyperactivity problem? I'm sure there are plenty of rowdy, noisy little girls, but I'm not just talking about rowdiness and noise. I'm talking about some sort of primal physicalness that causes the walls of my house to pulsate on rainy days. I'm talking about something inexplicable that makes my sons fall into a mad, scrambling, pull-your-ears-off-kick-your-teeth-in heap just before bedtime, when they're not even mad at each other. I mean something that causes them to climb the doorjamb with honey and peanut butter on their hands while giving me a synopsis of *Star Wars* that contains only five intelligible words: "And this this guy, he 'pssshhhhhhh.' And then this thing went 'vrongggggg.' But this little guy said, 'Nong-neee-nonh-nee.' " When Jack and Drew are not kicking a soccer ball or each other, they are kicking the chair legs, the cat, the baby's silver rattle, and, inadvertently, Baby William himself, whom they have affectionately dubbed "Tough Eddy." Staying put in a chair for the duration of a one-course meal is torturous for these boys. They compensate by never quite putting both feet under the table. They sit with one leg doubled under them while the other leg extends to one side. The upper half of the body appears committed to the task at hand—eating—but the lower extremities are poised to lunge should a more compelling distraction present itself. From this position, I have observed, one brother can trip a haughty dessert-eating sibling who is flaunting the fact he ate all his "sweaty little pease." Although we have civilized them to the point that they dutifully mumble, "May I be excused, please?" their abrupt departure from the table invariably overturns at least one chair or whatever milk remains. This sort of constant motion just doesn't lend itself to lessons in thoughtfulness and gentleness.

Despite my encouragement, my sons refuse to invite little girls to play 15 anymore. Occasionally friends leave their small daughters with us while they run errands. I am always curious to see what these females will find of interest in my sons' roomful of Tonka trucks and soccer balls. One morning the boys suggested that the girls join them in playing Emergency with the big red fire trucks and ambulance. The girls were delighted and immediately designated the ambulance as theirs. The point of Emergency, as I have seen it played countless times with a gang of little boys, is to make as much noise with the siren as possible and to crash the trucks into each other or into the leg of a living-room chair before you reach your destination.

The girls had other ideas. I realized why they had selected the ambulance. 16 It contained three dolls: a driver, a nurse, and sick man on the stretcher. My boys have used that ambulance many times, but the dolls were always secondary to the death-defying race with the fire trucks; they were usually just thrown in the back of the van as an afterthought. The girls took the dolls out, stripped and re-dressed them tenderly, and made sure that they were seated in their appropriate places for the first rescue. Once the fire truck had been lifted off the man's leg, the girls required a box of Band-Aids and spent the next half hour making a bed for the patient and reassuring him that he was going to be all right. These little girls and my sons had seen the same NBC *Emergency* series, but the girls had apparently picked up on the show's nurturing aspects, while Jack and Drew were interested only in the equipment, the fast driving, and the sirens. . . .

17   Of course, I want my sons to grow up knowing that what's inside a woman's head is more important than her appearance, but I'm sure they're getting mixed signals when I delay our departure for the swimming pool to put on lipstick. I also wonder what they make of their father, whose favorite aphorism is "beautiful women rule the world." I suppose what we want for these sons and the women they may marry someday is a sensitivity that enables them to be both flexible and at ease with their respective roles, so that marriage contracts are unnecessary. When my sons bring me the heads of two purple irises from the neighbor's yard and ask, "Are you really the most beautiful mama in the whole world like Daddy says, and did everyone want to marry you?" do you blame me if I keep on waffling?

▼ TOPICAL CONSIDERATIONS

1. Mackintosh discusses what raising a family has taught her about the differences in the way boys and girls behave. She includes a number of amusing illustrations. What are some of these examples? Do the scenes she describes sound like any you've experienced in your own home?

2. Reread Mackintosh's description (paragraph 15) of how her sons and their little girl visitors played *Emergency*. What is significant about this illustration? Do you think its implications are always true? For example, do nurturing qualities belong exclusively to girls? Is aggressiveness typical only of boys? Give examples to support your answer.

3. What do you think of the efforts Mackintosh and her friends have made to keep their children from assuming stereotypical sex roles? Would you raise your children the same way or differently? Explain your answer.

4. Mackintosh's essay encourages a healthy acceptance of the fact that boys and girls act differently when they are growing up and that these differences are inherent. Can you also think of some qualities or traits that boys and girls have in common? Or some that could be expressed by either?

5. Mackintosh implies that boys don't need to be encouraged to be nurses, just to avoid stereotypical sex roles. Is it necessarily true, though, that a man wouldn't want to be a nurse? Or a secretary? Or

a kindergarten teacher? Or that he wouldn't have a natural aptitude for these careers? Is Mackintosh implying that a woman naturally wouldn't want to be a lawyer? Would you agree if this were the assumption? Give reasons for your answer.

▼ RHETORICAL CONSIDERATIONS

1. Where does Mackintosh state her thesis? Is it implicit or explicit?
2. What is the primary rhetorical strategy Mackintosh uses to develop her essay? Cite individual passages to substantiate your answer.
3. Find five sentences that demonstrate Mackintosh's use of concrete detail. Revise the sentences by replacing these specifics with generalities. Read the two versions aloud. What is the difference in effect?
4. Examine Mackintosh's first and last paragraphs. Explain how the last paragraph ties in with the first to unify the essay and bring it to a conclusive finish.

▼ WRITING ASSIGNMENTS

1. What was it like growing up in your home? Were you encouraged to assume a stereotypical sex role? Or did your parents try to avoid this? In an essay, discuss these questions.
2. Identify a career that tends to be either male-oriented or female-oriented. Write an essay in which you discuss why this is true. Analyze whether you think it should or will continue to be this way.

▼ FEMINIST

Anna Quindlen

Anna Quindlen remembers life before the feminist revolution. An ardent feminist, she joined the struggle for women's equality 20 years ago and now enjoys its benefits. But in this piece, she worries that today's women, beneficiaries of feminism but never foot soldiers in the cause, may let their sense of entitlement lure them into a false sense of security. She fears that old stereotypes and limitations may reemerge unless today's self-described "generation of individualists" works as a group for women's rights. Anna Quindlen's nationally syndicated column "Public and Private" appears in *The New York Times* and other newspapers around the country. She was a reporter and editor with the *Times* from 1977 to 1986 when she created the popular column, "Life in the 30's" where this essay first appeared in 1988. *Living Out Loud* is a collection of those essays. Her first novel, *Object Lessons,* was published in 1991. Ms. Quindlen is married and the mother of two sons and a daughter.

1   I would like to say that I became a feminist to make the world better for women everywhere, but in truth it was to make the world better for me. This was almost twenty years ago, and altruism was not my strong suit; to paraphrase Rhett Butler, the only cause I believed in was me. Nor was I struck by the rank injustice of sex discrimination. It just seemed like men got all the good stuff.

2   I grew up in a city run by men, in a church run by men, in a household run by a man. Men had comfortable shoes, a life outside the home, and money in their wallets. Women had children, who are wonderful but not sufficient unto themselves, at least for me. The best job you could get as a woman then involved a lifetime vow of chastity, which was not my thing. I figured either life was going to be considerably different for me than it was for my mother, or I was going to be angry all the time. I jumped on the bandwagon. I've never gotten off.

3   As I watched the convention of the National Organization for Women on television the other night, I realized my only real political identification has been with womens' rights. It is the only cause I have ever believed in that has improved the world. Life for many women is not the same as it was when I was young, and I do not believe it will ever be so again. I do not believe that ever again will there be a handful of token women in the graduating class at Harvard Law School. I do not believe that ever again will there be a handful of female New York City police officers.

4   Change is exceedingly slow, but somehow sure. My friend the female rabbi still meets up with the occasional father of the bride who will not pay for the wedding if she officiates. To write that sentence alone is a measure of the shock of the new, and the stubborn strength of the old. On the one hand, the father of the bride and his wallet. On the other, a rabbi who is a woman.

5   I went to a women's college. Not long ago I was asked what it was like. At

the time I was speaking at a college that until 1969 had been all-male and fiercely proud to be so. I said it was a little like learning to swim while holding on to the side of the pool; I didn't learn the arm movements until after I graduated, but by that time I was one hell of a kicker.

When I began school there were still marks on the university buildings made 6 by student demonstrators. Perhaps that was why some of us were happy to view our own feminism as a liberal and not a radical political movement. A liberal movement is precisely what we got. We were permitted limited access to the world of men provided that to some considerable extent we mimicked their behavior but did not totally alter our own.

I suppose we sometimes feel disappointed with our circumstances today 7 because now that the liberal movement has taken place, now that women are performing cardiac surgery and becoming members of the welders' unions, it has become clearer than ever that what we really needed was a radical movement. We have given the word an ominous connotation, but in fact it means only a root change. We needed a root change in the way things work: in the way everyone approached work, in the way everyone approached the care of children, in the way everyone, male and female, approached the balance of life and work and obligations and inclinations. I do not think this really came about.

Everyone now accepts that men, too, can cry, but women still often have 8 more reason to. "We must fight for parental leaves for mothers and fathers," one feminist told me, and I knew she was right, except that I didn't know many men who were going to take paternity leaves if they were offered. I suppose we must fight to raise sons who will take them.

We still find ourselves dependent on the kindness of strangers, from Su- 9 preme Court justices to husbands and lovers. I do not believe that we are likely to go back to a time when patients refuse to be treated by female doctors, but I think we could go back to a time when doctors of both sexes are forbidden by law to perform abortions. I think that institutions run by men, with a sprinkling of women in high places, may begin to feel self-congratulatory and less enthusiastic about hiring and promotion efforts about which they have always been ambivalent.

It is difficult to communicate some of the terror of this to young women who 10 have grown up with a sense of entitlement, who were born in the year in which a bin was filled with undergarments on the Atlantic City boardwalk in protest of the Miss America pageant, who grew up knowing that they could go to Princeton or rabbinical school or the moon if they worked at it hard enough, who have never been asked how fast they typed.

Some have told me that they do not think of themselves as feminists, that 11 they are a generation of individualists who do not align themselves with a group cause, particularly one which represents battles they believe have been largely won.

Perhaps it was a particularly female thing about me, but I did not feel 12 qualified, when I was young, to be an individualist. I felt that by birth I was part of a group, and that the single hallmark of that group was that they were denied access to money and power by virtue of biology. That seemed overwhelming to me at seventeen, and it seemed to present me with two choices. One was to distinguish myself from other women. The other was to stand up for the rights of women as a group. I wasn't capable of going it alone. Luckily, I didn't have to. I had my sisters.

▼ TOPICAL CONSIDERATIONS

1. What does Quindlen mean when she says in paragraph 3 that her "only real political identification has been with women's rights"?
2. Have you ever had any strong political identifications? What have you identified with? What actions have you taken to help support those causes? How satisfying was this political identification for you?
3. What, according to Quindlen, is the difference between liberal feminism and radical feminism? Which does Quindlen prefer and why? Which do you prefer and why?
4. In paragraph 8 Quindlen writes, "men, too, can cry, but women still often have more reason to." Do you agree or disagree with this statement? What examples from your own experiences can you think of to support your stance?
5. Do you think that women of your age group have any rights left to fight for? If so, what are these? If not, why not?
6. What, according to Quindlen, is the "single hallmark" of being female? Do you agree with this?
7. Do you think of yourself as a feminist? Why or why not?

▼ RHETORICAL CONSIDERATIONS

1. How effective is the title of this essay for you? Did it make you want to read the article or not? Why did you feel this way?
2. Does the first paragraph of this article attract you or put you off? Why? What tone or attitude does this first paragraph set?
3. Quindlen's article contains many short, terse sentences. How does she use these in her article? How effective is this device for you?
4. Explain the rhetorical effect of the repetition in paragraph 2: "I grew up in a city run by men, in a church run by men, in a household run by a man." Where else do you find such repetition? Explain its effect, too.

▼ WRITING ASSIGNMENTS

1. To what extent do you consider yourself to be a feminist? Write a paper in which you explore this question. Give specific reasons for your answer.

2. Do you think that it is easier to be a feminist if you are a female, or do you think that males are just as capable of understanding and supporting feminist issues? In supporting your point of view, write about famous people or people you know who exemplify what you are saying.
3. Quindlen states that she did not become a feminist to save the world; she became a feminist to please herself. What have you done in your life strictly to please yourself? Were you pleased by it? Did you feel any guilt? Are you glad, now, that you did this, or do you have any regrets?

▼ THE FAILURE OF FEMINISM
Kay Ebeling

Like Anna Quindlen, Kay Ebeling is a writer and mother. Like Quindlen, Ebeling joined the feminist revolution when she was younger. Unlike Quindlen, Ebeling has little praise for what the feminist movement has accomplished in the past twenty years. While others celebrate women's hard-won victories in education, employment, and reproduction, the author of this provocative essay calls feminism "The Great Experiment That Failed." Given the biological reality that women have babies not men, Ebeling says that all the movement has produced is "frenzied and over-worked women dropping kids off at daycare centers." Only men have been liberated by feminism. A single mother, Ebeling is a free-lance writer from Humboldt County, California. This tough and spirited essay first appeared in *Newsweek* in November 1990.

The other day I had the world's fastest blind date. A Yuppie from Eureka penciled me in for 50 minutes on a Friday and met me at a watering hole in the rural northern California town of Arcata. He breezed in, threw his jammed daily planner on the table and shot questions at me, watching my reactions as if it were a job interview. He eyed how much I drank. Then he breezed out to his next appointment. He had given us 50 minutes to size each other up and see if there was any chance for romance. His exit was so fast that as we left he let the door slam back in my face. It was an interesting slam. 1

Most of our 50-minute conversation had covered the changing state of male-female relationships. My blind date was 40 years old, from the Experimental Generation. He is "actively pursuing new ways for men and women to interact now that old traditions no longer exist." That's a real quote. He really did say that, when I asked him what he liked to do. This was a man who'd read *Ms.* Magazine and believed every word of it. He'd been single for 16 years but 2 had lived with a few women during that time. He was off that evening for a ski weekend, meeting someone who was paying her own way for the trip.

3   I too am from the Experimental Generation, but I couldn't even pay for my own drink. To me, feminism has backfired against women. In 1973 I left what could have been a perfectly good marriage, taking with me a child in diapers, a 10-year-old Plymouth and Volume 1, Number One of Ms. Magazine. I was convinced I could make it on my own. In the last 15 years my ex has married or lived with a succession of women. As he gets older, his women stay in their 20s. Meanwhile, I've stayed unattached. He drives a BMW. I ride buses.

4   Today I see feminism as the Great Experiment That Failed, and women in my generation, its perpetrators, are the casualties. Many of us, myself included, are saddled with raising children alone. The resulting poverty makes us experts at cornmeal recipes and ways to find free recreation on weekends. At the same time, single men from our generation amass fortunes in CDs and real-estate ventures so they can breeze off on ski weekends. Feminism freed men, not women. Now men are spared the nuisance of a wife and family to support. After childbirth, if his wife's waist doesn't return to 20 inches, the husband can go out and get a more petite woman. It's far more difficult for the wife, now tied down with a baby, to find a new man. My blind date that Friday waved goodbye as he drove off in his RV. I walked home and paid the sitter with laundry quarters.

5   The main message of feminism was: woman, you don't need a man; remember, those of you around 40, the phrase: "A woman without a man is like a fish without a bicycle?" That joke circulated through "consciousness raising" groups across the country in the '70s. It was a philosophy that made divorce and cohabitation casual and routine. Feminism made women disposable. So today a lot of females are around 40 and single with a couple of kids to raise on their own. Child-support payments might pay for a few pairs of shoes, but in general, feminism gave men all the financial and personal advantages over women.

6   What's worse, we asked for it. Many women decided: you don't need a family structure to raise your children. We packed them off to day-care centers where they could get their nurturing from professionals. Then we put on our suits and ties, packed our briefcases and took off on this Great Experiment, convinced that there was no difference between ourselves and the guys in the other offices.

7   'Biological thing': How wrong we were. Because like it or not, women have babies. It's this biological thing that's just there, these organs we're born with. The truth is, a woman can't live the true feminist life unless she denies her childbearing biology. She has to live on the pill, or have her tubes tied at an early age. Then she can keep up with the guys with an uninterrupted career and then, when she's 30, she'll be paying her own way on ski weekends too.

8   The reality of feminism is a lot of frenzied and overworked women dropping kids off at day-care centers. If the child is sick, they just send along some children's Tylenol and then rush off to underpaid jobs that they don't even like. Two of my working-mother friends told me they were mopping floors and folding laundry after midnight last week. They live on five hours of sleep, and it shows in their faces. And they've got husbands! I'm not advocating that

women retrogress to the brainless housewives of the '50s who spent afternoons baking macaroni sculptures and keeping Betty Crocker files. Post–World War II women were the first to be left with a lot of free time, and they weren't too creative in filling it. Perhaps feminism was a reaction to that Brainless Betty, and in that respect, feminism has served a purpose.

Women should get educations so they can be brainy in the way they raise **9** their children. Women can start small businesses, do consulting, write freelance out of the home. But women don't belong in 12-hour-a-day executive office positions, and I can't figure out today what ever made us think we would want to be there in the first place. As long as that biology is there, women can't compete equally with men. A ratio cannot be made using disproportionate parts. Women and men are not equal, we're different. The economy might even improve if women came home, opening up jobs for unemployed men, who could then support a wife and children, the way it was, pre-feminism.

Sometimes on Saturday nights I'll get dressed up and go out club-hopping **10** or to the theater, but the sight of all those other women my age, dressed a little too young, made up to hide encroaching wrinkles, looking hopefully into the crowds, usually depresses me. I end up coming home, to spend my Saturday night with my daughter asleep in her room nearby. At least the NBC Saturday-night lineup is geared demographically to women at home alone.

▼ TOPICAL CONSIDERATIONS

1. What are the main objections Ebeling makes about the impact of feminism on her life? Do you have any objections about the impact of feminism on your own life? Discuss.
2. What does the "Experimental Generation" value according to Ebeling? Does she also value these ideas? Do you? Why or why not?
3. What attitude does the "Yuppie from Eureka" have that Ebeling objects to? Would you have objected? Why or why not?
4. How does Ebeling use the fact that "like it or not, women have babies" to further argue that feminism has failed women? Do you agree with her? Why or why not?
5. What solutions to the failure of feminism does Ebeling offer? What other solutions can you think of that might help Ebeling's situation?
6. How do the arguments presented here affect your thinking about divorce? Explain your answer in detail.

▼ RHETORICAL CONSIDERATIONS

1. Ebeling begins and ends her essay with anecdotes about dating. How does this framing device serve her argument?
2. Throughout the essay, Ebeling uses short, terse sentences ("He

drives a BMW. I ride buses." "How wrong we were.") to drive home her points. How effective is this device for you as a reader?

3. Look at the words that Ebeling capitalizes in her article. How does this naming device serve her argument?

▼ WRITING ASSIGNMENTS

1. Write an essay in which you explain your own views about the failure or success of feminism. Use examples from the lives of people you know to support your argument.

2. Research the laws in your state that explain the legal responsibilities of fathers and mothers. Write a detailed letter to your congressman or congresswoman explaining how you feel about the fairness of these laws. Suggest any changes that you think should be made in these laws. (By law, your congressional representative must answer your letter.)

3. Ebeling's essay explores some of the painful results of a society that increasingly values individuality over social responsibility. Write an essay in which you explore the conflict between individual rights and social responsibility in your own life. How, and in what ways, do you establish your individuality? What social responsibilities do you have? Which of these takes up more of your time and why?

▼ REQUIEM FOR A SOLDIER
Linda Bird Francke

To many feminists, the military has been a model for change. During the Persian Gulf War, 35,000 women earned their stripes on the minefields of the Saudi and Kuwaiti deserts. At the bases, daycare centers have become standard issue. And in July of 1991 Congress began debate of the final barrier—a bill allowing females combat equality with men. Despite these advances, many Americans find themselves in confusion over the traditional view of women's nurturing nature and the brave new militarism. One such person is author Linda Bird Francke whose essay "The Ambivalence of Abortion" appears in Chapter 1 of this text. The occasion for her ambivalence here is the funeral of Major Marie T. Rossi, one of the eleven women to die during Operation Desert Storm. Though her emotions are mixed, Francke, the mother of a teenage daughter, finds it harder to bury a fallen female soldier than a fallen man. This essay first appeared in The New York Times in April 1991.

The American flag was draped over the gunmetal-gray coffin at a funeral home in Oradell, N.J. On a table to the left of the coffin was an 8-by-10 photo of a smiling, somewhat shy-looking woman wearing a soft pastel suit and pearls. On the right was quite another photograph, of a leaner-faced woman with a cocky grin, hands on the hips of her desert camouflage uniform, an Army helicopter of the Second Battalion, 159th Aviation immediately behind her.

I drove three hours to Maj. Marie T. Rossi's wake and returned the next day for her funeral. I'd never met the chopper pilot whose helicopter had hit a microwave tower near a Saudi pipeline, the commanding officer of Company B who'd clung to civilized living in the desert by laying a "parquet" floor of half-filled sandbags in her tent, the woman who, after Sunday services, invited the chaplain back to share the Earl Grey tea her mother had sent her.

I was planning to interview Major Rossi when she returned to the States, to try to understand why she and so many other bright and thoughtful women were choosing careers in the military. Like many other civilians, I had been stunned to learn the numbers of women serving in the armed forces. If there hadn't been a war, I never would have known. Because there'd been a war, I'd now never know Major Rossi.

Watching the war on television, I'd vacillated between feelings of awe and uneasiness at women in their modern military roles. It was jolting to see young women loading missiles on planes and aching to fly fighter jets in combat. On the other hand, I admired these military women for driving six-wheel trucks and shinnying in and out of jet engine pods. A final barrier seemed to be breaking down between the sexes. But at what cost? Looking at the military funeral detachment as it wheeled Major Rossi's coffin into St. Joseph's Church, I tried to summon up pride for a fallen soldier, but instead felt sadness for a fallen sister.

5   As Major Rossi's friends and relatives spoke, I recalled an August evening soon after the Iraqi invasion of Kuwait when my daughters were home on vacation and several of their male friends dropped by. The young men, juniors and seniors in college, were pale and strained, talking anxiously about the possibility of a military draft. My daughters, 19 and 21 years old, were chattering on about their hopes for interesting jobs after graduation. It hadn't seemed fair. Here were my girls—healthy, strong graduates of Outward Bound, their faces still flushed from a pre-dinner run—talking freely about the future. And here were the boys whose futures suddenly seemed threatened.

6   I didn't know what to think. I still don't. As a feminist and my own sort of patriot, I feel that women and men should share equally in the burdens and the opportunities of citizenship. But the new military seems to have stretched equality to the breaking point. The surreal live television hookup between a family in the States and a mother in the desert reminding them where the Christmas ornaments were stored smacked of values gone entirely awry. Yet this woman, like the 29,000 others in the gulf, had voluntarily signed on to serve. What siren song had the military sung to them?

7   To ground myself in this growing phenomenon, I'd taken my younger daughter to a recruiting station in Riverhead, L.I. Each branch of the military had an office—the Army, the Navy, the Air Force, the Marines. The recruiters were very persuasive. "When you graduate, do you think any employer is going to be banging on your door in this economy?" the Marine recruiter asked her. "Think about it. You're out of college. Your Mom breaks your plate. Your Dad turns your bedroom into a den. You're on your own. Now what do you do?" He gave me a decal: "My daughter is a United States Marine."

8   The Air Force recruiter was easier to resist. "Have you ever had problems with the law?" he grilled my daughter. "Have you ever been arrested, ever gotten a traffic ticket? Have you ever sold, bought, trafficked, brought drugs into the country, used drugs?" Instead of a decal, he gave us a copy of "High Flight," the romantic World War II poem President Reagan had used to eulogize the crew of the Challenger. "Oh, I have slipped the surly bonds of earth and danced the skies on laughter-silvered wings" it begins. The Air Force recruiter did not mention the fact that the poem's author, John Gillespie Magee Jr., had died in the war at the age of 19.

9   There is no talk of death in recruiting offices, no talk of danger or war or separation from families. The operative words are "opportunity," "education," "technical skills" and "training." The Marine recruiter added another military carrot by pulling out a sheet of paper with newspaper want ads Scotch-taped to it. "Every job opening requires skills. But how do you get them? We give them to you." My daughter's face began to flush. "If we don't get out of here in 30 seconds, I'm going to sign up," she muttered.

10   Those in the military know about death, of course. They get on-the-job training. Major Rossi's husband, Chief Warrant Officer John Anderson Cay-

ton, told the mourners at her funeral that he had prayed hard for his wife's safety while he was serving in Kuwait. His were not the prayers that come on Hallmark cards. "I prayed that guidance be given to her so that she could command the company, so she could lead her troops in battle," said the tall young man in the same dress blue Army uniform he'd worn to their wedding just nine months before. "And I prayed to the Lord to take care of my sweet little wife."

Habits fade away slowly, just like old soldiers. When I called Arlington National Cemetery to confirm the time of Major Rossi's burial, I was told "he" was down for 3 P.M. on March 11.   **11**

"She," I corrected the scheduler gently.   **12**

"His family and friends will gather at the new administration building," the scheduler continued.   **13**

"Her family and friends," I said more firmly. "Major Rossi is a woman."   **14**

"Be here at least 15 minutes early," she said. "We have a lot of burials on Monday."   **15**

Hundreds of military women turned out at Arlington, wearing stripes and ribbons and badges indecipherable to most civilians. I caught a ride with three members of the Women Auxiliary Service Pilots, the Wasps, who flew during World War II. One was wearing her husband's shirt under her old uniform. The shirts sold at the PX with narrow enough shoulders, she explained, don't fit over the bust.   **16**

No one knows how many women are buried in their own military right under the 220,000 pristine headstones at Arlington. The cemetery's records do not differentiate between genders or among races and religions.   **17**

"If the women were married, you could walk around and count the headstones that say 'Her husband,' rather than 'His wife,' " suggested an Arlington historian. "I've seen a few and always noticed them." Arlington is going to run out of room by the year 2035; a columbarium will provide 100,000 niches for the ashes of 21st century soldiers. How many of them will be women?   **18**

The military pageant of death, no doubt, will remain the same. Six black horses pulled the caisson carrying Major Rossi's coffin. Seven riflemen fired the 21-gun salute, the band softly played "America the Beautiful" and a solitary bugler under the trees blew taps. Major Rossi's husband threw the first spadeful of dirt on his wife's coffin, her brother, the second. It was a scene we're going to have to get used to in this new military of ours, as we bury our sisters, our mothers, our wives, our daughters.   **19**

▼ TOPICAL CONSIDERATIONS

1. What does Francke mean when she says in paragraph 6 that "the new military seems to have stretched equality to the breaking point"? Do you agree?
2. How does Francke feel about women in the military? What lan-

guage from her essay suggests this? Has she convinced you? Explain your answer.

3. Do you think that this article is more poignant or less so because it is about the death of a *female* soldier? What makes you think this? Explain your answer.

4. Do you know women who are in the military or planning a military career? What are your feelings about their going into combat?

5. How do you feel about the military women who participated in the Persian Gulf War? Do you think they should have been able to participate more fully in military combat, or do you feel they were contributing all they should have?

6. Even though women have made great advancements in the military, very few of them occupy command positions. These positions are almost exclusively held by white males. Do you think that these commanders alone should decide whether or not women should go into combat?

7. Traditionally, women have been some of the strongest supporters of antiwar movements. Do you think that women are naturally pacifists and that men are naturally more aggressive? What makes you think this?

▼ RHETORICAL CONSIDERATIONS

1. Francke begins this article with a description of Rossi's coffin and the two pictures on either side of it. In your opinion, how effective is this beginning?

2. Several times Francke contrasts Marie Rossi's military side with her feminine side. Identify some of these contrasts. What rhetorical purpose does this contrasting serve?

3. How would you describe the tone of this article? Is it confused? Conciliatory? Angry? What language suggests this? Does Francke come to a resolution at the end?

4. Why do you think Francke includes the story of her daughter's visits to recruiting offices in this article about the death of Major Rossi?

▼ WRITING ASSIGNMENTS

1. Do you think that women should be allowed to participate in the military to the same extent that men are? What about combat? What about on the decision-making levels? Write an essay that clearly expresses your viewpoint. Be sure to explore all sides of the issue.

2. Many of the articles in this section suggest that, in addition to gaining new freedoms, women who want gender equality must also be prepared to take on new responsibilities. What are some of these new responsibilities? Refer to the other articles in this section for ideas.

3. Do you think that there is anything (apart from biological functions) that one gender should do that the other should not do? Or, do you think that total equality is an achievable goal? This is a very sensitive issue, so be sure to back up your answers with strong proof.

▼ THE BEAUTY MYTH
Naomi Wolf

"Mirror, mirror on the wall, who's the fairest of them all?" If Naomi Wolf is correct, this is a question women don't leave behind in childhood but continue to ask themselves all their lives. But why is that so more than two decades after the birth of the women's movement that supposedly raised consciousness and won women rights? In her controversial book *The Beauty Myth* (1991) from which this essay was taken, Ms. Wolf passionately argues that women are in a "violent backlash against feminism that uses images of female beauty as a political weapon against women's advancement." Whether or not one agrees with the wide-ranging implications put forth here, Wolf raises some disturbing issues about women and appearances. Naomi Wolf graduated from Yale University and is completing a doctorate from New College, Oxford, as a Rhodes scholar. Her journalism, poetry, and book reviews have appeared in various American and British journals.

At last, after a long silence, women took to the streets. In the two decades of radical action that followed the rebirth of feminism in the early 1970s, Western women gained legal and reproductive rights, pursued higher education, entered the trades and the professions, and overturned ancient and revered beliefs about their social role. A generation on, do women feel free?

The affluent, educated, liberated women of the First World, who can enjoy freedoms unavailable to any women ever before, do not feel as free as they want to. And they can no longer restrict to the subconscious their sense that this lack of freedom has something to do with apparently frivolous issues, things that really should not matter. Many are ashamed to admit that such trivial concerns—to do with physical appearance, bodies, faces, hair, clothes—matter so much. But in spite of shame, guilt, and denial, more and more women are wondering if it isn't that they are entirely neurotic and alone but rather that something important is indeed at stake that has to do with the relationship between female liberation and female beauty.

3   The more legal and material hindrances women have broken through, the more strictly and heavily and cruelly images of female beauty have come to weigh upon us. Many women sense that women's collective progress has stalled; compared with the heady momentum of earlier days, there is a dispiriting climate of confusion, division, cynicism, and above all, exhaustion. After years of much struggle and little recognition, many older women feel burned out; after years of taking its light for granted, many younger women show little interest in touching new fire to the torch.

4   During the past decade, women breached the power structure; meanwhile, eating disorders rose exponentially and cosmetic surgery became the fastest-growing medical specialty. During the past five years, consumer spending doubled, pornography became the main media category, ahead of legitimate films and records combined, and thirty-three thousand American women told researchers that they would rather lose ten to fifteen pounds than achieve any other goal. More women have more money and power and scope and legal recognition than we have ever had before; but in terms of how we feel about ourselves *physically,* we may actually be worse off than our unliberated grandmothers. Recent research consistently shows that inside the majority of the West's controlled, attractive, successful working women, there is a secret "underlife" poisoning our freedom; infused with notions of beauty, it is a dark vein of self-hatred, physical obsessions, terror of aging, and dread of lost control.

5   It is no accident that so many potentially powerful women feel this way. We are in the midst of a violent backlash against feminism that uses images of female beauty as a political weapon against women's advancement: the beauty myth. It is the modern version of a social reflex that has been in force since the Industrial Revolution. As women released themselves from the feminine mystique of domesticity, the beauty myth took over its lost ground, expanding as it waned to carry on its work of social control.

6   The contemporary backlash is so violent because the ideology of beauty is the last one remaining of the old feminine ideologies that still has the power to control those women whom second wave feminism would have otherwise made relatively uncontrollable: It has grown stronger to take over the work of social coercion that myths about motherhood, domesticity, chastity, and passivity, no longer can manage. It is seeking right now to undo psychologically and covertly all the good things that feminism did for women materially and overtly.

7   This counterforce is operating to checkmate the inheritance of feminism on every level in the lives of Western women. Feminism gave us laws against job discrimination based on gender; immediately case law evolved in Britain and the United States that institutionalized job discrimination based on women's appearances. Patriarchal religion declined; new religious dogma, using some of the mind-altering techniques of older cults and sects, arose around age and weight

to functionally supplant traditional ritual. Feminists, inspired by Friedan, broke the stranglehold on the women's popular press of advertisers for household products, who were promoting the feminine mystique; at once, the diet and skin care industries became the new cultural censors of women's intellectual space, and because of their pressure, the gaunt, youthful model supplanted the happy housewife as the arbiter of successful womanhood. The sexual revolution promoted the discovery of female sexuality; "beauty pornography"—which for the first time in women's history artificially links a commodified "beauty" directly and explicitly to sexuality—invaded the mainstream to undermine women's new and vulnerable sense of sexual self-worth. Reproductive rights gave Western women control over our own bodies; the weight of fashion models plummeted to 23 percent below that of ordinary women, eating disorders rose exponentially, and a mass neurosis was promoted that used food and weight to strip women of that sense of control. Women insisted on politicizing health; new technologies of invasive, potentially deadly "cosmetic" surgeries developed apace to re-exert old forms of medical control of women.

Every generation since about 1830 has had to fight its version of the beauty myth. "It is very little to me," said the suffragist Lucy Stone in 1855, "to have the right to vote, to own property, etcetera, if I may not keep my body, and its uses, in my absolute right." Eighty years later, after women had won the vote, and the first wave of the organized women's movement had subsided, Virginia Woolf wrote that it would still be decades before women could tell the truth about their bodies. In 1962, Betty Friedan quoted a young woman trapped in the Feminine Mystique: "Lately, I look in the mirror, and I'm so afraid I'm going to look like my mother." Eight years after that, heralding the cataclysmic second wave of feminism, Germaine Greer described "the Stereotype": "To her belongs all that is beautiful, even the very word beauty itself . . . she is a doll . . . I'm sick of the masquerade." In spite of the great revolution of the second wave, we are not exempt. Now we can look out over ruined barricades: A revolution has come upon us and changed everything in its path, enough time has passed since then for babies to have grown into women, but there still remains a final right not fully claimed. **8**

The beauty myth tells a story: The quality called "beauty" objectively and universally exists. Women must want to embody it and men must want to possess women who embody it. This embodiment is an imperative for women and not for men, which situation is necessary and natural because it is biological, sexual, and evolutionary: Strong men battle for beautiful women, and beautiful women are more reproductively successful. Women's beauty must correlate to their fertility, and since this system is based on sexual selection, it is inevitable and changeless. **9**

None of this is true. "Beauty" is a currency system like the gold standard. Like any economy, it is determined by politics, and in the modern age in the West it is the last, best belief system that keeps male dominance intact. In assigning value to women in a vertical hierarchy according to a culturally **10** imposed physical standard, it is an expression of power relations in which women must unnaturally compete for resources that men have appropriated for themselves.

11   "Beauty" is not universal or changeless, though the West pretends that all ideals of female beauty stem from one Platonic Ideal Woman; the Maori admire a fat vulva, and the Padung, droopy breasts. Nor is "beauty" a function of evolution: Its ideals change at a pace far more rapid than that of the evolution of species, and Charles Darwin was himself unconvinced by his own explanation that "beauty" resulted from a "sexual selection" that deviated from the rule of natural selection; for women to compete with women through "beauty" is a reversal of the way in which natural selection affects all other mammals. Anthropology has overturned the notion that females must be "beautiful" to be selected to mate: Evelyn Reed, Elaine Morgan, and others have dismissed sociobiological assertions of innate male polygamy and female monogamy. Female higher primates are the sexual initiators; not only do they seek out and enjoy sex with many partners, but "every nonpregnant female takes her turn at being the most desirable of all her troop. And that cycle keeps turning as long as she lives." The inflamed pink sexual organs of primates are often cited by male sociobiologists as analogous to human arrangements relating to female "beauty," when in fact that is a universal, nonhierarchical female primate characteristic.

12   Nor has the beauty myth always been this way. Though the pairing of the older rich men with young, "beautiful" women is taken to be somehow inevitable, in the matriarchal Goddess religions that dominated the Mediterranean from about 25,000 B.C.E. to about 700 B.C.E., the situation was reversed: "In every culture, the Goddess has many lovers. . . . The clear pattern is of an older woman with a beautiful but expendable youth—Ishtar and Tammuz, Venus and Adonis, Cybele and Attis, Isis and Osiris . . . their only function the service of the divine 'womb.' " Nor is it something only women do and only men watch: Among the Nigerian Wodaabes, the women hold economic power and the tribe is obsessed with male beauty; Wodaabe men spend hours together in elaborate makeup sessions, and compete—provocatively painted and dressed, with swaying hips and seductive expressions—in beauty contests judged by women. There is no legitimate historical or biological justification for the beauty myth; what it is doing to women today is a result of nothing more exalted than the need of today's power structure, economy, and culture to mount a counteroffensive against women.

13   If the beauty myth is not based on evolution, sex, gender, aesthetics, or God, on what is it based? It claims to be about intimacy and sex and life, a celebration of women. It is actually composed of emotional distance, politics, finance, and sexual repression. The beauty myth is not about women at all. It is about men's institutions and institutional power.

14   The qualities that a given period calls beautiful in women are merely symbols of the female behavior that that period considers desirable: *The beauty myth is always actually prescribing behavior and not appearance.* Competition

between women has been made part of the myth so that women will be divided from one another. Youth and (until recently) virginity have been "beautiful" in women since they stand for experiential and sexual ignorance. Aging in women is "unbeautiful" since women grow more powerful with time, and since the links between generations of women must always be newly broken: Older women fear young ones, young women fear old, and the beauty myth truncates for all the female life span. Most urgently, women's identity must be premised upon our "beauty" so that we will remain vulnerable to outside approval, carrying the vital sensitive organ of self-esteem exposed to the air.

Though there has, of course, been a beauty myth in some form for as long as there has been patriarchy, the beauty myth in its modern form is a fairly recent invention. The myth flourishes when material constraints on women are dangerously loosened. Before the Industrial Revolution, the average woman could not have had the same feelings about "beauty" that modern women do who experience the myth as continual comparison to a mass-disseminated physical ideal. Before the development of technologies of mass production—daguerrotypes, photographs, etc.—an ordinary woman was exposed to few such images outside the Church. Since the family was a productive unit and women's work complemented men's, the value of women who were not aristocrats or prostitutes lay in their work skills, economic shrewdness, physical strength, and fertility. Physical attraction, obviously, played its part; but "beauty" as we understand it was not, for ordinary women, a serious issue in the marriage marketplace. The beauty myth in its modern form gained ground after the upheavals of industrialization, as the work unit of the family was destroyed, and urbanization and the emerging factory system demanded what social engineers of the time termed the "separate sphere" of domesticity, which supported the new labor category of the "breadwinner" who left home for the workplace during the day. The middle class expanded, the standards of living and of literacy rose, the size of families shrank; a new class of literate, idle women developed, on whose submission to enforced domesticity the evolving system of industrial capitalism depended. Most of our assumptions about the way women have always thought about "beauty" date from no earlier than the 1830s, when the cult of domesticity was first consolidated and the beauty index invented. **15**

For the first time new technologies could reproduce—in fashion plates, daguerreotypes, tintypes, and rotogravures—images of how women should look. In the 1840s the first nude photographs of prostitutes were taken; advertisements using images of "beautiful" women first appeared in mid-century. Copies of classical artworks, postcards of society beauties and royal mistresses, Currier and Ives prints, and porcelain figurines flooded the separate sphere to which middle-class women were confined. **16**

Since the Industrial Revolution, middle-class Western women have been controlled by ideals and stereotypes as much as by material constraints. This situation, unique to this group, means that analyses that trace "cultural conspiracies" are uniquely plausible in relation to them. The rise of the beauty myth was just one of several emerging social fictions that masqueraded as natural **17** components of the feminine sphere, the better to enclose those women inside it. Other such fictions arose contemporaneously: a version of childhood that required continual maternal supervision; a concept of female biology that required middle-class women to act out the roles of hysterics and hypochondriacs; a conviction that respectable women were sexually anesthetic; and a definition of women's work that occupied them with repetitive, time-consuming, and painstaking tasks such as needlepoint and lacemaking. All such Victorian inventions as these served a double function—that is, though they were encouraged as a means to expend female energy and intelligence in harmless ways, women often used them to express genuine creativity and passion.

18   But in spite of middle-class women's creativity with fashion and embroidery and child rearing, and, a century later, with the role of the suburban housewife that devolved from these social fictions, the fictions' main purpose was served: During a century and a half of unprecedented feminist agitation, they effectively counteracted middle-class women's dangerous new leisure, literacy, and relative freedom from material constraints.

19   Though these time- and mind-consuming fictions about women's natural role adapted themselves to resurface in the postwar Feminine Mystique, when the second wave of the women's movement took apart what women's magazines had portrayed as the "romance," "science," and "adventure" of homemaking and suburban family life, they temporarily failed. The cloying domestic fiction of "togetherness" lost its meaning and middle-class women walked out of their front doors in masses.

20   So the fictions simply transformed themselves once more: Since the women's movement had successfully taken apart most other necessary fictions of femininity, all the work of social control once spread out over the whole network of these fictions had to be reassigned to the only strand left intact, which action consequently strengthened it a hundredfold. This reimposed onto liberated women's faces and bodies all the limitations, taboos, and punishments of the repressive laws, religious injunctions and reproductive enslavement that no longer carried sufficient force. Inexhaustible but ephemeral beauty work took over from inexhaustible but ephemeral housework. As the economy, law, religion, sexual mores, education, and culture were forcibly opened up to include women more fairly, a private reality colonized female consciousness. By using ideas about "beauty," it reconstructed an alternative female world with its own laws, economy, religion, sexuality, education, and culture, each element as repressive as any that had gone before.

21   Since middle-class Western women can best be weakened psychologically now that we are stronger materially, the beauty myth, as it has resurfaced in the last generation, has had to draw on more technological sophistication and reactionary fervor than ever before. The modern arsenal of the myth is a dissemination of millions of images of the current ideal; although this barrage is generally seen as a collective sexual fantasy, there is in fact little that is sexual about it. It is summoned out of political fear on the part of male-dominated institutions threatened by women's freedom, and it exploits female guilt and

apprehension about our own liberation—latent fears that we might be going too far. This frantic aggregation of imagery is a collective reactionary hallucination willed into being by both men and women stunned and disoriented by the rapidity with which gender relations have been transformed: a bulwark of reassurance against the flood of change. The mass depiction of the modern woman as a "beauty" is a contradiction: Where modern women are growing, moving, and expressing their individuality, as the myth has it, "beauty" is by definition inert, timeless, and generic. That this hallucination is necessary and deliberate is evident in the way "beauty" so directly contradicts women's real situation.

And the unconscious hallucination grows ever more influential and pervasive because of what is now conscious market manipulation: powerful industries—the $33-billion-a-year diet industry, the $20-billion cosmetics industry, the $300-million cosmetic surgery industry, and the $7-billion pornography industry—have arisen from the capital made out of unconscious anxieties, and are in turn able, through their influence on mass culture, to use, stimulate, and reinforce the hallucination in a rising economic spiral.   22

This is not a conspiracy theory; it doesn't have to be. Societies tell themselves necessary fictions in the same way that individuals and families do. Henrik Ibsen called them "vital lies," and psychologist Daniel Goleman describes them working the same way on the social level that they do within families: "The collusion is maintained by directing attention away from the fearsome fact, or by repackaging its meaning in an acceptable format." The costs of these social blind spots, he writes, are destructive communal illusions. Possibilities for women have become so open-ended that they threaten to destabilize the institutions on which a male-dominated culture has depended, and a collective panic reaction on the part of both sexes has forced a demand for counterimages.   23

The resulting hallucination materializes, for women, as something all too real. No longer just an idea, it becomes three-dimensional, incorporating within itself how women live and how they do not live: It becomes the Iron Maiden. The original Iron Maiden was a medieval German instrument of torture, a body-shaped casket painted with the limbs and features of a lovely, smiling young woman. The unlucky victim was slowly enclosed inside her; the lid fell shut to immobilize the victim, who died either of starvation or, less cruelly, of the metal spikes embedded in her interior. The modern hallucination in which women are trapped or trap themselves is similarly rigid, cruel, and euphemistically painted. Contemporary culture directs attention to imagery of the Iron Maiden, while censoring real women's faces and bodies.   24

Why does the social order feel the need to defend itself by evading the fact of real women, our faces and voices and bodies, and reducing the meaning of women to these formulaic and endlessly reproduced "beautiful" images? Though unconscious personal anxieties can be a powerful force in the creation of a vital lie, economic necessity practically guarantees it. An economy that depends on slavery needs to promote images of slaves that "justify" the institu-   25 tion of slavery. Western economies are absolutely dependent now on the continued underpayment of women. An ideology that makes women feel "worth less" was urgently needed to counteract the way feminism had begun to make us feel worth more. This does not require a conspiracy; merely an atmosphere. The contemporary economy depends right now on the representation of women within the beauty myth. Economist John Kenneth Galbraith offers an economic explanation for "the persistence of the view of homemaking as a 'higher calling' ": the concept of women as naturally trapped within the Feminine Mystique, he feels, "has been forced on us by popular sociology, by magazines, and by fiction to disguise the fact that woman in her role of consumer has been essential to the development of our industrial society. . . . Behavior that is essential for economic reasons is transformed into a social virtue." As soon as a woman's primary social value could no longer be defined as the attainment of virtuous domesticity, the beauty myth redefined it as the attainment of virtuous beauty. It did so to substitute both a new consumer imperative and a new justification for economic unfairness in the workplace where the old ones had lost their hold over newly liberated women.

26   Another hallucination arose to accompany that of the Iron Maiden: The caricature of the Ugly Feminist was resurrected to dog the steps of the women's movement. The caricature is unoriginal; it was coined to ridicule the feminists of the nineteenth century. Lucy Stone herself, whom supporters saw as "a prototype of womanly grace . . . fresh and fair as the morning," was derided by detractors with "the usual report" about Victorian feminists: "a big masculine woman, wearing boots, smoking a cigar, swearing like a trooper." As Betty Friedan put it presciently in 1960, even before the savage revamping of that old caricature: "The unpleasant image of feminists today resembles less the feminists themselves than the image fostered by the interests who so bitterly opposed the vote for women in state after state." Thirty years on, her conclusion is more true than ever: That resurrected caricature, which sought to punish women for their public acts by going after their private sense of self, became the paradigm for new limits placed on aspiring women everywhere. After the success of the women's movement's second wave, the beauty myth was perfected to checkmate power at every level in individual women's lives. The modern neuroses of life in the female body spread to woman after woman at epidemic rates. The myth is undermining—slowly, imperceptibly, without our being aware of the real forces of erosion—the ground women have gained through long, hard, honorable struggle.

27   The beauty myth of the present is more insidious than any mystique of femininity yet: A century ago, Nora slammed the door of the doll's house; a generation ago, women turned their backs on the consumer heaven of the isolated multiapplianced home; but where women are trapped today, there is no door to slam. The contemporary ravages of the beauty backlash are destroying women physically and depleting us psychologically. If we are to free ourselves from the dead weight that has once again been made out of femaleness, it is not ballots or lobbyists or placards that women will need first; it is a new way to see.

▼ TOPICAL CONSIDERATIONS

1. Describe in your own words the beauty myth that Wolf is talking about. What, according to Wolf, is the purpose of this beauty myth?

2. In paragraph 3, Wolf states that "the more legal and material hindrances women have broken through, the more strictly and heavily and cruelly images of female beauty have come to weigh upon us." What examples from today's society can you think of that support this statement?

3. How does the beauty myth work to control women?

4. In paragraph 11, Wolf asserts that the *ideals* of the beauty myth, what is called beautiful, change very rapidly. Can you think of how the concept of female beauty has changed in just your lifetime? What used to be valued as beautiful that no longer is? What is considered beautiful today that would have been ignored ten years ago?

5. What does Wolf mean in paragraph 13 when she writes that "the beauty myth is not about women at all. It is about men's institutions and institutional power"?

6. In paragraph 14 Wolf states that "the qualities that a given period calls beautiful in women are merely symbols of the female behavior that the period considers desirable." What are the qualities of a woman that we call beautiful today? What female behaviors do you think these qualities are symbolizing?

7. What roles does the "development of technologies of mass production" (paragraph 15) play in the promotion of the beauty myth?

8. In paragraph 17, Wolf mentions other "social fictions" that were meant to keep women in the domestic sphere during the Industrial Revolution. Which of these are still true today? What modern-day "social fictions" can you think of that work with the beauty myth to keep women out of positions of power in society?

9. What aspects of the beauty myth does your mother and other women of her generation adhere to?

10. Do you know women who are obsessed with beauty? Describe their efforts to be beautiful. What do you think they are hoping to gain with their beauty?

11. In paragraphs 21–23, Wolf explains why *women* as well as men feel the need to promote the beauty myth as well as participate in it. What reasons does she give? Can you think of any other reasons why women would want to promote the beauty myth?

12. Put into your own words an answer to the question Wolf poses at the beginning of paragraph 25—"Why does the social order feel the need to defend itself by evading the fact of real women, our faces

and voices and bodies, and reducing the meaning of women to these formulaic and endlessly reproduced 'beautiful' images?"

13. Wolf contends that "woman in her role of consumer has been essential to the development of our industrial society" (paragraph 25). Do you think that women do more of the buying in today's society than men do? What makes you think this?

14. When Wolf states in paragraph 25 that "behavior that is essential for economic reasons is transformed into a social virtue," she is explaining how the virtues a society values are actually myths or fictions created to make the society run more smoothly. In addition to the beauty myth, can you think of other myths or fictions our society promotes to make things run more smoothly? What, for instance, might be some myths about men's behavior?

▼ RHETORICAL CONSIDERATIONS

1. It is not until paragraph 5 that Wolf states the thesis of her article— "We are in the midst of a violent backlash against feminism that uses images of female beauty as a political weapon against women's advancement: the beauty myth." Look at all of the other information that Wolf gives before she gives us her thesis statement. Why do you suppose such a controversial thesis would need to be introduced in this way?

2. Both paragraph 4 and paragraph 7 are catalogues of contrasting facts about women's accomplishments versus the beauty myth. How effective is this contrasting catalogue for you? Add some other contrasting facts to the ones Wolf lays out.

3. If you had to change the title of this article to reflect how Wolf feels about the beauty myth, what would you change it to? Do you think this would have been a more or less effective title for this article than the one Wolf used?

4. How does Wolf use the metaphor of the Iron Maiden to support her thesis?

5. What does it mean to *colonize* something? What does Wolf mean when she says in paragraph 20 that "a private reality colonized female consciousness"? Is Wolf using this term in a positive or a negative sense?

▼ WRITING ASSIGNMENTS

1. Look at the articles by Mackintosh, Quindlen, and Wolf to see what each one says about where gender role stereotyping comes from. Write an essay that explores all of the possible aspects of society

that help to shape our concepts of gender roles. Be sure to include your own observations in this essay.

2. In her article, Wolf states that advancements in the media have helped to promote the beauty myth. What other myths or social fictions have benefitted from advances in the media? Write an essay that explores the role that the media plays in keeping society's myths and fictions valued and believable.

3. Wolf notes in paragraph 20 that "the women's movement had successfully taken apart most other necessary fictions of femininity." What, in addition to the beauty myth, are some other "necessary fictions of femininity"? If there were another feminist movement today, what aspects of social control would feminists seek to do away with?

4. Toys and games are some of the earliest "socializing" devices females interact with. How do toys and games help to support the beauty myth? Choose some toys and games that are popular with little girls today and analyze what behavior these items are seeking to promote in little girls.

5. Think about some of your favorite musical groups and songs. Are they promoting the beauty myth in any way? Write an essay that focuses on one musical group or a small number of songs and explains to what extent these are promoting the beauty myth.

MEN AS SUCCESS OBJECTS

Warren Farrell

"With all the focus on discrimination against women, few understand the sexism directed against men." Such is the claim of author Warren Farrell who examines the roots of men's anxiety about themselves in this essay. Farrell's focus is on men's unequal responsibility to succeed in the workplace, to prove their worth by making money, to be, as the author puts it, "a wallet." Warren Farrell is a psychologist and author of the 1986 bestseller, *Why Men Are the Way They Are.* This article first appeared in *Family Therapy Network* in the 1988 November/December issue.

1   For thousands of years, marriages were about economic security and survival. Let's call this Stage I in our culture's conception of marriage. Beginning in the 1950s, marriages became focused on personal fulfillment and we entered into the era of the Stage II relationship. In Stage II, love was redefined to include listening to each other, joint parenting, sexual fulfillment, and shared decision-making. As a result, many traditional marriages consummated in Stage I failed under the new Stage II expectations. Thus we had the great surge of divorces beginning in the '60s.

2   The increasing incidence of divorce altered the fundamental relationship between women, men, and the workplace. Before divorce became common, most women's income came from men, so discrimination in favor of a woman's husband benefited her. But, as the divorce rate mushroomed, the same discrimination often hurt her. Before divorce became a common expectation, we had two types of inequality—women's experience of unequal rights in the workplace and men's experience of unequal responsibility for succeeding in the workplace. To find a woman to love him, a man had to "make his mark" in the world. As women increasingly had to provide for themselves economically, we confined our examination of inequality between the sexes to inequality in the workplace. What was ignored was the effect of inequality in the homeplace. Also ignored was a man's feeling that no woman would love him if he volunteered to be a full-time househusband instead of a full-time provider. As a result, we falsely assumed that the experience of inequality was confined to women.

3   Because divorces led to a change in the pressures on women (should she *become* a doctor, marry a doctor, or have a career and marry a doctor?), that change became "news" and her new juggling act got attention in the media. Because the underlying pressures on men did not change (women still married men who earned more than they did), the pressure on men to succeed did not change, and, therefore, received no attention. With all the focus on discrimination against women, few understood the sexism directed against men.

4   The feminist perspective on relationships has become like fluoride in water—we drink it without being aware of its presence. The complaints about men, the idea

that "men are jerks," have become so integrated into our unconscious that even advertisers have caught on. After analyzing 1,000 commercials in 1987, researcher Fred Hayward found that when an ad called for a negative portrayal in a male-female interaction, an astonishing 100 percent of the time the "bad guy" was the man.

This anti-male bias isn't confined to TV commercials. A sampling of the   5
cards in the "Love and Friendship" section of a greeting card store revealed these gems:

> "If they can send one man to the moon, why can't they send them all?"
> "When you unzip a man's pants . . . his brains fall out."
> "If we can make penicillin out of moldy cheese . . . maybe we can make men out of the low-lifes in this town."

A visit to the bookstore turns up titles like *No Good Men*. Imagine *No Good*   6
Women or *No Good Jews*. And what do the following titles have in common? *Men Who Can't Love; Men Who Hate Women and the Women Who Love Them; Smart Women/Foolish Choices; Successful Women, Angry Men; Peter Pan Syndrome.*

Feminism-as-fluoride has left us acknowledging the working mother ("Su-   7
perwoman") without even being aware of the working father. It is by now well recognized that, even among men who do more housework or more childcare than their wives, almost never does the man truly share the 24-hour-a-day psychological responsibility of ministering to everyone's needs, egos, and schedules.

But it is not so widely recognized that, despite the impact feminism has had   8
on the contemporary family, almost every father still retains 24-hour-a-day psychological responsibility for the family's financial well-being. Even women who earn more than their husbands tell me that they know their husbands would support their decision to earn as much or as little as they wish. If a woman marries a successful man, then she knows she will have an option to work or not, but not an obligation. Almost all men see bringing home a healthy salary as an obligation, not an option.

A woman today has three options.   9

> *Option 1:* Full-time career.
> *Option 2:* Full-time family.
> *Option 3:* Some combination of career and family.

A man sees himself as having three "slightly different" options: 10

> *Option 1:* Work full time.
> *Option 2:* Work full time.
> *Option 3:* Work full time.

The U.S. Bureau of the Census explains that full-time working males work   11
an average of eight hours more per week on their jobs than full-time working females.

Since many women now earn substantial incomes, doesn't this relieve the   12
pressure on men to be a wallet? No. Why? Because successful women do exactly what less-successful women do—"marry up," that is, marry a man whose

income is greater than her own. According to statistics, if a woman cannot marry up or marry someone with a high wage-earning potential, she does not marry at all. Therefore, a man often reflexively backs away from a woman he's attracted to when he discovers she's more successful than he is because he senses he's only setting himself up for rejection. Ultimately, she'll dump him for a more successful man. She may sleep with him, or live with him, but not marry him unless she spots "potential." Thus, of top female executives, 85 percent don't get married; the remaining 15 percent almost all marry up. Even successful women have not relaxed the pressure on men to succeed.

13 Ask a girl in junior high or high school about the boy whom she would "absolutely love" to ask her out to the prom and chances are almost 100 percent that she would tell you her fantasy boy is *both* good-looking *and* successful (a jock or student leader, or someone who "has potential"). Ask a boy whom he would absolutely love to ask out to the prom and chances are almost 100 percent his fantasy girl is good-looking. Only about 25 percent will also be interested in a girl's "strong career potential" (or her being a top female jock). His invisible curriculum, then, taught him that being good-looking is not enough to attract a good-looking girl—he must be successful *in addition* to being good-looking. This was his experience of inequality: "Good-looking boy does not equal good-looking girl." Why are boys willing to consider themselves unequal to girls' attention until they hit their heads against 21 other boys on a football field?

14 In part, the answer is because boys are addicted. In all cultures, boys are addicted to the images of beautiful women. And in American culture this is enormously magnified. Boys are exposed to the images of beautiful women about 10 million times per year via television, billboards, magazines, etc. In the process, the naturally beautiful girl becomes a *genetic celebrity*. Boys become addicted to the image of the quasi-anorexic female. To be the equal of this genetic celebrity, the adolescent boy must become an *earned celebrity* (by performing, paying on dates, etc.) Until he is an earned celebrity, he feels like a groupie trying to get a celebrity's attention.

15 Is there an invisible curriculum for girls and boys growing up? Yes. For girls, "If you want to have your choice among boys, you had better be beautiful." For boys, it's "You had better be handsome *and* successful." If a boy wants a romantic relationship with a girl he must not only be successful and perform, he must pay and pursue—risk sexual rejection. Girls think of the three Ps—performing, paying, and pursuing—as male power. Boys see the three Ps as what they must do to earn their way to female love and sexuality. They see these not as power, but as compensations for powerlessness. This is the adolescent male's experience of inequality.

▼ TOPICAL CONSIDERATIONS

1. What arguments does Farrell present to prove that the increase in the number of divorces has "altered the fundamental relationship

between women, men, and the workplace" (paragraph 2)? Do you agree with his points? Why or why not?

2. How do Farrell's views on the effect of divorce on men and women compare with Ebeling's? How do you account for the differences in these two viewpoints?

3. Do you agree or disagree with Farrell when he writes in paragraph 4 that "complaints about men, the idea that 'men are jerks,' have become so integrated into our unconscious that even advertisers have caught on"? Describe some recent advertisements that support your stance.

4. What are the differences between men's and women's options, according to Farrell? Looking back over your own experience and the experiences of people you know, does what Farrell says ring true to you? How so? If not, where does your experience differ?

5. In paragraph 13, Farrell claims that junior-high and high-school girls' "fantasy boy" is *"both* good-looking *and* successful" while boys' "fantasy girl" is simply "good-looking." From your experience, is this claim true? Have you ever been dated because of your looks and/or "earned celebrity"?

6. What do you think Farrell hoped his readers would learn from this article? How do you think he wants them to respond? On what do you base your answers? Has this article made you more aware of the unfair pressures our culture puts on males and females? Explain.

▼ RHETORICAL CONSIDERATIONS

1. What are the strengths and weaknesses of Farrell's use of statistics in his article?

2. Look at the language Farrell uses to talk about feminism. How would you describe his attitude toward feminism? Is he angry? Dismissive? Supportive? Use his language to support your answer.

3. How would you describe Farrell's voice in this article? What sense do you get of Farrell as an individual? Use passages from the article to support your answers.

▼ WRITING ASSIGNMENTS

1. Write a conversation between Farrell and Ebeling about the relationship between women, men, and the workplace. In this conversation, be sure to write about the points that these authors agree upon, as well as the points where they differ. As a conclusion, have Farrell and Ebeling decide to write an article they both would agree upon. What would this article be about?

2. This article as well as the next article by Allis talk about the diffi-

culties of being male today. Have these pieces sensitized you to issues you've never really considered before? If so, do you think you now regard male roles in a different light? Enough as to consider changing your behavior? If so, write a paper explaining how you have been affected by the arguments presented in these three articles, and how your thinking/behavior might be affected.

3. Conduct a survey of both men and women in your age group, asking them to list at least five qualities of an ideal mate. What seem to be predominant qualities that both sexes want in a mate? Do the statistics you have gathered break down along gender lines, as Farrell suggests? What do men want? What do women want? Write an essay that summarizes the findings of your survey and then goes on to make some conclusions about the gender role expectations of the group you have surveyed.

4. There are many other aspects of our culture that contribute to our definitions of what it means to be female or male. How do rock music, advertising, and movies contribute to stereotypes of females as sex objects and men as success objects? Write an essay that explores how these three aspects of our culture (or any others you may wish to include) shape our notions of gender.

▼ WHAT DO MEN REALLY WANT?
Sam Allis

Might the 1990s turn out to be the decade of the Men's Movement? Some say the time is right. Angered by the incessant criticism of their inadequacies as lovers, husbands, and fathers, exhausted by the demands of the workplace, and confused over what it means to be a man today, many men seek new roles and identities. In this piece, Sam Allis, a *Time* magazine correspondent, lets us eavesdrop on men struggling with a need to define themselves the way women did about twenty years ago. This essay first appeared in *Time* in 1990.

1 Freud, like everyone else, forgot to ask the second question: What do *men* really want? His omission may reflect the male fascination with the enigma of woman over the mystery of man. She owns the center of his imagination, while the fate of man works the margins. Perhaps this is why so many men have taken the Mafia oath of silence about their hopes and fears. Strong and silent remain de rigueur.

2 But in the wake of the feminist movement, some men are beginning to pipe

up. In the intimacy of locker rooms and the glare of large men's groups, they are spilling their bile at the incessant criticism, much of it justified, from women about their inadequacies as husbands, lovers, fathers. They are airing their frustration with the limited roles they face today, compared with the multiple options that women seem to have won. Above all, they are groping to redefine themselves on their own terms instead of on the performance standards set by their wives or bosses or family ghosts. "We've heard all the criticism," says New York City–based television producer Tom Seligson. "Now we'll make our own decisions."

In many quarters there is anger. "The American man wants his manhood   **3**
back. Period," snaps John Wheeler, a Washington environmentalist and former chairman of the Vietnam Veterans Memorial Fund. "New York feminists [a generic term in his lexicon] have been busy castrating American males. They poured this country's testosterone out the window in the 1960s. The men in this country have lost their boldness. To raise your voice these days is a worse offense than urinating in the subway."

Even more prevalent is exhaustion. "The American man wants to stop   **4**
running; he wants a few moments of peace," says poet Robert Bly, one of the gurus of the nascent men's movement in the U.S. "He has a tremendous longing to get down to his own depths. Beneath the turbulence of his daily life is a beautiful crystalline infrastructure"—a kind of male bedrock.

Finally, there is profound confusion over what it means to be a man today.   **5**
Men have faced warping changes in role models since the women's movement drove the strong, stoic John Wayne–type into the sunset. Replacing him was a new hero: the hollow-chested, sensitive, New Age man who bawls at Kodak commercials and handles a diaper the way Magic Johnson does a basketball. Enter Alan Alda.

But he, too, is quickly becoming outdated. As we begin the '90s, the zeitgeist   **6**
has changed again. Now the sensitive male is a wimp and an object of derision to boot. In her song *Sensitive New Age Guys,* singer Christine Lavin lampoons, "Who carries the baby on his back? Who thinks Shirley MacLaine is on the inside track?" Now it's goodbye, Alan Alda; hello, Mel Gibson, with your sensitive eyes and your lethal weapon. Hi there, Arnold Schwarzenegger, the devoted family man with terrific triceps. The new surge of tempered macho is everywhere. Even the male dummies in store windows are getting tougher. Pucci Manikins is producing a more muscular model for the new decade that stands 6 ft. 2 in. instead of 6 ft. and has a 42-in. chest instead of its previous 40.

What's going on here? Are we looking at a backlash against the pounding   **7**
men have taken? To some degree, yes. But it's more complicated than that. "The sensitive man was overplayed," explains Seattle-based lecturer Michael Meade, a colleague of Bly's in the men's movement. "There is no one quality intriguing enough to make a person interesting for a long time." More important, argues Warren Farrell, author of the 1986 best seller *Why Men Are the Way They Are,* women liked Alan Alda not because he epitomized the sensitive man but be- cause he was a multimillionaire superstar success who also happened to be

sensitive. In short, he met all their performance needs before sensitivity ever entered the picture. "We have never worshiped the soft man," says Farrell. "If Mel Gibson were a nursery school teacher, women wouldn't want him. Can you imagine a cover of TIME featuring a sensitive musician who drives a cab on the side?"

8   The women's movement sensitized many men to the problems women face in society and made them examine their own feelings in new ways. But it did not substantially alter what society expects of men. "Nothing fundamental has changed," says Farrell. Except that both John Wayne and Alan Alda have been discarded on the same cultural garbage heap. "First I learned that an erect cock was politically incorrect," complains producer Seligson. "Now it's wrong not to have one."

9   As always, men are defined by their performance in the workplace. If women don't like their jobs, they can, at least in theory, maintain legitimacy by going home and raising children. Men have no such alternative. "The options are dismal," says Meade. "You can drop out, which is an abdication of power, or take the whole cloth and lose your soul." If women have suffered from being sex objects, men have suffered as success objects, judged by the amount of money they bring home. As one young career woman in Boston puts it, "I don't want a Type A. I want an A-plus." Chilling words that make Farrell wonder, "Why do we need to earn more than you to be considered worthy of you?"

10   This imbalance can be brutal for a man whose wife tries life in the corporate world, discovers as men did decades ago that it is no day at the beach, and heads for home, leaving him the sole breadwinner. "We're seeing more of this 'You guys can have it back. It's been real,'" observes Kyle Pruett, a psychiatrist at the Yale Child Studies Center. "I have never seen a case where it has not increased anxiety for the man."

11   There has been a lot of cocktail-party talk about the need for a brave, sensitive man who will stand up to the corporate barons and take time off to watch his son play Peter Pan in his school play, the fast track be damned. This sentiment showed up in a 1989 poll, conducted by Robert Half International, in which about 45% of men surveyed said they would refuse a promotion rather than miss time at home. But when it comes to trading income for "quality time," how many fathers will actually be there at the grade-school curtain call?

12   "Is there a Daddy Track? No," says Edward Zigler, a Yale psychologist. "The message is that if a man takes paternity leave, he's a very strange person who is not committed to the corporation. It's very bleak." Says Felice Schwartz, who explored the notion of a Mommy Track in a 1989 article in the *Harvard Business Review:* "There isn't any forgiveness yet of a man who doesn't really give his all." So today's working stiff really enjoys no more meaningful options than did his father, the pathetic guy in the gray flannel suit who was pilloried as a professional hamster and an emotional cripple. You're still either a master of the universe or a wimp. It is the cognitive dissonance between the desire for change and the absence of ways to achieve it that has reduced most men who even think about the subject to tapioca.

Robert Rackleff, 47, is one of the rare men who have stepped off the   **13**
corporate treadmill. Five years ago, after the birth of their third child, Rackleff
and his wife Jo-Ellen fled New York City, where he was a well-paid corporate
speechwriter and she a radio-show producer. They moved to his native Florida,
where Rackleff earns a less lavish living as a free-lance writer and helps his wife
raise the kids. The drop in income, he acknowledges, "was scary. It put more
pressure on me, but I wanted to spend more time with my children." Rackleff
feels happy with his choice, but isolated. "I know only one other guy who left
the fast track to be with his kids," he says. "Men just aren't doing it. I can still
call up most of them at 8 P.M. and know they will be in the office."

Men have been bombarded with recipes to ripen their personal lives, if not   **14**
their professional ones. They are now Lamaze-class regulars and can be found
in the delivery room for the cosmic event instead of pacing the waiting-room
floor. They have been instructed to bond with children, wives, colleagues and
anyone else they can find. Exactly how remains unclear. Self-help books, like
Twinkies, give brief highs and do not begin to address the uneven changes in
their lives over the past 20 years. "Men aren't any happier in the '90s than they
were in the '50s," observes Yale psychiatrist Pruett, "but their inner lives tend
to be more complex. They are interested in feeling less isolated. They are
stunned to find out how rich human relationships are."

Unfortunately, the men who attempt to explore those riches with the   **15**
women in their lives often discover that their efforts are not entirely welcome.
The same women who complain about male reticence can grow uncomfortable
when male secrets and insecurities spill out. Says Rackleff: "I think a lot of
women who want a husband to be a typical hardworking breadwinner are
scared when he talks about being a sensitive father. I get cynical about that."

One might be equally cynical about men opening up to other men. Atlanta   **16**
psychologist Augustus Napier tells of two doctors whose lockers were next to
each other in the surgical dressing room of a hospital. For years they talked
about sports, money and other safe "male" subjects. Then one of them learned
that the other had tried to commit suicide—and had never so much as mentioned the attempt to him. So much for male bonding.

How can men break out of the gender stereotypes? Clearly, there is a need   **17**
for some male consciousness raising, yet men have nothing to rival the giant
grass-roots movement that began razing female stereotypes 25 years ago. There
is no male equivalent for the National Organization for Women or *Ms.* magazine. No role models, other than the usual megabillionaire success objects.

A minute percentage of American males are involved in the handful of   **18**
organizations whose membership ranges from men who support the feminist
movement to angry divorcés meeting to swap gripes about alimony and child-
custody battles. There is also a group of mostly well-educated, middle-class men
who sporadically participate in a kind of male spiritual quest. Anywhere from
Maine to Minnesota, at male-only weekend retreats, they earnestly search for
some shard of ancient masculinity culled from their souls by the Industrial
Revolution. At these so-called warrior weekends, participants wrestle, beat

drums and hold workshops on everything from ecology to divorce and incest. They embrace, and yes, they do cry and confide things they would never dream of saying to their wives and girlfriends. They act out emotions in a safe haven where no one will laugh at them.

19 At one drumming session in the municipal-arts center of a Boston suburb, about 50 men sit in a huge circle beating on everything from tom-toms to cowbells and sticks. Their ages range from the 20s to the 60s. A participant has brought his young son with him. Drummers nod as newcomers appear, sit down and start pounding away. Before long, a strong primal beat emerges that somehow transcends the weirdness of it all. Some men close their eyes and play in a trance. Others rise and dance around the middle of the group, chanting as they move.

20 One shudders to think what *Saturday Night Live* would do with these scenes. But there is no smirking among the participants. "When is the last time you danced with another man?" asks Paul, a family man who drove two hours from Connecticut to be there. "It tells you how many walls there are still out there for us." Los Angeles writer Michael Ventura, who has written extensively about men's issues, acknowledges the obvious: much of this seems pretty bizarre. "Some of it may look silly," he says. "But if you're afraid of looking silly, everything stops right there. In our society, men have to be contained and sure of themselves. Well, f____ that. That's not the way we feel." The goal, continues Ventura, is to rediscover the mystery of man, a creature capable of strength, spontaneity and adventure. "The male mystery is the part of us that wants to explore, that isn't afraid of the dark, that lights a fire and dances around it."

21 One thing is clear: men need the support of other men to change, which is why activities like drumming aren't as dumb as they may look. Even though no words are exchanged, the men at these sessions get something from other men that they earnestly need: understanding and acceptance. "The solitude of men is the most difficult single thing to change," says Napier. These retreats provide cover for some spiritual reconnaissance too risky to attempt in the company of women. "It's like crying," says Michael Meade. "Men are afraid that if they start, they'll cry forever."

22 Does the search for a lineal sense of masculinity have any relevance to such thorny modern dilemmas as how to balance work and family or how to talk to women? Perhaps. Men have to feel comfortable with themselves before they can successfully confront such issues. This grounding is also critical for riding out the changes in pop culture and ideals. John Wayne and Alan Alda, like violence and passivity, reflect holes in a core that needs fixing. But men can get grounded in many ways, and male retreats provide just one stylized option, though not one necessarily destined to attract most American men.

23 What do men really want? To define themselves on their own terms, just as women began to do a couple of decades ago. "Would a women's group ask men if it was O.K. to feel a certain way?" asks Jerry Johnson, host of the San Francisco–based KCBS radio talk show *Man to Man*. "No way. We're still looking for approval from women for changes, and we need to get it from the male camp."

That's the point. And it does not have to come at women's expense. "It is **24** stupid to conclude that the empowerment of women means the disempowerment of men," says Robert Moore, a psychoanalyst at the C. G. Jung Institute in Chicago. "Men must also feel good about being male." Men would do well, in fact, to invite women into their lives to participate in these changes. It's no fun to face them alone. But if women can't or won't, men must act on their own and damn the torpedoes. No pain, no gain.

▼ TOPICAL CONSIDERATIONS

1. According to the author, what changes have taken place in the role models men look up to? What has caused these changes? Do Allis's claims here jive with your own observations. How or how not?
2. How, according to Allis, have men reacted to these changing role models? How do you feel about these changing definitions of what it means to be a male in our society?
3. Who are some of the male role models you admire today? What traits do they have that are admirable? What traits do these men have in common? What can you generalize about the traits of the "90's" male?
4. Do you agree or disagree with Allis when he says in paragraph 9 that "men are defined by their performance in the workplace"? Why or why not?
5. How do you feel about Allis's comment in paragraph 11 about "trading income for 'quality time' "? Do you think that it is easier for women to do this than men? Do you think women *should* do this more often than men do? Explain your answers.
6. What does Allis mention as possible remedies to the dilemma of shifting definitions of what it means to be a male? What other solutions can you suggest?
7. In paragraph 2, Allis states that men are "airing their frustration with the limited roles they face today, compared with the multiple options that women seem to have won." Do you think that men's opportunities today are *more* limited than women's opportunities or *less* limited? Give examples to support your answer.
8. In paragraph 2, Allis contends that women have won "multiple options" as a result of the women's movement. What, in your opinion, have women won as a result of the women's movement? Which of these opportunities might men benefit from?

▼ RHETORICAL CONSIDERATIONS

1. Look at the figurative language Allis uses in paragraphs 5 and 6 to describe different types of men. Do you think Allis accurately and

fairly describes each type of man, or does his language suggest that he has a preference for some types over others?

2. Compare the tone of this essay to the tone Ebeling uses in her article. How are they the same? How are they different? What accounts for these similarities and/or differences?

3. How is the information in this essay organized? Do you think this organization is effective? Why or why not?

▼ WRITING ASSIGNMENTS

1. Write an essay explaining what you think men really want. Draw from the men you know, as well as the information in Allis's article to flesh out your essay.

2. Gather together all of the solutions the class suggested for question 6 in Topical Considerations. Write an essay about solutions to the male dilemma, using the class's information as well as your own. Think about what would be the best combination of actions to help resolve this dilemma.

3. Allis, Farrell, and Ebeling all write about the difficulties of working for a living and raising a family at the same time. Write an essay that summarizes their various points of view about these difficulties. Then go on to explain your own views on this. Propose some solutions you think might ease at least some of the difficulties you talk about.

4. Quindlen, Ebeling, and Sanders all use examples from their own experiences to support the points they are making in their articles. Farrell and Allis use examples from the general society to support the points they are making. Which do you prefer to use when you write? Do you think that any essay would benefit from examples of personal experience being placed in it, or are there some kinds of writing that need to remain more formal? Explore this issue by thinking back over papers you have written and the uses you have made in these of personal experiences and of examples from more general society.

5 ▼ RACE AND CLASS

Every essay in this section reveals something of what it is like to be a member of a minority in a white-dominated America. And a theme common to each is the struggle to determine one's identity while torn between two cultures and two races.

By the next century, one-third of our nation will be made up of people of color. In many states, African-Americans, Latin-Americans, Asian-Americans, and Native Americans will comprise the majority of the population. In the opening essay, "America: The Multinational Society," Ishmael Reed surveys the rapidly changing complexion of the contemporary American landscape.

The next essay examines issues of identity for black Americans, the largest of our nation's minorities. In "The Struggle is Ours," Joan Morgan appeals to other young middle-class black professionals not to become so self-satisfied in their gains that they abandon the very traditions that made possible their progress. The next piece, "Black Men and Public Space" is a subdued protest against the stereotype that casts all black men as villains. Brent Staples captures the pain and isolation he has endured since first discovering at "the ripe old age of twenty-two," that his mere presence in public places can arouse fear and suspicion in others.

The next two selections examine how Hispanic Americans—the fastest growing minority in America today—deal with the pressures of assimilation in America. In "Your Parents Must Be Very Proud" Richard Rodriguez makes it clear that he yearned for Americanization. Embarrassed by his poor command of English when he first entered school, he tells of how he quickly grasped onto opportunities his parents never had as Mexican immigrants—opportunities that would later distance him from his heritage. By contrast, the author of the next piece suffered neither confusion nor embarrassment over the two cultures of his heritage. On the contrary, born black and raised in Spanish Harlem, Roberto Santiago celebrates his twin identities in "Black *and* Latino."

For Asian-Americans problems of being a minority are no different from what other people of color experience as we see in the next two pieces. "To Be an All-American Girl," is a powerful memoir of Elizabeth Wong who made every effort to deny her Chinese roots. Shanlon Wu, on the other hand, accepted his Chinese heritage. His boyhood crisis was the lack of Asian role models in mainstream American culture. "In Search of Bruce Lee's Grave" is a poignant reflection on his quest for identity in a martial-arts screen idol.

For Native Americans "Indian Bones" is a quest for a different sort of definition—respect as human beings whether alive or dead. In this final essay, Clara Spotted Elk presents an impassioned appeal for Federal agencies, museums, and other institutions to return for proper burial the physical remains of thousands of ancestors secreted away in "specimen" drawers.

▼ AMERICA: THE MULTINATIONAL SOCIETY

Ishmael Reed

America is a union of like-minded moral values and political and economic self-interest. But, lest we forget, America is also a country of immigrants— of people of different races, ethnic identities, religions, and languages. It is a nation whose motto, *e pluribus unum* ("one out of many") bespeaks the pride in its multicultural heritage. In the opening piece, Ishmael Reed looks around at the constant reminders of how once distinctly foreign cultural styles have now become part of the American landscape. Ishmael Reed is regarded as one of the most provocative and thoughtful black satirists writing today. He is the author of several novels, plays, books of poetry, and essay collections. He has taught at Harvard, Yale, Dartmouth, and the University of California at Berkeley. The essay below was taken from his latest collection, *Writin' Is Fightin'* (1990).

At the annual Lower East Side Jewish Festival yesterday, a Chinese woman ate a pizza slice in front of Ty Thuan Duc's Vietnamese grocery store. Beside her a Spanish-speaking family patronized a cart with two signs: "Italian Ices" and "Kosher by Rabbi Alper." And after the pastrami ran out, everybody ate knishes.

THE NEW YORK TIMES, 23 June 1983

On the day before Memorial Day, 1983, a poet called me to describe a city 1
he had just visited. He said that one section included mosques, built by the Islamic people who dwelled there. Attending his reading, he said, were large numbers of Hispanic people, forty thousand of whom lived in the same city. He was not talking about a fabled city located in some mysterious region of the world. The city he'd visited was Detroit.

A few months before, as I was leaving Houston, Texas, I heard it an- 2
nounced on the radio that Texas's largest minority was Mexican-American, and though a foundation recently issued a report critical of bilingual education, the taped voice used to guide the passengers on the air trams connecting terminals in Dallas Airport is in both Spanish and English. If the trend continues, a day will come when it will be difficult to travel through some sections of the country without hearing commands in both English and Spanish; after all, for some western states, Spanish was the first written language and the Spanish style lives on in the western way of life.

Shortly after my Texas trip, I sat in an auditorium located on the campus 3
of the University of Wisconsin at Milwaukee as a Yale professor—whose original work on the influence of African cultures upon those of the Americas has

led to his ostracism from some monocultural intellectual circles—walked up and down the aisle, like an old-time southern evangelist, dancing and drumming the top of the lectern, illustrating his points before some serious Afro-American intellectuals and artists who cheered and applauded his performance and his mastery of information. The professor was "white." After his lecture, he joined a group of Milwaukeeans in a conversation. All of the participants spoke Yoruban, though only the professor had ever traveled to Africa.

4   One of the artists told me that his paintings, which included African and Afro-American mythological symbols and imagery, were hanging in the local McDonald's restaurant. The next day I went to McDonald's and snapped pictures of smiling youngsters eating hamburgers below paintings that could grace the walls of any of the country's leading museums. The manager of the local McDonald's said, "I don't know what you boys are doing, but I like it," as he commissioned the local painters to exhibit in his restaurant.

5   Such blurring of cultural styles occurs in everyday life in the United States to a greater extent than anyone can imagine and is probably more prevalent than the sensational conflict between people of different backgrounds that is played up and often encouraged by the media. The result is what the Yale professor, Robert Thompson, referred to as a cultural bouillabaisse, yet members of the nation's present educational and cultural Elect still cling to the notion that the United States belongs to some vaguely defined entity they refer to as "Western civilization," by which they mean, presumably, a civilization created by the people of Europe, as if Europe can be viewed in monolithic terms. Is Beethoven's Ninth Symphony, which includes Turkish marches, a part of Western civilization, or the late nineteenth- and twentieth-century French paintings, whose creators were influenced by Japanese art? And what of the cubists, through whom the influence of African art changed modern painting, or the surrealists, who were so impressed with the art of the Pacific Northwest Indians that, in their map of North America, Alaska dwarfs the lower forty-eight in size?

6   Are the Russians, who are often criticized for their adoption of "Western" ways by Tsarist dissidents in exile, members of Western civilization? And what of the millions of Europeans who have black African and Asian ancestry, black Africans having occupied several countries for hundreds of years? Are these "Europeans" members of Western civilization, or the Hungarians, who originated across the Urals in a place called Greater Hungary, or the Irish, who came from the Iberian Peninsula?

7   Even the notion that North America is part of Western civilization because our "system of government" is derived from Europe is being challenged by Native American historians who say that the founding fathers, Benjamin Franklin especially, were actually influenced by the system of government that had been adopted by the Iroquois hundreds of years prior to the arrival of large numbers of Europeans.

8   Western civilization, then, becomes another confusing category like Third World, or Judeo-Christian culture, as man attempts to impose his small-screen view of political and cultural reality upon a complex world. Our most publicized

novelist recently said that Western civilization was the greatest achievement of mankind, an attitude that flourishes on the street level as scribbles in public restrooms: "White Power," "Niggers and Spic Suck," or "Hitler was a prophet," the latter being the most telling, for wasn't Adolph Hitler the archetypal monoculturalist who, in his pigheaded arrogance, believed that one way and one blood was so pure that it had to be protected from alien strains at all costs? Where did such an attitude, which has caused so much misery and depression in our national life, which has tainted even our noblest achievements, begin? An attitude that caused the incarceration of Japanese-American citizens during World War II, the persecution of Chicanos and Chinese-Americans, the near-extermination of the Indians, and the murder and lynchings of thousands of Afro-Americans.

Virtuous, hardworking, pious, even though they occasionally would wander off after some fancy clothes, or rendezvous in the woods with the town prostitute, the Puritans are idealized in our schoolbooks as "a hardy band" of no-nonsense patriarchs whose discipline razed the forest and brought order to the New World (a term that annoys Native American historians). Industrious, responsible, it was their "Yankee ingenuity" and practicality that created the work ethic. They were simple folk who produced a number of good poets, and they set the tone for the American writing style, of lean and spare lines, long before Hemingway. They worshiped in churches whose colors blended in with the New England snow, churches with simple structures and ornate lecterns.   **9**

The Puritans were a daring lot, but they had a mean streak. They hated the theater and banned Christmas. They punished people in a cruel and inhuman manner. They killed children who disobeyed their parents. When they came in contact with those whom they considered heathens or aliens, they behaved in such a bizarre and irrational manner that this chapter in the American history comes down to us as a late-movie horror film. They exterminated the Indians, who taught them how to survive in a world unknown to them, and their encounter with the calypso culture of Barbados resulted in what the tourist guide in Salem's Witches' House refers to as the Witchcraft Hysteria.   **10**

The Puritan legacy of hard work and meticulous accounting led to the establishment of a great industrial society; it is no wonder that the American industrial revolution began in Lowell, Massachusetts, but there was the other side, the strange and paranoid attitudes toward those different from the Elect.   **11**

The cultural attitudes of that early Elect continue to be voiced in everyday life in the United States: the president of a distinguished university, writing a letter to the *Times,* belittling the study of African civilizations; the television network that promoted its show on the Vatican art with the boast that this art represented "the finest achievements of the human spirit." A modern up-tempo state of complex rhythms that depends upon contacts with an international community can no longer behave as if it dwelled in a "Zion Wilderness" surrounded by beasts and pagans.   **12**

When I heard a schoolteacher warn the other night about the invasion of the American educational system by foreign curriculums, I wanted to yell at the   **13** television set, "Lady, they're already here." It has already begun because the world is here. The world has been arriving at these shores for at least ten thousand years from Europe, Africa, and Asia. In the late nineteenth and early twentieth centuries, large numbers of Europeans arrived, adding their cultures to those of the European, African, and Asian settlers who were already here, and recently millions have been entering the country from South America and the Caribbean, making Yale Professor Bob Thompson's bouillabaisse richer and thicker.

14   One of our most visionary politicians said that he envisioned a time when the United States could become the brain of the world, by which he meant the repository of all of the latest advanced information systems. I thought of that remark when an enterprising poet friend of mine called to say that he had just sold a poem to a computer magazine and that the editors were delighted to get it because they didn't carry fiction or poetry. Is that the kind of world we desire? A humdrum homogeneous world of all brains and no heart, no fiction, no poetry; a world of robots with human attendants bereft of imagination, of culture? Or does North America deserve a more exciting destiny? To become a place where the cultures of the world crisscross. This is possible because the United States is unique in the world: The world is here.

▼ TOPICAL CONSIDERATIONS

1. What would you say is the basic point of Reed's essay? Where does he make his thesis statement? Does the essay prove this thesis? Do you agree with Reed's assessment of America as a multicultural environment?

2. Consider Yale professor Robert Thompson's term "cultural bouillabaisse" (paragraph 5). Why does Reed favor this term over the familiar label, "melting pot," or "Western civilization"?

3. In paragraph 5, Reed discusses various influences on "Western" art. How, according to the author, does art blur cultural lines? Did his examples open your eyes to the narrowness of the label "Western culture"?

4. Explain the term "monoculturalist" in paragraph 8. How according to Reed has this philosophy affected America? Do you think monoculturalism is prevalent in your immediate environment? How about when you were growing up?

5. Consider the "street level scribbles" in paragraph 8. Thinking of this graffiti as actual text, try to determine what kind of power it has?

6. Comment on Reed's revisionist description of the founding of America (paragraph 9). What is his point here? How does it add to the theme of the essay? Have you ever been exposed to this side of the Puritans before? If not, how does it make you regard your early "schoolbook" concept of America's founding?

7. Reed writes in his final paragraph, "Or does North America deserve a more exciting destiny?" What kind of destiny does Reed envision?

▼ RHETORICAL CONSIDERATIONS

1. What does "the Elect" (with a capital *E*) mean in paragraph 11?
2. The essay is written in first person. Do you consider the narrator an authority on this subject? If so, how are you convinced of his expertise?
3. Does this essay convince you that "the world is here"? Explain where the essay is most effective and where it is lacking.
4. Consider the number of different locales Reed mentions throughout his essay. What is the rhetorical purpose of including the names of all these places?

▼ WRITING ASSIGNMENTS

1. Reed writes (in paragraph 10) of the Puritans, "When they came in contact with those whom they considered heathens or aliens, they behaved in such a bizarre and irrational manner that this chapter in the American history comes down to us as a late-movie horror film." Investigate some facet of early American history that is like a horror movie. Perhaps look at captivity narratives, letters, diaries, and the like that present new information to you. Juxtapose your findings with a standard "factual" account in a history textbook. Write a paper that focuses on a single event and compare the two accounts. Try to decide where the truth lies.
2. Explore the idea of a "cultural bouillabaisse." Does America as the Melting Pot accept nonwestern people as an ingredient, or is ours a discriminating bouillabaisse?
3. In the final paragraph, Reed asks if Americans desire "a humdrum homogeneous world of all brains and no heart, no fiction, no poetry; a world of robots with human attendants bereft of imagination, of culture? Or does North America deserve a more exciting destiny?" Write a paper in which you construct America's destiny. Include Reed's argument for multiculturalism and predict the route America has taken.
4. How does Reed's vision of a "Multinational Society" compare to popular culture's picture of America? Consider Spike Lee's *Do the Right Thing* and *Jungle Fever,* John Singleton's *Boyz 'N the Hood,* Public Enemy, and other segments of the media that address these issues.
5. Write a letter to Ishmael Reed telling him what you think of his essay—whether or not he was convincing; whether or not the essay

made you more aware of the true makeup of our society, its history, and destiny. Also comment on the effectiveness of his writing.

▼ THE STRUGGLE IS OURS
Joan L. Morgan

Joan Morgan is very happy being a young black woman in today's America. She says that in spite of reports of "impending doom" for black people, African-Americans in the span of a generation have made stunning progress in the areas of education, employment, politics, culture and housing. Today, a thriving black middle class boasts a higher percentage of college degrees, higher-wage jobs, better housing, and greater political clout than ever before. However, she warns that black Americans are in danger of losing hard-won gains because of the apathy and self-satisfaction that has come with social and economic progress. In the article below, Morgan calls on young black Americans to uncompromisingly embrace traditional Afrocentric values in combating the forces of homelessness, poverty, drugs, AIDS, and black redefinition. Joan L. Morgan writes and teaches high school in New York City. Focusing on rap music and popular culture, Morgan's articles have appeared in various publications including the *Village Voice, Spin, The New York Times, The Source,* and *Interview.* This essay first appeared in *Essence* magazine in May 1990.

1   These days I'm real happy about being a Black woman in my early twenties. In spite of the dismal statistics that proclaim Black folks' impending and inevitable doom, I believe in my generation's ability to continue our tradition of struggle *and* survival.

2   But first we have to come to grips with some hard truths. The end of the eighties represents the end of a mythology for my generation. Many of us grew up believing that we had, for all intents and purposes, overcome.

3   We grew fat and comfortable on the sacrifices made by those before us. We attended colleges—good colleges—got high-paying jobs and joined the seemingly swelling ranks of the Black middle class. Our Ivy League degrees, credit cards and newfound Buppiedom became badges of emotional armor against the pain and drain of racism. We needed desperately to believe that it no longer existed in a form that could debilitate us. Many of our parents needed to believe in the myth, too. They stopped reminding us, stopped telling us their stories. Their silence let us become apathetic and apolitical. We became the first generation to grow up with all of the benefits of the Civil Rights Movement—and the first to lose them. What we considered our inalienable right to privilege and upward mobility is quickly slipping away.

Now what was once flippantly dismissed as "political" has become intensely 4 personal. The urgency of the times has forced even the most apathetic among us to evaluate our existence in a more communal way. It's no longer as simple a matter as turning off the news and turning on the VCR.

Ignoring homelessness and poverty once meant turning a blind eye to the 5 occasional outstretched hand. Today it means walking over other Black bodies—literally—many times a day. Sisters I know who used to spend hours "conversatin' " about the lack of good Black men now discuss what can be done about the brothers we lose yearly to jail, drugs or AIDS. (It seems that lonely nights have led us to internalize the stats.) Meanwhile, the rapid reversal of civil-rights rulings makes it clear that our position as even second-class citizens is tenuous.

The challenge to my generation is to develop a value system that is uncom- 6 promisingly Afrocentric—one that not only embraces those traditions that have worked for us historically (family, extended family, community, spirituality, education and protest, to name a few), but one that also lets us embrace the uniqueness of our experience as young African-Americans. We are not the same as our parents. Developing this value system is a challenge to which we are slowly rising. The disillusionment of the eighties is being replaced by the powerful and sometimes painful process of redefinition.

There is evidence of it all around us. Lee Atwater felt it when he saw his 7 nomination to Howard University's board of trustees nipped in the bud by a stunning display of student activism. Political leaders David Dinkins and Jesse Jackson could not have accomplished as much as they have without the support of the young, Black and degreed. Filmmakers Euzhan Palcy and Spike Lee are at the forefront of the battle to gain control of our images. Word warriors Queen Latifah, Look Moe Dee, Public Enemy, Boogie Down Productions and the Jungle Brothers are among the rappers who bring our youth positive messages in stereo. Young writers and visual and performing artists are using their art to challenge outmoded assumptions about Black identity.

Our clothing and hairstyles reflect our growing Afrocentrism. Gold slave 8 chains are replaced by African medallions. Malcolm X is resurging as a symbol of pride, strength and promise. We are not only continuing the struggle; we are also defining it for ourselves, learning who we are. So don't count us out of the race yet. Instead, prepare to meet us at the finish.

▼ TOPICAL CONSIDERATIONS

1. With details from the essay explain Morgan's statement "Now what was once flippantly dismissed as 'political' has become intensely personal" (paragraph 4).
2. What is Morgan's challenge to blacks?
3. Looking ahead, how is Morgan's message similar to those of the other black authors in this chapter (Reed, Santiago, Staples)? Ex-

plain the extent to which these other authors convey a message to African-Americans that is as positive as Morgan's: "Don't count us out of the race yet. Instead, meet us at the finish."

4. According to Morgan, what do people like Jesse Jackson, Spike Lee, Public Enemy, and Malcolm X represent for African-Americans? Do you feel they are all positive images? Do you feel they all contribute to the benefits of black Americans?

5. What power did and can the "young, Black, and degreed" have in American society? Do you agree that the privileges of the Civil Rights movement are "quickly slipping away"?

6. Is there a difference between the "Afrocentrism" described in paragraph 6 and the monoculturalism that Reed warns us against in his essay? Use examples from each essay.

7. Who are the empowered black Americans Morgan sites in her essay? What are the gender roles Morgan attributes to blacks in America in the 1990s? What powerful black women could she have named as visionaries?

▼ RHETORICAL CONSIDERATIONS

1. What is "Buppiedom"? Considering "Buppiedom," what do you think of Santiago's charge in "Black *and* Latino" (p. 208) that America loves to categorize?

2. How is this essay rhetorically structured? What techniques does Morgan use to persuade her audience?

3. In the final paragraph, Morgan writes, "So don't count us out of the race yet." Comment on the meaning(s) of *race* in the statement.

4. Paragraph 2 states, "The end of the eighties represents the end of a mythology for my generation." What is the connotation of *mythology?* Give examples of other personal or societal mythologies from your own experience.

▼ WRITING ASSIGNMENTS

1. Write an essay in which you evaluate Joan L. Morgan's challenge to young African-Americans. Explain how it might inspire her audience to "develop a value system that is uncompromisingly Afrocentric."

2. Choose one of the figures Morgan mentions or a prominent African-American whom you admire. Research his or her contributions to strengthening the Afrocentric identity.

3. In many of the essays in this chapter on race and class, we find the

language of struggle. Discuss the different ways the language of struggle works and for what end. Quote from at least three essays.

4. To what extent has the search for an Afrocentric identity for black Americans invaded pop-culture? Consider television, film, music and music videos, magazines, and so on. Write a paper that explains how far this movement has come. Do you think white America is aware of this movement?

▼ BLACK MEN AND PUBLIC SPACE

Brent Staples

Brent Staples, born in Chester, Pennsylvania in 1951, is first assistant metropolitan editor of the *New York Times*. In the piece below, Staples tells of a shocking realization he had at the age of 22: that because he was a black male, he could "alter public space in ugly ways." Forever a suspect, Staples describes the alienation and danger he suffers from such a perception—a perception he has learned to deal with. This essay appeared in *Harper's* in December 1987.

My first victim was a woman—white, well dressed, probably in her early twenties. I came upon her late one evening on a deserted street in Hyde Park, a relatively affluent neighborhood in an otherwise mean, impoverished section of Chicago. As I swung onto the avenue behind her, there seemed to be a discreet, uninflammatory distance between us. Not so. She cast back a worried glance. To her, the youngish black man—a broad six feet two inches with a beard and billowing hair, both hands shoved into the pockets of a bulky military jacket—seemed menacingly close. After a few more quick glimpses, she picked up her pace and was soon running in earnest. Within seconds she disappeared into a cross street.

That was more than a decade ago, I was twenty-two years old, a graduate student newly arrived at the University of Chicago. It was in the echo of that terrified woman's footfalls that I first began to know the unwieldy inheritance I'd come into—the ability to alter public space in ugly ways. It was clear that she thought of herself the quarry of a mugger, a rapist, or worse. Suffering a bout of insomnia, however, I was stalking sleep, not defenseless wayfarers. As a softy who is scarcely able to take a knife to a raw chicken—let alone hold one to a person's throat—I was surprised, embarrassed, and dismayed all at once. Her flight made me feel like an accomplice in tyranny. It also made it clear that

I was indistinguishable from the muggers who occasionally seeped into the area from the surrounding ghetto. That first encounter, and those that followed, signified that a vast, unnerving gulf lay between nighttime pedestrians—particularly women—and me. And I soon gathered that being perceived as dangerous is a hazard in itself. I only needed to turn a corner into a dicey situation, or crowd some frightened, armed person in a foyer somewhere, or make an errant move after being pulled over by a policeman. Where fear and weapons meet— and they often do in urban America—there is always the possibility of death.

3   In that first year, my first away from my hometown, I was to become thoroughly familiar with the language of fear. At dark, shadowy intersections, I could cross in front of a car stopped at a traffic light and elicit the *thunk, thunk, thunk, thunk* of the driver—black, white, male, or female—hammering down the door locks. On less traveled streets after dark, I grew accustomed to but never comfortable with people crossing to the other side of the street rather than pass me. Then there were the standard unpleasantries with policemen, doormen, bouncers, cabdrivers, and others whose business it is to screen out troublesome individuals *before* there is any nastiness.

4   I moved to New York nearly two years ago and I have remained an avid night walker. In central Manhattan, the near-constant crowd cover minimizes tense one-on-one street encounters. Elsewhere—in SoHo, for example, where sidewalks are narrow and tightly spaced buildings shut out the sky—things can get very taut indeed.

5   After dark, on the warrenlike streets of Brooklyn where I live, I often see women who fear the worst from me. They seem to have set their faces on neutral, and with their purse straps strung across their chests bandolier-style, they forge ahead as though bracing themselves against being tackled. I understand, of course, that the danger they perceive is not a hallucination. Women are particularly vulnerable to street violence, and young black males are drastically overrepresented among the perpetrators of that violence. Yet these truths are no solace against the kind of alienation that comes of being ever the suspect, a fearsome entity with whom pedestrians avoid making eye contact.

6   It is not altogether clear to me how I reached the ripe old age of twenty-two without being conscious of the lethality nighttime pedestrians attributed to me. Perhaps it was because in Chester, Pennsylvania, the small, angry industrial town where I came of age in the 1960s, I was scarcely noticeable against a backdrop of gang warfare, street knifings, and murders. I grew up one of the good boys, had perhaps a half-dozen fistfights. In retrospect, my shyness of combat has clear sources.

7   As a boy, I saw countless tough guys locked away; I have since buried several, too. They were babies, really—a teenage cousin, a brother of twenty-two, a childhood friend in his mid-twenties—all gone down in episodes of bravado played out in the streets. I came to doubt the virtues of intimidation early on. I chose, perhaps unconsciously, to remain a shadow—timid, but a survivor.

8   The fearsomeness mistakenly attributed to me in public places often has a

perilous flavor. The most frightening of these confusions occurred in the late 1970s and early 1980s, when I worked as a journalist in Chicago. One day, rushing into the office of a magazine I was writing for with a deadline story in hand, I was mistaken for a burglar. The office manager called security and, with an ad hoc posse, pursued me through the labyrinthine halls, nearly to my editor's door. I had no way of proving who I was. I could only move briskly toward the company of someone who knew me.

Another time I was on assignment for a local paper and killing time before   9 an interview. I entered a jewelry store on the city's affluent Near North Side. The proprietor excused herself and returned with an enormous red Doberman pinscher straining at the end of a leash. She stood, the dog extended toward me, silent to my questions, her eyes bulging nearly out of her head. I took a cursory look around, nodded, and bade her good night.

Relatively speaking, however, I never fared as badly as another black male   10 journalist. He went to nearby Waukegan, Illinois, a couple of summers ago to work on a story about a murderer who was born there. Mistaking the reporter for the killer, police officers hauled him from his car at gunpoint and but for his press credentials would probably have tried to book him. Such episodes are not uncommon. Black men trade tales like this all the time.

Over the years, I learned to smother the rage I felt at so often being taken   11 for a criminal. Not to do so would surely have led to madness. I now take precautions to make myself less threatening. I move about with care, particularly late in the evening. I give a wide berth to nervous people on subway platforms during the wee hours, particularly when I have exchanged business clothes for jeans. If I happen to be entering a building behind some people who appear skittish, I may walk by, letting them clear the lobby before I return, so as not to seem to be following them. I have been calm and extremely congenial on those rare occasions when I've been pulled over by the police.

And on late-evening constitutionals I employ what has proved to be an   12 excellent tension-reducing measure: I whistle melodies from Beethoven and Vivaldi and the more popular classical composers. Even steely New Yorkers hunching toward nighttime destinations seem to relax, and occasionally they even join in the tune. Virtually everybody seems to sense that a mugger wouldn't be warbling bright, sunny selections from Vivaldi's *Four Seasons*. It is my equivalent of the cowbell that hikers wear when they know they are in bear country.

▼ TOPICAL CONSIDERATIONS

1. What did Staples' episode with the fleeing woman in Hyde Park make him realize? How did it make him feel?
2. Staples learns that his being a black male is perceived as a danger to others. How could this perception be a hazard to him? How has this perception actually been hazardous to him?

3. How does Staples's personal background explain his unawareness of the threat he posed to nighttime pedestrians?
4. How does Staples explain the submergence of his rage at being "taken for a criminal"?
5. What are some of the ways Staples has tried to mitigate the threat he poses to other night pedestrians? If you were Staples, would you resort to these strategies or not bother at all?
6. Does Staples describe attitudes and fears to which you can relate?

▼ RHETORICAL CONSIDERATIONS

1. Comment on the effectiveness of the opening sentence of this essay. Why does Staples use the word "victim"? What is the woman a victim of?
2. Why does Staples choose to describe himself in the first paragraph?
3. Do you find any examples of humor in the essay? If so, do you think this humor adds to or detracts from the seriousness of the subject?

▼ WRITING ASSIGNMENTS

1. Have you ever felt threatened by a person or persons on a street at night? Write a paper in which you describe the experience and the threat you felt.
2. Have you ever been aware of the threat you might have posed to strangers in public places? If so, describe how you might have been perceived in such circumstances.
3. If you were Staples, how would you feel knowing that you were perceived as dangerous? Could you imagine yourself going through the measures he does, just to make those around you feel at ease? Write out your thoughts in an essay.

▼ YOUR PARENTS MUST BE VERY PROUD

Richard Rodriguez

Although he was born and raised in California, Richard Rodriguez knew almost no English when he entered grade school. His parents were Mexican immigrants who spoke Spanish almost exclusively at home. Linguistically handicapped, he entered grammar school and the English-speaking world. Yearning for total assimilation in the dominant culture, Rodriguez flourished as a student in the American system. And he made his parents very proud. But, as he explains in the poignant memoir below, that personal success came at a cost to the cultural identity he once shared with his family and the closeness. Richard Rodriguez, who holds degrees from Stanford, Columbia, and the University of California at Berkeley, is an editor at *Pacific News Service* in San Francisco. In addition to teaching college English, Rodriguez has written several articles for the *Saturday Review, American Scholar, Change,* and other magazines. This essay was taken from his autobiography, *Hunger of Memory* (1982). His latest book is *Mexico's Children* (1992).

1   "Your parents must be very proud of you." People began to say that to me about the time I was in sixth grade. To answer affirmatively, I'd smile. Shyly I'd smile, never betraying my sense of the irony: I was not proud of my mother and father. I was embarrassed by their lack of education. It was not that I ever thought they were stupid, though stupidly I took for granted their enormous native intelligence. Simply, what mattered to me was that they were not like my teachers.

2   But, "Why didn't you tell us about the award?" my mother demanded, her frown weakened by pride. At the grammar school ceremony several weeks after, her eyes were brighter than the trophy I'd won. Pushing back the hair from my forehead, she whispered that I had "shown" the *gringos.* A few minutes later, I heard my father speak to my teacher and felt ashamed of his labored, accented words. Then guilty for the shame. I felt such contrary feelings. (There is no simple roadmap through the heart of the scholarship boy.) My teacher was so soft-spoken and her words were edged sharp and clean. I admired her until it seemed to me that she spoke too carefully. Sensing that she was condescending to them, I became nervous. Resentful. Protective. I tried to move my parents away. "You both must be very proud of Richard," the nun said. They responded quickly. (They were proud.) "We are proud of all our children." Then this afterthought: "They sure didn't get their brains from us." They all laughed. I smiled.

3   Tightening the irony into a knot was the knowledge that my parents were always behind me. They made success possible. They evened the path. They sent their

children to parochial schools because the nuns "teach better." They paid a tuition they couldn't afford. They spoke English to us.

4   For their children my parents wanted chances they never had—an easier way. It saddened my mother to learn that some relatives forced their children to start working right after high school. To *her* children she would say, "Get all the education you can." In schooling she recognized the key to job advancement. And with the remark she remembered her past.

5   As a girl new to America my mother had been awarded a high school diploma by teachers too careless or busy to notice that she hardly spoke English. On her own, she determined to learn how to type. That skill got her jobs typing envelopes in letter shops, and it encouraged in her an optimism about the possibility of advancement. (Each morning when her sisters put on uniforms, she chose a bright-colored dress.) The years of young womanhood passed, and her typing speed increased. She also became an excellent speller of words she mispronounced. "And I've never been to college," she'd say, smiling, when her children asked her to spell words they were too lazy to look up in a dictionary.

6   Typing, however, was dead-end work. Finally frustrating. When her youngest child started high school, my mother got a full-time office job once again. (Her paycheck combined with my father's to make us—in fact—what we had already become in our imagination of ourselves—middle class.) She worked then for the (California) state government in numbered civil service positions secured by examinations. The old ambition of her youth was rekindled. During the lunch hour, she consulted bulletin boards for announcements of openings. One day she saw mention of something called an "anti-poverty agency." A typing job. A glamorous job, part of the governor's staff. "A knowledge of Spanish required." Without hesitation she applied and became nervous only when the job was suddenly hers.

7   "Everyone comes to work all dressed up," she reported at night. And didn't need to say more than that her co-workers wouldn't let her answer the phones. She was only a typist, after all, albeit a very fast typist. And an excellent speller. One morning there was a letter to be sent to a Washington cabinet officer. On the dictating tape, a voice referred to urban guerrillas. My mother typed (the wrong word, correctly): "gorillas." The mistake horrified the anti-poverty bureaucrats who shortly after arranged to have her returned to her previous position. She would go no further. So she willed her ambition to her children. "Get all the education you can; with an education you can do anything." (With a good education *she* could have done anything.)

8   When I was in high school, I admitted to my mother that I planned to become a teacher someday. That seemed to please her. But I never tried to explain that it was not the occupation of teaching I yearned for as much as it was something more elusive: I wanted to *be* like my teachers, to possess their knowledge, to assume their authority, their confidence, even to assume a teacher's persona.

9   In contrast to my mother, my father never verbally encouraged his children's academic success. Nor did he often praise us. My mother had to remind

him to "say something" to one of his children who scored some academic success. But whereas my mother saw in education the opportunity for job advancement, my father recognized that education provided an even more startling possibility: It could enable a person to escape from a life of mere labor.

In Mexico, orphaned when he was eight, my father left school to work as **10** an "apprentice" for an uncle. Twelve years later, he left Mexico in frustration and arrived in America. He had great expectations then of becoming an engineer. ("Work for my hands and my head.") He knew a Catholic priest who promised to get him money enough to study full time for a high school diploma. But the promises came to nothing. Instead there was a dark succession of warehouse, cannery, and factory jobs. After work he went to night school along with my mother. A year, two passed. Nothing much changed, except that fatigue worked its way into the bone; then everything changed. He didn't talk anymore of becoming an engineer. He stayed outside on the steps of the school while my mother went inside to learn typing and shorthand.

By the time I was born, my father worked at "clean" jobs. For a time he **11** was a janitor at a fancy department store. ("Easy work; the machines do it all.") Later he became a dental technician. ("Simple.") But by then he was pessimistic about the ultimate meaning of work and the possibility of ever escaping its claims. In some of my earliest memories of him, my father already seems aged by fatigue. (He has never really grown old like my mother.) From boyhood to manhood, I have remembered him in a single image: seated, asleep on the sofa, his head thrown back in a hideous corpselike grin, the evening newspaper spread out before him. "But look at all you've accomplished," his best friend said to him once. My father said nothing. Only smiled.

It was my father who laughed when I claimed to be tired by reading and **12** writing. It was he who teased me for having soft hands. (He seemed to sense that some great achievement of leisure was implied by my papers and books.) It was my father who became angry while watching on television some woman at the Miss America contest tell the announcer that she was going to college. ("Majoring in fine arts.") "College!" he snarled. He despised the trivialization of higher education, the inflated grades and cheapened diplomas, the half education that so often passed as mass education in my generation.

It was my father again who wondered why I didn't display my awards on **13** the wall of my bedroom. He said he liked to go to doctors' offices and see their certificates and degrees on the wall. ("Nice.") My citations from school got left in closets at home. The gleaming figure astride one of my trophies was broken, wingless, after hitting the ground. My medals were placed in a jar of loose change. And when I lost my high school diploma, my father found it as it was about to be thrown out with the trash. Without telling me, he put it away with his own things for safekeeping.

These memories slammed together at the instant of hearing that refrain familiar **14** to all scholarship students: "Your parents must be very proud. . . ." Yes, my parents were proud. I knew it. But my parents regarded my progress with more than mere pride. They endured my early precocious behavior—but with what private anger and humiliation? As their children got older and would come home to challenge ideas both of them held, they argued before submitting to the force of logic or superior factual evidence with the disclaimer, "It's what we were taught in our time to believe." These discussions ended abruptly, though my mother remembered them on other occasions when she complained that our "big ideas" were going to our heads. More acute was her complaint that the family wasn't close anymore, like some others she knew. Why weren't we close, "more in the Mexican style"? Everyone is so private, she added. And she mimicked the yes and no answers she got in reply to her questions. Why didn't we talk more? (My father never asked.) I never said.

15   I was the first in my family who asked to leave home when it came time to go to college. I had been admitted to Stanford, one hundred miles away. My departure would only make physically apparent the separation that had occurred long before. But it was going too far. In the months preceding my leaving, I heard the question my mother never asked except indirectly. In the hot kitchen, tired at the end of her workday, she demanded to know, "Why aren't the colleges here in Sacramento good enough for you? They are for your brother and sister." In the middle of a car ride, not turning to face me, she wondered, "Why do you need to go so far away?" Late at night, ironing, she said with disgust, "Why do you have to put us through this big expense? You know your scholarship will never cover it all." But when September came there was a rush to get everything ready. In a bedroom that last night I packed the big brown valise, and my mother sat nearby sewing initials onto the clothes I would take. And she said no more about my leaving.

16   Months later, two weeks of Christmas vacation: The first hours home were the hardest. ("What's new?") My parents and I sat in the kitchen for a conversation. (But, lacking the same words to develop our sentences and to shape our interests, what was there to say? What could I tell them of the term paper I had just finished on the "universality of Shakespeare's appeal"?) I mentioned only small, obvious things: my dormitory life; weekend trips I had taken; random events. They responded with news of their own. (One was almost grateful for a family crisis about which there was much to discuss.) We tried to make our conversation seem like more than an interview.

▼ TOPICAL CONSIDERATIONS

1. Summarize Rodriguez's conflicting feelings in the essay. When have you felt a similar conflict? With family? Friends?
2. Compare the parents in the Rodriguez essay to those in the Elizabeth Wong and Shanlon Wu pieces that follow later in this chapter. Are their similarities cross-cultural?
3. Education has several meanings in the essay. Compare the author's view of education to his mother's and his father's. Which view do you most agree with?

4. The author's mother complains in paragraph 14 "that the family wasn't close anymore." What has broken the family apart? What role does culture play in this?

▼ RHETORICAL CONSIDERATIONS

1. Rodriguez admits in paragraph 1, "I was not proud of my mother and father." Though he never states that he becomes proud of his parents, what phrases, if any, imply that as he grew older, he changed his mind?
2. Explain the metaphor in paragraph 2: "There is no simple roadmap through the heart of the scholarship boy."
3. The subject of Rodriguez's freshman English paper was the "universality of Shakespeare's appeal." Consider the author's relationship with his parents. What is ironic about his paper topic?
4. The beginning of paragraph 3 states, "Tightening the irony into a knot was the knowledge that my parents were always behind me." Link this statement to the essay's title and fully explain the irony that pervades the essay.
5. What do "soft hands" (paragraph 12), "high school diploma" (paragraph 10) mean to the author's father? How do these reflect the fact that the author's "father never verbally encouraged his children's academic success" (paragraph 9)?
6. Comment on the conclusion of the essay. Is it climactic? True to life? Effective?

▼ WRITING ASSIGNMENTS

1. Rodriguez in paragraph 5 writes, "As a girl new to America my mother had been awarded a high school diploma by teachers too careless or busy to notice that she hardly spoke English." Do you believe that language is power? Consider the Rodriguez essay and, perhaps, Elizabeth Wong's essay. Write a paper that develops your own view of the power of language in light of these two authors.
2. Several of the essays in this chapter are written from first-person retrospective. Much of what they have learned from looking back on their childhoods is concealed in subtle endings and implied hurts. Write a paper that traces this narrative perspective in three essays. Discuss the effectiveness of this approach and explain any weaknesses this point of view has.
3. Considering your own race, class, and ethnicity, write a first-person retrospective of your own. In your essay, tell what particular endings and hurts you have felt and what lessons you have learned from them.

4. In paragraph 12 Rodriguez says of his father, "He despised the trivialization of higher education, the inflated grades and cheapened diplomas, the half education that so often passed as mass education in my generation." Is this a fair assessment of education in the United States as you've experienced it? Write a paper in which you compare the father's viewpoint of education to your own. Consider socioeconomic backgrounds.

▼ BLACK *AND* LATINO
Roberto Santiago

Establishing one's own identity when caught between two cultures can create serious problems. As Richard Rodriguez has just illustrated, sometimes the struggle means the denial of one's own racial or ethnic heritage. But does one need to choose? Is it not possible to integrate a divided identity? The author of the following essay thinks so. Roberto Santiago, who is both black and Puerto Rican, tells how he shares none of the confusion that besets other people about who he is. He fully understands and accepts his duo-culture. Born in Spanish Harlem in 1963, Santiago is an editorial writer for *Emerge* magazine in New York City. He has written articles for various other publications including *Omni,* the *Village Voice,* and *New York Newsday.* He is currently working on a novel. This article first appeared in *Essence* magazine in November 1989.

1   "There is no way that you can be black and Puerto Rican at the same time." What? Despite the many times I've heard this over the years, that statement still perplexes me. I *am* both and always have been. My color is a blend of my mother's rich, dark skin tone and my father's white complexion. As they were both Puerto Rican, I spoke Spanish before English, but I am totally bilingual. My life has been shaped by my black and Latino heritages, and despite other people's confusion, I don't feel I have to choose one or the other. To do so would be to deny a part of myself.

2   There has not been a moment in my life when I did not know that I looked black—and I never thought that others did not see it, too. But growing up in East Harlem, I was also aware that I did not "act black," according to the African-American boys on the block.

3   My lighter-skinned Puerto Rican friends were less of a help in this department. "You're not black," they would whine, shaking their heads. "You're a *boriqua* [slang for Puerto Rican], you ain't no *moreno* [black]." If

that was true, why did my mirror defy the rules of logic? And most of all, why did I feel that there was some serious unknown force trying to make me choose sides?

Acting black. Looking black. Being a real black. This debate among us is almost a parody. The fact is that I am black, so why do I need to prove it? **4**

The island of Puerto Rico is only a stone's throw away from Haiti, and, no fooling, if you climb a palm tree, you can see Jamaica bobbing on the Atlantic. The slave trade ran through the Caribbean basin, and virtually all Puerto Rican citizens have some African blood in their veins. My grandparents on my mother's side were the classic *negro como carbón* (black as carbon) people, but despite the fact that they were as dark as can be, they are officially not considered black. **5**

There is an explanation for this, but not one that makes much sense, or difference, to a working-class kid from Harlem. Puerto Ricans identify themselves as Hispanics—part of a worldwide race that originated from eons of white Spanish conquests—a mixture of white, African, and *Indio* blood, which, categorically, is apart from black. In other words, the culture is the predominant and determinant factor. But there are frustrations in being caught in a duoculture, where your skin color does not necessarily dictate what you are. When I read Piri Thomas's searing autobiography, *Down These Mean Streets,* in my early teens, I saw that he couldn't figure out other people's attitudes toward his blackness, either. **6**

My first encounter with this attitude about the race thing rode on horseback. I had just turned six years old and ran toward the bridle path in Central Park as I saw two horses about to trot past. "Yea! Horsie! Yea!" I yelled. Then I noticed one figure on horseback. She was white, and she shouted, "Shut up, you f——g nigger! Shut up!" She pulled back on the reins and twisted the horse in my direction. I can still feel the spray of gravel that the horse kicked at my chest. And suddenly she was gone. I looked back and, in the distance, saw my parents playing Whiffle Ball with my sister. They seemed miles away. **7**

They still don't know about this incident. But I told my Aunt Aurelia almost immediately. She explained what the words meant and why they were said. Ever since then I have been able to express my anger appropriately through words or action in similar situations. Self-preservation, ego, and pride forbid men from ever ignoring, much less forgetting, a slur. **8**

Aunt Aurelia became, unintentionally, my source for answers I needed about color and race. I never sought her out. She just seemed to appear at my home during the points in my childhood when I most needed her for solace. "Puerto Ricans are different from American blacks," she told me once. "There is no racism between what you call white and black. Nobody even considers the marriages interracial." She then pointed out the difference in color between my father and mother. "You never noticed that," she said, "because you were not raised with that hang-up." **9**

10   Aunt Aurelia passed away before I could follow up on her observation. But she had made an important point. It's why I never liked the attitude that says I should be exclusive to one race.

11   My behavior toward this race thing pegged me as an iconoclast of sorts. Children from mixed marriages, from my experience, also share this attitude. If I have to beat the label of iconoclast because the world wants people to be in set categories and I don't want to, then I will.

12   A month before Aunt Aurelia died, she saw I was a little down about the whole race thing, and she said, "Roberto, don't worry. Even if—no matter what you do—black people in this country don't you can always depend on white people to treat you like a black."

▼ TOPICAL CONSIDERATIONS

1. The essay begins, "There is no way that you can be black and Puerto Rican at the same time." Does the author prove this statement wrong? What is your opinion?
2. In paragraph 3, Santiago asks, "Why did I feel that there was some serious unknown force trying to make me choose sides?" What do you think is the source of this unknown force? Have you ever felt such force working on you?
3. What is the debate at the heart of the essay? What does Santiago think of the debate? Do you think it's a debate worth considering?
4. Explain the definition (and its limitations) of "culture" in paragraph 6. Write your own definition of culture.
5. How did Santiago's "first encounter with this attitude about the race thing" affect him? Have you ever had such an encounter about your race or ethnicity? If so, describe it. Were you so affected?
6. What role does Aurelia play in the essay?
7. Compare the difference according to Santiago between Puerto Rican and American blacks. How can Santiago still develop a cultural identity with his black-Hispanic background?
8. Santiago writes that to choose being either Hispanic or black "would be to deny a part of myself." How is the theme of this essay somehow fundamental to being an American?

▼ RHETORICAL CONSIDERATIONS

1. What does direct dialogue add to the essay? Does it provide anything that narrative description could not?
2. Analyze paragraph 4. What purpose do the italicized phrases serve? Is the question at the end of the paragraph rhetorical or does it call

for an answer? What is your opinion of the controversy introduced in the paragraph?

3. In paragraph 5, Santiago describes his grandparents as "negro como carbón." How does this description reflect the essay's bicultural theme.

4. Comment on the ending of the essay. Did you find it powerful? Convincing? What does it reveal about Santiago's perception of society?

▼ WRITING ASSIGNMENTS

1. The authors in this chapter would probably be evenly divided for and against Santiago's bicultural openness. Create a dialogue selecting characters from four of the essays and discuss the notion of race and culture. Stay close to the style and personality of each speaker.

2. Santiago in paragraph 11 suggests that "the world wants people to be set in categories." Consider some of the essays in the section; consider also television, film, music, and politics. Write a paper discussing whether we are a society who wants to categorize or not.

3. Compare the image of the black male in Santiago's essay to that of Brent Staples's essay. How do they compare? How do their projections of black males jive with those projected by our media, movies, television, and literature. Do you feel that black males have been fairly or unfairly characterized? Explain in detail and with supporting evidence.

4. Have you ever felt forces pulling on you to assume one ethnic or racial identity over another? If so, write an essay in which you describe those forces and how, if possible, you have come to terms with those forces and your identity.

▼ TO BE AN ALL-AMERICAN GIRL
Elizabeth Wong

> Like Richard Rodriguez, Elizabeth Wong experienced a cultural conflict with her immigrant parents. Like Rodriguez, her native tongue was a source of embarrassment for her. And like Rodriguez, she was too caught up with becoming all-American. The essay below briefly chronicles Ms. Wong's rejection of all things Chinese in her campaign to redefine herself—a success she seems to celebrate until the very last line. This essay first appeared in the *Los Angeles Times* in 1989.

1   It's still there, the Chinese school on Yale Street where my brother and I used to go. Despite the new coat of paint and the high wire fence, the school I knew 10 years ago remains remarkably, stoically the same.

2   Every day at 5 P.M., instead of playing with our fourth- and fifth-grade friends or sneaking out to the empty lot to hunt ghosts and animal bones, my brother and I had to go to Chinese school. No amount of kicking, screaming, or pleading could dissuade my mother, who was solidly determined to have us learn the language of our heritage.

3   Forcibly, she walked us the seven long, hilly blocks from our home to school, depositing our defiant tearful faces before the stern principal. My only memory of him is that he swayed on his heels like a palm tree, and he always clasped his impatience twitching hands behind his back. I recognized him as a repressed maniacal child killer, and knew that if we ever saw his hands we'd be in big trouble.

4   We all sat in little chairs in an empty auditorium. The room smelled like Chinese medicine, an imported faraway mustiness. Like ancient mothballs or dirty closets. I hated that smell. I favored crisp new scents. Like the soft French perfume that my American teacher wore in public school.

5   There was a stage far to the right, flanked by an American flag and the flag of the Nationalist Republic of China, which was also red, white and blue but not as pretty.

6   Although the emphasis at the school was mainly language—speaking, reading, writing—the lessons always began with an exercise in politeness. With the entrance of the teacher, the best student would tap a bell and everyone would get up, kowtow, and chant, "Sing san ho," the phonetic for "How are you, teacher?"

7   Being ten years old, I had better things to learn than ideographs copied painstakingly in lines that ran right to left from the tip of a *moc but,* a real ink pen that had to be held in an awkward way if blotches were to be avoided. After all, I could do the multiplication tables, name the satellites of Mars, and write reports on "Little Women" and "Black Beauty." Nancy Drew, my favorite book heroine, never spoke Chinese.

The language was a source of embarrassment. More times than not, I had **8** tried to disassociate myself from the nagging loud voice that followed me wherever I wandered in the nearby American supermarket outside Chinatown. The voice belonged to my grandmother, a fragile woman in her seventies who could outshout the best of the street vendors. Her humor was raunchy, her Chinese rhythmless, patternless. It was quick, it was loud, it was unbeautiful. It was not like the quiet, lilting romance of French or the gentle refinement of the American South. Chinese sounded pedestrian. Public.

In Chinatown, the comings and goings of hundreds of Chinese on their **9** daily tasks sounded chaotic and frenzied. I did not want to be thought of as mad, as talking gibberish. When I spoke English, people nodded at me, smiled sweetly, said encouraging words. Even the people in my culture would cluck and say that I'd do well in life. "My, doesn't she move her lips fast," they would say, meaning that I'd be able to keep up with the world outside Chinatown.

My brother was even more fanatical than I about speaking English. He was **10** especially hard on my mother, criticizing her, often cruelly, for her pidgin speech—smatterings of Chinese scattered like chop suey in her conversation. "It's not 'What it is,' Mom," he'd say in exasperation. "It's 'What *is* it, what *is* it, what *is* it!" Sometimes Mom might leave out an occasional "the" or "a," or perhaps a verb of being. He would stop her in midsentence: "Say it again, Mom. Say it right." When he tripped over his own tongue, he'd blame it on her: "See, Mom, it's all your fault. You set a bad example."

What infuriated my mother most was when my brother cornered her on her **11** consonants, especially "r." My father had played a cruel joke on Mom by assigning her an American name that her tongue wouldn't allow her to say. No matter how hard she tried, "Ruth" always ended up "Luth" or "Roof."

After two years of writing with a *moc but* and reciting words with multiples **12** of meanings, I finally was granted a cultural divorce. I was permitted to stop Chinese school.

I thought of myself as multicultural. I preferred tacos to egg rolls; I enjoyed **13** Cinco de Mayo more than Chinese New Year.

At last, I was one of you; I wasn't one of them. **14**

Sadly, I still am. **15**

▼ TOPICAL CONSIDERATIONS

1. This essay is written from a first-person retrospective viewpoint. What has Elizabeth Wong learned between the time she went to Chinese school and now?

2. What does language represent in the essay? Use specific passages in the essay to describe what language means to Wong, her brother, and her mother. Compare learning English to speaking Chinese to listening to French.

3. Much has been written in child psychology about the Maternal Voice and the comfort it brings. Elizabeth Wong describes the

Grandmaternal Voice; but it is not comforting. How variously does Wong describe her grandmother's voice? What might it represent for the author?

4. Both Elizabeth Wong and Shanlon Wu are Asian-Americans. Read the next essay in this chapter and try to determine the difference in their choices of heroes.

5. The author writes that she hated the smell of "ancient mothballs or dirty closets," and she "favored new scents" (paragraph 4). How does her preference for *new scents* reflect the theme of the essay?

6. What does the author mean by "the phonetic for 'How are you, teacher?'" (paragraph 6)? How does this reflect the distance between the American and Chinese culture?

7. In paragraph 9, Wong writes, "Even the people in my culture would cluck and say that I'd do well in life." What is Wong's definition of *culture* in this statement and throughout the essay? Compare Wong's definition of culture to your own.

8. Are Wong's feelings toward Chinese school specific to Chinese-Americans? If not, what is universal about her feelings? Can you relate to her?

9. Discuss the theme of rejection in the essay. Take into consideration not just Elizabeth Wong's attitudes, but those of her father and brother.

▼ RHETORICAL CONSIDERATIONS

1. At what point in the essay do we know how Elizabeth Wong really feels about her experience at Chinese school? Does this make the essay more effective?

2. What connotation do "pedestrian" and "public" have in paragraph 8? Explain.

3. In paragraph 10, Wong's brother corrects his mother, "It's not 'What it is, Mom.'" Why is correct grammar so important to Elizabeth and her brother? Do you feel correct grammar is as important as the Wong's consider it to be?

4. Wong writes in paragraph 12, "I finally was granted a cultural divorce." Consider the literal meaning of divorce. What is the full implication of her statement?

5. Explain the simile in paragraph 10: "for her pidgin speech—smatterings of Chinese spread like chop suey in her conversation."

▼ WRITING ASSIGNMENTS

1. Wong in paragraph 13 writes, "I thought of myself as multicultural. I preferred tacos to egg rolls." Ishmael Reed describes our nation

as a "cultural bouillabaisse." Think about your own multicultural experience in America. How much of it is rooted in food? Write a paper discussing the effect food has on cultural awareness.

2. Wong finishes her essay, "Sadly, I still am." Although she has Asian features, she feels completely American. Write a paper discussing one's social environment versus cultural heritage. Consider Wu's, Santiago's, Rodriguez's, Morgan's essays and your own experiences.

3. Write a paper discussing how the language barrier affects parent-child relationships. Consider how a parent's learning English as a second language might be a source of embarrassment for a child. If you have had any such experiences because of your own race or ethnicity, try to capture them in a paper.

▼ IN SEARCH OF BRUCE LEE'S GRAVE

Shanlon Wu

As an Asian boy growing up in America, Shanlon Wu had no healthy role models in pop-culture to emulate. While his American classmates had baseball players, movie stars, political leaders, and singers, Wu had no Asian males to grow up to be like. None, that is, except a TV houseboy and Bruce Lee, the martial-arts movie hero. Rejecting the servile Asian stereotype, Wu embraced the image of Bruce Lee who always had battles to fight and win. But unlike his hero, Shanlon Wu's battles were internal struggles at self-definition. Today Shanlon Wu is a judicial clerk for the United States Court of Appeals for the Ninth Circuit. He is completing a novel based on his first visit to China. This article first appeared in *The New York Times* in April 1990.

It's Saturday morning in Seattle, and I am driving to visit Bruce Lee's grave. I have been in the city for only a couple of weeks and so drive two blocks past the cemetery before realizing that I've passed it. I double back and turn through the large wrought-iron gate, past a sign that reads: "Open to 9 P.M. or dusk, whichever comes first."   1

It's a sprawling cemetery, with winding roads leading in all directions. I feel silly trying to find his grave with no guidance. I think that my search for his grave is similar to my search for Asian heroes in America.   2

I was born in 1959, an Asian-American in Westchester County, N.Y. During my childhood there were no Asian sports stars. On television, I can recall   3 only that most pathetic of Asian characters, Hop Sing, the Cartwright family houseboy on "Bonanza." But in my adolescence there was Bruce.

4   I was 14 years old when I first saw "Enter the Dragon," the grandaddy of martial-arts movies. Bruce had died suddenly at the age of 32 of cerebral edema, an excess of fluid in the brain, just weeks before the release of the film. Between the ages of 14 and 17, I saw "Enter the Dragon" 22 times before I stopped counting. During those years I collected Bruce Lee posters, putting them up at all angles in my bedroom. I took up Chinese martial arts and spent hours comparing my physique with his.

5   I learned all I could about Bruce: that he had married a Caucasian, Linda; that he had sparred with Kareem Abdul-Jabbar; that he was a buddy of Steve McQueen and James Coburn, both of whom were his pallbearers.

6   My parents, who immigrated to America and had become professors at Hunter College, tolerated my behavior, but seemed puzzled at my admiration of an "entertainer." My father jokingly tried to compare my obsession with Bruce to his boyhood worship of Chinese folk-tale heroes.

7   "I read them just like you read American comic books," he said.

8   But my father's heroes could not be mine; they came from an ancient literary tradition, not comic books. He and my mother had grown up in a land where they belonged to the majority. I could not adopt their childhood and they were wise enough not to impose it upon me.

9   Although I never again experienced the kind of blind hero worship I felt for Bruce, my need to find heroes remained strong.

10   In college, I discovered the men of the 442d Regimental Combat Team, a United States Army all-Japanese unit in World War II. Allowed to fight only against Europeans, they suffered heavy casualties while their families were put in internment camps. The motto was "Go for Broke."

11   I saw them as Asians in a Homeric epic, the protagonists of a Shakespearean tragedy; I knew no Eastern myths to infuse them with. They embodied my own need to prove myself in the Caucasian world. I imagined how their American-born flesh and muscle must have resembled mine: epicanthic folds set in strong faces nourished on milk and beef. I thought how much they had proved where there was so little to prove.

12   After college, I competed as an amateur boxer in an attempt to find my self-image in the ring. It didn't work. My fighting was only an attempt to copy Bruce's movies. What I needed was instruction on how to live. I quit boxing after a year and went to law school.

13   I was an anomaly there: a would-be Asian litigator. I had always liked to argue and found I liked doing it in front of people even more. When I won the first-year moot court competition in law school, I asked an Asian classmate if he thought I was the first Asian to win. He laughed and told me I was probably the only Asian to even compete.

14   The law-firm interviewers always seemed surprised that I wanted to litigate.

15   "Aren't you interested in Pacific Rim trade?" they asked.

16   "My Chinese isn't good enough," I quipped.

My pat response seemed to please them. It certainly pleased me. I thought **17** I'd found a place of my own—a place where the law would insulate me from the pressure of defining my Asian maleness. I sensed the possibility of merely being myself.

But the pressure reasserted itself. One morning, the year after graduating **18** from law school, I read the obituary of Gen. Minoru Genda—the man who planned the Pearl Harbor attack. I'd never heard of him and had assumed that whoever did that planning was long since dead. But the general had been alive all those years—rising at 4 every morning to do his exercises and retiring every night by 8. An advocate of animal rights, the obituary said.

I found myself drawn to the general's life despite his association with the **19** Axis powers. He seemed a forthright, graceful man who died unhumbled. The same paper carried a front-page story about Congress's failure to pay the Japanese-American internees their promised reparation money. The general, at least, had not died waiting for reparations.

I was surprised and frightened by my admiration for General Genda, by my **20** still-strong hunger for images of powerful Asian men. That hunger was my vulnerability manifested, a reminder of my lack of place.

The hunger is eased this gray morning in Seattle. After asking directions **21** from a policeman—Japanese—I easily locate Bruce's grave. The headstone is red granite with a small picture etched into it. The picture is very Hollywood— Bruce wears dark glasses—and I think the calligraphy looks a bit sloppy. Two tourists stop but leave quickly after glancing at me.

I realize I am crying. Bruce's grave seems very small in comparison to his **22** place in my boyhood. So small in comparison to my need for heroes. Seeing his grave, I understand how large the hole in my life has been, and how desperately I'd sought to fill it.

I had sought an Asian hero to emulate. But none of my choices quite fit me. **23** Their lives were defined through heroic tasks—they had villains to defeat and wars to fight—while my life seemed merely a struggle to define myself.

But now I see how that very struggle has defined me. I must be my own hero **24** even as I learn to treasure those who have gone before.

I have had my powerful Asian male images: Bruce, the men of the 442d and **25** General Genda; I may yet discover others. Their lives beckon like fireflies on a moonless night, and I know that they—like me—may have been flawed by foolhardiness and even cruelty. Still, their lives were real. They were not houseboys on "Bonanza."

▼ TOPICAL CONSIDERATIONS

1. Why does Shanlon Wu have a need for Asian heroes?
2. Who are Shanlon Wu's heroes? What qualities about each of them does he find most attractive? What qualities do you think make a hero heroic?

218 ▼ RACE AND CLASS

3. What is the relationship between each of Wu's heroes and America? What would you say is Wu's view of America, its culture and history? Do you see America through the same lens? Do you agree with Wu's likes and dislikes?

4. Wu writes in paragraph 11 that he saw his heroes as figures in a Homeric epic or a Shakespearean tragedy because he "knew no Eastern myths to infuse them with." What does he mean by this? Consider your own education. Do you think that an American student's education should be rooted solely in Western Civilization? Explain your feelings on this question.

5. What does Wu see as the fundamental difference between himself and his heroes? Considering such differences, how have your childhood and adolescent heroes influenced your life?

6. Why is it impossible for Wu and his father to share the same heroes? Compare your heroes to a parent's or older relative's. Do your heroes share any common qualities? If so, what qualities?

7. Wu writes of the 442d unit, "I imagined how their American-born flesh and muscle must have resembled mine: epicanthic folds set in strong faces nourished on milk and beef" (paragraph 11). Fully explain this statement. Do your heroes physically resemble you?

8. In its thematic and historical context explain Wu's statement in paragraph 19: "The general, at least, had not died waiting for reparations." How does this bitterness shape the rest of the essay? In what context have you shared these feelings?

9. Can you identify with Wu's yearning for heroic images from his own race? Do you feel American society lacks pop-culture idols from your own race? Do young Asian-Americans today look up to any Asian heroes? If so, who for instance? If not, have they adopted non-Asian pop-culture idols? Do you think the lack of, say, movie or sports heroes of the same race creates identity problems for young people? Explain your answer.

▼ RHETORICAL CONSIDERATIONS

1. Where is Shanlon Wu's thesis? Explain how he proves or falls short of proving this.

2. In paragraph 12 Wu writes, "I competed as an amateur boxer in an attempt to find my self-image in the ring." Explain how this statement fits into the overall clash between external and internal battles that Wu is struggling with.

3. Consider the title, "In Search of Bruce Lee's Grave." Why is Wu looking for his grave? What does he discover by finding it?

4. Consider Wu's lead. How does his opening draw the reader in? Does it have any thematic connection to the essay or is it fluff?

5. Consider the concluding paragraph. How does it serve to wrap up the thematic development of the essay? Did you find it an effective one?

▼ WRITING ASSIGNMENTS

1. When "Enter the Dragon" first hit the cinemas, it was a box office smash among inner-city nonwhites. Audiences finally saw an Asian martial-arts hero in action (as opposed to all the Chuck Norris films). Write a paper discussing who some of our culture's heroes are today. Are blacks, Hispanics, Asians, and women on the list of viable heroes?

2. Did you have heroes as a child? If so, who were they? Have your heroes changed as you grew up? How? What values did your new heroes have in common with the older ones. Write a paper in which you discuss the value of having heroes and how they have helped shape your ideals of yourself.

3. Reread Ishmael Reed's "America: The Multinational Society." Assuming the perspective of Reed, write a critique of Wu's essay.

4. Ishmael Reed writes of America, "The world is here." Do you agree or disagree with this statement on both a literal and metaphorical level? Address this question by writing an objective portrait of America as you believe it to be experienced by first-generation Americans. Use the essays by Ishmael Reed, Richard Rodriguez, and Shanlon Wu as your research. Consider cultural conflicts in the family, school, and media.

5. Assume the perspective of a sociologist. Discuss the parent-child relationships in the Richard Rodriguez essay and the Wu essay. One family is Hispanic-American, the other Chinese-American. Use your relationship with your parents as a third case study. Are parent-child relationships shaped by culture or the individuals? Does the search for self play into any parent-child conflicts?

▼ INDIAN BONES

Clara Spotted Elk

The history of Native Americans since the European migration to this continent is a disturbing study in oppression. With Columbus and his followers, the various peoples of the New World in spite of their linguistic and tribal differences were all dubbed "Indians." Renamed and classified as "savages," the native inhabitants proceeded to suffer centuries of enslavement, torture, and slaughter at the hands of the white invaders. The essay that follows is a protest of the continued dehumanization of Native Americans—not those who remain, but those who have long died. Clara Spotted Elk is a consultant to the U.S. government in Washington, where she represents Native American affairs. This article first appeared in *The New York Times* in 1989.

1 Millions of American Indians lived in this country when Columbus first landed on our shores. After the western expansion, only about 250,000 Indians survived. What happened to the remains of those people who were decimated by the advance of the white man? Many are gathering dust in American museums.

2 In 1985, I and some Northern Cheyenne chiefs visited the attic of the Smithsonian's Natural History Museum in Washington to review the inventory of their Cheyenne collection. After a chance inquiry, a curator pulled out a drawer in one of the scores of cabinets that line the attic. There were the jumbled bones of an Indian. "A Kiowa," he said.

3 Subsequently, we found that 18,500 Indian remains—some consisting of a handful of bones, but mostly full skeletons—are unceremoniously stored in the Smithsonian's nooks and crannies. Other museums, individuals and Federal agencies such as the National Park Service also collect the bones of Indian warriors, women and children. Some are on display as roadside tourist attractions. It is estimated that another *600,000* Indian remains are secreted away in locations across the country.

4 The museum community and forensic scientists vigorously defend these grisly collections. With few exceptions, they refuse to return remains to the tribes that wish to rebury them, even when grave robbing has been documented. They want to maintain adequate numbers of "specimens" for analysis and say they are dedicated to "the permanent curation of Indian skeletal remains."

5 Indian people are tired of being "specimens." The Northern Cheyenne word for ourselves is "tsistsistas"—human beings. Like people the world over, one of our greatest responsibilities is the proper care of the dead.

6 We are outraged that our religious views are not accepted by the scientific community and that the graves of our ancestors are desecrated. Many tribes are

willing to accommodate some degree of study for a limited period of time—provided that it would help Indian people or mankind in general. But how many "specimens" are needed? We will not accept grave robbing and the continued hoarding of our ancestors' remains.

Would this nefarious collecting be tolerated if it were discovered that it affected other ethnic groups? (Incidentally, the Smithsonian also collects skeletons of blacks.) What would happen if the Smithsonian had 18,500 Holocaust victims in the attic? There would be a tremendous outcry in this country. Why is there no outcry about the Indian collections? **7**

Indians are not exotic creatures for study. We are human beings who practice living religions. Our religion should be placed not only on a par with science when it comes to determining the disposition of our ancestors but on a par with every other religion practiced in this country. **8**

To that end, Sen. Daniel K. Inouye will soon reintroduce the "Bones Bill" to aid Indians in retrieving the remains of their ancestors from museums. As in the past, the "Bones Bill" will most likely be staunchly resisted by the collectors of Indian skeletons—armed with slick lobbyists, lots of money and cloaked in the mystique of science. **9**

Scientists have attempted to defuse this issue by characterizing their opponents as radical Indians, out of touch with their culture and with little appreciation of science. Armed only with a moral obligation to our ancestors, the Indians who support the bill have few resources and little money. **10**

But, in my view, the issue should concern all Americans—for it raises very disturbing questions. American Indians want only to reclaim and rebury their dead. Is this too much to ask? **11**

▼ TOPICAL CONSIDERATIONS

1. Why, according to the author, is it important for the Indian remains to be returned from the museum? Do you think this is specific to Native American culture?

2. Summarize the author's argument. Do you see any gaps in the information needed to strengthen her argument? If so, name them.

3. According to the author, why does the Smithsonian want 18,500 "Indian bones"? Do you think the museum has a valid reason for this collection? What would you think if the Smithsonian had the remains of thousands of your ethnic ancestors? How might you respond to the Smithsonian's justification?

4. What does author Clara Spotted Elk and her essay have in common with the other writers in this chapter? What common struggles do you see?

5. The author writes in paragraph 10 that American Indians are "Armed only with a moral obligation to our ancestors." What are those against the Bones Bill armed with? Does Spotted Elk specify

the kind of burial she and others so morally obligated wish to give their ancestors?

6. How does the first paragraph reinforce one of Ishmael Reed's points?

▼ RHETORICAL CONSIDERATIONS

1. Both Clara Spotted Elk and Ishmael Reed write as first-person observers. Which essay do you think is more effective? Why?

2. The beginning of paragraph 9 reads, "To that end, Sen. Daniel K. Inouye will soon reintroduce the 'Bones Bill.' " This bill is important to the author. Is it important to the reader to know why the bill didn't pass the first time?

3. In paragraph 7 how does the analogy to Holocaust victims work? Is it an effective strategy? Why is the inclusion of the collection of the skeletal remains of blacks in parentheses? And why does the sentence begin "Incidentally?" (Is this a loaded word?)

4. Explain the metaphor "cloaked in the mystique of science" (paragraph 9). How effective is it to project just the right image and meaning?

5. Paragraph 3 states Indian bones "are unceremoniously stored in the Smithsonian's nooks and crannies." What does the word *unceremoniously* suggest about Native Americans' standard burial? Do you wish the author gave some details of Native American burial ceremonies? Would such have added to the impact of the essay?

6. Comment on the conclusion of the essay. To whom is the author appealing?

▼ WRITING ASSIGNMENTS

1. Assume the position of the curator of the Smithsonian's Natural History Museum in Washington. Sen. Daniel K. Inouye (D. Hawaii) calls you for your final statement on the Bones Bill before he presents it to Congress. Write a statement either justifying your collection or conceding to Inouye. Use information from the text as your research.

2. Did this essay heighten your sensitivity to the needs of Native Americans in any way? If so, write an essay in which you explore this new awareness.

3. Compare your fourth grade understanding of the founding of America to your current understanding. Use evidence from Reed's

essay and "Indian Bones" to make the comparison. Also, how do we determine the truth of American history?

4. Write an essay in which you compare the moral obligation Clara Spotted Elk feels toward the Cheyenne with that Joan L. Morgan ("The Struggle Is Ours") feels to young African-Americans.

5. "Like people the world over, one of our greatest responsibilities is the proper care of the dead" (paragraph 5). Drawing from your own experience and what you have read, write an essay exploring this statement.

6. Fundamental to Spotted Elk's lament is how Native Americans have been dehumanized by the white-dominated culture. Consider, for instance, the projection of them as savages in cowboy and Indian movies of the past. In a paper, try to assess what recent changes you have noticed in such images from recent movies, television programs, media stories, books, and so on. You might consider, for instance, the highly popular 1991 film, *Dances with Wolves*.

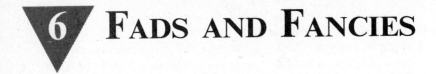

6 ▼ FADS AND FANCIES

Each essay in this book sheds some light on our contemporary culture—on the habits and values we share. While many of the selections focus on the more weighty issues of our era—race and class, gender roles, and the pros and cons of abortion, for example—this chapter is devoted to a lighter side of popular culture. Surprisingly, even the latest fad can tell us a lot about what we value and who we are.

We open with Madonna—one of the supreme icons of popular culture. Since her rise to superstardom in the 1980s, she has been the subject of feminist debates, sociopolitical interpretations, and college psychology courses. But in "What's Madonna Teaching Us?" Lynne Layton wonders if this mystifying and bedeviling entertainer who seems to scorn all categories from virgin to whore is little more than a woman capitalizing on outrageousness.

And, speaking of material girls, we turn next to "Ode to a Tyrannical Muse (or, Why I Love and Hate Fashion)." In this amusing piece, Johanna McGeary confesses that although fashion is ephemeral, agonizing, irrational, and expensive, she's hooked.

The next piece addresses the fitness craze sweeping America. In "Work That Body!" Sally B. Donnelly applauds the vigorous shakeup in women's attitudes toward physical fitness. As she reports, women all across the country are pumping and jogging their bodies into temples of health.

The reading habits of Americans reveals much about our culture. One of the hottest genres in commercial fiction today is horror, made popular by such superstars as Stephen King, Ann Rice, and Dean Koontz. As humorist Dave Barry confesses, he, too, has gotten caught up in the dark appeal. In "The Fear Lobe Meets 'The Brainsucker' " he admits, however, that a grown man should know better than to go to bed with a book about knife-wielding psychopaths.

The next essay is a touching personal narrative about an obsession that lasted for decades. As a boy, author Bill Boggs vowed that when he grew up he would get himself his dream car, a 1956 Plymouth Fury. He never stopped looking, and when at last he found one, he faced a moment of crisis that took him 30 years back. More than a simple quest to fulfill a childhood obsession, "Finding the Fury" is a story of breaking lifelong patterns, seizing the moment, and recapturing a little of what's passed.

To some people backpacking is a sport; to others it's the latest rage. In our final piece, "The Backpacker," Patrick F. McManus takes a humorous look at what oldtime mountain climbing has become today with all the newfangled high-tech lightweight materials and those newcomers who don't know the experience of a double hernia.

▼ WHAT'S MADONNA TEACHING US?

Lynne Layton

Madonna entertains, mystifies, and bedevils. As an icon of popular culture, she is relished by her fans, studied at universities, and debated among feminists. Admirers, including avant-garde feminists, credit her with banishing stereotypes limiting women, while her critics see her as a fashion plate who merely inspires teenage girls to be better shoppers. In this piece, Lynne Layton, a clinical psychologist and lecturer in women's studies at Harvard University, surveys the current thinking about Madonna. This article first appeared in the *Boston Globe* in June 1990.

1 "I teach Madonna," I told an acquaintance, an intellectual who hastily concluded I must be rather superficial. What he apparently didn't know is that Madonna is not only a subject of feminist scholarly debate but that discussion of Madonna in academe has become a minor industry.

2 In recent years, the elitist view that only "high art" is worthy of study has been challenged. It is now felt that all cultural productions, high or low, are worthy of examination because all texts equally reveal the social meanings of our world. Thus intellectuals who have ashamedly kept their love for pop culture hidden now get the chance to explicate with students the diverse meanings of Cosmo, "Married . . . with Children," "Batman," and Madonna.

3 Madonna is aware that intellectuals and feminists debate her social and political meaning. In a recent Vanity Fair interview, she said, "It's flattering to me that people take the time to analyze me and that I've so infiltrated their psyches that they have to intellectualize my very being. I'd rather be on their minds than off."

4 The Madonna fan might wonder what is being debated? Sheryl Garratt's title, "How I learned to stop worrying and love Madonna," illustrates feminist ambivalence about the brashly sexual pop queen. It seems that the puritanical strain in '70s feminism has made it difficult for the old guard to see Madonna as anything but a sex object making money from her own exploitation.

5 On the other side, an avant-garde feminism protests that what makes Madonna different is that she revels in her own sexuality, over which she, not the ubiquitous male gaze of classical popular culture, wields control. Madonna's self-enjoyment empowers younger girls, our culture's most invisible and least powerful group, to love their bodies, to play to each other and to themselves rather than to boys. As Judith Williamson, a British culture critic has written, ". . . she retains all the bravado and exhibitionism that most girls start off with, or feel inside, until the onset of 'womanhood' knocks it out of them."

6 I was ready to jump on the puritanical bandwagon after viewing the Ma-

donna cassette of her early videos. "Lucky Star," in particular, had, I thought, the unmistakable look of woman-as-sex-object-of-male-held-camera. Then I read John Fiske, professor of communication arts at the University of Wisconsin-Madison, whose chapters on Madonna in "Reading Popular Culture" convinced me that Madonna was in full control of the shoot.

My skepticism faded when I read that Madonna is enamored of her bellybutton, which she feels is perfect. Madonna, in fact, proudly claims that she could pick her bellybutton out in a lineup of a hundred bellybuttons. A look at the video reveals, indeed, that the most frequent shots are of her bellybutton, which does suggest that Madonna's doing it all for herself, not for the boys. (In fact, a recent poll showed that, when asked if they would want to sleep with Madonna, 60 percent of guys declined; a powerful female in control of her own sexuality may be more popular with the girls than with the boys.) **7**

Fiske and others interview young girls and find that the Madonna wannabes are most taken with her assertive self-enjoyment, her seeming indifference to men. Since much recent culture criticism maintains that the meaning of a film, video, song or star is not in the individual text but in what the audience makes of it, Madonna's empowerment of girls becomes a feminist phenomenon. **8**

A BLURRING OF GENDER IDENTITIES

Madonna is a darling of postmodern feminist critics. E. Ann Kaplan of Rutgers University, in "Rocking Around the Clock: Music Television, Postmodernism, and Counterculture," argues than when an artist succeeds in blurring any of the traditional boundaries that limit an individual's full range of experience, it is potentially liberating. **9**

Madonna's shows, videos and interviews upset rigid opposites such as fantasy/reality, viewer/viewed, commercialism/art, and, most important to feminists, male/female. More than any other pop icon, with the exception of David Bowie, Madonna refuses to be trapped in one identity, in one gender. For example, academic fan Fiske underscores the way Madonna's dress mixes the lace gloves of the bordello with the church crucifix. When Madonna wrenches out of their context the cultural artifacts that have played their part in fixing women in the rigid categories of either virgin or whore, she makes popular culture a point of struggle between those who have always controlled meaning (read white, upper-class men) and those who would like to challenge that control (read women and minorities). *Like* a virgin, Madonna scorns the virgin/whore dichotomy by mocking it; she will not be fixed in someone else's meaning system. **10**

So why am I not convinced that I have seen the revolution and it is Madonna? Why am I drawn to another critic's perception that Madonna as fashion grab bag merely empowers girls to be better shoppers? Partly, I am disturbed precisely by what the audience makes of her. Many of my younger students, for example, like the fact that Madonna toys with boys, that she **11** reverses the power balance of traditional gender roles. But role reversals don't seem to me to be what feminists have fought for these last 20 years.

"... A CONSTANT STRUGGLE OF POWER"

12 Madonna's songs, videos and interviews center over and over again on relationships of domination and submission, another traditional, debilitating dichotomy that she does not challenge and that is the lived reality of all too many people in our culture. While some might argue that it matters whether the person on top is male or female, it seems to me that real liberation lies in mutuality and not in one-upmanship. It's great to see a sister doin' it for herself and taking pleasure in the doing, but it's disturbing when this pleasure relies on the domination of another or the subjugation of oneself.

13 An early video, "Burning Up," is a case in point. It features Madonna in various poses of submission, culminating in a scene where she sits in the road waiting to be run over by the car of the indifferent lover for whose love she is burning up. In the final scene (often omitted in MTV versions), Madonna is driving the car and adopts the same indifferent gaze that the lover had.

14 The "is it sexist?/is it feminist?" debate might find critics arguing over whether or not the final scene has the power to negate the masochism of the rest of the video. Some critics would short-circuit the debate and assert that, like most texts of popular culture, the video contains messages that both legitimize a sexist status quo and speak to the utopian longings of a female audience for an end to male domination. From my perspective, the video and its ending are equally problematic in that neither challenges the common-sense view that a person is either in a position of power or a position of weakness.

15 Madonna does not keep her love of power or her pleasure in manipulating people a secret. In Vanity Fair, she expresses her philosophy that, in relationships as well as career, "there's a constant struggle for power." This philosophy is reiterated in several songs/videos of the recent album, "Like A Prayer." For example, one part of "Express Yourself" has Madonna in a neck collar and chains (an image that harks back to "Burning Up"), while the lyrics exhort the female listener not to settle for second best.

16 Two songs on the album do, however, begin to question relations of domination, "Till Death Do Us Part," which may be about her marriage to Sean Penn, and "Oh Father," which is about an abusive father-daughter relationship. The former describes a physicaly and verbally abusive marriage, where the heroine understands that her spouse's rage at her stems from self-hatred. Despite her knowledge of what is going on, she is unable to escape, not because of her masochism but because of her love. In this song, Madonna stops playing with domination and submission, stops reveling in it. She abandons her "survival of the fittest" stance and shows awareness that there are painful underlying causes and painful consequences of such relations, that domination and submission are two sides of the same lack of self-esteem.

When Madonna begins to question relations of domination and submis- **17**
sion, her art approaches what I would consider feminist popular culture. But
what keeps Madonna in the news is controversy, outrageousness and unpre-
dictability, not good politics. And so we have the scandals surrounding the
latest of her "down on my knees" hits, "Hanky Panky," where she asks to be
spanked.

I suppose it is difficult to be both outrageous and thoughtful. Abby Hoff- **18**
man perhaps succeeded at both; Madonna falls short.

Despite my concerns, however, I will continue to teach Madonna, for **19**
among all her other achievements, she has become the subject of hotly contested
social and psychological meanings, dividing generations of feminists and drawing to her the most elite of theories and theoreticians. She succeeds again at what
she does best, staying on the most diverse of people's minds.

▼ TOPICAL CONSIDERATIONS

1. Why are Madonna and other pop idols analyzed by academics now,
   although they were not in the past? Do you feel that Madonna
   merits such analysis? Why or why not? What attitude does Madonna herself seem to take toward her critics?
2. Explain how the 1970s feminists and the avant-garde feminists
   differ in their views of Madonna? Before reading this article which
   view did you take? Has your opinion changed? Explain why or why
   not.
3. The author refers us to John Fiske's analysis of the virgin/whore
   dichotomy in Madonna's music. Summarize this interpretation in
   your own words. In your opinion, does this interpretation have
   merit? How does the author regard Fiske's interpretation, and
   where in the essay does she state her opinion? Can you identify
   other dichotomies that you have noticed in Madonna's music?
4. How is Madonna's theme of domination and submission expressed
   in her music and videos? What is the author's response to Madonna's treatment of this theme? Do you feel that Madonna's
   treatment of this theme has a liberating effect, or do you feel these
   songs reinforce sexist views of women?
5. Throughout the essay the author grapples with her own conflicting
   feelings about Madonna. What conclusions does she finally reach
   regarding Madonna's worth? Do you agree or disagree with her?
6. Why has Layton chosen to continue teaching Madonna? If you
   were designing a college curriculum would you include a study of
   Madonna? Of other pop idols? Why or why not?
7. Considering the ideas presented in this article as well as your own
   experiences, would you argue that Madonna's music is art, entertainment, trash, simple fun? How would you categorize her music?

▼ RHETORICAL CONSIDERATIONS

1. How does the author in the introductory paragraph prepare the reader for an analytical piece rather than an entertainment piece that might be expected? Does the introduction intrigue you or turn you off? Is it an effective hook, or not? Does it make you want to read on? Why or why not?

2. Consider the author's voice in this essay. What sense do you get of the author as an individual? Refer to specific passages in the piece that give you your impressions. Does the voice the author establishes contribute to or diminish your confidence in her ability to handle her subject?

3. How does Layton use contrast to develop her argument? Since Layton's opinion about Madonna was ambivalent, was this the best method of organization to select?

4. What kinds of authorities does Layton quote or summarize in this piece? Do you feel she relies too heavily on quotations or summaries of other peoples' ideas? Cite a paragraph where this works well or poorly.

5. Do Layton's concluding remarks satisfy? Has she reached a conclusion? Or does she hold the same view she began with?

6. What part of the essay was most interesting to you? The least interesting? Can you explain the differences?

7. What do you make of paragraph 7? Is Layton being sincere or sarcastic here?

▼ WRITING ASSIGNMENTS

1. Write your own essay answering the question, "What's Madonna Teaching Us?" Refer to her music and videos. You might also consult any interviews with her.

2. Select another pop figure who, like Madonna, generates controversy and consternation. Write an essay sifting through positive and negative reactions to the star or the group and conclude by formulating your own opinion.

3. Write a letter to the curriculum committee of your school in which you argue that pop culture idols such as Madonna should or should not be taught at the college level.

4. Interview a number of people you consider feminists to find out if Madonna's themes are consistent with their feminist convictions. Write an essay on your findings.

▼ ODE TO A TYRANNICAL MUSE (OR, WHY I LOVE AND HATE FASHION)

Johanna McGeary

Every rational argument mitigates against fashion. By its very nature, fashion is ephemeral and expensive. Yet, many of us are so hooked, we cannot resist its allure. In the amusing piece below, Johanna McGeary, a self-confessed addict, analyzes the pull of fashion and comes to terms with a love she can neither abandon nor ignore. This article first appeared in *Time* magazine in the Fall of 1990.

1 A passion for fashion is a dangerous thing. It can, if you're not careful, fool the eye into betraying the body. Just when you think it might be safe to go out in a thigh-high mini, the fashion oracles say it's the year of the catsuit. I'm going to wear a neck-to-toe unitard in public? No way. I have only to think ladies' room (worse: airplane lavatory) to dismiss such a pernicious garment from my wardrobe. What sensible woman wants to reveal her every—and I do mean every—curve and bulge? And who wants to look at them?

2 Let me confess: I love fashion. I study the magazines; I shop; I spend more than I should. To look chic is to feel great. No matter how we women yearn to be valued for other qualities, we invest a considerable amount of our psychic selves in our appearance. We're not all born beautiful, but we can make the most of what we've got. That's the art of style: improving on nature. Fashion helps us shape that sense of style, give it definition, freshness, sparkle, zing.

3 But I hate fashion too. It's a tyrannical muse, demanding time, energy, money, discomfort. There are mornings when I look at my well-stocked closets and have nothing to wear. My husband can't understand this. The only time he has nothing to wear is when all his shirts are at the laundry. There is something so enviously simple about male dressing: a suit, a shirt, a tie. Our notions of how these should look don't change much with the seasons, and barely with the generations. So how wrong can a man go? How unattractive can he feel?

4 Female fashion is exhausting. All that variety from which to choose the few items that will transform you into a knockout. All those racks in all those stores: it takes hours and days to find the perfect thing. Once home, the garments crowd the closet, challenging you to put together the right pieces for the right occasion—and the right mood. There's a mutability to clothes that makes them appealing one day, appalling the next.

5 All that agonizing choice is made no easier by vast expense. I try to keep up with the mode, and it costs—just ask my husband. But the skyrocketing prices are pushing fashion beyond the reach of willing buyers like me. I was

leafing through a fall fashion magazine the other day, plotting my seasonal purchases. There was a charming outfit by a no-name designer in delicious shades of pink and red (this is the year of color, remember): mohair coat, $725; cropped jacket, $575; knit dress, $230. The total for the ensemble: $1,530. That's not including the $68 wool scarf, $15 ribbed tights or the who-knows-how-much gloves. I bought a pair of stretch velvet leggings last year for $80—not exactly dirt cheap but top-notch fashion for the money. When I see stretch velvet leggings in the magazines for $500, I wonder what the other $420 is for. That's not style, that's trying to sucker me.

6   Maybe it happens every fin de siècle, but lately fashion seems to slide further and further from reality. Most women I know have two kinds of clothes: work clothes and play clothes, in evening and weekend varieties. If women are not tending children at home, the clothes for work outnumber all the rest. So why is it that most designers of any fame produce garments intended for some weird fantasy life? I'm looking at a crotch-length strapless tweed dress topped by a blazer. Even in the permissive world of journalism, where am I going to wear this number? To interview the Secretary of State? I understand fashion's need for the new, but it gets less and less possible to find something modish I can actually wear.

7   Fashion is painful. Women suffer pinching, scratching, binding, twisting in the name of chic. Push-up bras give you the lush bosom of the '90s, but the underwire cuts into your rib cage. Panty hose are hot and, frankly, sweaty. High heels give your hips an alluring tilt, but after a 10-minute walk, your feet scream. Short skirts are young and kicky. But how young do you want to look when you can't sit comfortably?

8   I have learned from experience to say no to fashion. We're stuck with bras until a kinder form of support comes along. I liked long skirts because I could wear knee-high stockings underneath. And I simply refuse to wear hose in summer. So what if the oracles say I'm not properly dressed? I won't buy a catsuit this season, and I bet few other women will. While I refuse to trade in my pumps for Reeboks, I don't buy shoes with heels higher than an inch or two, and I still manage to have fashionable feet. (Pointy toes long ago revamped my metatarsals.)

9   But however hardened I've become, I succumb to fashion's lure. I swore I wouldn't wear short skirts again: I have photos from the last age of miniskirts; I remember trying to bend and sit without total exposure, and I remember how cold it was. And yet, as I dragged out my winter clothes, my hems looked downright dowdy. I'm busy shortening them again. See what a betrayer is the fashion muse? I hate it. I love it.

▼ TOPICAL CONSIDERATIONS

1. In what, if any, way did this piece change the way you think about the fashion industry? About your own personal involvement with

fashion? Could you identify with the author's love-hate relationship with fashion or not?

2. Do you find that your gender strongly influenced the way you responded to question 1? If a marked difference occurs between male and female responses to this question, what does that reveal about cultural values?

3. In paragraph 3 the author says, "There is something so enviously simple about male dressing. . . . How wrong can a man go? How unattractive can he feel?" Do you take exception to any part of this statement? Explain.

4. McGreary discusses the "mutability of clothes," the quality that makes them "appealing one day, appalling the next" (paragraph 4). Brainstorm a list of styles for both men and women that were considered high style at one time but ludicrous at another. Make a list, too, of hairstyles for men and women which have moved in and out of style. What conclusions about the purpose or function of style do you draw?

5. Would the author buy the outfit she describes in paragraph 5? Why or why not? If you could afford clothing in this price range, would you buy those items? Do you have any ethical problem with an individual paying exorbitant prices for designer fashions?

6. In her book *Femininity* (Fawcett, 1985), Susan Brownmiller wrote, "Feminine clothing has never been designed to be functional, for that would be a contradiction in terms. Functional clothing is a masculine privilege and practicality is a masculine virtue. To be truly feminine is to accept the handicap of restraint and restriction, and to come to adore it." Explain with specific references your reaction to this quotation. Does it reflect your experiences? Does it apply to some groups but not all depending on age, sex, income, job status?

7. After reading this piece, who do you think is in charge: The "tyrannical muse" or the author?

▼ RHETORICAL CONSIDERATIONS

1. Did the title capture you interest? Were the terms "ode" and "muse" effective?

2. Would you agree that without its sense of humor, this essay would be flat? If so, and if you found the essay amusing, try to find examples of the three or four different humorous devices McGeary uses in the piece. You could consider, overstatement, understatement, pithy parallel statements, contrasting high and low diction, loaded rhetorical questions, and self-satirizing remarks.

3. Rewrite one or two paragraphs of this essay without benefit of the

humorous devices McGeary uses. What do you end up with? Could the substitution of another voice or tone redeem your rewritten version?

4. In paragraph 5, McGeary says, "I try to keep up with the mode, and it costs—just ask my husband." Does this reference and others to her husband undercut McGeary's authority in the piece?

5. Which is most important in this piece: the style of the author's prose or the substance of her ideas? Can such a separation be made?

▼ WRITING ASSIGNMENTS

1. Leaf through a fashion magazine for men or women. Based on an ad or series of ads, use your imagination to capture the person in the ad. Write about the lifestyle, interests, income, profession, and so forth, that are projected in the ad. You can assume a serious or humorous tone.

2. Write an essay entitled "Why I Love or Hate Fashion."

3. Research the styles of dress of another culture such as Saudi Arabia, China, or India. Analyze the cultural values and attitudes toward males and females reinforced by the style of dress.

4. Imagine it is the year 2010. Write an essay describing the current fashion trends and explain why they are so popular.

▼ WORK THAT BODY!

Sally B. Donnelly

The prototypes of female beauty have come a long way over the years: From the full and fleshy forms of a Rubens canvas to the curvaceous and busty screen stars of the fifties to the lean and leggy magazine models of the seventies. And for the 1990s, the new norm is more muscles, fewer curves. As reported in this article, women of today are "grunting and sweating" their way to a revolutionary ideal of female attractiveness in gyms and health clubs all over America. And the benefits are not only reflected in mirrors. The "sweat-soaked revolution" has pumped up a greater sense of self-esteem, independence, and general well-being. This article first appeared in the Fall of 1990 in *Time* magazine.

I am strong. I am invincible. I am woman.
   —I Am Woman

When Helen Reddy belted out her 1972 hit, she had no idea it would pump up women. Not only did the song become the unofficial anthem of the feminist movement, but women and girls seemed to take the words literally and headed off to the gym. In the two decades since, female attitudes toward fitness and athletics have undergone a vigorous shake-up. Across the country, women are working out, running hard, even pumping iron. And they are doing it not just to look attractive but also to gain strength and a sense of self-sufficiency. They have discovered the secret pleasures long enjoyed by athletic men: the heady, sweaty, solitary joy of hard physical exercise and the rosy, relaxed afterglow that follows it. "Sports and exercise make you feel better," says Gail Weldon, who runs the Women's Traac Health Club in Los Angeles. "Women want to be more in control of their bodies." 1

All the sweating and grunting has redefined the cultural parameters of female attractiveness—away from soft curves toward a more athletic body. For proof, just compare pop icon Madonna to her prototype, Marilyn Monroe. On her Blond Ambition tour, Madonna flashed chiseled biceps and deltoids, so impressing one Los Angeles critic that he wrote that instead of the customary audience call for "Author! Author!" the cry from Madonna's fans should be "Fitness trainer! Fitness trainer!" Tennis ace Martina Navratilova also notes the changing standards. When the Czechoslovak-born athlete defected to the U.S. in 1975, she was so embarrassed by her powerful build that she favored baggy, concealing clothes. "I was always covering up my arms because I have these big veins," she recalls, "and I didn't want anyone to see my shoulders." Now that muscles are in, Navratilova doesn't hesitate to appear in a tank top. "I don't seem as big anymore because other women are bigger!" 2

3   The sweat-soaked revolution is borne out by statistics: more than 62% of women over age 18 exercise regularly. According to a 1990 survey by the Melpomone Institute in St. Paul, which studies females and exercise, women also make up more than half the participants in the eight most popular sports in the U.S., including 95% of the 15 million people who do aerobics.

4   Baby boomers led the change. Growing up with the feminist movement, they wanted not only to work alongside men on the trading-room floor but also to play alongside them on the gym floor. "I started working out to get stronger," explains Sidney Perry, 39, a Portland, Ore., wardrobe stylist. "I wanted to be my own person." Other previously nonathletic women were swept up by the more general fitness movement. "I used to think there were two classes of people: athletes and the rest of us," says Nancy Crichlow, 29, a sales assistant in Houston who now works out regularly. Improved health is another motivator; regular exercise helps prevent osteoporosis and other age-related ailments.

5   Though it came too late for most boomers, the U.S. government gave a boost to women's athletics with the 1972 Title IX Amendment, which prohibited sex discrimination in federally funded educational institutions. The act helped encourage girls to go into sports by providing college scholarships and spurring the organization of girls' athletic teams. Since 1975, the number of girls' track-and-field competitors has grown sixfold. By 1989 there were 130,000 women competing in collegiate sports throughout the U.S., in contrast to 32,000 in 1972.

6   Encouraging as that sounds, there are some troubling gaps in the fitness boom. Exercise continues to be primarily a concern of the well off and well educated. A federal study this past summer reported that only 7% of low-income Americans exercise regularly. Nor have the workouts trimmed the obesity rate: 1 in 4 U.S. women age 35 to 64 is obese. And as much as the ideal body image has changed, there is still a lingering fear that women will begin to look like Arnold Schwarzenegger. Sports columnist Ira Berkow, for instance, wrote approvingly in the New York *Times* that tennis star Jennifer Capriati is "ladylike" and "nicely toned without looking muscular."

7   Such antiquated ideas are going the way of the vibrating-band contraption our mothers once used to battle the bulge. Women are working those bodies as never before, and not so much to impress a man as to impress the person flexing in the mirror. "Working out is a way of life for me," says Lorri Sparks, 37, athletic director of New York City's Downtown Athletic Club. "Sometimes I'd rather work out with a man than even have sex." Not everyone adopts that hard-core approach, but many are sympathetic: they are women; they are getting strong; and they feel damn near invincible.

▼ TOPICAL CONSIDERATIONS

1. According to this article, what motivates women to work out today? Are these reasons convincing to you? How do women's

motives for working out today differ from those of a generation ago?

2. How are Madonna and Martina Navratilova examples of the new definition of female attractiveness? What is your reaction to this new definition?

3. Do you think a new trend "away from soft curves toward a more athletic body" really exists, or is this media hype? Does this new "trend" seem a good thing for the average woman, or does it just set more trivial and unattainable goals for women to waste time pursuing?

4. How do you think Naomi Wolf ("The Beauty Myth" in Chapter 4) would react to this essay? Explain.

5. What was the purpose of the 1972 Title IX Amendment? What measurable effect has it had on college sports? Are you aware of athletic opportunities at your school that were made possible by the Title IX Amendment? If not, contact the Office of the Director of Athletics at your school and inquire.

6. Do you agree with the following statement from paragraph 7: "Women are working those bodies as never before, and not so much to impress a man as to impress the person flexing in the mirror"?

7. The last paragraph mentions the "vibrating-band contraption our mothers once used to battle the bulge." List other exercise devices for men as well as women that were once the rage but are now outmoded. What generalizations can we make about exercise fads?

▼ RHETORICAL CONSIDERATIONS

1. How is Helen Reddy's hit "I am Woman" used in this piece? Does it serve its purpose well?

2. In two sections of the piece statistics are used to illustrate points. Do you find the statistics convincing, compelling, or thin? Which seems to be more effective? Which the least effective? Explain the difference.

3. Most of the individuals quoted in this piece are either athletic directors of prestigious athletic clubs or exercise enthusiasts. Does this strengthen or weaken your confidence in their comments?

4. How would you describe the purpose of the concluding statement of the essay? Is it effective?

▼ WRITING ASSIGNMENTS

1. Keep a record for a week documenting your exercise regimen. Then write an essay explaining what you personally get out of exercise.

2. Write a speech on the benefits of physical fitness that you will deliver at the National Convention of Couch Potatoes. Have some fun with this.
3. Are you tired of the whole fitness craze? Write a humorous piece extolling the virtues of the sedentary life-style.

▼ THE FEAR LOBE MEETS "THE BRAINSUCKER"

Dave Barry

We can all recall scenes from a horror flick we'd much rather forget. We've all reminded ourselves around 2 A.M. that the Stephen King novel we're clutching is "only make-believe." Famous newspaper columnists are no different. In this amusing piece, Dave Barry abashedly admits to such irrational fears. With some hilarious anecdotes, the author shows what can happen when "the fear lobe" takes over. When not shuddering through horror novels, Dave Barry is making millions of people laugh with his Pulitzer Prize–winning *Miami Herald* column syndicated in more than 200 publications. Collections of his essays have been published in several books including *Babies and Other Hazards of Sex* (1984), *Dave Barry Turns Forty* (1990), and, *Dave Barry's Only Travel Guide You'll Ever Need* (1991). This essay first appeared in his column in May 1990.

1 Recently I've been reading horror novels at bedtime. I'm talking about those paperbacks with names like "The Brainsucker," full of scenes such as this:

2 "As Marge stepped through the doorway into the darkening mansion, she felt a sense of foreboding, caused, perhaps, by the moaning of the wind, or the creaking of the door, or possibly the Kentucky Fried Chicken bucket full of eyeballs."

3 Of course, if Marge had the intelligence of paint, she'd stop right here. "Wait a minute," she'd say. "I'm getting the hell out of this novel." Then she'd leap off the page, sprint across my bedspread, and run into my son's bedroom to become a character in a safe book like "Horton Hears a Who."

4 But Marge, in the hallowed horror-novel-character tradition, barges straight ahead, down gloomy corridors where she has to cut through the foreboding with a machete, despite the obvious fact that something hideous is about to happen, probably involving the forced evacuation of her skull cavity by a demonic being with the underworld Roto-Rooter franchise. So I'm flinching as I turn each page, thinking, "What a moron this woman is!" And Marge is

thinking: "Well, I may be a moron, but at least I'm not stupid enough to be *reading* this."

And, of course, Marge is right. I should know better than to read horror 5
books, or watch horror movies, because—this is not easy for a 42-year-old male
to admit—*I believe them.* I have always believed them. When I was a child, I was
routinely terrified by horror movies, even the comically inept ones where, when
Lon Chaney turned into a werewolf, you could actually see the makeup person's
hand darting into the picture to attach more fake fur to his face.

When I was 17—this is a true anecdote—I had to explain to my father one 6
Sunday morning that the reason our car was missing was that the night before,
I had taken my date to see "Psycho," and afterward I had explained to her that
it made more sense for *her* to drive *me* home, because of the strong possibility
that otherwise I would be stabbed to death by Anthony Perkins.

For years, after I saw "The Exorcist," I felt this need to be around priests. 7
Friends would say, "What do you want to do tonight?" And I'd say, "Let's take
in a Mass!"

I'm still this way, even though I'm a grown-up parent, constantly reassuring 8
my son about his irrational fears, telling him don't be silly, there aren't any
vampires in the guest bathroom. Part of my brain—the rational part, the part
that took the SAT tests, actually believes this; but a much more powerful part,
the Fear Lobe, takes the possibility of bathroom vampires far more seriously
than it takes, for example, the US trade deficit.

And, so, late at night, when I finish my horror novel and take the dogs out 9
into the yard, which is very dark, I am highly alert. My brain's SAT Sector,
trying to be cool, is saying, "Ha ha! This is merely your yard!" But the Fear
Lobe is saying: "Oh yes, this is exactly the kind of place that would attract The
Brainsucker. For The Brainsucker, this is Walt Disney World."

And so I start sauntering back toward the house, trying to look as casual 10
as possible considering that every few feet I suddenly whirl around to see if
anything's behind me. Soon I am sauntering at upwards of 35 miles per hour,
and the Fear Lobe is screaming *"It's coming!"* and even the SAT Sector has
soaked its mental armpits and now I'm openly sprinting through the darkness,
almost to the house, and *what's that noise behind me, oh no, please, aaaiiieeee
whump* I am struck violently in the back by Earnest, our Toyota-sized main dog,
who has located a cache of valuable dog poo and shrewdly elected to roll in it,
and is now generously attempting to share the experience with me.

Thus, the spell of horror is broken, and my SAT Sector reasserts control 11
and has a good laugh at what a silly goose I was, and I walk calmly back inside
and close the door, just seconds before the tentacle reaches it.

▼ TOPICAL CONSIDERATIONS

1. List some horror novels you've read or some horror films you've
   seen. As best you can, try to explain your attraction and reactions

to them. Do you share any of Barry's reactions? If you have never read a horror story or seen a horror movie, explain your avoidance.

2. What criticisms of the book, "The Brainsucker," and its main character, "Marge," does Barry make? If the book is so bad, why is Barry reading it? Have you read a horror novel you considered poorly written but irresistible? What was the attraction? Can you name a well-written horror novel that you would consider a respectable piece of literature? Explain your answer.

3. What movie scared Barry as a child? As an adult? Do you take his fears seriously, or is he just kidding? Can you think of a particular movie that scared you as a child? As an adult?

4. How does fear track Barry into his own backyard?

▼ RHETORICAL CONSIDERATIONS

1. Where does Barry make his thesis statement? Is it stated directly, or is it implied?

2. How does Barry employ narrative and personification to make the struggle between reason and fear humorous and entertaining?

3. An anecdote is a brief and entertaining account of an event. Mention two or three which you thought were most effective in this piece. Is the abbreviated form of these stories effective, or would you prefer it if Barry had expanded them?

4. What is the effect on the reader of Barry's concluding phrase, "just seconds before the tentacle reaches it"? What is this ending an allusion to?

5. This essay is filled with contemporary references of people, places, and things. List a few items a person needs to be familiar with to fully appreciate the ideas and humor of the essay. Does this limit the essay's audience? Does it detract from the value or stature of the essay? How would you characterize Barry's audience?

▼ WRITING ASSIGNMENTS

1. The major thrust of Barry's humor here is self-deprecation, that is, making fun of himself. Try writing some self-deprecating humor of your own by describing some irrational fears you may have. As does Barry, use exaggeration, irony, overstatement, understatement, and other humorous strategies.

2. Write an essay explaining the appeal of horror to you and your friends. Try to analyze some of the specific qualities of the genre that draw you to it.

▼ FINDING THE FURY
Bill Boggs

> The essay below is the story of an obsession that lasted for 30 years. It is told by a man who as a boy fell in love with a car that he could neither afford nor drive—a car that over the decades haunted him like a restless ghost. But more than that, it is a moving statement about growing up and looking back. Bill Boggs is a television personality and producer. This essay first appeared in *The New York Times Magazine* in 1987.

There were 10 minutes to kill before I had to leave for the Police Athletic League baseball game. I sat on the side of my bed to look through Popular Mechanics magazine. When I reached the article on the new 1956 Plymouth Fury, my heart started to pound. It would be years before I defined the experience as a *coup de foudre;* later on, I would meet a woman and fall in love at first sight. But that day in Philadelphia I was 14 years old, and the object of my passion was a car. 1

I'd never seen a car with something that looked like a lightning bolt shooting along its side. Actually, the eggshell-white Fury sported a unique anodized gold aluminum trim on each side, giving the design a thrilling sense of motion. It was the most beautiful car I'd ever seen. 2

It cost $2,800. I had a measly $235 saved up from neighborhood jobs and Christmas gifts. Buying the Fury was as out of reach as playing with the Phillies. Besides, I didn't even have a driver's license. But someday, I vowed, I would get a '56 Fury. 3

I pedaled my bicycle to Plymouth showrooms all over Philadelphia. My Uncle John drove me to far-away dealerships in the suburbs. But we never found a Fury. It was a special production model, and only 4,485 were manufactured. Rich people with $2,800 had ordered them all. 4

A year would pass before I even saw one. My father and I were out driving, and coming toward us was a '56 Fury. Could the Lone Ranger have been more thrilled on seeing the great horse Silver for the first time? "That's it, Dad!" I yelled. My father glanced at the gleaming car and let out a loud "Hmmm" of admiration. In the 30 years since, I have seen a '56 Fury only three other times. 5

During my freshman year at the University of Pennsylvania, I bought a used 1956 Plymouth Belvedere convertible. It was as close as I could get to the Fury. Two more owner's cards passed through my wallet before I bought the car I still drive today, a 1968 Mercury Parklane convertible. The Merc has taken me 148,000 miles over nearly 20 years. It has driven Hubert Humphrey to the airport, whisked me away on two honeymoons, raced my dying dog to the vet and endured years of living outside that people said would kill it. 6

But I could never find a '56 Fury. For 15 years, I have checked the antique and classic car ads. In the early 1980's, I placed ads myself. No callers. I've told 7 everyone from gas station attendants to strangers on airplanes what I was looking for. Once, interviewing the race car driver Richard Petty on television, I blurted out that I craved a '56 Fury. Surely that will do it, I thought. During my years as a television host, viewers have sent me unsolicited items that ranged from handknitted cat costumes to a 100-year-old corncob stripper, but this time there was no response.

8   Then, finally, in Hemmings Motor News, I saw the words: "Plymouth: 1956 Fury, superb condition, all original and complete."

9   I was working in Los Angeles, but I made an immediate call to the advertiser in Seattle. A voice on the telephone assured me that the car had been restored to perfect condition.

10   Would a small deposit hold it for two weeks, when I'd have a break in my schedule and could go see it?

11   No. A buyer from Kansas was seriously interested.

12   I hung up. If I don't get this Fury, I rationalized, I'll find another one some other time.

13   Then I laughed out loud at myself.

14   How easy it has been for me to postpone important decisions. I've delayed making commitments to good relationships until I ruined them and waited far too long to get out of bad ones. I've put off having a child for years, always thinking I wasn't ready, only to discover that fatherhood is my greatest source of joy. I've postponed buying a home and taking vacations as if there were some guarantee there will always be enough time, as if I expected to live two lives instead of one.

15   I canceled everything I had scheduled for the next 48 hours and flew to Seattle. When the garage door swung open and I saw the Fury, I let out a long "Hmmmm" and remembered that day with my father.

16   "I like to take old beat-up things and make them beautiful again," said Bob Dally, the owner, who had been working on the car for seven years. He had succeeded. Under a full moon in the clear Seattle sky, the Fury seemed to glow in the dark. "Let's go for a ride," he said. I slid the car into first gear, slowly released the clutch and depressed the accelerator. We roared into the darkness.

17   "It's still fast," I thought. When we pulled into a gas station, we were quickly surrounded by teen-agers looking at us as if we'd just driven off the set of "Back to the Future."

18   Less than an hour later, we were back at Bob's house. I had piloted the Fury through the quiet streets, and it had performed perfectly. But when I turned off the engine, I had a feeling I would never have anticipated. My fantasy seemed fulfilled; I didn't have to buy the car. I was like a man who pursues a woman, finally makes love to her and then doesn't want to take the responsibility of seeing her again. Finding the car had been wonderful, but I was afraid to commit to ownership. Bob Dally seemed surprised when I told him I had to do some thinking and wanted to walk around the block.

19   Could I handle the responsibility of realizing my childhood fantasy? Adult experience told me that owning this car was totally impractical. To start with,

where would I put it? I travel back and forth between New York and Los Angeles, and I have no garage in either place.

I have no mechanical ability and would have to depend on others to track 20 down out-of-stock parts and fix the car. The Fury is perfect now. Would each inevitable scratch drive me into a rage? Would a stolen hubcap turn me into a bounty hunter?

It all boiled down to asking myself this: did I really need to own the Fury 21 to enjoy it any more than I already had? A younger voice inside me said, "Yes."

"But," I argued with myself, "is this really the best time to get it? Maybe 22 I should wait."

The 14-year-old voice said, "Today is the someday." 23

I bought the Fury. I drove it from Seattle down the Pacific Coast Highway 24 to Los Angeles. I took my time along Big Sur. I'd planned all my life to make that trip.

▼ TOPICAL CONSIDERATIONS

1. How did Boggs first discover the Fury? What was so special about this particular model?
2. Why do you suppose Boggs still drives his 20-year-old Mercury Parklane? What does this say about the man?
3. What kind of measures did the author go through trying to locate a Fury? How did he actually find the one he bought?
4. When Boggs learns that a buyer from Kansas was "seriously interested" in the Fury, he rationalizes that since he can't find the time to fly off to Seattle, he'd have to "find another one some other time." What realization about himself finally convinces him to drop everything and act?
5. How does Boggs almost talk himself out of buying the car? What practical reasons does he come up with?
6. What ultimately moves Bill Boggs to buy his Fury?

▼ RHETORICAL CONSIDERATIONS

1. Comment on the appropriateness of the title of Boggs's essay. What different meanings might it have?
2. When Boggs at last lays eyes on the dream Fury, he lets out a long "Hmmmm" the way his father did years ago. Why would the author include this little detail? How is it appropriate? What effect does it create?
3. When he drives the Fury into a gas station, Boggs says (in paragraph 17) that the car was "quickly surrounded by teenagers look-

ing at us as if we'd just driven off the set of *Back to the Future."*
Discuss the appropriateness of this little detail.
4. Toward the end of the essay Boggs resorts to quoting the voices in
his head. Why does he do this instead of just summarizing his
thoughts? What do the direct quotations add to the overall effect of
the essay?
5. What effect did the essay's last line have on you?
6. How well did Boggs maintain the element of suspense in this essay?
In other words, did he have you guessing right to the end as to
whether or not he'd actually buy his dream car?

▼ WRITING ASSIGNMENTS

1. Write Bill Boggs a letter congratulating him on buying the Fury and
in it, specify your reasons.
2. The 1956 Plymouth Fury was the object of young Bill Boggs's
passion. Describe an object of your passion—some material thing
that once took hold of you, something that you someday would like
to own, or now do own. Describe the object and your obsession.
Describe the fulfillment you've derived or hope to derive from it.

▼ THE BACKPACKER
Patrick F. McManus

In the old days before backpacking became fashionable, you'd hoof your way up a mountain with a plywood-and-canvas pack that was your own weight plus that of the kitchen range. Your sleeping bag was a rolled-up mattress full of "sawdust, horsehair, and No. 6 bird shot." Today, with the sport refined by high technology, the packs come in almost weightless magnesium; the sleeping bags are filled with "the down of unborn goose"; and the tents are made of "waterproof smoke." So writes Patrick F. McManus in this hilarious look at a current craze. For years, McManus has been regaling readers of such magazines as *Field and Stream, Reader's Digest,* and *Sports Illustrated* with his witty exposes of the "pleasures and rewards" of the Great Outdoors. This essay comes from his popular collection *A Fine and Pleasant Misery* (1981).

1 Strange, the things that suddenly become fashionable. Take backpacking for instance.

2 I know people who five years ago had never climbed anything higher than a tall barstool. Now you can scarcely name a mountain within three hundred miles they haven't hoofed up in their Swiss-made waffle-stompers.

3 They used to complain about the price of sirloin steak. Now they complain about the price of beef jerky (which is about three times that of Maine lobster in Idaho).

4 Their backpacking is a refined sport, noted for lightness. The gear consists of such things as silk packs, magnesium frames, dainty camp stoves. Their sleeping bags are filled with the down of unborn goose, their tents are made of waterproof smoke. They carry two little packets from which they can spread out a nine-course meal. One packet contains the food and the other a freeze-dried French chef.

5 Well, it wasn't like that back in the old days, before backpacking became fashionable. These latecomers don't know what real backpacking was like.

6 The rule of thumb for the old backpacking was that the weight of your pack should equal the weight of yourself and the kitchen range combined. Just a casual glance at a full pack sitting on the floor could give you a double hernia and fuse four vertebrae. After carrying the pack all day, you had to remember to tie one leg to a tree before you dropped it. Otherwise, you would float off into space. The pack eliminated the need for any special kind of ground-gripping shoes, because your feet would sink a foot and a half into hard-packed earth, two inches into solid rock. Some of the new breed of backpackers occasionally wonder what caused a swath of fallen trees on the side of a mountain. That is where one of the old backpackers slipped off a trail with a full pack.

7   My packboard alone met the minimum weight requirement. It was a canvas and plywood model, surplus from the Second World War. These packboards apparently were designed with the idea that a number of them could be hooked together to make an emergency bridge for Sherman tanks. The first time you picked one up you thought maybe someone had forgotten to remove his tank.

8   My sleeping bag looked like a rolled-up mattress salvaged from a fire in a skid row hotel. Its filling was sawdust, horsehair, and No. 6 bird shot. Some of today's backpackers tell me their sleeping bags are so light they scarcely know they're there. The only time I scarcely knew my sleeping bag was there was when I was in it at 2 A.M. on a cold night. It was freckled from one end to the other with spark holes, a result of my efforts to stay close enough to the fire to keep warm. The only time I was halfway comfortable was when it was ablaze. It was the only sleeping bag I ever heard of which you could climb into in the evening with scarcely a mark on you and wake up in the morning bruised from head to toe. That was because two or three times a night my companions would take it upon themselves to jump up and stomp out my sleeping-bag fires—in their haste neglecting to first evacuate the occupant. Since I was the camp cook, I never knew whether they were attempting to save me from immolation or getting in a few last licks for what they thought might be terminal indigestion.

9   Our provisions were not distinguished by variety. Dehydrated foods were considered effeminate. A man could ruin his reputation for life by getting caught on a pack trip with a dried apple. If you wanted apples, brother, you carried them with the water still in them. No one could afford such delicacies as commercial beef jerky. What you carried was a huge slab of bacon. It was so big that if the butcher had left on the legs, it could have walked behind you on a leash.

10   A typical meal consisted of fried bacon, potatoes and onions fried in bacon grease, a pan of beans heated in bacon grease, bacon grease gravy, some bread fried in bacon grease, and cowboy coffee (made by boiling an old cowboy in bacon grease). After meals, indigestion went through our camp like a sow grizzly with a toothache. During the night coyotes sat in nervous silence on surrounding hills and listened to the mournful wailing from our camp.

11   There were a few bad things, too, about backpacking in the old style, but I loved all of it. I probably would never have thought of quitting if it hadn't been for all those geophysical changes that took place in the Western Hemisphere a few years ago.

12   The first thing I noticed was a distinct hardening of the earth. This occurred wherever I happened to spread out my sleeping bag, so I knew that the condition was widespread. (Interestingly enough, my children, lacking their father's scientific training, were unable to detect the phenomenon.)

13   A short while later it became apparent to me that the nights in the mountains had become much colder than any I could remember in the past. The chill would sink its fangs into my bones in the pre-dawn hours and hang on like a terrier until the sun was high. I thought possibly that the drop in temperature was heralding a new ice age.

Well, I could put up with the hard and the cold but then the air started **14** getting thinner. The only way you could get sufficient oxygen to lug a pack the size of an adolescent pachyderm was by gasping and wheezing. (Some of my wheezes were sufficient to strip small pine trees bare of their needles.) My trail speed became so slow it posed a dangerous threat to my person. If we were in fact at the onset of a new ice age, there was a good chance I might be overtaken and crushed by a glacier.

The final straw was the discovery that a trail I had traveled easily and often **15** in my youth had undergone a remarkable transformation. In the intervening years since I had last hiked it, the damn thing had nearly doubled in length. I must admit that I was puzzled, since I didn't know that trails could stretch or grow. The fact that it now took me twice as long to hike it, however, simply did not allow for any other explanation. I asked a couple of older friends about it, and they said that they had seen the same thing happen. They said probably the earth shifted on its axis every once in a while and caused trails to stretch. I suggested that maybe that was also the cause for the ground getting harder, the nights colder, and the air thinner. They said that sounded like a plausible theory to them. (My wife had another theory, but it was so wild and farfetched that I won't embarrass her by mentioning it here.)

Anyway, one day last fall while I was sitting at home fretting about the **16** environment, a couple of friends telephoned and invited me along on a pack trip they were taking into the Cascades. Both of them are of the new school of backpacking, and I thought I owed it to them to go along. They could profit considerably by watching an old trail hand in action.

When I saw the packs R.B. and Charley showed up with I almost had to **17** laugh. Neither pack was large enough to carry much more than a cheese sandwich. I carried more bicarbonate of soda than they had food. I didn't know what they planned to sleep in, but it certainly couldn't be in those tidy little tote bags they had perched on top of their packs. Anyway, I didn't say anything. I just smiled and got out my winch and they each got a pry pole and before you knew it we had my pack out of the car and on my shoulders. As we headed up the trail I knew it was going to be a rough trip. Already a few flakes of snow had fallen on my eyeballs.

The environment on that trip was even harsher than I had remembered. The **18** trails were steeper, the air thinner, the ground harder, the nights colder. Even my trail speed was slower. Several porcupines shot past me like I was standing still.

R.B. and Charley showed obvious signs of relief when I made it into camp **19** that first night.

"You probably thought I wouldn't make it with all the food," I chided **20** them.

"No," R.B. said. "It was just that for a moment there we didn't recognize **21** you. We thought we were being attacked by a giant snail."

I explained to them that we old-time backpackers made a practice of travel- **22** ing the last mile or so on our hands and knees in order to give our feet a rest.

23   It was disgusting to see them sitting there so relaxed and cheerful after a hard day's hike. They didn't seem to have any notion at all what backpacking was about. I could hardly stand it when they whipped out a little stove and boiled up some dried chunks of leather and sponge for supper. It probably would have hurt their feelings if I had got out the slab of bacon, so I didn't mention it. I just smiled and ate their food—four helpings in fact, just to make my act convincing. I never told them, but the Roast Baron of Beef was not quite rare enough for my taste and they had forgotten the cream sauce for the asparagus tips. And I have certainly tasted better Baked Alaska in my day, too.

24   Well, they can have their fashionable new-school backpacking if they want it. I'm sticking with the old way. Oh, I'm making a few concessions to a harsher environment, but that's all. When I got back from that trip, I did order a new pack frame. It was designed by nine aeronautical engineers, three metallurgists, and a witch doctor, and weighs slightly less than the down of a small thistle. My new sleeping bag weighs nine ounces, including the thermostatic controls. If I want to sleep in, my new cook kit gets up and puts on the coffee. Then I bought a few boxes of that dried leather and sponge. But that's all. I'm certainly not going to be swept along on the tides of fashion.

▼ TOPICAL CONSIDERATIONS

1. What contrasts between the backpacking of the "old days" and today does McManus point out?
2. Why did the author resist the new backpacking gear and defend the old?
3. In a tongue-in-cheek manner, McManus cites several "geophysical changes that took place in the Western Hemisphere a few years ago." What are these changes? What transformation in McManus do they explain?
4. What concessions to the harsher environment does McManus finally make?

▼ RHETORICAL CONSIDERATIONS

1. Much humor in this piece depends on exaggeration. Examine paragraph 6 and cite some examples of the author's exaggeration.
2. Find an example of humor through repetition.

▼ WRITING ASSIGNMENTS

1. Select a sport or pastime you enjoy and write a tongue-in-cheek defense of it in a style similar to the author's here. For humorous

effects, try to employ irony, exaggeration, repetition, and other devices.

2. Write an essay describing someone you know who prefers to do something "the old-fashioned way"—someone who rejects the latest conveniences and efficiencies.

3. Write an essay explaining the values of doing something "the old-fashioned way"—for instance, using a manual typewriter instead of a word processor, a traditional oven instead of a microwave, or an adding machine instead of a calculator.

7 ▼ TELEVISION

Television is the prime mover of American culture. It is the foremost source of entertainment and news. More than any other medium, it regulates commerce, life-styles, and social values. In this chapter we will explore some of the various ways this extraordinary entity has become part of our lives—for better or worse.

We open with a glimpse of pre-TV childhood. In "What Did Kids Do Before Television was Invented?" Peter C. Kratcoski recalls how kids created their own fantasies instead of living them through screen characters.

While some critics complain that TV takes kids away from creative play, others worry that TV intrudes on family life. In "The Plug-In Drug" Marie Winn argues that television is replacing traditional family rituals and interfering with the formation of family bonds.

According to a 1991 report by the National Coalition on Television Violence, the average American child will have seen 200,000 violent acts on TV by the age of 18, including 40,000 murders. Since television shapes our behavior and attitudes, such heavy exposure to mayhem on the screen threatens to desensitize viewers, especially young ones, while prompting real violence. What concerns Ellen Goodman in "The Violence Is Fake, the Impact Is Real" is not just that television depicts too much violence, but that it fails to depict the consequences of violence—pain and suffering.

And now for a look at the news—or, more precisely, the nonnews. The next piece, "Now . . . This," argues that the "entertainment values" of broadcast news have corrupted our knowledge of world affairs. With its heavy reliance on dynamic images and pleasing personalities, says Neil Postman, news has been packaged to suit the requirements of show biz not the dissemination of information.

So far, we have heard how bad television is: the low-grade shows, the violence, the deleterious effects on children, the undermining of the family. Some reviewers, however, have made peace with the tube. In "Don't Blame TV," Jeff Greenfield contends that critics get carried away trying to pin all our social woes on television. Point for point he attempts to debunk their claims.

We close this chapter with a few chuckles from P. J. O'Rourke. "Why I Quit Watching TV" is the humorous confession of a man who decided to do something about all the grim reports of how TV has no artistic or social value, how it rots our brains, how it turns us into zombies. He got rid of his set. But as O'Rourke discovers, life without television was like . . . well, keep reading.

▼ WHAT DID KIDS DO BEFORE TELEVISION WAS INVENTED?

Peter C. Kratcoski

Television is the primary source of entertainment for Americans. It is also the prime target of many psychologists and sociologists who see television as dangerous to health. The lead piece in this section reflects one major criticism—that television threatens the creative activity of children. Peter C. Kratcoski is an editor for *USA Today* and a professor of sociology and criminal justice at Kent State University. His criticism here is not leveled at the quality of television, as is the criticism of others in this section, but at the passive nature of the experience. His essay also gives a glimpse of how kids filled their time before television. This first appeared in *USA Today* in 1981.

1 When adults who grew up in the 1940's or early 1950's describe the days of their youth to their children, they paint a Norman Rockwell–style portrait of life. Hats went off as the flag passed by; days were filled with fishing, swimming, playing ball, or chatting with kindly adults; and parents' dreams for their children could be attained within the town limits—a good report card, a date for the prom, a romance with the boy next door. No matter how rosy the picture is painted, however, the question inevitably comes back: "Yes, but what did you do without television?" With television currently taking a good deal of criticism for its violence, suggestiveness, and debunking of authority figures in children's lives, it seems appropriate to recall the sorts of pastimes in which children of a small-town background engaged in the pre-television era.

2 One of our particular favorite activities was playing in the cemetery. Although children seen roaming unsupervised in a cemetery today would probably be viewed suspiciously as potential vandals, we spent quite a few hours walking among the markers, commenting on the age and life status of the deceased and speculating on the character of those whose stones were particularly ornate. The children buried in the cemetery were most intriguing to us. We would talk about what dread disease might have finished them off and how old they would be today if they had lived; they even were sometimes included as imaginary playmates in our games.

3 This rather ghoulish preoccupation with the other-worldly also extended to our favorite holiday, Halloween. "Trick or treat," rather than being a one-night affair, extended for two or more weeks before the haunting day. A group of children disguised as hobos, ghosts, scarecrows, or gypsies might descend on a household at any time, and the hauntee had to be ready with treats or face the penalty of having his or her windows "soaped" (coated over with swirls and squiggles of bar soap). A code of "soaping" ethics existed—"nice" kids used bar

soap, never pieces of wax, which had to be scraped from the window with a razor blade. The climax of the Halloween season came with the town parade, in which every kid who could walk or be carried participated. Many adults also joined in the fun, and prizes were awarded. One of the oddities of our particular area was the custom of fashioning costumes from suits of long underwear and then stuffing pillows into every possible inch of the material to produce droopy, horrendous-looking, fatty creatures. *Buying* a costume was unthinkable. Some mothers took this as the yearly opportunity to show off their sewing skills and fashioned elaborate crepe-paper costumes for their pretty, curly haired daughters. Those of us not so blessed uttered secret prayers for rain during the parade, in the hope that these strutting beauties would be reduced to dripping, runny nothings. Hours were spent talking about what this year's costume would be, pretending we were going to dress another way to keep others from stealing our prize-winning idea, and spying on friends to find out what they were *really* going to wear.

Some of our pastimes centered about the church and the parochial school, but were not necessarily inspirational in intent. Holy Saturday was a day of great rejoicing, because at noon on that day Lent ended and we could again eat candy, read comic books, drink pop, or return to whatever other vice our parents had helped us promise to give up for the past 40 days. We would gravely prepare the forbidden fruit and wait for the signal of the church bell tolling at noon before gleefully digging in. Another important day was Aug. 15, the Feast of the Assumption, when the nuns who taught in the school received their assignments for the following year. It was a clear case of fate intervening in our lives. A word from the Mother Superior on that day would send a particularly feared presence from among us, never to be seen again, or would commit us to another year of toeing the line. The 8 A.M. Mass was crowded, rumors flew, and we would intently study the faces of the nuns for any sign that a packed suitcase was waiting in the convent. When the news came out, it would spread like wildfire, and then a period of relief or resignation followed. **4**

It seemed that we did a good deal more reading than children do today, but the adventure themes we favored were not unlike those of television escapism. Nancy Drew was frowned upon by the town librarian, a fact which made her even more appealing to the girls. The older boys' interest ran to novels smuggled from their parents' collections or paperbacks purchased at the drugstore. All of the "juicy" parts were marked for rereading and discussion. **5**

These few examples seem to suggest that, even without television, we were preoccupied in our early lives with the same themes of violence, rather ghoulish aspects of the supernatural, testing and disrespect for authority, vandalism, a desire to shock adults, and references to things considered "taboo" which we now object to in television fare available to children. The apparent difference is the level and visibility of these themes. A good deal of the rebellious or aberrant activity of the past occurred only in the imaginations of the youths of that time, in contrast to the graphic visual presentation of these themes on television. In addition, a good deal of the testing of limits or rebelliousness was expressed in **6** activities of which adults were unaware. In contrast to television programming—which is prepared, produced, and projected by adults—the testing activities engaged in years ago had an element of social control by the children themselves. Parents were not seen as friends or buddies, and the kids' world was closed to them. Adults seemed comfortable with this idea and kept a hands-off attitude unless behavior became blatantly rebellious, disruptive, or destructive. One possible answer, then, to the question, "What did kids do before television was invented?" seems to be that they acted out their fantasies themselves, rather than depending on film characters to do it for them.

▼ TOPICAL CONSIDERATIONS

1. What are the implications in the question asked of adults: "But what did you do without television?"
2. According to Kratcoski, how did his childhood activities differ from those of kids today?
3. Did your own Halloween experiences differ much from those of the author? In what ways? In general, how have Halloween activities changed since the days of Kratcoski's childhood?
4. How does the author answer the question in the title?

▼ RHETORICAL CONSIDERATIONS

1. Explain the allusion in paragraph 1 to "a Norman Rockwell–style portrait of life." How does the author characterize such a portrait?
2. Comment on the tone of Kratcoski's word choice, "finished them off," when he refers to the children buried in the cemetery (paragraph 2).
3. Does this essay have an organizing scheme? Outline it according to paragraphs.
4. Where is the thesis statement in this piece? What is the rhetorical strategy of placing it where it is? How well does Kratcoski support that statement in the essay?

▼ WRITING ASSIGNMENTS

1. Kratcoski's complaint is aimed not at the quality of television but at the nature of the experience itself, which he says is passive. Before television, kids used to act out their own fantasies, but today they depend on programs produced by adults to do it for them. Do you agree with Kratcoski? Write a paper evaluating his claim, and use

your own childhood memories as evidence. Did you have a free and active fantasy life?

2. One of the arguments people make against television is that children read less because of it. Evaluate the effects television has had on your own reading experience. Did you like to read as a child? What did you read? Did you prefer television to books?

3. Part of Kratcoski's essay centers on his pretelevision activities, such as his memories of Halloween. Write your own recollection of Halloweens past. What kinds of preparations did you make? Did you design and create your own costumes, or did you buy them? What trick-or-treat experiences did you have? In a narrative, try to capture some of the things you did.

▼ THE PLUG-IN DRUG
Marie Winn

For years, the harmful effects of television, particularly on children, have been the professional interest of social commentator and writer Marie Winn. She is author of *The Plug-In Drug: TV* (1985), from which this essay has been adapted, and *Children Without Childhood* (1983). She says that home and family life have changed considerably—and in ways we may not care to imagine—since the invention of television. She makes a strong case against television, accusing it of being a prime force in the warping of children and in the disintegration of the American family.

Less than forty years after the introduction of television into American society, a period that has seen the medium become so deeply ingrained in American life that in at least one state the television set has attained the rank of a legal necessity, safe from repossession in case of debt along with clothes, cooking utensils, and the like, television viewing has become an inevitable and ordinary part of daily life. Only in the early years of television did writers and commentators have sufficient perspective to separate the activity of watching television from the actual content it offers the viewer. In those early days writers frequently discussed the effects of television on family life. However, a curious myopia afflicted those early observers: almost without exception they regarded television as a favorable, beneficial, indeed, wondrous influence upon the family. 1

"Television is going to be a real asset in every home where there are children," predicts a writer in 1949. 2

"Television will take over your way of living and change your children's 3 habits, but this change can be a wonderful improvement," claims another commentator.

4 "No survey's needed, of course, to establish that television has brought the family together in one room," writes *The New York Times'* television critic in 1949.

5 Each of the early articles about television is invariably accompanied by a photograph or illustration showing a family cozily sitting together before the television set, Sis on Mom's lap, Buddy perched on the arm of Dad's chair, Dad with his arm around Mom's shoulder. Who could have guessed that twenty or so years later Mom would be watching a drama in the kitchen, the kids would be looking at cartoons in their room, while Dad would be taking in the ball game in the living room?

6 Of course television sets were enormously expensive in those early days. The idea that by 1982 more than half of all American families would own two or more sets seemed preposterous. The splintering of the multiple-set family was something the early writers could not foresee. Nor did anyone imagine the number of hours children would eventually devote to television, the changes television would effect upon child-rearing methods, the increasing domination of family schedules by children's viewing requirements—in short, the *power* of television to dominate family life.

7 After the first years, as children's consumption of the new medium increased, together with parental concern about the possible effects of so much television viewing, a steady refrain helped to soothe and reassure anxious parents. "Television always enters a pattern of influences that already exist: the home, the peer group, the school, the church and culture generally," wrote the authors of an early and influential study of television's effects on children. In other words, if the child's home life is all right, parents need not worry about the effects of all that television watching.

8 But television did not merely influence the child; it deeply influenced that "pattern of influences" everyone hoped would ameliorate the new medium's effects. Home and family life have changed in important ways since the advent of television. The peer group has become television-oriented, and much of the time children spend together is occupied by television viewing. Culture generally has been transformed by television. Therefore it is improper to assign to television the subsidiary role its many apologists (too often members of the television industry) insist it plays. Television is not merely one of a number of important influences upon today's child. Through the changes it has made in family life, television emerges as *the* important influence in children's lives today.

THE QUALITY OF FAMILY LIFE

9 Television's contribution to family life has been an equivocal one. For while it has, indeed, kept the members of the family from dispersing, it has not served to bring them *together*. By its domination of the time families spend together,

it destroys the special quality that distinguishes one family from another, a quality that depends to a great extent on what a family *does,* what special rituals, games, recurrent jokes, familiar songs, and shared activities it accumulates.

"Like the sorcerer of old," writes Urie Bronfenbrenner, "the television set 10 casts its magic spell, freezing speech and action, turning the living into silent statues so long as the enchantment lasts. The primary danger of the television screen lies not so much in the behavior it produces—although there is danger there—as in the behavior it prevents: the talks, the games, the family festivities and arguments through which much of the child's learning takes place and through which his character is formed. Turning on the television set can turn off the process that transforms children into people."

Yet parents have accepted a television-dominated family life so completely 11 that they cannot see how the medium is involved in whatever problems they might be having. A first-grade teacher reports:

"I have one child in the group who's an only child. I wanted to find out 12 more about her family life because this little girl was quite isolated from the group, didn't make friends, so I talked to her mother. Well, they don't have time to do anything in the evening, the mother said. The parents come home after picking up the child at the baby-sitter's. Then the mother fixes dinner while the child watches TV. Then they have dinner and the child goes to bed. I said to this mother, 'Well, couldn't she help you fix dinner? That would be a nice time for the two of you to talk,' and the mother said, 'Oh, but I'd hate to have her miss "Zoom." It's such a good program!' "

Even when families make efforts to control television, too often its very 13 presence counterbalances the positive features of family life. A writer and mother of two boys aged 3 and 7 described her family's television schedule in an article in *The New York Times:*

> We were in the midst of a full-scale War. Every day was a new battle and every program was a major skirmish. We agreed it was a bad scene all around and were ready to enter diplomatic negotiations. . . . In principle we have agreed on 2½ hours of TV a day, "Sesame Street," "Electric Company" (with dinner gobbled up in between) and two half-hour shows between 7 and 8:30 which enables the grown-ups to eat in peace and prevents the two boys from destroying one another. Their pre-bedtime choice is dreadful, because, as Josh recently admitted, "There's nothing much on I really like." . . . Clearly there is a need for first-rate children's shows at this time. . . .

Consider the "family life" described here: Presumably the father comes 14 home from work during the "Sesame Street"—"Electric Company" stint. The children are either watching television, gobbling their dinner, or both. While the parents eat their dinner in peaceful privacy, the children watch another hour of television. Then there is only a half-hour left before bedtime, just enough time for baths, getting pajamas on, brushing teeth, and so on. The children's evening is regimented with an almost military precision. They watch their favorite programs, and when there is "nothing much on I really like," they watch whatever else is on—because *watching* is the important thing. Their mother does not see anything amiss with watching programs just for the sake of watching; she only wishes there were some first-rate children's shows on at those times.

15   Without conjuring up memories of the Victorian era with family games and long, leisurely meals, and large families, the question arises: isn't there a better family life available than this dismal, mechanized arrangement of children watching television for however long is allowed them, evening after evening?

16   Of course, families today still do *special* things together at times: go camping in the summer, go to the zoo on a nice Sunday, take various trips and expeditions. But their *ordinary* daily life together is diminished—that sitting around at the dinner table, that spontaneous taking up of an activity, those little games invented by children on the spur of the moment when there is nothing else to do, the scribbling, the chatting, and even the quarreling, all the things that form the fabric of a family, that define a childhood. Instead, the children have their regular schedule of television programs and bedtime, and the parents have their peaceful dinner together.

17   The author of the article in the *Times* notes that "keeping a family sane means mediating between the needs of both children and adults." But surely the needs of the adults are being better met than the needs of the children, who are effectively shunted away and rendered untroublesome, while their parents enjoy a life as undemanding as that of any childless couple. In reality, it is those very demands that young children make upon a family that lead to growth, and it is the way parents accede to those demands that builds the relationships upon which the future of the family depends. If the family does not accumulate its backlog of shared experiences, shared *everyday* experiences that occur and recur and change and develop, then it is not likely to survive as anything other than a caretaking institution.

FAMILY RITUALS

18   Ritual is defined by sociologists as "that part of family life that the family likes about itself, is proud of and wants formally to continue." Another text notes that "the development of a ritual by a family is an index of the common interest of its members in the family as a group."

19   What has happened to family rituals, those regular, dependable, recurrent happenings that gave members of a family a feeling of *belonging* to a home rather than living in it merely for the sake of convenience, those experiences that act as the adhesive of family unity far more than any material advantages?

20   Mealtime rituals, going-to-bed rituals, illness rituals, holiday rituals—how many of these have survived the inroads of the television set?

21   A young woman who grew up near Chicago reminisces about her childhood and gives an idea of the effects of television upon family rituals:

"As a child I had millions of relatives around—my parents both come from **22** relatively large families. My father had nine brothers and sisters. And so every holiday there was this great swoop-down of aunts, uncles, and millions of cousins. I just remember how wonderful it used to be. These thousands of cousins would come and everyone would play and ultimately, after dinner, all the women would be in the front of the house, drinking coffee and talking, all the men would be in the back of the house, drinking and smoking, and all the kids would be all over the place, playing hide and seek. Christmas time was particularly nice because everyone always brought all their toys and games. Our house had a couple of rooms with go-through closets, so there were always kids running in a great circle route. I remember it was just wonderful.

"And then all of a sudden one year I remember becoming suddenly aware **23** of how different everything had become. The kids were no longer playing Monopoly or Clue or the other games we used to play together. It was because we had a television set which had been turned on for a football game. All of that socializing that had gone on previously had ended. Now everyone was sitting in front of the television set, on a holiday, at a family party! I remember being stunned by how awful that was. Somehow the television had become more attractive."

As families have come to spend more and more of their time together **24** engaged in the single activity of television watching, those rituals and pastimes that once gave family life its special quality have become more and more uncommon. Not since prehistoric times, when cave families hunted, gathered, ate, and slept, with little time remaining to accumulate a culture of any significance, have families been reduced to such a sameness.

REAL PEOPLE

It is not only the activities that a family might engage in together that are **25** diminished by the powerful presence of television in the home. The relationships of the family members to each other are also affected, in both obvious and subtle ways. The hours that children spend in a one-way relationship with television people, an involvement that allows for no communication or interaction, surely affect their relationships with real-life people.

Studies show the importance of eye-to-eye contact, for instance, in real-life **26** relationships, and indicate that the nature of one's eye-contact patterns, whether one looks another squarely in the eye or looks to the side or shifts one's gaze from side to side, may play a significant role in one's success or failure in human relationships. But no eye contact is possible in the child-television relationship, although in certain children's programs people purport to speak directly to the child and the camera fosters this illusion by focuing directly upon the person being filmed. (Mister Rogers is an example, telling the child, "I like you, you're special," etc.). How might such a distortion of real-life relationships affect a child's development of trust, of openness, of an ability to relate well to other *real* people?

27   Bruno Bettelheim writes:

> Children who have been taught, or conditioned, to listen passively most of the day to the warm verbal communications coming from the TV screen, to the deep emotional appeal of the so-called TV personality, are often unable to respond to real persons because they arouse so much less feeling than the skilled actor. Worse, they lose the ability to learn from reality because life experiences are much more complicated than the ones they see on the screen. . . .*

28   A teacher makes a similar observation about her personal viewing experiences:

29   "I have trouble mobilizing myself and dealing with real people after watching a few hours of television. It's just hard to make that transition from watching television to a real relationship. I suppose it's because there was no effort necessary while I was watching, and dealing with real people always requires a bit of effort. Imagine, then, how much harder it might be to do the same thing for a small child, particularly one who watches a lot of television every day."

30   But more obviously damaging to family relationships is the elimination of opportunities to talk, and perhaps more important, to argue, to air grievances, between parents and children and brothers and sisters. Families frequently use television to avoid confronting their problems, problems that will not go away if they are ignored but will only fester and become less easily resolvable as time goes on.

31   A mother reports:

32   "I find myself, with three children, wanting to turn on the TV set when they're fighting. I really have to struggle not to do it because I feel that's telling them this is the solution to the quarrel—but it's so tempting that I often do it."

33   A family therapist discusses the use of television as an avoidance mechanism:

34   "In a family I know the father comes home from work and turns on the television set. The children come and watch with him and the wife serves them their meal in front of the set. He then goes and takes a shower, or works on the car or something. She then goes and has her own dinner in front of the television set. It's a symptom of a deeper-rooted problem, sure. But it would help them all to get rid of the set. It would be far easier to work on what the symptom really means without the television. The television simply encourages a double avoidance of each other. They'd find out more quickly what was going on if they weren't able to hide behind the TV. Things wouldn't necessarily be better, of course, but they wouldn't be anesthetized."

35   The decreased opportunities for simple conversation between parents and

---

*Bruno Bettelheim (1903–1991) was a world-renowned child psychologist and author of many books on the development of children's imaginations and identities. (Editor's note)

children in the television-centered home may help explain an observation made by an emergency room nurse at a Boston hospital. She reports that parents just seem to sit there these days when they come in with a sick or seriously injured child, although talking to the child would distract and comfort him. "They don't seem to know *how* to talk to their own children at any length," the nurse observes. Similarly, a television critic writes in the *New York Times:* "I had just a day ago taken my son to the emergency ward of a hospital for stitches above his left eye, and the occasion seemed no more real to me than Maalot or 54th Street, south-central Los Angeles. There was distance and numbness and an inability to turn off the total institution. I didn't behave at all; I just watched. . . . "

A number of research studies substantiate the assumption that television **36** interferes with family activities and the formation of family relationships. One survey shows that 78 percent of the respondents indicate no conversation taking place during viewing except at specified times such as commercials. The study notes: "The television atmosphere in most households is one of quiet absorption on the part of family members who are present. The nature of the family social life during a program could be described as 'parallel' rather than interactive, and the set does seem to dominate family life when it is on." Thirty-six percent of the respondents in another study indicated that television viewing was the only family activity participated in during the week.

In a summary of research findings on television's effect on family interac- **37** tions James Garbarino states: "The early findings suggest that television had a disruptive effect upon interaction and thus presumably human develop- ment. . . . It is not unreasonable to ask: 'Is the fact that the average American family during the 1950's came to include two parents, two children and a tele- vision set somehow related to the psychosocial characteristics of the young adults of the 1970's?' "

UNDERMINING THE FAMILY

In its effect on family relationships, in its facilitation of parental withdrawal **38** from an active role in the socialization of their children, and in its replacement of family rituals and special events, television has played an important role in the disintegration of the American family. But of course it has not been the only contributing factor, perhaps not even the most important one. The steadily rising divorce rate, the increase in the number of working mothers, the decline of the extended family, the breakdown of neighborhoods and communities, the growing isolation of the nuclear family—all have seriously affected the family.

As Urie Bronfenbrenner suggests, the sources of family breakdown do not **39** come from the family itself, but from the circumstances in which the family finds itself and the way of life imposed upon it by those circumstances. "When those circumstances and the way of life they generate undermine relationships of trust and emotional security between family members, when they make it difficult for parents to care for, educate and enjoy their children, when there is no support or recognition from the outside world for one's role as a parent and when time spent with one's family means frustration of career, personal fulfillment and peace of mind, then the development of the child is adversely affected," he writes.

40   But while the roots of alienation go deep into the fabric of American social history, television's presence in the home fertilizes them, encourages their wild and unchecked growth. Perhaps it is true that America's commitment to the television experience masks a spiritual vacuum, an empty and barren way of life, a desert of materialism. But it is television's dominant role in the family that anesthetizes the family into accepting its unhappy state and prevents it from struggling to better its condition, to improve its relationships, and to regain some of the richness it once possessed.

41   Others have noted the role of mass media in perpetuating an unsatisfactory *status quo.* Leisure-time activity, writes Irving Howe, "must provide relief from work monotony without making the return to work too unbearable; it must provide amusement without insight and pleasure without disturbance—as distinct from art which gives pleasure through disturbance. Mass culture is thus oriented towards a central aspect of industrial society: the depersonalization of the individual." Similarly, Jacques Ellul rejects the idea that television is a legitimate means of educating the citizen: "Education . . . takes place only incidentally. The clouding of his consciousness is paramount. . . . "

42   And so the American family muddles on, dimly aware that something is amiss but distracted from an understanding of its plight by an endless stream of television images. As family ties grow weaker and vaguer, as children's lives become more separate from their parents', as parents' educational role in their children's lives is taken over by television and schools, family life becomes increasingly more unsatisfying for both parents and children. All that seems to be left is love, an abstraction that family members *know* is necessary but find great difficulty giving each other because the traditional opportunities for expressing love within the family have been reduced or destroyed.

43   For contemporary parents, love toward each other has increasingly come to mean successful sexual relations, as witnessed by the proliferation of sex manuals and sex therapists. The opportunities for manifesting other forms of love through mutual support, understanding, nurturing, even, to use an unpopular word, *serving* each other, are less and less available as mothers and fathers seek their independent destinies outside the family.

44   As for love of children, this love is increasingly expressed through supplying material comforts, amusements, and educational opportunities. Parents show their love for their children by sending them to good schools and camps, by providing them with good food and good doctors, by buying them toys, books, games, and a television set of their very own. Parents will even go further and express their love by attending PTA meetings to improve their children's schools, or by joining groups that are acting to improve the quality of their children's television programs.

But this is love at a remove, and is rarely understood by children. The more   **45**
direct forms of parental love require time and patience, steady, dependable,
ungrudgingly given time actually spent *with* children, reading to them, comforting them, playing, joking, and working with them. But even if parents were
eager and willing to demonstrate that sort of direct love to their children today,
the opportunities are diminished. What with school and Little League and piano
lessons and, of course, the inevitable television programs, a day seems to offer
just enough time for a good-night kiss.

▼ TOPICAL CONSIDERATIONS

1. According to Winn, in what specific ways does television destroy "the special quality that distinguishes one family from another" (paragraph 9)? What family behavior is dangerously "prevented"?
2. How does television threaten family unity and closeness, according to the author?
3. What does Winn say about the quality of television programs?
4. In what specific ways does television affect children's play and creativity?
5. What evidence does Winn present to support her claim that TV has endangered family rituals?
6. How can television adversely affect the way people—including children—relate to one another?
7. In paragraph 41, Irving Howe is quoted as saying that the mass media, including television, "must provide amusement without insight and pleasure without disturbance." Do you think this is a fair assessment of the nature of network television? Do you think this is what the general American public wants? What it needs? What about public television? How would Howe assess PBS programs?

▼ RHETORICAL CONSIDERATIONS

1. In what ways is television a "plug-in drug"? Is this a fair metaphor?
2. Winn says that people today are so dominated by the television set "that they cannot see how the medium is involved in whatever problems they might be having" (paragraph 11). How well does she illustrate that claim?
3. What would you say Winn's attitude is toward the American television public? Cite some passages in her essay to support your statement.
4. In paragraph 44, Winn speaks of love of children, stating that its expression has been reduced to material display. Do you think she oversimplifies? Does she offer much evidence? Need she?

5. Evaluate the kind and amount of evidence Winn summons to support her thesis in the essay. Is some of it excessive? Is it lacking in other places?

▼ WRITING ASSIGNMENTS

1. Did television play a prominent role in your home? Did you and your family watch it regularly as you were growing up? If so, try to evaluate any negative effects television had on your family and your upbringing. Consider how it might have functioned as a babysitter for you and how it affected communication between family members, rituals, and creativity.
2. Winn calls television a "plug-in drug." The use of a drug often leads to some effort to shake the habit. Write a paper in which you explore the difficulties some people you know would have in adjusting to life without television. Consider the rigid patterns that might have evolved over the years with television.
3. Imagine what life might be like 20 years from now, given the rapid development and spread of cable television across America. Consider that television might someday have hundreds of channels broadcasting twenty-four hours a day. Consider also possible developments in interactive television where viewers can shop, order movies, or instantly be polled on political issues and candidates. Create a scenario of the total-television family of the future, extrapolating from some of Winn's observations.
4. In paragraph 13, Winn refers to the plight of a mother who tries to "control television" in her home. Write this woman a letter in which you suggest how she can creatively reorganize her family's day around activities other than television and still gets things accomplished.

▼ THE VIOLENCE IS FAKE, THE IMPACT IS REAL

Ellen Goodman

Perhaps the most common concern among critics of television is the effect of violence on children. Many studies by private institutions and by the government conclude that children do, in fact, learn aggressive behavior from what they see on the screen, despite the disclaimers of broadcasters. The issue Ellen Goodman raises here is what television violence fails to teach kids about the consequences of real violence. Ellen Goodman is a widely syndicated, Pulitzer Prize–winning columnist for the *Boston Globe*. Collections of her columns have been published in *At Large* (1983), *Keeping in Touch* (1985) and, *Making Sense* (1989). This article first appeared in 1977 in the *Boston Globe*.

1   I don't usually think of television executives as being modest, shy and retiring. But for a decade or two, the same souls who have bragged about their success in selling products have been positively humble about their success in selling messages.

2   Yes indeed, they would tell advertisers, children see, children do . . . do buy candy bars and cereals and toys. But no, no, they would tell parents, children see, but children don't . . . imitate mangling and mayhem.

3   But now the government has released another study on TV and violence. The predictable conclusion is that "violence on television does lead to aggressive behavior by children and teenagers who watch the programs." After analyzing 2500 studies and publications since 1970, the "overwhelming" scientific evidence is that "excessive" violence on the screen produces violence off the screen.

4   Somehow or other, I feel like I have been here before. By now, the protestations of the networks sound like those of the cigarette manufacturers who will deny the link between cigarettes and lung disease to their (and our) last breath. By now, studies come and go, but the problem remains.

5   Today the average kid sits in front of the tube for 26 hours a week. The kids don't begin with a love of violence. Even today, one runaway favorite in the Saturday morning line-up is about the benign "Smurfs." But eventually they learn from grown-ups.

6   In the incredible shrinking world of kidvid, there is no regularly scheduled program for kids on any of the three networks between the hours of 7 A.M. and 6 P.M. A full 80 percent of the programs kids watch are adult television. For those who choose adventures, the broadcaster offer endless sagas of terror, chase, murder, rescue.

7   As Peggy Charren, who has watched this scene for a long time as head of Action for Children's Television, puts it: "Broadcasters believe that the more

violent the problems, the more attractive the adventure to audiences in terms of sitting there and not turning it off. The ultimate adventure is doing away with someone's life. The ultimate excitement is death."

8   The government, in its report, listed some theories about why there is this link between violence on TV and violence in kids' behavior. One theory was that TV is a how-to lesson in aggression. Children learn "how to" hit and hurt from watching the way they learn how to count and read. Another theory is that kids who see a world full of violence accept it as normal behavior.

9   But I wonder whether violence isn't accepted because it is normalized—sanitized and packaged. We don't see violence on television in terms of pain and suffering, but in terms of excitement. In cartoons, characters are smashed with boulders, and dropped from airplanes only to get up unscathed. In adventure shows, people are killed all the time, but they are rarely "hurt."

10   As Charren put it, "There is no feeling badly about violence on television." We don't bear witness to the pain of a single gunshot wound. We don't see the broken hand and teeth that come from one blow to the jaw. We don't share the blood or the guilt, the anguish or the mourning. We don't see the labor of rebuilding a car, a window, a family.

11   Our television stars brush themselves off and return same time, same station, next week without a single bruise. Cars are replaced. The dead are carted off and forgotten.

12   In Japan, I am told there is an unwritten rule that if you show violence on television, you show the result of that violence. Such a program is, I am sure, much more disturbing. But maybe it should be. Maybe that's what's missing.

13   In the real world, people repress aggression because they know the consequences. But on television, there are no consequences. In the end kids may be less affected by the presence of violence than by the absence of pain. They learn that violence is okay. That nobody gets hurt.

14   So, if the broadcasters refuse to curb their profitable adventures in hurting, their national contribution to violence, then let them add something to the mix: equal time for truth and consequences.

▼ TOPICAL CONSIDERATIONS

1. What is Goodman's major criticism of television broadcasters? How are they like cigarette manufacturers?
2. What, according to the author, are some of the problems with network television for children?
3. What is Goodman's central complaint about the way violence is portrayed on television? Is it just that it is too graphic?
4. How does the Japanese treatment of television violence differ from the American treatment?
5. What suggestions does Ellen Goodman make about portrayal of violence on television? Would you make the same suggestions?

▼ RHETORICAL CONSIDERATIONS

1. Where is the thesis statement in this essay? Would you have placed it elsewhere? Explain your answer.
2. Explain Goodman's use of the word "sanitized" in describing television violence in paragraph 9. What does the word mean, and how good a choice is it?
3. What is the rhetorical effect of the parallel sentence structures in paragraph 10?
4. How does paragraph 12 fit Goodman's thesis?

▼ WRITING ASSIGNMENTS

1. Do you agree with Goodman's claim that pain and suffering are missing from television's treatment of violence? Using your own knowledge of television, write a paper in which you answer this question. You may want to watch a few shows in which violence and its consequences are dramatized.
2. Watch a typical Saturday morning cartoon show and make note of the way violence is handled. Then write a paper in which you analyze just how violence is depicted and how it might be interpreted by children. Does cartoon violence seem normal? Are people hurt? Are children left feeling that violence is okay? (You may first want to read Kathi Maio's essay "Hooked on Hate?" on page 358.)
3. Have you ever seen a television program or a made-for-TV movie in which both the "truth and consequences" of violence were fairly portrayed? If so, write a paper in which you defend the accuracy of the portrayal of the pain and suffering that follow violence.

▼ "NOW . . . THIS"

Neil Postman

Television is a visual medium whose fast-paced and dynamic images account for viewing pleasure. Consequently, discourse on television takes the form of entertainment. Simply put, the medium has little tolerance for argument, hypothesis, or explanation—it is all performance, Neil Postman says. And that includes broadcast news. In this essay he argues persuasively that the nightly news is a mindless entertainment package that creates the illusion of keeping the public informed. On the contrary, Postman says the news creates public ignorance by destroying critical faculties and the ability to process or evaluate all the information bits.

Neil Postman is a critic, writer, communication theorist, and professor of communication arts and sciences at New York University. He is editor of *Et cetera,* a journal of general semantics. His sixteen books include *Teaching as a Subversive Activity, The Soft Revolution, The Disappearance of Childhood,* and *Amusing Ourselves to Death* (1985) from which this essay comes.

1 The American humorist H. Allen Smith once suggested that of all the worrisome words in the English language, the scariest is "uh oh," as when a physician looks at your X rays and with knitted brow says, "Uh oh." I should like to suggest that the words which are the title of this chapter are as ominous as any, all the more so because they are spoken without knitted brow—indeed, with a kind of idiot's delight. The phrase, if that's what it may be called, adds to our grammar a new part of speech, a conjunction that does not connect anything to anything but does the opposite: separates everything from everything. As such, it serves as a compact metaphor for the discontinuities in so much that passes for public discourse in present-day America.

2 "Now . . . this" is commonly used on radio and television newscasts to indicate that what one has just heard or seen has no relevance to what one is about to hear or see, or possibly to anything one is ever likely to hear or see. The phrase is a means of acknowledging the fact that the world as mapped by the speeded-up electronic media has no order or meaning and is not to be taken seriously. There is no murder so brutal, no earthquake so devastating, no political blunder so costly—for that matter, no ball score so tantalizing or weather report so threatening—that it cannot be erased from our minds by a newscaster saying, "Now . . . this." The newscaster means that you have thought long enough on the previous matter (approximately forty-five seconds), that you must not be morbidly preoccupied with it (let us say, for ninety seconds), and that you must now give your attention to another fragment of news or a commercial.

3 Television did not invent the "Now . . . this" world view. . . . It is the

offspring of the intercourse between telegraphy and photography. But it is through television that it has been nurtured and brought to a perverse maturity. For on television, nearly every half hour is a discrete event, separated in content, context, and emotional texture from what precedes and follows it. In part because television sells its time in seconds and minutes, in part because television must use images rather than words, in part because its audience can move freely to and from the television set, programs are structured so that almost each eight-minute segment may stand as a complete event in itself. Viewers are rarely required to carry over any thought or feeling from one parcel of time to another.

Of course, in television's presentation of the "news of the day," we may see 4 the "Now . . . this" mode of discourse in its boldest and most embarrassing form. For there, we are presented not only with fragmented news but news without context, without consequences, without value, and therefore without essential seriousness; that is to say, news as pure entertainment.

Consider, for example, how you would proceed if you were given the 5 opportunity to produce a television news show for any station concerned to attract the largest possible audience. You would, first, choose a cast of players, each of whom has a face that is both "likable" and "credible." Those who apply would, in fact, submit to you their eight-by-ten glossies, from which you would eliminate those whose countenances are not suitable for nightly display. This means that you will exclude women who are not beautiful or who are over the age of fifty, men who are bald, all people who are overweight or whose noses are too long or whose eyes are too close together. You will try, in other words, to assemble a cast of talking hairdo's. At the very least, you will want those whose faces would not be unwelcome on a magazine cover.

Christine Craft has just such a face, and so she applied for a co-anchor 6 position on KMBC-TV in Kansas City. According to a lawyer who represented her in a sexism suit she later brought against the station, the management of KMBC-TV "loved Christine's look." She was accordingly hired in January 1981. She was fired in August 1981 because research indicated that her appearance "hampered viewer acceptance." What exactly does "hampered viewer acceptance" mean? And what does it have to do with the news? Hampered viewer acceptance means the same thing for television news as it does for any television show: Viewers do not like looking at the performer. It also means that viewers do not believe the performer, that she lacks credibility. In the case of a theatrical performance, we have a sense of what that implies: The actor does not persuade the audience that he or she is the character being portrayed. But what does lack of credibility imply in the case of a news show? What character is a co-anchor playing? And how do we decide that the performance lacks verisimilitude? Does the audience believe that the newscaster is lying, that what is reported did not in fact happen, that something important is being concealed?

It is frightening to think that this may be so, that the perception of the truth 7 of a report rests heavily on the acceptability of the newscaster. In the ancient world, there was a tradition of banishing or killing the bearer of bad tidings. Does the television news show restore, in a curious form, this tradition? Do we banish those who tell us the news when we do not care for the face of the teller? Does television countermand the warnings we once received about the fallacy of the ad hominem argument?

8   If the answer to any of these questions is even a qualified "Yes," then here is an issue worthy of the attention of epistemologists. Stated in its simplest form, it is that television provides a new (or, possibly restores an old) definition of truth: The credibility of the teller is the ultimate test of the truth of a proposition. "Credibility" here does not refer to the past record of the teller for making statements that have survived the rigors of reality testing. It refers only to the impression of sincerity, authenticity, vulnerability or attractiveness (choose one or more) conveyed by the actor/reporter.

9   This is a matter of considerable importance, for it goes beyond the question of how truth is perceived on television news shows. If on television, credibility replaces reality as the decisive test of truth-telling, political leaders need not trouble themselves very much with reality provided that their performances consistently generate a sense of verisimilitude. I suspect, for example, that the dishonor that now shrouds Richard Nixon results not from the fact that he lied but that on television he looks like a liar. Which, if true, should bring no comfort to anyone, not even veteran Nixon-haters. For the alternative possibilities are that one may look like a liar but be telling the truth; or even worse, look like a truth-teller but in fact be lying.

10   As a producer of a television news show, you would be well aware of these matters and would be careful to choose your cast on the basis of criteria used by David Merrick and other successful impresarios. Like them, you would then turn your attention to staging the show on principles that maximize entertainment value. You would, for example, select a musical theme for the show. All television news programs begin, end, and are somewhere in between punctuated with music. I have found very few Americans who regard this custom as peculiar, which fact I have taken as evidence for the dissolution of lines of demarcation between serious public discourse and entertainment. What has music to do with the news? Why is it there? It is there, I assume, for the same reason music is used in the theater and films—to create a mood and provide a leitmotif for the entertainment. If there were no music—as is the case when any television program is interrupted for a news flash—viewers would expect something truly alarming, possibly life-altering. But as long as the music is there as a frame for the program, the viewer is comforted to believe that there is nothing to be greatly alarmed about; that, in fact, the events that are reported have as much relation to reality as do scenes in a play.

11   This perception of a news show as a stylized dramatic performance whose content has been staged largely to entertain is reinforced by several other features, including the fact that the average length of any story is forty-five seconds. While brevity does not always suggest triviality, in this case it clearly does. It is simply not possible to convey a sense of seriousness about any event if its implications are exhausted in less than one minute's time. In fact, it is quite obvious that TV news has no intention of suggesting that any story *has* any

implications, for that would require viewers to continue to think about it when it is done and therefore obstruct their attending to the next story that waits panting in the wings. In any case, viewers are not provided with much opportunity to be distracted from the next story since in all likelihood it will consist of some film footage. Pictures have little difficulty in overwhelming words and short-circuiting introspection. As a television producer, you would be certain to give both prominence and precedence to any event for which there is some sort of visual documentation. A suspected killer being brought into a police station, the angry face of a cheated consumer, a barrel going over Niagara Falls (with a person alleged to be in it), the President disembarking from a helicopter on the White House lawn—these are always fascinating or amusing and easily satisfy the requirements of an entertaining show. It is, of course, not necessary that the visuals actually document the point of a story. Neither is it necessary to explain why such images are intruding themselves on public consciousness. Film footage justifies itself, as every television producer well knows.

It is also of considerable help in maintaining a high level of unreality that 12 the newscasters do not pause to grimace or shiver when they speak their prefaces or epilogs to the film clips. Indeed, many newscasters do not appear to grasp the meaning of what they are saying, and some hold to a fixed and ingratiating enthusiasm as they report on earthquakes, mass killings and other disasters. Viewers would be quite disconcerted by any show of concern or terror on the part of newscasters. Viewers, after all, are partners with the newscasters in the "Now . . . this" culture, and they expect the newscaster to play out his or her role as a character who is marginally serious but who stays well clear of authentic understanding. The viewers, for their part, will not be caught contaminating their responses with a sense of reality, any more than an audience at a play would go scurrying to call home because a character on stage has said that a murderer is loose in the neighborhood.

The viewers also know that no matter how grave any fragment of news may 13 appear (for example, on the day I write a Marine Corps general has declared that nuclear war between the United States and Russia is inevitable), it will shortly be followed by a series of commercials that will, in an instant, defuse the import of the news, in fact render it largely banal. This is a key element in the structure of a news program and all by itself refutes any claim that television news is designed as a serious form of public discourse. Imagine what you would think of me, and this book, if I were to pause here, tell you that I will return to my discussion in a moment, and then proceed to write a few words in behalf of United Airlines or the Chase Manhattan Bank. You would rightly think that I had no respect for you and, certainly, no respect for the subject. And if I did this not once but several times in each chapter, you would think the whole enterprise unworthy of your attention. Why, then, do we not think a news show similarly unworthy? The reason, I believe, is that whereas we expect books and even other media (such as film) to maintain a consistency of tone and a continuity of content, we have no such expectation of television, and especially television news. We have become so accustomed to its discontinuities that we are no longer struck dumb, as any sane person would be, by a newscaster who having just reported that a nuclear war is inevitable goes on to say that he will be right back after this word from Burger King; who says, in other words, "Now . . . this." One can hardly overestimate the damage that such juxtapositions do to our sense of the world as a serious place. The damage is especially massive to youthful viewers who depend so much on television for their clues as to how to respond to the world. In watching television news, they, more than any other segment of the audience, are drawn into an epistemology based on the assumption that all reports of cruelty and death are greatly exaggerated and, in any case, not to be taken seriously or responded to sanely.

14 I should go so far as to say that embedded in the surrealistic frame of a television news show is a theory of anticommunication, featuring a type of discourse that abandons logic, reason, sequence and rules of contradiction. In aesthetics, I believe the name given to this theory is Dadaism; in philosophy, nihilism; in psychiatry, schizophrenia. In the parlance of the theater, it is known as vaudeville.

15 For those who think I am here guilty of hyperbole, I offer the following description of television news by Robert MacNeil, executive editor and co-anchor of the "MacNeil-Lehrer Newshour." The idea, he writes, "is to keep everything brief, not to strain the attention of anyone but instead to provide constant stimulation through variety, novelty, action, and movement. You are required . . . to pay attention to no concept, no character, and no problem for more than a few seconds at a time." He goes on to say that the assumptions controlling a news show are "that bite-sized is best, that complexity must be avoided, that nuances are dispensable, that qualifications impede the simple message, that visual stimulation is a substitute for thought, and that verbal precision is an anachronism."

16 Robert MacNeil has more reason than most to give testimony about the television news show as vaudeville act. The "MacNeil-Lehrer Newshour" is an unusual and gracious attempt to bring to television some of the elements of typographic discourse. The program abjures visual stimulation, consists largely of extended explanations of events and in-depth interviews (which even there means only five to ten minutes), limits the number of stories covered, and emphasizes background and coherence. But television has exacted its price for MacNeil's rejection of a show business format. By television's standards, the audience is minuscule, the program is confined to public-television stations, and it is a good guess that the combined salary of MacNeil and Lehrer is one-fifth of Dan Rather's or Tom Brokaw's.

17 If you were a producer of a television news show for a commercial station, you would not have the option of defying television's requirements. It would be demanded of you that you strive for the largest possible audience, and, as a consequence and in spite of your best intentions, you would arrive at a production very nearly resembling MacNeil's description. Moreover, you would include some things MacNeil does not mention. You would try to make celebrities of your newscasters. You would advertise the show, both in the press and on

television itself. You would do "news briefs," to serve as an inducement to viewers. You would have a weatherman as comic relief, and a sportscaster whose language is a touch uncouth (as a way of his relating to the beer-drinking common man). You would, in short, package the whole event as any producer might who is in the entertainment business.

The result of all this is that Americans are the best entertained and quite   **18**
likely the least well-informed people in the Western world. I say this in the face of the popular conceit that television, as a window to the world, has made Americans exceedingly well informed. Much depends here, of course, on what is meant by being informed. I will pass over the now tiresome polls that tell us that, at any given moment, 70 percent of our citizens do not know who is the Secretary of State or the Chief Justice of the Supreme Court. Let us consider, instead, the case of Iran during the drama that was called the "Iranian Hostage Crisis." I don't suppose there has been a story in years that received more continuous attention from television. We may assume, then, the Americans know most of what there is to know about this unhappy event. And now, I put these questions to you: Would it be an exaggeration to say that not one American in a hundred knows what language the Iranians speak? Or what the word "Ayatollah" means or implies? Or knows any details of the tenets of Iranian religious beliefs? Or the main outlines of their political history? Or knows who the Shah was, and where he came from?

Nonetheless, everyone had an opinion about this event, for in America   **19**
everyone is entitled to an opinion, and it is certainly useful to have a few when a pollster shows up. But these are opinions of a quite different order from eighteenth- or nineteenth-century opinions. It is probably more accurate to call them emotions rather than opinions, which would account for the fact that they change from week to week, as the pollsters tell us. What is happening here is that television is altering the meaning of "being informed" by creating a species of information that might properly be called *disinformation.* I am using this word almost in the precise sense in which it is used by spies in the CIA or KGB. Disinformation does not mean false information. It means misleading information—misplaced, irrelevant, fragmented or superficial information—information that creates the illusion of knowing something but which in fact leads one away from knowing. In saying this, I do not mean to imply that television news deliberately aims to deprive Americans of a coherent, contextual understanding of their world. I mean to say that when news is packaged as entertainment, that is the inevitable result. And in saying that the television news show entertains but does not inform, I am saying something far more serious than that we are being deprived of authentic information. I am saying we are losing our sense of what it means to be well informed. Ignorance is always correctable. But what shall we do if we take ignorance to be knowledge?

Here is a startling example of how this process bedevils us. A *New York*   **20**
Times article is headlined on February 15, 1983:

REAGAN MISSTATEMENTS GETTING LESS ATTENTION

The article begins in the following way:

> President Reagan's aides used to become visibly alarmed at suggestions that he had given mangled and perhaps misleading accounts of his policies or of current events in general. That doesn't seem to happen much anymore.
>
> Indeed, the President continues to make debatable assertions of fact but news accounts do not deal with them as extensively as they once did. In the view of White House officials, the declining news coverage mirrors a *decline in interest by the general public.* (my italics)

21   This report is not so much a news story as a story about the news, and our recent history suggests that it is not about Ronald Reagan's charm. It is about how news is defined, and I believe the story would be quite astonishing to both civil libertarians and tyrants of an earlier time. Walter Lippmann, for example, wrote in 1920: "There can be no liberty for a community which lacks the means by which to detect lies." For all of his pessimism about the possibilities of restoring an eighteenth- and nineteenth-century level of public discourse, Lippmann assumed, as did Thomas Jefferson before him, that with a well-trained press functioning as a lie-detector, the public's interest in a President's mangling of the truth would be piqued, in both senses of that word. Given the means to detect lies, he believed, the public could not be indifferent to their consequences.

22   But this case refutes his assumption. The reporters who cover the White House are ready and able to expose lies, and thus create the grounds for informed and indignant opinion. But apparently the public declines to take an interest. To press reports of White House dissembling, the public has replied with Queen Victoria's famous line: "We are not amused." However, here the words mean something the Queen did not have in mind. They mean that what is not amusing does not compel their attention. Perhaps if the President's lies could be demonstrated by pictures and accompanied by music the public would raise a curious eyebrow. If a movie, like *All the President's Men,* could be made from his misleading accounts of government policy, if there were a break-in of some sort or sinister characters laundering money, attention would quite likely be paid. We do well to remember that President Nixon did not begin to come undone until his lies were given a theatrical setting at the Watergate hearings. But we do not have anything like that here. Apparently, all President Reagan does is *say* things that are not entirely true. And there is nothing entertaining in that. . . .

23   My point is that we are by now so thoroughly adjusted to the "Now . . . this" world of news—a world of fragments, where events stand alone, stripped of any connection to the past, or to the future, or to other events—that all assumptions of coherence have vanished. And so, perforce, has contradiction. In the context of *no context,* so to speak, it simply disappears. And in its absence, what possible interest could there be in a list of what the President says *now* and what he said *then*? It is merely a rehash of old news, and there is nothing interesting or entertaining in that. The only thing to be amused about is the

bafflement of reporters at the public's indifference. There is an irony in the fact that the very group that has taken the world apart should, on trying to piece it together again, be surprised that no one notices much, or cares.

For all his perspicacity, George Orwell would have been stymied by this situation; there is nothing "Orwellian" about it. The President does not have the press under his thumb. *The New York Times* and *The Washington Post* are not *Pravda;* the Associated Press is not Tass. And there is no Newspeak here. Lies have not been defined as truth nor truth as lies. All that has happened is that the public has adjusted to incoherence and been amused into indifference. Which is why Aldous Huxley would not in the least be surprised by the story. Indeed, he prophesied its coming. He believed that it is far more likely that the Western democracies will dance and dream themselves into oblivion than march into it, single file and manacled. Huxley grasped, as Orwell did not, that it is not necessary to conceal anything from a public insensible to contradiction and narcoticized by technological diversions. Although Huxley did not specify that television would be our main line to the drug, he would have no difficulty accepting Robert MacNeil's observation that "Television is the *soma* of Aldous Huxley's *Brave New World.*" Big Brother turns out to be Howdy Doody. **24**

I do not mean that the trivialization of public information is all accomplished *on* television. I mean that television is the paradigm for our conception of public information. As the printing press did in an earlier time, television has achieved the power to define the form in which news must come, and it has also defined how we shall respond to it. In presenting news to us packaged as vaudeville, television induces other media to do the same, so that the total information environment begins to mirror television. **25**

For example, America's newest and highly successful national newspaper, *USA Today,* is modeled precisely on the format of television. It is sold on the street in receptacles that look like television sets. Its stories are uncommonly short, its design leans heavily on pictures, charts and other graphics, some of them printed in various colors. Its weather maps are a visual delight; its sports section includes enough pointless statistics to distract a computer. As a consequence, *USA Today,* which began publication in September 1982, has become the third largest daily in the United States (as of July 1984, according to the Audit Bureau of Circulations), moving quickly to overtake the *Daily News* and the *Wall Street Journal.* Journalists of a more traditional bent have criticized it for its superficiality and theatrics, but the paper's editors remain steadfast in their disregard of typographic standards. The paper's Editor-in-Chief, John Quinn, has said: "We are not up to undertaking projects of the dimensions needed to win prizes. They don't give awards for the best investigative paragraph." Here is an astonishing tribute to the resonance of television's epistemology: In the age of television, the paragraph is becoming the basic unit of news in print media. Moreover, Mr. Quinn need not fret too long about being deprived of awards. As other newspapers join in the transformation, the time cannot be far off when awards will be given for the best investigative sentence. **26**

It needs also to be noted here that new and successful magazines such as **27**

People and *Us* are not only examples of television-oriented print media but have had an extraordinary 'ricochet" effect on television itself. Whereas television taught the magazines that news is nothing but entertainment, the magazines have taught television that nothing but entertainment is news. Television programs, such as "Entertainment Tonight," turn information about entertainers and celebrities into "serious" cultural content, so that the circle begins to close: Both the form and content of news become entertainment.

28   Radio, of course, is the least likely medium to join in the descent into Huxleyan world of technological narcotics. It is, after all, particularly well suited to the transmission of rational, complex language. Nonetheless, and even if we disregard radio's captivation by the music industry, we appear to be left with the chilling fact that such language as radio allows us to hear is increasingly primitive, fragmented, and largely aimed at invoking visceral response; which is to say, it is the linguistic analogue to the ubiquitous rock music that is radio's principal source of income. As I write, the trend in call-in shows is for the "host" to insult callers whose language does not, in itself, go much beyond humanoid grunting. Such programs have little content, as this word used to be defined, and are merely of archeological interest in that they give us a sense of what a dialogue among Neanderthals might have been like. More to the point, the language of radio newscasts has become, under the influence of television, increasingly decontextualized and discontinuous, so that the possibility of anyone's knowing about the world, as against merely knowing *of* it, is effectively blocked. In New York City, radio station WINS entreats its listeners to "Give us twenty-two minutes and we'll give you the world." This is said without irony, and its audience, we may assume, does not regard the slogan as the conception of a disordered mind.

29   And so, we move rapidly into an information environment which may rightly be called trivial pursuit. As the game of that name uses facts as a source of amusement, so do our sources of news. It has been demonstrated many times that a culture can survive misinformation and false opinion. It has not yet been demonstrated whether a culture can survive if it takes the measure of the world in twenty-two minutes. Or if the value of its news is determined by the number of laughs it provides.

▼ TOPICAL CONSIDERATIONS

1. In your own words briefly summarize Postman's argument in this essay.
2. Why does the author find so "ominous" the two words that make up the title of this piece?
3. Has this reading changed your thinking? Has it affected your perception of broadcast news? If so, explain how. If not, why not?
4. Postman speaks of broadcast news as "pure entertainment." In what different ways is the news made to be entertaining? Do you agree with this claim?

5. How might "viewer credibility" replace "reality as the decisive test of truth-telling"? What dangers does Postman see in this? Do you share his concern?

6. Do you take for granted the "musical theme" of your favorite news show? Could you readily distinguish it from other networks' news themes? Do you like one over the others? If so, what are the reasons? Have you even wondered what music has to do with the news? Would you watch a news show if it had no music? Do you agree with the author's explanation of why news shows have musical themes?

7. "Viewers would be quite disconcerted by any show of concern or terror on the part of newscasters," says the author (paragraph 12). What does he mean by this? Do you agree with his explanation? Have you ever seen a newscaster do anything to violate the neutral approach to a story—for instance, "pause to grimace or shiver" or shake a head?

8. How does the "Now . . . this" structure of news programs reduce their seriousness according to Postman? Do you agree with this assessment? Do you agree with his claims of the damage done to young viewers? Would you restructure news shows if you could? Why or why not?

9. Do you agree or disagree that television "is altering the meaning of 'being informed' " (paragraph 19)? Can you give examples of your own?

10. How has television affected the format of other media? What other examples can you come up with? Going the other way, how has television adopted magazine formats? What other examples can you come up with? Do Postman's observations here jive with your own? Explain how they do or do not.

▼ RHETORICAL CONSIDERATIONS

1. Consider Postman's voice in this article. What sense do you get of him as an individual? Is he someone you'd like to spend some time with? Why or why not? Point to some details in the writing to support your answers.

2. Postman's vocabulary in places is quite sophisticated. Did any of the terms get in the way of your reading? Did you have to look up many? Which ones? What does the level of language here say about the intended audience for the essay?

3. In paragraph 10 Postman invites the reader to pretend he or she is a producer of a TV news show. In fact, he addresses the reader directly as "you." Trace how far this device is used in the essay. Why do you suppose he makes use of the second-person point of view? How effective is this strategy?

4. Explain the references to George Orwell and Aldous Huxley in paragraph 24. How are they used to support Postman's arguments? How effective are these references?
5. Writers at times have difficulty integrating outside sources into their discussion. Choose a paragraph in which Postman cites outside sources. Just how successfully does he incorporate these into the paragraph?

▼ WRITING ASSIGNMENTS

1. In paragraph 19 Postman says that we Americans are "losing our sense of what it means to be well informed." Do you agree with this statement, or do you think that Postman is overstating the issue? Gather some evidence of your own and write an essay in which you present your own views on whether we are well informed by the media. You might consider, for instance, the TV coverage of the war with Iraq.
2. Although Postman does not include slogans as one of the features in the entertainment package of broadcast news, some shows make use of them. Consider the slogan for CNN's headline news: "Around the world in thirty minutes." How does this promo line capture Postman's contention that "television is altering the meaning of 'being informed' "? Write out your views in a paper using supporting details.
3. Postman cites the "MacNeil-Lehrer Newshour" as a superior news program. Over the next few evenings tune in to that program and try to evaluate what makes it so different from network news shows. Consider the proportion of visual presentation to verbal, the level of language, the quality and depth of the coverage, the number and kinds of stories covered, the format and the newscasters. How many "entertainment" features do you find? If you were not familiar with the program, would you now consider being a steady viewer? Why or why not?
4. Postman complains in paragraph 28 that the language of radio talk shows has declined to an "increasingly primitive, fragmented" level "aimed at invoking visceral response." Listen to some local talk shows. Does the language you hear warrant such complaints? In a paper write up your findings.

▼ DON'T BLAME TV

Jeff Greenfield

Television has been indicted for nearly all our social ills—the rise in crime, increased divorce rate, lower voter turnout, falling SAT scores, the rise in sexual promiscuity, the collapse of family life. Indeed, television has been cited as the cause of the decline of Western Civilization. Now a word from the defense: Jeff Greenfield, a correspondent for ABC's "Nightline" and "Evening News" and a syndicated columnist. What follows is some criticism of the critics of television—or, more exactly, an attack on their knee-jerk assumptions that every American social and political ill can be blamed on television. This article first appeared in *TV Guide* in January 1986.

1 One of the enduring pieces of folk wisdom was uttered by the 19th-century humorist Artemus Ward, who warned his readers: "It ain't what you don't know that hurts you; it's what you know that just ain't so."

2 There's good advice in that warning to some of television's most vociferous critics, who are certain that every significant change in American social and political life can be traced, more or less directly, to the pervasive influence of TV.

3 It has been blamed for the decline of scores on scholastic achievement tests, for the rise in crime, for the decline in voter turnout, for the growth of premarital and extramarital sex, for the supposed collapse of family life and the increase in the divorce rate.

4 This is an understandable attitude. For one thing, television is the most visible, ubiquitous device to have entered our lives in the last 40 years. It is a medium in almost every American home, it is on in the average household some seven hours a day, and it is accessible by every kind of citizen from the most desperate of the poor to the wealthiest and most powerful among us.

5 If so pervasive a medium has come into our society in the last four decades, and if our society has changed in drastic ways in that same time, why not assume that TV is the reason why American life looks so different?

6 Well, as any philosopher can tell you, one good reason for skepticism is that you can't make assumptions about causes. They even have an impressive Latin phrase for that fallacy: *post hoc, ergo propter hoc.* For instance, if I do a rain dance at 5 P.M. and it rains at 6 P.M., did my dance bring down the rains? Probably not. But it's that kind of thinking, in my view, that characterizes much of the argument about how television influences our values.

7 It's perfectly clear, of course, that TV *does* influence some kinds of behavior. For example, back in 1954, *Disneyland* launched a series of episodes on the life of Davy Crockett, the legendary Tennessee frontiersman. A song based on that series swept the hit parade, and by that summer every kid in America was wearing a coonskin cap.

8   The same phenomenon has happened whenever a character on a prime-time television show suddenly strikes a chord in the country. Countless women tried to capture the Farrah Fawcett look a decade ago when *Charlie's Angels* first took flight. Schoolyards from Maine to California picked up—instantly, it seemed—on such catch phrases as "Up your nose with a rubber hose!" (*Welcome Back, Kotter*), "Kiss my grits!" (*Alice*) and "Nanu-nanu!" (*Mork & Mindy*). Today, every singles bar in the land is packed with young men in expensive white sports jackets and T-shirts, trying to emulate the macho looks of *Miami Vice's* Don Johnson.

9   These fads clearly show television's ability to influence matters that do not matter very much. Yet, when we turn to genuinely important things, television's impact becomes a lot less clear.

10   Take, for example, the decline in academic excellence, measured by the steady decline in Scholastic Aptitude Test scores from 1964 to 1982. It seemed perfectly logical to assume that a younger generation spending hours in front of the TV set every day with Fred Flintstone and Batman must have been suffering from brain atrophy. Yet, as writer David Owen noted in a recent book on educational testing, other equally impassioned explanations for the drop in scores included nuclear fallout, junk food, cigarette smoking by pregnant women, cold weather, declining church attendance, the draft, the assassination of President Kennedy and fluoridated water.

11   More significant, SAT scores stopped declining in 1982; they have been rising since then. Is TV use declining in the typical American home? On the contrary, it is increasing. If we really believed that our societal values are determined by new media, we might conclude that the birth of MTV in 1981 somehow caused the test scores to rise.

12   Or consider the frequently heard charge that the increase in TV violence is somehow responsible for the surge in crime. In fact, the crime rate nationally has been dropping for three straight years. It would be ludicrous to "credit" television for this; explanations are more likely to be found in the shift of population away from a "youth bulge" (where more crimes are committed) and improved tracking of career criminals in many big cities.

13   But why, then, ignore the demographic factors that saw in America an enormous jump in teen-agers and young adults in the 1960s and 1970s? Why *assume* that television, with its inevitable "crime-does-not-pay" morality, somehow turned our young into hoodlums? The same kind of problem bedevils those who argue that TV has triggered a wave of sexually permissive behavior. In the first place, television was the most sexually conservative of all media through the first quarter-century of its existence. While Playboy began making a clean breast of things in the mid-1950s, when book censorship was all but abolished in the "Lady Chatterly's Lover" decision of 1958, when movies began showing it all in the 1960s, television remained an oasis—or desert—of twin beds, flannel nightgowns and squeaky-clean dialogue and characters.

14   In fact, as late as 1970, CBS refused to let Mary Tyler Moore's Mary Richards character be a divorcee. The audience, they argued, would never accept it. Instead, she was presented as the survivor of a broken relationship.

Why, then, do we see so many broken families and divorces on television **15** today? Because the networks are trying to denigrate the value of the nuclear family? Hardly. As *The Cosby Show* and its imitators show, network TV is only too happy to offer a benign view of loving husbands, wives and children.

The explanation, instead, lies in what was happening to the very fabric of **16** American life. In 1950, at the dawn of television, the divorce rate was 2.6 per 1000 Americans. By 1983, it had jumped to five per thousand; nearly half of all marriages were ending in divorce. The reasons range from the increasing mobility of the population to the undermining of settled patterns of work, family, and neighborhood.

What's important to notice, however, is that it was not television that made **17** divorce more acceptable in American society; it was changes in American society that made divorce more acceptable on television. (Which is why, in her new sitcom, Mary Tyler Moore can finally play a divorced woman.) In the mid 1980s, divorce has simply lost the power to shock.

That same argument, I think, undermines much of the fear that television **18** has caused our young to become sexually precocious. From my increasingly dimming memory of youthful lust, I have my doubts about whether young lovers really need the impetus of *Dallas* or *The Young and the Restless* to start thinking about sex. The more serious answer, however, is that the spread of readily available birth control was a lot more persuasive a force in encouraging premarital sex than the words and images on TV.

We can measure this relative impotence of television in a different way. All **19** through the 1950s and early 1960s, the images of women on TV were what feminists would call "negative"; they were portrayed as half-woman, half-child, incapable of holding a job or balancing a checkbook or even running a social evening. (How many times did Lucy burn the roast?) Yet the generation of women who grew up on television was the first to reject forcefully the wife-and-home-maker limitations that such images ought to have encouraged. These were the women who marched into law schools, medical schools and the halls of Congress.

The same was true of the images of black Americans, as TV borrowed the **20** movie stereotypes of shiftless handymen and relentlessly cheerful maids. We didn't begin to see TV blacks as the equal of whites until Bill Cosby showed up in *I Spy* in 1966. Did the generation weaned on such fare turn out to be indifferent to the cause of black freedom in America? Hardly. This was the generation that organized and supported the civil-rights sit-ins and freedom rides in the South. Somehow, the reality of second-class citizenship was far more powerful than the imagery of dozens of television shows.

I have no argument with the idea that television contains many messages **21** that need close attention; I hold no brief for shows that pander to the appetite for violence or smarmy sexuality or stereotyping. My point is that these evils ought to be fought on grounds of taste and common decency. We ought not to try and prove more than the facts will bear. Television, powerful as it is, has shown precious little power over the most fundamental values of Americans. Given most of what's on TV, that's probably a good thing. But it also suggests that the cries of alarm may be misplaced.

▼ TOPICAL CONSIDERATIONS

1. What are some of the social ills television has been blamed for, according to the author? Why?
2. What does Greenfield say is wrong with the thinking of those critical of television?
3. How does Greenfield counter the argument that television was the main cause of the decline in SAT scores from 1964 to 1982?
4. How does Greenfield answer the charges that television violence is responsible for the rise in crime rates?
5. How does Greenfield seek to refute the claim that television is to blame for the rise in sexual promiscuity?
6. How does Greenfield answer the charge that television is responsible for the increased divorce rate?
7. According to Greenfield, how has television affected the image of women and black Americans?

▼ RHETORICAL CONSIDERATIONS

1. How well does the Artemus Ward quotation in the opening paragraph establish Greenfield's line of argument?
2. Which of Greenfield's arguments seems the strongest and most convincing? Which seems the weakest and least convincing?
3. Paragraph 13 consists of two rhetorical questions. How effective are these questions in making Greenfield's point? Would straight statements have been more effective, given his argument?

▼ WRITING ASSIGNMENTS

1. Do you agree with Greenfield that television gets too much of the blame for our social problems? Using your own knowledge of television, write a paper in which you answer this question.
2. Do you disagree with any of Greenfield's views here? In other words, do you feel that television contributes to social problems such as violence, sexual promiscuity, the divorce rate, and the collapse of family life? Write a paper in which you explain your feelings.
3. At the end of his essay, Greenfield admits that "television contains many messages that need close attention"—messages that "pander to the appetite for violence or smarmy sexuality or stereotyping." What problems of "taste and common decency" do you find with television? Specify by singling out certain shows.

▼ WHY I QUIT WATCHING TELEVISION

P. J. O'Rourke

"Well, I was nuzzling her ear, making little kissy noises . . . Then, all of a sudden, I experienced one of those devastating realizations: She was watching a *Star Trek* rerun over my shoulder." So laments P. J. O'Rourke, recalling when he decided that he had had it with television. Television was dumb. It was a waste of time. It kept him from more worthwhile activities. But as the author discovered in this humorous little essay, the lack of a television has severe aftereffects. P. J. O'Rourke was the editor of the *National Lampoon* during the late 1970s. His work has since appeared in a variety of magazines. Currently, he is "investigative humorist" for *Rolling Stone*. Collections of his essays include *Republican Party Reptile* (1987) and *Parliament of Whores* (1991). This article first appeared in *Parade* magazine in December 1985.

I remember the exact moment I quit watching television. It was 10 years ago. I had a girlfriend who was a compulsive viewer. We were at her apartment on a Sunday afternoon, sitting on the couch, and I was . . . Well, I was nuzzling her ear, making little kissy noises, and generally acting like a boyfriend. Then, all of a sudden, I experienced one of those devastating realizations: She was watching a *Star Trek* rerun over my shoulder.

We had a big fight. I'm still wondering where our relationship went wrong. She's still wondering if Captain Kirk got beamed up in time to escape from the Klingons.

I was tired of watching television anyway. TV was too dumb. And TV was too much trouble. Not too much trouble to watch, of course, but there was too much trouble on the screen. Every show seemed to be about murder, theft, car chases or adultery. I was living in Manhattan at the time, and if I wanted to see those things, I could look out my window. Even comedy shows like *M*A*S*H* were about people getting blown apart. I figured there was enough real tragedy every day. Why get four more hours of it on TV every night? I gave my television set away.

TV is such a waste of time, I thought. I never considered how else I'd fill my evenings and weekends. It turns out there are worse things to do with time than waste it; more expensive things, anyway.

In my newfound leisure hours, I fixed up my apartment. This cost $12,000—$600 for the do-it-yourself remodeling and $11,400 for the carpenters, painters and plasterers to repair the damage I'd done. I also took up downhill skiing and paid $1500 for equipment when I probably could have gotten somebody to break my leg for free. And I began to read. This sounds worthwhile, but anyone who worries about the lewdness and mayhem on TV ought to peek into *The Satyricon* by Petronius or *Gargantua and Pantagruel* by Rabelais or some Shakespeare plays or even the Old Testament. Most of my reading, though, wasn't quite so brainy. I read paperbacks like *Murder for Brunch.* It's hard to call these more intellectual than *The Gong Show.*

6   Without a TV set (and with a new girlfriend), I had time for conversation. But a lot of conversations, if they go on long enough, turn into arguments. What's dumber—watching *Family Feud* or arguing about whether to get a TV so we *could* watch *Family Feud?*

7   Not having a TV is supposed to bring families closer together. I didn't have a family, so this didn't help me.

8   Not having a TV turns out to be more strange than virtuous. I don't see any trend-setting shows like *Miami Vice,* so I don't know what to wear. I still dress like John Cameron Swayze. Without TV advertising, I don't understand new consumer products. Styling mousse, for instance—is it edible? And since, as a spectator, I'm limited to home teams, I've lost interest in most professional sports. I'm honestly not sure what the Seattle Seagulls are. They may be a girls' field hockey team, for all I know. (Editor's note: They're the Sea*hawks*—a football team.)

9   *People* magazine, newspaper gossip columns and friends' conversations are filled with names that mean nothing to me—"Prince," "Sting," "Peewee," "Appollonia." Sounds like a litter of puppies. And the celebrities I do recognize are mystifying. Imagine Mr. T completely out of *The A-Team* context: What kind of character could he possibly play?

10   Lack of a television set has more severe effects too. No TV means no VCR. That is, I actually paid to see *Flashdance* and couldn't even fast-forward through the parts where Jennifer Beals has all her clothes on. Furthermore, I'm getting fat. When you don't have to wait for a commercial to get up and get a sandwich and a beer, you can get up and get a lot more beer and sandwiches.

11   So maybe television isn't so bad for us as it's supposed to be. To research this story, I borrowed my next-door neighbor's TV—or, rather, I borrowed his whole TV room, since televisions are connected to cables now, so you can get 100 silly channels instead of five or six. I watched some shows at the start of the new season: *Hell Town, Hometown, Crazy Like a Fox, Stir Crazy,* etc. There were a few surprises. On MTV, I saw the video of a song I thought was a tender love ballad. It turns out to be sung by guys in leather underwear chasing a girl through a sewer.

12   But, mostly, television was just the same. It was kind of comforting to see Johnny Carson again, a little grayer but with the same slack gags. Most of the shows are still violent, but I live in New Hampshire these days, and we don't have as much murder, theft or car-chasing (and not even as much adultery) as some might like. The shows are still dumb, but I'm 10 years older, and I've forgotten how perfect everything is in the television world. The people are all pretty. The pay phones all work. And all the endings are hopeful. That's not so bad. Most of us real people are a bit homely, and lots of our endings are

hopeless. TV's perfect world was a relief. So I was sitting, comfortable as a pig, in my neighbor's armchair, punching remote-control buttons with my snout.

But I didn't enjoy it. No, sir. Not me. I've spent a whole decade acting 13 superior to everybody because I don't watch television. I'm not about to back down and start liking it now. (Though I might drop in next door about 8 tonight. That's when *Amazing Stories* comes on.)

▼ TOPICAL CONSIDERATIONS

1. Why did O'Rourke quit watching television?
2. The author complains that after giving up television what he did to fill his time turned out to be worse. What were some of those things, and why were they worse than watching television?
3. According to O'Rourke, what are some of the drawbacks of not having a television?
4. What changes in television does the author discover after a ten-year hiatus? What has stayed the same? Why does he say the "shows are still dumb"?
5. This essay is satirical, of course. What is O'Rourke mainly satirizing here? What does he actually suggest is wrong with television?
6. In paragraph 12, O'Rourke mentions "how perfect everything is in the television world." Then, he adds "That's not so bad." How does television create an illusion of a perfect world? Do you agree that such an illusion is "not so bad"? Can that illusion of a perfect world create problems for viewers?

▼ RHETORICAL CONSIDERATIONS

1. One means of creating a humorous effect is irony. Find some examples of irony in this essay.
2. Consider the structure of this essay. Can you find a clear beginning, middle, and end? Where would you make the cuts, and why?
3. How well does the final paragraph illustrate the central point of this essay?

▼ WRITING ASSIGNMENTS

1. Could you ever stop watching television? Write an essay in which you explore this possibility. Could you live without it? What might you miss? What could you afford to miss? What would you do to fill your leisure time (be realistic)?
2. O'Rourke humorously suggests that his girlfriend's addiction to

television helped break up their relationship. Write a paper in which you describe how people's lives are governed by television schedules and how television intrudes on relationships.

3. "No TV means no VCR." So says the author who complains that he actually had to pay to see the movie *Flashdance* (paragraph 10). From your own perspective, what are the advantages and disadvantages of watching movies on VCRs instead of in movie houses? Do you think VCRs will be the death of movie houses?

4. O'Rourke says that coming back to TV after ten years he still finds the shows "dumb." Write a paper in which you talk about what's "dumb" about television. You might consider analyzing a particular show—its characters and situations, its treatment of the real world and real people, and its messages, both subtle and obvious.

5. O'Rourke also says, "Most of the shows are still violent (paragraph 12)." Write a paper about television violence, analyzing a particular show or series. Is the violence realistic? Is it overdone? Do you think the violence is damaging to viewers? Do you agree with Ellen Goodman's claim (see "The Violence Is Fake, the Impact Is Real") that pain and suffering are missing from television violence?

8 ▼ ADVERTISING

Most of us are so accustomed to the incessant roar of advertising that we hear it without listening, we see it without looking. But if we stopped to examine how it works, we may be amazed at just how powerful and complex a psychological force advertising is. In this chapter we examine how a simple page in a magazine or a fifteen-second TV spot feeds our fantasies and fears with the sole intention of separating us from our money.

The first three essays, written by professional advertisers, provide some inside views of the craft. In "A Word from Our Sponsor" Patricia Volk confesses that there is only one rule in writing ads: "There are no rules." By contrast, Charles O'Neill, also an ad writer, praises the craft and the craftiness that have gone into some familiar commercials and print ads. While admitting to the seductive appeal, his "The Language of Advertising" argues that no ad forces consumers to lay their money down. The title of Carol Moog's essay makes clear her focus. "Sex, Sin, and Suggestion" takes a hard and close look at the sexy images that forge a short circuit from our psyches to our wallets.

As in print ads, television commercials rely less on language now and more on visuals. But as communications professor Jay Rosen observes in "The Presence of the Word in TV Advertising," language is not disappearing from the ads but functioning on a deeper lever—one that you can hear best when the sound is turned off.

The final two pieces examine specific ads. In "How Now Dow?" Mark Crispin Miller analyzes the subtle messages in a recent Dow Chemical TV commercial—an ad that tries to humanize the image of a huge, impersonal manufacturer of insecticides. And "Who Brews Up These Ads?" is an amusing look at Folger's coffee commercials—the ones that boast how you too can trick your friends by serving them instant coffee instead of the real brew.

We end this chapter with a series of ten recently published magazine ads each followed by a set of questions to help you analyze how ads work their appeal on us. Our hope is that by inviting you to apply a critical eye, some of the power of advertising might be unraveled and dispelled.

▼ A WORD FROM OUR SPONSOR
Patricia Volk

> The following piece, which originally appeared in the "On Language" column of *The New York Times Magazine,* was written by a professional advertising copywriter. However, Patricia Volk is anything but defensive of the practices of her profession. While demonstrating some of the jargon of the trade, Volk confesses that the language of advertising is a language "without rules," a language with "little to protect it." Ad people, she explains, will stop at nothing to make a product that the world neither wants nor needs sound wonderful. Besides being a copywriter, Patricia Volk is author of the award-winning short-story collection *The Yellow Banana and Other Stories* (1985) and the novel *White Light* (1987).

1 Linguistically speaking (and that's still the preferred way), there is only one rule in advertising: There are no rules. "We try harder," lacks parallelism. "Nobody doesn't like Sara Lee," is a double negative. And "Modess. Because. . . . " Because . . . why? My friends didn't know. My mother wouldn't tell. My sister said, like Mount Everest, because it was there. The word "creme" on a product means there's no cream in it. "Virtually," as in "Virtually all our cars are tested," means in essence, not in fact. Even a casual "Let's have lunch," said in passing on Mad Ave. means "Definitely, let's not."

2 Language without rules has little to protect it. Some of the most familiar lines would disappear like ring-around-the-collar if you put a mere "Says who?" after them. "Coke is it." Says who? "Sony. The one and only." Oh, yeah?

3 Still, one word in advertising has virtually limitless power. It gives "permission to believe." It inspires hope. It is probably (disclaimer) the oldest word in advertising.

4 What "new" lacks in newness, it makes up for in motivation. Unfortunately, new gets old fast. Legally, it's usable for only six months after a product is introduced. As in, say, "Introducing New Grippies. The candy that sticks to "the woof of your mouf."

5 Once Grippies are six months old, unlike newlyweds, who get a year, and the New Testament which has gotten away with it for who knows how long, Grippies are reduced to just plain Grippies. That's when you improve them and say "Introducing New Improved Grippies." Now they really stick like cwazy to that woof.

6 Had you named your product "New" to start with, as in "New Soap. The soap that cleans like new," you'd never have to worry about your product sounding old. Introduced as "New New Soap," six months down the road it segues into "New Improved New Soap." Or you could avoid the six-month thing entirely and just call it "The Revolutionary New Soap" from day one.

PITCHING GLUE

7   How do you get the Grippies account in the first place? You "pitch" it in a flurry of work called a "push." A creative team works weekends and sleeps in the office. It's intense.

8   A successful pitch winds up in a "win," and you've "landed" the account. By the end of the week, everyone in the agency has a free box of Grippes and work begins. This is the "honeymoon period."

9   Everybody loves everybody else. You take the factory tour. You eat Grippies till your molars roll. And you attend "focus groups," i.e., meetings between researchers and preselected members of your "target audience," the people you hope will love Grippies.

10   You sit behind a two-way mirror and watch people eat Grippies. You take notes. You start hating the man who scratches the exposed area of his leg between the top of his sock and the bottom of his pants. "Look! He's doing it! He's doing it *again!*" And what you learn in the focus group, you use to build "share," which is the percentage of the population using your *kind* of product that buys yours in particular.

11   It gives you some idea of how large this country is when you realize that if you can raise Forever Glue's .01 share of market (one person per thousand) to .03, Forever Glue will be a dazzling success. So you do the "Nothing lasts like Forever" campaign, complete with "The Big Idea." You find a small town in a depressed area upstate and glue it back together. Brick by brick, clapboard by clapboard, you actually (favorite ad word) glue a town together and restore it in a classic "demo" with "product as hero." You get a corner office and a Tizio lamp.

12   Forever is stickier. Grippies are grippier. But what if your product is "parity," a "me-tooer"? What if it has no "unique selling point" or "exclusivity"? What if the world is not waiting for Mega-Bran, the cereal that tastes like Styrofoam pellets and gets soggy in the bowl?

13   Some folks "make it sing." It's what everybody thinks people in advertising do anyway, as in, "Oh, you're in advertising! You must write jingles!" So you write new words to Bon Jovi's "Never Say Good-bye," only the client doesn't want to spend $2 million for the rights. So you check out the P.D.'s, public domain songs, songs with lapsed copyrights that are at least 75 years old. You just have to hope the Mega-Bran lyrics work to the tune of "Ach, the Moon Climbs High," "Jim Crack Corn," or "Whoopee Ti Yi Yo—Git Along Little Dogies."

14   At last the new Mega-Bran campaign is ready to crawl through all the "loops" in the "approval cycle," from your client's kids to the network's lawyers. Everybody "signs off" on it.

15   In "pretest," you get "rich verbatims"—a lot of people who remember everything about your commercial. You go for it. You shoot a finished "spot." You spend $250,000 on production, "net net," and $3 million on network and uh-oh, nobody buys the bran. Your commercial has failed to generate "trial" and "brand awareness." It's the Edsel of brans.

Quick, you do another "execution," a celebrity endorsement using someone **16** with a high "Q" (familiarity and popularity) score. (Bill Cosby has the highest.) You try "image advertising," which says almost nothing, but leaves the viewer feeling good about your product. (Soft drinks do it all the time.)

Still, no one remembers Mega-Bran. It's a case of "vampire video"—what **17** people saw in your ad was so strong that it sucked the blood out of your message. The account becomes "shaky." "Doomers and gloomers" worry all over your carpet. They "bail." Bailers are people in a room who sniff out with whom the power lies; whatever that person says, the bailer agrees. The fastest bailer I ever knew was an account man who told me every time he was asked his opinion, he saw his mortgage float in front of his eyes.

The account goes from shaky to the ICU. Then it's "out the door." There **18** is no funeral, no period of mourning because every loss presents an opportunity, a chance to roll up your sleeves, grease up your elbow and pitch again.

BODY PARTS

Clients like to find "niches" for their products. A niche is a special place no **19** other product can fit. Sometimes you find the niche before you find the product and then you have to find a product to fill the niche you found.

Body parts are always good, though by now almost everything has been **20** spoken for. There are still the navel and the philtrum. If you can do "exploratories" and with a little prodding make consumers aware that their philtrums sweat too much, smell funny or have unwanted hair, you're in business. You create a new form of consumer anxiety and cure it in a single stroke. You launch "Creme de Philtrum," with no cream in it, and have "preemptiveness." You're hot.

You don't have to go to school to write great copy. The best writers I know **21** wrap fish in the Elements of Style. Schools say they can teach it, but you either have it or you don't. It's like perfect pitch, good gums, or being able to sit on the floor with your ankles around your neck. They use language to convince, persuade, and, at its best, educate. They twist and twiddle words and understand their power. They make people do things they hadn't thought of doing before. They make them change.

One of the best writers ever had a great line: "The only thing we have to **22** fear is fear itself." It led a whole country out of Depression. Imagine what he could have done with detergent.

▼ TOPICAL CONSIDERATIONS

1. How is the language of advertising a language "without rules"? Can you think of some current ads that illustrate this claim? What rules of grammar or meaning are being broken?
2. According to Volk, the advertiser's word "inspires hope" (para-

graph 3). Do you agree? How do claims of "newness" appeal to the consumer? Have you ever been seduced into buying a product because it's "new" or "improved"? Can you think of any other potent "hope" words?

3. How does the author, who is an advertising copywriter, characterize her profession? Would you want to be an ad writer? Why or why not?

4. What strategies do ad writers resort to if their "product is 'parity,' " if it has no " 'unique selling point' "?

5. What special power of advertising does Volk's hypothetical "Creme de Philtrum" illustrate (paragraph 20)? Can you think of any real products that this might describe?

6. Why does Volk say, "You don't have to go to school to write great copy" (paragraph 21)?

▼ RHETORICAL CONSIDERATIONS

1. Volk says that the language of advertising has no rules. How well does she illustrate this assertion in her essay? Can you think of other examples?

2. How would you characterize Volk's attitude toward advertising claims?

3. Throughout the essay, Volk resorts to ad industry jargon highlighted in quotation marks. What would you say her purpose is here? How do you evaluate her attitude toward the jargon? What do you think of some of the expressions? Any strike you as particularly amusing?

4. Explain the effectiveness of the final paragraph. What point is being made? How does the paragraph summarize the theme of the essay? How consistent is her tone here with the rest of the piece?

▼ WRITING ASSIGNMENTS

1. Can you think of any ads whose claims particularly irritate you? Which ones? And what bothers you about them?

2. Volk says in paragraph 3 that there is "limitless power" in the words of advertising because what is being sold is hope. Select a familiar ad and write a paper analyzing how its language—verbal and visual—inspires hope.

3. Has this essay in any way changed your attitude toward advertising? Has it sensitized you to the power of advertising language? Has it made you more wary of the claims in ads? Discuss the article's effect on you in an essay.

4. Would you like to be a professional copywriter? In an essay explain why you would or would not want to write ad copy for a living.

▼ THE LANGUAGE OF ADVERTISING
Charles A. O'Neill

The language of advertising is very special. Charming and seductive, it is a language calculated to separate consumers from their money. Charles O'Neill has been a marketing executive for many years. In this essay, he explains just what advertising language does and how it does it. He examines some familiar TV commercials and magazine ads and explains their continued prominence in those media. While admitting to some of the craftiness of his profession, O'Neill defends advertising language against critics who see it as a distorter of language and reality.

Toward the end of her concert in a downtown park in Manchester, New Hampshire—not far, as the wind blows, from the long-suffering nuclear power plant at Seabrook—Bonnie Raitt, the rock star, looked out over her audience and noticed the Marlboro and Dunkin' Donuts signs in the distance. "If you think Marlboro country and donuts are where the flavor is, I've got news: it's not." She proceeded to tell the sympathetic, energized late-evening crowd that "where it is" was somewhere between a thing called love and a nonprofit group she supported, International Physicians for the Prevention of Nuclear War.

Ms. Raitt said nothing to indicate that she really had anything against Dunkin' Donuts—or, for that matter, cigarettes. And if she had anything against Miller beer, one of the sponsors of the event, she didn't say. Ms. Raitt's midconcert comments were, after all, not meant to start a debate. But she was, in her own way, commenting on one aspect of something we in America have long accepted as part of our culture; something pervasive, often taken for granted but often criticized: advertising.

If Marlboro is not truly "where the flavor is," it's not for lack of effort. Perhaps they have not convinced Ms. Raitt, but the architects of "Marlboro country" know how to reach into millions of smokers' heads and touch the desired motivational lever: the one labelled "buy!" The "real truth" doesn't matter, for advertising is not about truth, virtue, love or positive social values; it is about making money. When the writers of Marlboro's ads sat down in front of their word processors, they set in motion a sequence of events that changed the buying habits of millions of people. The final test of any advertising program (whether for donuts, cigarettes, nonprofit groups, detergents, cereals, life insurance, or pantyhose) is simply the degree to which it creates that impulse, the impulse to buy.

4   What creates the impulse? The strategy may call for billboards in a city in New Hampshire, full-page ads in Rolling Stone, 30-second spots on the CBS Evening News, T-shirts imprinted with a corporate logo, music videos—or, for that matter, Ms. Raitt at the microphone. Whatever the strategy, advertisements derive their power from a purposeful, directed combination of images. Images can take several forms: words—spoken or written—or visuals; or, most powerfully, a combination of the two. The precise formula is determined by the creative concept and the medium chosen. The combination is the language of advertising.

5   Everyone who grows up in the Western world soon learns that advertising language is different from other languages. Most children would be unable to explain how such lines as "With Nice 'n Easy, it's color so natural, the closer he gets the better you look!" (the famous ad for Clairol's Nice 'n Easy hair coloring product) or Marlboro's "come to where the flavor is" differs from ordinary language, but they would be able to tell you, "It sounds like an ad." Whether printed on a page, blended with music on the radio or smoothly whispered on the sound track of a television commercial, advertising language is "different."

6   Over the years, the texture of advertising language has frequently changed. Styles and creative concepts come and go. But there are at least four distinct general characteristics of the language of advertising that make it different from other languages; characteristics that, taken together, lend advertising its persuasive power:

1. The language of advertising is edited and purposeful.
2. The language of advertising is rich and arresting; it is specifically intended to attract and hold our attention.
3. The language of advertising involves us; in effect, *we* complete the message.
4. The language of advertising holds no secrets from us; it is a simple language.

EDITED AND PURPOSEFUL

7   One easy way to develop a feeling for the basic difference between advertising language and other languages is to transcribe a television talk show. An examination of such a transcript will show the conversation skipping from one topic to another, even though the guest and the host may attempt to stick to a specific subject. The conversation also is rife with repetition. After all, informal, conversational language transactions are not ordinarily intended to meet specific objectives. Advertising language cannot afford to be so desultory. It *does* have a specific purpose—to sell us something.

8   In *Future Shock,* Alvin Toffler draws a distinction between normal "coded"

messages and "engineered" messages. As an example of an uncoded message, Toffler writes about a random, unstructured experience:

> A man walks along a street and notices a leaf whipped along a sidewalk by the wind. He perceives this event through his sensory apparatus. He hears a rustling sound. He sees movement and greenness. He feels the wind. From these sensory perceptions he somehow forms a mental image. We can refer to these sensory signals as a message. But the message is not, in any ordinary sense of [the] term, man-made. It is not designed by anyone to communicate anything, and the man's understanding of it does not depend directly on a social code—a set of agreed-upon signs and definitions.[1]

The talk show conversation, however, is coded; the guests' ability to exchange information with their host, and our ability to understand it, depend, as Toffler puts it, upon social conventions. **9**

Beyond coded and uncoded messages there is another kind—the engineered message—a variation of the coded message. The language of advertising is a language of finely engineered, ruthlessly purposeful messages. By Toffler's calculation,[2] the average adult American is assaulted by at least 560 advertising messages a day. Not one of these messages would reach us, to attract and hold our attention, if it were completely unstructured. Advertising messages have a clear purpose; they are intended to trigger a specific response.

RICH AND ARRESTING

Advertisements—no matter how carefully "engineered" and packed with information—cannot succeed unless they capture our attention in the first place. Of the hundreds of advertising messages in store for us each day, very few (Toffler estimates seventy-six) will actually obtain our conscious attention.[3] The rest are screened out. The people who design and write ads know about this screening process; they anticipate and accept it as a basic premise of their business. They expend a great deal of energy to guarantee that their ads will make it past the defenses and distractions that surround us. The classic, all-time favorite device used to penetrate the barrier is sex. The desire to be attractive to the opposite sex is an ages-old instinct, and few drives are more powerful. Whether it takes this approach or another, every successful advertisement contains a "hook." The hook can take the form of strong visuals (photos or illustrations with emotional value) or a disarming, unexpected—even incongruous—set of words: **10**

"Reeboks let U B U"	(Reebok)
"My chickens eat better than you do."	(Perdue Chickens)

"Introducing the ultimate
   concept in air freight.
   Men that fly."   (Emery Air Freight)
"Look deep into our ryes."   (Wigler's bakery products)
"Me. 4 U."   (The State of Maine)
"If gas pains persist, try
   Volkswagen."   (Volkswagen)

11   Even if the text contains no incongruity and does not rely on a pun for its impact, every effective ad needs a creative strategy based on some striking concept or idea. In fact, the concept and execution are often so good that many successful ads entertain while they sell.

12   For example, consider the campaigns created by Ally and Gargano for Federal Express. A campaign was developed to position Federal Express as the company that would deliver packages, not just "overnight," but "by 10:30 A.M." the next day. The plight of the junior executive in "Presentation," one ad in the campaign, is stretched for dramatic purposes, but it is, nonetheless, all too real: the young executive, who is presumably trying to climb his way up the corporate ladder, is shown calling another parcel delivery service and all but begging for assurance that he will have his slides in hand by 10:30 the next morning. "No slides, no presentation," he pleads. Only a viewer with a heart of stone can watch without feeling sympathetic, as the next morning our junior executive struggles to make his presentation *sans* slides. He is so lost without them that he is reduced to using his hands to perform imitations of birds and animals in shadows on the movie screen. What does the junior executive *viewer* think when he or she sees the ad?

1. Federal Express guarantees to deliver packages "absolutely, positively over- night."
2. Federal Express packages arrive early in the day.
3. What happened to that fellow in the commercial will absolutely not happen to me, now that I know what package delivery service to call.

A sound creative strategy supporting a truly innovative service idea sold Federal Express. But the quality of execution and imagination doesn't really matter. An ad for Merit Ultra Lights (August 1990) made use of one slang word in its headline: "Yo!" Soft drink and fast food companies often take another ap- proach. "Slice of life" ads (so-called because they purport to provide glimpses of people in "real life" situations), replete with beautiful babies frolicking at family picnics or Fourth of July parades, seduce us into thinking that if we drink the right beverage or eat the right hamburger, we'll fulfill our deep yearning for a world where old folks and young folks live together in perfect suburban bliss. Lifestyle—and the natural affiliation of a particular lifestyle with a product— has also been used effectively as an advertising strategy for other types of merchandise. This TV spot for Levi's Corduroys was produced by Foote, Cone & Belding (1985):

Music up. (Open on quick shot of saxophone player. Cut to man at sink drying his face with a towel. Reflection seen in mirror.)

MALE SINGER: Gotta be there at eight. Gotta luminate.

(Cut to two women at a table in a 24-hour diner. A man tries to coax them.)

MALE SINGER: Got to be lookin' much better than great.

(Cut to man and woman walking down the street.)

MALE SINGER: Grab a flash of color, add a little more style . . .

(Cut to shot of two different women at a table. Man does a quick turn landing on a chair. He laughs. The women get up to leave.)

MALE SINGER: . . . Looks like Levi's Corduroy night.

(Cut to shot of large neon sign "Levi's Cords Tonight.")

MALE SINGER WITH GROUP SINGERS: Levi's Corduroy night.

(Cut back to last man on chair. He shrugs.)

MALE SINGER: Lookin' good . . .

(Quick cut to neon sign. Camera pulls back.)

MALE SINGER WITH GROUP SINGERS: It's a Levi's Corduroy night.

(Cut to two women at phone booth. One is talking on phone, other waits impatiently.)

MALE SINGER: Looks like it's gonna be another Levi's Corduroy night/ Levi's . . .

(Cut back to first man at the mirror. He taps the mirror and walks away.)

GROUP SINGERS: Corduroy night.

SUPER: Levi's batwing. Quality never goes out of style. Music fade out.

13 Of course, the printed word cannot begin to capture the pace or ambiance of this ad; nonetheless, it is clear that this effort doesn't appeal to everyone, and that's just the point. It *will* appeal to the young people identified by Levi's marketing research as the prime target market for the product. The ad encourages the viewer to make a connection: "I'm a flexible, luminous, streetwise kind of guy, just like the man in the mirror. Levi's Corduroys are O.K. Better buy some soon."

14 The prominence of ads containing puns or cleverly constructed headlines would seem to suggest that ads emerge, like Botticelli's Venus from the sea, flawless and full grown. Usually they do not. The idea that becomes the platform for an effective creative strategy is most often developed only after exhaustive research. The product is examined for its potential, and the prospective buyers are examined for their habits, characteristics and preferences.

15 "Who will be interested in our product? How old are they? Where do they live? How much money do they earn? What problem will our product solve?" Answers to these questions provide the foundation on which the creative strategy is built.

16 The creative people in the advertising business are well aware that consumers do not watch television or read magazines in order to see ads. Ads have to earn the right to be seen, read, and heard.

INVOLVING

17 We have seen that the language of advertising is carefully engineered; we have seen that it uses various devices to get our attention. Frank Perdue has us looking at a photo of his chickens at a dinner table. Sneaker companies have us watching athletes at work, Marlboro has us looking at a cowboy on an outdoor billboard. Now that they have our attention, advertisers present information intended to show us that the product they are offering for sale fills a need and, in filling this need, differs from the competition. The process is called "product positioning." Once our attention has been captured, it is the copywriter's responsibility to express such product differences and to exploit and intensify them.

18   What happens when product differences do not exist? Then the writer must glamorize the superficial differences (for example, difference of color, packaging, or other qualities without direct bearing on the product's basic function) or else *create* differences. As long as the ad is trying to get our attention, the "action" is mostly in the ad itself, in the words and visual images. But as we read an ad or watch it on television, we become more deeply involved. The action starts to take place in *us.* Our imagination is set in motion, and our individual fears and aspirations, our little quirks and insecurities, superimpose themselves on that tightly engineered, attractively packaged message.

19   Consider, for example, the running battle among the low-calorie soft drinks. The cola wars have spawned many "look-alike" advertisements, because the product features and consumer benefits are generic, applying to all products in the category. Substitute one product name for another, and the messages are often identical, right down to the way the cans are photographed in the closing sequence. This strategy relies upon mass saturation and exposure for impact. In contrast, consider the way sneaker companies have attempted to create a "sense" of product differentiation where few significant differences exist. Reebok said their sneakers were different—meriting their high price tag—because "Reeboks Let U B U" (presumably, other brands of footwear failed to deliver this benefit.) To further underscore the difference between their brands and those of competitors, some sneaker companies in 1990 offered such "significant" innovations as inflatable air bladders, possibly in order to bring the wearer to a new state of walking ecstasy heretofore unavailable to mortals . . . but more likely in an effort to differentiate the product in a crowded, competitive field. Interestingly, competitors "rebelled," against Reebok's "innovation" (thus making themselves appear to be different). As reported in the *Boston Globe* (August 13, 1990), a print ad for Keds is to show a Reebok shoe, adjacent to its $65 price tag, with the headline, "U Gotta B Kidding." Not to be outdone, Puma ran ads depicting a sneaker they described as "too much," replete with bells, a whistle, electric sockets, wings and an air pump! (Guess whose sneaker, in contrast, is depicted as offering "just enough?") Sneakers are shoes, but they are also, in effect, "lifestyle indicators," or symbols: If I think of myself as somewhat rebellious, with a clear sense of independent spirit, I'll go with the Reeboks, since, after all, they'll Let me B Me; if I'm the practical sort—un-

swayed by technical hype—perhaps I'll go with the "practical" Keds or Pumas.

Symbols have become important elements in the language of advertising in other ways, too; not so much because they carry meanings of their own but because we bring a meaning to them: we charge them with significance. Symbols are efficient, compact vehicles for the communication of an advertising message; they are pervasive and powerful. **20**

One noteworthy example of symbolism at work is provided by the campaign begun in 1978 by Somerset Importers for Johnnie Walker Red Scotch. Sales of Johnnie Walker Red had been trailing sales of Johnnie Walker Black, and Somerset Importers needed to position Red as a fine product in its own right. The Smith/Greenland Agency produced ads which made heavy use of the color red. One ad, often printed as a two-page spread, is dominated by a close-up photo of red autumn leaves. At lower right, the copy reads, "When their work is done, even the leaves turn to red." Another ad—also suitably dominated by a photograph in the appropriate color—reads: "When it's time to quiet down at the end of the day, even a fire turns to Red." *Red.* Warm. Experienced. Seductive. A perfect symbol to use in a liquor advertisement; all the more for the fact that it offers great possibilities for graphic design and copywriting: more fuel for the advertiser's creative art. **21**

From time to time, many people believe, a more disturbing form of symbolism is also used—the "hidden message" symbol. Take a close, hard look at liquor ads and occasionally you will see, reflected in the photograph of a glass of spirits, peculiar, demonlike shapes. Are these shapes merely the product of one consumer's imagination or an accident of photography? Were they deliberately superimposed onto the product photograph by the careful application of ink and airbrush? **22**

The art of advertising contains many such ambiguities. Some are charged, like this one, with multiple shades of meaning. The demons may be taken to represent the problems and cares which one can presumably chase away through consumption of the advertised product. Or they can, just as easily, be taken as representations of the playful spirits which will be unleashed once the product has been consumed. The advertising creative director did not create the need to relax, or to get away from the stresses of daily life; he or she merely took advantage of these common human needs in developing a promotion strategy for the product. **23**

Another human desire advertising writers did not invent (although they liberally exploit it) is the desire to associate with successful people. All of us tend to admire or in some way identify ourselves with famous or successful people. We are therefore already primed for the common advertising device of the testimonial or personality ad. Once we have seen a famous person in an advertisement, we associate the product with the person. "I like Mr. X. If Mr. X likes (endorses) this product, I would like it too." The logic is faulty, but we fall for it just the same. That is how Joe DiMaggio sold Mr. Coffee. The people who write testimonial ads did not create our trust in famous personalities. They merely recognize our inclinations and exploit them. **24**

The language of advertising is different from other languages because we **25** participate in it; in fact, we—not the words we read on the magazine page or the pictures flashing before us on the television screen—charge the ads with most of their power.

A SIMPLE LANGUAGE

26 Clip a typical story from the publication you read most frequently. Calculate the number of words in an average sentence. Count the number of words of three or more syllables in a typical 100-word passage, omitting words that are capitalized, combinations of two simple words, or verb forms made into three-syllable words by the addition of -ed or -es. Add the two figures (the average number of words per sentence and the number of three-syllable words per 100 words), then multiply the result by .4. According to Robert Gunning, if the resulting number is seven, there is a good chance that you are reading *True Confessions.*[4] He developed this formula, the "Fog Index," to determine the comparative ease with which any given piece of written communication can be read. Here is the complete text of a typical cigarette advertisement:

> I demand two things from my cigarette. I want a cigarette with low tar and nicotine. But, I also want taste. That's why I smoke Winston Lights. I get a lighter cigarette, but I still get a real taste. And real pleasure. Only one cigarette gives me that: Winston Lights.

27 The average sentence in this ad runs seven words. *Cigarette* and *nicotine* are three-syllable words, with *cigarette* appearing four times; *nicotine,* once. Considering *that's* as two words, the ad is exactly fifty words long, so the average number of three-syllable words per 100 is ten.

$$
\begin{array}{r}
7 \text{ words per sentence} \\
+\ 10 \text{ three-syllable words}/100 \\
\hline
17 \\
\times\ .4 \\
\hline
6.8 \text{ Fog Index}
\end{array}
$$

28 According to Gunning's scale, this particular ad is written at about the seventh grade level, comparable to most of the ads found in mass circulation magazines.[5] It's about as sophisticated as *True Confessions;* harder to read than a comic book, but easier than *Ladies Home Journal.*

29 Of course, the Fog Index cannot evaluate the visual aspect of an ad. The headline, "I demand two things from my cigarette," works with the picture (that of an attractive woman) to arouse consumer interest. The text reinforces the image. It is unlikely that many consumers actually take the trouble to read the entire text, but it is not necessary for them to do so in order for the ad to work.

30 Since three-syllable words are harder to read than one- or two-syllable words, and since simple ideas are more easily transferred from one human to

another than complex ideas, advertising copy tends to use even simpler language all the time. Toffler speculates:

> If the [English] language had the same number of words in Shakespeare's time as it does today, at least 200,000 words—perhaps several times that many—have dropped out and been replaced in the intervening four centuries. The high turnover rate reflects changes in things, processes, and qualities in the environment from the world of consumer products and technology.[6]

It is no accident that the first terms Toffler uses to illustrate his point ("fastback," "wash-and-wear," and "flashcube") were invented not by engineers, or journalists, but by advertising copywriters.

Advertising language is simple language; in the engineering process, difficult words or images (which could be used in other forms of communication to lend color or fine shades of meaning) are edited out and replaced by simple words or images not open to misinterpretation. **31**

WHO IS RESPONSIBLE?

Some critics view the entire advertising business as a cranky, unwelcomed child of the free enterprise system, a noisy, whining, brash kid who must somehow be kept in line, but can't just yet be thrown out of the house. Because advertising mirrors the fears, quirks, and aspirations of the society that creates it (and is, in turn, sold by it), it is wide open to parody and ridicule. **32**

Perhaps the strongest, most authoritative critic of advertising language in recent years is journalist Edwin Newman. In his book *Strictly Speaking,* he poses the question, "Will America be the death of English?" Newman's "mature, well thought out judgment" is that it will. As evidence, he cites a number of examples of fuzzy thinking and careless use of the language, not just by advertisers, but by many people in public life, including politicians and journalists: **33**

> The federal government has adopted the comic strip character Snoopy as a symbol and showed us Snoopy on top of his doghouse, flat on his back, with a balloon coming out of his mouth, containing the words, "I believe in conserving energy," while below there was this exhortation: savEnergy.
>
> savEnergy. An entire letter e at the end was savd. In addition, an entire space was savd. Perhaps the government should say onlYou can prevent forest fires. . . . Spelling has been assaulted by Duz, E-Z Off, Fantastik, Kook, Kleen . . . and by products that make you briter, so that you will not be left hi and dri at a parti, but made welkom. . . . Under this pressure, adjectives become adverbs; nouns become adjectives; prepositions disappear; compounds abound.[7]

In this passage, Newman presents three of the charges most often levied against advertising:

1. Advertising debases English.
2. Advertising downgrades the intelligence of the public.
3. Advertising warps our vision of reality, implanting in us groundless fears and insecurities. (He cites, as examples of these groundless fears, "tattletale gray," "denture breath," "morning mouth," "unsightly bulge," "ring around the collar.")

34   Other charges have been made from time to time. They include:

1. Advertising sells daydreams; distracting, purposeless visions of lifestyles beyond the reach of most of the people who are most exposed to advertising.
2. Advertising feeds on human weaknesses and exaggerates the importance of material things, encouraging "impure" emotions and vanities.
3. Advertising encourages bad, even unhealthy habits like smoking.
4. Advertising perpetuates racial and sexual stereotypes.

35   What can be said in advertising's defense? Advertising is only a reflection of society; slaying the messenger (and just one of the messengers, at that) would not alter the fact—if it is a fact—that "America will be the death of English." A case can be made for the concept that advertising language is an acceptable stimulus for the natural evolution of language. (At the very least, advertising may stimulate debate about what current trends in language are "good" and "bad.") Another point: is "proper English" the language most Americans actually speak and write, or is it the language we are told we should speak and write, the language of *The Elements of Style* and *The Oxford English Dictionary?*

36   What about the charge that advertising debases the intelligence of the public? Those who support this particular criticism would do well to ask themselves another question: Exactly how intelligent is the public? How many people know the difference between adverbs and adjectives? How many people *want* to know? The fact is that advertisements are effective, not because agencies say they are effective, but because they sell products.

37   Advertising attempts to convince us to buy products; we are not forced to buy something because it is heavily advertised. Who, for example, is to be blamed for the success, in the mid-70s, of a nonsensical, nonfunctional product—"Pet Rocks"? The people who designed the packaging, those who created the idea of selling ordinary rocks as pets, or those who bought the product?

38   Perhaps much of the fault lies with the public, for accepting advertising so readily. S. I. Hayakawa finds "the uncritical response to the incantations of advertising . . . a serious symptom of a widespread evaluational disorder." He does not find it "beyond the bounds of possibility" that "today's suckers for national advertising will be tomorrow's suckers for the master political propagandist who will, by playing up the 'Jewish menace,' in the same way as national advertisers play up the 'pink toothbrush menace,' and by promising us national glory and prosperity, sell fascism in America."[8]

Fascism in America is fortunately a far cry from Pet Rocks, but the point **39**
is well taken. In the end, advertising simply attempts to change behavior. It is
a neutral tool, just as a gun is a neutral tool, but advertising at least has not been
known to cause accidental deaths. Like any form of communication, it can be
used for positive social purposes, neutral commercial purposes, or for the most
pernicious kind of paranoid propaganda. Accepting, for the purpose of this
discussion, that propaganda is, at heart, an extension of politics and therefore
is materially different from commercial advertising as practiced in the United
States of America, circa 1990, *do* advertisements sell distracting, purposeless
visions? Occasionally. But perhaps such visions are necessary components of the
process through which our society changes and improves.

And recognize this: advertising is a mirror. It is not perfect; sometimes it **40**
distorts. When we view ourselves in it, we're not always pleased with what we
see. Perhaps, all things considered, that's the way it should be.

▼ NOTES

1. Alvin Toffler, *Future Shock* (New York: Random House, 1970), p. 146.
2. Ibid., p. 149
3. Ibid.
4. Curtis D. MacDougall, *Interpretive Reporting* (New York: Macmillan, 1968), p. 94
5. Ibid., p. 95
6. Toffler, *Future Shock,* p. 151.
7. Edwin Newman, *Strictly Speaking* (Indianapolis: Bobbs-Merrill, 1974), p. 13.
8. S. I. Hayakawa, *Language in Action* (New York: Harcourt, Brace, 1941), p. 235.

▼ TOPICAL CONSIDERATIONS

1. The author uses the phrases "advertising language" and "other languages." What assumptions about language is he making? Are they valid? Why or why not?
2. O'Neill describes several ways in which the language of advertising differs from other kinds of language. Briefly list the different ways he mentions. Can you think of any other characteristics of advertising language that set it apart?
3. In paragraphs 33 and 34, O'Neill presents several of the most frequent charges levied against advertising language. What are they? What does he say in defense of advertising? Which set of arguments carries more strength?

4. "Symbols are efficient, compact vehicles for the communication of an advertising message" (paragraph 20). What symbols from the advertising world do you associate with your own life? Are they effective symbols for selling?

5. Patricia Volk, author of the previous essay, is a professional advertiser as is Charles O'Neill. It's clear that they both see advertising language as charged and seductive, but how do their attitudes toward advertising generally differ? What differences, moral or otherwise, can you determine?

▼ RHETORICAL CONSIDERATIONS

1. What introductory technique does O'Neill use in this piece? Why do you think he chose this particular approach? What tone is established in the introduction, and what does it reveal about O'Neill's attitude toward Bonnie Raitt? Toward the subject of advertising?

2. O'Neill is an advertising professional. Does his writing style reflect the advertising techniques he describes? Cite examples to support your answer.

3. Describe the author's point of view about advertising. Does he ever tell us how he feels? Does his style indicate his attitude?

▼ WRITING ASSIGNMENTS

1. The author believes that advertising language "mirrors the fears, quirks, and aspirations of the society that creates it." Do you agree or disagree with this statement? Explain in a brief essay.

2. Choose a brand-name product you use regularly and one of its competitors—one whose differences are negligible, if they exist at all. Examine some advertisements for each brand. Write a short paper explaining what really makes you prefer your brand.

3. Write a description of a common object in "formal standard English." Now write an advertisement for the same object. Analyze what has happened to the language in your writing.

4. Write a paper on sexism or racism in advertising. Use specific examples from current ads and commercials.

▼ SEX, SIN, AND SUGGESTION

Carol Moog

Does sex in advertising sell? Does sex in advertising attract attention? Does sex in advertising influence people? What are we really buying—a product or a compelling image of ourselves? The essay below answers these questions and raises many others. Drawing on her training as a psychologist, Dr. Carol Moog guides us through several recent print ads and campaigns pointing out the subtle and not-so-subtle symbols that shape our psyches and consumer behavior. Carol Moog is a clinical psychologist and advertising consultant. She has taught at the Charles Morris Price School of Advertising and Journalism. Her articles have appeared in *Advertising Age, Art Direction, Adweek,* and other publications. This essay was excerpted from Ms. Moog's book, *Are They Selling Her Lips?* (1990)

Sex *is* rampant in advertising. And no other type of psychological imagery hits people closer to where they really live. Advertisers didn't create the need for men and women to feel sexually viable, and advertisers didn't create the insecurities people have about being able to love. These are core issues in human development that cut right through to the heart of self-esteem, where people are most vulnerable. And advertisers, because they're in the business of making money, have long dangled the lure of enhanced sexuality to motivate consumers to buy. 1

Does sex in advertising sell? Sometimes. 2

Does sex in advertising attract attention? Yes. Does sex in advertising influence people? Yes. And vice versa. 3

Some of the most pervasive, and persuasive, sexual imagery in advertising is more symbolic than blatant, although the connotations are often far from subtle. The ad for Chanel lipstick by Doyle Dane Bernbach (Milan) shows a woman with her upturned, open mouth grasping a tube of the product between her teeth. The red lipstick is fully extended, her eyes are closed, and her face shows pleasure. The image is visually arresting, clearly evocative of fellatio, and symbolically links the cosmetic with the promise of sexual allure. 4

What Chanel is selling here isn't simply lipstick; the imagery sends a message to the unconscious, granting permission to fulfill sexual wishes and points the way to an attractor that can facilitate the encounter. But she's also thumbing her nose—symbolically sticking her tongue out—at conventional refinement. She's playful, arrogant, and Chanel uses that message (intentionally or not) as a way of poking fun at its own reserved image. 5

Seagram's Extra Dry Gin ad, created by Ogilvy & Mather, is on a direct line to the male unconscious with its imagery. Dominating the center of the page is a huge Spanish olive, its nearly neon-red pimiento pushing out at the viewer as it is engulfed by a clear, viscous liquid. Presumably, the fluid is Seagram's Extra 6

Dry Gin, an elixir that, the headline claims, can "Arouse an Olive." Metaphorically speaking, this is a very sexy imperative and a very sexy product benefit. The archetypal shape, signifying the female, which has endured since the Paleolithic Era, is round. À la olive. And this one, with its bulging scarlet center, is suggestive both of a tumescent clitoris or nipple—and essentially of a woman in a state of arousal. The invitation "Arouse an Olive," written in a classic masculine typeface, is psychologically directed to men, and delivers a message that promises, and then visually delivers, a sexual seduction, complete with a climactic outpouring of liquid.

7   Psychological analysis aside, it's gut-level obvious what the advertiser's up to here. "Arouse" is not a word generally applied to an olive.

8   The sexual message Seagram's Extra Dry Gin symbolizes in its "Olive" ad is sent, but more overtly, in a different ad for the same product. In the upper right is a picture of an upright bottle (male) overlapping the rounded edge of an orange (female)—a graphic echo of the lower-right image of a couple in heated embrace. As if there could be any doubt about the advertiser's imbuing Seagram's Gin with aphrodisiac powers, the copy reads like a litany of praises for the product's capabilities, which ends with the line, positioned as being spoken by the lovers, "They also say it could turn a 'maybe' into . . . 'again.' " Interpreted at its most basic level, the ad's message about the link between the product and sexuality would appear to be "Get her drunk and get her in bed."

9   It's easier for consumers to dismiss the transparent seduction of the "Maybe" Seagram's ad than the symbolic, indirect sexual message of the "Arouse" piece. Symbolic communications bypass the layers of logic and cultural appropriateness and head straight for the unconscious, which is then free to find an equivalence between what is symbolized, in this case sexual arousal, and the brand, Seagram's Extra Dry Gin.

12   . . . The pressures to be sexy, stay sexy, and get sexier are enormous. We are a driven culture, and the fuel firing the more-is-always-better machine is internal as well as external. Madison Avenue's *pressure* to measure up is only matched in intensity by the level of *need* to measure up that people bring to the relationship. And that need boils down to the need to love and be loved.

11   People who are secure enough to develop an enduring, mutual, affectionate relationship with another person have accomplished an extraordinarily difficult psychological task. Too often, people get stuck in their insecurities; in their desperate determination not to expose their insecurities, they frantically try to fill up a sense of emptiness with cultural facsimiles of love. And the culture—with advertisers ranking right up there, our sergeant-at-arms of imagery—holds up an endless array of tempting surrogates in designer packaging: popularity, prestige, glamour, sexiness.

12   What's vicious about this particular cycle is that the more people try to fill themselves up by propping up the *outside,* the more terrified they are about exposing who they really are on the *inside.* The discrepancy becomes too great, and the investment in the decoy self becomes too high to risk losing whatever security it does provide. Probably the single biggest barrier to love is the fear of

psychological exposure, of being found out and found lacking. When advertisers link products with sexuality, they lock in with people's deepest fears of being unlovable; they offer their products and images as the tickets to love, when what they're really providing are more masks for people to hide behind. . . .

Cheesy sexual-power games are recurrent themes in [a] long-standing cigarette campaign. Newport, a product of Lorillard, Inc., has been successfully profiting from associating cigarettes with themes of sexual dominance and submission for a decade. Targeted to a young market, the campaign's slogan is "Alive with pleasure!" What Newport's imagery suggests, in ad after ad, is that its smokers will become *sexually* alive with pleasure. The gist of the campaign is that if it feels good, do it, an insidiously shrewd strategy for a product that invites people to sell their birthrights to health for a bowl of momentary pleasure. **13**

In one vivid example of the ravishing sexual adventures young singles *could* have if they started smoking Newports, two men are carrying a long pole between them from which is hanging, in deer-bounty fashion, their female prey. All three are having a great time as her head hangs down exactly at one man's crotch level, while her up-ended legs expose her rear to the opposite man—at just about the right level for a soft-porn ménage à trois. Just as the primary acceptable justification today's smokers can feed themselves is simply that they *like* to smoke, sexual entanglements like the merry threesomes are justified as worthy of pursuit as long as they're fun. As Newport puts it in the ad's closing tag line, "After all, if smoking isn't a pleasure, why bother?" **14**

There's nothing wrong with a fun fantasy, except that while the sexy scene can remain solely in consumers' imaginations, smoking and its medical sequelae are very real indeed. The advertiser's imagery isn't intended to get consumers to *fantasize* about Newports, it's designed to get consumers to *smoke* Newports. All the persuasive copy and visuals going into pushing the *pleasure* of Newports are just as busy pushing the pleasure of sexuality, a human drive that needs no advertising support. The unconscious doesn't separate the product from the passion, and sexual *expectations* get sold just as hard as the brand. **15**

Men in this culture feel just as pressured to exude sexual prowess and proficiency as women, and advertisers provide steady, compelling reinforcement of these expectations. There is no dearth of ads offering men groaning boards heaped with tasty images of available young women, designed to whet their appetites for associated consumer goods. But does it work? Does sex sell? **16**

Women perceive romantic imagery and even symbolic metaphors (like the Chanel ad) as sexy; to men, nudity means sexiness. While women can look at ads with considerable sexual content and still remember what brand is being promoted, when men are faced with overtly sexual imagery, they can't remember *anything*—often they can't even describe what was in the ad, let alone name the product! Sexy ads *do* rivet a man's attention, but the intellectual circuits can get overloaded fast and, at that point, all that gets marketed is food for fantasies. And that's no cause for a bottom-line celebration. If their consumer target can't ask for it by name, the advertiser has just squandered a bundle. For men **17** in this culture trying to grow up, to move from sexual preoccupations into committed relationships, advertisers' sexual preoccupations help keep them stuck in the crippling quicksand of adolescence. And that's no cause for psychological celebration. . . .

18   In the world of primitive cultures, New Guinea tribesmen attach foot-long tubes to their penises. In the world of civilized advertisers, Pierre Cardin man's cologne, shaped unmistakably like a phallus, is shown in an ad as a dominance display object of a superior male who is admired by his subordinates: "You wear it well."

19   In this case, hyperphallic packaging combines with power-message advertising. The guy is visibly a big player. (Comfortable in a tux.) Hardworking, smart, suave. (Reading his speech? Briefing himself for a diplomatic reception? Prepping for tomorrow's contest with Manly Power in a Man's World?) He has nouveaux tastes. (Checker-patterned linoleum—*very* classy.) Could be married or single. (The ring finger is neatly concealed.) Nothing particularly effeminate, but no women to be seen either.

20   And that's important, because this phallic-shaped bottle of men's perfume should hit two markets, straight and gay, if all goes well. The phallic symbol, for anyone for whom it resonates, stands up and says precisely what it is without any embarrassment about what it's doing. If the straight male prefers to ignore the blatant hard-on in the foreground, the ad gives him permission to do so. If the gay male responds to the obvious suggestiveness, that's okay too. It's a clever male-manipulation ad, not least of all because it allows both markets to get their own messages without catering to either specifically.

21   Guess Jeans is one of those advertisers with a huge stake in the attraction of some women to the sadomasochistic side of sexuality, and the women it's after are young. Until quite recently, the campaign featured highly provocative black-and-white photos of porcelain-skinned girls in a string of seemingly endless encounters with salacious older men, labeled only by the scribbled red-lipsticked script "Georges Marciano" or "Guess Jeans."

22   Some of the more notorious scenes in Guess ads along the way include an aging Mafioso-type wearing sunglasses, in postures of sexual dominance toward young, semibuttoned women with apathetic expressions. One has us facing the kneeling rear of a woman looking up at the crotch of a man standing above her, arms folded expectantly. Although she *is* wearing a Guess jeans jacket, what is actually being advertised here? In most of the Guess ads, the advertiser's product is simply a prop for the center-stage interplay between the fragile, loosened-clothing, exposed vulnerability of a nubile female and a possessive, unsavory Daddy-like male, as we see in one of the car scenes. Evocative of Louis Malle's 1978 film *Pretty Baby,* or Elia Kazan's earlier *Baby Doll* (1956), Guess is associating an edge of danger with its brand name, a strategy that plays directly on the urgency and ambivalence of adolescents' sexual impulses. Much of the time, the Guess girls look like runaways photographed in distasteful situations their mothers would never approve of.

23   Irresponsible? Guess jeans sell. The advertiser has gone to whatever lengths

it takes to get noticed by its market and has been handsomely rewarded by the public. Some teenagers, like my daughter Julie's friend Alison, buy Guess jeans because "they're comfortable." But for others, the imagery does more than persuade them to wear the brand; the broader effects of this kind of advertising fall outside of the narrow realm of marketing and into the larger universe of moral issues. The psychological messages sent by Guess imagery strongly imply that girls can use their sexuality to free themselves from parental constraints. The ads create the illusion that being possessed by a powerful, older man can be a glamorous identity for a confused, angry adolescent. Being used sexually, or running away, isn't portrayed as being either self-destructive or hostile; it's presented as a daring walk on the rebel side of the tracks. The perfect counter to the ruling party of adults. The latest from Guess? Young women are still often portrayed as sexually submissive and dominated in ads, but now the man strong-arming her from behind while she straddles him and his motorcycle is as young as she.

In Revlon's internally produced ad for its Trouble fragrance, the psychological message isn't one of female submission, but rather one of equality between the sexes—both are equally ignorant. In plunging black décolletage, she smiles dreamily, conspiratorially, at her audience. The object of her designs leans on a bar in the shadows, wearing black, a fashionably decadent stubble, and slightly narrowed eyes. The headline titles this scene "He's Trouble, But He's Finally Met His Match." What qualities does she bring to this sexual showdown? If she's sufficiently doused herself with Trouble, she's unhinged whatever mental apparatus might have stopped her from stepping into a story designed to come to a ruinous end. With Revlon's help, she'll match him in destructiveness. Trouble, the imagery tells consumers, can loosen the bothersome intellectual controls that so often interfere with romantic meetings at bars. As the copy explains, Trouble is "The fragrance for those times when your better judgment is better off ignored. After all, a little Trouble keeps life interesting." **24**

How can all these images of sexual entanglings be going on in the eighties? Hasn't anyone told advertisers about AIDS? Over the years, I've frequently had the opportunity of being asked to comment on trends in advertising. The effect of the AIDS tragedy on the culture has been one of the year's hottest topics. Often, conclusions come to me masquerading as questions such as: What do you think about the new trend in advertising toward love and romance? What I think is that, given the sheer magnitude of print and broadcast messages, advertising "trends" are more often created by the media feeding off its own perceptions than reflecting a true groundswell of change in the industry. **25**

While it is true that some advertisers have modified their explicitly young-and-sexual imagery to better reach maturing baby boomers engaged in long-term, committed romantic relationships, these instances can easily be counter-balanced by examples of advertisers calling for attention on the same old hormone hotline. There is little doubt that a combination of AIDS and aging has intensified the desire of people in our culture for lasting, substantive relationships, where two people fall in love and grow old together. Hollywood has **26** jumped on this bandwagon and produced rashes of films, such as *Baby Boom, Three Men and a Baby, For Keeps,* and *She's Having a Baby*—that not only deemphasize the joys of promiscuity, but elevate to near-mythic wonder the pleasures of child rearing. These movies reflect a natural consequence of the inevitable winding down of the prolonged adolescence of the sixties. Again, while there are some noticeable recent changes in the culture's images of relationships, I believe that these do not eclipse the emphasis on sexuality that has been so pervasive in the media; instead, they provide some balance in a cultural marketing mix long skewed toward the sexual sell. . . .

27   One psychological development cropping up increasingly in ad imagery has little to do with romance in the traditional, interpersonal sense of the word. Some people find it safer to relate simply to themselves—and the monstrosity of AIDS looms as a conveniently unassailable reason to stay isolated. The myth of Narcissus lives.

28   Handsome Narcissus was extraordinarily enamored of his beauty. Although young maidens loved him, he paid no attention to any of them. Echo, a lovely nymph, was so pained by his coldness that she faded away, leaving only her voice, hopelessly repeating the last syllables of words it heard. The gods, angry at Narcissus because Echo was their favorite, punished him by making him fall in love with his own reflection in a pool. Despairing because he could never possess what he loved, he killed himself with a knife. The narcissus flower grew from the drops of his blood.

29   Calvin Klein's ad for Calvin Klein fragrance for men is a perfect contemporary rendition of the classical myth of Narcissus. Shot in black-and-white, sleekly oblong, the product has the form of a brick bullion—the same kind of gold that gilds the frame of the mirror in the photo—a mirror into which the transfixed, mesmerized face of a man enraptured by his own image is staring. He looks as if he could stay there forever. Clearly, this is the face of a man in love—and he only has eyes for himself. Homoerotic undertones aside, this is what narcissistic self-absorption is all about. Psychologically, it's a dead-end street.

30   At the root of this kind of narcissism are feelings of worthlessness, the inability to live up to unattainable expectations coupled with an insatiable need to extract admiration from others. Legions of advertisers use imagery that is ostensibly designed to be sexually provocative but that actually sets up a self-perpetuating cycle of narcissistic needs.

31   People in desperate need of validation from others are caught in a media avalanche of narcissistic images of people who essentially feel empty and unlovable beneath their grandiose postures. The sole purpose of these images is to persuade people that the way to achieve the sexual and personal power reflected by a commercial model is to buy the associated product. Consumers buy the product unconsciously hoping that they will win the admiration they covet, but since they're still trying to measure up to somebody else's expectations, they feel just as empty as ever on the inside. The process continues to fuel the quest for approval, which, in turn, fuels the sales of products selling a promise of narcissistic gratification. . . .

Harper's Bazaar uses narcissistic self-absorption to interest female consumers in buying the magazine. The campaign, using no copy at all, focuses on pictures of women so locked into reading a copy of *Bazaar* that they are completely oblivious to the activities of the man, however unusual, in the same room. In one, a nude man is shown in the shower, vainly kissing the glass door—talk about protection!—to get the attention of a young woman in pearls and cocktail dress, engrossed in reading the magazine. The campaign, created by Margeotes-Fertitta & Weiss, Inc., is intended to be provocative, startling, slick, alienated, and ironic. But what is most arresting to me about the imagery is the level of narcissism and distance displayed by the women. The men might as well be pieces of furniture for all the interest they stir. **32**

Even perfume advertising, which, given the nature of the product's intrinsic sensuality, has appropriately featured traditional imagery suggestive of romantic or sexually charged interludes, abounds with examples of pure self-indulgence and smug egocentricity rather than relationships. Elizabeth Arden is the sublicenser of Fendi perfume, and its advertising is dominated by a luminous photograph of a beautiful woman, eyes closed in the passion of the moment, kissing the marble lips of a sculptured male bust. No risk of messy intimate exposure with this packaged smell. The message is resoundingly clear on the subject of emotional closeness: Don't do it. Stick with statues and cozy up to a healthy hunk of alabaster and you won't get hurt. Here, any sexuality resides exclusively on Fantasy Island, an island inhabited by the very embodiment of a nonthreatening male with no needs of his own: a Roman statue. . . . **33**

Although Calvin Klein Cosmetic Corporation's use of sexual imagery in advertising, from the earlier Obsession through the more recent Eternity brands of fragrances, appears, on the surface, to have moved from uncommitted, self-centered couplings toward visions of mature, mutual relationships, underneath the seemingly disparate images runs a common thread that sends a consistent message to the public. Despite Calvin Klein's assiduous efforts to package the personalities of Obsession and Eternity differently, the advertiser's family album of brands is still filled with people who appear incapable of having a relationship with a person separate from themselves. **34**

Consider Calvin Klein's Obsession perfume. When it's ménage-à-many ads first broke, the intentionally scandalous, enormously successful campaign was met with a combination of titillation and outrage, depending on how well the imagery fit into the sexual fantasies of the viewer. Grainy, chiaroscuro nudes of all genders, sensuously coupled in all configurations, formed the backdrop for the print ads; commercials ended with a man's voice achingly murmuring, "Ah! The smell of it!" The use of the word "smell," with its primitive biological connotations, rather than the more usual "scent" or "fragrance," cued even more basic sexuality for Obsession, creating a brand personality built on the free expression of basic human lust. **35**

Obsession's smell is strongly musky, a scent categorized by perfumers as "animalic" because of its organic source, and is quite recognizable on the wearer. I am regularly struck by the range of women I pass during a day whose choice of perfume message to send is Obsession's. Many are far from young, and **36** far from the media-based definition of sexy, but they're doused with a scent-image that reveals their underlying fantasies of themselves—fantasies nourished by advertising.

37   Not long ago, I was in a Saks Fifth Avenue and an unmistakable current of Obsession wafted by, trailed by an energetic, pink-haired, cosmetic-laden matron with hat and gloves. While it is true that, demographically, women of her age tend to wear heavier fragrances, that's not the whole show. Perfume advertising is all image—that's what drives the product category. At some level, here was a woman with a fantasy of herself as a femme fatale—a lascivious consort—in secret longing.

38   After the mating-hydra approach to selling Obsession, a shift occurs in the brand's advertising imagery. What do we have next? A bunch of naked people who studiously avoid contact of any kind with each other. In one ad for Obsession, four muscular men and two well-toned women organize their oiled, nude bodies into approximate pairs—not all of which include one member of the opposite sex—on and about a tall, aggressively angled white obelisk. Any sign of emotion, let alone sexual passion, has been eradicated. The people are turned stiffly away from each other, posturing states of grand boredom—noses hoisted in the air as if listening to a private muse. These people have no more feelings or thoughts going on than the phallic prop they surround. What's being sold here is an elaborate image of self-control through psychological detachment. It's as if only two poles of the erotic continuum can be conceptualized by Obsession's advertiser—unbounded promiscuity or asexual androidism. The real obsession is again with the self, which is certainly one way of pulling back from messy, possibly even disease-carrying, relationships, with no expectations of closeness that counts. That's a fairly discouraging cultural mirror.

39   Calvin Klein's Eternity, the advertiser's latest fragrance entry, uses advertising that creates the impression that the image of this product is radically different from the type of flagrant sexual displays associated with Obsession—and they are, but only on the surface. In one of the introductory print ads, a married couple, ring glinting in evidence, rest against one another, beneath the word "Eternity," written in classic typeface; in others, the couple are joined by their children in tranquil settings. Squeakily wholesome commitment and tender romance look like the new name of the game, until the characters play out a bizarre view of what their relationship might really be about in Eternity's *television* campaign.

40   In Eternity's series of surrealistic, technically superb spots, a man and woman voice their fears of being engulfed and consumed by the fervor of their cravings for each other. Speaking in the hollow, hurried flatness of an Ingmar Bergman film, the lovers engage in ardent psychological jargon about the frightening nature of their hopelessly enmeshed relationship. They say things like "We haven't hurt each other yet, but we soon will. . . . "; "Help me destroy me—become me until there's nothing left but you. . . . "; "I destroy everything I love. . . . "; "I don't know where I end and you begin . . . would you still love me if I were a woman?"; and the familiar narcissistic refrain, "When I look at you, I feel like I'm looking in a mirror."

This isn't love, and it isn't romance; this is an *obsession,* an addiction. With   **41**
this type of psychological message, the advertiser's imagery may be moving
away from multiple naked sex partners, but the model of narcissistic self-
involvement is just as entrenched as ever. The romantic potential of these ads
is mired in the fears of the emotional risks of closeness, fears that are often
rooted in a poorly defined self-identity. For the commercials' heroes, spending
an eternity together—Eternity's promise—would be tantamount to a hereafter
in Sartre's *No Exit.*

Advertisers aren't the cause of people's problems with true intimacy, but   **42**
neither are they the passive, neutral reflectors of how our society views relationships. In their frenzied bids for attention, advertisers frequently wave sexual
imagery at consumers, hoping to be remembered. Some are; many are not. But
what goes get set in the collective memory of the culture are portraits of stunted
sexual development, portraits of sexual-status displays, narcissistic glorification,
and crude innuendo, portraits that are sold along with products pledging to help
consumers put themselves in the power positions promoted by the advertiser as
enviable.

Because these portraits reflect essentially insecure identities, the images   **43**
promoted point the way toward more, rather than less, emotional emptiness.
When Madison Avenue's idea of a loving relationship includes mutual self-
destruction, the measuring-up game can become downright crippling. Ideally,
relationships are strongest when both partners play with a full deck, with a sense
of security and solid identity. Barring that, it's a safe bet to play with fewer cards
than to borrow advertisers' pictures and try to build a winning hand from them.

▼ TOPICAL CONSIDERATIONS

1. Why, according to the author, is sexual imagery used so extensively
   in advertising?
2. Why are ads with symbolic or indirect sexual messages, such as the
   Seagram's "Arouse an Olive" (paragraphs 6 and 7), more effective
   than ads with more straightforward and transparent messages, such
   as the Seagram's "Maybe" ad (paragraph 8)?
3. How is the theme of dominance-and-submission used to sell cigarettes? Include an explanation of the connection established between sexual passion and smoking cigarettes. Can you think of
   other products that are advertised using this approach? Will your
   awareness of this theme change your attitude toward the products
   being advertised?
4. According to this piece, do men and women react differently to
   sexual imagery in advertisements? Do you agree, or do you feel
   Moog's analysis reflects commonly held stereotypes about men and
   women?
5. Describe the kinds of images commonly found in Guess Jeans' ads.
   Do you agree that the "psychological messages sent by Guess imag-

ery strongly imply that girls can use their sexuality to free themselves from parental constraints" (paragraph 23)? Based on your personal experiences, can you make any generalizations about the kinds of people who are attracted to, turned off by, or indifferent to these ads?

6. Do you feel that ads such as that for Trouble are irresponsible in the age of AIDS? Explain your answer.

7. How does the myth of Narcissus live on in advertising? Why does Moog say of this narcissistic self-absorption, "Psychologically, it's a dead-end street" (paragraph 29).

8. Do you feel advertisers should avoid sexual imagery that may promote psychologically undesirable themes (i.e., narcissism, alienation, domination, and submission)? Or should they feel free to incorporate any themes that the culture will tolerate to sell products?

9. According to Moog, what kind of impact does the sexual sell have on one's emotional development? Do you agree or disagree?

▼ RHETORICAL CONSIDERATIONS

1. We could not reproduce the various visuals for the ads Moog discusses. However, are her descriptions vivid enough for you? Are they persuasive and engaging?

2. Ms. Moog is a clinical psychologist and an advertising consultant. Does her expertise in these fields come through in this essay? Cite some examples as evidence.

3. Since Ms. Moog is an ad consultant the reader may question her objectivity. Does her professional connection with the advertising world seem to compromise her analysis of the way sex is used in ads? In other words, does she act as an apologist for advertising?

4. Are there instances in the essay where you feel Moog read things into ads that were not there? Explain your answer with examples.

▼ WRITING ASSIGNMENTS

1. In paragraph 25, Moog asks, "How can all these images of sexual entanglings be going on in the eighties? Hasn't anyone told advertisers about AIDS?" Write an essay expressing your feelings about the use of sexual imagery to sell in an age when the consequences of a sexual alliance can be deadly.

2. Interview some acquaintances to determine what they think of particular ads using the kind of sexual imagery described here. Write an essay giving an overview of their reactions. In your conclu-

sion try to determine whether Moog's concern about psychological messages were warranted or not.

3. Write an essay defending the sexual sell. You might take as your slant the fact that advertisers are in business to make money not regulate morality.

4. Peruse a current magazine and select three or four ads that use symbolic sexual imagery to sell a product. As Moog does, analyze the imagery, the psychological message, and the potential impact on the viewer of the ad.

5. In paragraph 37, Moog describes a "matron with hat and gloves" wearing Obsession, an "animalic" scent. Moog finds this an incompatible combination. Write an essay describing someone who has purchased a product whose ad image does not fit the person. What conclusions can you make about the power of the ads and what might have motivated the purchaser?

▼ THE PRESENCE OF THE WORD IN TV ADVERTISING
Jay Rosen

We have looked at the language of advertising claims and promises. In critical detail, we have seen the lengths to which advertisers will go to sell their wares. We have also heard a persuasive defense of advertisers against claims that they distort language and reality. What follows is an analysis of the language of TV commercials, but not the kind of *language* we've been talking about. As explained below, Jay Rosen has discovered the existence of a deeper language in TV ads—a language that is best understood when the sound is turned off. It's then you can hear what's really being said.

Jay Rosen is an assistant professor of journalism and communications at New York University. He is also a writer and contributing editor of *Channels* magazine. This article first appeared in *Et cetera* in the Summer of 1987.

It is safe to say that most inquiries into the language of television advertising would look at the sort of language actually used in the ads. I could imagine, for example, a rather interesting article on how an advertising slogan like "Where's the Beef?" became almost instantly part of the American language in the summer of 1984. Indeed, in a journal like *Et cetera* there could easily be an entire issue devoted to the "Where's the Beef?" slogan. For cultural observers, then, there is quite a lot of material in the language employed by television advertising. But that is not the direction I want to take in this article.

2   I would like to begin by observing the following fact. All over America there are people who have discovered a new way of watching television. The advertising industry calls them "flippers," people who drift restlessly around the dial by remote control, changing the channel at the slightest provocation—the appearance on screen of Angie Dickinson, for example. I know one man—not an academic, as it turns out—who says he hits the button as soon as he feels the smallest hint of content coming on. My own habits are not quite so severe, but I am, I confess, a flipper. (By the way, most flippers are male, something no one has thought to study yet.) If the advertising industry is concerned about flippers, it would be doubly concerned about me. For I am not only a flipper, but I often flip with the sound off. I find it easier to recognize patterns that way, and pattern recognition is, so to speak, my profession.

3   Now, flipping with the sound off is a good way of investigating television ads. Frequently I find myself asking, "what is this ad about?" as I watch the images float by. "What is this ad about?" is a different question, of course, from "what *product* is this an ad for?" To ask what an ad is "about" is to inquire into the underlying message of the ad. . . . Deodorant ads, as almost everyone knows, are about shame and the body, no matter what they seem to be saying. The art of flipping makes it easier to recognize such things, and I recommend it to everyone as an inexpensive research tool.

4   You don't have to be a flipper to recognize that one trend in television advertising is toward increasing visualization—more images, arriving at a faster clip, and packing more of a punch. Often they are accompanied by music, and frequently this music is borrowed or adapted from hit songs on the radio. MTV is thus an obvious influence on this sort of advertising, but there's an important difference. A certain vagueness or incoherence is possible, even desirable, in a music video. As a result, it is often impossible to say what music videos are really about, despite the presence of a lot of striking images. In advertising there is not as much license. The images must succeed, not only in grabbing attention, but in communicating a single concept or theme which can then be linked to the product. This is what I mean by "deep structure" in TV advertising.

5   A good example is a new series of ads for Michelob beer. You may recall that Michelob's slogan used to be "Weekends Were Made for Michelob." In the new campaign the line is, "The Night Belongs to Michelob," suggesting that in the 1990s, Michelob has colonized the entire week. In any event, the ads now feature a series of images, very well shot, all of which vivify life in the big city at night. Well-dressed women step out of cabs, skylines twinkle and glow, performers take the stage in smoky nightclubs, couples kiss on the street, backlit by the headlights of cars. These are not only images *of* the night; they are *about* the night as an idea or myth. Their goal is to create a swirl of associations around the word "night," which is actually heard in the ad if you have the sound on. Phil Collins of the rock band Genesis sings a song in which the word "tonight" is repeated over and over.

6   But what's interesting about the ads is that neither the lyrics of Phil Collins

nor the slogan, "The Night Belongs to Michelob," are necessary to get the message. The word "night" comes through in the very texture of the images. It's there even when the sound is off and no language is being heard. What Walter Ong once called "the presence of the word" does not, in this case, depend on the presence of language. For example, a singer is shown silhouetted in a spotlight on stage at a night club. This is not merely a picture *taken* at night, in a place associated *with* the night. It is almost an abstract diagram of the concept of night. The beam of the spotlight, because it is visible, demonstrates the presence of darkness all around. The singer appears as a silhouette, a black shape who is in, of, and surrounded by the night. The spotlight, then, is the very principle of intelligibility at work: It lights up the night, not in order to obliterate it, but to give it form, to demonstrate what "night" is, almost like a Sesame Street vocabulary lesson. This giving of form to an abstract concept is the logic behind a number of ads on television.

Levi's, for example, has created a series of ads about the idea of "blue." **7** Naturally they are shot in blue tones on city streets. They also feature blues songs being strummed in the background. And, of course, the actors are all wearing blue jeans. But blue is communicated on a deeper level, as well. The feeling of blue—the meaning blue has taken on in popular culture—is brought out in the way a girl walks wistfully down the street, blowing soap bubbles into the air. In these ads, blue would come through without the sound of blues songs or the product name—Levi's 501 blues. Indeed, I am tempted to say that blue would come through even on a black and white set. Why? Because the director has found images which "mean" blue at the deepest cultural level. It is not the surfaced presence of the *color* blue that matters, but a kind of inner architecture of blue, on top of which blue scenes, blue jeans and blues songs have been placed.

This may seem easy enough with a concept, like blue, that is primarily **8** visual. But what about notions that are essentially verbal? The Hewlett-Packard company has attempted something along these lines. It is now running a series of ads whose slogan is "What if . . . ?" In these ads, Hewlett-Packard people are seen pondering difficult problems, hitting upon a possible answer, and rushing to their colleagues to announce, "I've got it: What if . . . " and the sound fades out.

Of course, if you turn the sound off, there is no "what if" to be heard and **9** no fade out. And yet the idea of "what if" is not necessarily gone. Picture this: An intelligent-looking woman in glasses is shown alone in her office, tapping a pencil and sort of looking skyward, as if contemplating a majestic possibility. Here the attempt is to produce a visual image of "what-if-ness," a notion ordinarily expressed in words or mathematical symbols. It has often been said that pictures have no tense. But Hewlett-Packard is attempting to prove that a tense—in this case, the conditional—can in fact be a visual idea—borrowed from language, but expressed in images. Perhaps we will soon see ads visualizing a host of ideas we ordinarily think of as linguistic. How about a series of pictures about the concept of "nevertheless" or "because"?

What I am trying to point out is a certain irony in the trend toward **10** increased visualization. As TV ads become shorter, they become more visual, as a way of saying more in a smaller amount of time. But as they become more visual, the ads seem to be about concepts which are inescapably verbal. Advertising may appear to be relying less on language, but language is simply functioning on a deeper level. It has not, in any sense, gone away. And a final irony is this: In order to discover this deeper level of language it is necessary to ignore the language on the surface. In a strange way, turning the sound off allows you to hear what's really being said.

▼ TOPICAL CONSIDERATIONS

1. The ad industry has a name for a certain type of viewer—"flipper." Just what is a "flipper"? Are you one? Why are advertisers concerned about flippers?
2. Slogans such as "Where's the beef?" became part of American language in the summer of 1984. Are there any ad slogans that have more recently become part of our language? Can you think of slogans that you heard before seeing the ad? Has any slogan gotten you to buy a product? If so, what was it, and how do you explain your decision to buy?
3. Rosen says in paragraph 3 that deodorant ads are "about shame and the body." What ads for other products have this same message? How do they differ in their handling of the message? Which are more subtle, which more blunt?
4. In paragraph 6, what is meant by the claim that " 'the presence of the word' " in some commercials does not "depend on the presence of language"? Can you think of other examples currently being aired?
5. Rosen says that some commercials capture abstract concepts without the use of language. Can you think of any current commercials that do that? Do any operate with visual images alone—that is, no spoken words? Describe how the visuals create the abstract messages.
6. Did you learn anything from this essay? Did it make you more aware of the power of television commercials? of the " 'presence of the word' " in commercials? of how they work on us?

▼ RHETORICAL CONSIDERATIONS

1. What would you say is the author's purpose in writing this essay: to inform, to educate, to persuade, to entertain? Some of each? Explain.
2. To better understand how Rosen organized his discussion, make an

outline of the essay. Which paragraphs serve as the beginning, middle and end? Is there a solid unity here? Explain.

3. What part of this essay struck you as the most interesting? What reasons can you offer for your selection: the quality of language, the use of details, examples, humor, interesting observations?

4. Reread the concluding paragraph. In your own words, summarize the point Rosen is making. How well does this unify and round off the discussion? Do you find this conclusion satisfying? Why or why not?

▼ WRITING ASSIGNMENTS

1. Select an ad campaign currently running on television. With the sound off, record how you think the visual images relay the language and meaning behind the concept. (You might even try to count the number of different camera cuts.) What are the messages? How do the actors, scenery and/or action help support those messages? Is spoken language necessary for the ad's concept to work? Consider these questions and write a paper stating your conclusions.

2. Although it is said that pictures lack tense (paragraph 9), Rosen points to the Hewlett-Packard ad as an example of "the conditional." Taking up the challenge, try to think of a series of pictures about "yesterday." How about "tomorrow"? Or Rosen's own challenge: "nevertheless" and "because." In a paper, describe just what pictures you have in mind. Can you think of products to fit these pictures?

3. Rosen says that viewers flip through channels with different frequency and for different reasons. He also claims that there are more male flippers than female. Quietly observe family and friends over the next week for signs of flipping. Who does all the flipping? As best as you can tell, when do they flip, and why? Feel free to be creative in your report.

▼ HOW NOW DOW?
Mark Crispin Miller

This essay is a focused analysis of the kinds of hidden messages Jay Rosen just talked about. It is also a good illustration of how you might go about critically analyzing TV commercials or magazine ads such as those reprinted at the end of this chapter. The particular commercial Mark Crispin Miller examines is a corporate-image TV spot Dow Chemical put together for Earth Day 1990. Like so many other "green ads" then and since, this particular piece was aimed at promoting a proenvironment image—in this case, for the huge manufacturer of pesticides, fertilizers, and Styrofoam. Miller is a journalist who has written widely on cinema, television, rock music, and advertising. His material has appeared in the *Nation, Mother Jones,* and the *New Republic. Boxed In: The Culture of TV* (1988) is a recent collection of some of his essays. The essay below first appeared in the September 1990 issue of *Esquire* magazine.

---

1   "That's my Dad." In the pre-teen voice there's just the trace of an apologetic chuckle. It's understandable. The "Dad" in this commercial is an overt dork. Pitching at a (Dow) company softball game, he gives up a base hit, then tries to block it with his foot.

2   "Good thing he's got a *real* job!" jokes Dad's young son, ". . . at Dow!" As the subject shifts from softball to the corporation, this cherub drops the mild, ironic tone and starts promoting Dow's environmentalism in a kind of earnest kidspeak. Dad is (spoken haltingly) "a . . . plastics . . . recycling . . . engineer!" Dad "figures out ways" to turn plastic trash "into neat stuff like those picnic tables—and Brad's bat 'n' ball!"

3   With this last phrase, there appears tiny "Brad," apparently a baby brother, whacking a home run—and then there's Dad again, oafishly striking out: "My Dad may be a lousy ballplayer," his son concludes, "but he's a *neat guy!*" The boy then grasps Dad's hand and gazes up, with filial pathos, into the engineer's weak, boyish face, sighing, "I'm *real proud* o' ya, Dad!" *"Proud* of me?" Dad gasps, and the camera cranes up and back to reveal the father-son communion amid the Dow-sponsored gaiety, as that hearty female voice, so reminiscent of "the sixties" (the Seekers), breaks, as usual, into the jingle: "Dow . . . *lets* you do *great thiiiings!"*

4   Devised for Earth Day, this ad, like most "green ads," tries to dim our awareness of foul air, mounting garbage, ozone depletion. Implicitly, Dow's sponsorship of this old-fashioned sunny fete assures us that Dow, prolific maker of (among other goodies) Styrofoam, pesticide, and chemical fertilizer, wants us all to live as we did before the rise of agri-business, freeways, and fast food. The child, too, is reassuring. If this cool young kid is so moved by Dad's daily

responsibilities, then Dad/Dow must be doing a heroic job indeed, with that "plastic recycling."

Not that plastic poses any danger! Certainly, each and every one of us **5** should go on using tons of it: Dad is there to help Dow make *more* plastics.

And Dow's TV spots work to sanitize not just its wares but its very image. **6** In this ad Dow seems not huge and lethal, but goofily benign, like that awkward boy/dad in his special hat and corporate colors. By softening "Dad," our usual symbol of authority, Dow appears also to champion the weak and innocent: "Brad" belts a homer while Dad strikes out—just as, in other Dow ads, the effectual one is not some steel-gray CEO, but a slightly rumpled backpacker; a lanky college student grinning on a humble bike; a slim and saintly Ph.D. gone home to save her grandpa's farm.

What Dow is selling here, then, is not just a profitable myth about plastics **7** but the sense (which will become *our* sense, if we don't watch out) that certain dissident impulses of the past have been absorbed—by Dow. In its ads, the young are on Dow's side—not like, say, 20 years ago. Back then, one of Dow's products—napalm—made the company notorious, through horrifying images of children burned and screaming. Those who saw those images, and haven't forgotten, may not feel comforted by Dow's knowing hikers, tykes, and Ph.D.'s. Younger viewers, on the other hand, have no way of spotting the lie, since TV, thanks to Dow and others, has no memory.

▼ TOPICAL CONSIDERATIONS

1. What do you think Miller hoped his readers would learn from his essay? How do you think he wants them to respond? On what do you base your answers?
2. Even if you have not seen this particular Dow commercial, from Miller's descriptions of it, do you agree with his criticism? Do you disagree with any of his points?
3. At the end of the essay, Miller warns about "certain dissident impulses of the past . . . [having] been absorbed—by Dow." Explain his warning here. How might Dow be more effective with young viewers in selling "the lie"?
4. Has Miller's analysis changed your thinking about such "green ads"? If so, in what ways? Do you think your attitudes and behavior will be altered any? How might the analysis and arguments presented here affect your thinking about commercials in general?
5. Can you think of other "green ads" that try to take the viewer's mind off of environmental dangers? What do they have in common with the Dow ad? What kinds of corporate images are being projected? Are these ads effective? Convincing? Obviously propagandistic?

▼ RHETORICAL CONSIDERATIONS

1. Consider the title Miller chose for this piece. What exactly does it mean? Given the thrust of the essay, can you think of any associations or connotations that make it a particularly appropriate one?
2. At what point in the essay does Miller make his focus clear? Does this lead capture your attention? What device does he use to cue you to his purpose?
3. What aspects of Miller's writing do you think were most effective? The least effective?
4. This essay has a clear beginning, middle, and end. Outline it by paragraphs. Does this outline more clearly help you see how the various parts of the essay are related? Is this a structure you might consider following in papers?

▼ WRITING ASSIGNMENTS

1. Miller's discussion of the Dow Chemical commercial is a good example of how to analyze a piece of advertising. Try doing your critical analysis of a current "green ad." As Miller does, try to point out subtle messages and symbols. Consider the scenes, the actors, how they dress, their life-styles, the audience targeted, the visual styles and motifs, the music, etc. What are the messages of the ads? Who are the figures of "authority"? What causes are being championed? What are the "lies"?
2. Both Naomi Wolf ("The Beauty Myth") and Carol Moog above, among others, reprimanded advertisers for sexually exploiting women in ads and commercials. As Miller points out, Dow projects an adult male as "an overt dork." Is this "male-as-dork" a new trend in advertising? See if you can find other commercials that project men as "goofily benign," "awkward" or "oafish." Then write a paper analyzing the ads or trend if you detect one. Consider the following questions: What do the ads have in common? How are the men imaged? What are the intentions of the ads? How do they target the audience? Are the men forgiveable for their dorkiness? How are the females in the ads portrayed?

▼ WHO BREWS UP THESE ADS?

Diane White

Thus far, the essays in this chapter have been aimed at sharpening our critical eyes and ears when it comes to advertising. To that end, we've examined the slick images, the slyly crafted claims, and the psychological designs and effects. This closing piece is a humorous warning that perhaps too much thinking about ads can be a dangerous thing. As Diane White explains here, one can too easily become obsessed with reading between the lines and behind the scenes of commercials we've seen a million times. Diane White is a humor columnist for the *Boston Globe*. This essay first appeared in November 1990.

1 "The best part of waking up is Folgers in your cup!"

2 I'd seen the ad, or one like it, a million times, give or take a hundred thousand. But for some reason, on this particular morning, I actually started to think about it. The ad, I mean, what it was saying.

3 The best part of waking up is Folgers in your cup. It's depressing to think that for some people it may be true, that there are those whose lives are so benighted that the best part of waking up might very well be a cup of Folgers. It might even be the high point of the day.

4 I've had plenty of mornings when the best reason, maybe the only good reason, to get out of bed was the prospect of a cup of coffee. Of course, that might not have been the case if Folgers had been all I had to look forward to.

5 Sitting there, drinking non-Folgers coffee, I began to think about how I might feel if I had dragged myself out of bed hoping for a decent cup of coffee, only to find that some stinker had slipped one over on me in the form of Folgers Instant.

6 Because that's what's happening, all over America. People are pussyfooting around kitchens in the early hours of the day shamelessly tricking their friends and loved ones by substituting Folgers Instant for the brewed coffee that, as human beings, they have a right to expect.

7 Apparently, the people who run Folgers are encouraging them in this treachery by soliciting these tales of deception and betrayal to use in their advertising. They've been running a new series of ads featuring dramatizations of stories sent in by people dying to brag about how they put one over on friends, relatives, co-workers, wedding guests.

8 There's even a nun in one. She gleefully describes how she conned her fellow sisters—sister sisters?—by filling the convent coffeepot with Folgers Instant instead of the real stuff. Imagine, a nun actually boasting in public about being so underhanded. What's the world coming to?

9 Once you start thinking about ads, it's hard to stop. Of course, there are

some ads I try very hard not to think about. The Preparation H ad with the people playing musical chairs. That woman who wants me to join the Sine-Aid Society. The countless ads for nostrums and supplements designed to promote "regularity." Anybody who still thinks baseball is the national pastime hasn't seen enough of these.

10   But there are other ads I can't stop thinking about. One in particular has obsessed me lately, that one in which they bake the pearls made of denture material into the blueberry pie.

11   The idea, I guess, is to demonstrate how Efferdent will clean false teeth of something as seemingly indelible as blueberry pie. Somehow, though, whenever I see this ad, and I see it a lot, my mind veers sharply away from the merits of the product and I begin thinking: Who in the world ever thought of this? How much did they get paid? If I had false teeth, would I see it in a different light? Should Agent Cooper look into this?

12   I try to imagine the meeting at which the creative team from the ad agency first pitched the idea to the client: "First we'll bake a string of pearls made of denture material into a blueberry pie . . . "

13   Did the Efferdent people say, "Swell concept!" Did they say, "What are you, nuts?" Did they say, "Why blueberry? Why not cherry?" Or "How about mincemeat?" Did it occur to them that after seeing this ad, some people might never dare eat blueberry pie again for fear of chomping on a string of pearls made of denture material, or maybe even a set of false teeth? What do the blueberry growers think of it? Has it cut into their sales?

14   It's probably not a good idea to think about ads too much. You can see where it leads.

▼ TOPICAL CONSIDERATIONS

1. Summarize Diane White's feelings about the recent Folger's ads. Are the ads familiar to you? If so, do you share her sentiments about them? Explain your answer.

2. Are you a coffee drinker? Do you wake up hankering for your first cup? If so, is it the taste, the caffeine kick, or both? Consider the success of the Folgers ads in appealing to consumer desires. Do you think they are effective in selling the product? Have the ads made you want to try Folgers? How about Folgers Instant? If so, do you prefer it to fresh brewed coffee? How does it compare to other instant coffees?

3. Explain White's statement in paragraph 9, "there are some ads I try very hard not to think about." Do you feel the same way? If so, which ads do you not want to think about, and why? Do you think the creators of such ads want you not to think probingly about them, or just the opposite? Explain your thoughts here.

4. There are other ads that White admits she cannot stop thinking

about. What is there about the Efferdent ad that captures her imagination? If you're familiar with the ad, have you had the same thoughts? If not, did White make you question the kinds of thinking that goes into brewing up such creations? Can you think of commercials not mentioned by White that seem a little bizarre or foolish to you?

5. What do you think Diane White hoped her readers would learn from her essay? How do you think she wants them to respond? On what do you base your answer? Has she changed the way you think about television commercials in general?

▼ RHETORICAL CONSIDERATIONS

1. Comment on the opening sentence of the essay. How does it capture your attention? Is it effective in making you want to read on? How does it forecast what is to follow?

2. White ends paragraph 8 with the rhetorical question, "What's the world coming to?" How would you describe the tone of this question? Does she mean it seriously? Is she just trying to be funny? Or does its intent lie someplace in between? Explain.

3. Comment on White's writing style. Is it formal or informal? Conversational? Friendly? Is it a style you could adopt for your own essays?

4. Did you find this essay humorous in places? If so, try to describe the humorous effects?

5. White does not come right out and say what she thinks about the Efferdent commercial, but it's clear she has strong feelings. What techniques does she use to convey her opinion of it?

6. Consider the closing paragraph in the essay. Was it satisfying for you? Did it succinctly capture the tone, slant, and emphasis of the essay? Does it make a clear point? Explain your answer.

▼ WRITING ASSIGNMENTS

1. If you're familiar with a current Folgers commercial (regular or instant), write a paper in which you analyze its effectiveness in wooing the consumer into switching brands. Consider the "message" and pitch as well as the visuals, music, scenes, the tone of the ad, its cinematic techniques, style, and so forth.

2. Are there certain television commercials that just bug you? If so, which ones are they, and what is it about them that gets to you? Write a paper in which you describe some particularly annoying commercials, then analyze what you find obnoxious about them.

Would you purposely avoid buying such products because of the ads?

3. Some advertisers defend annoying commercials by claiming that they are most successful because they draw the most attention. Do you agree with this, or is it the other way around? Analyze some television commercials that do and do not draw attention to themselves. Which seem the most successful?

4. At the end of her essay, White imagines what might have been said by the creative team members of the ad agency that dreamed up the Efferdent commercial. Think of a product—perhaps, a familiar one on the market—and write a dialogue of the ad team brainstorming to come up with a catchy new commercial. Have some fun with this.

▼ SAMPLE ADS AND STUDY QUESTIONS

Here we reproduced ten recently published magazine ads—familiar pitches for cereal, liquor, condoms, long-distance telephone service, photographic film, clothing, and the National Rifle Association. The ads are as diversified in their products as in their selling strategies. Some are nearly all graphics with no hard-sell copy, while others are informative, even chatty. To demonstrate the wide variety in advertising strategies and styles, three of the ads are for the same product—whiskey. Following each of the ten ads is a set of questions to assist you in analyzing how the ads work their appeal on us—how they subtly and not-so-subtly try to convince us that their product is worth our money.

▼ "THEY'RE IN A HURRY."

1. What would you say is the main appeal of this ad's visuals? Try to explain how that appeal works.
2. The statement of this ad is "They're in a hurry." What different messages does this convey? How do these messages appeal to our emotions? How do these messages help promote Kellogg's cereals?
3. How would the impact of the ad be affected were the children not smiling? What would be the impact if the girl was taller than the boy? What if their clothes were less stylish or formal? What if their postures and hand positions were different?
4. Why do you suppose the advertisers chose not to include a particular box of Kellogg's cereal in the ad?
5. Does this ad make you want to purchase Kellogg's cereal? Why, or why not?

They're in a hurry.
(But we're not.)

When you're young, it seems to take forever to grow up. And sometimes, you're tempted to try to speed up the process.
Of course, good things need time to grow, and nobody knows better than Kellogg's. We've been in the growing business for more than 75 years.
In that time, we have grown from a small cornflakes com-

pany to a worldwide manufacturer of a variety of products. So we know a little bit about growing up. For us, it takes time to make grains into great-tasting, nutritious ready-to-eat breakfast cereals for your family.
So, if they are in a hurry to grow up, it's all right. But at Kellogg's we're in no hurry. We know that good things take time.

Kellogg's

® Kellogg Company © 1983 Kellogg Company

Courtesy Kellogg's

▼ "SEAGRAM'S V.O. THE REWARD."

1. According to the ad, why do Steve Wade and Ernest Paine deserve "the reward" of Seagram's V.O.?
2. What image of men does the ad project? Consider the men's clothes, physical condition, expressions, age, and the locale. Do they look like the kinds of men who fit the copy? Do they strike you as extraordinary looking? Ordinary looking? Would the male model in the Polo ad be right for this ad? Why or why not?
3. How would the ad be affected if the two men were holding glasses of Seagram's V.O. in their hands? How would the ad be affected if the men were smiling with their arms around each other's shoulders?
4. Consider the setting of the ad. How do the distant rugged mountains add to the appeal and message of the ad? What about the flat plains and the animals grazing behind the fence?
5. What is the strategy of laying the bottle of Seagram's V.O. on it's side? What about the way the bottle divides the copy?

Reprinted courtesy of Seagram Distillers Company

▼ "WHEN YOU LIVE A CUTTY ABOVE."

1. In his essay, "The Language of Advertising," Charles O'Neill made the point that much of an ad's appeal depends upon the consumer's identification with the image projected. Consider the two models in this Cutty Sark ad. What image is projected by the following: their clothing? their hair? the setting? their ages? the expressions on their faces? their general appearances? How do these images help sell the product?

2. Judging from the setting and the men's apparel, what might be the occasion of the photograph? How does this help support the statement in the ad's brief copy, "When you live a Cutty above"?

3. Consider the line, "When you live a Cutty above." Why was it positioned where it is in the ad? Do you find the line catchy? Do you think the pun is intended to stick in one's mind? Is it likely to become a familiar phrase such as other commercial slogans?

4. How do the visual images coordinate with the copy: "When you live a Cutty above"? How do the visual images coordinate with the copy: "Uncommon Quality"? How do the visuals help sell Cutty Sark?

5. Consider the attitude of the two men. What kind of exchange might be going on between them? Is it clear which man made the remark they are laughing about? What is the "message" of their laughing and how does it relate to the product? How would the ad be affected if the two men were looking seriously at each other?

6. Consider the "body messages" of the two models. What do their poses say about their relationship? How would the message be altered were their poses reversed—that is, were the older man's head bowed and his arm resting on the younger man's shoulder? Now consider the message in the positions of the men's glasses.

7. How old would you say the two models are? Why do you suppose the advertisers chose an older and younger man rather than two of the same generation?

8. Do you find this ad appealing? If so, why? If not, why?

Courtesy the Buckingham Wile Company

▼ "DEWAR'S PROFILE: HENRY THREADGILL"

1. For years Dewar's has run "profiles" featuring men and women of differing age, profession, race, income bracket, and life-style. Which segments of the alcohol-drinking population are being targeted in this profile? Which segments are being excluded? Is this an effective approach to selling Dewar's in your estimation?

2. Henry Threadgill chose as his "quote" the following: "Tradition is a background of ingredients; in itself it's nothing. If you can't make something out of it, the world can do without it." What do these words mean? What do they say about the kind of man Henry Threadgill is? How might this philosophy have determined his being chosen for the ad?

3. At first glance, what is the most arresting aspect of this ad? In other words, what grabbed your attention, and why?

4. Compare and contrast the images of men projected in this ad and that for Cutty Sark and Seagram's. Which is more appealing to you and why?

5. Setting is very important in ads because it helps make associations and project images. What about the setting here—or lack of it? How would this ad be altered were it shot "on location"—as was the Cutty Sark—instead of in a studio?

6. Draw up a Dewar's profile of yourself. In it list some of your latest accomplishments, the last book read, your hobbies, a choice quotation of yours, and why you do what you do. Do you think your profile would sell "White Label"? Why, or why not?

Courtesy Schenley Imports Company

▼ "TROJAN BRAND LATEX CONDOMS: FOR ALL THE RIGHT REASONS"

1. What first caught your attention about this ad? Was it the photographs of the models? Was it the ad copy? Was it the large-type Trojan name at the bottom?
2. The makers of Trojan brand latex condoms want to associate their product with particular values and images. Consider the two models in this ad. What images are projected by the man and the woman? Consider their ages, appearances, clothes, hair styles, expressions, attractiveness, the positions of their heads, and the way they are looking at the camera. Do they seem to be the kind of people who would listen to the Surgeon General? Would they practice "safety regarding sex"?
3. What kind of audience does this ad appeal to?
4. How would the impact, message, images, and values be altered if the ad had just the male model speaking? How would these things be altered with just the female model speaking?
5. Consider the phrase "safety regarding sex." Why do you think this particular wording was chosen? What kind of "safety" do the manufacturers want you to think about? What other kind of "safety" is implied, but intentionally avoided in the ad? Why?
6. National magazines began running ads for condoms in the mid-1980s. Why do you suppose they had not been run before then? Why are they being run today? How has the authority of the Surgeon General been enlisted here to sell condoms?
7. Consider the first guarantee of safe sex claimed by the makers of Trojan brand latex condoms: "a faithful marriage to a healthy person." How would the message be altered were it worded: "marriage to a healthy person"? or, "a faithful relationship with a healthy person"? or, "a relationship with a healthy person"? or, "relationships with healthy persons"?
8. What do you make of the second "guarantee"—"abstinence"? What is the message here?
9. Consider the next paragraph: "In all other cases, as the Surgeon General of the United States says, 'An individual must be warned to use the protection of a condom.' " What might "all other cases" cover? Would sex in marriage be one of the cases? What about premarital sex? What about extramarital sex? What about sex between gays? Does the direct quote from the Surgeon General imply that he is endorsing the use of condoms as opposed to other means of "protection"?
10. How might the Catholic Church react to this ad?

"Someone I respect has been urging me to use condoms. He's the Surgeon General."

"I've heard what the Surgeon General is saying about condoms. And believe me, I'm listening."

The makers of Trojan latex condoms would like you to know that there are really only two ways to be absolutely sure of safety regarding sex.

One is a faithful marriage to a healthy person.

And the other is abstinence.

In all other cases, as the Surgeon General of the United States says, "An individual must be warned to use the protection of a condom."

Trojan latex condoms, America's most widely used and trusted brand, help reduce the risk of spreading many sexually transmitted diseases.

We urge you to use them in any situation where there is any possibility of sexually transmitted disease.

Look at it this way. You have nothing to lose. And what you stand to save is your life.

TROJAN
BRAND LATEX CONDOMS
For all the right reasons.   © 1987 Carter-Wallace, Inc.

Courtesy of Carter-Wallace, Inc.

▼ "ALL YOU NEED TO REACH OUT."

1. Consider the copy, "I just feel like they care. And it shows—it's in the way that they talk to me. They treat me the way I want to be treated." What is being sold here, a feeling or a product? How does this copy relate to the slogan "All you need to reach out"?

2. What is the purpose of specifying the young woman's name and place of residence at the top of the ad?

3. Again, looking at the copy, who do you think "they" might be? AT&T? Do you see other possibilities? If so, what is the purpose of this ambiguity?

4. The ad consists of little copy and lots of white space. What is the effect of this minimalist style?

5. Studying the photographs, what conclusions are we meant to draw about the age, background, life-style and temperament of the young woman? How does this characterization fit into the strategy of the ad? What audience is being appealed to? What characteristics is the viewer meant to identify with?

6. AT&T uses here the familiar advertising technique of personal testimony. How do the size and placement of the photographs, the photographic angles and hand gestures help create this effect?

7. Do you think this ad is free of sexist stereotypes? Explain your answer.

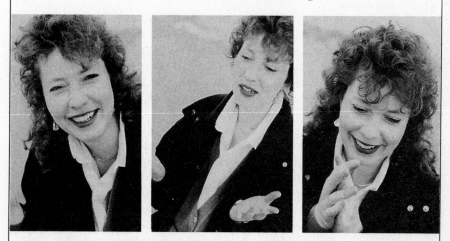

*I just feel like they care. And it shows—
it's in the way that they talk to me. They
treat me the way I want to be treated.*

AT&T Long Distance.
All you need to reach out." 1 800 222-0300.

Courtesy AT&T

▼ "HE JUST SLAYED HIS LAST DRAGON."

1. Many ads appeal to our desires. How does this ad for Kodak film appeal to our emotions? Consider the appearance of the little boy, his clothes, what he has in his hands, what he seems to be doing, the setting (a field of green grass), the backdrop (dark green woods), and so on.

2. Although most of this ad consists of a photograph, there is some copy, set in three different sizes of print. What is the strategy behind heading the copy with a line in the largest type reading, "He just slayed his last dragon"? What is the first message this line conveys to you? Do you sense a subtle, more ominous message in the wording? Do you find any ominous message elsewhere in the ad copy? In the visuals?

3. The middle-sized print is at the bottom: "Kodak film. Because time goes by." What is the strategy of placing it at the bottom and in the next largest size type? What is the subtle strategy of printing it in the same style of type as the first line, "He just slayed his last dragon"?

4. Consider how the wording in the smallest print continues to work on an emotional level. What particular emotions are subtly addressed in this block of copy?

5. How does the actual layout of the ad suggest the way Kodak can help stop time?

Reprinted courtesy of Eastman Kodak Company

▼ "POLO RALPH LAUREN"

1. As Charles O'Neill pointed out in his essay, image is everything. Much of an ad's appeal depends upon the consumer's identification with the image projected. Consider these Polo models. What image is projected by the following: the models' facial expressions? their body poses? their ages? their general appearances?
2. What image is projected by the man's outfit—in particular, the tweed top coat over a denim jacket? What about the scarf and shoestring tie and buckle?
3. What image is projected by the woman's outfit—in particular, the suede jacket over an open blouse? What about the leather gloves?
4. How would the effect of the ad be altered if the man were alone or if the woman were alone? If the woman were not holding the man by his jacket front? If the man's hand were on the woman's jacket?
5. What kind of people would identify with the images of these models? Explain your answer.
6. Both Seagram's and Polo use male models to sell their products. Compare the different images of men that are projected. Would the same man attracted to the Seagram's ad be attracted to the Polo ad?
7. Do you find this ad appealing? If so, why? If not, why?
8. The only copy in this ad is the label: "Polo Ralph Lauren." What products are actually being advertised here? Men's clothing, women's clothing, or both? Do you suppose all of the items have the Polo label? How important is label recognition?

© 1986 PFI Photograph by permission of Polo/Ralph Lauren. Photograph by Bruce Weber.

▼ GUESS?

1. A highly suggestive yet ambiguous scenario is created in this ad. Fill in the details and explain the situation in this ad. Who are these men? Who is the woman with them? What is going on among these three people?
2. What Guess clothing items are being sold? What image is being projected by the men's outfits? In particular—the hats and the scarves? Why are the men holding bottles of beer? Are they meant to be celebrating something?
3. What is the image projected by the woman's outfit? In particular— the blouse and exposed brassiere? Why do you suppose the woman is not holding a beer bottle? Why isn't she smiling as are the men?
4. What might be the subtle message in the fact that the men are wearing boots and the woman is barefoot?
5. Consider the placement of the models. How is the concept of domination and submission being introduced here?
6. What comments would Carol Moog (see "Sex, Sin, and Suggestion") make about this piece?
7. Why would this ad make someone want to buy Guess jeans?
8. This magazine ad originally appeared in black and white. Why this choice instead of color? Consider the effect of light, color, and texture.

Courtesy Guess, Inc.

▼ "I'M THE NRA."

1. For several years the National Rifle Association has been running "I'm the NRA" in national magazines and newspapers. Most often the ad subjects are adults, but on occasion children are used. Do you find the photo of Casey Steenburgen holding a shotgun particularly provocative? Why, or why not? Why do you think the NRA used a 9-year-old boy?
2. How does the ad want you to perceive the NRA? Explain your answer from specifics in the ad.
3. Why do you think the NRA chose to use Casey Steenburgen's own words in describing his feelings about hunting rather than paraphrase them?
4. How would you describe the image Casey Steenburgen projects? Does he appear to be the kind of boy responsible enough to own a shotgun? To be a member of the NRA? Consider his position, the way he holds his shotgun, the expression on his face, his attire, his gender and race. In general, what kind of image does the NRA ad want to project of the young hunter?
5. How is the theme of safe gun handling variously emphasized in the ad?
6. Gun control has been a controversial issue in America for years. How does this ad express the position of the NRA in different ways?
7. The copy mentions Casey's father and grandfather. Why did the advertiser want to mention them? What is the message here?
8. If you are someone who has never had much interest in guns, does this ad provoke your interest in them at all? In gun owners or hunters? Did it alter your attitude toward the NRA? Did it make you consider the possibility of joining someday? Explain your answer.

CASEY STEENBURGEN: 4th Grader, Hunter, Graduate
of Hunter Safety Course,
Member of the National Rifle Association.

"I'm nine years old. I was seven when I started
hunting with my dad and grandpa. I got a shotgun about a year
ago, but it just sat in the closet until I passed
my state's Hunter Safety Course. We spent a lot of time in
classes, then took a test. I got a 98 score.

"My dad and brother and I like to hunt together. We went dove
hunting for my first real hunt. It was a lot of fun. I also
like to hunt squirrels, rabbits and ducks. When ducks fly over I can
hear them coming, even when I'm in class at school.

"I joined the NRA right after I passed the safety
course. My dad signed me up. I like the NRA because they
make sure you can keep your guns and hunt.

"I like football, baseball and soccer, but
hunting is my favorite. It's more exciting." **I'm the NRA.**

Each year NRA-certified instructors teach hundreds of thousands of young people
safe gun handling and basic marksmanship skills. If you would like to join the NRA or want
more information about our programs and benefits, write Harlon Carter,
Executive Vice President, P.O. Box 37484, Dept. CS-13, Washington, D.C. 20013.
Paid for by the members of the National Rifle Association of America. Copyright 1985

Reprinted courtesy of the National Rifle Association

▼ WRITING ASSIGNMENTS

1. Look over the ten ads in our collection. Try to determine which ad you thought was the most effective and which was the least effective. Explain your choices as fully as you can.
2. Select one of the ads and revise its copy and/or visuals so that it appeals to a completely different audience. For example, try to redo the Seagram's V.O. ad so that it appeals to the swinging yuppie set.
3. Using the ads printed here and others you have seen for illustration, write a paper in which you discuss some of the ways advertisers project images of women. Do you find any of these images offensive?
4. Do the same as the previous question, but for men.

9 ▼ On Violence
in America

The United States is "the most violent and self-destructive nation on earth," declared the Senate Judiciary Committee in a 1991 report. Americans are killing, raping, and robbing one another at a rate greatly surpassing every other country that keeps crime statistics. In 1991 there were nearly 24,000 murders committed in the United States, or nearly three an hour, as well as a record number of rapes, robberies, and assaults. While debates rage over issues of criminal justice and gun control, the violence increases and threatens the very nature of American life.

We open this chapter with a plea for nonviolence by one of this century's most courageous opponents of violence, Martin Luther King, Jr. Though "Pilgrimage to Nonviolence" was meant as an inspiration for American blacks struggling for racial equality during the most turbulent days of the civil rights movement, Dr. King's philosophy of nonviolence outlined here has universal appeal.

The next selection is Martin Gansberg's famous award-winning article, "38 Who Saw Murder Didn't Call the Police." What makes this a remarkable piece of journalism is its vivid and shocking realism. It is as much a story of the brutal killing of Kitty Genovese as an indictment of her neighbors who were too afraid, indifferent, or tired to pick up a phone to save a life.

The violence against women in America is truly shocking. The rape rate in the United States is 8 times higher than in France, 15 times higher than in England, 23 times higher than in Italy, and 26 times higher than in Japan, according to the Senate Judiciary report. Even more appalling, rape and assaults on women are rising faster than other crimes. The three pieces that follow address violence against women, each from a different slant—cultural, personal, and social.

In "Hooked on Hate?" Kathi Maio says we need not look far to see why our culture breeds such violence against women. Sexual brutality makes up much of today's popular entertainment. Misogynistic comedians, tabloid television, pornography, rap and rock music, fright films, and video games—these staples of pop culture project messages that women are sexual objects to be used and abused by men, argues the author.

"An Incident in the Park" is not about the infamous assault and rape of a Central Park jogger that filled the media in the early 1990s. In fact, this incident never made the papers. One reason is the sexual assault on the author Aileen Hefferren did not result in physical injury. "It was no big deal," she was told. But that's just the point of her story: What kind of a society considers an assault on a woman an ordinary event?

The next piece looks at a growing problem on our college campuses and in society at large: acquaintance or date rape. Fueled by the notorious 1991 Palm Beach case involving William Kennedy Smith and a woman who accused him of sexual assault, "When Is It Rape?" explores the murky area where a man's advance is a woman's rape.

Our final selection is "Why I Bought a Gun." As the title suggests, the author, Gail Buchalter, explains why a sensitive, intelligent woman from a liberal upper-middle-class background would be driven to purchase a handgun.

▼ PILGRIMAGE TO NONVIOLENCE

Martin Luther King, Jr.

We open this section with an essay by one of America's most prominent and charismatic opponents of violence, Dr. Martin Luther King, Jr. Written at a time when American blacks were suffering racial injustice, sometimes violently, this essay served as a call for social change through peaceful means. King was a clergyman and a prominent civil rights leader. In 1957, he organized the Southern Christian Leadership Conference to extend his nonviolent efforts toward equality and justice for his people. In 1964, he was awarded the Nobel Peace Prize. Four years later, while supporting striking sanitation workers in Memphis, King was shot and killed. The following statement comes from his *Stride Toward Freedom* (1958).

When I went to Montgomery as a pastor, I had not the slightest idea that I would later become involved in a crisis in which nonviolent resistance would be applicable. I neither started the protest nor suggested it. I simply responded to the call of the people for a spokesman. When the protest began, my mind, consciously or unconsciously, was driven back to the Sermon on the Mount, with its sublime teachings on love, and the Gandhian method of nonviolent resistance. As the days unfolded, I came to see the power of nonviolence more and more. Living through the actual experience of the protest, nonviolence became more than a method to which I gave intellectual assent; it became a commitment to a way of life. Many of the things that I had not cleared up intellectually concerning nonviolence were now solved in the sphere of practical action. 1

Since the philosophy of nonviolence played such a positive role in the Montgomery Movement, it may be wise to turn to a brief discussion of some basic aspects of this philosophy. 2

First, it must be emphasized that nonviolent resistance is not a method for cowards; it does resist. If one uses this method because he is afraid or merely because he lacks the instruments of violence, he is not truly nonviolent. This is why Gandhi often said that if cowardice is the only alternative to violence, it is better to fight. He made this statement conscious of the fact that there is always another alternative: no individual or group need submit to any wrong, nor need they use violence to right the wrong; there is the way of nonviolent resistance. This is ultimately the way of the strong man. It is not a method of stagnant passivity. The phrase "passive resistance" often gives the false impression that this is a sort of "do-nothing method" in which the resister quietly and passively accepts evil. But nothing is further from the truth. For while the nonviolent resister is passive in the sense that he is not physically aggressive toward his opponent, his mind and emotions are always active, constantly seeking to 3 persuade his opponent that he is wrong. The method is passive physically, but strongly active spiritually. It is not passive nonresistance to evil, it is active nonviolent resistance to evil.

4   A second basic fact that characterizes nonviolence is that it does not seek to defeat or humiliate the opponent, but to win his friendship and understanding. The nonviolent resister must often express his protest through noncooperation or boycotts, but he realizes that these are not ends themselves; they are merely means to awaken a sense of moral shame in the opponent. The end is redemption and reconciliation. The aftermath of nonviolence is the creation of the beloved community, while the aftermath of violence is tragic bitterness.

5   A third characteristic of this method is that the attack is directed against forces of evil rather than against persons who happen to be doing the evil. It is evil that the nonviolent resister seeks to defeat, not the persons victimized by evil. If he is opposing racial injustice, the nonviolent resister has the vision to say that the basic tension is not between races. As I like to say to the people in Montgomery: "The tension in this city is not between white people and Negro people. The tension is, at bottom, between justice and injustice, between the forces of light and the forces of darkness. And if there is a victory, it will be a victory not merely for fifty thousand Negroes, but a victory for justice and the forces of light. We are out to defeat injustice and not white persons who may be unjust."

6   A fourth point that characterizes nonviolent resistance is a willingness to accept suffering without retaliation, to accept blows from the opponent without striking back. "Rivers of blood may have to flow before we gain our freedom, but it must be our blood," Gandhi said to his countrymen. The nonviolent resister is willing to accept violence if necessary, but never to inflict it. He does not seek to dodge jail. If going to jail is necessary, he enters it "as a bridegroom enters the bride's chamber."

7   One may well ask: "What is the nonviolent resister's justification for this ordeal to which he invites men, for this mass political application of the ancient doctrine of turning the other cheek?" The answer is found in the realization that unearned suffering is redemptive. Suffering, the nonviolent resister realizes, has tremendous educational and transforming possibilities. "Things of fundamental importance to people are not secured by reason alone, but have to be purchased with their suffering," said Gandhi. He continues: "Suffering is infinitely more powerful than the law of the jungle for converting the opponent and opening his ears which are otherwise shut to the voice of reason."

8   A fifth point concerning nonviolent resistance is that it avoids not only external physical violence but also internal violence of spirit. The nonviolent resister not only refuses to shoot his opponent but he also refuses to hate him. At the center of nonviolence stands the principle of love. The nonviolent resister would contend that in the struggle for human dignity, the oppressed people of the world must not succumb to the temptation of becoming bitter or indulging in hate campaigns. To retaliate in kind would do nothing but intensify the existence of hate in the universe. Along the way of life, someone must have sense

enough and morality enough to cut off the chain of hate. This can only be done by projecting the ethic of love to the center of our lives.

In speaking of love at this point, we are not referring to some sentimental or affectionate emotion. It would be nonsense to urge men to love their oppressors in an affectionate sense. Love in this connection means understanding, redemptive good will. Here the Greek language comes to our aid. There are three words for love in the Greek New Testament. First, there is *eros*. In Platonic philosophy *eros* meant the yearning of the soul for the realm of the divine. It has come now to mean a sort of aesthetic or romantic love. Second, there is *philia*, which means intimate affection between personal friends. *Philia* denotes a sort of reciprocal love; the person loves because he is loved. When we speak of loving those who oppose us, we refer to neither *eros* nor *philia;* we speak of a love which is expressed in the Greek word *agape. Agape* means understanding, redeeming good will for all men. It is an overflowing love which is purely spontaneous, unmotivated, groundless, and creative. It is not set in motion by any quality or function of its object. It is the love of God operating in the human heart.

Agape is disinterested love. It is a love in which the individual seeks not his own good, but the good of his neighbor (I Cor. 10:24). *Agape* does not begin by discriminating between worthy and unworthy people, or any qualities people possess. It begins by loving others *for their sakes.* It is entirely "neighbor-regarding concern for others," which discovers the neighbor in every man it meets. There, *agape* makes no distinction between friend and enemy; it is directed toward both. If one loves an individual merely on account of friendliness, he loves him for the sake of the benefits to be gained from the friendship, rather than for the friend's own sake. Consequently, the best way to assure oneself that Love is disinterested is to have love for the enemy-neighbor from whom you can expect no good in return, but only hostility and persecution.

Another basic point about *agape* is that it springs from the *need* of the other person—his need for belonging to the best in the human family. The Samaritan who helped the Jew on the Jericho Road was "good" because he responded to the human need that he was presented with. God's love is eternal and fails not because man needs his love. St. Paul assures us that the loving act of redemption was done "while we were yet sinners"—that is, at the point of our greatest need for love. Since the white man's personality is greatly distorted by segregation, and his soul is greatly scarred, he needs the love of the Negro. The Negro must love the white man, because the white man needs his love to remove his tensions, insecurities, and fears.

Agape is not a weak, passive love. It is love in action. *Agape* is love seeking to preserve and create community. It is insistence on community even when one seeks to break it. *Agape* is a willingness to sacrifice in the interest of mutuality. *Agape* is a willingness to go to any length to restore community. It doesn't stop at the first mile, but it goes the second mile to restore community. It is a willingness to forgive, not seven times, but seventy times seven to restore community. The cross is the eternal expression of the length to which God will go in order to restore broken community. The resurrection is a symbol of God's triumph over all the forces that seek to block community. The Holy Spirit is the continuing community creating reality that moves through history. He who works against community is working against the whole of creation. Therefore, if I respond to hate with a reciprocal hate I do nothing but intensify cleavage in broken community. I can only close the gap in broken community by meeting hate with love. If I meet hate with hate, I become depersonalized, because creation is so designed that my personality can only be fulfilled in the context of community. Booker T. Washington was right: "Let no man pull you so low as to make you hate him." When he pulls you that low he brings you to the point of working against community; he drags you to the point of defying creation, and thereby becoming depersonalized.

13   In the final analysis, *agape* means a recognition of the fact that all life is interrelated. All humanity is involved in a single process, and all men are brothers. To the degree that I harm my brother, no matter what he is doing to me, to that extent I am harming myself. For example, white men often refuse federal aid to education in order to avoid giving the Negro his rights; but because all men are brothers they cannot deny Negro children without harming their own. They end, all efforts to the contrary, by hurting themselves. Why is this? Because men are brothers. If you harm me, you harm yourself.

14   Love, *agape,* is the only cement that can hold this broken community together. When I am commanded to love, I am commanded to restore community, to resist injustice, and to meet the needs of my brothers.

15   A sixth basic fact about nonviolent resistance is that it is based on the conviction that the universe is on the side of justice. Consequently, the believer in nonviolence has deep faith in the future. This faith is another reason why the nonviolent resister can accept suffering without retaliation. For he knows that in his struggle for justice he has cosmic companionship. It is true that there are devout believers in nonviolence who find it difficult to believe in a personal God. But even these persons believe in the existence of some creative force that works for universal wholeness. Whether we call it an unconscious process, an impersonal Brahman, or a Personal Being of matchless power and infinite love, there is a creative force in this universe that works to bring the disconnected aspects of reality into a harmonious whole.

▼ TOPICAL CONSIDERATIONS

1. From reading King's essay, what kind of education would you say King had as a young man? How is this training reflected in the essay?
2. King was strongly influenced by Mahatma Gandhi, political activist and leader of the Indian people in the first half of this century. What do you know about Gandhi and his civil disobedience movement?

3. During the Vietnam War, thousands of young men fled to Canada and Europe to avoid being drafted. Would you call them nonviolent resisters? Consider the motives and aims of both types of protestors. Are conscientious objectors the same as nonviolent resisters, as described by Dr. King?

4. King refers to the Sermon on the Mount. What similarities do you see between its teachings and King's definition of nonviolent resistance? What differences do you see?

5. Is King's philosophy practical in today's world in which there is so much terrorism and violence? Give reasons for your answer.

6. When King defines *agape,* he discusses how it promotes community responsibility. Identify citizen groups in your community or on your campus that demonstrate the kind of love King defines here. What other evidence of *agape* do you find in our society?

7. Do you agree with King's philosophy? Could you practice it? Describe a situation in which you might find yourself wanting to resist. Explain how you would deal with the crisis. How would it be the same or different from King's approach?

8. King was a charismatic figure of the early sixties. Is there anything about this essay that would suggest why this was true?

▼ RHETORICAL CONSIDERATIONS

1. Did King's opening capture your interest immediately? Was it an effective way to introduce his subject matter? Explain your reactions.

2. What is King's thesis? Is it stated explicitly or implicitly?

3. What primary rhetorical strategy does King use in developing his essay?

4. What transitional devices does King use when moving from one idea to another? How does he achieve variety so that he is not repeating the same words and phrases too often?

5. What do you think of King's conclusion? Does he need to summarize the points he made in his essay? Or has he successfully brought the essay to a close without the need for this? How would you have ended it?

▼ WRITING ASSIGNMENTS

1. In paragraph 1, King remarks: "Many of the things I had not cleared up intellectually concerning nonviolence were now solved in the sphere of practical action." King's practical experiences molded his philosophy. In an essay, write about an experience you have had

that taught you something about your own standards of behavior in society.

2. Were the young men who fled to Canada and Europe during the Vietnam War nonviolent resisters? In an essay, compare and contrast this type of resistance with the type King describes.

3. Identify a community action group in your community or on your campus that is involved in demonstrating *agape*. Write an essay describing the goals and actions of the group. Explain how the group demonstrates the kind of community responsibility King discusses in his essay.

▼ 38 WHO SAW MURDER DIDN'T CALL THE POLICE

Martin Gansberg

Martin Gansberg has been a reporter and editor for *The New York Times* since 1942. The article reprinted here was written in 1964, just a few days after Kitty Genovese was murdered in full view of dozens of people. The incident shocked the nation and became a springboard for countless editorials and articles—even a television movie—about public indifference and fear. Has anything changed in three decades? This article won Gansberg several awards for best feature and news story of the year.

1   For more than half an hour 38 respectable, law-abiding citizens in Queens watched a killer stalk and stab a woman in three separate attacks in Kew Gardens.

2   Twice their chatter and the sudden glow of their bedroom lights interrupted him and frightened him off. Each time he returned, sought her out, and stabbed her again. Not one person telephoned the police during the assault; one witness called after the woman was dead.

3   That was two weeks ago today.

4   Still shocked is Assistant Chief Inspector Frederick M. Lussen, in charge of the borough's detectives and a veteran of 25 years of homicide investigations. He can give a matter-of-fact recitation on many murders. But the Kew Gardens slaying baffles him—not because it is a murder, but because the "good people" failed to call the police.

5   "As we have reconstructed the crime," he said, "the assailant had three chances to kill this woman during a 35-minute period. He returned twice to

complete the job. If we had been called when he first attacked, the woman might not be dead now."

This is what the police say happened beginning at 3:20 A.M. in the staid, middle-class, tree-lined Austin Street area: **6**

Twenty-eight-year-old Catherine Genovese, who was called Kitty by almost everyone in the neighborhood, was returning home from her job as manager of a bar in Hollis. She parked her red Fiat in a lot adjacent to the Kew Gardens Long Island Rail Road Station, facing Mowbray Place. Like many residents of the neighborhood, she had parked there day after day since her arrival from Connecticut a year ago, although the railroad frowns on the practice.   **7**

She turned off the lights of her car, locked the door, and started to walk the 100 feet to the entrance of her apartment at 82-70 Austin Street, which is in a Tudor building, with stores in the first floor and apartments on the second.   **8**

The entrance to the apartment is in the rear of the building because the front is rented to retail stores. At night the quiet neighborhood is shrouded in the slumbering darkness that marks most residential areas.   **9**

Miss Genovese noticed a man at the far end of the lot, near a seven-story apartment house at 82-40 Austin Street. She halted. Then, nervously, she headed up Austin Street toward Lefferts Boulevard, where there is a call box to the 102nd Police Precinct in nearby Richmond Hill.   **10**

She got as far as a street light in front of a bookstore before the man grabbed her. She screamed. Lights went on in the 10-story apartment house at 82-67 Austin Street, which faces the bookstore. Windows slid open and voices punctuated the early-morning stillness.   **11**

Miss Genovese screamed: "Oh, my God, he stabbed me! Please help me! Please help me!"   **12**

From one of the upper windows in the apartment house, a man called down: "Let that girl alone!"   **13**

The assailant looked up at him, shrugged, and walked down Austin Street toward a white sedan parked a short distance away. Miss Genovese struggled to her feet.   **14**

Lights went out. The killer returned to Miss Genovese, now trying to make her way around the side of the building by the parking lot to get to her apartment. The assailant stabbed her again.   **15**

"I'm dying!" she shrieked. "I'm dying!"   **16**

Windows were opened again, and lights went on in many apartments. The assailant got into his car and drove away. Miss Genovese staggered to her feet. A city bus, O-10, the Lefferts Boulevard line to Kennedy International Airport, passed. It was 3:35 A.M.   **17**

The assailant returned. By then, Miss Genovese had crawled to the back of the building, where the freshly painted brown doors to the apartment house held out hope for safety. The killer tried the first door; she wasn't there. At the second door, 82-62 Austin Street, he saw her slumped on the floor at the foot of the stairs. He stabbed her a third time—fatally.   **18**

19   It was 3:50 by the time the police received their first call, from a man who was a neighbor of Miss Genovese. In two minutes they were at the scene. The neighbor, a 70-year-old woman, and another woman were the only persons on the street. Nobody else came forward.

20   The man explained that he had called the police after much deliberation. He had phoned a friend in Nassau County for advice and then he had crossed the roof of the building to the apartment of the elderly woman to get her to make the call.

21   "I didn't want to get involved," he sheepishly told the police.

22   Six days later, the police arrested Winston Moseley, a 29-year-old business-machine operator, and charged him with homicide. Moseley had no previous record. He is married, has two children and owns a home at 133-19 Sutter Avenue, South Ozone Park, Queens. On Wednesday, a court committed him to Kings County Hospital for psychiatric observation.

23   When questioned by the police, Moseley also said that he had slain Mrs. Annie May Johnson, 24, of 146-12 133d Avenue, Jamaica, on Feb. 29 and Barbara Kralik, 15, of 174-17 140th Avenue, Springfield Gardens, last July. In the Kralik case, the police are holding Alvin L. Mitchell, who is said to have confessed that slaying.

24   The police stressed how simple it would have been to have gotten in touch with them. "A phone call," said one of the detectives, "would have done it." The police may be reached by dialing "O" for operator or SPring 7-3100.

25   Today witnesses from the neighborhood, which is made up of one-family homes in the $35,000 to $60,000 range with the exception of the two apartment houses near the railroad station, find it difficult to explain why they didn't call the police.

26   A housewife, knowingly if quite casually, said, "We thought it was a lovers' quarrel." A husband and wife both said, "Frankly, we were afraid." They seemed aware of the fact that events might have been different. A distraught woman, wiping her hands in her apron, said, "I didn't want my husband to get involved."

27   One couple, now willing to talk about that night, said they heard the first screams. The husband looked thoughtfully at the bookstore where the killer first grabbed Miss Genovese.

28   "We went to the window to see what was happening," he said, "but the light from our bedroom made it difficult to see the street." The wife, still apprehensive, added: "I put out the light and we were able to see better."

29   Asked why they hadn't called the police, she shrugged and replied: "I don't know."

30   A man peeked out from a slight opening in the doorway to his apartment and rattled off an account of the killer's second attack. Why hadn't he called the police at the time? "I was tired," he said without emotion. "I went back to bed."

31   It was 4:25 A.M. when the ambulance arrived to take the body of Miss Genovese. It drove off. "Then," a solemn police detective said, "the people came out."

▼ TOPICAL CONSIDERATIONS

1. Suppose you had been one of the 38 witnesses who heard Kitty Genovese scream. What would you have done?
2. What do you think of the reasons the witnesses gave for not calling the police? Are any of the reasons justifiable?
3. What does the article reveal about Kitty Genovese's neighborhood? Is there anything about it that would suggest that it is particularly crime-prone? Is it surprising that such a crime would happen in it?
4. How would you have felt if the victim had been your best friend? Your sister? Your girlfriend? How would you have felt toward her neighbors?
5. What impact do you think this article had when it was first published in 1964? What impact did it have on you?

▼ RHETORICAL CONSIDERATIONS

1. Gansberg gives specific times, addresses, and ages in his article. He even lists the phone number for the police department. Why does he do this? How would the article be affected if he didn't include these specifics?
2. What is Gansberg's aim in writing this article? What impact do you think he intended to have on his audience? Do you think he was successful?
3. Although this article is written in an objective, journalistic style, Gansberg's own bias often reveals itself. For example, why does he describe the Austin Street area as "staid" and "middle-class" (paragraph 6)? Why does he point out that it is a neighborhood of "one-family homes in the $35,000 to $60,000 range" (paragraph 25)? What does this tell you about his point of view? What other revealing clues do you see?
4. How effective is Gansberg's use of dialogue? Would the article have a greater impact without it? Give reasons for your answers.
5. Does Gansberg's conclusion tie in with his thesis? Is it an effective conclusion? Why or why not? What does it reveal about the author's point of view?

▼ WRITING ASSIGNMENTS

1. Have you ever been a victim of a crime? If so, write a narrative account of what happened to you. Include a description of how witnesses to the crime came or failed to come to your aid.
2. How do you think a newscaster would have reported the Kitty

Genovese crime? Write a brief news blurb that could be used on a nightly TV news program. Include many of the details Gansberg provides in his article.

3. Gansberg's article is written from the point of view of the victim. Adopt another point of view—that of a witness, the murderer, a bus driver, a police officer—and write two brief papers. In the first, describe your own response to what happened the night of the crime. In the second, describe how you felt two weeks later, when Gansberg's article was published.

▼ HOOKED ON HATE?
Kathi Maio

People have long debated whether the violence in popular entertainment is more than just a reflection of what goes on in society. Some, in fact, have loudly protested that popular culture contributes to violent attitudes and behavior. The author of the following piece forcefully argues that American popular culture is brutally antifemale. Unfunny comedians, sadomasochistic MTV videos, tabloid television, rock and rap musicians, slasher films, porn movies, Saturday morning cartoons, even Nintendo games—they subtly and not-so-subtly exploit violence against women sometimes even "under the guise of social advocacy," she argues. Kathi Maio is the film editor for *Sojourner*. Her first collection of film essays, *Feminist in the Dark*, was published in 1988. This article first appeared in *Ms.* magazine in September 1990.

1   It starts with the Saturday morning slugfests that pass for children's shows these days. Then there are comic books that eroticize the violence with colorful images of female victims (wearing little more than panties and push-up bras) being violated by supervillains before they are rescued by the superhero. Nintendo games like "The Adventures of Bayou Billy" promote woman as passive victim. And "adult" video games present graphic sexual violence for sickies of all ages (a "joystick" can't check ID). The most infamous of these was "Custer's Revenge," a racist bit of fun that shows a naked General Custer raping an Indian woman tied to a post. U.S. popular culture, along with much of our high culture, glories in a not-so-subtle blend of sex and the brutalizing of women.

2   The structure of the wildly popular slasher film of the eighties is, in fact, modeled after pornography. Instead of repeated episodes of anonymous sex, we are treated to repeated episodes of anonymous violence. Slasher films rely on "slice 'n' dice" weapons as phallic stand-ins. Power drills and chain saws are popular items. And for monster men on the move who don't own a portable

generator, there are always old-fashioned low-tech weapons like the machete and the butcher knife that can go anywhere in search of a victim.

Men do die in slasher movies, but the majority of victims—whether in "classic" series like *Halloween, Friday the 13th,* and *Nightmare on Elm Street,* or in their even lower-budget, generic equivalents—are young women. The audience viewpoint—the "gaze," as film theorists call it—is both male and voyeuristic. First comes the arousal of watching a young woman undress or soap up in a shower for us, showing off a body of centerfold nubility. Then there's the "come shot"—the euphoric release the male killer (and vicariously his audience) achieves by murdering a woman.   3

It's a telling example of women's lack of empowerment in film that when a man is an evil monster, he never stays dead. Popular slashers return from apparent annihilation again and again. Try to picture a female slasher monster who kills man after man after man. Now imagine that character making millions for an independent production company in eight sequels (each more gruesome than the last). Picture her image dominating video store displays and home screens, and spawning hundreds of licensed products: dolls, greeting cards, masks, and plastic replicas of her favorite weapon. Then imagine all the little girls of the U.S.A. begging to costume themselves as that character for Halloween.   4

Can't picture it? Neither can I. Male-directed violence coming from a woman will never play in Peoria. This is true not just in horror films or thrillers, but in shock comedies as well. In this year's *A Shock to the System,* Michael Caine murdered his wife and lived happily ever after. Conversely, Tracey Ullman, who has more reason for anger in *I Love You to Death,* never manages to kill her husband—but she suffers plenty for trying.   5

Less obvious, but no less disturbing, are "respectable" movies that target a woman as a social evil who must be destroyed. While watching Adrian Lyne's *Fatal Attraction* I was dumbfounded by the hatred directed at Glenn Close's single, successful character. I don't mean Lyne's slick on-screen misogyny, but the woman-hatred the same director who brought us *9½ Weeks* was able to whip up in his audience. During the two key scenes in which Michael Douglas gets a chance to avenge himself on his one-night-stand-from-hell lover, the audience screamed "Kill her! Kill her!" And when Alex Forrest is finally shot down, the audience applauded and cheered. Slasher or schlemiel—we are meant to bond with a male character.   6

One movie fan told me she avoided films that glorify violence against women by attending only critic-approved "art house" films. The intelligentsia has long been enamored of Woody Allen, a misogynist who usually expresses his fear and loathing of women in nonviolent terms. But in *Crimes and Misdemeanors,* one woman is bound and shit on by a new lover, and another is murdered by hit men an old lover hires. In both cases the male perps get away with it. Allen may well be protesting the moral decay of modern society in his film, but by allowing his film's protagonist to kill a woman and prosper, he delivers a mixed message.   7

Stanley Kubrick *(A Clockwork Orange, The Shining)* and Brian DePalma   8

(Dressed to Kill, Body Double) recently made Vietnam movies that allowed them to have their bloodshed and decry it, too, by focusing on the torture and murder of a young Vietnamese woman. DePalma milks the abduction, gang rape, and slaughter of an innocent village girl in *Casualties of War.* Kubrick saves it for the big finale of *Full Metal Jacket.* Both would claim that they are horrified by violence against the innocent, and maybe they are. But they are in love with it, too.

9   Last year, *Henry: Portrait of a Serial Killer,* a cult movie featuring lots of scenes of women being slaughtered, was embraced as an art film by male critics far and wide, even though writer/director John McNaughton admitted it was originally meant to be a "horror movie." McNaughton is but the latest inductee into the sick puppy school of intellectual filmmaking, joining directors like Spain's Pedro Almodovar *(Tie Me Up! Tie Me Down!),* Canada's David Cronenberg *(Dead Ringers),* and the U.S.'s own David Lynch *(Blue Velvet)* in casting modern woman as victim of sadomasochistic scenarios.

10   Now Lynch is behind what is being touted as "the year's best show" on television: *Twin Peaks,* a bizarre nighttime soap centered on an investigation into the torture-murder of a small-town homecoming queen. The characters include one battering husband who beats his wife with a sap made from a bar of soap in a wet sock, and threatens to "snap [her] neck like a twig"; and another killer hubby who, from behind bars, can keep half the women in town trembling with the telephoned parting shot "Catch you later."

11   Television also exploits violence against women under the guise of social advocacy. Outrage-of-the-week TV movies frequently focus on wife battering, acquaintance rape, and spousal murder. After shamelessly graphic depictions of the subject matter, the number of a battered women's hotline or victims' aid agency flashes up at the end. (At least these portraits of violence usually show women as survivors, not just victims.) Similarly, TV's many tabloid shows *(Unsolved Mysteries, A Current Affair, America's Most Wanted,* and so on) rake over rapes and murders, often "reenacting" the crime, but this too is claimed to serve justice and victims' rights. The advocacy is presented so salaciously, though, that the shows' high motives become questionable.

12   Even if the depictions of violence against women aren't intentionally exploitive, audiences conditioned to "enjoy" such fare are almost certain to identify with the sadism. When I saw the film *The Accused,* a group of young boys broke into the theater at the point that the rape of Jodie Foster's character is finally shown, and verbalized their relish for the gang-bang. I do not think that Jonathan Kaplan, whom I respect as a filmmaker, *meant* the rape of Foster's character to attract "prurient interest." *But it did.*

13   Antiwoman violence is also endemic to popular music. White racist and homophobe Axl Rose, of heavy metal Guns N' Roses, brags that "I used to love her, but I had to kill her. . . . And now I'm happier this way" in one song, and discusses rape as a surefire cure for his boredom in another. Rap masters like Ice T may brag about raping a woman with a flashlight, or suggest, like Easy-E, that a woman be "smoked" with an Uzi, extending the example set by the

Rolling Stones, those middle-aged "Under My Thumb" boys whose notorious billboard, showing a bruised woman bound to a chair, was captioned "I'm black and blue from the Rolling Stones . . . and I Love It!"

Ironically, MTV has a "Stereotypes Suck" promo campaign (meant to foster racial harmony). Yet that very popular cable network promotes damaging stereotypes of women in almost every video it airs. In most, women are portrayed as passive, scantily clad sex objects. But then you notice videos in which those same garter-belted cuties are shown behind bars or in chains. Female stars like Madonna (see her recent "Express Yourself" video) are not exactly innocent bystanders, but most of the worst images come from male groups. **14**

Comics like Eddie Murphy and Andrew Dice Clay view women as "bitches," "pussies," and "w(ho)res" to be abused and discarded at will. Clay's "Diceman" character, a homophobe and racist invested with Clay's hatred of women, boasts in a 1989 release that he'll burn a woman with a cigarette if she doesn't screw him with enough enthusiasm. **15**

It is cause for alarm that young teens experience more women-victimizing fare than any other group, through video rentals, cable "premium" stations, and syndicated TV shows like *Freddy's Nightmares* and *Friday the 13th: The Series*. Several recent studies support what we've all known in our hearts to be true: slasher movies desensitize young men to real-life violence against women. A 1987 United Press International story reported that a boy of five who stabbed a two-year-old girl 17 times stated his fascination with Jason and Freddy Krueger. And in Massachusetts a year later, after an 18-year-old man (dubbed "The Halloween Killer") murdered a 19-year-old female acquaintance by stabbing her more than 30 times, police found in his room over 100 horror tapes and slasher memorabilia that included hockey masks, an ax, and a hunting knife. **16**

Therese Stanton of the National Anti-Pornography Civil Rights Organization told me that 24-hour-a-day, at-home access to 900-number "dial-a-porn" and personal computer smut has lowered the mean age of males accessing hard-core pornography "down to about fourteen." Also coordinator of the Brooklyn Women's Anti-Rape Exchange, she is documenting the fact that rapists are getting younger. Furthermore, she's hearing about "gang rapes of high school girls thrown into a van . . . a videotape running while [the rape] is happening." Rapists now have a profit motive, since this violent, real-life, camcorder-made porn can be sold for $5,000. She theorizes that many of the serial killers of prostitutes are actually snuff pornographers. **17**

Many women, myself included, try not to think about the reality of snuff pornography, and to block out make-believe mutilations that surround us on radio, television, and movie screens, in order to cope—and survive. But the fact is that many women are not surviving. **18**

Women need to say no to family members who bring slasher films into our homes, or who want the company of an abusive "shock DJ" on the morning commute, or who switch on an Andrew Dice Clay "comedy" special on cable and expect us to lie back and enjoy it. Nora Dunn had the right idea when she **19** refused to work on *Saturday Night Live* while Clay was guest host.* Dunn cited Dice's "joke" about incest—it's okay for men to have sex with their daughters because they pay their tuition—as an example of why she refused to "be part of providing an arena for him to make himself legitimate." Dunn's decision to oppose Clay's work in a strong and highly visible way should inspire us all to similar action.

▼ TOPICAL CONSIDERATIONS

1. What is Maio's assessment of Saturday morning cartoons, comic books, and video games? Do you agree or disagree with this assessment? Is it fair to judge them all categorically? List any exceptions you can think of.
2. List some "slasher" films you have seen or heard about. Why might they be so popular? How do you respond to Maio's critique of them?
3. In paragraph 2, Maio writes, "The structure of the wildly popular slasher film . . . is . . . modeled after pornography." Have you ever made this connection between the genres? Do you see the "blend of sex and the brutalizing of women" that Maio raises in the first paragraph of her essay?
4. What does the scenario in paragraph 4 suggest about accepted societal roles for men and women? What might it suggest about acceptable male fantasies as opposed to female fantasies? Explain why you answered the way you did.
5. In her discussion of the film, *Fatal Attraction,* Maio writes, "Slasher or schlemiel—we are meant to bond with a male character" (paragraph 6). Is this generally true about all films? Can you think of any exceptions to the rule?
6. What do you think of Maio's claim that film makers like Kubrick, Allen, and DePalma send mixed messages in their films? Think of the types of music you listen to and the videos you watch. Are any of them sending mixed messages about violence against women?
7. Maio turns her argument away from film and toward other texts of popular culture: television, music, music video, and stand-up comedy. Do you agree or disagree with her analysis of these genres? List specific examples to back up your answer.

*Editor's Note: Dunn's protest was followed by that of the singer Sinéad O'Conner, who canceled her appearance on that same show. A few weeks later, Starr Parodi, keyboardist on the *Arsenio Hall Show,* also refused to appear the night Clay was a scheduled guest; Parodi claimed that since she didn't have the option of switching channels, she could at least avoid being on the same stage with Clay.

8. In paragraph 16, Maio writes, "slasher movies desensitize young men to real-life violence against women." Do you agree with this claim? Does Maio tell us how slasher films affect young women? Are there other issues that need to be considered besides the gender of the viewer?

▼ RHETORICAL CONSIDERATIONS

1. In your own words, what is Maio's thesis? Does she convince you of her argument?
2. Why might Maio use phrases like "Saturday morning slugfests" (paragraph 1), "slice 'n' dice' weapons" (paragraph 2), and "sick puppy school" (paragraph 9)? What purpose might these words serve in the context of her argument?
3. How did Maio catch your attention? What was your initial reaction to the essay? Explain why you think you reacted the way you did. Does your prior opinion affect the way you read the essay?
4. Describe the tone of Maio's piece? Is it both effective and consistent throughout her argument?
5. How do Maio's references to "misogynist" Woody Allen (paragraph 7), "white racist homophobe" Axl Rose (paragraph 13), and "homophobe and racist" Andrew Dice Clay (paragraph 15) influence your reading of the piece? Does they reinforce her thesis?
6. What are the solutions that Maio offers at the conclusion of her essay?

▼ WRITING ASSIGNMENTS

1. You are on a local committee that is trying to regulate the distribution of violent films. Paying special attention to your audience, draft a proposal to present to local officials.
2. Create a dialogue between Maio and Michael Ventura, author of "On Kids and Slasher Movies" (p. 103). How might they respond to each other's arguments?
3. You are a producer of "slasher" films or violent cartoons. Write an essay defending your "art" to Maio. Can you find faults with her argument? Where might she find faults with yours?
4. Write an essay in which you consider what type of advice Martin Luther King, Jr., would give to Maio.

▼ AN INCIDENT IN THE PARK

Aileen C. Hefferren

What follows is a very personal narrative of "an incident." No battering. No sexual assault. No Kitty Genovese killing. Nothing that made the newspapers. Just a minor interlude between the author jogging in a park and a 12-year-old boy on a bike who touched her. But as small as the incident seems, the traumatic ramifications were large enough for the author to raise some tough questions about what our society has come to tolerate. Aileen Hefferren is assistant managing editor of the *National Interest*. This article first appeared in *Newsweek* in December 1990.

1   I realize that, with most U.S. cities awash in violent crime, my story will strike some readers as very mild. But I have learned the hard way that even a minor, unreported incident can have profound effect. Early one evening last August, I was running on a well-used pathway in Washington, D.C.'s, Rock Creek Park. Finishing a six-mile run, I headed north from the P Street bridge toward Calvert Street when I heard a bicycle behind me. Suddenly, I felt a hand on my buttocks. Alongside rode a young male—I learned later he was only 12 years old— wearing a brightly colored jersey. I started to yell and reached out toward him. He skidded his bicycle into me, jumping aside as he did so. My hands, head, hip, elbow and shoulder hit the cement with great force; my leg hit his bicycle.

2   The boy, fists up, danced around me like a boxer. Crying and badly shaken, I shouted at him. People gathered. A woman on a bike said she saw the whole thing. Another boy, apparently his friend, stood aimlessly about, saying nothing.

3   Amid the confusion, my assailant rode off. A man on a 10-speed went after him. Several minutes later the boy returned and extended his hand to me. Sorry, he said, it was an accident. I couldn't shake his hand: it was not an accident. A runner said, "No, kid, it's not that easy." The runner signaled a Secret Service police car that was passing by. The boy promptly hopped on his bike again and rode away as we watched.

4   The Secret Service man, out of his jurisdiction, radioed for help. A fire chief, who happened to be driving by in one of those red station wagons, stopped to take my blood pressure and pulse, and cover my wounds. He asked over and over: "What day is today? Where are you? Did you lose consciousness?" My lower leg had begun to develop a contorted swelling. I was nauseated and shaking uncontrollably. The fire chief covered me with a blanket. District and Park police came and more people stopped. It began to get dark. My assailant's friend was taken in a police car, his bicycle in the trunk, to identify the assailant's house.

5   I was taken to the emergency room. Dehydrated and in shock, my body still

shook. My leg was X-rayed for fractures; my head checked for concussion; my wounds cleaned and dressed. It was after midnight by the time I got home. During the next few days, I couldn't turn my head or raise my arms above waist level. I couldn't hold or lift anything with my hands. I could walk but only slowly and with great care. It was more than a month before I ran. Even now, every time I step off a curb pain shoots through my lower leg.

As a woman I have always been conscious of my surroundings, especially **6** at night. To avoid or minimize risks, I have walked purposefully, carried house keys between my fingers, crossed the street when I saw a threatening person. But I was assaulted during the daylight with plenty of people around. My attacker was not a large man, he was not suspicious looking. The old rules no longer apply. Now I must fear boys. It is difficult to cope with this new vulnerability. When I see groups of kids, I find myself looking for my assailant among them. I am relieved when he is not there, but then I become anxious because other, unknown ones might be just like him.

Friends say, quite innocently, Why don't you run with someone, and only **7** go during the daylight? But they don't understand what is lost. Running has always been an important part of my life. In school, I ran cross-country, even a marathon. As an adult I've run in road races. The long runs give me time to be alone, time to think. Now I must find other people to run with—at mutually convenient times, for mutually convenient distances, at a mutually convenient pace or forgo it altogether. But when I run with another person, I still jump if my elbow touches a bush or if someone moves unexpectedly. Even a walk to the grocery store creates tension. Now I find myself looking away as people pass, trying to appear solemn, tough, never smiling. I have been forced to create a hard shell. Inside I am left compromised and insecure.

In the days following the assault I had to decide whether to press charges. **8** Part of me wanted to settle the score, wanted the boy to be frightened, taken down to the station and fingerprinted. I also felt an obligation to other women and other runners to register his name with the police.

Of course, pressing charges might be a waste of time. My case was not **9** unusual: one of the men who waited with me for the ambulance that night had been recently assaulted while running. The kid went unpunished.

In the end, I didn't have to decide. The detective told me he was going to **10** go after the kid. The weeks went by and nothing happened. The few times the detective called I found myself expressing anger: how could it be taking so long? The police knew where the boy lived and that, as it turns out, he had a case pending from July, involving a stolen car. Finally the detective told me the prosecutor wouldn't sign an arrest warrant for "a case like this," meaning it was too minor to bother about.

As I said in the beginning, I know my story is no big deal the way things **11** go these days. Compared to what happened to the Central Park jogger, I was lucky. That's why, it seems to me, my case is also significant. A 12-year-old boy touched a stranger in a sexual way in a public place during the daylight and then struck her when she protested. The boy goes unpunished. The woman is thought to be "lucky" to have "only" suffered bad cuts and bruises, humiliation and a shattering loss of confidence. That such a sequence of events barely merits public notice says more about the way we live now than does the occasional outrage evoked by more extreme events. Is not the measure of a society's condition what it accepts as ordinary and dismisses, rather than what it considers clearly exceptional?

▼ TOPICAL CONSIDERATIONS

1. Have you or someone you know ever experienced a "minor" incident like the one Hefferren describes? How did it affect you?
2. In paragraph 6, Hefferren writes, "As a woman I have always been conscious of my surroundings." Why does she emphasize her gender? Is her "incident" limited by gender? Do you feel conscious of your surroundings? How does your answer make you feel?
3. Look ahead to Nancy Gibbs's essay on rape. Is what Hefferren went through a form of rape? Defend your answer.
4. What does Hefferren mean when she writes, "The old rules no longer apply" (paragraph 6)? Think of examples to back up or refute her point.
5. What are the consequences of Hefferren's attack? Does she lose or gain anything by it?
6. Contrast Hefferren's narrative with Martin Gansberg's essay on Kitty Genovese. Why might the witnesses' reactions be different?
7. Have you ever been in a situation that made you feel vulnerable? What methods did you devise to overcome the vulnerability?

▼ RHETORICAL CONSIDERATIONS

1. Hefferren's essay is very personal. Is this narrative method effective? Can you think of cases where such a style might not be effective?
2. Why does Hefferren put words like " 'lucky' " and " 'only' " (paragraph 11) in quotation marks?
3. When is a rhetorical question effective? Consider the conclusion of Hefferren's essay. Why does she end her essay with such a question? Have you ever used this strategy?
4. Does the title of Hefferren's piece, "An Incident in the Park," prepare you for her narrative? How did you react to the title of Kathi Maio's essay, "Hooked on Hate?" Compare the two titles. Based on these titles, what were your expectations of each piece?
5. Hefferren's piece reads like a story, but a main point is inferred throughout her narrative. In your own words, explain Hefferren's main idea.

▼ WRITING ASSIGNMENTS

1. After witnessing Hefferren's attack, you write a letter to the editor of the local newspaper. What issues will you raise? What solutions will you offer?
2. Consider the title of Maio's essay, "Hooked on Hate?" Is the incident Hefferren explains a result of this hate? Write a paper considering both pieces.
3. You are the detective who took care of Hefferren's attack. Based on the information provided in Hefferren's piece, write an objective analysis of the incident for police files.

▼ WHEN IS IT RAPE?
Nancy Gibbs

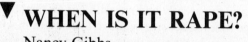

On the evening of Good Friday 1991 in Palm Beach, Florida, William Kennedy Smith, nephew of Senator Edward Kennedy, met a woman at a bar, invited her to his home later that night and apparently had sex with her on the lawn. She says it was rape, he says it was not. Eventually the court found Kennedy innocent of the charges, but the case raised the question in the title of this *Time* magazine cover story. *Date rape*, which seems a contradiction in terms, is the name given to this increasingly disturbing issue—and one that has raised a clamor on America's college campuses. Women say date rape is a widespread yet hidden crime. Men claim it's difficult to prevent a crime they can't define. Where is the line drawn between his date and her rape? This article appeared in the June 3, 1991, issue of *Time* magazine.

Be careful of strangers and hurry home, says a mother to her daughter, knowing that the world is a frightful place but not wishing to swaddle a child in fear. Girls grow up scarred by caution and enter adulthood eager to shake free of their parents' worst nightmares. They still know to be wary of strangers. What they don't know is whether they have more to fear from their friends.   **1**

Most women who get raped are raped by people they already know—like the boy in biology class, or the guy in the office down the hall, or their friend's brother. The familiarity is enough to make them let down their guard, sometimes even enough to make them wonder afterward whether they were "really raped." What people think of as "real rape"—the assault by a monstrous stranger lurking in the shadows—accounts for only 1 out of 5 attacks.   **2**

So the phrase "acquaintance rape" was coined to describe the rest, all the cases of forced sex between people who already knew each other, however   **3** casually. But that was too clinical for headline writers, and so the popular term is the narrower "date rape," which suggests an ugly ending to a raucous night on the town.

4 These are not idle distinctions. Behind the search for labels is the central mythology about rape: that rapists are always strangers, and victims are women who ask for it. The mythology is hard to dispel because the crime is so rarely exposed. The experts guess—that's all they can do under the circumstances— that while 1 in 4 women will be raped in her lifetime, less than 10% will report the assault, and less than 5% of the rapists will go to jail.

5 When a story of the crime lodges in the headlines, the myths have a way of cluttering the search for the truth. The tale of Good Friday in Palm Beach landed in the news because it involved a Kennedy, but it may end up as a watershed case, because all the mysteries and passions surrounding date rape are here to be dissected. William Kennedy Smith met a woman at a bar, invited her back home late at night and apparently had sex with her on the lawn. She says it was rape, and the police believed her story enough to charge him with the crime. Perhaps it was the bruises on her leg; or the instincts of the investigators who found her, panicked and shaking, curled up in the fetal position on a couch; or the lie-detector tests she passed.

6 On the other side, Smith has adamantly protested that he is a man falsely accused. His friends and family testify to his gentle nature and moral fiber and insist that he could not possibly have committed such a crime. Maybe the truth will come out in court—but regardless of its finale, the case has shoved the debate over date rape into the minds of average men and women. Plant the topic in a conversation, and chances are it will ripen into a bitter argument or a jittery sequence of pale jokes.

7 Women charge that date rape is the hidden crime; men complain it is hard to prevent a crime they can't define. Women say it isn't taken seriously; men say it is a concept invented by women who like to tease but not take the consequences. Women say the date-rape debate is the first time the nation has talked frankly about sex; men say it is women's unconscious reaction to the excesses of the sexual revolution. Meanwhile, men and women argue among themselves about the "gray area" that surrounds the whole murky arena of sexual relations, and there is no consensus in sight.

8 In court, on campus, in conversation, the issue turns on the elasticity of the word *rape,* one of the few words in the language with the power to summon a shared image of a horrible crime.

9 At one extreme are those who argue that for the word to retain its impact, it must be strictly defined as forced sexual intercourse: a gang of thugs jumping a jogger in Central Park, a psychopath preying on old women in a housing complex, a man with an ice pick in a side street. To stretch the definition of the word risks stripping away its power. In this view, if it happened on a date, it wasn't rape. A romantic encounter is a context in which sex *could* occur, and so what omniscient judge will decide whether there was genuine mutual consent?

Others are willing to concede that date rape sometimes occurs, that sometimes   10
a man goes too far on a date without a woman's consent. But this infraction,
they say, is not as ghastly a crime as street rape, and it should not be taken as
seriously. The New York *Post,* alarmed by the Willy Smith case, wrote in a
recent editorial, "If the sexual encounter, *forced or not,* has been preceded by a
series of consensual activities—drinking, a trip to the man's home, a walk on
a deserted beach at 3 in the morning—the charge that's leveled against the
alleged offender should, it seems to us, be different than the one filed against,
say, the youths who raped and beat the jogger."

This attitude sparks rage among women who carry scars received at the   11
hands of men they knew. It makes no difference if the victim shared a drink or
a moonlit walk or even a passionate kiss, they protest, if the encounter ended
with her being thrown to the ground and forcibly violated. Date rape is not
about a misunderstanding, they say. It is not a communications problem. It is
not about a woman's having regrets in the morning for a decision she made the
night before. It is not about a "decision" at all. Rape is rape, and any form of
forced sex—even between neighbors, co-workers, classmates and casual
friends—is a crime.

A more extreme form of that view comes from activists who see rape as a   12
metaphor, its definition swelling to cover any kind of oppression of women.
Rape, seen in this light, can occur not only on a date but also in a marriage, not
only by violent assault but also by psychological pressure. A Swarthmore College training pamphlet once explained that acquaintance rape "spans a spectrum of incidents and behaviors, ranging from crimes legally defined as rape to
verbal harassment and inappropriate innuendo."

No wonder, then, that the battles become so heated. When innuendo quali-   13
fies as rape, the definitions have become so slippery that the entire subject sinks
into a political swamp. The only way to capture the hard reality is to tell the
story.

A 32-year-old woman was on business in Tampa last year for the Florida   14
supreme court. Stranded at the courthouse, she accepted a lift from a lawyer
involved in her project. As they chatted on the ride home, she recalls, "he was
saying all the right things, so I started to trust him." She agreed to have dinner,
and afterward, at her hotel door, he convinced her to let him come in to talk.
"I went through the whole thing about being old-fashioned," she says. "I was
a virgin until I was 21. So I told him talk was all we were going to do."

But as they sat on the couch, she found herself falling asleep. "By now, I'm   15
comfortable with him, and I put my head on his shoulder. He's not tried
anything all evening, after all." Which is when the rape came. "I woke up to find
him on top of me, forcing himself on me. I didn't scream or run. All I could
think about was my business contacts and what if they saw me run out of my
room screaming rape.

"I thought it was my fault. I felt so filthy, I washed myself over and over   16
in hot water. Did he rape me?, I kept asking myself. I didn't consent. But who's

gonna believe me? I had a man in my hotel room after midnight." More than a year later, she still can't tell the story without a visible struggle to maintain her composure. Police referred the case to the state attorney's office in Tampa, but without more evidence it decided not to prosecute. Although her attacker has admitted that he heard her say no, maintains the woman, "he says he didn't know that I meant no. He didn't feel he'd raped me, and he even wanted to see me again."

17   Her story is typical in many ways. The victim herself may not be sure right away that she has been raped, that she had said no and been physically forced into having sex anyway. And the rapist commonly hears but does not heed the protest. "A date rapist will follow through no matter what the woman wants because his agenda is to get laid," says Claire Walsh, a Florida-based consultant on sexual assaults. "First comes the dinner, then a dance, then a drink, then the coercion begins." Gentle persuasion gives way to physical intimidation, with alcohol as the ubiquitous lubricant. "When that fails, force is used," she says. "Real men don't take no for an answer."

18   The Palm Beach case serves to remind women that if they go ahead and press charges, they can expect to go on trial along with their attacker, if not in a courtroom then in the court of public opinion. The *New York Times* caused an uproar on its own staff not only for publishing the victim's name but also for laying out in detail her background, her high school grades, her driving record, along with an unattributed quote from a school official about her "little wild streak." A freshman at Carleton College in Minnesota, who says she was repeatedly raped for four hours by a fellow student, claims that she was asked at an administrative hearing if she performed oral sex on dates. In 1989 a man charged with raping at knife point a woman he knew was acquitted in Florida because his victim had been wearing lace shorts and no underwear.

19   From a purely legal point of view, if she wants to put her attacker in jail, the survivor had better be beaten as well as raped, since bruises become a badge of credibility. She had better have reported the crime right away, before taking the hours-long shower that she craves, before burning her clothes, before curling up with the blinds down. And she would do well to be a woman of shining character. Otherwise the strict constructionist definitions of rape will prevail in court. "Juries don't have a great deal of sympathy for the victim if she's a willing participant up to the nonconsensual sexual intercourse," says Norman Kinne, a prosecutor in Dallas. "They feel that many times the victim has placed herself in the situation." Absent eyewitnesses or broken bones, a case comes down to her word against his, and the mythology of rape rarely lends her the benefit of the doubt.

20   She should also hope for an all-male jury, preferably composed of fathers with daughters. Prosecutors have found that women tend to be harsh judges of one another—perhaps because to find a defendant guilty is to entertain two grim realities: that anyone might be a rapist, and that every woman could find herself a victim. It may be easier to believe, the experts muse, that at some level the victim asked for it. "But just because a woman makes a bad judgment, does that

give the guy a moral right to rape her?" asks Dean Kilpatrick, director of the Crime Victim Research and Treatment Center at the Medical University of South Carolina. "The bottom line is, Why does a woman's having a drink give a man the right to rape her?"

Last week the Supreme Court waded into the debate with a 7-to-2 ruling **21** that protects victims from being harassed on the witness stand with questions about their sexual history. The Justices, in their first decision on "rape shield laws," said an accused rapist could not present evidence about a previous sexual relationship with the victim unless he notified the court ahead of time. In her decision, Justice Sandra Day O'Connor wrote that "rape victims deserve heightened protection against surprise, harassment and unnecessary invasions of privacy."

That was welcome news to prosecutors who understand the reluctance of **22** victims to come forward. But there are other impediments to justice as well. An internal investigation of the Oakland police department found that officers ignored a quarter of all reports of sexual assaults or attempts, though 90% actually warranted investigation. Departments are getting better at educating officers in handling rape cases, but the courts remain behind. A New York City task force on women in the courts charged that judges and lawyers were routinely less inclined to believe a woman's testimony than a man's.

The present debate over degrees of rape is nothing new: all through history, **23** rapes have been divided between those that mattered and those that did not. For the first few thousand years, the only rape that was punished was the defiling of a virgin, and that was viewed as a property crime. A girl's virtue was a marketable asset, and so a rapist was often ordered to pay the victim's father the equivalent of her price on the marriage market. In early Babylonian and Hebrew societies, a married woman who was raped suffered the same fate as an adulteress—death by stoning or drowning. Under William the Conqueror, the penalty for raping a virgin was castration and loss of both eyes—unless the violated woman agreed to marry her attacker, as she was often pressured to do. "Stealing an heiress" became a perfectly conventional means of taking—literally—a wife.

It may be easier to prove a rape case now, but not much. Until the 1960s **24** it was virtually impossible without an eyewitness; judges were often required to instruct jurors that "rape is a charge easily made and hard to defend against; so examine the testimony of this witness with caution." But sometimes a rape was taken very seriously, particularly if it involved a black man attacking a white woman—a crime for which black men were often executed or lynched.

Susan Estrich, author of *Real Rape,* considers herself a lucky victim. This **25** is not just because she survived an attack 17 years ago by a stranger with an ice pick, one day before her graduation from Wellesley. It's because police, and her friends, believed her. "The first thing the Boston police asked was whether it was a black guy," recalls Estrich, now a University of Southern California law professor. When she said yes and gave the details of the attack, their reaction was, "So, you were really raped." It was an instructive lesson, she says, in understanding how racism and sexism are factored into perceptions of the crime.

26   A new twist in society's perception came in 1975, when Susan Brownmiller published her book *Against Our Will: Men, Women and Rape*. In it she attacked the concept that rape was a sex crime, arguing instead that it was a crime of violence and power over women. Throughout history, she wrote, rape has played a critical function. "It is nothing more or less than a conscious process of intimidation, by which *all men* keep *all women* in a state of fear."

27   Out of this contention was born a set of arguments that have become politically correct wisdom on campus and in academic circles. This view holds that rape is a symbol of women's vulnerability to male institutions and attitudes. "It's sociopolitical," insists Gina Rayfield, a New Jersey psychologist. "In our culture men hold the power, politically, economically. They're socialized not to see women as equals."

28   This line of reasoning has led some women, especially radicalized victims, to justify flinging around the term rape as a political weapon, referring to everything from violent sexual assaults to inappropriate innuendos. Ginny, a college senior who was really raped when she was 16, suggests that false accusations of rape can serve a useful purpose. "Penetration is not the only form of violation," she explains. In her view, rape is a subjective term, one that women must use to draw attention to other, nonviolent, even nonsexual forms of oppression. "If a woman did falsely accuse a man of rape, she may have had reasons to," Ginny says. "Maybe she wasn't raped, but he clearly violated her in some way."

29   Catherine Comins, assistant dean of student life at Vassar, also sees some value in this loose use of "rape." She says angry victims of various forms of sexual intimidation cry rape to regain their sense of power. "To use the word carefully would be to be careful for the sake of the violator, and the survivors don't care a hoot about him." Comins argues that men who are unjustly accused can sometimes gain from the experience. "They have a lot of pain, but it is not a pain that I would necessarily have spared them. I think it ideally initiates a process of self-exploration. 'How do I see women?' 'If I didn't violate her, could I have?' 'Do I have the potential to do to her what they say I did?' Those are good questions."

30   Taken to extremes, there is an ugly element of vengeance at work here. Rape is an abuse of power. But so are false accusations of rape, and to suggest that men whose reputations are destroyed might benefit because it will make them more sensitive is an attitude that is sure to backfire on women who are seeking justice for all victims. On campuses where the issue is most inflamed, male students are outraged that their names can be scrawled on a bathroom-wall list of rapists and they have no chance to tell their side of the story.

31   "Rape is what you read about in the New York *Post* about 17 little boys raping a jogger in Central Park," says a male freshman at a liberal-arts college, who learned that he had been branded a rapist after a one-night stand with a friend. He acknowledges that they were both very drunk when she started

kissing him at a party and ended up back in his room. Even through his haze, he had some qualms about sleeping with her: "I'm fighting against my hormonal instincts, and my moral instincts are saying, 'This is my friend and if I were sober, I wouldn't be doing this.'" But he went ahead anyway. "When you're drunk, and there are all sorts of ambiguity, and the woman says 'Please, please' and then she says no sometime later, even in the middle of the act, there still may very well be some kind of violation, but it's not the same thing. It's not rape. If you don't hear her say no, if she doesn't say it, if she's playing around with you—oh, I could get squashed for saying it—there is an element of say no, mean yes."

The morning after their encounter, he recalls, both students woke up hung over and eager to put the memory behind them. Only months later did he learn that she had told a friend that he had torn her clothing and raped her. At this point in the story, the accused man starts using the language of rape. "I felt violated," he says. "I felt like she was taking advantage of me when she was very drunk. I never heard her say 'No!,' 'Stop!', anything." He is angry and hurt at the charges, worried that they will get around, shatter his reputation and force him to leave the small campus. **32**

So here, of course, is the heart of the debate. If rape is sex without consent, how exactly should consent be defined and communicated, when and by whom? Those who view rape through a political lens tend to place all responsibility on men to make sure that their partners are consenting at every point of a sexual encounter. At the extreme, sexual relations come to resemble major surgery, requiring a signed consent form. Clinical psychologist Mary P. Koss of the University of Arizona in Tucson, who is a leading scholar on the issue, puts it rather bluntly: "It's the man's penis that is doing the raping, and ultimately he's responsible for where he puts it." **33**

Historically, of course, this has never been the case, and there are some who argue that it shouldn't be—that women too must take responsibility for their behavior, and that the whole realm of intimate encounters defies regulation from on high. Anthropologist Lionel Tiger has little patience for trendy sexual politics that make no reference to biology. Since the dawn of time, he argues, men and women have always gone to bed with different goals. In the effort to keep one's genes in the gene pool, "it is to the male advantage to fertilize as many females as possible, as quickly as possible and as efficiently as possible." For the female, however, who looks at the large investment she will have to make in the offspring, the opposite is true. Her concern is to "select" who "will provide the best set up for their offspring." So, in general, "the pressure is on the male to be aggressive and on the female to be coy." **34**

No one defends the use of physical force, but when the coercion involved is purely psychological, it becomes hard to assign blame after the fact. Journalist Stephanie Gutmann is an ardent foe of what she calls the date-rape dogmatists. "How can you make sex completely politically correct and completely safe?" she asks. "What a horribly bland, unerotic thing that would be! Sex is, by nature, a risky endeavor, emotionally. And desire is a violent emotion. These people in **35** the date-rape movement have erected so many rules and regulations that I don't know how people can have erotic or desire-driven sex."

36   Nonsense, retorts Cornell professor Andrea Parrot, co-author of *Acquaintance Rape: The Hidden Crime.* Seduction should not be about lies, manipulation, game playing or coercion of any kind, she says. "Too bad that people think that they only way you can have passion and excitement and sex is if there are miscommunications, and one person is forced to do something he or she doesn't want to do." The very pleasures of sexual encounters should lie in the fact of mutual comfort and consent: "You can hang from the ceiling, you can use fruit, you can go crazy and have really wonderful sensual erotic sex, if both parties are consenting."

37   It would be easy to accuse feminists of being too quick to classify sex as rape, but feminists are to be found on all sides of the debate, and many protest the idea that all the onus is on the man. It demeans women to suggest that they are so vulnerable to coercion or emotional manipulation that they must always be escorted by the strong arm of the law. "You can't solve society's ills by making everything a crime," says Albuquerque attorney Nancy Hollander. "That comes out of the sense of overprotection of women, and in the long run that is going to be harmful to us."

38   What is lost in the ideological debate over date rape is the fact that men and women, especially when they are young, and drunk, and aroused, are not very good at communicating. "In many cases," says Estrich, "the man thought it was sex, and the woman thought it was rape, and they are both telling the truth." The man may envision a celluloid seduction, in which he is being commanding, she is being coy. A woman may experience the same event as a degrading violation of her will. That some men do not believe a woman's protests is scarcely surprising in a society so drenched with messages that women have rape fantasies and a desire to be overpowered.

39   By the time they reach college, men and women are loaded with cultural baggage, drawn from movies, television, music videos and "bodice ripper" romance novels. Over the years they have watched Rhett sweep Scarlett up the stairs in *Gone With the Wind;* or Errol Flynn, who was charged twice with statutory rape, overpower a protesting heroine who then melts in his arms; or Stanley rape his sister-in-law Blanche du Bois while his wife is in the hospital giving birth to a child in *A Streetcar Named Desire.* Higher up the cultural food chain, young people can read of date rape in Homer or Jane Austen, watch it in *Don Giovanni* or *Rigoletto.*

40   The messages come early and often, and nothing in the feminist revolution has been able to counter them. A recent survey of sixth- to ninth-graders in Rhode Island found that a fourth of the boys and a sixth of the girls said it was acceptable for a man to force a woman to kiss him or have sex if he has spent money on her. A third of the children said it would not be wrong for a man to rape a woman who had had previous sexual experiences.

41   Certainly cases like Palm Beach, movies like *The Accused* and novels like

Avery Corman's *Prized Possessions* may force young people to re-examine assumptions they have inherited. The use of new terms, like acquaintance rape and date rape, while controversial, has given men and women the vocabulary they need to express their experiences with both force and precision. This dialogue would be useful if it helps strip away some of the dogmas, old and new, surrounding the issue. Those who hope to raise society's sensitivity to the problem of date rape would do well to concede that it is not precisely the same sort of crime as street rape, that there may be very murky issues of intent and degree involved.

On the other hand, those who downplay the problem should come to realize that date rape is a crime of uniquely intimate cruelty. While the body is violated, the spirit is maimed. How long will it take, once the wounds have healed, before it is possible to share a walk on a beach, a drive home from work or an evening's conversation without always listening for a quiet alarm to start ringing deep in the back of the memory of a terrible crime? **42**

▼ TOPICAL CONSIDERATIONS

1. What distinction does Gibbs make between "real" rape and "date" rape? Consider historical issues such as rapes "that mattered and those that did not" (paragraph 23). How do these classifications affect your answer?

2. What myths about rape are dispelled in the beginning of the essay? Why do you think that people have accepted these myths for so long?

3. Why is date rape termed the "hidden crime" (paragraph 7)?

4. Can you think of any reasons a rape victim might not want to press charges against the rapist?

5. There is an ongoing controversy surrounding the issue of the rape victim's anonymity (paragraph 18). Do you think the victim's name should be made public? Explain your answer.

6. What does Gibbs mean when she reports that "racism and sexism are factored into perceptions of the crime" (paragraph 25)? How do these two issues affect the crime of rape?

7. Consider the implications of false accusations against men? Should the people who make these accusations be punished by law? How would you treat false accusations against women (i.e., "she's a slut or a tease")?

8. Can you think of any factors that might influence our society's conceptions of and ideas about rape? Look at Kathi Maio's essay, "Hooked on Hate?" Is there a relationship between seeing representations of rape and raping?

9. Explain the mythology, "she was asking for it."

▼ RHETORICAL CONSIDERATIONS

1. Is Gibbs's essay objective? Can you find her opinions anywhere? Does this strengthen or reduce her analysis?
2. Look at the question that concludes the essay. Is it meant to be answered? Is it an effective way of closing the piece? Why or why not?
3. Gibbs provides readers with a lot of information in her essay. How well does she move from one idea to the next? Are her transitions smooth?
4. Gibbs presents many opinions. Which one(s) do you find more convincing than others? Why?

▼ WRITING ASSIGNMENTS

1. Write an essay in which you discuss "celluloid seduction" (paragraph 38). Is there a connection between media representation and date rape? Can you think of any media representations that show date rape? Is it glamorized? Romanticized? Critiqued? Look at Kathi Maio's essay, "Hooked on Hate?" How might she respond to the term?
2. Write an essay investigating the issue of men as victims of rape.
3. You are the Dean of Student Affairs at your university. Draft a proposal for a rape-awareness meeting to be attended by incoming students.
4. You are a judge at a rape trial. A witness testifies that the victim was drunk and willingly agreed to go to the alleged rapist's room. How does this evidence affect your judgment? Write an essay explaining your decision.

▼ WHY I BOUGHT A GUN
Gail Buchalter

Why would an intelligent, sensitive, liberal woman purchase a handgun? That was the question posed to writer Gail Buchalter, who after years of resistance bought a gun. Her article that follows is not intended to argue for or against any particular gun control legislation, or even to debate whether anyone should purchase a handgun. Rather, it is an attempt to understand why a person might feel the need to own a pistol and to explore the root causes of such a profound decision. Buchalter, who lives with her young son in a middle-class section of Los Angeles, is one of more than 12 million women in the United States who own guns. This essay was first published in *Parade* magazine in February 1988.

I was raised to wear black and cultured pearls in one of Manhattan's more desirable neighborhoods. My upper-middle-class background never involved guns. If my parents felt threatened, they simply put another lock on the door.

By high school, I had traded in my cashmere sweaters for a black arm band. I marched for Civil Rights, shunned Civil Defense drills and protested the Vietnam war. It was easy being 18 and a peacenik. I wasn't raising an 11-year-old child then.

Today, I am typical of the women whom gun manufacturers have been aiming at as potential buyers—and one of the millions who have succumbed: Between 1983 and 1986, there was a 53 percent increase in female gun-owners in the U.S.—from 7.9 million to 12.1 million, according to a Gallup Poll paid for by Smith & Wesson, the gun manufacturer.

Gun enthusiasts have created ad campaigns with such snappy slogans as "You Can't Rape a .38" or "Should You Shoot a Rapist Before He Cuts Your Throat?" While I was trying to come to a rational decision, I disliked these manipulative scare tactics. They only inflamed an issue that I never even dreamed would touch me.

I began questioning my beliefs one Halloween night in Phoenix, where I had moved when I married. I was almost home when another car nearly hit mine head-on. With the speed of a New York cabbie, I rolled down my window and screamed curses as the driver passed me. He instantly made a U-turn, almost climbing on my back bumper. By now, he and his two friends were hanging out of the car windows, yelling that they were going to rape, cut and kill me.

I already had turned into our driveway when I realized my husband wasn't home. I was trapped. The car had pulled in behind me. I drove up to the back porch and got into the kitchen, where our dogs stood waiting for me. The three men spilled out of their car and into our yard.

My adrenaline was pumping faster than Edwin Moses' legs clearing a hurdle. I grabbed the collars of Jack, our 200-pound Irish wolfhound, and his 140-pound malamute buddy, Slush. Then I kicked open the back door—I was so scared that I became aggressive—and actually dared the three creeps to keep coming. With the dogs, the odds had changed in my favor, and the men ran back to the safety of their car, yelling that they'd be back the next day to blow me away. Fortunately, they never returned.

8   A few years and one divorce later, I headed for Los Angeles with my 3-year-old son, Jordan (the dogs had since departed). When I put him in preschool a few weeks later, the headmistress noted that I was a single parent and immediately warned me that there was a rapist in my new neighborhood.

9   I called the police, who confirmed this fact. The rapist had no *modus operandi*. Sometimes he would be waiting in his victim's house; other times he would break in while the person was asleep. Although it was summer, I would carefully lock my windows at night and then lie there and sweat in fear. Thankfully, the rapist was caught, but not before he had attacked two more women.

10   Over some time, at first imperceptibly, my suburban neighborhood became less secure. A street gang took over the apartment building across from my house, and flowers and compact cars gave way to graffiti and low-riders.

11   Daytime was quiet, but these gang members crawled out like cockroaches after dark. Several nights in a row they woke me up. It was one of the most terrifying times in my life. I could hear them talking and laughing as they leaned against our fence, tossing their empty beer cans into our front yard. I knew that they were drinking, but were they also using violence-inducing drugs such as PCP and crack? And if they broke in, could I get to the police before they got to me?

12   I found myself, to my surprise, wishing that I had a loaded pistol under my pillow. In the clear light of day, I found this reaction shocking and simply decided to move to a safer neighborhood, although it cost thousands of dollars more. Luckily, I was able to afford it.

13   Soon the papers were telling yet another tale of senseless horror. Richard Ramirez, who became known as "The Walk-In Killer," spent months crippling and killing before he was caught. His alleged crimes were so brutal and bizarre, his desire to inflict pain so intense, that I began to question my beliefs about the sanctity of human life—his, in particular. The thought of taking a human life is repugnant to me, but the idea of being someone's victim is worse. And how, I began to ask myself, do you talk pacifism to a murderer or a rapist?

14   Finally, I decided that I would defend myself, even if it meant killing another person. I realized that the one-sided pacifism I once so strongly had advocated could backfire on me and, worse, on my son. Reluctantly, I concluded that I had to insure the best option for our survival. My choices: to count on a cop or to own a pistol.

15   But still I didn't go out and buy a gun. Everything about guns is threatening. My only exposure to them had been in movies; owning one, I feared, would bring all that violence off of the screen and into my home.

16   So, instead, I called up my girlfriend (who has begged to remain nameless)

and told her I had decided to buy a gun. We were both surprised that I didn't know she already had one. She was held up at gunpoint several years ago and bought what she said was a .37. We figured out it must be either a .38 or a .357. I was horrified when she admitted that not only had she no idea what type of gun she owned, but she also had never even shot it. It remains in her drawer, loaded and unused.

Upset, I hung up and called another friend. He was going to the National 17 Rifle Association convention that was being held in Reno and suggested I tag along. My son's godmother lives there, so I figured I could visit her and kill two birds with one stone.

My first night in Reno, I attended the Handgun Hunters' Awards dinner 18 and sat next to a contributing editor for one of the gun magazines. He bitterly complained that killing elephants had been outlawed, although there were thousands still running around Africa. Their legs, he explained, made wonderful trash baskets. I felt like Thumper on opening day of the hunting season, and my foot kept twitching under the table.

The next day at the convention center, I saw a sign announcing a seminar 19 for women on handguns and safety. I met pistol-packing grandmas, kids who were into competitive shooting and law-enforcement agents. I listened to a few of them speak and then watched a video, "A Woman's Guide to Firearms." It explained everything from how guns worked to an individual's responsibilities as a gun owner.

It was my kind of movie, since everything about guns scares me—especially 20 owning one. Statistics on children who are victims of their parents' handguns are overwhelming: About 300 children a year—almost a child a day—are killed by guns in this country, according to Handgun Control, Inc., which bases its numbers on data from the National Safety Council. Most of these killings are accidental.

As soon as I returned to Los Angeles, I called a man I had met a while ago 21 who, I remembered, owned several guns. He told me he had a Smith & Wesson .38 Special for sale and recommended it, since it was small enough for me to handle yet had the necessary stopping power.

I bought the gun. That same day, I got six rounds of special ammunition 22 with plastic tips that explode on impact. These are not for target practice; these are for protection.

For about $50, I also picked up the metal safety box that I had learned 23 about in the video. Its push-button lock opens with a touch if you know the proper combination, possibly taking only a second or two longer than it does to reach into a night-table drawer. Now I knew that my son, Jordan, couldn't get his hands on it while I still could.

When I brought the gun home, Jordan was fascinated by it. He kept picking 24 it up, while I nervously watched. But knowledge, I believe, is still our greatest defense. And since I'm in favor of education for sex, AIDS and learning to drive, I couldn't draw the line at teaching my son about guns.

Next, I took the pistol and my son to the target range. I rented a .22 caliber 25 pistol for Jordan. (A .38 was too much gun for him to handle.) I was relieved when he put it down after 10 minutes—he didn't like the feel of it.

26   But that didn't prevent him from asking me if he should use the gun if someone broke into our house while I wasn't home. I shrieked "no!" so loud, we both jumped. I explained that, if someone ever broke in, he's young and agile enough to leap out the window and run for his life.

27   Today he couldn't care less about the gun. Every so often, when we're watching television in my room, I practice opening the safety box, and Jordan times me. I'm down to three seconds. I'll ask him what's the first thing you do when you handle a gun, and he looks at me like I'm a moron, saying for the umpteenth time: "Make sure it's unloaded. But I know I'm not to touch it or tell my friends about it." Jordan's already bored with it all.

28   I, on the other hand, look forward to Mondays—"Ladies' Night" at the target range—when I get to shoot for free. I buy a box of bullets and some targets from the guy behind the counter, put on the protective eye and ear coverings and walk through the double doors to the firing lines.

29   Once there, I load my gun, look down the sights of the barrel and adjust my aim. I fire six rounds into the chest of a life-sized target hanging 25 feet away. As each bullet rips a hole through the figure drawn there, I realize I'm getting used to owning a gun and no longer feeling faint when I pick it up. The weight of it has become comfortable in my hand. And I am keeping my promise to practice. Too many people are killed by their own guns because they don't know how to use them.

30   It took me years to decide to buy a gun, and then weeks before I could load it. It gave me nightmares.

31   One night I dreamed I woke up when someone broke into our house. I grabbed my gun and sat waiting at the foot of my bed. Finally, I saw him turn the corner as he headed toward me. He was big and filled the hallway—an impossible target to miss. I aimed the gun and froze, visualizing the bullet blowing a hole through his chest and spraying his flesh all over the walls and floor. I didn't want to shoot, but I knew my survival was on the line. I wrapped my finger around the trigger and finally squeezed it, simultaneously accepting the intruder's death at my own hand and the relief of not being a victim. I woke up as soon as I decided to shoot.

32   I was tearfully relieved that it had only been a dream.

33   I never have weighed the consequences of an act as strongly as I have that of buying a gun—but, then again, I never have done anything with such deadly repercussions. Most of my friends refuse even to discuss it with me. They believe that violence begets violence.

34   They're probably right.

▼ TOPICAL CONSIDERATIONS

1. How does Buchalter's decision to purchase a handgun contradict her upbringing and attitudes as a young woman?

2. What was the turning point for the author's attitude regarding handguns? What event or events made her question her pacifist beliefs? What finally convinced Buchalter to buy a gun?
3. Why had Buchalter's nameless woman friend purchased her handgun?
4. What does Buchalter learn at the National Rifle Association? How did her experience there make it easier for her to buy her own gun?
5. What reason does Buchalter give for teaching her young son about guns?
6. Do you sympathize with Buchalter's decision to purchase a gun? Would you have bought one if you were she?

▼ RHETORICAL CONSIDERATIONS

1. Where does Buchalter state the thesis of her essay?
2. At the Handgun Hunters' Award dinner, Buchalter sits next to a man who complains about elephant-hunting laws. What is the function of this little detail? How does it comment on the change taking place in her? Explain her comment about feeling like "Thumper on opening day of the hunting season."
3. Comment on the effect of the concluding line of the article. What's the author's strategy behind making it a one-line paragraph? How do you interpret the meaning of this final comment?

▼ WRITING ASSIGNMENTS

1. Do you or anyone you know own a handgun? If so, write a paper explaining how you feel about owning a handgun or how your friend feels about owning one.
2. Write a letter to Gail Buchalter in which you express your support for her decision to purchase a handgun.
3. Write a letter to Gail Buchalter in which you express your disappointment that she broke down and bought a handgun.
4. This essay brings up the question of gun control. What are your feelings on this issue? Do you think that there should be stronger gun control laws?

10 CONTEMPORARY ISSUES: PROS AND CONS

Abortion. Gun control. Euthanasia. Capital punishment. Freedom of expression.

These are the hottest issues in contemporary American society—issues that never seem to go away, that echo year after year in the media, the courts of justice, the halls of academe, and on Capitol Hill. Whether or not you've taken firm stands on them, you may not be aware of some complexities of the problems—the emotional as well as ethical, moral, political, and legal implications. So, we have chosen to present these five controversial topics by pitting opponents in a pro-and-con debate on each issue. By sensitizing you to slants you may not have considered, we hope to invite you into the debates. Also, we hope that in recognizing the strengths, weaknesses, and strategies of an argument you will learn how to write strong arguments of your own.

As we saw in the last chapter, the soaring rate of violent crime is America's most disturbing social issue. As public fear increases, so does the talk about crime prevention; inevitably, the talk turns to the subject of handguns. According to the Bureau of Justice, some 70 million handguns are in the possession of private citizens. The real issue is what to do about preventing guns from falling into the hands of the criminally minded or mentally unbalanced who account for the 13,000 handgun murders, 15,000 rapes, 250,000 robberies, and 500,000 assaults each year. And that is the heart of our first debate. Arguing for stronger gun control measures including a mandatory waiting period for handgun purchases is Sarah Brady, head of Handgun Control Inc. and wife of former presidential press secretary James Brady who was incapacitated by a would-be assassin's bullet in an attempt on the life of Ronald Reagan on March 30, 1981. Representing the other side is Warren Cassidy the executive vice president of the National Rifle Association who argues that a mandatory waiting period will not stop criminals from getting guns but only penalize law-abiding buyers.

Abortion is not an issue that most people are neutral about. It is highly charged because it revolves around the definition of life itself—a definition that has moral, religious, political, legal ramifications. A definition scientists and lawmakers still grapple with. On one side, antiabortionists argue that abortion is murder. On the other side, prochoice advocates argue that a woman has a right to control her own body. More often than not, the voices we hear in the major media are those of white men and women. We thought it would be illuminating to listen to what black women have to say. Though the debate is addressed to African-Americans, universal are the arguments of Faye Wattleton ("Which Way Black America?—Pro-Choice"), past president of Planned Parenthood Federation of America, and Pamela Carr ("Which Way Black America?—Anti-Abortion"), spokesperson for Black Americans for Life.

Medical science can be both a blessing and a curse when it comes to prolonging life. In the next selections, we address the subject of euthanasia. But instead of pitting abstract theories and arguments against each other, we have reprinted an article from the *Journal of the American Medical Association* that set off a firestorm of controversy. "It's Over, Debbie" is an anonymously written confession of a physician who decided to help end the life of a young woman dying painfully of cancer. Representing the extraordinary response to that piece are three letters to the editor of *JAMA* that argue the ethics of ending Debbie's life.

Is the death penalty the ultimate deterrent and a fitting punishment for crime, or is it a cruel eye-for-an-eye retribution that our society should rise above? Those are the questions raised in the next two debates. Arguing for capital punishment is Edward Koch past mayor of New York City, and a man who believes that execution helps affirm life while deterring crime. Representing the opposition is David Bruck, chief attorney at the South Carolina Office of Appellate Defense. Bruck contends that capital punishment is a desperate symbol of the government's helplessness in fighting crime.

One of the more difficult challenges to higher education has to do with the First Amendment. Does the right to freedom of expression prevent universities from curbing certain forms of speech on campus—namely, racist, sexist, and other offensive discourse? In "Regulating Racist Speech on Campus," Charles R. Lawrence argues that allowing people to demean other members of a college community violates student victims' rights to education. Taking the opposing side in "Free Speech on Campus," Nat Hentoff says that censorship of the language of hate threatens the very nature of a university and the spirit of academic freedom while making more dangerous the forces of hate.

▼ THE CASE AGAINST FIREARMS

Sarah Brady

While the crime rate in America climbs, one of the debates that continues to rage is what to do about firearms. Some people cry for stronger gun control—even a ban—while others argue that gun control will not reduce crime since criminals will always find a means to kill. Sarah Brady, head of Handgun Control, knows firsthand about gun violence. Her own future was partly destroyed on March 31, 1981, when would-be assassin John W. Hinckley Jr.'s bullets wounded President Ronald Reagan and permanently disabled her husband, James Brady, then White House press secretary. Seeking to reduce gun violence in America, gun control advocates have lobbied for passage of the so-called Brady Bill, which calls for a mandatory waiting period on handgun purchases. Supported by Ronald Reagan, this bill, which is tied to a larger anticrime package including the ban on the sale and domestic production of semiautomatic weapons, is the first attempt by the federal government to restrict handgun sales since the 1960s. At this printing this anticrime package still has not become law. This article first appeared in *Time* magazine in January 1990.

1   As America enters the next decade, it does so with an appalling legacy of gun violence. The 1980s were tragic years that saw nearly a quarter of a million Americans die from handguns—four times as many as were killed in the Viet Nam War. We began the decade by witnessing yet another President, Ronald Reagan, become a victim of a would-be assassin's bullet. That day my husband Jim, his press secretary, also became a statistic in America's handgun war.

2   Gun violence is an epidemic in this country. In too many cities, the news each night reports another death by a gun. As dealers push out in search of new addicts, Smalltown, U.S.A., is introduced to the mindless gun violence fostered by the drug trade.

3   And we are killing our future. Every day a child in this country loses his or her life to a handgun. Hundreds more are permanently injured, often because a careless adult left within easy reach a loaded handgun purchased for self-defense.

4   Despite the carnage, America stands poised to face an even greater escalation of bloodshed. The growing popularity of military-style assault weapons could turn our streets into combat zones. Assault weapons, designed solely to mow down human beings, are turning up at an alarming rate in the hands of those most prone to violence—drug dealers, gang members, hate groups and the mentally ill.

5   The Stockton, Calif., massacre of little children was a warning to our policymakers. But Congress lacked the courage to do anything. During the year

of inaction on Capitol Hill, we have seen too many other tragedies brought about by assault weapons. In Louisville an ex-employee of a printing plant went on a shooting spree with a Chinese-made semiautomatic version of the AK-47, gunning down 21 people, killing eight and himself. Two Colorado women were murdered and several others injured by a junkie using a stolen MAC-11 semiautomatic pistol. And Congress votes itself a pay raise.

6   The National Rifle Association, meanwhile, breathes a sigh of relief, gratified that your attention is now elsewhere. The only cooling-off period the N.R.A. favors is a postponement of legislative action. It counts on public anger to fade before such outrage can be directed at legislators. The N.R.A. runs feel-good ads saying guns are not the problem and there is nothing we can do to prevent criminals from getting guns. In fact, it has said that guns in the wrong hands are the "price we pay for freedom." I guess I'm just not willing to hand the next John Hinckley a deadly handgun. Neither is the nation's law-enforcement community, the men and women who put their lives on the line for the rest of us every day.

7   Two pieces of federal legislation can make a difference right now. First, we must require a national waiting period before the purchase of a handgun, to allow for a criminal-records check. Police know that waiting periods work. In the 20 years that New Jersey has required a background check, authorities have stopped more than 10,000 convicted felons from purchasing handguns.

8   We must also stop the sale and domestic production of semiautomatic assault weapons. These killing machines clearly have no legitimate sporting purpose, as President Bush recognized when he permanently banned their importation.

9   These public-safety measures are supported by the vast majority of Americans—including gun owners. In fact, these measures are so sensible that I never realized the campaign to pass them into law would be such an uphill battle. But it can be done.

10   Jim Brady knows the importance of a waiting period. He knows the living hell of a gunshot wound. Jim and I are not afraid to take on the N.R.A leaders, and we will fight them everywhere we can. As Jim said in his congressional testimony, "I don't question the rights of responsible gun owners. That's not the issue. The issue is whether the John Hinckleys of the world should be able to walk into gun stores and purchase handguns instantly. Are you willing and ready to cast a vote for a commonsense public-safety bill endorsed by experts—law enforcement?"

11   Are we as a nation going to accept America's bloodshed, or are we ready to stand up and do what is right? When are we going to say "Enough"? We can change the direction in which America is headed. We can prevent the 1990s from being bloodier than the past ten years. If each of you picks up a pen and writes to your Senators and Representative tonight, you would be surprised at how quickly we could collect the votes we need to win the war for a safer America.

12   Let us enter a new decade committed to finding solutions to the problem of gun violence. Let your legislators know that voting with the gun lobby—and

against public safety—is no longer acceptable. Let us send a signal to lawmakers that we demand action, not excuses.

▼ TOPICAL CONSIDERATIONS

1. What argument does Brady introduce in the opening paragraph and carry through the entire essay? Is this a strong and convincing argument? Do you agree with Brady?
2. In the first paragraph, Brady cites "yet another" presidential attack by "a would-be-assassin's bullet". Do you think that political assassinations or such attempts should impel us to take a firmer stand against handguns? Why or why not?
3. What specific legislations is Sarah Brady asking for? What evidence does she give that such measures will make a difference in the violence in this country? Do you agree with her reasoning? Do you find her appeals convincing? Enough to change peoples' attitudes?
4. Brady points out that the National Rifle Association is part of the reason our country has no effective national gun control legislation. Why is this? What is your opinion of the N.R.A. campaign against gun control? Why do you think it has so much influence?
5. If the author of this piece were not the wife of Jim Brady, would it be as effective an appeal for gun control? Why or why not?

▼ RHETORICAL CONSIDERATIONS

1. In the opening paragraph, Brady says that the decade of the 1980s left us an "appalling legacy of gun violence." How does she communicate this idea?
2. What do you remember best about the writing in this essay? How was it effective in presenting the arguments? How was it convincing and persuasive?
3. How would you characterize the tone of this essay—reasoned and objective? Angry and bitter? Resigned and frustrated? Explain your answer.
4. Consider the last sentence in paragraph 5: "And Congress votes itself a pay raise." Does this sentence effectively resolve any points of the paragraph? What point does it make? What is the tone here?

▼ WRITING ASSIGNMENTS

1. If all the laws on the books prohibiting theft of property and drug abuse haven't aided enforcement, what is the likelihood that one or

two more gun control laws will curb violence? Write an essay in which you offer a rebuttal to Sarah Brady's arguments for gun control legislation.

2. Write a paper in which you argue that requiring a national waiting period before purchasing a handgun does not compromise N.R.A. members' right to own and use guns. Nor does it violate the Bill of Rights or Americans' freedom to hunt, target shoot, or protect themselves.

3. Do you own a gun? If so, and if you do not use it for hunting or target-shooting, explain why you own it.

4. If you are not a gun owner, do you think you ever could be? Can you imagine circumstances in which you might feel compelled to purchase a gun?

GUN CONTROL–CON

▼ THE CASE FOR FIREARMS
Warren Cassidy

The opposing argument is made by Warren Cassidy who argues that gun control will not reduce crime since gangsters can always get guns illegally. Furthermore, any gun control laws will only deny law-abiding citizens their constitutional right to bear arms. Guns, he argues, help keep decent Americans free. Mr. Cassidy is the executive vice president of the National Rifle Association. This article first appeared in *Time* magazine in January 1990.

1   The American people have a right "to keep and bear arms." This right is protected by the Second Amendment to the Constitution, just as the right to publish editorial comment in this magazine is protected by the First Amendment. Americans remain committed to the constitutional right to free speech even when their most powerful oracles have, at times, abused the First Amendment's inherent powers. Obviously the American people believe no democracy can survive without a free voice.

2   In the same light, the authors of the Bill of Rights knew that a democratic republic has a right—indeed, a need—to keep and bear arms. Millions of American citizens just as adamantly believe the Second Amendment is crucial to the maintenance of the democratic process. Many express this belief through membership in the National Rifle Association of America.

3   Our cause is neither trendy nor fashionable, but a basic American belief that spans generations. The N.R.A.'s strength has never originated in Washington

but instead has reached outward and upward from Biloxi, Albuquerque, Concord, Tampa, Topeka—from every point on the compass and from communities large and small. Those who fail to grasp this widespread commitment will never understand the depth of political and philosophical dedication symbolized by the letters N.R.A.

Scholars who have devoted careers to the study of the Second Amendment agree in principle that the right to keep and bear arms is fundamental to our concept of democracy. No high-court decision has yet found grounds to challenge this basic freedom. Yet some who oppose this freedom want to waive the constitutionality of the "gun control" question for the sake of their particular—and sometimes peculiar—brand of social reform. **4**

In doing so they seem ready, even eager, to disregard a constitutional right exercised by at least 70 million Americans who own firearms. Contrary to current antigun evangelism, these gun owners are not bad people. They are hardworking, law abiding, tax paying. They are safe, sane and courteous in their use of guns. They have never been, nor will they ever be, a threat to law-and-order. **5**

History repeatedly warns us that human character cannot be scrubbed free of its defects through vain attempts to regulate inanimate objects such as guns. What has worked in the past, and what we see working now, are tough, N.R.A.-supported measures that punish the incorrigible minority who place themselves outside the law. **6**

As a result of such measures, violent crimes with firearms, like assault and robbery, have stabilized or are actually declining. We see proof that levels of firearm ownership cannot be associated with levels of criminal violence, except for their deterrent value. On the other hand, tough laws designed to incarcerate violent offenders offer something gun control cannot: swift, sure justice meted out with no accompanying erosion of individual liberty. **7**

Violent crime continues to rise in cities like New York and Washington even after severe firearm-control statutes were rushed into place. Criminals, understandably, have illegal ways of obtaining guns. Antigun laws—the waiting periods, background checks, handgun bans, et al.—only harass those who obey them. Why should an honest citizen be deprived of a firearm for sport or self-defense when, for a gangster, obtaining a gun is just a matter of showing up on the right street corner with enough money? **8**

Antigun opinion steadfastly ignores these realities known to rank-and-file police officers—men and women who face crime firsthand, not police administrators who face mayors and editors. These law-enforcement professionals tell us that expecting firearm restrictions to act as crime-prevention measures is wishful thinking. They point out that proposed gun laws would not have stopped heinous crimes committed by the likes of John Hinckley Jr., Patrick Purdy, Laurie Dann or mentally disturbed, usually addicted killers. How can such crimes be used as examples of what gun control could prevent? **9**

There are better ways to advance our society than to excuse criminal behavior. The N.R.A. initiated the first hunter-safety program, which has trained millions of young hunters. We are the shooting sports' leading safety organiza- **10** tion, with more than 26,000 certified instructors training 750,000 students and trainees last year alone. Through 1989 there were 9,818 N.R.A.-certified law-enforcement instructors teaching marksmanship to thousands of peace officers.

11   Frankly, we would rather keep investing N.R.A. resources in such worthwhile efforts instead of spending our time and members' money debunking the failed and flawed promises of gun prohibitionists.

12   If you agree, I invite you to join the N.R.A.

▼ TOPICAL CONSIDERATIONS

1. Do you own a gun? If so, what are your reasons? If not, what circumstances would make you consider buying one? Explain your answer.

2. What does Cassidy see as the motives behind those who call for gun control? Is this a fair characterization of their motives? Can you think of others?

3. Citing scholarly interpretations of the Second Amendment, Cassidy argues that in a democracy the individual has the constitutional right to bear arms. Why does he believe gun control is unconstitutional? Does he make a valid point? Do you agree with him, or not? Do you know the original intention of the Second Amendment? If not, it might be a good idea to investigate this before you answer.

4. In the battle against crime, what does Cassidy offer as an alternative to gun control legislation? What evidence does he give that such alternatives work? What evidence is there that it is not working?

5. According to Cassidy, how will antigun measures prove useless in preventing crime? How will such measures "harass" law-abiding gun owners? Do you agree with his arguments here? Explain your answer.

6. Cassidy is clearly opposed to any legislation that will prevent gun owners from owning guns. What do you think he would say about legislation against the import and sale of assault rifles? What are your feelings about such legislation?

7. After you read the essay that follows, if you were judging a debate between Cassidy and Brady, who would you decide had won? Consider how well each of them address the issues and whether either one successfully argues a point that the other fails to note.

▼ RHETORICAL CONSIDERATIONS

1. How would you characterize the tone of this essay—reasoned and objective? Emotional and flag-waving? Angry and bitter? Resigned and frustrated?

2. What do you think was the intention (or intentions) of Mr. Cassidy in this article? Was he trying to make a case against gun control, for firearms, or for joining the N.R.A.? Or, all three?

3. In paragraph 11, Cassidy refers to waisting N.R.A. resources and time "debunking the failed and flawed promises of gun prohibition-ists." Do you think he successfully debunked the arguments of gun prohibitionists in his essay? Did he convince you their promises have "failed" or were "flawed?" Explain.

▼ WRITING ASSIGNMENTS

1. Do you agree with Cassidy that people in our democracy have "a right—indeed, a need—to keep and bear arms" (paragraph 2)? Write a paper in which you explore the constitutionality of the gun control issue. Before you do, check the Second Amendment and the circumstances under which it was drafted and its original intentions.

2. Write a letter to Warren Cassidy telling him what you thought of his case for firearms. Cite his specific points of argument.

3. Write a paper in which you argue for or against gun control measures such as waiting periods, background checks, handgun bans, and so forth. Use the arguments you find in either Cassidy's essay or Sarah Brady's that you believe are most convincing.

4. Have you ever witnessed a gun-related crime? If so, write a narrative description of the incident. Comment on how it influenced your views (if at all) on gun control.

5. Cassidy argues that the N.R.A.'s hunter-safety programs and civil-ian and police training along with its support for mandatory sen-tences for criminal use of firearms do more for society than the gun prohibitionists. Write a paper in which you support or counter this claim.

ABORTION–PRO

▼ WHICH WAY BLACK AMERICA?—PRO-CHOICE

Faye Wattleton

In 1989 the Supreme Court passed a controversial ruling in the case of *Webster* v. *Reproductive Health Services* allowing states to impose new restrictions on a woman's right to have an abortion. The decision set off renewed debates between those who believe a woman has a legal right to an abortion and those who wish to restrict or outlaw abortion. While many of the legal and moral arguments are relevant to all Americans, the two pieces that follow focus the debate on the black community. Representing the prochoice stand is Faye Wattleton, past president of Planned Parenthood Federation of America. In her essay Ms. Wattleton argues that legal restrictions on a woman's access to abortion services will have dangerous effects on all women. But, she says, on black women the consequences will be devastating. This article first appeared in the October 1989 issue of *Ebony*.

---

1   It is ironic. As we celebrate the bicentennial of the Bill of Rights that guarantees Americans protection against the tyranny of the legislative process, we confront a serious threat to one of our most fundamental rights—our right to make independent reproductive decisions.

2   For eight years the Reagan administration wages a protracted war against both family planning programs and legal abortion. While the administration was unsuccessful in eliminating either, it was successful in shaping a federal court system that alarmingly reflects Mr. Reagan's vision of Americans' constitutional protections. Increasingly, decisions are being handed down by the federal courts that reflect a narrow and restricted interpretation of the Constitution and that threaten the future of many rights that Americans today take for granted.

3   Nowhere is this more explicitly demonstrated than in the Supreme Court's recent decision in *Webster* v. *Reproductive Health Services,* which allows states to impose severe restrictions on access to abortion services, particularly for poor women.

4   This decision has profound implications for the health and survival of the Black community. Black women are disproportionately poor, and poor Black women already have great difficulty in gaining access to reproductive health care information and services. Consider the following:

- Black women are twice as likely to experience unintended pregnancy and to seek abortions than White women.
- Black women are twice as likely to bear low birth–weight babies.

- The Black infant mortality rate is twice as high as that for White infants.
- 52% of all women with AIDS and 53% of all children with AIDS are Black.

The danger looms even larger when we consider the high incidence of **5** pregnancy among Black teenagers. Clearly, we fail miserably in providing our children with the ways and means of preventing pregnancy. The rates of pregnancy, childbirth and pregnancy among Black teens in this country are double the rates for White teens. The impact of this tragedy is devastating. It threatens the lives and future of our children for generations to come and seriously undermines the structure of the family in our communities.

Any restrictions placed on the availability of family planning and abortion **6** for young people will only exacerbate the problem. Young people need to be helped to seek the support and guidance of their loved ones when making sexual decisions. But when this is not possible, barriers such as parental consent and notification requirements must not be erected. They only force teenagers away from safe and reliable sources of reproductive health services and into the hands of unsafe and uncaring opportunists.

The affluent always have had the means to circumvent restrictions on **7** contraceptive and abortion services. Poor Black women have not. Poor Black women have borne the brunt of the virtual cutoff of Medicaid funding for abortion and will certainly be the first to be forced to seek unsafe abortions if legal and safe abortions once again are restricted. Black women will be the first to be injured and the first to die.

There is strong support among key Black leaders and major Black and **8** minority organizations for the right to keep abortion safe and legal. These include the National Council of Negro Women and the National Urban League. In addition to my own organization, two other national organizations that were instrumental in organizing support for the April 9 pro-choice march in Washington, D.C., are headed by Black women—the Religious Coalition for Abortion Rights, headed by Patricia Tyson, and the YWCA, headed by Gwendolyn Calvert Baker.

It has been charged that few Black women actually marched in that massive **9** demonstration in support of women's health and women's rights. The fact is that demonstrations requiring personal expense and travel have traditionally been made up largely of middle-class persons who have such means. Nevertheless, the number of Blacks among the marchers was reasonably close to the proportionate numbers of middle-class Blacks in America. Many who share our views simply could not be present.

Finally, when violent, extremist anti-abortion demonstrators had the au- **10** dacity to compare their tactics of intimidation and harassment of women to the civil rights demonstrations of the 1960s, America's civil rights leaders stepped forward to condemn such notions. Among these leaders were Julian Bond, James Farmer, Dorothy Height, the Rev. Jesse Jackson, John Jacob, Vernon Jordan, Barbara Jordan, Andrew Young, as well as several congressional representatives and leaders in law, business and education.

Black Americans, indeed *all* Americans, must realize that the courts can no **11** longer be relied upon to protect our most precious rights to reproductive privacy, and the profile of Black women is being inalterably shaped by the erosion of these rights. We must refuse to be put off track in our efforts to make progress—socially, economically and privately. We must be *suspicious* when social problems are oversimplified or when quick fixes are proposed. We must remember: Without the right to take charge of our personal lives and our destinies, our other rights are virtually *meaningless.*

▼ TOPICAL CONSIDERATIONS

1. What is the connection between family planning and abortion? Why might Wattleton link the two? Do you see them as being related?
2. In your own words, describe the implications of the information Wattleton gives readers on health care for black women.
3. What is the "tragedy" (paragraph 5) to which Wattleton refers? Do you agree with her word choice?
4. Do you think that "parental consent" and "notification" laws are helpful or harmful for women? What do you think is a good age for a young woman to make up her own mind without the consent of her parents? How might your parents respond to your answer?
5. In paragraph 7, Wattleton writes, "Black women will be the first to be injured and the first to die." Why might this be the case? Is her argument contingent solely upon race? Consider other issues such as gender, class, and age.
6. Do you find Wattleton's argument persuasive? Why?

▼ RHETORICAL CONSIDERATIONS

1. Is Wattleton's tone effective? How does Wattleton's invocation of "facts" (paragraph 4) influence how you see her argument? Do these "facts" validate the essay?
2. What is the difference between calling Wattleton's stance *prochoice* or *proabortion?* How is this difference significant to how you read the article?
3. Consider the final sentence of the essay. How does this quote relate to the issues Wattleton addresses? Can you think of specific rights that might become *"meaningless"?*
4. How does Wattleton make the transition from a discussion of poor women to a discussion of black women? Do you follow her logic?
5. How does Wattleton's shift from "Black Americans" to *"all* Americans" (paragraph 11) affect how you think about the issue? In the

same paragraph, Wattleton moves toward the use of "we." Do you feel a part of this "we"?

▼ WRITING ASSIGNMENTS

1. You are on a committee in charge of funding for Planned Parenthood. How do you respond to Wattleton's argument? What questions would you like to ask her before you grant or deny funding?
2. Write an essay agreeing or disagreeing with Wattleton's analysis. Consider issues of race, gender, and class in your analysis. Does Wattleton speak to *"all* Americans" (paragraph 11) as she claims to do?
3. Consider the role of audience in Wattleton's essay. How would you change her essay to convince a different audiences of her argument?

ABORTION–CON

▼ WHICH WAY BLACK AMERICA?—ANTI-ABORTION
Pamela Carr

Representing the antiabortion position is Pamela Carr, spokesperson for Black Americans for Life. Like Faye Wattleton, in the previous piece, Carr presents some sobering statistics in her arguments; she also cites key black leaders in an effort to bolster her position. But unlike Ms. Wattleton, Pamela Carr draws a personal element into her debate: The experience of her own abortion which, she says, taught her firsthand that abortion is no solution to the problems that plague black America. This article first appeared in the October 1989 issue of *Ebony.*

I am often asked why I, a young professional woman, am pro-life. I am pro-life because of my knowledge, both personal and scientific, that every abortion involves the taking of a human life. For the Black community, that means 1,000 African-Americans killed every day by abortion—more than 400,000 each year. The future of Black America is being threatened, our hope—through our children—destroyed in the name of convenience.

Is abortion a solution to break the poverty cycle? Will it enable young women and men to overcome unplanned obstacles to their education and career successes, and thus the success of the whole Black community?

3   No, abortion is not a solution, because it undermines the very ideals previous Black leaders stood for—the belief that each life is valuable and has something to contribute; whether Black or White, born or unborn.

4   Through my own abortion experience, I learned firsthand that abortion is no solution to the problems of the Black community.

5   On the verge of entering college, with a bright hope of educational and career success before me, I was horrified to learn my life plans were threatened by a small group of multiplying cells within me. I was pregnant. I panicked! I couldn't believe that it happened to me. How would I face my family and friends? I reluctantly asked my boyfriend to give me the money to get an abortion. He was hesitant because he wanted the baby.

6   It is important to know that I epitomized what was good and right in my community as a young Black woman. I was headed for success, allowing nothing from the past to hinder me. No obstacle would stop me from achieving my goals.

7   I had it all together. I was 17 and in my junior year of high school in Queens, New York. I believed in myself, my ability to make my own decisions, and my right to do so. I was an enterprising young woman ready to make my mark on the world. I had plans to graduate the following year with the hopes of attending one of the top Black colleges in the country. Nothing or no one could interfere with the plans I had made for my life.

8   I had been dating my boyfriend for about a year. We were well informed about sex education and the necessity of birth control. We were considered decent, intelligent and good students among our peers. We decided to become sexually active several months prior to the pregnancy.

9   Eventually, I contacted an older family friend in whom I confided. She informed my family about my pregnancy. My parents were hurt, but never ceased to remain concerned about me.

10   I had the 'procedure'' the following morning.

11   With my fears of a lost future and destroyed reputation behind me, I immediately faced a worse fear that I knew instinctively to be true. I had removed more than a "blob of tissue" or "the products of conception." I had killed my baby.

12   The anguish and the guilt I felt were unbelievable. I became deeply depressed. I no longer felt like that confident, jubilant young woman everyone knew me to be. Extreme feelings of insecurity followed me daily. My life took on new burdens. I could not have cared less about graduating from high school, or for that matter, attending college.

13   Over time, I was able to forgive myself and go on with my life, but always with the knowledge that I had swept away a part of my future which could never be recovered.

14   Abortion is offered as a solution to help young Blacks to forge forward to overcome present hindrances and to strive for brighter tomorrows. Yet, abortion only darkened my future. It took me many years to rise above the tide of confusion and guilt that flooded my life.

15   By allowing 400,000 Black babies to be systematically killed every year, we

as African-Americans have strayed from the path of the leaders who fought so hard for our freedom. They would be alarmed today at how we forfeit the lives of our children, and, as a result, our future.

In the United States today, Black people only make up 12 percent of the population. Yet Black women have 25 percent of the abortions performed in our nation every year. For every three Black babies born, two die from abortion. It seems a silent genocide is taking place. **16**

Teenage pregnancies, drugs, poverty and a lack of quality education are some of the problems that plague Black America. Abortion eliminates children, not these complex social problems. We shortchange ourselves when we buy the lie that we can improve the quality of our lives by terminating the lives of our children. How many more of them have to die before we realize that abortion is not a solution but another, more troubling, problem plaguing our community? **17**

The solutions for the problems faced by the Black community will not be easy—they will require the effort of all of us working together. Let's take the first step by giving our children life because our children are our future. **18**

Brave, positive leaders such as Harriet Tubman, Frederick Douglass, Martin Luther King Jr. and others have paved the way for the freedoms we possess today as Black Americans. **19**

We cannot accept something so deeply wrong and injust as abortion as a solution to the problems that still plague us. We cannot gain our freedom and our rights by taking away the lives of other members of the Black community. If we do, we have cheated ourselves of a future and betrayed the leaders who came before us and struggled so hard for our lives. **20**

In the words of the great leader Martin Luther King Jr.: "Injustice anywhere is a threat to justice everywhere." **21**

▼ TOPICAL CONSIDERATIONS

1. In paragraph 6, Carr writes, "It is important to know that I epitomized what was good and right in my community." Why is this "important"? How does Carr's own experience with abortion convince you or fail to convince you of her point? What was your stand on the issue before you read this essay?

2. When does Carr begin to focus her discussion on the African-American community? How is this approach different from Wattleton's? Why might she have chosen this approach?

3. Carr insists that she and her boyfriend were well educated on birth control, but Wattleton in the preceding essay writes, "we fail miserably in providing our children with the ways and means of preventing pregnancy" (paragraph 5). Discuss the ways in which these contradictory statements might coexist.

4. Carr suggests that abortion is a betrayal of "the leaders who came before us and struggled so hard for our lives" (paragraph 20). What

does she mean by this? Can you think of leaders outside the black community who would also feel this "betrayal"?

5. In your own words, describe what Carr means by "a silent genocide is taking place" (paragraph 16)? Do you agree with this analysis? What connotations can you think of for a word like *genocide?*

6. What is "the lie" (paragraph 17) to which Carr refers?

7. Do you think Carr wants all women to stop having abortions? Does she want to outlaw abortion? Why do you answer the way you do?

8. How might someone from a different race respond to this essay? What other positions might affect a reader's understanding of Carr's argument? For example, does gender, age, socioeconomic class, religious or ethnic background make a difference in engaging Carr's essay?

▼ RHETORICAL CONSIDERATIONS

1. Carr begins her essay in the first person, but in paragraph 15, she moves her narrative to the third person. Why? Is this an effective strategy for convincing you of her argument? Consider her shift from specific/subjective to general/objective. Would you consider using this strategy to write a persuasive essay? Look at Faye Wattleton's essay—how is it different?

2. Pay specific attention to the way that language constructs an issue such as abortion. What is the difference between calling Carr's stance *antiabortion* or *prolife?* How does she describe pregnancy? Abortion? What purpose might these words serve in the context of Carr's argument?

3. Why does Carr mention famous leaders such as Harriet Tubman, Frederick Douglass, and Martin Luther King, Jr.? How do these references add to or detract from the essay's effectiveness? Can you think of other instances when naming famous people is a persuasive strategy?

4. Consider that final sentence of the essay. In your own words, put this sentence in the context of Carr's argument. Compare it to the conclusion of Wattleton's argument.

5. How did Carr catch your attention? What was your initial reaction to the essay? Explain why you think you reacted the way you did. Does your prior opinion affect the way you read the essay?

▼ WRITING ASSIGNMENTS

1. Abortion is one of the most controversial issues facing the United States today. It has been debated on many levels—personally and

politically. Imagine you are a Supreme Court Justice, and Carr has given this testimony to the Court. Write an essay responding to her argument. What questions would you like to ask her?

2. Write an essay agreeing or disagreeing with Carr's analysis of the effect of abortion on the African-American community. Is the "procedure" unique to African-Americans? Consider issues of race, gender, and class in your analysis. How might a poor Asian woman respond to Carr's argument? A rich white man?

3. Carr writes that "abortion is no solution to the problems of the Black community" (paragraph 4). She also says that the solutions "will not be easy" (paragraph 18). Imagine you are a leader of a black community; draft a proposal indicating some "solutions" to the "problem." How does abortion fit into your proposal?

4. Consider how abortion affects your own community and write an addendum or a rebuttal to Carr's piece.

5. Imagine yourself in a conversation with Carr and Wattleton. Set the scene, and create a dialogue between the two women and yourself.

6. Write a paper discussing the roles that Wattleton's and Carr's essays had in forming or altering your views on the plight of black women and abortion.

EUTHANASIA–PRO

▼ IT'S OVER, DEBBIE

Anonymous

> The *Journal of the American Medical Association* is not known as a hotbed
> of controversy. Most of its articles are highly technical; and any debates
> found on its pages are cool exchanges in arcane language between medi-
> cal specialists. Nevertheless, in 1988 the editors of *JAMA* created an
> uproar by publishing an article by an unidentified doctor describing how he
> or she had ended the life of a young woman dying painfully of cancer.
> According to the author, a resident physician, the only words from the
> woman were "Let's get this over with." A few minutes later the doctor gave
> the woman a lethal dose of morphine. The story of "Debbie" touched off
> widespread debate on the ethics of euthanasia. It also brought down con-
> siderable criticism of the *Journal* for not publishing the author's name
> (withheld by request) and for not including a clear statement of the AMA's
> opposition to mercy killing. Some of the hundreds of letters to the editors
> defended the doctor's action, courage, and compassion; but more ex-
> pressed outrage. Reprinted here is "It's Over, Debbie" as it originally
> appeared in *JAMA* in January 1988. On the following pages are three of the
> several letters subsequently published.

1   The call came in the middle of the night. As a gynecology resident rotating
through a large, private hospital, I had come to detest telephone calls, because
invariably I would be up for several hours and would not feel good the next day.
However, duty called, so I answered the phone. A nurse informed me that a
patient was having difficulty getting rest, could I please see her. She was on 3
North. That was the gynecologic-oncology unit, not my usual duty station. As
I trudged along, bumping sleepily against walls and corners and not believing
I was up again, I tried to imagine what I might find at the end of my walk.
Maybe an elderly woman with an anxiety reaction, or perhaps something partic-
ularly horrible.

2   I grabbed the chart from the nurses station on my way to the patient's
room, and the nurse gave me some hurried details: a 20-year-old girl named
Debbie was dying of ovarian cancer. She was having unrelenting vomiting
apparently as the result of an alcohol drip administered for sedation. Hmmm,
I thought. Very sad. As I approached the room I could hear loud, labored
breathing. I entered and saw an emaciated, dark-haired woman who appeared
much older than 20. She was receiving nasal oxygen, had an IV, and was sitting
in bed suffering from what was obviously severe air hunger. The chart noted her
weight at 80 pounds. A second woman, also dark-haired but of middle age,
stood at her right, holding her hand. Both looked up as I entered. The room
seemed filled with the patient's desperate effort to survive. Her eyes were hollow,
and she had suprasternal and intercostal retractions with her rapid inspirations.

She had not eaten or slept in two days. She had not responded to chemotherapy and was being given supportive care only. It was a gallows scene, a cruel mockery of her youth and unfulfilled potential. Her only words to me were, "Let's get this over with."

I retreated with my thoughts to the nurses station. The patient was tired and needed rest. I could not give her health, but I could give her rest. I asked the nurse to draw 20 mg of morphine sulfate into a syringe. Enough, I thought, to do the job. I took the syringe into the room and told the two women I was going to give Debbie something that would let her rest and to say good-bye. Debbie looked at the syringe, then laid her head on the pillow with her eyes open, watching what was left of the world. I injected the morphine intravenously and watched to see if my calculations on its effects would be correct. Within seconds her breathing slowed to a normal rate, her eyes closed, and her features softened as she seemed restful at last. The older woman stroked the hair of the now-sleeping patient. I waited for the inevitable next effect of depressing the respiratory drive. With clocklike certainty, within four minutes the breathing rate slowed even more, then became irregular, then ceased. The dark-haired woman stood erect and seemed relieved.

It's over, Debbie.

Name Withheld by Request

▼ TOPICAL CONSIDERATIONS

1. In your opinion, which description best fits the doctor's reaction to Debbie's plight—aggravation or sympathy?
2. While in the nurses' station the doctor comes to the following conclusion: "The patient was tired and needed rest. I could not give her health, but I could give her rest." Do you think this represents an adequate analysis of the situation? What factors does the doctor consider? What factors does the doctor ignore?
3. According to the doctor, Debbie's only words were "Let's get this over with." How did the doctor interpret her remark? What other possible interpretations could have been made from her remark?
4. What details suggest that Debbie and her companion knew and approved of what the doctor was doing? Do you find them convincing?
5. If you were the doctor, what would you have done for Debbie?

▼ RHETORICAL CONSIDERATIONS

1. What do you think the doctor's purpose was in the first paragraph? How does it enhance or detract from our opinion of the doctor and the actions taken?

2. How does the doctor's statement, "It was a gallows scene, a cruel mockery of her youth and unfulfilled potential," encapsulate the doctor's point of view and interpretation of the situation?

3. In the style or tone of this letter, is there any clue as to the gender of the doctor? Do you think the doctor was a man or a woman? Explain your reasoning.

▼ WRITING ASSIGNMENTS

1. Write your own letter to the editors of *JAMA* responding to the doctor's story.

2. Try to imagine how Debbie might have felt in the last moments of her life. In an essay, attempt to create from her point of view her encounter with the doctor.

3. Why do you think the doctor chose to write about the death of Debbie anonymously? Does this suggest a fear of possible repercussions or, perhaps, the doctor's own doubts about the propriety of the action? Write a paper in which you explore the doctor's choice of anonymity.

4. In a paper, write your own feelings about mercy killing. What specific conditions would you say have to be met for euthanasia to be practiced?

▼ RESPONSE TO *IT'S OVER, DEBBIE*

The extraordinary response to the publication of "It's Over, Debbie" showed a clear split between the medical profession and the public. While doctors were concerned with the preservation of life, the public was more interested in dying with minimal suffering and pain. At the heart of the debate is a question of ethics: What is more humane, prolonging the misery of a terminally ill patient or ending it with a lethal injection? The letter from Susan D. Wilson to the editor of *JAMA* represents one of the several responses from lay people who defended the physician's decision to end Debbie's suffering.

To the Editor.—I read with a great deal of interest the article entitled "It's Over, Debbie." 1

My father, age 85 years, has been in a nursing home for more than a year. 2 He is incontinent, has lost his memory and ability to comprehend and reason, and is hospitalized periodically for pneumonia, urinary tract infection, dehydration, and so on.

He has now lost his ability to swallow, and since Christmas he has been fed 3 through a tube inserted in his nose. Because he tries to remove the tube, his hands are tied at all times to the bed rails. He is not comatose but he does not recognize his family and he has no understanding of why he is being forced to lie in bed under these circumstances. I believe that if I were asked to make a list of ways in which to torture people, this would have to be placed somewhere near the top.

I am fully aware that a physician's duty is to treat and heal, but when 4 healing is clearly not possible, should not mercy killing be allowed? Humaneness is also a definitive part of the medical profession, and it seems that something should be done to prevent so many people from existing for sustained periods of time in a living hell. The technology we have today is wonderful, but it cannot and should not be used in every instance.

Susan D. Wilson
Glen Ellyn, Ill

▼ TOPICAL CONSIDERATIONS

1. Susan D. Wilson describes her aged father's condition and concludes, "The technology we have today is wonderful, but it cannot

and should not be used in every instance." Do you agree that it should not be used in her father's case? Why or why not?

2. How might the physician who terminated Debbie's life react to this letter from Susan D. Wilson? Do you think the physician would be willing to end the man's suffering?

3. If you were a doctor treating Wilson's father, how would you react to her appeal?

▼ RHETORICAL CONSIDERATION

1. Do you consider Susan Wilson's letter too emotional an appeal? Why or why not?

▼ WRITING ASSIGNMENT

1. Suppose there was a movement in your state to put on the ballot a measure allowing a terminally ill patient the right to request a lethal injection from a physician. Write an editorial supporting or condemning this movement.

EUTHANASIA–CON

▼ RESPONSE TO *IT'S OVER, DEBBIE*

The following two letters to the editors of *JAMA* condemn the action taken by the anonymous physician to end Debbie's life. The first letter is from a member of the medical community, Harold Y. Vanderpool, who raises some troubling questions about professional ethics. The second letter, from Don C. Shaw, expresses the disapproval from the Hemlock Society, which advocates legalized doctor-assisted death only in conformation with specific requirements.

To the Editor.—The story entitled "It's Over, Debbie" raises profoundly troubling ethical issues—the more so because its sentimental surface masks a dark and worrisome underside. **1**

On the surface of the story, a hassled but resolutely caring resident physician ends the hollow-eyed suffering of a young woman named Debbie by putting a stop to the cruel, "gallows"-like technology that mocks her youth and former vitality. **2**

Just beneath the surface of these heartwarming themes lies the real point of the story—that in cases like this it is ethical for physicians to kill patients. Unfortunately, "It's Over, Debbie" only disguises and distorts the debate and clarification that are necessary for a moral assessment of mercy killing. First, the story's rhetoric (which is equated with the way the physician thinks) masks the act of killing Debbie with such euphemisms as doing one's "job," giving Debbie the "rest" she needs, and enabling her "to say goodbye." Second, the physician's premeditated manslaughter is associated only with such positive themes as heroically resisting a blind technological imperative within medicine or displaying unique empathy for this cancer patient's plight. Debbie's physician never struggles with opposing moral issues, such as whether this action could be generalized or whether killing constitutes a betrayal of one's promises to self and peers or what would happen if the term "physician" is also associated with putting persons to death. In fact, the resident kills Debbie with no moral qualms whatsoever. **3**

Even more problematic than the morality of premeditated manslaughter per se, however, are the terribly murky grounds for killing in this instance. The physician's database on this new patient was gathered entirely while walking toward the patient's room (when the chart was scanned and as the nurse was talking), followed by a single visit to the patient. The one sentence uttered by the patient at the time, "Let's get this over with," was taken to be a firm request for a painless death from a fully competent adult. There are no consultations, no further conversations with anyone, no sophistication regarding pain relief as **4** a beginning point, and no worries that Debbie's intentions may well have been misread and that the physician may be committing murder in the second degree. The story ends with the physician observing that the "older woman" standing next to the patient the whole time "seemed relieved" when the morphine overdose (quickly supplied by the nurse) ends Debbie's life. Anything but relieved, I believe "It's Over, Debbie" needs a sequel entitled "It's Not Over, Doctor."

Harold Y. Vanderpool, PhD
Institute for the Medical Humanities
University of Texas Medical Branch
Galveston

1   *To the Editor.*—Hemlock of Illinois is grateful to *JAMA* for publishing "It's Over, Debbie." In so doing, *JAMA* has contributed substantially to the dialogue on the important and unresolved issue of physician aid-in-dying.

2   The Debbie story is the opposite of what the Hemlock Society espouses. It is also the perfect story for what those supporting the right to life perceive as the dangers of legalizing physician aid-in-dying.

3   We condemn the Debbie case as both illegal and unethical, both by present law and ethics and by the law we hope to achieve in the near future. The Hemlock Society firmly believes in legalized physician aid-in-dying only when it conforms to the following requirements:

1. There must be adequate legal documentation that the euthanasia was requested by the patient well in advance of its occurring.
2. The physician who aids the patient in dying must have known the patient and must have been fully aware of his/her medical history and desire for aid-in-dying in the event of terminal illness.
3. The physician must have a second opinion from another qualified physician that affirms that the patient's condition is indeed terminal.
4. The rights of physicians who cannot in good conscience perform aid-in-dying are to be fully respected, providing they in no way obstruct the practice of physicians who in good conscience give such aid.

4   There is indeed danger of abuse in euthanasia, just as there is in everything from issuing drivers' licenses to selling alcohol and over-the-counter medications and, indeed, as there is in keeping "brain dead" comatose patients alive for long periods of time by the dogmatic use of modern technology. In the case of Debbie, there was simply the illegal and unethical killing of a patient by a resident physician.

Don C. Shaw
Hemlock of Illinois
Chicago

▼ TOPICAL CONSIDERATIONS

1. How, according to Vanderpool, does the physician use language to paint the lethal injection as "heroic" action? What terms does Vanderpool use to describe the physician's action? How does the language used by each writer influence the readers' responses?
2. Are you convinced by Vanderpool that the decision to end Debbie's life was done on "terribly murky grounds"?
3. How do the guidelines set down by the Hemlock Society for "aid-in-dying" guard against abuse by euthanasia?
4. Don C. Shaw warns of the "dangers of abuse in euthanasia." What are some possible dangers you might imagine?

▼ RHETORICAL CONSIDERATIONS

1. Harold Y. Vanderpool ends his letter with the statement, "Anything but relieved, I believe 'It's Over, Debbie,' needs a sequel entitled 'It's Not Over, Doctor.'" What attitude does this statement convey about the doctor? What are the implications of "It's Not Over, Doctor"?
2. Don C. Shaw says that there is "danger of abuse in euthanasia" likening it to dangers in issuing drivers' licenses and selling alcohol and over-the-counter drugs. Is his analogy accurate and effective?

▼ WRITING ASSIGNMENT

1. One of the hundreds of letters received by the editors of *JAMA* in response to "It's Over, Debbie" described the physician in question as "jury, judge, and executioner of this young patient." Another called the doctor "a brave, caring, and progressive member" of the medical profession. Write an essay explaining which view you take of the doctor.

CAPITAL PUNISHMENT–PRO

▼ DEATH AND JUSTICE: HOW CAPITAL PUNISHMENT AFFIRMS LIFE

Edward I. Koch

There are more murders committed in New York than in any other American city. From 1978 to 1990, Edward Koch, a long active Democrat, served as mayor of New York City. In those years he established a reputation as a hard-driving, no-nonsense, and feisty leader. In the piece below, originally published in the *New Republic* in March 1985, Koch argues that the death penalty is the only just recourse we have to "heinous crimes of murder." In building his case, he examines the arguments most frequently voiced by opponents to capital punishment. Koch is the author of *Mayor: An Autobiography* (1984) written with William Rauch.

1   Last December a man named Robert Lee Willie, who had been convicted of raping and murdering an 18-year-old woman, was executed in the Louisiana state prison. In a statement issued several minutes before his death, Mr. Willie said: "Killing people is wrong. . . . It makes no difference whether it's citizens, countries, or governments. Killing is wrong." Two weeks later in South Carolina, an admitted killer named Joseph Carl Shaw was put to death for murdering two teenagers. In an appeal to the governor for clemency, Mr. Shaw wrote: "Killing is wrong when I did it. Killing is wrong when you do it. I hope you have the courage and moral strength to stop the killing."

2   It is a curiosity of modern life that we find ourselves being lectured on morality by cold-blooded killers. Mr. Willie previously had been convicted of aggravated rape, aggravated kidnapping, and the murders of a Louisiana deputy and a man from Missouri. Mr. Shaw committed another murder a week before the two for which he was executed, and admitted mutilating the body of the 14-year-old girl he killed. I can't help wondering what prompted these murderers to speak out against killing as they entered the deathhouse door. Did their newfound reverence for life stem from the realization that they were about to lose their own?

3   Life is indeed precious, and I believe the death penalty helps to affirm this fact. Had the death penalty been a real possibility in the minds of these murderers, they might well have stayed their hand. They might have shown moral awareness before their victims died, and not after. Consider the tragic death of Rosa Velez, who happened to be home when a man named Luis Vera burglarized her apartment in Brooklyn. "Yeah, I shot her," Vera admitted. "She knew me, and I knew I wouldn't go to the chair."

During my twenty-two years in public service, I have heard the pros and cons of capital punishment expressed with special intensity. As a district leader, councilman, congressman, and mayor, I have represented constituencies generally thought of as liberal. Because I support the death penalty for heinous crimes of murder, I have sometimes been the subject of emotional and outraged attacks by voters who find my position reprehensible or worse. I have listened to their ideas. I have weighed their objections carefully. I still support the death penalty. The reasons I maintain my position can be best understood by examining the arguments most frequently heard in opposition. **4**

1. The death penalty is "barbaric." Sometimes opponents of capital punishment horrify with tales of lingering death on the gallows, of faulty electric chairs, or of agony in the gas chamber. Partly in response to such protests, several states such as North Carolina and Texas switched to execution by lethal injection. The condemned person is put to death painlessly, without ropes, voltage, bullets, or gas. Did this answer the objections of death penalty opponents? Of course not. On June 22, 1984, the *New York Times* published an editorial that sarcastically attacked the new "hygienic" method of death by injection, and stated that "execution can never be made humane through science." So it's not the method that really troubles opponents. It's the death itself they consider barbaric. **5**

Admittedly, capital punishment is not a pleasant topic. However, one does not have to like the death penalty in order to support it any more than one must like radical surgery, radiation, or chemotherapy in order to find necessary these attempts at curing cancer. Ultimately we may learn how to cure cancer with a simple pill. Unfortunately, that day has not yet arrived. Today we are faced with the choice of letting the cancer spread or trying to cure it with the methods available, methods that one day will almost certainly be considered barbaric. But to give up and do nothing would be far more barbaric and would certainly delay the discovery of an eventual cure. The analogy between cancer and murder is imperfect, because murder is not the "disease" we are trying to cure. The disease is injustice. We may not like the death penalty, but it must be available to punish crimes of cold-blooded murder, cases in which any other form of punishment would be inadequate and, therefore, unjust. If we create a society in which injustice is not tolerated, incidents of murder—the most flagrant form of injustice—will diminish. **6**

2. No other major democracy uses the death penalty. No other major democracy—in fact, few other countries of any description—are plagued by a murder rate such as that in the United States. Fewer and fewer Americans can remember the days when unlocked doors were the norm and murder was a rare and terrible offense. In America the murder rate climbed 122 percent between 1963 and 1980. During that same period, the murder rate in New York City increased by almost 400 percent, and the statistics are even worse in many other cities. A study at M.I.T. showed that based on 1970 homicide rates a person who lived in a large American city ran a greater risk of being murdered than an American soldier in World War II ran of being killed in combat. It is not surprising that **7** the laws of each country differ according to differing conditions and traditions. If other countries had our murder problem, the cry for capital punishment would be just as loud as it is here. And I daresay that any other major democracy where 75 percent of the people supported the death penalty would soon enact it into law.

8   3. *An innocent person might be executed by mistake.* Consider the work of Hugo Adam Bedau, one of the most implacable foes of capital punishment in this country. According to Mr. Bedau, it is "false sentimentality to argue that the death penalty should be abolished because of the abstract possibility that an innocent person might be executed." He cites a study of the 7,000 executions in this country from 1893 to 1971, and concludes that the record fails to show that such cases occur. The main point, however, is this. If government functioned only when the possibility of error didn't exist, government wouldn't function at all. Human life deserves special protection, and one of the best ways to guarantee that protection is to assure that convicted murderers do not kill again. Only the death penalty can accomplish this end. In a recent case in New Jersey, a man named Richard Biegenwald was freed from prison after serving 18 years for murder; since his release he has been convicted of committing four murders. A prisoner named Lemuel Smith, who, while serving four life sentences for murder (plus two life sentences for kidnapping and robbery) in New York's Green Haven Prison, lured a woman corrections officer into the chaplain's office and strangled her. He then mutilated and dismembered her body. An additional life sentence for Smith is meaningless. Because New York has no death penalty statute, Smith has effectively been given a license to kill.

9   But the problem of multiple murder is not confined to the nation's penitentiaries. In 1981, 91 police officers were killed in the line of duty in this country. Seven percent of those arrested in the cases that have been solved had a previous arrest for murder. In New York City in 1976 and 1977, 85 persons arrested for homicide had a previous arrest for murder. Six of these individuals had two previous arrests for murder, and one had four previous murder arrests. During those two years the New York police were arresting for murder persons with a previous arrest for murder on the average of one every 8.5 days. This is not surprising when we learn that in 1975, for example, the median time served in Massachusetts for homicide was less than two and a half years. In 1976 a study sponsored by the Twentieth Century Fund found that the average time served in the United States for first-degree murder is ten years. The median time served may be considerably lower.

10   4. *Capital punishment cheapens the value of human life.* On the contrary, it can be easily demonstrated that the death penalty strengthens the value of human life. If the penalty for rape were lowered, clearly it would signal a lessened regard for the victims' suffering, humiliation, and personal integrity. It would cheapen their horrible experience, and expose them to an increased danger of recurrence. When we lower the penalty for murder, it signals a lessened regard for the value of the victim's life. Some critics of capital punishment, such as columnist Jimmy Breslin, have suggested that a life sentence is

actually a harsher penalty for murder than death. This is sophistic nonsense. A few killers may decide not to appeal a death sentence, but the overwhelming majority make every effort to stay alive. It is by exacting the highest penalty for the taking of human life that we affirm the highest value of human life.

5. *The death penalty is applied in a discriminatory manner.* This factor no **11** longer seems to be the problem it once was. The appeals process for a condemned prisoner is lengthy and painstaking. Every effort is made to see that the verdict and sentence were fairly arrived at. However, assertions of discrimination are not an argument for ending the death penalty but for extending it. It is not justice to exclude everyone from the penalty of the law if a few are found to be so favored. Justice requires that the law be applied equally to all.

6. *Thou Shalt Not Kill.* The Bible is our greatest source of moral inspiration. **12** Opponents of the death penalty frequently cite the sixth of the Ten Commandments in an attempt to prove that capital punishment is divinely proscribed. In the original Hebrew, however, the Sixth Commandment reads "Thou Shalt Not Commit Murder," and the Torah specifies capital punishment for a variety of offenses. The biblical viewpoint has been upheld by philosophers throughout history. The greatest thinkers of the 19th century—Kant, Locke, Hobbes, Rousseau, Montesquieu, and Mill—agreed that natural law properly authorizes the sovereign to take life in order to vindicate justice. Only Jeremy Bentham was ambivalent. Washington, Jefferson, and Franklin endorsed it. Abraham Lincoln authorized executions for deserters in wartime. Alexis de Tocqueville, who expressed profound respect for American institutions, believed that the death penalty was indispensable to the support of social order. The United States Constitution, widely admired as one of the seminal achievements in the history of humanity, condemns cruel and inhuman punishment, but does not condemn capital punishment.

7. *The death penalty is state-sanctioned murder.* This is the defense with **13** which Messrs. Willie and Shaw hoped to soften the resolve of those who sentenced them to death. By saying in effect, "You're no better than I am," the murderer seeks to bring his accusers down to his own level. It is also a popular argument among opponents of capital punishment, but a transparently false one. Simply put, the state has rights that the private individual does not. In a democracy, those rights are given to the state by the electorate. The execution of a lawfully condemned killer is no more an act of murder than is legal imprisonment an act of kidnapping. If an individual forces a neighbor to pay him money under threat of punishment, it's called extortion. If the state does it, it's called taxation. Rights and responsibilities surrendered by the individual are what give the state its power to govern. This contract is the foundation of civilization itself.

Everyone wants his or her rights, and will defend them jealously. Not **14** everyone, however, wants responsibilities, especially the painful responsibilities that come with law enforcement. Twenty-one years ago a woman named Kitty Genovese was assaulted and murdered on a street in New York. Dozens of neighbors heard her cries for help but did nothing to assist her. They didn't even call the police. In such a climate the criminal understandably grows bolder. In the presence of moral cowardice, he lectures us on our supposed failings and tries to equate his crimes with our quest for justice.

15   The death of anyone—even a convicted killer—diminishes us all. But we are diminished even more by a justice system that fails to function. It is an illusion to let ourselves believe that doing away with capital punishment removes the murderer's deed from our conscience. The rights of society are paramount. When we protect guilty lives, we give up innocent lives in exchange. When opponents of capital punishment say to the state, "I will not let you kill in my name," they are also saying to murderers: "You can kill in your *own* name as long as I have an excuse for not getting involved."

16   It is hard to imagine anything worse than being murdered while neighbors do nothing. But something worse exists. When those same neighbors shrink back from justly punishing the murderer, the victim dies twice.

▼ TOPICAL CONSIDERATIONS

1. What would you say is Koch's key reason for supporting the death penalty? Does his argument seem convincing? Has it changed your attitude on the issue?
2. In the debates over capital punishment Koch distinguishes two issues: punishment and deterrence. Which of the arguments against his opposition are rooted in punishment? Which are rooted in deterrence?
3. What is Koch's argument against opponents' claim that the death penalty makes great the risk of putting to death innocent people? How sound is his stand?
4. In paragraph 4, Koch says that he supports capital punishment for "heinous crimes of murder." Do you think he is distinguishing different kinds of murder? In other words, do you think he is arguing capital punishment for special cases of murder? If so, what might be the criteria Koch suggests? Which criteria would you consider?
5. Of the seven opposition arguments Koch counters, which do you find the strongest? Which do you find the weakest? Why? Which of Koch's counter-arguments did you find to be the most convincing? Which did you find the least convincing? Why?
6. Can you think of any arguments against the death penalty that Koch fails to address? Can you think of any arguments for the death penalty that Koch may have missed?

▼ RHETORICAL CONSIDERATIONS

1. Where exactly does Koch make his thesis statement in this essay?
2. In paragraph 6, Koch likens murder to cancer and the death penalty to cancer treatment. How apt is this analogy?

3. Koch has built his case against the abolition of capital punishment by appeals to logic, emotions, and ethics. Reread the essay and find examples of each of these different appeals. Which were the most effective? Which were the least effective? Explain your answers.
4. How would you describe the tone of Koch's writing?

▼ WRITING ASSIGNMENTS

1. Suppose that your state legislature is considering a bill to abolish capital punishment. Write a letter to your state representative urging him or her to oppose the bill. Use the arguments from Koch's essay that you feel will be most convincing.
2. There are many opponents of capital punishment who say that the death penalty is "cruel and unusual punishment" and argue that the government should not be in the business of taking human lives. What is your feeling about this particular argument? Do you think the government has the right to take lives? Do you think that capital punishment reduces the government to the level of those who murder?

▼ THE DEATH PENALTY

David Bruck

In April 1985, a month after the *National Review* published Mayor Koch's defense of capital punishment, it published the following response by David Bruck. Questioning the basis of Koch's defense argument and finding it morally dangerous, Bruck goes on to suggest that Koch has made the electric chair a campaign platform. Frustrated and enraged by violent crime and the inability of government to stop it, the public, of course, supports the call for blood, says Bruck—even if the measure doesn't work. Bruck is a lawyer in the South Carolina Office of Appellate Defense. Many of his defendants are prisoners under the death sentence.

1   Mayor Ed Koch contends that the death penalty "affirms life." By failing to execute murderers, he says, we "signal a lessened regard for the value of the victim's life." Koch suggests that people who oppose the death penalty are like Kitty Genovese's neighbors, who heard her cries for help but did nothing while an attacker stabbed her to death.

2   This is the standard "moral" defense of death as punishment: even if executions don't deter violent crime any more effectively than imprisonment, they are still required as the only means we have of doing justice in response to the worst of crimes.

3   Until recently, this "moral" argument had to be considered in the abstract, since no one was being executed in the United States. But the death penalty is back now, at least in the southern states, where every one of the more than 30 executions carried out over the last two years has taken place. Those of us who live in those states are getting to see the difference between the death penalty in theory, and what happens when you actually try to use it.

4   South Carolina resumed executing prisoners in January with the electrocution of Joseph Carl Shaw. Shaw was condemned to death for helping to murder two teenagers while he was serving as a military policeman at Fort Jackson, South Carolina. His crime, propelled by mental illness and PCP, was one of terrible brutality. It is Shaw's last words ("Killing was wrong when I did it. It is wrong when you do it. . . .") that so outraged Mayor Koch: he finds it "a curiosity of modern life that we are being lectured on morality by cold-blooded killers." And so it is.

5   But it was not "modern life" that brought this curiosity into being. It was capital punishment. The electric chair was J. C. Shaw's platform. (The mayor mistakenly writes that Shaw's statement came in the form of a plea to the governor for clemency: actually Shaw made it only seconds before his death, as he waited, shaved and strapped into the chair, for the switch to be thrown.) It

was the chair that provided Shaw with celebrity and an opportunity to lecture us on right and wrong. What made this weird moral reversal even worse is that J. C. Shaw faced his own death with undeniable dignity and courage. And while Shaw died, the TV crews recorded another "curiosity" of the death penalty—the crowd gathered outside the deathhouse to cheer on the executioner. Whoops of elation greeted the announcement of Shaw's death. Waiting at the penitentiary gates for the appearance of the hearse bearing Shaw's remains, one demonstrator started yelling, "Where's the beef?"

For those who had to see the execution of J. C. Shaw, it wasn't easy to keep **6** in mind that the purpose of the whole spectacle was to affirm life. It will be harder still when Florida executes a cop-killer named Alvin Ford. Ford has lost his mind during his years of death-row confinement, and now spends his days trembling, rocking back and forth, and muttering unintelligible prayers. This has led to litigation over whether Ford meets a centuries-old legal standard for mental competency. Since the Middle Ages, the Anglo-American legal system has generally prohibited the execution of anyone who is too mentally ill to understand what is about to be done to him and why. If Florida wins its case, it will have earned the right to electrocute Ford in his present condition. If it loses, he will not be executed until the state has first nursed him back to some semblance of mental health.

We can at least be thankful that this demoralizing spectacle involves a **7** prisoner who is actually guilty of murder. But this may not always be so. The ordeal of Lenell Jeter—the young black engineer who recently served more than a year of a life sentence for a Texas armed robbery that he didn't commit— should remind us that the system is quite capable of making the very worst sort of mistake. That Jeter was eventually cleared is a fluke. If the robbery had occurred at 7 P.M. rather than 3 P.M., he'd have had no alibi, and would still be in prison today. And if someone had been killed in that robbery, Jeter probably would have been sentenced to death. We'd have seen the usual execution-day interviews with state officials and the victim's relatives, all complaining that Jeter's appeals took too long. And Jeter's last words from the gurney would have taken their place among the growing literature of death-house oration that so irritates the mayor.

Koch quotes Hugo Adam Bedau, a prominent abolitionist, to the effect that **8** the record fails to establish that innocent defendants have been executed in the past. But this doesn't mean, as Koch implies, that it hasn't happened. All Bedau was saying was that doubts concerning executed prisoners' guilt are almost never resolved. Bedau is at work now on an effort to determine how many wrongful death sentences may have been imposed: his list of murder convictions since 1900 in which the state eventually *admitted* error is some 400 cases long. Of course, very few of these cases involved actual executions: the mistakes that Bedau documents were uncovered precisely because the prisoner was alive and able to fight for his vindication. The cases where someone is executed are the very cases in which we're least likely to learn that we got the wrong man.

I don't claim that executions of entirely innocent people will occur very **9** often. But they will occur. And other sorts of mistakes already have. Roosevelt Green was executed in Georgia two days before J. C. Shaw. Green and an accomplice kidnapped a young woman. Green swore that his companion shot her to death after Green had left, and that he knew nothing about the murder. Green's claim was supported by a statement that his accomplice made to a witness after the crime. The jury never resolved whether Green was telling the truth, and when he tried to take a polygraph examination a few days before his scheduled execution, the state of Georgia refused to allow the examiner into the prison. As the pressure for symbolic retribution mounts, the courts, like the public, are losing patience with such details. Green was electrocuted on January 9, while members of the Ku Klux Klan rallied outside the prison.

10   Then there is another sort of arbitrariness that happens all the time. Last October, Louisiana executed a man named Ernest Knighton. Knighton had killed a gas station owner during a robbery. Like any murder, this was a terrible crime. But it was not premeditated, and is the sort of crime that very rarely results in a death sentence. Why was Knighton electrocuted when almost everyone else who committed the same offense was not? Was it because he was black? Was it because his victim and all 12 members of the jury that sentenced him were white? Was it because Knighton's court-appointed lawyer presented no evidence on his behalf at his sentencing hearing? Or maybe there's no reason except bad luck. One thing is clear: Ernest Knighton was picked out to die the way a fisherman takes a cricket out of a bait jar. No one cares which cricket gets impaled on the hook.

11   Not every prisoner executed recently was chosen that randomly. But many were. And having selected these men so casually, so blindly, the death penalty system asks us to accept that the purpose of killing each of them is to affirm the sanctity of human life.

12   The death penalty states are also learning that the death penalty is easier to advocate than it is to administer. In Florida, where executions have become almost routine, the governor reports that nearly a third of his time is spent reviewing the clemency requests of condemned prisoners. The Florida Supreme Court is hopelessly backlogged with death cases. Some have taken five years to decide, and the rest of the Court's work waits in line behind the death appeals. Florida's death row currently holds more than 230 prisoners. State officials are reportedly considering building a special "death prison" devoted entirely to the isolation and electrocution of the condemned. The state is also considering the creation of a special public defender unit that will do nothing else but handle death penalty appeals. The death penalty, in short, is spawning death agencies.

13   And what is Florida getting for all of this? The state went through almost all of 1983 without executing anyone: its rate of intentional homicide declined by 17 percent. Last year Florida executed eight people—the most of any state, and the sixth highest total for any year since Florida started electrocuting people back in 1924. Elsewhere in the U.S. last year, the homicide rate continued to decline. But in Florida, it actually rose by 5.1 percent.

14   But these are just the tiresome facts. The electric chair has been a centerpiece of each of Koch's recent political campaigns, and he knows better than

anyone how little the facts have to do with the public's support for capital punishment. What really fuels the death penalty is the justifiable frustration and rage of people who see that the government is not coping with violent crime. So what if the death penalty doesn't work? At least it gives us the satisfaction of knowing that we got one or two of the sons of bitches.

Perhaps we want retribution on the flesh and bone of a handful of convicted murderers so badly that we're willing to close our eyes to all of the demoralization and danger that come with it. A lot of politicians think so, and they may be right. But if they are, then let's at least look honestly at what we're doing. This lottery of death both comes from and encourages an attitude toward human life that is not reverent, but reckless. **15**

And that is why the mayor is dead wrong when he confuses such fury with justice. He suggests that we trivialize murder unless we kill murderers. By that logic, we also trivialize rape unless we sodomize rapists. The sin of Kitty Genovese's neighbors wasn't that they failed to stab her attacker to death. Justice does demand that murderers be punished. And common sense demands that society be protected from them. But neither justice nor self-preservation demands that we kill men whom we have already imprisoned. **16**

The electric chair in which J. C. Shaw died earlier this year was built in 1912 at the suggestion of South Carolina's governor at the time, Cole Blease. Governor Blease's other criminal justice initiative was an impassioned crusade in favor of lynch law. Any lesser response, the governor insisted, trivialized the loathsome crimes of interracial rape and murder. In 1912 a lot of people agreed with Governor Blease that a proper regard for justice required both lynching and the electric chair. Eventually we are going to learn that justice requires neither. **17**

▼ TOPICAL CONSIDERATIONS

1. Compare Bruck's account of J. C. Shaw's crime with that of Koch's account. Does knowing the circumstances—that is, the crime being "propelled by mental illness and PCP"—strengthen Bruck's argument against capital punishment? Do these details weaken Koch's argument? How about the fact that Shaw's words, coming moments before his execution, were not, as Koch suggests, an appeal for clemency? Do these details change your stand on capital punishment?

2. What would you say forms the basis of Bruck's opposition to the death penalty? How does it compare with the basis of Koch's advocacy for the death penalty?

3. What is the heart of Bruck's counter-argument against Edward Koch? Do you agree or disagree with Bruck's view?

4. How does Bruck use the Lenell Jeter case? In your estimation, is this a convincing argument for the abolition of the death penalty? Why or why not?

5. How does Bruck make use of the research of abolitionist Hugo

Adam Bedau who is cited as support in Koch's essay? Do you think Bruck is successful in undermining Koch's own use of Bedau?

6. If not capital punishment, what form of justice do you think Bruck would see fit for "heinous crimes of murder"? What punishment(s) do you see fit?

7. In paragraph 10, Bruck brings up the case of Ernest Knighton executed for a murder that was not premeditated. What do you think Koch would say about this case?

8. In paragraph 14, Bruck says that the public's support of capital punishment is fueled by the "frustration and rage of people who see that government is not coping with violent crime." Do you agree with this claim? Do you agree with the rationalization that even "if the death penalty doesn't work," at least "we got one or two of the sons of bitches."

▼ RHETORICAL CONSIDERATIONS

1. Where exactly does Bruck state his thesis?

2. What is the point of letting the reader know about the crowd's reaction to the execution of J. C. Shaw? How do these details add to the arguments the author is making?

3. In the previous essay, Koch says that the Bible, "our greatest source of moral inspiration" (paragraph 12), takes the eye-for-an-eye view of justice: The punishment for murder is death. How does Bruck counter this stand and how effective is his argument against it?

▼ WRITING ASSIGNMENTS

1. Adopt the point of view of a supporter of capital punishment who has just read Bruck's essay. Write a letter to the author in which you offer a rebuttal to his argument. Include some emotional appeals and try to show some fallacies in Bruck's reasoning.

2. Suppose that your state legislature is considering a bill to abolish capital punishment. Write a letter to your state representative asking that he or she support the bill. Include the arguments in Bruck's essay that you feel will be most convincing.

3. Suppose you were on a panel of judges presiding over a debate between Edward Koch and David Bruck. Having heard their arguments in these essays, who would you decide had won the debate? Write an essay in which you defend your decision.

▼ REGULATING RACIST SPEECH ON CAMPUS

Charles R. Lawrence III

The last few years has seen a disturbing rise in racist and sexist language on college campuses. Some administrations have dealt with the problem by outright banning such offensive language on the grounds that racial slurs are violent verbal assaults that interfere with students' rights to an education. Others fear that putting sanctions on racist speech violates the First Amendment guarantee of free expression. In the following essay, a professor of law argues for the restricting of free speech by appealing to the U.S. Supreme Court's landmark decision in the case of *Brown* v. *Board of Education*. Charles R. Lawrence teaches law at Stanford University and the University of California at Los Angeles. He is the author of many articles on law and coauthor of the book, *The Bakke Case: The Politics of Inequality* (1979). A longer version of this article appeared in the February 1990 issue of *Duke Law*.

I have spent the better part of my life as a dissenter. As a high-school student, I was threatened with suspension for my refusal to participate in a civil-defense drill, and I have been a conspicuous consumer of my First Amendment liberties ever since. There are very strong reasons for protecting even racist speech. Perhaps the most important of these is that such protection reinforces our society's commitment to tolerance as a value, and that by protecting bad speech from government regulation, we will be forced to combat it as a community.

But I also have a deeply felt apprehension about the resurgence of racial violence and the corresponding rise in the incidence of verbal and symbolic assault and harassment to which blacks and other traditionally subjugated and excluded groups are subjected. I am troubled by the way the debate has been framed in response to the recent surge of racist incidents on college and university campuses and in response to some universities' attempts to regulate harassing speech. The problem has been framed as one in which the liberty of free speech is in conflict with the elimination of racism. I believe this has placed the bigot on the moral high ground and fanned the rising flames of racism.

Above all, I am troubled that we have not listened to the real victims, that we have shown so little understanding of their injury, and that we have abandoned those whose race, gender, or sexual preference continues to make them second-class citizens. It seems to me a very sad irony that the first instinct of civil libertarians has been to challenge even the smallest, most narrowly framed efforts by universities to provide black and other minority students with the protection the Constitution guarantees them.

4   The landmark case of *Brown* v. *Board of Education* is not a case that we normally think of as a case about speech. But *Brown* can be broadly read as articulating the principle of equal citizenship. *Brown* held that segregated schools were inherently unequal because of the *message* that segregation conveyed—that black children were an untouchable caste, unfit to go to school with white children. If we understand the necessity of eliminating the system of signs and symbols that signal the inferiority of blacks, then we should hesitate before proclaiming that all racist speech that stops short of physical violence must be defended.

5   University officials who have formulated policies to respond to incidents of racial harassment have been characterized in the press as "thought police," but such policies generally do nothing more than impose sanctions against intentional face-to-face insults. When racist speech takes the form of face-to-face insults, catcalls, or other assaultive speech aimed at an individual or small group of persons, it falls directly within the "fighting words" exception to First Amendment protection. The Supreme Court has held that words which "by their very utterance inflict injury or tend to incite an immediate breach of the peace" are not protected by the First Amendment.

6   If the purpose of the First Amendment is to foster the greatest amount of speech, racial insults disserve that purpose. Assaultive racist speech functions as a preemptive strike. The invective is experienced as a blow, not as a proffered idea, and once the blow is struck, it is unlikely that a dialogue will follow. Racial insults are particularly undeserving of First Amendment protection because the perpetrator's intention is not to discover truth or initiate dialogue but to injure the victim. In most situations, members of minority groups realize that they are likely to lose if they respond to epithets by fighting and are forced to remain silent and submissive.

7   Courts have held that offensive speech may not be regulated in public forums such as streets where the listener may avoid the speech by moving on, but the regulation of otherwise protected speech has been permitted when the speech invades the privacy of the unwilling listener's home or when the unwilling listener cannot avoid the speech. Racist posters, fliers, and graffiti in dormitories, bathrooms, and other common living spaces would seem to clearly fall within the reasoning of these cases. Minority students should not be required to remain in their rooms in order to avoid racial assault. Minimally, they should find a safe haven in their dorms and in all other common rooms that are a part of their daily routine.

8   I would also argue that the university's responsibility for insuring that these students receive an equal educational opportunity provides a compelling justification for regulations that insure them safe passage in all common areas. A minority student should not have to risk becoming the target of racially assaulting speech every time he or she chooses to walk across campus. Regulating vilifying speech that cannot be anticipated or avoided would not preclude announced speeches and rallies—situations that would give minority-group

members and their allies the chance to organize counter-demonstrations or avoid the speech altogether.

The most commonly advanced argument against the regulation of racist speech proceeds something like this: we recognize that minority groups suffer pain and injury as the result of racist speech, but we must allow this hate mongering for the benefit of society as a whole. Freedom of speech is the lifeblood of our democratic system. It is especially important for minorities because often it is their only vehicle for rallying support for the redress of their grievances. It will be impossible to formulate a prohibition so precise that it will prevent the racist speech you want to suppress without catching in the same net all kinds of speech that it would be unconscionable for a democratic society to suppress. **9**

Whenever we make such arguments, we are striking a balance on the one hand between our concern for the continued free flow of ideas and the democratic process dependent on that flow, and, on the other, our desire to further the cause of equality. There can be no meaningful discussion of how we should reconcile our commitment to equality and our commitment to free speech until it is acknowledged that there is real harm inflicted by racist speech and that this harm is far from trivial. **10**

To engage in a debate about the First Amendment and racist speech without a full understanding of the nature and extent of that harm is to risk making the First Amendment an instrument of domination rather than a vehicle of liberation. We have not known the experience of victimization by racist, misogynist, and homophobic speech, nor do we equally share the burden of the societal harm it inflicts. We are often quick to say that we have heard the cry of the victims when we have not. **11**

The *Brown* case is again instructive because it speaks directly to the psychic injury inflicted by racist speech by noting that the symbolic message of segregation affected "the hearts and minds" of Negro children "in a way unlikely ever to be undone." Racial epithets and harassment often cause deep emotional scarring and feelings of anxiety and fear that pervade every aspect of a victim's life. **12**

Brown also recognized that black children did not have an equal opportunity to learn and participate in the school community if they bore the additional burden of being subjected to the humiliation and psychic assault contained in the message of segregation. University students bear an analogous burden when they are forced to live and work in an environment where at any moment they may be subjected to denigrating verbal harassment and assault. The same injury was addressed by the Supreme Court when it held that sexual harassment that creates a hostile or abusive work environment violates the ban on sex discrimination in employment of Title VII of the Civil Rights Act of 1964. **13**

Carefully drafted university regulations would bar the use of words as assault weapons and leave unregulated even the most heinous of ideas when those ideas are presented at times and places and in manners that provide an opportunity for reasoned rebuttal or escape from immediate injury. The history **14** of the development of the right to free speech has been one of carefully evaluating the importance of free expression and its effects on other important societal interests. We have drawn the line between protected and unprotected speech before without dire results. (Courts have, for example, exempted from the protection of the First Amendment obscene speech and speech that disseminates official secrets, that defames or libels another person, or that is used to form a conspiracy or monopoly.)

15   Blacks and other people of color are skeptical about the argument that even the most injurious speech must remain unregulated because, in an unregulated marketplace of ideas, the best ones will rise to the top and gain acceptance. Our experience tells us quite the opposite. We have seen too many good liberal politicians shy away from the issues that might brand them as being too closely allied with us.

16   Whenever we decide that racist speech must be tolerated because of the importance of maintaining societal tolerance for all unpopular speech, we are asking blacks and other subordinated groups to bear the burden for the good of all. We must be careful that the ease with which we strike the balance against the regulation of racist speech is in no way influenced by the fact that the cost will be borne by others. We must be certain that those who will pay that price are fairly represented in our deliberations and that they are heard.

17   At the core of the argument that we should resist all government regulation of speech is the ideal that the best cure for bad speech is good, that ideas that affirm equality and the worth of all individuals will ultimately prevail. This is an empty ideal unless those of us who would fight racism are vigilant and unequivocal in that fight. We must look for ways to offer assistance and support to students whose speech and political participation are chilled in a climate of racial harassment.

18   Civil rights lawyers might consider suing on behalf of blacks whose right to an equal education is denied by a university's failure to insure a nondiscriminatory educational climate or conditions of employment. We must embark upon the development of a First Amendment jurisprudence grounded in the reality of our history and our contemporary experience. We must think hard about how best to launch legal attacks against the most indefensible forms of hate speech. Good lawyers can create exceptions and narrow interpretations that limit the harm of hate speech without opening the floodgates of censorship.

19   Everyone concerned with these issues must find ways to engage actively in actions that resist and counter the racist ideas that we would have the First Amendment protect. If we fail in this, the victims of hate speech must rightly assume that we are on the oppressors' side.

▼ TOPICAL CONSIDERATIONS

1. What reasons does Lawrence offer for protecting racist speech from governmental restrictions? Do you agree? How else can a community fight such speech?

2. According to the author, how in the debate over racist language does the fight against racism conflict with the fight for free speech? What fundamental problem does Lawrence have with this conflict? Are his reasons convincing to you? Why or why not?

3. According to the author, how can the case of *Brown* v. *Board of Education* be interpreted to cover protection of victims of racist speech?

4. Why, according to Lawrence, is racist speech "undeserving of First Amendment protection" (paragraph 6)? Do you agree? If not, why not? If so, can you think of any circumstances when racist speech should be protected?

5. What legal measures does Lawrence suggest for the protection of black students against hate speech?

6. Has this article affected your thinking on the subject of free speech and censorship? Has it changed your mind about the use of racially or sexually abusive language? Explain your answer.

7. Have you ever been the victim of abusive speech—speech that victimized you because of your race, gender, religion, ethnicity, or sexual preference? If so, do you agree with Lawrence's argument about the "psychic injury" (paragraph 12) such speech can cause? Did you experience such injury? Explain your answer.

8. Is there any racial tension on your campus? If so, do you see a link between racial tension and racist speech? What suggestions would you make to school officials to deal with such tension? Do you think that banning hate speech might lessen racial tension and violence? How about in society at large? Explain your reasoning.

▼ RHETORICAL CONSIDERATIONS

1. Where in the essay do you get a clear focus on Lawrence's line of argument? What are the first signals that he sends to clue the reader? Can you point to a thesis statement?

2. Lawrence opens his essay saying that he has a long history as a "dissenter." What would you say is his strategy here? What kinds of assumptions does he make of his audience? What does his refusing to participate in a civil-defense drill have to do with the essay's central issues?

3. How convincingly does Lawrence argue that racist speech should not be protected by the First Amendment? What is the logic of his argument? What evidence does he offer as support?

4. Select one of Lawrence's arguments that you think is especially strong or especially weak, and explain why you regard it so.

5. Consider the author's voice in this essay. What sense do you get of Charles R. Lawrence III as an individual? In a paragraph, try to

characterize him. Take into consideration his stand here as well as the style and tone of his writing.

▼ WRITING ASSIGNMENTS

1. As Lawrence points out, many university officials—as well as legal scholars—view the outlawing of hate speech as contrary to the democratic spirit of pluralism and tolerance. Write a paper in which you argue that hate speech should be protected if we are to remain a legitimate democracy. In your discussion, explain just where you would draw the line on the protection, if at all.

2. Taking the opposite stand from above, and using some of your own ideas, write a paper in which you argue that racist (and/or sexist) speech should be outlawed because it can only contribute to the victimization of people and the already-tense social conditions in America. In your discussion, explain just what kinds of hate speech you would want to see banned, and why. Also explain why you think such speech could be controlled by regulation.

3. Suppose that a leader of a known hate group were invited to your campus, someone certain to speak in inflammatory racist language. Would you defend that person's right to address the student body? Why or why not? Should that person be protected under the First Amendment? Would you attend? Why or why not?

4. What if a condition of acceptance to your school was signing an agreement that you would refrain from using racist, sexist, or otherwise abusive language on campus—an agreement that could lead to suspension. Weighing the social benefits against the restrictions on freedom of expression, write a paper in which you explain why you would sign or not sign the agreement.

▼ FREE SPEECH ON CAMPUS
Nat Hentoff

Representing the opposing side of the freedom-of-speech argument, Nat Hentoff argues that instituting sanctions on hate speech seriously mocks the pluralistic nature of a university and academic freedom and inquiry. He warns that preventing or punishing offensive language could lead to Orwellian nightmares. Nat Hentoff is a staff writer for the *New Yorker*, the *Village Voice* and a columnist for the *Washington Post*. Much of his writing focuses on the subject of freedom of expression including his recent book, *The First Freedom: The Tumultuous History of Free Speech in America* (1989). He is also author of *American Heroes: In and Out of School* (1987) and *Boston Boy: A Memoir* (1988). This article first appeared in the May 1989 issue of the *Progressive*.

A flier distributed at the University of Michigan some months ago proclaimed that blacks "don't belong in classrooms, they belong hanging from trees." 1

At other campuses around the country, manifestations of racism are becoming commonplace. At Yale, a swastika and the words WHITE POWER! were painted on the building housing the University's Afro-American Cultural Center. At Temple University, a White Students Union has been formed with some 130 members. 2

Swastikas are not directed only at black students. The Nazi symbol has been spray-painted on the Jewish Student Union at Memphis State University. And on a number of campuses, women have been signled out as targets of wounding and sometimes frightening speech. At the law school of the State University of New York at Buffalo, several women students have received anonymous letters characterized by one professor as venomously sexist. 3

These and many more such signs of the resurgence of bigotry and know-nothingism throughout the society—as well as on campus—have to do solely with speech, including symbolic speech. There have also been physical assaults on black students and on black, white, and Asian women students, but the way to deal with physical attacks is clear: call the police and file a criminal complaint. What is to be done, however, about speech alone—however disgusting, inflammatory, and rawly divisive that speech may be? 4

At more and more colleges, administrators—with the enthusiastic support of black students, women students, and liberal students—have been answering that question by preventing or punishing speech. In public universities, this is a clear violation of the First Amendment. In private colleges and universities, suppression of speech mocks the secular religion of academic freedom and free inquiry. 5

6   The Student Press Law Center in Washington, D.C.—a vital source of legal support for student editors around the country—reports, for example, that at the University of Kansas, the student host and producer of a radio news program was forbidden by school officials from interviewing a leader of the Ku Klux Klan. So much for free inquiry on that campus.

7   In Madison, Wisconsin, the *Capital Times* ran a story in January about Chancellor Sheila Kaplan of the University of Wisconsin branch at Parkside, who ordered her campus to be scoured of "some anonymously placed white supremacist hate literature." Sounding like the legendary Mayor Frank ("I am the law") Hague of Jersey City, who booted "bad speech" out of town, Chancellor Kaplan said, "This institution is not a lamppost standing on the street corner. It doesn't belong to everyone."

8   Who decides what speech can be heard or read by everyone? Why, the Chancellor, of course. That's what George III used to say, too.

9   University of Wisconsin political science professor Carol Tebben thinks otherwise. She believes university administrators "are getting confused when they are acting as censors and trying to protect students from bad ideas. I don't think students need to be protected from bad ideas. I think they can determine for themselves what ideas are bad."

10   After all, if students are to be "protected" from bad ideas, how are they going to learn to identify and cope with them? Sending such ideas underground simply makes them stronger and more dangerous.

11   Professor Tebben's conviction that free speech means just that has become a decidedly minority view on many campuses. At the University of Buffalo Law School, the faculty unanimously adopted a "Statement Regarding Intellectual Freedom, Tolerance, and Political Harassment." Its title implies support of intellectual freedom, but the statement warned students that once they enter "this legal community," their right to free speech must become tempered "by the responsibility to promote equality and justice."

12   Accordingly, swift condemnation will befall anyone who engages in "remarks directed at another's race, sex, religion, national origin, age, or sex preference." Also forbidden are "other remarks based on prejudice and group stereotype."

13   This ukase is so broad that enforcement has to be alarmingly subjective. Yet the University of Buffalo Law School provides no due-process procedures for a student booked for making any of these prohibited remarks. Conceivably, a student caught playing a Lenny Bruce, Richard Pryor, or Sam Kinison album in his room could be tried for aggravated insensitivity by association.

14   When I looked into this wholesale cleansing of bad speech at Buffalo, I found it had encountered scant opposition. One protester was David Gerald Jay, a graduate of the law school and a cooperating attorney for the New York Civil Liberties Union. Said the appalled graduate: "Content-based prohibitions constitute prior restraint and should not be tolerated."

15   You would think that the law professors and adminstration at this public university might have known that. But hardly any professors dissented, and

among the students only members of the conservative Federalist Society spoke up for free speech. The fifty-strong chapter of the National Lawyers Guild was on the other side. After all, it was more important to go on record as vigorously opposing racism and sexism than to expose oneself to charges of insensitivity to these malignancies.

The pressures to have the "right" attitude—as proved by having the "right" language in and out of class—can be stifling. A student who opposes affirmative action, for instance, can be branded a racist. **16**

At the University of California at Los Angeles, the student newspaper ran an editorial cartoon satirizing affirmative action. (A student stops a rooster on campus and asks how the rooster got into UCLA. "Affirmative action," is the answer.) After outraged complaints from various minority groups, the editor was suspended for violating a publication policy against running "articles that perpetuate derogatory or cultural stereotypes." The art director was also suspended. **17**

When the opinion editor of the student newspaper at California State University at Northridge wrote an article asserting that the sanctions against the editor and art director at UCLA amounted to censorship, he was suspended too. **18**

At New York University Law School, a student was so disturbed by the pall of orthodoxy at that prestigious institution that he wrote to the school newspaper even though, as he said, he expected his letter to make him a pariah among his fellow students. **19**

Barry Endick described the atmosphere at NYU created by "a host of watchdog committees and a generally hostile classroom reception regarding any student comment right of center." This "can be arguably viewed as symptomatic of a prevailing spirit of academic and social intolerance of . . . any idea which is not 'politically correct.'" **20**

He went on to say something that might well be posted on campus bulletin boards around the country, though it would probably be torn down at many of them: "We ought to examine why students, so anxious to wield the Fourteenth Amendment, give short shrift to the First. Yes, Virginia, there are racist assholes. And you know what, the Constitution protects them, too." **21**

Not when they engage in violence or vandalism. But when they speak or write, racist assholes fall right into this Oliver Wendell Holmes definition— highly unpopular among bigots, liberals, radicals, feminists, sexists, and college administrators: "If there is any principle of the Constitution that more imperatively calls for attachment than any other, it is the principle of free thought—not free only for those who agree with us, but freedom for the thought we hate." **22**

The language sounds like a pietistic Sunday sermon, but if it ever falls wholly into disuse, neither this publication nor any other journal of opinion— right or left—will survive. **23**

Sometimes, college presidents and administrators sound as if they fully understand what Holmes was saying. Last year, for example, when the *Daily Pennsylvanian*—speaking for many at the University of Pennsylvania—urged that a **24** speaking invitation to Louis Farrakhan be withdrawn, University President Sheldon Hackney disagreed.

25 "Open expression," said Hackney, "is the fundamental principle of a university." Yet consider what the same Sheldon Hackney did to the free-speech rights of a teacher at his own university. If any story distills the essence of the current decline of free speech on college campuses, it is the Ballad of Murray Dolfman.

26 For twenty-two years, Dolfman, a practicing lawyer in Philadelphia, had been a part-time lecturer in the Legal Studies Department of the University of Pennsylvania's Wharton School. For twenty-two years, no complaint had ever been made against him; indeed his student course evaluations had been outstanding. Each year students competed to get into his class.

27 On a November afternoon in 1984, Dolfman was lecturing about personal-service contracts. His style somewhat resembles that of Professor Charles Kingsfield in *The Paper Chase*. Dolfman insists that students he calls on be prepared—or suffer the consequences. He treats all students this way—regardless of race, creed, or sex.

28 This day, Dolfman was pointing out that no one can be forced to work against his or her will—even if a contract has been signed. A court may prevent the resister from working for someone else so long as the contract is in effect but, Dolfman said, there can "be nothing that smacks of involuntary servitude."

29 Where does this concept come from? Dolfman looked around the room. Finally, a cautious hand was raised: "The Constitution?"

30 "Where in the Constitution?" No hands. "The Thirteenth Amendment," said the teacher. So, what does *it* say? The students were looking everywhere but at Dolfman.

31 "We will lose our liberties," Dolfman often told his classes, "if we don't know what they are."

32 On this occasion, he told them that he and other Jews, as ex-slaves, spoke at Passover of the time when they were slaves under the Pharaohs so that they would remember every year what it was like not to be free.

33 "We have ex-slaves here," Dolfman continued, "who should know about the Thirteenth Amendment." He asked black students in the class if they could tell him what was in that amendment.

34 "I wanted them to really think about it," Dolfman told me recently, "and know its history. You're better equipped to fight racism if you know all about those post–Civil War amendments and civil rights laws."

35 The Thirteenth Amendment provides that "neither slavery nor involuntary servitude . . . shall exist within the United States."

36 The black students in his class did not know what was in that amendment, and Dolfman had them read it aloud. Later, they complained to university officials that they had been hurt and humiliated by having been referred to as ex-slaves. Moreover, they said, they had no reason to be grateful for a constitutional amendment which gave them rights which should never have been denied them—and gave them precious little else. They had not made these points in class, although Dolfman—unlike Professor Kingsfield—encourages rebuttal.

Informed of the complaint, Dolfman told the black students he had in- **37**
tended no offense, and he apologized if they had been offended.

That would not do—either for the black students or for the administration. **38**
Furthermore, there were mounting black-Jewish tensions on campus, and someone had to be sacrificed. Who better than a part-time Jewish teacher with no
contract and no union? He was sentenced by—George Orwell would have loved
this—the Committee on Academic Freedom and Responsibility.

On his way to the stocks, Dolfman told President Sheldon Hackney that if **39**
a part-time instructor "can be punished on this kind of charge, a tenured
professor can eventually be booted out, then a dean, and then a president."

Hackney was unmoved. Dolfman was banished from the campus for what **40**
came to be a year. But first he was forced to make a public apology to the entire
university and then he was compelled to attend a "sensitivity and racial awareness" session. Sort of like a Vietnamese reeducation camp.

A few conservative professors objected to the stigmatization of Murray **41**
Dolfman. I know of no student dissent. Indeed, those students most concerned
with making the campus more "sensitive" to diversity exulted in Dolfman's
humiliation. So did most liberals on the faculty.

If my children were still of college age and wanted to attend the University **42**
of Pennsylvania, I would tell them this story. But where else could I encourage
them to go?

▼ TOPICAL CONSIDERATIONS

1. In your own words, summarize the argument Nat Hentoff is making here. What would you say his purpose is in the essay?
2. How are college and university administrators dealing with the
   recent rise in incidents of verbal abuse on American campuses?
   What is Hentoff's reaction to their handling of such problems?
3. With regard to the First Amendment, Hentoff distinguishes between physical assaults and those that are verbal and/or symbolic.
   What distinctions does he make? How does Charles R. Lawrence
   III in the previous essay distinguish between the two? Explain the
   different interpretations between the two authors.
4. If a leader of the Ku Klux Klan was barred from speaking at your
   school, would you protest? How about a member of the American
   Nazi party? The PLO? What about Louis Farrakhan? Explain your
   reasons.
5. In paragraph 9, the author quotes Professor Carol Tebben who
   states, "I don't think students need to be protected from bad ideas."
   Do you agree with Professor Tebben? Do you feel that students can
   "determine for themselves what ideas are bad"? What constitutes a
   bad idea to you? Can you imagine any *bad ideas* that you feel should
   be censored? What would they be, and under what circumstances?
6. Hentoff argues that many people who concur with sanctions on free

speech do so to avoid being considered sexist or racist. Does this describe people you know? Do you think a person who opposes sexism and racism can still support freedom of speech? Or, do you think it's racist and sexist to be opposed to sanctions on racist and sexist speech? Explain your answers.

7. What problems does Hentoff have with University of Buffalo Law School's "Statement Regarding Intellectual Freedom, Tolerance, and Political Harassment"? What explanation does he offer for the wide acceptance of and "scant opposition" to that "ukase"? What are your feelings about such a Statement?

8. Would Hentoff agree that "sticks and stones will break my bones, but names will never hurt me?" What about Charles R. Lawrence III? What about you?

9. In paragraph 17, Hentoff cites the case of the UCLA student newspaper which ran an editorial cartoon satirizing affirmative action. From Hentoff's description, does the cartoon sound offensive to you? As described, how might it have been offensive to minority students? Do you think the administration was morally and legally justified in suspending the editor and art director? If this happened on your campus, how would you react? Explain why.

10. What do you make of the Dolfman case that Hentoff discusses in the last half of the essay? From what we're told, do you think that Dolfman was insensitive to the black students in his class? Do you think the black students were justified in their complaints? Do you think the administration was right in suspending Dolfman? Explain your answers.

▼ RHETORICAL CONSIDERATIONS

1. Consider the title of this essay. What different meanings can it have? How does it forecast Hentoff's position in the essay? Do you think it's an effective title?

2. Where in the essay does Hentoff's line of argument begin to take focus? Is his line of argument carried clearly throughout the essay? Where does he state his thesis?

3. Consider the case of the editorial cartoon in the UCLA student newspaper (paragraphs 17 and 18). What about the cartoon does Hentoff want you to believe? Is his description of it satisfying to you? Would you prefer to actually see it before passing judgment on its offensiveness? Suppose you learned that Hentoff left out some particularly offensive details in the cartoon, say, a racist caricature of the rooster, how would that affect the impact of his argument?

4. Find two or three of Hentoff's sentences that you find particularly effective as examples of persuasive writing, then explain why they are effective.

5. Explain the meaning of the aside reference to George Orwell in paragraph 38. How is it an appropriate remark?
6. What do you make of the conclusion of this essay? What is the strategy of ending it with the question he asks? What's Hentoff's message here? Is his conclusion consistent with the development of his argument?

▼ WRITING ASSIGNMENTS

1. In paragraph 10, Hentoff claims, "Sending such [bad] ideas underground simply makes them stronger and more dangerous." Explore this claim in a paper in which you try to imagine how certain "bad ideas" could become stronger and more dangerous were they censored.
2. Suppose your school had such a "Statement" as that at the University of Buffalo Law School (paragraph 11). Weighing the social benefits against the restrictions to the freedom of speech, would you be willing to sign a pledge of allegiance to it? Write a paper in which you explain your decision.
3. Where does *offensive* language end and *racist* and *sexist* language begin. Write a paper in which you try to determine these distinctions. Give clear examples to support your arguments.
4. Take another look at Charles Lawrence's essay. Which of the two arguments on the free speech issue seems the most persuasive? Explain exactly why you feel that way? Try to support your answer with specific evidence from each of the essays.
5. Write a letter to Nat Hentoff arguing that hate speech—racist, sexist and otherwise—should be regulated because it can only contribute to the already-tense social conditions in America.

11 ▼ NATURE AND THE ENVIRONMENT

Our magnificent planet has endured for 4.5 billion years of evolution, but its future is clouded by humankind's reckless ways: overpopulation, pollution, the depletion of resources, and the destruction of natural habitats. While some essays here celebrate the glories of nature others lament its redefinition.

Although brief, the opening piece grapples with universal questions about the natural world. Why do evil things happen? Why are there devastating earthquakes, floods, droughts, and wars? Is there an all-powerful, all-good God ruling creation, or is the universe a cold mechanistic system ruled by chance? In "A Cruel Universe, but the Only One Where Humans Could Exist," Gwynne Dyer explains why nature is nonmoral—why the universe does not seem to care about human life. If nature has been created by divinity, it could not be made any less cruel even if God had so wanted it.

Edward Hoagland, naturalist and essayist, has the remarkable ability to draw profound insights from the most common scenes. His essay that follows, "The Courage of Turtles," tightens the focus to a single remarkable species. In beautifully vivid descriptions, he captures the primitive majesty of these creatures. And, yet, he reminds us of their shrinking environment and numbers.

"Toward a Warmer World" addresses a looming ecological crisis that only recently has been brought to light—the so-called greenhouse effect. Here, climatologist Charles Tyler objectively examines the evidence that the gaseous byproducts of modern life are raising the temperature of the earth. Should the evidence prove true, deserts will flood, farmlands will wither, and coastlines will need to be redrawn. Could human society prepare itself? Could anything be done to reverse the process?

This last question is the incentive behind the final two selections. In response to the greenhouse warnings, "A Path of More Resistance" by naturalist Bill McKibben suggests a radical change in life-style—one stripped down to bare essentials. In order to live with nature he explains how he and his wife have pruned their desires, made sacrifices, and learned the pleasures of self-reliance.

A radically different approach, to say the least, is what Edward Abbey calls for in a spirited and controversial piece, "Eco-Defense." Lamenting the assault on the American wilderness by developers and industry, and outraged that our government allows the pillage to continue, the late author and nature-activist suggests that we fight back with hammers and nails. It's "illegal but ethically imperative." And, he adds, "it's good for the trees."

▼ A CRUEL UNIVERSE, BUT THE ONLY ONE WHERE HUMANS COULD EXIST

Gwynne Dyer

Most of us have wondered at times why the natural universe seems so cruel and unjust a place. Just look at some of the brutal headlines over the past few years—the thousands of innocents lost to famine, earthquakes, volcanic eruptions, and diseases. Or consider the death of a child. As Gwynne Dyer says, even nonbelievers often wish the universe were a kinder, more forgiving environment. But, as he explains, it can't be and still be natural. Mr. Dyer is a columnist specializing in foreign affairs and creator of the 1985 PBS television series "War." This article first appeared in the *Boston Globe* in November 1985.

1   Why do babies die? Why do people starve to death in famines? Why is the universe so cruel, taking some people's lives away before they even had a chance to enjoy life, while others have long, happy lives and die peacefully in bed?

2   Religious people call it "the problem of evil." If God is all-powerful, why does he allow such horror and pain in his universe? A god who deliberately allowed Auschwitz and the killing fields of Cambodia to happen would not deserve our love, or even our respect—and if he couldn't prevent them, then he isn't all-powerful.

3   Cardinal Basil Hume, an English clergyman, was recently asked why God permitted such things by a journalist as they both stood in the middle of an Ethiopian refugee camp. Hume had the honesty to answer that he had "no idea." More sophisticated men of religion, whether Christian, Muslim or Jewish, might give longer answers that sounded plausible—but they are all answers that go round in circles.

4   If you don't believe in God, of course, then there is no philosophical problem. The universe is impersonal, human beings are on their own, and terrible things happen to them for the same reason they happen to fruit flies: no reason at all, except blind chance. But even non-believers often wish the universe were a kinder, more forgiving environment. And the answer is: it can't be.

5   It is an answer that applies equally to a universe created by a loving God and to a Godless universe which doesn't care about people at all. Any universe which could conceivably be a habitat for human beings must be one in which events have predictable consequences—even if those consequences include terrible tragedies for human beings.

6   Imagine, for a moment, a universe in which tragedies didn't happen. When the engines of a jet airliner fail on takeoff, it does not crash at the end of the

runway and burn 150 people to death. Instead, it just wafts gently to the ground, because God loved the passengers and chose to save them.

But if that were all that happened when aircraft engines failed, there would **7** be no need for aircraft maintenance. Indeed, there would be no need for engines, or even wings—and people could safely step off the edge of cliffs and walk on air. The law of gravity would be suspended whenever it endangered human lives.

So would all the other laws of nature. Whenever children's lives were at risk **8** from disease, biochemistry would change its rules to save them. If an earthquake were going to kill thousands of people, continental drift would simply have to stop: so much for geology. And if someone tried to kill somebody else, the gun wouldn't work, or the bullet wouldn't fly straight, or it would turn into a marshmallow before it struck the victim.

In such a universe, there could be no science or technology, because there **9** would be no fixed natural laws on which we could base them. The strength of steel and the temperature of boiling water would vary depending on whether human lives were threatened by a given value. There could not even be logic, since the same causes would not invariably have the same effects. It would be an entirely magical universe.

It is all a package, and quite indivisible. Either you have a magical Garden **10** of Eden where non-human creatures closely resembling angels, with no hard choices to make and no penalties to pay, browse idly on lotus leaves. Or else you get the remorselessly logical universe we live in, where actions have consequences and you pay dearly for your own mistakes (and those of others).

I know there is little consolation in all this for those who have had to watch **11** helplessly while their child died, or for the millions whose loves and hopes lie 40 years buried with the last world war. It is a cruel universe, and knowing why does not make it less cruel. But even God could not have made it any different if he wanted it to be an appropriate home for human beings.

It's cold comfort, but maybe there is some consolation to be had in the fact **12** that we're extremely fortunate to have been able to visit the universe even briefly. At the instant of your conception and mine, a million other potential men and women lost their only chance to see the place at all.

▼ TOPICAL CONSIDERATIONS

1. In paragraph 5, the author writes: "Any universe which could conceivably be a habitat for human beings must be one in which events have predictable consequences." In your own words explain what he means by this.
2. Why does Dyer say that "Hume had the honesty to answer that he had 'no idea'" (paragraph 3) when asked why God permits bad things to happen? What answer would you give?
3. If God prevented tragedies from happening in the universe, why would that mean there could be no science or technology?

4. According to Dyer, what consolation can we derive from recognizing that we live in a cruel universe?

▼ RHETORICAL CONSIDERATIONS

1. What rhetorical strategy is Dyer using when he begins his essay with questions?
2. How well does Dyer illustrate his argument that the universe by necessity must be a cruel place for human habitation?
3. How does the final paragraph encourage appreciation of the universe as we know it? How does it reflect back on the opening paragraph?

▼ WRITING ASSIGNMENTS

1. Write an essay supporting Dyer's thesis, using three examples from your own experience.
2. In paragraph 3, we are told that Cardinal Basil Hume, an English clergyman, said he had no idea why God permitted terrible things to occur. In a well-documented essay, write your own answer to the journalist's question.

▼ THE COURAGE OF TURTLES
Edward Hoagland

Edward Hoagland is one of the great essayists of our time. Although he has published novels and travel books, he is perhaps best known for his essays on nature. Here he evokes both the perseverence and the vulnerability of a creature of primordial majesty. Whether describing the turtle's appearance or diet or temperament, Hoagland displays an uncanny ability of making scenes come alive while drawing profound insights from the most common details. Here he captures some remarkable characteristics of turtles. And, yet, in his rich descriptions he sounds a darker note also, for like so many creatures turtles are suffering a loss of habitat. In an understated indictment of our callous age, Hoagland does not exclude himself as you will see in the haunting last lines of this essay. Edward Hoagland is the author of thirteen books, including *Cat Man, African Calliope: A Journey to the Sudan,* and *Walking the Dead Diamond River.* This essay comes from his collection, *The Courage of Turtles* (1985).

Turtles are a kind of bird with the governor turned low. With the same attitude of removal, they cock a glance at what is going on, as if they need only to fly away. Until recently they were also a case of virtue rewarded, at least in the town where I grew up, because, being humble creatures, there were plenty of them. Even when we still had a few bobcats in the woods the local snapping turtles, growing up to forty pounds, were the largest carnivores. You would see them through the amber water, as big as greeny wash basins at the bottom of the pond, until they faded into the inscrutable mud as if they hadn't existed at all.

When I was ten I went to Dr. Green's Pond, a two-acre pond across the road. When I was twelve I walked a mile or so to Taggart's Pond, which was lusher, had big water snakes and a waterfall; and shortly after that I was bicycling way up to the adventuresome vastness of Mud Pond, a lake-sized body of water in the reservoir system of a Connecticut city, possessed of cat-backed little islands and empty shacks and a forest of pines and hardwoods along the shore. Otters, foxes and mink left their prints on the bank; there were pike and perch. As I got older, the estates and forgotten back lots in town were parceled out and sold for nice prices, yet, though the woods had shrunk, it seemed that fewer people walked in the woods. The new residents didn't know how to find them. Eventually, exploring, they did find them, and it required some ingenuity and doubling around on my part to go for eight miles without meeting someone. I was grown by now, I lived in New York, and that's what I wanted on the occasional weekends when I came out.

Since Mud Pond contained drinking water I had felt confident nothing untoward would happen there. For a long while the developers stayed away, until the drought of the mid-1960s. This event, squeezing the edges in, convinced the local water company that the pond really wasn't a necessity as a catch basin, however; so they bulldozed a hole in the earthen dam, bulldozed the banks to fill in the bottom, and landscaped the flow of water that remained to wind like an English brook and provide a domestic view for the houses which were planned. Most of the painted turtles of Mud Pond, who had been inaccessible as they sunned on their rocks, wound up in boxes in boys' closets within a matter of days. Their footsteps in the dry leaves gave them away as they wandered forlornly. The snappers and the little musk turtles, neither of whom leave the water except once a year to lay their eggs, dug into the drying mud for another siege of hot weather, which they were accustomed to doing whenever the pond got low. But this time it was low for good; the mud baked over them and slowly entombed them. As for the ducks, I couldn't stroll in the woods and not feel guilty, because they were crouched beside every stagnant pothole, or were slinking between the bushes with their heads tucked into their shoulders so that I wouldn't see them. If they decided I had, they beat their way up through the screen of trees, striking their wings dangerously, and wheeled about with that headlong, magnificent velocity to locate another poor puddle.

4   I used to catch possums and black snakes as well as turtles, and I kept dogs and goats. Some summers I worked in a menagerie with the big personalities of the animal kingdom, like elephants and rhinoceroses. I was twenty before these enthusiasms began to wane, and it was then that I picked turtles as the particular animal I wanted to keep in touch with. I was allergic to fur, for one thing, and turtles need minimal care and not much in the way of quarters. They're personable beasts. They see the same colors we do and they seem to see just as well, as one discovers in trying to sneak up on them. In the laboratory they unravel the twists of a maze with the hot-blooded rapidity of a mammal. Though they can't run as fast as a rat, they improve on their errors just as quickly, pausing at each crossroads to look left and right. And they rock rhythmically in place, as we often do, although they are hatched from eggs, not the womb. (A common explanation psychologists give for our pleasure in rocking quietly is that it recapitulates our mother's heartbeat *in utero*.)

5   Snakes, by contrast, are dryly silent and priapic. They are smooth movers, legalistic, unblinking, and they afford the humor which the humorless do. But they make challenging captives; sometimes they don't eat for months on a point of order—if the light isn't right, for instance. Alligators are sticklers too. They're like war-horses, or German shepherds, and with their bar-shaped, vertical pupils adding emphasis, they have the *idée fixe* of eating, eating, even when they choose to refuse all food and stubbornly die. They delight in tossing a salamander up towards the sky and grabbing him in their long mouths as he comes down. They're so eager that they get the jitters, and they're too much of a proposition for a casual aquarium like mine. Frogs are depressingly defenseless: that moist, extensive back, with the bones almost sticking through. Hold a frog and you're holding its skeleton. Frogs' tasty legs are the staff of life to many animals—herons, raccoons, ribbon snakes—though they themselves are hard to feed. It's not an enviable role to be the staff of life, and after frogs you descend down the evolutionary ladder a big step to fish.

Turtles cough, burp, whistle, grunt and hiss, and produce social judgments. **6**
They put their heads together amicably enough, but then one drives the other
back with the suddenness of two dogs who have been conversing in tones too
low for an onlooker to hear. They pee in fear when they're first caught, but
exercise both pluck and optimism in trying to escape, walking for hundreds of
yards within the confines of their pen, carrying the weight of that cumbersome
box on legs which are cruelly positioned for walking. They don't feel that the
contest is unfair; they keep plugging, rolling like sailorly souls—a bobbing,
infirm gait, a brave, sea-legged momentum—stopping occasionally to study the
lay of the land. For me, anyway, they manage to contain the rest of the animal
world. They can stretch out their necks like a giraffe, or loom underwater like
an apocryphal hippo. They browse on lettuce thrown on the water like a cow
moose which is partly submerged. They have a penguin's alertness, combined
with a build like a Brontosaurus when they rise up on tiptoe. Then they hunch
and ponderously lunge like a grizzly going forward.

Baby turtles in a turtle bowl are a puzzle in geometrics. They're as decora- **7**
tive as pansy petals, but they are also self-directed building blocks, propping
themselves on one another in different arrangements, before upending the
tower. The timid individuals turn fearless, or vice versa. If one gets a bit
arrogant he will push the others off the rock and afterwards climb down into the
water and cling to the back of one of those he has bullied, tickling him with his
hind feet until he bucks like a bronco. On the other hand, when this same
milder-mannered fellow isn't exerting himself, he will stare right into the face of
the sun for hours. What could be more lionlike? And he's at home in or out of
the water and does lots of metaphysical tilting. He sinks and rises, with an
infinity of levels to choose from; or, elongating himself, he climbs out on the
land again to perambulate, sits boxed in his box, and finally slides back in the
water, submerging into dreams.

I have five of these babies in a kidney-shaped bowl. The hatchling, who is **8**
a painted turtle, is not as large as the top joint of my thumb. He eats chicken
gladly. Other foods he will attempt to eat but not with sufficient perseverance
to succeed because he's so little. The yellow-bellied terrapin is probably a
yearling, and he eats salad voraciously, but no meat, fish or fowl. The Cumberland terrapin won't touch salad or chicken but eats fish and all of the meats
except for bacon. The little snapper, with a black crenelated shell, feasts on any
kind of meat, but rejects greens and fish. The fifth of the turtles is African. I
acquired him only recently and don't know him well. A mottled brown, he
unnerves the green turtles, dragging their food off to his lairs. He doesn't seem
to want to be green—he bites the algae off his shell, hanging meanwhile at
daring, steep, head-first angles.

The snapper was a Ferdinand until I provided him with deeper water. Now **9**
he snaps at my pencil with his downturned and fearsome mouth, his swollen face
like a napalm victim's. The Cumberland has an elliptical red mark on the side
of his green-and-yellow head. He is benign by nature and ought to be as elegant
as his scientific name *(Pseudemys scripta elegans),* except he has contracted a
disease of the air bladder which has permanently inflated it; he floats high in the

water at an undignified slant and can't go under. There may have been internal bleeding, too, because his carapace is stained along its ridge. Unfortunately, like flowers, baby turtles often die. Their mouths fill up with a white fungus and their lungs with pneumonia. Their organs clog up from the rust in the water, or diet troubles, and, like a dying man's, their eyes and heads become too prominent. Toward the end, the edge of the shell becomes flabby as felt and folds around them like a shroud.

10   While they live they're like puppies. Although they're vivacious, they would be a bore to be with all the time, so I also have an adult wood turtle about six inches long. Her shell is the equal of any seashell for sculpturing, even a Cellini shell; it's like an old, dusty, richly engraved medallion dug out of a hillside. Her legs are salmon-orange bordered with black and protected by canted, heroic scales. Her plastron—the bottom shell—is splotched like a margay cat's coat, with black ocelli on a yellow background. It is convex to make room for the female organs inside, whereas a male's would be concave to help him fit tightly on top of her. Altogether, she exhibits every camouflage color on her limbs and shells. She has a turtleneck neck, a tail like an elephant's, wise old pachydermous hind legs and the face of a turkey—except that when I carry her she gazes at the passing ground with a hawk's eyes and mouth. Her feet fit to the fingers of my hand, one to each one, and she rides looking down. She can walk on the floor in perfect silence, but usually she lets her shell knock portentously, like a footstep, so that she resembles some grand, concise, slow-moving lid. But if an earthworm is presented, she jerks swiftly ahead, poises above it and strikes like a mongoose, consuming it with wild vigor. Yet she will climb on my lap to eat bread or boiled eggs.

11   If put into a creek, she swims like a cutter, nosing forward to intercept a strange turtle and smell him. She drifts with the current to go downstream, maneuvering behind a rock when she wants to take stock, or sinking to the nether levels, while bubbles float up. Getting out, choosing her path, she will proceed a distance and dig into a pile of humus, thrusting herself to the coolest layer at the bottom. The hole closes over her until it's as small as a mouse's hole. She's not as aquatic as a musk turtle, not quite as terrestrial as the box turtles in the same woods, but because of her versatility she's marvelous, she's everywhere. And though she breathes the way we breathe, with scarcely perceptible movements of her chest, sometimes instead she pumps her throat ruminatively, like a pipe smoker sucking and puffing. She waits and blinks, pumping her throat, turning her head, then sets off like a loping tiger in slow motion, hurdling the jungly lumber, the pea vine and twigs. She estimates angles so well that when she rides over the rocks, sliding down a drop-off with her rugged front legs extended, she has the grace of a rodeo mare.

12   But she's well off to be with me rather than at Mud Pond. The other turtles have fled—those that aren't baked into the bottom. Creeping up the brooks to sad, constricted marshes, burdened as they are with that box on their backs, they're walking into a setup where all their enemies move thirty times faster than they. It's like the nightmare most of us have whimpered through, where we are

weighted down disastrously while trying to flee; fleeing our home ground, we try to run.

I've seen turtles in still worse straits. On Broadway, in New York, there is a penny arcade which used to sell baby terrapins that were scrawled with bon mots in enamel paint, such as KISS ME BABY. The manager turned out to be a wholesaler as well, and once I asked him whether he had any larger turtles to sell. He took me upstairs to a loft room devoted to the turtle business. There were desks for the paper work and a series of racks that held shallow tin bins atop one another, each with several hundred babies crawling around in it. He was a smudgy-complexioned, serious fellow and he did have a few adult terrapins, but I was going to school and wasn't actually planning to buy; I'd only wanted to see them. They were aquatic turtles, but here they went without water, presumably for weeks, lurching about in those dry bins like handicapped citizens, living on gumption. An easel where the artist worked stood in the middle of the floor. She had a palette and a clip attachment for fastening the babies in place. She wore a smock and a beret, and was homely, short and eccentric-looking, with funny black hair, like some of the ladies who show their paintings in Washington Square in May. She had a cold, she was smoking, and her hand wasn't very steady, although she worked quickly enough. The smile that she produced for me would have looked giddy if she had been happier, or drunk. Of course the turtles' doom was sealed when she painted them, because their bodies inside would continue to grow but their shells would not. Gradually, invisibly, they would be crushed. Around us their bellies—two thousand belly shells—rubbed on the bins with a mournful, momentous hiss.

Somehow there were so many of them I didn't rescue one. Years later, however, I was walking on First Avenue when I noticed a basket of living turtles in front of a fish store. They were as dry as a heap of old bones in the sun; nevertheless, they were creeping over one another gimpily, doing their best to escape. I looked and was touched to discover that they appeared to be wood turtles, my favorites, so I bought one. In my apartment I looked closer and realized that in fact this was a diamondback terrapin, which was bad news. Diamondbacks are tidewater turtles from brackish estuaries, and I had no sea water to keep him in. He spent his days thumping interminably against the baseboards, pushing for an opening through the wall. He drank thirstily but would not eat and had none of the hearty, accepting qualities of wood turtles. He was morose, paler in color, sleeker and more Oriental in the carved ridges and rings that formed his shell. Though I felt sorry for him, finally I found his unrelenting presence exasperating. I carried him, struggling in a paper bag, across town to the Morton Street Pier on the Hudson. It was August but gray and windy. He was very surprised when I tossed him in; for the first time in our association, I think, he was afraid. He looked afraid as he bobbed about on top of the water, looking up at me from ten feet below. Though we were both accustomed to his resistance and rigidity, seeing him still pitiful, I recognized that I must have done the wrong thing. At least the river was salty, but it was also bottomless; the waves were too rough for him, and the tide was coming in, bumping him against the pilings underneath the pier. Too late, I realized that he wouldn't be able to swim to a peaceful inlet in New Jersey, even if he could figure out which way to swim. But since, short of diving in after him, there was nothing I could do, I walked away.

▼ TOPICAL CONSIDERATIONS

1. What would you say is the main idea in Hoagland's essay? Is he trying to convince you of something? If so, what?
2. Why might Hoagland write, "I couldn't stroll in the woods and not feel guilty" (paragraph 3)? Have you ever felt a similar guilt involving animals or nature?
3. The author tells readers why he keeps turtles as pets. Can you summarize these reasons? Point to specific passages to explain your answer.
4. Why might Hoagland think that it is important to tell the reader what different kinds of turtles like to eat?
5. Hoagland describes turtles in a variety of ways. For example, he writes that they are "a puzzle in geometrics," "decorative," and "self-directed building blocks" (paragraph 7). Why might he choose these descriptions?
6. In paragraph 12, Hoagland describes the "nightmare most of us have whimpered through." Why does he describe this nightmare?
7. What is the purpose of the story about the penny arcade? What impression does Hoagland want you to take away after reading it? How does the description of the artist painting the turtles' shells contribute to the thesis of the essay?
8. What does Hoagland mean by the line, "They were aquatic turtles, but here they went without water, presumably for weeks, lurching about in those dry bins like handicapped citizens living on gumption" (paragraph 13)?
9. How does Hoagland's conclusion relate to his main point? Might it be a metaphor for something? What were your feelings as you finish the essay?

▼ RHETORICAL CONSIDERATIONS

1. In paragraph 2 Hoagland writes, "though the woods had shrunk, it seemed that fewer people walked in the woods. The new residents didn't know how to find them." What does he mean by this remark? How would you describe the tone here?
2. Why might Hoagland have named this essay, "The Courage of

Turtles"? What particularly courageous qualities of turtles does he point to?

3. What is the intended effect of the statement, "Turtles cough, burp, whistle, grunt and hiss, and produce social judgments" (paragraph 6)? What do all of these habits have in common?

4. Hoagland describes the shell of his adult wood turtle as an "old, dusty, richly engraved medallion dug out of a hillside" (paragraph 10). Analyze each element of the description—the modifiers, the dug-up engraved medallion analogy—and explain how the particular words contribute to the overall image projected. Did the description successfully capture for you the turtle?

5. Hoagland in paragraph 6 says that turtles "manage to contain the rest of the animal world." How does he back up this claim? Name some of the animals he compares turtles to. In what different ways does he say turtles are like human beings?

6. Why might Hoagland choose to write very specifically about his adult wood turtle (paragraphs 10 and 11)?

7. In paragraph 12, Hoagland echoes some of his introductory remarks about turtles "baked" into the bottom of Mud Pond. What is his purpose in returning to this image of "entombment" (paragraph 3)?

8. The first line of Hoagland's conclusion reads, "Somehow there were so many of them I didn't rescue one" (paragraph 14). What is the effect of this line? Do you think this conclusion is appropriate given what went before?

▼ WRITING ASSIGNMENTS

1. Write an essay in which you develop thoughts about an animal in nature as Hoagland does. Include facts, details, and information about the habits and characteristics of the creature. What particular qualities, human or otherwise, do you attribute to the animal? Can your animal serve as a metaphor for something?

2. Hoagland makes some wonderfully vivid and insightful observations of turtles. Write your own observations but reverse the point of view. That is, describe humans through the eyes of a turtle or some other creature of the wild.

3. Would you have written a different ending to Hoagland's essay? If so, what would it have been? Write a letter to Mr. Hoagland explaining your changes and the reasons for them.

4. Write an essay in which you discuss the joys and rewards you've experienced exploring nature. Pick a particular experience you have had, and use specific details to make it come alive.

5. Write an essay in which you argue the need to protect endangered species even at the expense of industrial and economic growth.

6. Extinction is an irrefutable law of nature as evidenced by the thousands of different species preserved in fossils. Write an essay arguing that attempts to protect endangered species are costly and vain efforts to reverse a natural process.

▼ TOWARD A WARMER WORLD
Charles Tyler

Over the last few years scientist have gathered evidence that our world is becoming warmer. And the cause, it appears, is our technological way of life—in particular, the billions of tons of so-called greenhouse gases (methane, chlorofluorocarbons, and, most notably, carbon dioxide) that are released into the atmosphere each year by industry and the burning of fossil fuels. If the warming trend continues—and it seems to—scientists worry that the map of the earth will need to be redrawn as the polar caps shrink and coastlines are washed further inland. What will such cataclysmic environmental changes mean for human life? With a scientist's objective eye, climatologist Charles Tyler addresses that sobering question while raising some others. This article first appeared in *Geographical* magazine in 1990.

1 There is now no doubt that the world is getting warmer. Data from both the Southern and Northern Hemispheres shows an upward trend in average temperatures over the last hundred years. At the moment most scientists are not prepared to stick their necks out and attribute a cause to this trend. It is possible that it represents a natural climatic change caused by a gradual increase in the sun's radiation output. But these same scientists are painfully aware that recent temperature changes are at the limit of known natural fluctuations: it seems increasingly likely that the cause is an enhanced greenhouse effect.

2 The basic theory of the greenhouse effect is quite simple. The earth's atmosphere consists mainly of oxygen and nitrogen, but there are small concentrations of various "greenhouse" gases—notably carbon dioxide (CO_2), water vapour, methane, and chlorofluorocarbons (CFCs)—which play a very important role in maintaining the planet's "heat balance." As their name suggests these gases have a similar effect to glass in a greenhouse: They let heat from the sun in, and keep it in.

3 The atmosphere is more or less transparent to the visible solar radiation which warms the earth (ground or oceans) on which it falls. Because it has been heated, the earth is warmer than space and gives off energy in the form of invisible long-wave infra-red radiation. (This accounts for nighttime cooling.)

Greenhouse gases absorb some of this long-wave radiation, and reradiate it in the lower atmosphere.

The gases therefore act rather like a blanket by preventing some infra-red   **4**
radiation from leaving the earth-atmosphere system. Within certain limits, the more greenhouse gases present, the more infra-red radiation will become trapped, and the higher the surface temperature of the earth.

Theoretical calculations suggest that if there were no greenhouse gases   **5**
present in the atmosphere, the average surface temperature of the earth would be about $-15°C$ as all the infra-red radiation would be lost to outer space. Clearly, they are vital to the well-being of life on the earth. But over the last hundred years the amount of CO_2 in the atmosphere has increased by nearly 25 percent from 280 ppmv (parts per million by volume) to the current level of around 340 ppmv. This is almost entirely due to Man's burning of fossil fuels. The cutting down and burning of huge areas of temperate and tropical forest has also contributed.

Though present in much smaller quantities than CO_2, the concentrations of   **6**
other greenhouse gases have increased even more dramatically. Methane, for example, is currently increasing by 1 percent per year, while CFCs are increasing at a rate of six percent per year. This is worrying, since molecule for molecule, CFCs are up to 20,000 times more efficient at trapping infra-red radiation than carbon dioxide.

It is very difficult to predict how the concentrations of these gases will   **7**
change in the coming decades. Following the 1987 Montreal Protocol now in force, it is hoped that CFC concentrations will not continue to increase at such an alarming rate.

Unfortunately, man is so dependent on fossil fuels, that it is hard to see   **8**
much of a reduction in the five billion tonnes of carbon as CO_2 pumped out of chimneys and exhaust pipes each year. Even if the developed world becomes more energy-efficient, the Third World's appetite for fossil fuels is growing continually. The burning of tropical forests is also continuing apace, which may contribute a further one billion tonnes of carbon as CO_2 each year.

The outlook for reducing emissions of methane is also limited. There is a   **9**
close relationship between methane and the growth of agriculture, which itself is linked to population: Two major sources of methane are rice paddies and livestock, both of which have grown in line with population. It also seems that methane is not being broken down in the atmosphere as rapidly because of increased levels of carbon monoxide (CO)—another product of combustion.

Future emission levels of greenhouse gases is not the only uncertainty in   **10**
trying to establish the changes in climate that we might expect. For any given increase in the concentration of these gases, it is relatively easy to calculate the increased heating effect in watts/square meter—but that is only the tip of the problem.

Unfortunately, once warming has started, it is likely to affect the earth-   **11**
atmosphere system in such a way as to encourage further warming. Several such positive-feedback systems have been identified. Again, the impact these will

have remains uncertain. Increased surface temperature will undoubtedly increase evaporation from the oceans and put more water vapour into the air. Water vapour is often overlooked as a greenhouse gas. In fact, it is the main contributor to the current greenhouse effect—and is far more important than CO_2.

12   More water vapour in the air suggests that there will also be more cloud cover in a warmer world. In fact, recent research by Ann Henderson-Sellers shows that global cloud-cover has increased by ten per cent since the turn of the century. But it's not entirely clear whether clouds cool the earth by reflecting solar radiation or warm it by trapping infra-red radiation. It seems that the former effect is dominant with low cloud; the latter with high cloud. Inevitably, with global warming, snow- and ice-cover over the North and South of the globe will retreat toward the poles. Thus instead of reflecting away solar energy, these areas will absorb it and may further increase the warming.

13   There are a number of other potential positive feedbacks, which have not generally been included in modelling effects of an enhanced greenhouse effect. For example, there is concern about the response of oceans to an increase in temperature. The oceans and the organisms in them currently absorb about half of the CO_2 released into the air. Cold waters can absorb more gas than warm water, so it is probable that as the oceans warm up they will absorb less CO_2 from the atmosphere.

14   Investigators also believe that they have found a new vast reservoir of methane, held in lattice-like geological structures called clathrates on the seabed at depths of several hundred metres. These methane "deposits" are physically bound to the water in nodules, and kept stable by the pressure of water on top of them. Small changes in temperature or pressure will alter the compound's stability. A warming of the oceans could unleash much of this methane.

15   In addition to this the observed warming effect is likely to lag behind what might be expected, because the oceans are so vast that they take time to respond to higher air temperatures. This "thermal inertia" means that we will not feel the full effects of the warming associated with any particular level of greenhouse gases until twenty to sixty years later.

16   Over the last century, the world has warmed by approximately 0.5°C, which is less than might be expected for the 30 percent increase in CO_2 over the same period. It's believed that even if all emissions ceased today, we are committed to a further warming of up to 1°C before equilibrium is reached, given the current concentrations of greenhouse gases in the atmosphere.

17   It is largely because there are so many uncertainties about feedback mechanisms that it is difficult to make any clear predictions. "Until we reduce the uncertainty in the equilibrium warming, there is limited value in using vast computing resources to make detailed predictions about the future climate," said John Mitchell, a modeller at the Meteorological Office. "We are still at the stage of looking at mechanisms rather than making quantitative forecasts."

18   The models employed to predict future changes are known as "surprise-free

scenarios"—that is, they assume that the ocean-atmosphere-biosphere systems keep functioning in the same way they do now. This is not necessarily a correct assumption; should something unexpected occur, it would not be the first time scientists have been surprised by the behaviour of the atmosphere—nobody predicted the ozone hole over Antarctica, for example.

Wallace Broecker of Columbia University is one of several researchers **19** worried about this. ". . . The earth's climate does not respond to forcing in a smooth and gradual way. Rather it responds in sharp jumps which involve large-scale reorganization of the Earth's systems. . . ." "We must consider the possibility that the main responses of the system to our provocation of the atmosphere will come in jumps whose timing and magnitude are unpredictable."

Amidst all the models, and the talk, has it been conclusively shown that the **20** greenhouse effect will change the climate? Has it already caused the 0.5°C rise in global temperatures over the last century? The favoured phrase used by climatologists at the moment seems to be that the observed changes are "not inconsistent" with models of the greenhouse effect.

"It will take a number of years' more data before anyone will come out and **21** say categorically that one is due to the other," said Dr. Phil Jones of the Climatic Research Unit. "Obviously, the warmer the world gets, the more difficult it will be to deny the greenhouse effect on climate." It is true that in terms of average global temperatures, the five warmest years since records began have all occurred in the 1980s (1980, 1983, 1987, 1988).

Dr. James Hansen of NASA has been rather more outspoken on the sub- **22** ject. Last summer he told a news conference that it was time to "stop waffling and admit that there is considerable evidence that the greenhouse effect is here. . . . We have to anticipate big climatic changes. The policymakers have to know that."

And that is really the crux of the issue. In itself, the greenhouse effect is not **23** necessarily a bad thing. Certainly, it is a more desirable state of the world, from the human point of view, than the onset of a new Ice Age might be. What is desperately important is the way human society responds to this environmental challenge during the coming decades. It is a question of being prepared to change—not only in developing ways to deal with the effects of a warmer world, but also in reducing future emissions of greenhouse gases.

Some countries will benefit from an enhanced greenhouse effect, while **24** others will suffer. Nobody, for example, is likely to be very disappointed if winters get milder in Britain. But a continuing rise in sea-levels could spell disaster for low-lying countries like Bangladesh. Some parts of the world will get wetter; others dryer. That means that patterns of agriculture will have to change if we are to continue to produce anything like enough food to feed everyone.

What we do not know is how the adverse effects will be balanced by **25** beneficial effects in a warmer world. In a sense we are conducting an uncontrolled experiment on a global scale by changing the composition of the atmosphere. And that is a potentially disastrous state of affairs. As Senator Bennett Johnson of Louisiana put it: "We have only one planet. If we screw it up we have no place to go."

▼ TOPICAL CONSIDERATIONS

1. What would you say is Tyler's main point? Does he persuade you to form an opinion about the warmer world?
2. What reason does Tyler offer for his statement that "most scientists are not prepared to stick their necks out and attribute a cause" (paragraph 1) to our warmer world?
3. In your own words, can you describe the "greenhouse effect"? Why does it bear the name it does? What are the effects of "greenhouse" gases? Are they all negative? Where does the major production of these gases come from? Think of your own life-style; do you contribute to their increase in any way?
4. In paragraph 8, Tyler writes, "Unfortunately, man is so dependent on fossil fuels." Do you agree with his statement? Do you see any ways that "man" is trying to alleviate this dependency? What are other solutions to the burning of fossil fuels?
5. Tyler talks about the cyclical nature of the warming problem. How does this cycle work?
6. In paragraph 15, Tyler writes, "we will not feel the full effects of the warming associated with any particular level of greenhouse gases until twenty to sixty years later." Does this statement worry you? Explain your feelings.
7. Is it Tyler's intention to convince you that the possible "greenhouse effect" is a negative thing? What is "the crux of the issue" (paragraph 23)?
8. What does Tyler mean when he says "we are conducting an uncontrolled experiment" (paragraph 25)? Do you agree with him?
9. Refer back to "The Courage of Turtles." How are Hoagland and Tyler talking about similar things? How do they differ in their concern over the natural world?

▼ RHETORICAL CONSIDERATIONS

1. How does Tyler's introductory sentence affect how you read the rest of his piece?
2. Does Tyler's explanation of scientific matters make sense to you? What particular areas of the essay are clear? Are any unclear? Refer to specific areas that contain particularly difficult language.
3. Tyler writes that the gas concentration is "very difficult to predict"

(paragraph 7). He tells us that impacts are "uncertain" (paragraph 11) and that "it's not entirely clear whether clouds cool the earth" (paragraph 12). In addition, he writes that "there are so many uncertainties" (paragraph 17). How do all of these phrases of "uncertainty" affect how you interpret the piece? Are these effective tools in presenting his argument?

4. In his concluding paragraph, Tyler moves away from scientific language and restates his case in very basic terms. What is the function of this paragraph?

5. How would you characterize Tyler's tone throughout his piece? Does it shift at any point? Does Tyler's analysis ever become subjective?

6. When describing the greenhouse effect, Tyler uses the image of a "blanket" (paragraph 4) that "traps" the radiation in our atmosphere. How do these terms color the tone of his discussion?

7. There is a tone shift that occurs around paragraph 23. What purpose does it serve?

8. Compare and contrast the overall tone of Hoagland's "The Courage of Turtles" with that of Tyler's essay. How do they differ?

▼ WRITING ASSIGNMENTS

1. You are speaking to a group of middle school children who have no idea what the "greenhouse effect" is. With that audience in mind, draft a speech explaining Tyler's argument as clearly as possible. Be sure to provide plenty of examples.

2. In a well-organized essay, offer to a senate panel suggestions on curbing the greenhouse effect. What concrete examples can you offer to reduce the likelihood of drastic global change?

3. Write a letter to the scientists who "are not prepared to stick their necks out and attribute a cause" to global warming (paragraph 1). Explain what you think of their stance. Why do you agree or disagree with their hesitancy in classifying the issue?

4. Imagine a conversation between Hoagland and Tyler. Write an essay in which the two writers respond to the concerns raised by each other.

▼ A PATH OF MORE RESISTANCE
Bill McKibben

Confronted with the sobering realization that the world of nature is endangered by a life-style of accumulation and growth, Bill McKibben offers a solution—a voluntary simplification of life-styles. He sketches out a humble, simple alternative in which human happiness is secondary to the survival of the natural world. He suggests a life of reduced material possessions—a small wardrobe, few essentials, and almost no luxuries— of growing one's own food, and of burning as little fossil fuel as necessary. Could we conform to such a stripped-down life? Do we really have a choice? Bill McKibben has written many articles on nature which have appeared in the *New Yorker,* the *New York Review of Books* and *The New York Times.* He and his wife live in the Adirondack Mountains of New York. This piece was taken from his book *The End of Nature* published in 1989.

1   A half hour's hike brings my dog and me to the top of the hill behind my house. I know the hill well by now, each gully and small creek, each big rock, each opening around the edges. I know the places where the deer come, and the coyotes after them. It is no Bald Mountain, no unlogged virgin forest with trees ten feet around, but it is a deep and quiet and lovely place all the same.

2   Only the thought of what will happen as the new weather kicks in darkens my view: the trees dying, the hillside unable to hold its soil against the rainfall, the gullies sharpening, the deer looking for ever-scarcer browse. And, finally, the scrub and brush colonizing the slopes, clinging to what soil remains. Either that or the cemetery rows of perfect, heat-tolerant genetically improved pines.

3   From the top of the hill, if I stand on a certain ledge, I can see my house down below, white against the hemlocks. I can see my whole material life—the car, the bedroom, the chimney above the stove. I like that life, I like it enormously. But a choice seems unavoidable. Either that life down there changes, perhaps dramatically, or this life all around me up here changes—passes away.

4   That is a terrible choice. Two years ago, when I got married, my wife and I had the standard hopes and dreams, and their fulfillment seemed not so far away. We love to travel; we had set up our lives so that work wouldn't tie us down. Our house is nice and big—it seemed only a matter of time before it would fill with the racket of children.

5   As the consequences of the greenhouse effect have become clearer to us, though, we've started to prune and snip our desires. Instead of taking long vacation trips in the car, we ride our bikes on the road by the house. Instead of building a wood-fired hot tub for the backyard (the closest I've ever come to real decadence), we installed exciting new thermal-pane windows. Most of our other changes have been similarly small. We heat with our wood, and we try to keep

the house at 55 degrees. We drive much less frequently; we shop twelve times a year, and there are weeks when we do not venture out at all. Though I'm a lousy gardener, I try to grow more and more of our food.

Still, those are the easy things, especially if you live in the country. And they're as much pleasure as sacrifice. It may be icy in most of the house but it's warm cuddled by the stove. I like digging in the garden, though it makes me more nervous than it did when it was pure hobby: if a storm knocks down a tomato plant, I feel slightly queasy. If we don't travel great distances and constantly see new sights, we have come to know the few square miles around us in every season and mood. **6**

But there are harder changes, too, places where the constricting world has begun to bind and pinch. It is dawning on me and my wife that the world we inhabit is not the world we grew up in, the world where our hopes and dreams were formed. That responsibility may mean something new and sad. In other words, we try very hard not to think about how much we'd like a baby. **7**

And it may take even more. Sometimes I stand on top of the hill and wonder if someday we'll need to move away, perhaps live closer to other people. Probably that would be more energy-efficient. Would I love the woods enough to leave them behind? I stand up there and look out over the mountain to the east and the lake to the south and the rippling wilderness knolls stretching off to the west—and to the house below with the line of blue smoke trailing out of the chimney. One world or the other will have to change. **8**

And if it is the human world that changes—if this humbler idea begins to win out—what will the planet look like? Will it appeal only to screwballs, people who thrive on a monthly shower and no steady income? **9**

It's hard to draw a detailed picture—it's so much easier to picture the defiant future, for it is merely the extension of our current longings. I've spent my whole life wanting more, so it's hard for me to imagine "less" in any but a negative way. But that imagination is what counts. Changing the way we think is at the heart of the question. If it ever happens, the actions will follow. **10**

For example, to cope with the greenhouse problem, people may need to install more efficient washing machines. But if you buy such a machine and yet continue to feel that it's both your right and your joy to have a big wardrobe, then the essential momentum of our course won't be broken. For big wardrobes imply a world pretty much like our own, where people pile up possessions, and where human desire is the only measure that counts. Even if such a world somehow licks the greenhouse effect, it will still fall in a second for, say, the cornucopia of genetic engineering. On the other hand, you could slash your stock of clothes to a comfortable (or even uncomfortable) minimum and then chip in with your neighbors to buy a more efficient washing machine to which you would lug your dirty laundry. If we reached that point—the point where great closetfuls of clothes seemed slightly absurd, *unnatural*—then we might have begun to climb down from the tottering perch where we currently cling. **11**

"Absurd" and "unnatural" are different from "wrong" or "immoral." This **12** is not a moral argument. There are plenty of good reasons having to do with aesthetics or whimsy to own lots of sharp clothes. (And many more and much better reasons to, say, drive cars or raise large families.) But those reasons may be outweighed by the burden that such desires place on the natural world. And if we could see that clearly, then our thinking might change of its own accord.

13   In this particular example, the thinking is more radical than the action. If we decided against huge wardrobes (which is to say, against a whole way of looking at ourselves) and against every family's owning a washer (which is to say, against a pervasive individual consumerism), then taking your clothes down the street to wash them would be the most obvious idea in the world. If people *hadn't* changed their minds about such things, these would be obnoxious developments—you'd need to employ secret police to make sure they weren't washing in private. It wouldn't be worth it, and it wouldn't work. But if we had changed our minds, our current ways of life might soon seem as bizarre as the six thousand shoes of Imelda Marcos.

14   It's normal to imagine that this humbler world would resemble the past. Simply because the atmosphere was cleaner a century ago, though, there's no call to forget all that's been developed since. My wife and I just acquired a fax machine, for instance, on the premise that it makes for graceful, environmentally sound communication—an advanced way to do with less. But if communication prospered in a humbler world, transportation might well wither, as people began to live closer not only to their work but to their food supply. Oranges all year round—oranges at any season in the northern latitudes—might prove ambitious beyond our means, just as the tropics might have to learn to do without apples. We—or, at least, our grandchildren—might come to use the "appropriate technologies" of "sustainable development" that we urge on peasants through organizations like the Peace Corps—bicycle-powered pumps, solar cookstoves, and so on. And, as in a less developed country (a phrase that would probably turn into a source of some pride), more Westerners might find their work connected directly with their supper. That is to say, they would farm, which begins to sound a little quaint, a little utopian.

15   But conventional utopian ideas are not much help, either. Invariably they are designed to advance human happiness, which is found to be suffering as the result of crowding or stress or lack of meaningful work or not enough sex or too much sex. Machinery is therefore abolished, or cities abandoned, or families legislated against—but it's all in the name of man. Dirt under your nails will make you happier!

16   The humbler world I am describing is just the opposite. Human happiness would be of secondary importance. Perhaps it would be best for the planet if we all lived not in kibbutzes or on Jeffersonian farms, but crammed into a few huge cities like so many ants. I doubt a humbler worlds would be one big happy Pennsylvania Dutch colony. Certain human sadnesses might diminish; other human sadnesses would swell. But that would be beside the point. This is not an attempt at a utopia—as I said, I'm happy now. It's a stab at something else—an "atopia," perhaps—where our desires are not the engine.

The ground rules for such an atopia would be few enough. We would have **17** to conquer the desire to grow in numbers; the human population would need to get gradually smaller, though how much smaller is an open question. Some deep ecologists say the human population shouldn't exceed a hundred million, others a billion or two—roughly our population a century ago. And those people would need to use less in the way of resources—not just oil, but wood and water and chemicals and even land itself. Those are the essentials. But they are practical rules, not moral ones. Within them, a thousand cultures—vegetarian and hunter, communal and hermitic—could still exist.

A pair of California professors, George Sessions and Bill Devall, listed what **18** they saw as some of the principles of deep ecology in a book *(Deep Ecology)* they published several years ago. Although the work shows its West Coast origins at times (there is some discussion of how this philosophy could give us "joyous confidence to dance with the sensuous harmonies discovered through spontaneous, playful intercourse with the rhythms of our bodies, the rhythms of flowing water"), it is frank about the sharp contrast between the current worldview and their proposed replacement: instead of material and economic growth, "elegantly simple" material needs; instead of consumerism, "doing with enough." It is frank, too, in its acknowledgment that deep ecology—that humility—is an infant philosophy, with many questions yet to be asked, much less answered: Exactly how much is enough? Or, what about poor people?

Those are hard questions—but perhaps not beyond our imagination. When **19** we decided that accumulation and growth were our economic ideals, we invented wills and lending at interest and puritanism and supersonic aircraft. Why would we come up with ideas less powerful in an all-out race to do with less?

The difficulty is almost certainly more psychological than intellectual—less **20** that we can't figure out major alterations in our way of life than that we simply don't want to. Even if our way of life has destroyed nature and endangered the planet, it is so hard to imagine living in any other fashion. The people whose lives may point the way—Thoreau, say, or Gandhi—we dismiss as exceptional, a polite way of saying there is no reason we should be expected to go where they pointed. The challenge they presented with the physical examples of their lives is much more subversive than anything they wrote or said: if they could live those simple lives, it's no use saying we could not. I could, I suppose, get by on half the money I currently spend. A voluntary simplification of life-styles is not beyond our abilities, but it is probably outside our desires.

And our desires count. Nothing is necessarily going to force us to live humbly; **21** we are free to chance the other, defiant route and see what happens. The only thing we absolutely must do is cut back immediately on our use of fossil fuels. That is not an option; we need to do it in order to choose any other future. But there is no certainty we must simultaneously cut back on our material desires—not if we're willing to live in a world ever more estranged from nature. Both the defiant and the humble alternatives offer ways to adapt to the greenhouse effect, this total upheaval. They present us with a choice.

22   The obvious objection to this choice is that it does not exist: that man always pushes restlessly ahead, that it's inevitable, biological, part of "human nature." That is a cop-out, at least intellectually—that is, it maẏ be true, but those of us who have thought about the question still have the moral burden of making a choice. Anyway, there are examples of civilizations, chiefly Eastern ones, that by choice spent centuries almost suspended in time. I *can* imagine a world in which we decide not to conduct genetic experiments or to build new dams, just as a few people in the late nineteenth century began to imagine forests that were not logged and so preserved the Adirondacks. As I said, I'm not certain what that world would look like. Probably it would have to develop an enormously powerful social taboo against "progress" of the defiant kind—a religious or quasi-religious horror at the thought of "improved chickens" and large families. And I'm not saying I see the path from here to any of the possible theres; my point is merely that, for the purpose of argument, I can imagine such a world. Possession of a certain technology imposes on us no duty to use it.

23   A second obvious objection is that perhaps we needn't decide now, that surely we can leave it for some future generation to figure out. That is an attractive idea and a traditional one; we have been putting off this particular question since at least 1864, when George Perkins Marsh, the first modern environmentalist, wrote that by our tree cutting and swamp draining we were "breaking up the floor and wainscotting and doors and window-frames of our dwelling for fuel to warm our bodies."

24   I have tried to explain, though, why it cannot be put off any longer. We just happen to be living at the moment when the carbon dioxide has increased to an intolerable level. We just happen to be alive at the moment when if nothing is done before we die the world's tropical rain forests will become a brown girdle around the planet that will last for millennia. It's simply our poor luck; it might have been nicer to have been born in 1890 and died in 1960, confident that everything was looking up. We just happen to be living in the decade when genetic engineering is acquiring a momentum that will soon be unstoppable. The comforting idea that we could decide to use such technology to, in the words of Lewis Thomas, cure "most of the unsolved diseases on society's agenda" and then not use it to straighten trees or grow giant trout seems implausible to me: we're already doing those things.

25   One needs, obviously, to be wary of millennialism. And it's perhaps not fair that those of us currently alive should have to deal with these developments. On the other hand, it wasn't fair that our fathers had to go fight Hitler. The American Methodist Church has just adopted a new hymnal, and, along with the usual wrangles over sexism and militarism and so on, there was a dispute over a marvelous Civil War–era hymn by James Russell Lowell. "Once to Every Man and Nation," it begins, "comes the moment to decide, / In the strife of truth with falsehood, for the good or evil side. / Some great cause, God's new messiah, offering each the bloom or blight, / And the choice goes by forever, / 'Twixt the darkness and the light." The hymnal committee reportedly decided against the tune on the grounds that it was unsound theology—that once was

not enough, that it was never too late for a person to reform. But this was one of Martin Luther King's favorite hymns, and in terms of public policy, if not personal salvation, I fear it may be all too true.

Of these two paths which one will we choose? It's impossible to know for certain, but there's no question but that the momentum of our age ceaselessly hurries us ahead, making it horribly difficult to choose the humble path and incredibly easy to follow the defiant one.   **26**

I have a neighbor, a logger whom I'll call Jim Franklin. Jim honestly believes that the cause of acid rain in the Adirondacks is "too many trees," the result of environmentalists' setting too much land aside as wilderness. He has worked out a theory, something about the mat of pine needles accumulating on the ground, which I can't begin to repeat even though I have heard it several times. "I told it to the forest ranger and he just looked at me," says Jim, as if this were proof of the conspiracy. We believe things because we have a need to believe them. (That is not a novel insight, I realize.) Jim wants to log for economic reasons and for reasons that might be described as psychological or cultural, and he has constructed an idea to support his desire. But it is not a lie: he believes it to be true. Muir, on his thousand-mile stroll to the Gulf of Mexico, met a man in a particularly backward section of North Carolina who said to him: "I believe in Providence. Our fathers came into these valleys, got the richest of them, and skimmed the cream of the soil. The worn-out ground won't yield no roasting ears now. But the Lord foresaw this state of affairs and prepared something else for us. And what is it? Why, He meant us to bust open these copper mines and gold mines, so that we may have money to buy the corn we cannot raise." Though this argument has its obvious weaknesses, it is immensely appealing, just as the thought of a new genetically engineered cornucopia is appealing: it means we wouldn't have to change.   **27**

And we don't want to change. Jim wants to log as he always has. I want to be able to drive as I always have and go on living in the large house I live in and so on. The tidal force of biology continues to govern us, even when we realize (as no lemming can) that we're doing something stupid. This genetic inheritance from millions of years when it did make sense to grow and expand can't simply be shrugged off.   **28**

And the opposing forces are so weak. In a curious way, for example, some environmentalists have made it easier for people to ignore global threats. In the late 1960s and early 1970s, a spate of horror books came out—books filled with the direst predictions. "At the current rate of population increase, there will be a billion billion people on the face of the earth, or seventeen hundred for every square mile," wrote Paul Ehrlich. "Projecting this farther into the future, in about two thousand or three thousand years people would weigh more than the earth; in five thousand years everything in the visible universe would be converted into people, and their expansion would be at the speed of light." While this was technically true, it was also so unrealistic that we could safely ignore it. The greenhouse effect, he wrote, might raise ocean levels two hundred and   **29** fifty feet. "Gondola to the Empire State Building, anyone? he asked. "Lake Erie has died. . . . Lake Michigan will soon follow it into extinction."

30 But that didn't happen. Lake Erie rose again—still sick, of course, but not dead. The oil crisis eased and then turned into an oil glut. The greenhouse effect could realistically raise the sea level ten feet, which is plenty bad enough but sounds like nothing next to two hundred and fifty. With every unfulfilled apocalyptic projection, our confidence in the environmentalists has waned, our belief that we'll muddle through been bolstered.

31 We'll look for almost any reason not to change our attitudes; the inertia of the established order is powerful. If we can think of a plausible, or even implausible, reason to discount environmental warnings, we will. If a solitary scientist says, as S. Fred Singer did in a recent issue of the *Wall Street Journal,* that the greenhouse effect is a "Mixture of fact and fancy," we read it to mean that the whole business is nonsense. And if we can imagine a plausible reason to believe that it will all be okay—if someone tells us that we can "manage" the planet, for instance—the temptation is to believe him. In 1980, when Ronald Reagan ran for the presidency, he made his shrillest attacks on the idea that we might be living in an "age of limits." This notion, perhaps the first necessary recognition on the road to a new relationship with the earth, a first baby step on a thousand-mile journey toward deep ecology, had gained some small currency with Carter administration officials. But Reagan attacked it mercilessly. Occasionally, as when he announced that trees pollute, he got in a little trouble. But the country forgave him, because it wanted to believe him—wanted to believe that, even though the shadows seemed to be lengthening, it was "morning in America." Unfortunately, optimism didn't aid the ozone layer.

▼ TOPICAL CONSIDERATIONS

1. What is McKibben's main point? Is he trying to convince the reader of something? Did he convince you of anything? What is "the choice" that McKibben talks about in paragraphs 3 and 4?

2. In paragraph 4, McKibben talks about his "standard hopes and dreams." What are they? By whose standards is he weighing these "hopes and dreams"? Do you see certain assumptions from which he is writing the essay? Do your "hopes and dreams" differ from the standard? If so, how?

3. In paragraphs 5 and 11, McKibben writes about "the consequences of the greenhouse effect." Relate this analysis to Charles Tyler's discussion in "Toward a Warmer World."

4. What are the positive and the negative aspects of the life-style that McKibben describes in paragraph 5? What parts of your current life-style would have to change? Would you be willing to make such "sacrifices"? Explain.

5. Why does McKibben write, "This is not a moral argument" (paragraph 12)? Does McKibben anticipate a counter-argument?

6. What are the distinctions that McKibben makes between "utopia" and "atopia" (paragraphs 14–17)? Why are these important distinctions? What are his "ground rules for the 'atopia' " (paragraph 17)? Do you think that these are feasible goals? In your opinion, are any of them more feasible or more necessary than others?

7. McKibben admits the difficulty of carrying out his suggestions. Discuss his distinction between "ability" and "desire" that he discusses in paragraph 20.

8. In paragraph 22, McKibben writes, "Possession of a certain technology imposes on us no duty to use it." Do you agree or disagree with this statement? Can you think of particular technologies that McKibben might be referring to? Can you create your own list?

9. What technique does McKibben use to convince us to take action now?

10. Why might McKibben tell readers the story of "Jim Franklin" (paragraph 27)? How does the story contribute to his text? Did it change your attitude at all? Might it make you alter your behavior? Explain your answer.

11. McKibben writes, "some environmentalists have made it easier for people to ignore global threats" (paragraph 29). Why might he make this seemingly contradictory statement? Do you agree with him?

▼ RHETORICAL CONSIDERATIONS

1. What is the effect of the repetition in paragraph 1: "I know . . . I know"?

2. In paragraph 3, McKibben changes the vocabulary he uses. He writes, "this life all around me up here changes—passes away." Why does he alter his words from "changes" to "passes away"?

3. Why does McKibben use words like "constricting," "bind," and "pinch" (paragraph 7)?

4. Does McKibben manage to keep an objective outlook? Can you find any lapses into subjectivity?

5. Why might McKibben put words like "absurd," "unnatural," "wrong," and "immoral" (paragraph 12) in quotation marks?

6. How would you characterize McKibben's tone throughout the essay? Does it change at all?

7. How does McKibben's conclusion affect how you react to his subject matter? Why might he invoke the examples of Jimmy Carter and Ronald Reagan?

▼ WRITING ASSIGNMENTS

1. Try to imagine making some of the drastic changes in life-style that McKibben describes. Do you think you could adjust to the "sacrifices"—to the loss of luxuries, modern conveniences, and consumer commodities to which you have grown accustomed? Could you find satisfaction in growing your own food? Write up your ideas in a paper.

2. Do you think you could live the rest of your life without television and still be happy? Write an essay in which you explore that possibility. Examine whether you think your life would be changed for better or for worse.

3. For the good of the environment, would you be willing to switch from the automobile to a bicycle? Write a paper in which you answer this question. Try to imagine the circumstances which would so motivate you.

4. Consider the difference between a "utopia" and an "atopia." In a well-supported essay, discuss both of these ideas and describe the ideal human-centered world as opposed to the ideal world.

5. Imagine that you are serving on an environmental protection panel and are preparing a presentation to the Senate. The other members of your panel are Edward Hoagland, Charles Tyler, and Bill McKibben. What are the contents of this proposal?

6. One of the major causes of environmental decline is the burning of fossil fuels. Raising the gasoline tax from the current 9 cents per gallon to 59 cents per gallon over the next five years would spur conservation of fuel. Would you be willing to pay an extra 50 cents for a gallon of gasoline if it would help save the environment? Write an essay in which you answer this question and explore the reasons.

7. Write a letter to your congressman (or to the president) in which you call for increased funding for research on alternate energy sources, including solar power and safe designs for nuclear reactors.

8. Write a paper in which you argue for or against laws requiring households to sort garbage into recyclable and non-recyclable items.

9. Write a paper in which you argue for or against hypothetical tax laws penalizing married couples who have more than two children.

▼ ECO-DEFENSE
Edward Abbey

Edward Abbey was a sort of underground hero to the environmental movement. An impassioned environmentalist and irreverent writer, he dreamed
of seeing "the whole American West made into a wilderness." He was
born in Appalachia and worked off and on for both the National Park
Service and the U.S. Forest Service. He wrote essays and seven novels the
most famous of which is *The Monkey Wrench Gang* (1976) which told of a
group of environmentalists plotting to blow up Arizona's Glen Canyon
Dam. He wrote, he once said, to make a difference: "to oppose injustice,
to defy the powerful, to speak for the voiceless." Taken from *One Life at
a Time, Please* (1988), this brief essay does all of that. It is at once an attack
on the American government for selling out on the American wilderness
as well as a call for defensive action by those so outraged. Other collections include *Slumgullion Stew: An Edward Abbey Reader* (1984) and *Down
the River* (1982).

If a stranger batters your door down with an axe, threatens your family and **1**
yourself with deadly weapons, and proceeds to loot your home of whatever he
wants, he is committing what is universally recognized—by law and in common
morality—as a crime. In such a situation the householder has both the right and
the obligation to defend himself, his family, and his property by whatever means
are necessary. This right and this obligation is universally recognized, justified,
and praised by all civilized human communities. Self-defense against attack is
one of the basic laws not only of human society but of life itself, not only of
human life but of all life.

The American wilderness, what little remains, is now undergoing exactly **2**
such an assault. With bulldozer, earth mover, chainsaw, and dynamite the
international timber, mining, and beef industries are invading our public
lands—property of all Americans—bashing their way into our forests, mountains, and rangelands and looting them for everything they can get away with.
This for the sake of short-term profits in the corporate sector and multimillion-
dollar annual salaries for the three-piece-suited gangsters (MBA—Harvard,
Yale, University of Tokyo, et alia) who control and manage these bandit enterprises. Cheered on, naturally, by *Time, Newsweek,* and *The Wall Street Journal,*
actively encouraged, inevitably, by those jellyfish government agencies that are
supposed to *protect* the public lands, and as always aided and abetted in every
way possible by the compliant politicians of our Western states, such as Babbitt,
DeConcini, Goldwater, McCain, Hatch, Garn, Simms, Hansen, Andrus, Wal-
lop, Domenici and Co. Inc.—who would sell the graves of their mothers if
there's a quick buck in the deal, over or under the table, what do they care.

Representative government in the United States has broken down. Our **3** legislators do not represent the public, the voters, or even those who voted for them but rather the commercial-industrial interests that finance their political campaigns and control the organs of communication—the TV, the newspapers, the billboards, the radio. Politics is a game for the rich only. Representative government in the USA represents money, not people, and therefore has forfeited our allegiance and moral support. We owe it nothing but the taxation it extorts from us under threats of seizure of property, imprisonment, or in some cases already, when resisted, a violent death by gunfire.

4   Such is the nature and structure of the industrial megamachine (in Lewis Mumford's term) which is now attacking the American wilderness. That wilderness is our ancestral home, the primordial homeland of all living creatures including the human, and the present final dwelling place of such noble beings as the grizzly bear, the mountain lion, the eagle and the condor, the moose and the elk and the pronghorn antelope, the redwood tree, the yellow pine, the bristlecone pine, and yes, why not say it?—the streams, waterfalls, rivers, the very bedrock itself of our hills, canyons, deserts, mountains. For many of us, perhaps for most of us, the wilderness is more our home than the little stucco boxes, wallboard apartments, plywood trailer-houses, and cinderblock condominiums in which the majority are now confined by the poverty of an overcrowded industrial culture.

5   And if the wilderness is our true home, and if it is threatened with invasion, pillage, and destruction—as it certainly is—then we have the right to defend that home, as we would our private quarters, by whatever means are necessary. (An Englishman's home is his castle; the American's home is his favorite forest, river, fishing stream, her favorite mountain or desert canyon, his favorite swamp or woods or lake.) We have the right to resist and we have the obligation; not to defend that which we love would be dishonorable. The majority of the American people have demonstrated on every possible occasion that they support the ideal of wilderness preservation; even our politicians are forced by popular opinion to *pretend* to support the idea; as they have learned, a vote against wilderness is a vote against their own reelection. We are justified then in defending our homes—our private home and our public home—not only by common law and common morality but also by common belief. We are the majority; they—the powerful—are in the minority.

6   How best defend our homes? Well, that is a matter of the strategy, tactics, and technique which eco-defense is all about.

7   What is eco-defense? Eco-defense means fighting back. Eco-defense means sabotage. Eco-defense is risky but sporting; unauthorized but fun; illegal but ethically imperative. Next time you enter a public forest scheduled for chainsaw massacre by some timber corporation and its flunkies in the US Forest Service, carry a hammer and a few pounds of 60-penny nails in your creel, saddlebag, game bag, backpack, or picnic basket. Spike those trees; you won't hurt them; they'll be grateful for the protection; and you may save the forest. Loggers hate nails. My Aunt Emma back in West Virginia has been enjoying this pleasant

exercise for years. She swears by it. It's good for the trees, it's good for the woods, and it's good for the human soul. Spread the word.

▼ TOPICAL CONSIDERATIONS

1. Explain the reasoning behind Abbey's eco-defense plan. What are its merits? What problems might it cause? Would you be willing to try his suggestions? Why or why not?
2. Why is it important for Abbey to emphasize that the "householder" has "both the right and the obligation" to protect his family and property (paragraph 1).
3. What does Abbey mean when he says, "Representative government in the USA represents money, not people" (paragraph 3).
4. Abbey writes that eco-defense is "illegal but ethically imperative" (paragraph 6). What does he mean by this? Do you agree with the weight of importance that Abbey puts on eco-defense? Can you think of other instances where people felt morally compelled to break the law?
5. Can you offer any other suggestions for eco-defense that might be more effective than what Abbey suggests?
6. Consider the previous arguments and suggestions of Hoagland, Tyler, and McKibben. How does Abbey's suggestion for a better environment fit into the spectrum of advice from these other three men?

▼ RHETORICAL CONSIDERATIONS

1. Consider the opening line of the essay. Was it an effective "hook?" Did it capture your attention? Did it make you want to read on? Do you think you might use such a strategy to open a paper?
2. How does the introductory paragraph set the tone and argument for the rest of the essay?
3. Consider Abbey's choice of words and how they shape the reader's response. Pay particular attention to phrases such as "batters . . . threatens . . . proceeds to loot" (paragraph 1) and his references to "three-piece-suited gangsters" and "jellyfish government agencies" (paragraph 2). Abbey writes of "the taxation" that the government "extorts" from us (paragraph 3). What is the connotation of *extort?* How does this word help color the reader's view of government?
4. Paragraph 6 is the shortest in the essay. From a rhetorical point of

view, what is its function in the essay? What change in the discussion does it mark?

5. How would you describe the tone of Abbey's conclusion. How does it differ from the rest of the essay?

▼ WRITING ASSIGNMENTS

1. You serve on a college committee that is investigating the implications of eco-defense. Draft a proposal offering suggestions for preserving local forests. Be certain to invoke Abbey's argument either positively or negatively. Would you recommend that a group of students follow Abbey's agenda?
2. You are a judge who is hearing the following case. The defendant is Abbey's Aunt Emma who is charged with criminal trespass to land and assault. The plaintiff is a logger who was seriously injured when his chain saw hit a nail. Draft a clear and well-supported decision in favor of the logger or Aunt Emma.
3. Write a letter to Abbey telling him what you think of his suggestion, and plan to offer additional suggestions to his eco-defense.
4. Write an essay in which you compare and contrast the methods of Abbey and those of Bill McKibben.

12 Sports

Americans have a love affair with sports. Whether we're cheering from the stands or playing pickup ball on weekends, we crave the heat of competitive play. And, as each author here proclaims, that craving is healthy for the body and the collective psyche. In this section we explore the value of sports—what they do for us and what they mean.

We begin with an insightful overview, "Sport and the American Dream," in which Jeffrey Schrank explains how three popular American pastimes—football, baseball, and golf—ritualistically reflect all-American character and values.

In the next selection, "Attitude," humorist Garrison Keillor takes a look at the fundamental secret to being a sport: Attitude. Focusing on softball, he gives some fine tips for any man or woman, young or old, who wants to pick up a bat and feel like the pros "without getting beaned or having to run too hard."

There was a time when sports were all-male experiences. But, as we see in the next three pieces, a rush of women into athletic competition has been taking place on every level—secondary schools, college, Olympic games, professional sports, even Little League. In our second baseball essay, "Girls at Bat," Anna Quindlen celebrates liberated fields of play where girls and boys learn to handle a ball and competition equally. Women and basketball are the focus of "Playing to Win" in which Margaret A. Whitney describes how her daughter's inspiring intensity on the parquet court has overturned the forces of tradition. Although women's high school and college athletics have won growing support recently, professional female athletes have suffered one loss after another. Lack of sponsorship, fan support, and media coverage have all but killed past efforts to form professional leagues. According to Kate Rounds in "Why Men Fear Women's Teams," the problem has to do with continued sexual bias and homophobia.

In our final piece, "On the Bench," best-selling novelist Robert B. Parker takes us into a health club where men and women spend hours groaning and sweating as they pump chrome. With the characteristic wit and humor that have made his series of Spenser detective novels such a success, Mr. Parker explains why after 33 years he's still at it.

▼ SPORT AND THE AMERICAN DREAM
Jeffrey Schrank

Our opening piece serves as an overview of this chapter. In the essay, the author looks for meanings in the fields of play that lie hidden to most spectators. Focusing on three American sports—football, baseball, and golf—he explains how the players of the games are participating in ritual-istic enactments of all-American values and myths. Jeffrey Schrank has written widely on communications and popular culture. He is the author of several books, including *Snap, Crackle, and Popular Taste: The Illusion of Free Choice in America* (1977) from which this was taken.

Sport is a ritual, an acting out of a myth or series of myths. A sport that can be considered a national pastime can be expected to reflect national values and wishes. Sports that capture the national fancy are ritualistic enactments of the American Dream. Baseball is still called our national pastime but is rapidly being replaced by American football. That football should become our "national pastime" is understandable to those who can see sports as reflections of national character.

American football is passionately concerned with the gain and loss of land, of territory. The football field is measured and marked with all the care of a surveyor and the ball's progress noted to the nearest inch. Football is a precise game and its players are often trained like a military unit on a mission to gain territory for the mother country. The players are the popular heroes but the coaches and owners run the game, using the players to carry out their plans—there is comparatively little room for individual initiative. A score comes as the result of a strategic series of well-executed maneuvers and is bought on the installment plan, yard by yard.

The regulation and almost military precision of American football is a reflection of national psychology. Even the words we use to describe the game include throwing the bomb, marching downfield, game plan (which has become nearly a national phrase for any field, from selling toothpaste to covering up political scandals), guards, executions, blitz, zone, platoon, squad, drills, attack, drives, marching bands for entertainment, stars on helmets, lines that can be blasted through and even war paint. Much of the verbal similarity comes from the fact that war was originally the ultimate game played within the confines of certain rules agreed upon by both "teams."

Football, more than any other sport, is a game for spectators to watch superhuman, mythical heroes. Football is a sport that more people watch than play. The game requires too many people, too much space and is simply too dangerous for the weekend athlete. The size and speed of professional players and their uniforms make them into heroic figures capable of feats that invite admiration but not imitation. The football spectator is in awe of the armored monsters. The viewer of a golf match or even baseball or tennis dreams of going out the next day and doing likewise, but football is played only by the gods who can run the 100 yard dash in ten seconds, stand six feet three and weigh 260 pounds.

5   The demise of baseball as our national pastime reflects a change in national character. The change does not mean the disappearance of baseball, merely its relocation to a position as just another game rather than *the* game. Professor John Finlay of the University of Manitoba, writing in *Queen's Quarterlay,* compares baseball to an acting out of the robber baron stage of capitalism, whereas football more clearly reflects a more mature capitalism into which we are now moving. Hence, the rise in popularity of football and apparent decline in baseball. He notes that Japan, still in the early stages of capitalism, has taken avidly to baseball but not to football. It is not a question of Japanese physique serving as a determinant since rugby has a large Asian following. He predicts that when their capitalism moves into a higher stage, the Japanese will move on to football as have Americans.

6   Baseball is a game of a quieter age when less action was needed to hold interest, when going to the park was enjoyable (baseball is still played in ball parks while football is played in stadiums), when aggression was subservient to finesse. Baseball players did not need exposure as college players to succeed as football players do; they play a relatively calm game almost daily instead of a bruising gladiatorial contest weekly. Baseball has room for unique and colorful characters, while football stresses the more anonymous but effective team member. Baseball is a game in which any team can win at any given contest and there are no favorites; only football has real "upsets." Football's careful concern with time adds a tension to the game that is lacking in the more leisurely world of baseball.

7   Football has replaced baseball as the favorite American spectator sport largely because of television. A comparison between a telecast of a football game on one channel and a baseball game on another could reveal baseball as a game with people standing around seemingly with little to do but watch two men play catch. Football would appear as twenty-two men engaged in almost constant, frenzied action. To watch baseball requires identification with the home team; to watch football requires only a need for action or a week of few thrills and the need for a touch of vicarious excitement.

8   Baseball is a pastoral game, timeless and highly ritualized; its appeal is to nostalgia and so might enjoy periods of revitalization in comparison to football. But for now, the myth of football suits the nation better.

9   According to a 1974 Harris survey, baseball has already been statistically dethroned. In a sports survey a cross section of nearly fourteen hundred fans was asked, "Which of these sports do you follow?"

10   The decision to play or "follow" a certain sport is also the decision to live

a certain myth. The team violence of football, the craftiness of basketball, the mechanistic precision of bowling, the auto racer's devotion to machinery are all subworlds within the universe of sport.

Golf, for example, is a unique subworld, one of the few left as a sport (unlike hunting which does not involve scoring or teams) in which the game is played between man and nature. The winner of a match is one who has beaten the opponent, but the game itself is a person versus the environment. To understand the appeal of golf it is again necessary to consider the game as a ritual reenactment of an appealing myth.   **11**

Golf, perhaps more than any other sport, has to be played to be appreciated. Millions who never played football can enjoy the game on TV, but only a dedicated participant can sit through two hours of televised golf. Golf is growing in participation but still has the stigma of an upper-class game. Eighty percent of the nation's golfers must play on 20 percent of the nation's courses that are open to the public. The ratio of public to private facilities hurts public participation in the game but mirrors the inequities of society and provides a convenient status symbol for those who can afford club membership. Its TV audience is not the largest of any sport but it is the most well heeled.   **12**

Golf is a reenactment of the pioneer spirit. It is man versus a hostile environment in search of an oasis. The goal is a series of lush "greens," each protected by natural hazards such as water, sand and unmanageably long grass. The hazards are no threat to physicial life but they are to the achievement of success. Golf is a journey game with a constantly changing field. Golfers start the eighteen-hole journey, can rest at a halfway point and then resume until they return to near the point of origination.   **13**

The winner of the match is one who has fallen victim to the fewest hazards and overcome the terrain. Many golf courses have Indian names as if to remind the golfer of the frontier ethos. A local course called Indian Lakes invites golfers to use either one of two courses—the Iroquois trail or the Sioux trail.   **14**

Golf, like baseball, is a pastoral sport—with a high degree of tensions and drama but relatively little action. It is a game in which players are constantly in awe of the magic flight of the golf ball. To hit any kind of ball 100 or 200 or more yards with accuracy or to hit a small target from 150 yards is an amazing feat to be appreciated only by those who have at least tried the game. Golf is very likely the most difficult game to master, yet one in which the average player occasionally hits a shot as good as the best of any professional. It is this dream of magic results that keeps the golfer on course.   **15**

▼ TOPICAL CONSIDERATIONS

1. Why is watching a football, baseball, or golf game a ritualistic act? What myths are Americans acting out when they participate in this way?

2. How is football a reflection of the American character? In other words, what does the game of football reveal about ourselves, our life-styles, and our values as Americans?
3. What does "pastoral" mean? How are baseball and golf pastoral sports? Can you think of other sports that would fit this category? How is golf's television audience "well-heeled" (paragraph 12)?
4. Do you have a favorite sport? How does this preference reflect your personality?
5. According to Schrank, a 1974 Harris survey revealed that baseball has been "dethroned" (paragraph 9). How have we as Americans changed to cause the national pastime to shift from baseball to football?
6. What is a *robber baron?* How was the "robber baron stage of capitalism" (paragraph 5) a less mature capitalism than we have now? Why does Schrank feel that the Japanese, too, will eventually prefer football to baseball?

▼ RHETORICAL CONSIDERATIONS

1. What underlying idea links the descriptions of football, baseball, and golf together? Where in the essay is it introduced? Is this the thesis? Where else in the essay does Schrank rephrase, restate, or touch on this idea?
2. Outline the essay. Identify its major sections. Show how Schrank orders his ideas within each section. Cite the transitional words and phrases Schrank uses to move from one section to another.
3. Does Schrank use topic sentences effectively? Cite specific paragraphs to prove your answer.
4. Schrank begins four of his last five paragraphs with the word *golf.* Why does he do this? What effect does it have on the development of the essay?

▼ WRITING ASSIGNMENTS

1. What is your favorite sport? Write an essay showing how this sport is a reflection of your own personality.
2. Identify another leisure time activity that a majority of Americans like to either watch or participate in. In an essay, explain how it is a reflection of the American character.
3. Television programs and motion pictures also often portray ritualistic enactments of the American dream. Choose a television program or motion picture that does this and write about it. Show how it is "an acting out of a myth or series of myths."

▼ ATTITUDE

Garrison Keillor

Garrison Keillor did a remarkable thing in this television age. In 1974, he managed to pull two million Americans to their radio sets each Saturday night. He did that for a dozen years since creating and hosting the live variety show "Prairie Home Companion," from Minneapolis. What made Keillor's National Public Radio production so popular is just the kind of warm wit and wisdom that characterize the following article. In the essay he gives some thoughts about playing softball—particularly about attitude and how it might be the most important part of the game. This essay is taken from a collection of Keillor's pieces—most published in *The New Yorker*—*Happy to Be Here* (1982). Keillor is also the author of two best-selling novels *Lake Wobegon Days* (1985) and *Leaving Home* (1987), as well as *We Are Still Married: Stories and Letters* (1990).

Long ago I passed the point in life when major-league ballplayers begin to be younger than yourself. Now all of them are, except for a few aging trigenarians and a couple of quadros who don't get around on the fastball as well as they used to and who sit out the second games of double-headers. However, despite my age (thirty-nine), I am still active and have a lot of interests. One of them is slow-pitch softball, a game that lets me go through the motions of baseball without getting beaned or having to run too hard. I play on a pretty casual team, one that drinks beer on the bench and substitutes freely. If a player's wife or girlfriend wants to play, we give her a glove and send her out to right field, no questions asked, and if she lets a pop fly drop six feet in front of her, nobody agonizes over it.

Except me. This year. For the first time in my life, just as I am entering the dark twilight of my slow-pitch career, I find myself taking the game seriously. It isn't the bonehead play that bothers me especially—the pop fly that drops untouched, the slow roller juggled and the ball then heaved ten feet over the first baseman's head and into the next diamond, the routine singles that go through outfielder's legs for doubles and triples with gloves flung after them. No, it isn't our stone-glove fielding or pussyfoot base-running or limp-wristed hitting that gives me fits, though these have put us on the short end of some mighty ridiculous scores this summer. It's our attitude.

Bottom of the ninth, down 18-3, two outs, a man on first and a woman on third, and our third baseman strikes out. *Strikes out!* In slow-pitch, not even your grandmother strikes out, but this guy does, and after his third strike—a wild swing at a ball that bounces on the plate—he topples over in the dirt and lies flat on his back, laughing. *Laughing!*

Same game, earlier. They have the bases loaded. A weak grounder is hit toward our second baseperson. The runners are running. She picks up the ball, and she looks at them. She looks at first, at second, at home. We yell, "Throw it! Throw it!" and she throws it, underhand, at the pitcher, who has turned and run to back up the catcher. The ball rolls across the third-base line and under the bench. Three runs score. The batter, a fatso, chugs into second. The other team hoots and hollers, and what does she do? She shrugs and smiles ("Oh, silly me"); after all, it's only a game. Like the aforementioned strikeout artist, she treats her error as a joke. They have forgiven themselves instantly, which is unforgivable. It is *we* who should forgive them, who can say, "It's all right, it's only a game." They are supposed to throw up their hands and kick the dirt and hang their heads, as if this boner, even if it is their sixteenth of the afternoon— *this* is the one that really and truly breaks their hearts.

5   That attitude sweetens the game for everyone. The sinner feels sweet remorse. The fatso feels some sense of accomplishment; this is no bunch of rumdums he forced into an error but a team with some class. We, the sinner's teammates, feel momentary anger at her—dumb! dumb play!—but then, seeing her grief, we sympathize with her in our hearts (any one of us might have made that mistake or one worse), and we yell encouragement, including the shortstop, who, moments before, dropped an easy throw for a force at second. "That's all right! Come on! We got 'em!" we yell. "Shake it off! These turkeys can't hit!" This makes us all feel good, even though the turkeys now lead us by ten runs. We're getting clobbered, but we have a winning attitude.

6   Let me say this about attitude: Each player is responsible for his or her own attitude, and to a considerable degree you can *create* a good attitude by doing certain little things on the field. These are certain little things that ballplayers do in the Bigs, and we ought to be doing them in the Slows.

7   1. When going up to bat, don't step right into the batter's box as if it were an elevator. The box is your turf, your stage. Take possession of it slowly and deliberately, starting with a lot of back-bending, knee-stretching, and torso-revolving in the on-deck circle. Then, approaching the box, stop outside it and tap the dirt off your spikes with your bat. You don't have spikes, you have sneakers, of course, but the significance of the tapping is the same. Then, upon entering the box, spit on the ground. It's a way of saying, "This here is mine. This is where I get my hits."

8   2. Spit frequently. Spit at all crucial moments. Spit correctly. Spit should be *blown,* not ptuied weakly with the lips, which often results in dribble. Spitting should convey forcefulness of purpose, concentration, pride. Spit down, not in the direction of others. Spit in the glove and on the fingers, especially after making a real knucklehead play; it's a way of saying, "I dropped the ball because my glove was dry."

9   3. At the bat and in the field, pick up dirt. Rub dirt in the fingers (especially after spitting on them). Toss dirt, as if testing the wind for velocity and direction. Smooth the dirt. Be involved with dirt. If no dirt is available (e.g., in the outfield), pluck tufts of grass. Fielders should be grooming their areas constantly between plays, flicking away tiny sticks and bits of gravel.

4. Take your time. Tie your laces. Confer with your teammates about possible   **10**
situations that may arise and conceivable options in dealing with them.
Extend the game. Three errors on three consecutive plays can be humiliating
if the plays occur within the space of a couple of minutes, but if each error
is separated from the next by extensive conferences on the mound, lace-tying,
glove adjustments, and arguing close calls (if any), the effect on morale is
minimized.

5. Talk. Not just an occasional "Let's get a hit now" but continuous rhythmic   **11**
chatter, a flow of syllables: "Hey babe hey babe c'mon babe good stick now
hey babe long tater take him downtown babe . . . hey good eye good eye."

    Infield chatter is harder to maintain. Since the slow-pitch is required to   **12**
be a soft underhand lob, infielders hesitate to say, "Smoke him babe hey low
heat hey throw it on the black babe chuck it in there back him up babe no
hit no hit." Say it anyway.

6. One final rule, perhaps the most important of all: When your team is up and   **13**
has made the third out, the batter and the players who were left on base do
not come back to the bench for their gloves. *They remain on the field, and
their teammates bring their gloves out to them.* This requires some organization and discipline, but it pays off big in morale. It says, "Although we're
getting our pants knocked off, still we must conserve our energy."

    Imagine that you have bobbled two fly balls in this rout and now you have   **14**
just tried to stretch a single into a double and have been easily thrown out
sliding into second base, where the base runner ahead of you had stopped. It was
the third out and a dumb play, and your opponents smirk at you as they run
off the field. You are the goat, a lonely and tragic figure sitting in the dirt. You
curse yourself, jerking your head sharply forward. You stand up and kick the
base. How miserable! How degrading! Your utter shame, though brief, bears
silent testimony to the worthiness of your teammates, whom you have let down,
and they appreciate it. They call out to you now as they take the field, and as
the second baseman runs to his position he says, "Let's get 'em now," and tosses
you your glove. Lowering your head, you trot slowly out to right. There you do
some deep knee bends. You pick grass. You find a pebble and fling it into foul
territory. As the first batter comes to the plate, you check the sun. You get set
in your stance, poised to fly. Feet spread, hands on hips, you bend slightly at
the waist and spit the expert spit of a veteran ballplayer—a player who has
known the agony of defeat but who always bounces back, a player who has lost
a stride on the base paths but can still make the big play.

    This is *ball,* ladies and gentlemen. This is what it's all about.   **15**

▼ TOPICAL CONSIDERATIONS

1. What does Keillor believe is the wrong attitude to have toward
   playing softball? What does he believe is the right attitude? If it's
   just a game, why is attitude so important?

2. Why does Keillor encourage his teammates to tap the dirt off their spikes when they are only wearing tennis shoes without spiked soles? What other apparently unnecessary acts does he insist they perform? Why does he feel these acts are so essential to the way the game is played?

3. How could Keillor's thesis and his comments about how to approach a game of softball be related to other activities? How could it help a student pass a course? Earn a promotion on a job? Get along better with a girlfriend or boyfriend?

4. How familiar is Keillor with professional baseball practices? Is he writing from firsthand or little, if any, experience? Cite specific passages to prove your point.

5. In comparing football to baseball, Jeffery Schrank, in "Sport and the American Dream," remarks that baseball has more "finesse." If Schrank were to happen by one afternoon while Keillor and his team were playing a casual game of slow-pitch softball, do you think Keillor would be likely to invite him to play? Why or why not? While sitting on the bench with Schrank, what comments might Keillor make about baseball as a reflection of American character?

▼ RHETORICAL CONSIDERATIONS

1. Keillor introduces his thesis in installments. Where does he actually state it? Identify each of the stages that leads up to it.

2. Writers strive to use specifics to show their readers what they mean and to avoid speaking in vague generalities. Is Keillor successful in this? Cite specific passages that prove your point.

3. Keillor refers to the "Bigs" and the "Slows" (paragraph 6). He describes a member of the opposite team as a "fatso" and his team as "no bunch of rumdums" (paragraph 5). Given these examples, how would you characterize the diction of this essay? Can you cite other examples?

4. Keillor often uses verbs that create a vivid word picture. In paragraph 4 he states: "The batter, a fatso, chugs into second." What image does "chugs" convey? What other interesting verbs does Keillor use?

5. Reread Keillor's list of things to do to create a proper attitude toward playing softball. What kind of sentence does he use here? What effect does it have on the reading of the essay?

6. What does Keillor's last sentence remind you of? Why is this a good concluding line?

▼ WRITING ASSIGNMENTS

1. Write an essay in which you explain your own views on the proper attitude to take toward some other sport. Draw on ideas from Keillor's essay that you agree with. Select incidents and examples that illustrate the points you want to make.
2. Attitude is important for professional athletes, musicians, singers, actors, and other performers. Write an essay about the effect the right attitude has on a nonathletic activity such as playing a musical instrument, singing, or writing.

▼ GIRLS AT BAT

Anna Quindlen

In Chapter 4, Anna Quindlen's essay "Feminist" celebrated some of the progress made by women in the last 20 years of the feminist movement. Implied but not directly cited is how far females have come in sports. That is the subject of this essay—in particular, the "girls of summer." Although she had no option to play Little League as a girl, she is delighted that more girls today are at bat and more women are playing professionally. But, will they ever cry, "Mighty Stacie has struck out"? This essay first appeared in Quindlen's "Life in the 30's" column of *The New York Times* on June 2, 1988. Quindlen is the author of the novel *Object Lesson* (1990) and the collection of essays, *Living Out Loud* (1988). She is also married and the mother of two sons and a daughter.

I can't tell you what a kick I get out of Little League these days. It's not that I'm a mother now, and can place my own stifled competitive spirit in the little mitts of my sons. They are too young for baseball, and who knows if they will have much interest when they grow older? It's not even that Little League seems to have improved greatly since my brothers played: back then, most coaches seemed to feel that the point of the exercise was to humiliate children and ram their shortcomings down their throats.

One of my brothers told me the other day that his oldest boy is playing this year, and that he was amazed and cheered by the emphasis on sportsmanship, on having a good time, on doing the best you can and giving everyone a turn. He said that during the games the children keep asking for the score, and the coach keeps telling them the score is not that important. In contrast, when my brother was in Little League, the score could be stated in three words: Win or die.

• • •

3   That's all great, but what I like about Little League today is simpler: those sweet moments when the batter makes a clean hit, and the shortstop fields it nicely, and he runs as fast as he can to second base but she tags him out, just in the nick of time. Or when the pitcher has to stop and readjust her hat to keep her bangs out of her eyes. Or when the left fielder catches a high pop fly and the batter mutters, "Stupid girl."

4   If I ever have a daughter, she will be able to play baseball. If my sons play baseball, they will play with girls as a matter of course. We're not talking about the Supreme Court here, or the White House, but, my goodness, for a former girl like me, what a difference a couple of decades makes.

5   When we were the girls of summer, our lives were different. Making plaques of plaster with our handprints in them to take home from day camp. Weaving endless chains out of elaborately folded chewing-gum wrappers (I cannot, for the life of me now, remember the folding formula, or the point). Playing Baby in the Air and Monkey in the Middle in the street. Some nights the boys were there, and some nights they were at Little League practice, or even at actual games, proud as punch in their Central Plumbing or Downtown Hardware shirts and hats.

6   Strangely, I don't remember resenting it, unlike some women who are professional athletes now and who say they were galvanized by being excluded. Probably, secretly, I saw it as a blessing. I have the eye-hand coordination of a department-store dummy; I may be the only person who contrived to go to college in the 1970's and to never throw a Frisbee. When I compare notes with my husband, who was an indifferent athlete as a boy, I think his memories of not doing well are much more painful than my memories of not doing at all.

7   And I did play sports as a girl. I had no choice. But they were second-rate sports, it seemed to me; ephemeral sports; sports that were as important then in the real world as Baby in the Air was. Field hockey. Volleyball. Softball. Basketball was the exception and, not coincidentally, the sport I liked best, with its occasional suggestion of aggression and hostile body contact. But even that was girl's basketball. One summer I spent all my time playing on a park court with a group of tolerant boys—one or two thought the way to a girl's heart was to let her shoot from the outside—and I had to relearn all the rules. My teammates were stunned at the mishmash I had acquired from the women who coached me in gym. Still, I wasn't a half-bad guard.

8   But the boys played sports that were important: sports that people would show up to watch in the high school gym; sports that they would go on to play in college and, if they were terribly gifted, for large sums of money in professional athletics, which at some level passed for real life. The girls, of course, were cheerleaders, which required some athletic skill then and a good deal now, but which is really nothing more than a metaphor for traditional relationships between men and women, complete with short skirts and artificial smiles.

• • •

Perhaps my aspirations would have been different if I had grown up playing **9**
Little League, although I suspect not. I never think that if my life had not been
blighted by lack of opportunity, a public-address system in the Bronx would be
quavering, "Now playing third base for the New York Yankees . . ." with my
husband and my father cheering in the spousal seats. Lots of other women
managed to thrive despite the segregation: the tough-as-nails women who play
volleyball in the Olympic Games, the ones who have tried and failed and tried
again to make women's basketball as popular as men's, and the girls who have
insisted on going out for the high school football team.

It's nice that girls in Little League have become commonplace now, so that **10**
many people don't think much about it. Except for me. I think about it a lot,
fondly. I like to see the little girls go off, in their high socks and their hats and
their Central Hardware shirts, doing something that I was not allowed to do.
Who knows what they might grow up to be? Who knows what they might feel
capable of doing? Who knows whether one of them might, incredibly, be publicly maligned by George Steinbrenner in the decades to come?

▼ TOPICAL CONSIDERATIONS

1. According to Anna Quindlen, how do sports for children in the past
   contrast with sports for children today? From your own experience
   and observations, does her assessment ring true? Explain your answer.

2. Quindlen says that she does not remember resenting the fact that in
   her youth only boys played Little League. What reasons does she
   offer? By contrast, how did exclusion affect some of today's female
   professional athletes?

3. If you are a woman, did you experience exclusion from athletics as
   a girl? Or, do you know women who were excluded because of
   gender? If so, what were the effects? Do you know any women,
   yourself included, who play college or professional sports? How did
   their participation in, or exclusion from, athletics as girls affect their
   competition as adults?

4. If you are a male, did you play sports as a boy? If so, were there girls
   on the teams? Do you recall whether or not they participated
   equally or whether or not they were treated differently from boys?
   Explain.

5. Quindlen says that her husband's memories of not doing well are
   more painful than her memories of not playing sports at all. Do you
   think this is an accurate assessment of males and females today? Or,
   have times so changed since Quindlen's days?

6. Quindlen speaks of playing "second-rate sports" as a girl (paragraph 7). From you observation, are girl's sports today still "sec-

ond-rate," "ephemeral," and ultimately unimportant? If so, what
do you perceive are the problems? If not, what changes have been
made, and why? What about on the collegiate level? Do women's
athletics draw the same attention and support as do men's? What
differences, if any, can you explain?

7. In paragraph 8, Quindlen says that girls cheerleading "is really
nothing more than a metaphor for traditional relationships between men and women." What does she mean by this statement?
Do you agree with her? If so, why? If not, why not?

8. Did you ever play Little League? If so, do you recall active participation by girls? Were they treated the same as boys on the team?
Were they excluded or treated differently by coaches and/or teammates?

9. Do you think that people's aspirations have anything to do with
whether or not they played organized sports as kids? Do you think
this is true for both males and females? Can you think of any
individuals you know who bear out your observations?

▼ RHETORICAL CONSIDERATIONS

1. At what point in the essay do you know Quindlen's focus? How
does she cue her purpose?

2. Comment on the choice of pronouns in paragraph 3. What strategy
is Quindlen using? Had the gender of the pronouns been switched,
how would Quindlen's point have been altered?

3. What part of the essay did you find most interesting? Where was it
less interesting? What are the differences between the two?

4. How would you characterize the style and tone of the writing here?
(Consider, among other things, Quindlen's word choice, syntax,
specific observations and evaluations.) What kind of a personality
does the author project? Does she sound like somebody you would
like to know? Explain your answer.

5. What do you remember best about the actual writing of this essay?
Explain your answer.

6. Consider the concluding paragraph. Was this ending satisfying for
you? Did it capture the tone, slant, and emphasis of the essay?
Explain your answer.

▼ WRITING ASSIGNMENTS

1. Throughout the essay, Quindlen reflects on her own experience, or
lack of it, in sports. Try some reflection of your own. In a paper try
to recall your own experiences and/or observations of organized

sports from your youth. If you played, how would you assess your performance? What differences do you recall in the participation, performance and encouragement of boys versus girls? What differences, if any, in sportsmanship? Did your participation, or lack of it, have any effect on your aspirations and/or competitiveness today? Cite some specific recollections to support yourself.

2. If you attend a coed school, try to evaluate the differences between the men's and women's athletics in terms of sportsmanship and performance, as well as general support by the administration and student body. Try to explain any differences you see. Do you find any discrimination that you would cite as sexist? Explain.

3. Write a paper in which you explore whether or not women's baseball—collegiate or professional—will eventually enjoy the same sponsorship, exposure, fan support, and training as does men's.

▼ PLAYING TO WIN
Margaret A. Whitney

As Anna Quindlen points out in the previous piece, females are more active in athletics today than ever before. Girls on the Little League diamonds are a common sight. In high school and college, women's sports have experienced burgeoning growth. And across America millions of women swim, run, play golf, volleyball and do aerobics. But as women move onto playing fields traditionally ruled by men, questions of femininity, sexuality, power, and freedom arise. The following essay is an assessment of a young woman who as a high-school basketball player overcame family and the forces of tradition to sit still and be pretty. The essay was written by her mother who finds in the message of sports inspiration for her own midlife quest. Margaret A. Whitney is a writer and a doctoral candidate in technical communications at Rensselaer Polytechnic Institute. This article was first published in *The New York Times Magazine* in July 1988.

My daughter is an athlete. Nowadays, this statement won't strike many parents as unusual, but it does me. Until her freshman year in high school, Ann was only marginally interested in sport of any kind. When she played, she didn't swing hard, often dropped the ball, and had an annoying habit of tittering on field or court.

Indifference combined with another factor that did not bode well for a sports career. Ann was growing up to be beautiful. By the eighth grade, nature and orthodontics had produced a 5-foot-8-inch, 125-pound, brown-eyed beauty with a wonderful smile. People told her, too. And, as many young women know, it is considered a satisfactory accomplishment to be pretty and stay pretty. Then you can simply sit still and enjoy the unconditional positive regard. Ann loved the attention too, and didn't consider it demeaning when she was awarded "Best Hair," female category, in the eighth-grade yearbook.

3 So it came as a surprise when she became a jock. The first indication that athletic indifference had ended came when she joined the high-school cross-country team. She signed up in early September and ran third for the team within three days. Not only that. After one of those 3.1-mile races up hill and down dale on a rainy November afternoon, Ann came home muddy and be-draggled. Her hair was plastered to her head, and the mascara she had applied so carefully that morning ran in dark circles under her eyes. This is it, I thought. Wait until Lady Astor sees herself. But the kid with the best eighth-grade hair went on to finish the season and subsequently letter in cross-country, soccer, basketball and softball.

4 I love sports, she tells anyone who will listen. So do I, though my midlife quest for a doctorate leaves me little time for either playing or watching. My love of sports is bound up with the goals in my life and my hopes for my three daughters. I have begun to hear the message of sports. It is very different from many messages that women receive about living, and I think it is good.

5 My husband, for example, talked to Ann differently when he realized that she was a serious competitor and not just someone who wanted to get in shape so she'd look good in a prom dress. Be aggressive, he'd advise. Go for the ball. Be intense.

6 Be intense. She came in for some of the most scathing criticism from her dad, when, during basketball season, her intensity waned. You're pretending to play hard, he said. You like it on the bench? Do you like to watch while your teammates play?

7 I would think, how is this kid reacting to such advice? For years, she'd been told at home, at school, by countless advertisements, "Be quiet, Be good, Be still." When teachers reported that Ann was too talkative, not obedient enough, too flighty. When I dressed her up in frilly dresses and admonished her not to get dirty. When ideals of femininity are still, quiet, cool females in ads whose vacantness passes for sophistication. How can any adolescent girl know what she's up against? Have you ever really noticed intensity? It is neither quiet nor good. And it's definitely not pretty.

8 In the end, her intensity revived. At half time, she'd look for her father, and he would come out of the bleachers to discuss tough defense, finding the open player, squaring up on her jump shot. I'd watch them at the edge of the court, a tall man and a tall girl, talking about how to play.

9 Of course I'm particularly sensitive at this point in my life to messages about trying hard, being active, getting better through individual and team effort. Ann, you could barely handle a basketball two years ago. Now you're bringing the ball up against the press. Two defenders are after you. You must

dribble, stop, pass. We're depending on you. We need you to help us. I wonder if my own paroxysms of uncertainty would be eased had more people urged me—be active, go for it!

Not that dangers don't lurk for the females of her generation. I occasionally run this horror show in my own mental movie theater: an unctuous but handsome lawyer-like drone of a young man spies my Ann. Hmmm, he says unconsciously to himself, good gene pool, and wouldn't she go well with my BMW and the condo? Then I see Ann with a great new hairdo kissing the drone goodbyehoney and setting off to the nearest mall with splendid-looking children to spend money. **10**

But the other night she came home from softball tryouts at 6 in the evening. The dark circles under her eyes were from exhaustion, not makeup. I tried too hard today, she says. I feel like I'm going to puke. **11**

After she has revived, she explains. She wants to play a particular position. There is competition for it. I can't let anybody else get my spot, she says, I've got to prove that I can do it. Later we find out that she has not gotten the much-wanted third-base position, but she will start with the varsity team. My husband talks about the machinations of coaches and tells her to keep trying. You're doing fine, he says. She gets that I-am-going-to-keep-trying look on her face. The horror-show vision of Ann-as-Stepford-Wife fades. **12**

Of course, Ann doesn't realize the changes she has wrought, the power of her self-definition. I'm an athlete, Ma, she tells me when I suggest participation in the school play or the yearbook. But she has really caused us all to rethink our views of existence: her younger sisters who consider sports a natural activity for females, her father whose advocacy of women has increased, and me. Because when I doubt my own abilities, I say to myself, Get intense, Margaret. Do you like to sit on the bench? **13**

And my intensity revives. **14**

I am not suggesting that participation in sports is the answer for all young women. It is not easy—the losing, jealousy, raw competition and intense personal criticism of performance. **15**

And I don't wish to imply that the sports scene is a morality play either. Girls' sports can be funny. You can't forget that out on that field are a bunch of people who know the meaning of the word cute. During one game, I noticed that Ann had a blue ribbon tied on her ponytail, and it dawned on me that every girl on the team had an identical bow. Somehow I can't picture the Celtics gathered in the locker room of the Boston Garden agreeing to wear the same color sweatbands. **16**

No, what has struck me, amazed me and made me hold my breath in wonder and in hope is both the ideal of sport and the reality of a young girl not afraid to do her best. **17**

I watch her bringing the ball up the court. We yell encouragement from the stands, though I know she doesn't hear us. Her face is red with exertion, and her body is concentrated on the task. She dribbles, draws the defense to her, passes, **18** runs. A teammate passes the ball back to her. They've beaten the press. She heads toward the hoop. Her father watches her, her sisters watch her, I watch her. And I think, drive, Ann, drive.

▼ TOPICAL CONSIDERATIONS

1. How did Ann Whitney's beauty at first work against her sports career in high school?
2. Why did it come as a surprise to the author that her daughter became a jock?
3. What does the author mean by the statement, "I have begun to hear the message of sports" (paragraph 4). What is the "message of sports"? Do you agree the message "is good"?
4. What social forces were at work against Ann becoming a serious athlete? Do you see these forces working still? Have you ever had to confront such forces?
5. In paragraph 7, Whitney says that advertisements promote "quiet and cool" images of females "whose vacantness passes for sophistication." Do you find this observation to be generally true? Find some ads in magazines to support your answer. Can you find many ads in which such traditional female "ideals" are not projected—ads of active, competitive women?
6. The author says that she wishes when she was young she had been encouraged to be more active, to "go for it!" (paragraph 9). Why does she say this?
7. What "dangers" to her daughter's athletic career does Whitney fear? How does Ann allay her mother's fears?
8. This essay is more than just a celebration of the author's daughter. In your own words, what higher matters are celebrated?

▼ RHETORICAL CONSIDERATIONS

1. How do the opening two lines forecast the central conflicts of the essay?
2. In paragraph 4, the author relates her daughter's athletic drive to her own "midlife quest" for a doctorate. How well does the author weave this issue into her essay? Does it ever take away from the story of her daughter? Does it add to it?
3. What is the rhetorical purpose and effect of the sudden switch to a direct address of Ann in the present tense in paragraph 9? Where else does this switch in perspective appear?
4. Explain the "Lady Astor" allusion in paragraph 3. Explain the "Ann-as-Stepford-Wife" allusion in paragraph 12.

▼ WRITING ASSIGNMENTS

1. The author makes the point that female beauty works against female drive. Do you find this to be true? Do you think that women who are attractive are encouraged to be passive? Write an essay in which you explore this question. In it, address the same forces of school, family, and advertising.
2. Do you think females in sports receive the same quality of training as do males? Do they receive the same kind of encouragement? Write an essay examining any differences you have observed.
3. Do you see any difference in the athletic training females of your generation received and that of your parents? Talk to your parents about this, or someone from an older generation. Write an essay in which you compare the training of today's women with that of women from the past. Include personal experiences to illustrate the differences.
4. Write your own essay about "playing to win." Speak from either your own experience as an athlete or from the observation of athletes—male or female—you know or admire. Try to capture a sense of the drive and determination to excel in your essay.

▼ WHY MEN FEAR WOMEN'S TEAMS

Kate Rounds

A woman cannot be an athlete without raising questions of femininity, sexuality, power—and just how good she is compared to men. In the following essay, Kate Rounds examines the unfortunate state of professional women's athletics in America. The only kinds of female sporting events that get television coverage are bizarre spectacles such as jousting and beach volleyball, each played by women in scant attire. She argues that the lack of support for women's sports goes beyond economics to sexual bias and homophobia. Kate Rounds, a freelance writer, is a black belt in judo. This article first appeared in the January/February 1991 issue of *Ms.* magazine.

1   Picture this. You're flipping through the channels one night, and you land on a local network, let's say ABC. And there on the screen is a basketball game. The players are sinking three-pointers, slam-dunking, and doing the usual things basketball players do. They're high-fiving each other, patting one another on the butt, and then sauntering to the locker room to talk about long-term contracts.

2   Now imagine that the players aren't men. They're women, big sweaty ones, wearing uniforms and doing their version of what guys thrive on—bonding. So far, this scene is a fantasy and will remain so until women's professional team sports get corporate sponsors, television exposure, arenas, fan support, and a critical mass of well-trained players.

3   While not enough fans are willing to watch women play traditional team sports, they love to watch women slugging it out on roller-derby rinks and in mud-wrestling arenas. Currently popular is a bizarre television spectacle called *American Gladiators,* in which women stand on pastel pedestals, wearing Lycra tights and brandishing weapons that look like huge Q-Tips. The attraction obviously has something to do with the "uniforms."

4   The importance of what women athletes wear can't be underestimated. Beach volleyball, which is played in the sand by bikini-clad women, rates network coverage while traditional court volleyball can't marshal any of the forces that would make a women's pro league succeed.

5   It took a while, but women were able to break through sexist barriers in golf and tennis. Part of their success stemmed from the sports themselves—high-end individual sports that were born in the British Isles and flourished in country clubs across the U.S. The women wore skirts, makeup, and jewelry along with their wristbands and warm-up jackets. The corporate sponsors were hackers themselves, and the fan—even men—could identify with these women: a guy

thought that if he hit the ball enough times against the barn door, he too could play like Martina. And women's purses were equaling men's. In fact, number-one-ranked Steffi Graf's prize money for 1989 was $1,963,905 and number-one-ranked Stefan Edberg's was $1,661,491.

By contrast, women's professional team sports have failed spectacularly. Since the mid-seventies, every professional league—softball, basketball, and volleyball—has gone belly-up. In 1981, after a four-year struggle, the Women's Basketball League (WBL), backed by sports promoter Bill Byrne, folded. The league was drawing fans in a number of cities, but the sponsors weren't there, TV wasn't there, and nobody seemed to miss the spectacle of a few good women fighting for a basketball.   6

Or a volleyball, for that matter. Despite the success of bikini volleyball, an organization called MLV (Major League Volleyball) bit the dust in March of 1989 after nearly three years of struggling for sponsorship, fan support, and television exposure. As with pro basketball, there was a man behind women's professional volleyball, real estate investor Robert (Bat) Batinovich. Batinovich admits that, unlike court volleyball, beach volleyball has a lot of "visual T&A mixed into it."   7

What court volleyball does have, according to former MLV executive director Lindy Vivas, is strong women athletes. Vivas is assistant volleyball coach at San Jose State University. "The United States in general," she says, "has problems dealing with women athletes and strong, aggressive females. The perception is you have to be more aggressive in team sports than in golf and tennis, which aren't contact sports. Women athletes are looked at as masculine and get the stigma of being gay."   8

One former women's basketball promoter, who insists on remaining anonymous, goes further. "You know what killed women's sports?" he says. "Lesbians. This cost us in women's basketball. But I know there are not as many lesbians now unless I'm really blinded. We discourage it, you know. We put it under wraps."   9

People in women's sports spend a lot of time dancing around the "L" word, and the word "image" pops up in a way it never does in men's sports. Men can spit tobacco juice, smoke, and even scratch their testicles on national television and get away with it.   10

Bill Byrne, former WBL promoter, knows there isn't a whole lot women can get away with while they're beating each other out for a basketball. "In the old league," he says, "my partner, Mike Connors, from *Mannix*—his wife said, 'Let's do makeup on these kids.' And I knew that the uniforms could be more attractive. We could tailor them so the women don't look like they're dragging a pair of boxer shorts down the floor."   11

The response from the athletes to this boy talk is not always outrage. "Girls in women's basketball now are so pretty," says Nancy Lieberman-Cline. "They're image-conscious." The former Old Dominion star, who made headlines as Martina's trainer, played with the men's U.S. Basketball League, the Harlem Globe Trotters Tour (where she met husband Tim Cline), and with the   12

Dallas Diamonds of the old WBL. "Everyone used to have short hair," she says. "Winning and playing was everything. I wouldn't think of using a curling iron. Now there are beautiful girls out there playing basketball."

13 Lieberman-Cline says she doesn't mind making the concession. "It's all part of the process," she says. "You can't be defensive about everything."

14 Bill Byrne is so certain that women's professional basketball can work that he's organized a new league, the Women's Pro Basketball League, Inc. (WPBL), set to open its first season shortly. Byrne talks fast and tough, and thinks things have changed for the better since 1981 when the old league went under. "Exposure is the bottom word," he says. "If you get plenty of TV exposure, you'll create household names, and you'll fill arenas. It takes the tube. But I'll get the tube this time because the game of TV has changed. You have cable now. You have to televise home games to show people a product."

15 There's no doubt that many athletes in the women's sports establishment are leery of fast-talking guys who try to make a buck off women's pro sports, especially when the women themselves don't profit from those ventures. In the old league, finances were so shaky that some players claim they were never paid.

16 "We weren't getting the gate receipts," says Lieberman-Cline. "They'd expect 2,000, get only 400, and then they'd have to decide to pay the arena or pay the girls, and the girls were the last choice. There was a lot of mismanagement in the WBL, though the intent was good." She also has her doubts about the new league: "There are not enough things in place to make it happen, not enough owners, arenas, TV coverage, or players. It's going to take more than optimism to make it work."

17 Given the track record of women's professional team sports in this country, it's not surprising that the national pastime is faring no better. When Little League was opened to girls by court order in 1974, one might have thought that professional women's baseball could not be far behind. Baseball is a natural for women. It's not a contact sport, it doesn't require excessive size or strength— even little guys like Phil Rizzuto and Jose Lind can play it—and it's actually an individual sport masquerading as a team sport. Still, in recent years, no one's taken a serious stab at organizing a women's professional league.

18 In 1984, there was an attempt to field a women's minor-league team. Though the Sun Sox had the support of baseball great Hank Aaron, it was denied admission to the Class A Florida State League. The team was the brainchild of a former Atlanta Braves vice president of marketing, Bob Hope. "A lot of the general managers and owners of big-league clubs were mortified," Hope says, "and some players said they wouldn't compete against women. It was male ego or something."

19 Or something, says softball hall-of-famer Donna Lopiano. "When girls suffer harassment in Little League, that's not exactly opening up opportunities for women," she says. "Girls don't have the access to coaching and weight training that boys have. Sports is a place where physiological advantages give men power, and they're afraid of losing it. Sports is the last great bastion of male chauvinism. In the last eight years, we've gone backward, not only on gender equity but on civil rights."

Women of color still face barriers that European American women don't, **20** particularly in the areas of coaching and refereeing. But being a woman athlete is sometimes a bond that transcends race. "We're all at a handicap," says Ruth Lawanson, an African American who played volleyball with MLV. "It doesn't matter whether you're Asian, Mexican, black or white."

Historically, baseball and softball diamonds have not been very hospitable **21** to black men and any women. Despite the fact that even men's softball is not a crowd pleaser, back in 1976, Billie Jean King and golfer Jane Blalock teamed up with ace amateur softball pitcher Joan Joyce to form the International Women's Professional Softball Association (IWPSA). Five years later, without sponsorship, money, or television, the league was history.

Billie Jean King has her own special attachment to the team concept. As a **22** girl, she wanted to be a baseball player, but her father gave her a tennis racket, knowing that there wasn't much of a future for a girl in baseball. The story is especially touching since Billie Jean's brother, Randy Moffitt, went on to become a pitcher with the San Francisco Giants. But even as a tennis player, Billie Jean clung to the team idea. She was the force behind World TeamTennis, which folded in 1978, and is currently the chief executive officer of TeamTennis, now entering its eleventh season with corporate sponsorship.

On the face of it, TeamTennis is a bizarre notion because it takes what is **23** a bred-in-the-bones individual sport and tries to squeeze it into a team concept. It has the further handicap of not really being necessary when strong women's and men's professional tours are already in place.

In the TeamTennis format, all players play doubles as well as singles. Billie **24** Jean loves doubles, she says, because she enjoys "sharing the victory." What also distinguishes TeamTennis from the women's and men's pro tours is fan interaction. Fans are encouraged to behave as if watching a baseball or basketball game rather than constantly being told to shut up and sit down as they are at pro tour events like the U.S. Open. The sense of team spirit among the players—the fact that they get to root for one another—is also attracting some big names. Both Martina Navratilova and Jimmy Connors have signed on to play TeamTennis during its tiny five-week season, which begins after Wimbledon and ends just before the U.S. Open.

But you have to go back almost 50 years to find a women's professional **25** sports team that was somewhat successful—though the conditions for that success were rather unusual. During World War II, when half the population was otherwise engaged, women were making their mark in the formerly male strongholds of welding, riveting—and baseball. The All-American Girls Professional Baseball League (AAGPBL) fielded such teams as the Lassies, the Belles, and the Chicks on the assumption that it was better to have "girls" playing than to let the national pastime languish. The league lasted a whopping 12 years after its inception in 1943.

The success of this sandlot venture, plagued as it was by the simple-hearted **26** sexism of the forties (the women went to charm school at night), must raise nagging doubts in the mind of the woman team player of the nineties. Can she triumph only in the absence of men?

27   It may be true that she can triumph only in the absence of competition from the fiercely popular men's pro leagues, which gobble up sponsorship, U.S. network television, and the hearts and minds of male fanatics. The lack of male competition outside the United States may be partly responsible for the success of women's professional team sports in Europe, Japan, South America, and Australasia. Lieberman-Cline acknowledges that Europe provides a more hospitable climate for women's pro basketball. "Over there, they don't have as many options," she says. "We have Broadway plays, movies, you name it. We're overindulged with options."

28   Bruce Levy is a 230-pound bespectacled accountant who escaped from the Arthur Andersen accounting firm 11 years ago to market women's basketball. "It's pretty simple," he says. "People overseas are more realistic and enlightened. Women's basketball is not viewed as a weak version of men's. If Americans could appreciate a less powerful, more scientific, team-oriented game, we'd be two thirds of the way toward having a league succeed."

29   Levy, who represents many women playing pro basketball abroad, says 120 U.S. women are playing overseas and making up to $70,000 in a seven-month season. They include star players like Teresa Edwards, Katrina McClain, and Lynette Woodward. "A player like Teresa Weatherspoon, everybody recognizes her in Italy," he says. "No one in the U.S. knows her. If there were a pro league over here, I wouldn't be spending all day on the phone speaking bad Italian and making sure the women's beds are long enough. I'd just be negotiating contracts."

30   Levy claims that U.S. businesswomen aren't supporting women's team sports. "In Europe," he says, "the best-run and most publicized teams are run by women who own small businesses and put their money where their mouth is." Joy Burns, president of Sportswomen of Colorado, Inc., pleads no contest. "Businesswomen here are too conservative and don't stick their necks out," she says. MLV's Bat Batinovich, who says he's "disappointed" in U.S. businesswomen for not supporting women's team sports, figures an investor in MLV should have been willing to lose $200,000 a year for five years. Would Burns have done it? "If I'm making good financial investments, why should I?"

31   The prospects for women's professional team sports don't look bright. The reasons for the lack of financial support go beyond simple economics and enter the realm of deep-rooted sexual bias and homophobia. San Jose State's Lindy Vivas says men who feel intimidated by physically strong women have to put the women down. "There's always a guy in the crowd who challenges the women when he wouldn't think of going one-on-one with Magic Johnson or challenging Nolan Ryan to a pitching contest."

32   Softball's Donna Lopiano calls it little-boy stuff: "Men don't want to have a collegial, even-steven relationship with women. It's like dealing with cavemen."

▼ TOPICAL CONSIDERATIONS

1. Summarize Kate Round's complaint about the kinds of female sporting events that rate television coverage. Have you ever seen

these events? If so, do you agree with Round's argument? If not, why not?

2. What reasons does Rounds offer for the failure of women's professional team sports? What, according to the author, are promoters doing to turn things around for women's pro basketball, for instance? Do you think this is a step in the right direction? Why or why not?

3. In paragraph 10, the author argues, "Men can spit tobacco juice, smoke, and even scratch their testicles on national television and get away with it," but the image of "strong, aggressive females" works against women. What point is Rounds making here? Do you agree with her?

4. Why, according to Rounds, is baseball a "a natural for women" (paragraph 17)? Why even after the opening up of Little League to females in 1974 has women's professional baseball not gained official recognition?

5. How does Rounds explain the fact that women's professional team sports are more successful outside the United States than inside? Do you agree with the explanations offered?

6. Have you ever watched women's baseball or softball games? If so, did you get as caught up in the events as at men's games? Did the women show the same degree of competence, competitiveness and sporting behavior? Were they more impressive than you had expected? Explain your answer.

7. Has this essay made you more aware of the inequitable treatment professional sportswomen have suffered? Do you think that the general public is aware of all the efforts to establish women's professional sports leagues? If more people knew, do you think those efforts would be more successful? Or is society just too sexually biased to grant women's professional athletics official recognition and support? Explain your answer.

▼ RHETORICAL CONSIDERATIONS

1. Consider the effectiveness of the opening paragraph. How well did it capture your attention? What were the strategies behind the following: the two-word opening sentence; the direct address of the reader ("You're" and "you"); the use of sports jargon; the particular descriptions of the players? How well did the paragraph set up the discussion to follow?

2. Where exactly does the author make clear her intention in the essay?

3. Rounds claims in paragraph 6 that "women's professional team sports have failed spectacularly." How well does Rounds support her claim? What does she offer by way of examples, explanations,

testimony (statements of authorities), statistics, and so on? Did you find her support satisfying and convincing? Would you have wanted more?

4. Rounds claims that the lack of support for women's sports can be rooted, in part, to homophobia. Do you feel that this is an opinion Rounds is passing off as fact, or do you think she substantiates her claim well?

5. What part of this essay did you find most interesting? Where was it least interesting? What do you make of the differences between the two?

▼ WRITING ASSIGNMENTS

1. Has this essay sensitized you to the inequities women athletes experience in America? If so, do you think you will regard women in sports in a different light? If yes, write a paper explaining how you have been affected by the arguments Rounds presents here, and how your thinking has been changed.

2. If this piece has not changed your attitudes about the inequities women athlete's experience, write a paper just why and where Rounds' essay failed to convince you.

3. In paragraph 26, Rounds wonders, "Can she [the woman team player of the nineties] triumph only in the absence of men?" What do you think—can women's professional sports in America ever enjoy proper success given the fierce conmpetition from men's pro leagues? Write a paper exploring your thoughts on this question?

4. After having read this essay, are you convinced that men fear women's teams? Or, do you think there are other reasons women's team sports have met with such lack of fan support and sponsorship? Write an essay in which you explore your own thoughts in conjunction with those presented in this essay.

▼ ON THE BENCH

Robert B. Parker

There was a time when men who pumped iron were regarded as densely wadded muscle-freaks whose manhood was questionable. Over the last dozen years, however, weightlifting—and body building—not only has become popular, it is positively *au courant*. In nearly every city and suburb across America, you can find big, flossy health clubs full of physical-fitness-minded men and women on the benches of fancy weight machines pumping chrome. What follows is a humorous and insightful confession of a man who has been on the bench before it was fashionable. In his characteristic style, Robert B. Parker tells how he got interested in weightlifting, why he continued for over thirty years, and what it has done for his body and psyche. Since 1974, when he wrote his *Sports Illustrated Training with Weights* (with John R. Marsh), Parker has written nineteen novels about a tough, wisecracking private eye named Spenser—the most notable of which include the best-selling novels *Early Autumn* (1981), *Ceremony* (1982), and *Playmates* (1989). (Like Parker, Spenser is occasionally on the bench.) Parker is also the author of several non-Spenser books including *Wilderness* (1979) and *Love and Glory* (1983). His latest Spenser novel is *Double Deuce* (1992). "Spenser for Hire" was an American Broadcasting Corporation television series based on Parker's novels. This article first appeared in *Sportscape* in 1981, and the author has updated it for this edition.

When I came home from Korea in the early 1950s I weighed 148 pounds. While 1 I was cat-quick and a trained killer, I did have to hold onto my wife's arm in a strong wind, and the only reason people couldn't kick sand on me was that I stood sideways and they missed. Judicious management of food and drink helped me get up to 160 by the time my first son was born. But neither Pabst Blue Ribbon nor meatloaf sandwiches has much positive effect on biceps or pectoral muscle, and I remember thinking in the first rush of parenthood, a boy needs a strong father. So, at age 26 I got my first set of weights.

It was a big step, because when I was a boy, weightlifting was not fashion- 2 able. Only muscle-bound freaks lifted weights, and, while one would hesitate to actually tell a weightlifter that he was a muscle-bound freak, one knew it to be true. His manhood was open to speculation as well.

When I got my first set of weights I had my wife buy them for me. I hid in 3 the bedroom when they were delivered and she signed for them. After the delivery man left, I scurried out and assembled the weights and began to do the exercises described in the accompanying pamphlet. That was 33 years ago and I am still shoving away at the irons. The results have been mixed, but now when it's windy Joan holds onto *my* arm.

4   My first set of weights allowed me to lift a maximum of 110 pounds, if I put all the weights on the bar. I especially wanted to do bench presses. So I made a bench out of two-by-fours and plywood and added a rack for the barbell. I put the bar on the rack, put all the weights on the bar, lay on the bench on my back, feet on the ground, hands comfortably apart, grasped the bar firmly near each end, tested the balance, hoisted it off the bar and lowered it to my chest: step one of the bench press. Step two is to press the barbell back up to arm's length. Ah, there's the rub. The bar, resting with nice balance on my chest, would not move. After a manful struggle I faced the hopelessness of my situation and called for Joan. She arrived, helped me tip the barbell off my chest, smiled her Mona Lisa smile, and went away without comment.

5   I tried again with less weight until I could do one bench press, then several, then ten, and then three sets of ten. The muscles in my chest and arms got stronger. I added a little more weight and started the same routine again.

6   When I got too powerful for my 110-pound barbells, I graduated to the big York barbells at the local Y. York barbells are the kind they use in the Olympics. The poundage plates slide onto a 45-pound bar easily and needn't be locked in place. The 100-pound weight plates for a York set look like spare wheels for a McCormick reaper.

7   The trick to weight training is simple: you isolate one muscle, or muscle group, and exercise it repeatedly; then you exercise another, and another, voilà—Arnold Schwarzenegger. A good deal of ingenuity is required to find positions that will isolate, say, the upper abdominals, or the trapezius muscles.

8   After some regular congress with the Yorks (though I tended to eschew the 100-pound plates), I was presentable enough to go public at the Universal Trainer in the weight room at Northeastern University. During my Babylonian captivity, when I had access to the Universal, I more than doubled my earliest bench pressing efforts and was able to mingle with the weight room crowd undetected. No one suspected me of being an English teacher (this was, unfortunately, also true in the English Department).

9   One of the charms of the Universal is that it is a weight lifting machine with several lifting stations. The weights are fixed on pulleys or runners, and poundage can be adjusted by simply moving a pin. Now that I am no longer at Northeastern, the Universal is denied me. But, ever venturesome, I signed up to try the new Nautilus system at the Colonial in Lynnfield. Remember Yaz in '67? Next summer I tore up the Lynnfield Men's Softball League.

10   I didn't devote myself exclusively to the irons all this time. Joan and I had another son. Further motivated, I built up to 190 pounds of bone and sinew. At this writing there are still 190 pounds of bone and sinew. It is, however, almost entirely disguised by about 30 pounds of what could generously be called tissue. If you think weightlifting is sure to trim you down you haven't been watching the Russian weightlifters.

11   Why have I spent several hours each week for 33 years, straining to exercise, with weights, at the outer limits of my strength, and trying to do it again and again at the outer limits of my endurance? In 33 years I've had to thrash no

bullies on behalf of my sons. I have occasionally glared at someone who got uppity with Joan. But she needs my protection about as much as Mike Tyson does. I am good at picking up one end of something. Over the last twenty years my friend, John Marsh, and I have picked up and carried about an impressive assortment of refrigerators, pianos, sofas, washing machines, boulders, bag of Portland cement, stoves, timbers, and beer kegs. But that seems small recompense for 33 years of Ben-Gay.

There *are* drawbacks to all that lifting. I'm probably heavier (though not fatter) than I would have been if I hadn't started lifting. I have distorted my upper body so that I am nearly impossible to fit off the rack. Clothing salesmen blanch when I enter. At 5'10" I take a size 50 suit. The pants have to be shortened so much that the cuffs catch in the zipper.   **12**

You are also brought face-to-face with the validity of an old truth: never a horse that couldn't be rode; never a rider that couldn't be throw'd. If you can bench press 300 pounds you're certain to have a friend who can do 350, and he knows someone who can do 450. I'm fairly strong for a 59-year-old fat man. But in any weight room in the country there are twenty people (mostly men) who are stronger than I am and maybe one that's better looking. Weightlifting is very useful in understanding the inequality of nature's dispensation.   **13**

Of course it is embarrassing at first when you go into the weight room with your little potbelly and your skinny white arms wearing the brand new gym suit your spouse bought you at K-Mart; and there are a lot of people who look like the Great Blue Hill pumping iron with their sleeves cut off. But progress is rapid, and you can learn from watching others. Most of them will be preoccupied with the wall mirrors and won't notice you anyway.   **14**

For a man who makes his living sitting down, alone, all day, weightlifting has much to offer. It pays off promptly, it fits conveniently into my schedule, it provides exercise that my profession does not (helping to offset typists' hump), and, perhaps more to the point, it makes me sweat. I *like* to sweat. Inelegant, but true. I like the feeling of effort, of tension followed by release (Arnold Schwarzenegger has already pointed out the sexual parallels; I try to write only of what I know). I like the sense of work carried through to resolution, and I like the sense of near endless possibility in goals accomplished and new goals set.   **15**

But most simply I lift weights for the reason with which I began. I want to be strong. I want to be strong the way I want to be smart. So I study to be smart and lift to be strong. (Joan says I'm oh-for-two, but she's never admitted my resemblance to the young Olivier either.) In the case of strong, as in the case of smart, there are limits to what can be made of the raw material. Like study, exercise can only improve on the basics. It can't supply them.   **16**

But within the limits of how you start, it seems to me that the renaissance ideal of the warrior poet (Sir Philip Sidney, say) isn't a bad one. It needn't, of course, be weights. One of my sons is a dancer and he can do things with his body that no one else I know can do. It could be running. It could be gymnastics. Physical accomplishment doesn't have to include the ability to pick up the front end of a Buick. To be physically accomplished would seem as much a   **17** fulfillment of one's humanity as to be intellectually accomplished. To be both would seem most fully human.

▼ TOPICAL CONSIDERATIONS

1. What were Parker's original reasons for buying a set of weights? Back then, what was the general attitude toward men who were weightlifters, according to Parker?
2. What has 33 years of pumping iron done for Parker? How has it physically changed him? What has it done for his self-image? What drawbacks has he had to face as a result? How has it helped him?
3. What reasons does the author give for continuing to lift weights after 33 years? Is it for physical accomplishments alone?

▼ RHETORICAL CONSIDERATIONS

1. What is the organizing principle of this essay?
2. What is there about the first paragraph that makes you want to read on?
3. What kind of humor does Parker use in this piece? What is the source of his humor? How does his wife Joan serve his humorous effects?
4. Could you tell from this essay that Parker was once a professor of English? What literary allusions does he make directly and indirectly?
5. Could you tell from this essay that Parker is a successful novelist? If so, how?
6. Explain the following allusions and how they sustain the humorous tone of this essay: Mona Lisa, Mike Tyson, Ben-Gay, Arnold Schwarzenegger, Sir Philip Sidney.

▼ WRITING ASSIGNMENTS

1. Parker says that 33 years ago the attitude toward men who were weightlifters was not complimentary. What is the current attitude toward people who lift weights? Write a paper about how the general attitude toward weightlifters has changed.
2. If you lift weights regularly, write a report on how you got started. Try to capture the experience and explain how it has affected your physical development as well as your attitude.
3. If you are not a weightlifter but play a sport regularly, write a paper in which you tell how you first got interested in that sport, why you enjoy it, and what it has done for you physically and mentally.

13 EDUCATION

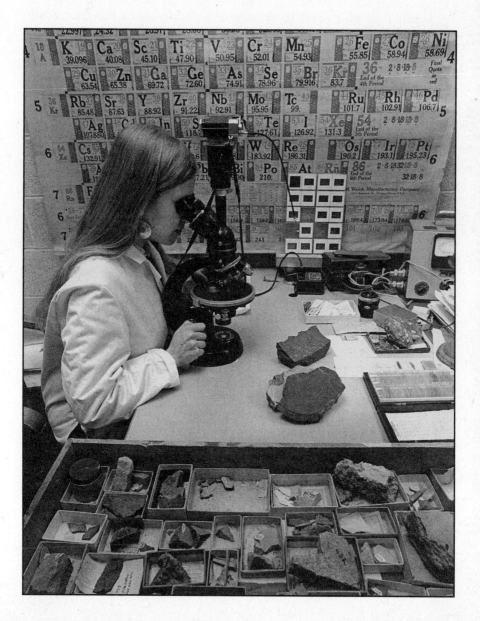

Education in 1990s America is at a turning point. Educators argue that students aren't learning the way they used to while students and parents complain that teachers and curricula aren't measuring up. What everybody agrees on is that changes from kindergarten through college better be made or we risk abandoning the future to chance. The essays in this chapter offer perspectives on what's wrong (and a little of what's right) with the state of education today.

Page Smith's "Killing the Spirit" looks critically at what you as students will come to know well in your college experience—the lecture. It has been estimated that almost 90 percent of all instruction at the university level is by the lecture method. Even if the lecturer is not dull, argues Professor Smith, without dialogue between student and instructor "there can be no genuine education."

The next selection addresses the declining interest in science in American schools and colleges. "Why My Kids Hate Science" was written by scientist Robert M. Hazen who blames schools and scientists for this illiteracy that, he says, dulls the capacity to appreciate the elegant principles governing the universe.

The questionable state of history education is the subject of the next piece. According to Jonathan Alter and Lydia Denworth in "A (Vague) Sense of History," too few high-school grads have mastered basic historic facts. The fear is that such national amnesia may affect our future as a democratic nation and as individuals. Unlike science or math, historical illiteracy cannot be linked to loss of international competitiveness. The problem is with the teaching of history. And as reported much is being done to reduce boredom and to incorporate multiculturalism in the curriculum.

We next turn to the subject of literature and the imbroglio over college course work. The focus of "Debate Between the Lines" is Victorian poet Matthew Arnold's famous poem, "Dover Beach"—an old chestnut in Freshman literature courses. The issue is why teach it? Gerald Graff's essay examines two very different views of the poem—views that encapsulate much of the national controversy over the *what* and *how* of teaching literature. A traditionalist older male professor defends "Dover Beach" as a Western world classic, while a young female professor argues that the poem is just another example of white-male propaganda.

On the subject of math education, we've taken a lighter approach. In "Can America be No. 1 in Math? You Bet Your Noogie," humorist Dave Barry recalls the formative experience of high-school math class to suggest how parents can do something about the "mathematical boneheadism" plaguing our nation.

Our final selection is an inspiring address on teaching and learning by best-selling author Robert Fulghum. In "A Bag of Possibles and Other Matters of the Minds," Fulghum calls on students to rediscover their natural creative talents and on educators to rekindle the self-esteem that kids lose between kindergarten and college.

▼ KILLING THE SPIRIT
Page Smith

Drawing on some thirty years of college teaching, Page Smith scrutinizes that hallmark of the university experience: the lecture. Before reading this essay, consider the number of hours you've spent listening to lectures in your college career. Take a moment to evaluate those lectures making a list of strong and weak points. Ask yourself what makes a lecturer a success or a failure. Once you've done that, you'll be ready to react to Smith's contention that "the lecture system is the most inefficient way of transmitting knowledge ever devised." Mr. Smith is the author of fifteen books, the most recent of which is *Killing the Spirit* (1990) from which this essay was taken.

I came away from my years of teaching on the college and university level with a conviction that enactment, performance, dramatization are the most successful forms of teaching. Students must be incorporated, made, so far as possible, an integral part of the learning process. The notion that learning should have in it an element of inspired play would seem to the greater part of the academic establishment merely frivolous, but that is nonetheless the case. Of Ezekiel Cheever, the most famous schoolmaster of the Massachusetts Bay Colony, his onetime student Cotton Mather wrote that he so planned his lessons that his pupils "came to work as though they came to play," and Alfred North Whitehead, almost three hundred years later, noted that a teacher should make his/her students "glad they were there."

Since, we are told, 80 to 90 percent of all instruction in the typical university is by the lecture method, we should give close attention to this form of education. There is, I think, much truth in Patricia Nelson Limerick's observation that "lecturing is an unnatural act, an act for which providence did not design humans. It is perfectly all right, now and then, for a human to be possessed by the urge to speak, and to speak while others remain silent. But to do this regularly, one hour and 15 minutes at a time . . . for one person to drone on while others sit in silence? . . . I do not believe that this is what the Creator . . . designed humans to do."

The strange, almost incomprehensible fact is that many professors, just as they feel obliged to write dully, believe that they should lecture dully. To show enthusiasm is to risk appearing unscientific, unobjective; it is to appeal to the students' emotions rather than their intellect. Thus the ideal lecture is one crammed with facts and read in an uninflected monotone. Witness the testimony of the eminent sociologist Daniel Bell.

When Bell gave a talk to the faculty and staff and some graduate students at the Leningrad State University during a trip to Russia, he spoke extemporaneously (which professors seldom do) and with evident emotion, which clearly moved his listeners profoundly but which left Bell feeling "an odd turbulence. . . . For years," he writes, "I had fought within myself against giving emotional speeches. They were easy, cheap, sentimental, lachrymose. . . . In the lectures I usually give . . . I have tried to be expository, illustrative . . . resenting the cheap jibes to get a rise out of the audience." Here, to his discomfort, he had let emotion get the best of him and, plainly, of his audience. I would only note that the kind of austerity and lack of emotion that Bell normally strove for is the classic mode of the American professor lecturing to his class.

5 The cult of lecturing dully, like the cult of writing dully, goes back, of course, some years. Edward Shils, professor of sociology and social thought at the University of Chicago, recalls the professors he encountered at the University of Pennsylvania in his youth. They seemed "a priesthood, rather uneven in their merits but uniform in their bearing; they never referred to anything personal. Some read from old lecture notes—one of them used to unroll the dog-eared lower corners of his foolscap manuscript and then haltingly decipher the thumb-worn last lines. Others lectured from cards that had served for years, to judge by the worn and furry edges. . . . The teachers began on time, ended on time, and left the room without saying a word more to their students, very seldom being detained by questioners. . . . Almost all male students wore suits, all wore neckties. . . . The classes were not large, yet there was no discussion. No questions were raised in class, and there were no office hours."

6 William Lyon Phelps described the Yale faculty in the 1890s thusly: "nearly all the members of the Faculty wore dark clothes, frock coats, high collars; in the classroom their manners had an icy formality. . . ." The clothes and manners have become informal, but the aloofness and impersonality, I fear, remain.

7 Karl Jaspers makes the point that the lecture, like research, must never become routine. It is the opportunity for the teacher to present in dramatic fashion, highlighted by his/her own insight and enthusiasm, material that cannot be conveyed with the same potency on the printed page. In the lecture the student must see *enacted* the power and excitement of ideas. The posture, gestures, and intonations of the lecturer carry as much force as the words themselves, words that, when reduced to notes, often lie quite inert on the page.

8 The lecture has a quasi-religious character about it, since exalted speech partakes of the sacred. Every lecture, listened to by dozens or hundreds of students, should partake of art (dramatic art being perhaps the closest). The lecturer who reads his notes dutifully is performing an act that the students can do better for themselves. Such an instructor gives up the very element of spontaneity which alone justifies the lecture as a form of teaching. The lecturer must *address* students. He/she is, after all, asking a good deal of them. If there are two hundred students in the class, the lecturer is saying to them, in effect: What I have to say is of such considerable consequence that I feel entitled to take up two hundred precious hours of your collective time in order to explain it to you, or, even better, in order to enlarge your sense of the possibilities of human existence in relation to this topic we are considering together. "Lectures which

aim to sum up an entire subject are in a class by themselves," Jaspers writes. "Such lectures should be given only by the most mature professors drawing upon the sum total of their life's work. . . . Such lectures belong to what is irreplaceable in tradition. The memory of outstanding scholars lecturing, accompanies one throughout life. The printed lecture, perhaps even taken down word for word, is only a pale residue." The inspired lecture evokes, again in Jaspers' words, "something from the teacher which would remain hidden without it. . . . He allows us to take part in his innermost intellectual being." The great lecture is thus a demonstration of something precious and essential in the life of the spirit and the mind, and the dramatic power that inheres in that unity. Such lectures link us with the sermons and political addresses that have played central roles in the "great chain of being" that links classes and generations and nations together in "the unity of spirit." Thus the casual, the perfunctory, the oft-repeated, the read lecture, the *dead* lecture, is a disservice both to the students and to the ideal of learning that presumably holds the whole venture together.

William Lyon Phelps at Yale was a "great teacher," in the classic tradition. 9 "If a teacher wishes success with pupils, he must inflame their imagination," he wrote. "The lesson should put the classroom under the spell of an illusion, like a great drama." The abstract should be avoided. "If a pupil feels the reality of any subject, feels it in relation to actual life, half the battle is gained. Terms must be clothed in flesh and blood . . . ," Phelps wrote. The modern professor often takes a contrary turn. The real things are the abstractions; the personal, the individual, the anecdotal are all distractions and indulgences. A professor may give the same course, covering the same material, year in and year out (it is, after all, his "field," and he is actively discouraged from stepping outside it). He/she may go so far as to incorporate in the lectures the latest "researchers," to the degree that they are relevant to undergraduate students, but unless he/she rethinks each lecture, reanimates it, *reappropriates* it, and thereby makes evident to his listeners why they should take their valuable time to listen, the lecturer is discrediting the lecture system and the process of learning that the lecture system represents. The lecturer is putting forward a "negative stereotype," as we say, not just of himself and of lectures in general, but of the whole edifice of higher education. If the lecturer is bored by the constant repetition of familiar material, he may be sure that his auditors are even more bored. The comedian Professor Irwin Corey had a popular routine in which he fell asleep while lecturing; it was invariably greeted with enthusiastic applause.

In his fourteen-week survey of the great universities in 1910, the journalist 10 Edwin Slosson attended more than a hundred classes. His strongest impression was "the waste of time and energy in the ordinary collegiate instruction." There was "no lack of industry, devotion, and enthusiasm on the part of the teachers, but the educational results," Slosson wrote, "are not commensurate with the opportunities afforded and the efforts expended." One's strongest impression was of "lost motion." There was "no general appreciation of the fact that the printing press had been invented in the years since the rise of the Medieval university." Most of the professors lectured poorly, and many did not "even take pains to speak distinctly enough so that they can be heard in their small classrooms without strained attention." Conveying information by ear was a strikingly inefficient way of transmitting it, especially to passive, note-taking students who often showed little comprehension of what they were hearing. "The lecture," Slosson concluded, "is useful for inspiration and demonstration, but not for information." It was apparent to Slosson that, despite its obvious and, in the main, undisputed shortcomings, the lecture was persisted in because it was the quickest and easiest way for a professor to discharge his nominal obligations as a teacher of undergraduate students. One of the unfortunate consequences was that the professor commonly indulged himself in excessively detailed information in the field of his academic specialty, often scanting or ignoring issues of the greatest importance and interest to his captive auditors.

11   I must confess that my own attitude toward lecturing was deeply influenced by my experience in teaching Dante's *Divine Comedy* in a seminar. When I suggested to my students that they devise some modern hells for modern sins, two students in the seminar offered interesting hells for professors-who-neglected-their-students. They proposed that the professors be required to listen to lectures for all eternity. The only point of dispute between them was whether it would be worse torment for professors to have to listen to their own lectures or to those of an especially dull colleague. I have never been able to feel the same way about lecturing since. Every time in the intervening years that I have undertaken to lecture, I have suffered from post-traumatic stress syndrome.

12   I think it is fair to say that the lecture system is the most inefficient way of transmitting knowledge ever devised. It would be much more effective, in most instances, simply to print up a lecturer's notes and distribute them to the students at the beginning of the course. Or students might be given reading lists of important books to pursue on their own initiative. In many instances it would be more useful to let the students give the lectures. All this is not to say, of course, that particularly inventive and enterprising professors can't overcome the most negative aspects of the lecture system, but only to point out that very few do. Indeed, it is the nature of things that there are only a few great lecturers. In the thirty-some years in which I had contact with the academic world, I knew only five or six. They were individuals who had passionately held views of life as well as deep knowledge of their subjects. They took every lecture with the greatest seriousness and spoke as though they realized that to speak was both a privilege and a responsibility. Eugen Rosenstock-Huessy, William Hitchcock, Mary Holmes, Norman O. Brown, Donald Nichol, and Paul Lee all fell into that category.

13   The most conclusive argument against the lecture system is that all true education must involve response. If there is no dialogue, written or spoken, there can be no genuine education. The student must be lured out of his or her instinctive passivity. This can only be done properly if an atmosphere of trust is built in the classroom or seminar. The professor cannot ask his students to expose their innermost hopes and feelings unless he is equally candid with them and allows them to see him as a fallable, searching individual.

The best discussion of the relationship between professors and their students (which, of course, is at the heart of all true teaching) is, I am pleased to say, by a former student of mine, Patricia Nelson Limerick, a professor of history at the University of Colorado. After describing a number of imaginative ways to involve students in classroom exercises designed to break down the barriers between "aloof professors" and "shy students," Limerick writes: "In all these exercises, my goals have been the same; to bump students out of passivity, and to bump myself out of self-consciousness and sometimes out of complacency. . . . By contrast, the more conventional tensions of the classroom cause students and professors to fear making fools of themselves. . . . The underlying reason for holding class, whatever the subject or the course, has to involve the project of inviting students to think for themselves, to ask their own questions, and to pursue the answers with both freedom of thought and discipline of argument." If a professor tries to promote such a notion in the conventional classroom, "there is such a disjunction between the medium and the message," Limerick writes, "that the project will work for only a few. . . . The trial and burden of adventurous teaching is that it never feels safe—you never sign a contract with the universe guaranteeing success in all your experiments." **14**

That, of course, is the essence of teaching—taking chances. And you can only do that if you are willing to come down from your perch as a professor of this or that and be as vulnerable (or almost as vulnerable) as your students. No professional vulnerability, no real teaching. **15**

Karl Jaspers wrote, "The reverence and love rendered to the master's person have something of worship in them," but Jaspers goes on to point out that the master must turn this "reverence and love" into the channels of learning in a manner perhaps akin to the analytic "transference," wherein the scrupulous analyst directs the patient's instinctive attachment to the analyst back toward the process of healing. Jaspers' ideal in the teaching relationship is the Socratic method, whereby teacher and student "stand on the same level. . . . No hard and fast educational system exists here, rather endless questioning and ultimate ignorance in the face of the absolute." **16**

The geologist Israel C. Russell wrote in the journal *Science* in 1904: "In the school of research . . . professor and student should be co-workers and mutually assist each other. From such comradeship, that intangible something which is transmitted from person to person by association and contact, but cannot be written or spoken—we may term it 'inspiration,' or personal magnetism, or perhaps the radium of the soul—is acquired by the student to a greater degree than at any previous time in his life after leaving the caressing arms of his mother." **17**

Alfred North Whitehead's wife, Evelyn, told Lucien Price: "When we first came to Harvard, Altie's [Whitehead's] colleagues in the department said, *'Don't let the students interfere with your work!'* Ten or fifteen minutes is long enough for any conference with them." Instead of following his colleagues' advice, Whitehead, who lectured three times a week, would give his students "a whole afternoon or a whole evening. . . . The traffic was two-way, for Whitehead felt that he needed contact with young minds to keep his own springs flowing. 'It **18** is all nonsense,' he said, 'to suppose that the old cannot learn from the young.' "

19   Contacts between professors and their students outside the classroom, ideally in walks or sports or social occasions, are as important as or perhaps more
important than classroom contacts, because they reveal something to the student about reality that can, I suspect, be learned no other way. Such contacts
demonstrate that ideas are "embodied." They do not exist apart from a person,
remote or near at hand, who enunciates, who takes responsibility for them by
declaring them, by speaking about them. It is not only that ideas have consequences; they are held, passionately or perhaps frivolously, by individuals;
otherwise they could not survive; they would die of inattention, and of course
many do. We are all dependent, in the last analysis, on readers or listeners (and
responders) who by responding remind us that we are talking to living souls.

20   In Woodrow Wilson's words: "The ideal college . . . should be a community, a place of close, natural, intimate association, not only of the young men
who are its pupils and novices in various lines of study but also of young men
with older men . . . of teachers with pupils, outside the classroom as well as
inside. . . ."

21   When it became evident beyond question or cavil that professors were
determined to ignore the "moral and spiritual" needs of their students, a new
academic order called "counselors" was created. Counselors were in essence
men and women employed to do what the traditional college education had
professed to do (but which it had seldom done)—that is to say, care for what
we would call today the psychological needs of the student, what, indeed, John
Jay Chapman's ladies and bishops and teas had done at Harvard: provide some
human contact, some counsel and advice. I suspect "ladies, Bishops and tea"
were a sounder remedy for the distress of undergraduates not simply ignored
but positively rebuffed by their instructors. The trouble was (and is) that most
of the students who find their way to counselors are near the end of their rope.
They have, as we say today, serious "problems." One can only speculate that
there might be far fewer such "problems" if faculty members were willing to
lend sympathetic ears to the trials and tribulations of the young men and women
they are supposed to teach. Their defense, as one might suspect, is that they are
not "experts" in matters pertaining to the psychological needs of students, they
are only experts in Sanskrit, or economics or abnormal psychology or chemistry. I have long maintained that Ionesco's *The Lesson* should be performed each
year for entering freshmen at our institutions of higher learning to prepare them
for the years ahead. The reader may recall that in *The Lesson* the student arrives
to interrupt the professor in his researches on the origin of ancient Spanish
verbs. While he is lecturing on the subject, she experiences acute pain from a
toothache. The professor ignores her cries until they become too obtrusive, at
which point he strangles her. The play ends as another student arrives.

22   Testimony to the bad consciences of universities about the sorry state of the
teaching function is the widespread practice of awarding, with much fanfare,
cash prizes to the "teacher-of-the-year." This is supposed to demonstrate the
institution's commitment to "excellence in teaching." What it does, in fact, is to

distort and demean the true nature of teaching. It is also often the case that untenured winners of such awards soon disappear from the scene, victims of the publish-or-perish rule. So often has this been the case on some campuses that there has been pressure from the administration to make the award only to faculty who have already attained tenure, thus sparing the university the embarrassment of firing someone who has just been recognized as an outstanding teacher. Moreover, although the awards doubtless go, in the main, to deserving individuals, the winners are often those lecturers whom the students simply find the most entertaining. William Arrowsmith, the classics scholar, has written: "At present the universities are as uncongenial to teaching as the Mojave Desert to a clutch of Druid priests. If you want to restore a Druid priesthood you cannot do it by offering prizes for Druid-of-the-year. If you want Druids, you must grow forests. There is no other way of setting about it." In other words, if you want good teaching, you have to create an academic atmosphere where good teaching is encouraged, recognized, and rewarded with something more substantial than "prizes."

It should also be said that one of the greatest obstacles to effective teaching **23** is the grading system ("de-grading system" would be a better name for it). It treats the students as isolated individuals. It pits them against each other and, in a sense, against their teachers in a competitive struggle for survival. Only the fittest survive. I have heard not a few professors boast of the severity of their grading. How many students flunked a course was a measure of their tough-mindedness. In addition to discouraging cooperation among students, grades falsify the relation between teacher and student. The teacher's task is to win the student's confidence and to create an air of trust congenial to learning, but over this rather tender relationship there hovers the cloud of that grade. Professors often fall into the habit of thinking of students less as people in need of help and guidance than as A students or C students, a very bad frame of mind indeed.

▼ TOPICAL CONSIDERATIONS

1. Do you think the author prefers the classic style of William Lyon Phelps or the modern one? Explain your answer using specific details. Which do you prefer? Which style have you seen more of in your school?
2. Do you agree with Smith's notion that 80 to 90 percent of all university instruction is lecture? In your response, discuss your own experience in college classes.
3. Smith begins with the point that "Students must be . . . an integral part of the learning process." Has this been true for you during your experience as a high school and college student? Explain your answer.
4. Many students have difficulty taking lecture notes, especially if the lecture is dull. Do you find it easy or difficult to record the impor-

tant information from a lecture? Describe your note-taking process during a lecture.

5. Has Smith's view of teaching changed your views, reinforced your views, or had no effect on your views of teaching? Explain your reasoning.

6. Alfred North Whitehead said, "It is all nonsense to suppose that the old cannot learn from the young" (paragraph 18). Do you agree or disagree? Why or why not?

7. Why does Smith think entering freshmen should view Ionesco's *The Lesson?* Do you agree? Why or why not?

8. Have you experienced classrooms where there is a dialogue between teacher and student? Describe how the class works and whether that method is advantageous. If you have not had such an experience, describe how you think it might work and whether that method would be advantageous.

▼ RHETORICAL CONSIDERATIONS

1. At the beginning of the essay, Smith uses first-person point of view giving his opinion and backing it with several examples. After he gives a definition of lecturing, what change of tone does he use in the next three paragraphs? Is it effective? Explain why or why not.

2. The author interjects his personal feelings at several points. Give an example and explain whether you think it is effective or not.

3. When each of us writes an essay, we pull from our own experiences for examples. From where does Smith get his examples?

4. Is his use of past and present day examples effective? Please use an example of each to agree or disagree.

5. Do you think this essay should end with paragraph 20, 21, or 22 rather than 23? Please support your decision with valid reasoning.

6. Consider the voice of the author. Describe the author as a teacher based on his voice in this essay. Be sure to use specific examples.

▼ WRITING ASSIGNMENTS

1. Has this essay influenced your view of college professors? If so, in a paper describe the influence of Smith's essay on your own views, atitudes and/or behavior.

2. We have all sat through lectures that bored us miserably. Think of a teacher or professor whose classes habitually put you to sleep or nearly so. In a paper try to analyze just what made that instructor's classes so dull. Aside from the material, consider his or her style of talking (i.e., intonation, volume, variation, accent), personal de-

portment, attitude, and the use or lack of anecdotes, humor, abstractions, specific details, visual aids, physical movement, gestures, facial expression, and so forth.
3. Design your own dull-lecturer's hell. In a paper try to describe what the experience should be like for outstandingly boring instructors. Try to come up with some original torments.
4. In a paper, describe a professor or teacher you have had who was truly an exception to the rule—one who was a " 'great teacher' in the classic tradition" (paragraph 9) as Smith calls it. In your paper, try to explain just what it was that made that person such an outstanding teacher.

▼ WHY MY KIDS HATE SCIENCE
Robert M. Hazen

From the White House to the corridors of academe, there is great concern over declining student interest in science. Fewer students are naming the sciences as college majors than in the past, and a diminishing number of graduates are science-literate. As the author argues here, this growing "illiteracy" is a threat to our survival as a nation. Without scientific knowledge, "informed decision can't be made about where we live, what we eat and how we treat our environment." In this essay, Robert M. Hazen, a scientist at the Carnegie Institution of Washington's Geophysical Laboratory and Robinson Professor at George Mason University, wants to know why our educational system is turning out scientifically illiterate graduates and who is to blame. He points a finger at professional scientists and offers ways to solve the problem. Hazen is the author of many scientific articles and eight books including *Science Matters: Achieving Scientific Literacy* (1991), coauthored with James Trefil.

Last year my sixth-grade daughter, Elizabeth, was subjected to science. Her 1
education, week after week, consisted of mindless memorization of big words like "batholith" and "saprophyte"—words that an average Ph.D. scientist wouldn't know. She recited the accomplishments of famous scientists who did things like "improved nuclear fusion"—never mind that she hasn't the vaguest notion of what nuclear fusion means. Elizabeth did very well (she's good at memorizing things). And now she hates science. My eighth-grade son, Ben, was also abused by science education. Week after week he had to perform canned laboratory experiments—projects with preordained right and wrong answers. Ben figured out how to guess the right answers, so he got good grades. Now he hates science, too.

2   Science can provide an exhilarating outlet for every child's curiosity. Science education should teach ways to ask questions, and create a framework for seeking answers. In elementary school, because of jargon and mathematical abstraction, my children got the mistaken impression that science is difficult, boring and irrelevant to their everyday interests. Year by year, class by class across America, the number of students who persevere with science education shrinks.

3   As a professional geologist who has tried to convey some of the wonder and excitement of science to nonscientists, I am saddened and angered to see "the great science turnoff." I know that science is profoundly important in our lives. Informed decisions can't be made about where we live, what we eat and how we treat our environment without basic knowledge about our physical world, the knowledge that constitutes scientific literacy. Yet studies and surveys prove that our educational system is turning out millions of scientifically illiterate graduates. What's gone wrong? Who is to blame?

4   Some people say the problem is too much TV, or lack of parental supervision, or the sometimes poor media image of scientists. Perhaps the fault lies in declining national standards of education, poorly trained teachers or inadequate resources. Maybe students are just too dumb. But I can't escape the truth. Blame for the scientific literacy crisis in America lies squarely at the feet of working scientists. Too often we have sacrificed general education for our own specialized interests. Why haven't children been taught the basics in science? Because most university scientists at the top of the educational hierarchy couldn't care less about teaching anyone but future scientists. To them, science education is a long process of elimination that weeds out and casts aside the unworthy. It's not surprising that scientists have guided science education in this way. All the good things in academic life—tenure, promotion, salary, prestige— hinge on one's reputation in specialized research. Educators focus on teaching advanced courses to students who are willing to run the laboratory. Time devoted to teaching, or even reading, general science is time wasted.

5   One amazing consequence of this emphasis is that working scientists are often as scientifically illiterate as nonscientists. I'm a good example. The last time I took a course in biology was in ninth grade, long before genetics had made it into the textbooks. In college I studied lots of earth science, even more in graduate school. But from that distant day in 1962 when I dissected a frog, to quite recently when as a teacher I was forced to learn about the revolution in our understanding of life, I was as illiterate in modern genetics as it was possible to be. The average Ph.D. scientist doesn't know enough to teach general science at any level.

6   Working physicists or geologists or biologists know a great deal about their specialties. That's why Americans win so many Nobel Prizes. But all that specialization comes at a price. National science leaders, who usually are the ones who have done the best playing the research game, have fostered an education policy more concerned with producing the next generation of specialized scientists than educating the average citizen. This policy has backfired by turning off students in unprecedented numbers.

The picture may seem bleak, but the solution is not all that difficult. First, **7** we need to recognize that science can be shared without jargon and complex mathematics. You don't have to be a scientist to appreciate the overarching scientific principles that influence every action of our lives. The central ideas of science are simple and elegant—together they form a seamless web of knowledge that ties together every aspect of our physical experience.

Then we need teachers who are able to convey this unified vision with **8** confidence and enthusiasm. Teachers can't give students a vision if no one has ever given it to them, so every college and university needs to institute general science courses. These courses should be required of all future teachers. Administrators at institutions of higher learning should be as quick to reward the gifted teachers of general science with raises and tenure as they have been to reward the gifted science researcher.

The science classroom, at least through junior high school, should be a **9** hands-on exploration of the universe. Textbooks that are daunting and boring should be burned. Standardized tests that bully teachers into creating a rigid curricula should be outlawed. Our children should be given the chance to explore backward in time, look outward through space and discover unity in the workings of the cosmos. Armed with that knowledge they will someday combat disease, create new materials and shape our environment in marvelous ways. Science will also give them the means to predict the consequences of their actions and perhaps, with wisdom, to save us from ourselves.

▼ TOPICAL CONSIDERATIONS

1. Summarize why Hazen's own children hate science.
2. Do Hazen's descriptions of the way his children were taught science remind you of your own experience? How? If not, explain how your experience differed.
3. Whom does Hazen blame for the scientific literacy crisis? Do you agree or disagree with him? Explain your answer.
4. What solutions to the problem does he offer?
5. Describe the difference between general education and specialized interests in relation to the study of science.
6. Compare Hazen's view of teaching with Page Smith's ("Killing the Spirit"). Would they wish for similar teaching methods or not?

▼ RHETORICAL CONSIDERATIONS

1. Hazen is critical of the scientific world. What gives him credibility as a critic? Do you think he practices what he preaches? Explain your answer.
2. What technique does the author use to develop his explanation of

why "our" educational system is turning out millions of scientifically illiterate graduates?

3. Describe the changes in point of view in the essay and why you
think he uses each.

4. Consider how this essay would work if it were written in third
person rather than first person. Do you think it would be better or
worse? Explain your answer.

5. When Hazen discusses the consequences of teaching specialized
interest in science, he uses himself as an example. Can you relate to
his own experience? If so, please explain. If not, explain how your
experience differed.

6. Does the title of this essay prepare you for a discussion of how to
handle scientific illiteracy? Explain your answer, referring to specific sections of the essay.

▼ WRITING ASSIGNMENTS

1. Hazen's daughter memorized words like "batholith" and "saprophyte" (paragraph 1). Did you ever have to memorize something in
school that you considered *mindless?* Describe the experience and
results of it. If not, describe what you considered to be *mindful*
memorization and why the experience was a good one.

2. Write a letter to Hazen from Page Smith. As Smith, describe how
science could be kept alive in the classroom today.

3. You are a science teacher. Write a response to this essay. Be sure to
deal with Hazen's specific comments on education.

4. Pretend you are a textbook publisher. What would you do to
publish books that are not "daunting and boring" (paragraph 9).
List and explain your plan.

▼ A (VAGUE) SENSE OF HISTORY

Jonathan Alter and Lydia Denworth

Too many American high-school graduates are unfamiliar with the major events of the Civil War and World War I. Too many cannot name the countries the United States fought in World War II. Too many students see the study of history as plowing through a "dull data dump." As the authors here point out, ignorance of history is a danger to the very future of our nation and its individuals. The blame for the high degree of historical illiteracy, they say, is the way history has been taught in American schools. A cause for optimism, this essay offers many exciting suggestions to reform and revitalize the teaching of history. Instead of making it the rote memorization of dates and names, educators should fashion their courses as the study of real people with a more balanced approach to multiculturalism. This article first appeared in *Newsweek* magazine in September 1990.

Historians tend to tell the same joke when they're describing history education in America. It's the one about the teacher standing in the schoolroom door waving goodbye to students for the summer and calling after them, "By the way, we won World War II." 1

The problem with the joke, of course, is that it's not funny. The surveys on historical illiteracy are beginning to numb: nearly one third of American 17-year-olds cannot even identify which countries the United States fought against in that war. One third have no idea what *Brown* v. *Board of Education* accomplished. One third thought Columbus reached the New World after 1750. Two thirds cannot correctly place the Civil War between 1850 and 1900. Even when they get the answers right, some (many?) are just guessing. 2

Unlike math or science, ignorance of history cannot be directly connected to loss of international competitiveness. But it does affect our future as a democratic nation and as individuals. "People without a sense of history are amnesiacs," says Diane Ravitch, professor of history and education at Columbia University Teachers College. "They wake up and don't know who they are." 3

The good news is that there's growing agreement on what's wrong with the teaching of history and what needs to be done to fix it. The steps are tentative and yet to be felt in most classrooms. And the debate over "multiculturalism"—the latest buzzword in broadening history's scope—has politicized the subject in often distracting ways. But beneath the rhetoric lies some evidence that educators are beginning to paddle in the same direction, with California taking the lead. 4

In the spirit of consensus, here are a few paths for reform that sensible people should be able to agree on: 5

6   **Recognize the Boredom Factor.** History itself isn't boring; it's just taught that way. As in science, the natural curiosity of students is snuffed out at an early age. The reasons aren't hard to figure. "Kids see it as going through dull data dumps," says Francie Alexander, who oversees curriculum for California's Department of Education. The image of the teacher asking his students to read page 454, then answer the questions on page 506, is enough to induce a yawn without even being in the classroom. The natural human fascination with good stories, which the entertainment industry understands so well, is missing from history, where that fascination originated. Admitting this as a problem—avoiding the usual defensiveness of the educational establishment—is the first step toward doing something about it.

7   **Rethink "Social Studies."** Many educators now see the transformation of history into social studies as the root of what's wrong. Social studies began in the 1930s as an effort to make the subject more "relevant." Paul Hanna, its original champion, wrote that children were failing to "face the realities of this world in which we live—they escape, they retreat to a romantic realm of yesterday." Social studies flowered fully in the 1960s and 1970s, when such romantic stories and legends (for instance, King Arthur and the Round Table) were frequently replaced in the lower grades by studying family and neighborhood life. In higher grades, social studies came to mean an interdisciplinary approach that threw history into an academic stew with psychology, anthropology, ethnic studies, civics and other subjects.

8   The results have been discouraging. The "romantic realm" Hanna denigrated turns out to have a narrative thrust and natural appeal far more memorable than soupy sociology, which is what social studies—however noble in theory—so often becomes. "Kids like history because it's the story of real people," says Elaine Reed of the Ohio-based Bradley Commission, which helps states reform their history programs. "There's some blood and gore in there, but also some love and caring."

9   Consider Arleen Chatman, a teacher at the 75th St. School in Los Angeles, who straps on an apron and takes her students on an imaginary covered-wagon ride across the country, complete with vivid first-person accounts of the arduous trip. The whole school (K-6) creates a time line by stringing a rope across the yard and attaching cards representing historical events. Chatman cites the fourth grade, which is usually the year that children study their state, as a good example of the differences between history and social studies. While the social-studies curriculum would focus that year on the (often dry) roles of various state offices, Chatman's fourth graders did a research project on William Mulholland, the "dream builder" who brought water to Los Angeles. A woman who had known Mulholland came to tea with the class. "This 90-year-old woman became so real to the kids," says Chatman. "She told them wonderful stories." Stories—the stuff of history—are what people of all ages crave. Properly told, they can bring any class alive.

10   As a practical matter in elementary school, there's just not enough time in the day to make history separate from civics, community issues and similar

topics. But the aim should be for history and geography to play a larger role in that mix. And from junior high on, it makes more sense to define the subject as history instead of social studies. Otherwise schools are providing what Gilbert T. Sewall of the New York-based American Textbook Council calls "escape hatches for uninterested students to satisfy their diploma requirements." As of 1987, 15 percent of high-school graduates took no American history in high school, and 50 percent studied no world history. When psychology or anthropology or even driver's education classes count as social studies it's no wonder so many students don't know anything about the Civil War.

Expand History's Place. One way to bridge the history gap is simply to teach   11
more of it. Three years ago, California adopted a new History-Social Science Framework which strongly recommends that every student be required to take at least three years of American history and three years of world history between grades five and 12. (Most states currently mandate only one year of American history.) In 1988, the Bradley Commission echoed California's plans, arguing that, properly taught, history would help develop certain "habits of the mind"—critical thinking, acceptance of uncertainty, appreciation of causation—that have been sadly lacking from many classrooms.

One of the obstacles to greater concentration on history is the National   12
Council on Social Studies (NCSS), which often downplays history in favor of what NCSS executive director Fran Haley calls "a more integrated approach." Over the years, social studies has fallen prey to trends—ethnic, demographic, environmental, women's and "peace" studies—that are unobjectionable, even commendable in themselves. But these subject areas too often crowd out basic historical literacy. Instead of being included in the broad sweep of history, they tend to replace it. Only this year have traditionalists organized to balance the NCSS with their own professional group, the National Council for History Education.

Put "Multiculturalism" in Perspective. Even after arriving at a consensus on   13
the importance of history, the debate still rages over *whose* history should be taught. In some ways, this is a diversion, like arguing calculus versus trigonometry when the students don't know how to add and subtract. But it is a passionate debate within the profession, and with minorities soon to make up one third of the public-school population, it will only grow in importance.

On one side are those who attack the traditional emphasis on American   14
history and Western civilization as "Eurocentric." They argue that such curricula—which stress the centrality of the transfer of European values and traditions to America—are not meaningful for many minority students; in fact, they suggest that a traditional approach can be downright harmful because it doesn't present positive enough views of nonwhite groups. This critique is fueled by a sense that curriculum is often too positive, downplaying, for instance, the horrors of slavery and the destruction of Indians. American history, these critics say, is often presented as a "parade of presidents." World history seems to be a story of Europe on top. "That's hard for kids attached to those nations that were subjugated," says Irene Segade, who teaches at San Diego High School.

15   The most extreme version of this view was contained in "A Curriculum of Inclusion," a highly controversial report issued last year by a New York task force assigned by Education Commissioner Thomas Sobol to review social studies. Sobol admits that he created the task force, which he says was preliminary and not responsible for curricular reform, essentially as a political gesture to minority groups upset by his appointment. (He is white.) He underestimated the potential for backlash. The report is a textbook case of what happens when education is treated as akin to a pork-barrel project, with bones thrown to constituency groups. Although the state's history curriculum was overhauled to make it more multicultural as recently as 1987, representatives of different ethnic groups each argued that their histories should be more heavily weighted.

16   The problem with the argument is that the contributions of different cultures have simply not been comparable. Like it or not, Europe has had the largest influence on this nation's values and institutions. "No one would say that Afro-Asian culture studies is not important. These parts of the world are relevant to us today," says Steve Houser, a history teacher at Horace Greeley High School in Chappaqua, N.Y. "But we have a problem with being [attacked as] 'Eurocentric.' We teach the good and the bad of European history—imperialism, world wars, the Holocaust. It's ridiculous to say that Europe hasn't had an inordinate influence over the modern world."

17   The "Europhobic" approach, says Diane Ravitch, "endorses the principle of collective guilt. It encourages a sense of rage and victimization in those who are the presumed descendants of victims and a sense of resentment in those who are the presumed descendants of oppressors. Instead of learning from history about the dangers of prejudging individuals by their color or religion, students learn that it is appropriate to think of others primarily in terms of their group identity." California Education Superintendent Bill Honig argues simply that the essential themes of history often transcend lines of race and national origin. He points to the Chinese students who raised the Statue of Liberty last year in Tiananmen Square. "They're quoting Montesquieu, Jefferson and Locke," he says. "In fact, they can quote [them] better than our people."

18   As bitter as this debate has become, there's a middle course between, say, portraying slavery as merely a minor episode and giving Benjamin Banneker equal weight to Benjamin Franklin. It is possible—even essential—to "step into the [minority group's] shoes, see it from their perspective" without letting that dominate a curriculum, as Sobol says. Primary source materials such as first-person accounts by slaves or Asian workers on the transcontinental railroad can achieve that end. So can classroom arguments about whether the West was "won" or "stolen." The creator of that exercise, Joseph Palumbo, a teacher at Stephens Junior High in Long Beach, Calif., also asks his students to view Columbus's landing in America from the Indians' point of view. This is multiculturalism with a human face, and it's easily achievable without harsh attacks and hand wringing.

19   **Demand Good Textbooks.** History textbooks are too often a crutch for

teachers and a club over their students. They are almost always too long and boring. A 1987 study by Columbia University's American History Textbooks project found these texts "generally to be mere catalogues of factual material about the past, not sagas peopled with heroic and remarkable individuals engaged in exciting and momentous events." The insightful texts favored in Gilbert Sewall's report, such as "A History of the United States" *(Ginn and Co., Lexington, Mass.)*, by Daniel Boorstin and Brooks Mather Kelly, all featured heavy participation by the distinguished authors.

Amazingly, this is rare in elementary and secondary history textbooks. **20** Most are written—badly—by unknown and often professionally unqualified firms subcontracted by publishing houses. (The "authors" whose names appear on the cover often merely review and amend the turgid text.) Beyond placing less faith in textbooks in general, teachers should insist on texts that have strong narrative voices instead of those that make kaleidoscopic attempts at comprehensiveness. The whole historical establishment should worry less about battling over exactly which details are mentioned or missing from textbooks and more about making these books convey the wonder of history.

Bring History Alive. This, after all, is the challenge. How to make Jefferson **21** or Roosevelt or Gandhi inhabit the minds of students? Good teachers know it's possible. Use primary sources. Use literature. Tell a story. Relate historical events to current events. Insist that they write essays instead of merely answering multiple-choice questions. Make kids take sides in debate. Make them establish connections between different historical ideas. Make them *think*.

Joe Palumbo's eighth-grade students in Long Beach know more than when **22** the Civil War took place. Last spring they spent class time using that war—and others they had studied—to debate the morality and complexity of conflict. Was it right for Northern troops to burn Southern crops and leave the population hungry? Was it right for Confederates to hold Northerners in squalid POW camps? When do the ends justify the means? By the time the bell rang, the students were not yet finished arguing the issues with one another. The conversations continued out in the hall, almost making them late for their next class. Palumbo would not be one of those waving goodbye to his students with the words, "By the way, the North won."

▼ TOPICAL CONSIDERATIONS

1. The authors bemoan the national problem of historical illiteracy in America. What specific examples do they offer as evidence?
2. Compare Robert A. Hazen's concern in "Why My Kids Hate Science" for the way science has been taught to Alter and Denworth's view of how history has been taught.
3. Have you ever taken a social studies course? If so, did your course have a "narrative thrust and natural appeal," or was it "soupy

sociology" (paragraph 8)? Explain your answer. If you have never taken a social studies course, how do you think such a course should be taught?

4. The authors offer several suggestions to solve the problem of historical illiteracy. Mention each in a one-sentence description.

5. How would Page Smith ("Killing the Spirit") respond to the teaching methods of Joseph Palumbo? Give specific examples.

▼ RHETORICAL CONSIDERATIONS

1. Note the authors' use of envelope structure. That is, the beginning and end of the essay are tied neatly together. There are no loose ends. Explain how the authors do this in the essay.

2. Why do you suppose the authors of this essay chose to use the third person point of view while Robert A. Hazen uses first person in his essay? Which technique do you prefer, and why?

3. The authors deal with some controversial ideas but manage to offer both sides of these issues. Give an example of a controversial point and tell how the authors handle it tactfully.

4. Does the title prepare the reader for what follows? Please explain your answer.

5. With each path to reform (boldfaced words, paragraphs 6–21) the authors give specific examples to support their point. Which path to reform would you agree with based on your history education? Explain using your own experience as a student of history.

▼ WRITING ASSIGNMENTS

1. Imagine that you are the supervisor of a history department in a high school. Write a letter to your teachers describing how they should teach history to their students. Base your ideas on those of Alter and Denworth.

2. Write a one-week lesson plan for the teaching of a particular unit of history—that is, America's entrance into World War II, the assassination of John Kennedy, civil rights reform. Explain how you would cover the subject by using the reform ideas of Alter and Denworth.

3. Think back to a history class that you had to take. Was the experience favorable or unfavorable? Write a letter to your high school principal describing why you think this course was effectively or ineffectively taught. Be sure to use at least one specific example in your letter.

4. The integration of multicultural history is a controversial one.

Write an essay in which you support a specific way of teaching multicultural history within the framework of the curriculum. You may refer to sources from this or other essays in your response.

▼ DEBATE BETWEEN THE LINES
Gerald Graff

Most undergraduates never hear their literature professors "talking shop." Most couldn't even imagine academic disputes breaking out in the confines of a faculty lounge let alone two professors getting into a full-fledged shouting match over the interpretation of a poem written a century ago. But that is what this piece does: It takes us behind the scenes of a university English department to witness some of the political "warfare currently agitating the educational world." The focus here: A favorite literary chestnut, "Dover Beach," a poem written by one of England's most famous Victorian poets, Matthew Arnold (1822–1888). The principals: An older male professor (OMP) who bemoans his students' inability to comprehend the poem; and, a young female professor (YFP) who, echoing the students' indifference, wonders why teach "Dover Beach" anyway. Their rift widens when OMP proclaims the poem a "great masterpiece of Western Civilization" and YFP attacks it as an example of "phallocentric discourse" in which male experience is presented as though it were universal. While some academics may decry such radical disagreement, Gerald Graff, the author of this piece and a professor of literature at Northwestern University, sees such controversy as a way to revitalize the teaching of literature—to make poetry "a live issue." This article first appeared in the Autumn 1990 issue of *New Literary History*. In its entirety, "Dover Beach" is reprinted at the end of this piece.

In the faculty lounge the other day, a dispute arose between a couple of my colleagues that typifies the warfare currently agitating the educational world. It began when one of our older male professors complained that he had just come from teaching Matthew Arnold's "Dover Beach" and had been appalled to discover that the poem was virtually incomprehensible to his class. Why, can you believe it, said the older male professor (let us call him OMP for short), my students were at a loss as to what to make of Arnold's famous concluding lines, which he proceeded to recite with slightly self-mocking grandiloquence:

Ah, love, let us be true
To one another! For the world, which seems
To lie before us like a land of dreams,
So various, so beautiful, so new,

> Hath really neither joy, nor love, nor light,
> Nor certitude, nor peace, nor help for pain;
> And we are here as on a darkling plain
> Swept with confused alarms of struggle and flight
> Where ignorant armies clash by night.

My other colleague, a young woman who has just recently joined our department (let us call her YFP), replied that she could appreciate the students' reaction. She recalled that she had been forced to study "Dover Beach" in high school and had consequently formed a dislike for poetry that had taken her years to overcome. Why teach "Dover Beach" anyway? YFP asked.

2   Furiously stirring his Coffee-mate, OMP replied that in *his* humble opinion—reactionary though he supposed it now was—"Dover Beach" was one of the great masterpieces of the Western tradition, a work that, until recently at least, every seriously educated person took for granted as part of the cultural heritage. YFP retorted that while that might be so, it was not altogether to the credit of the cultural heritage. Take those lines addressed to the woman by the speaker, she said: "Ah, love, let us be true / To one another . . . ," and so on. In other words, protect and console me, my dear—as we know it's the function of your naturally more spiritual sex to do—from the "struggle and flight" of politics and history that we men have regrettably been assigned the unpleasant duty of dealing with. YFP added that she would have a hard time finding a better example of what feminists mean when they speak of the ideological construction of the feminine as by nature private and domestic and therefore justly disqualified from sharing male power. Here, however, she paused and corrected herself: "Actually," she said, "we *should* teach 'Dover Beach.' We should teach it as the example of phallocentric discourse that it is."

3   OMP responded that YFP seemed to be treating "Dover Beach" as if it were a piece of political propaganda rather than a work of art. To take Arnold's poem as if it were a species of "phallocentric discourse," whatever that is, misses the whole point of poetry, OMP said, which is to rise above such local and transitory problems by transmuting them into universal structures of language and image. Arnold's poem is no more about gender politics, declared OMP, than *Macbeth* is about the Stuart monarchical succession.

4   But *Macbeth is* about the Stuart monarchical succession, retorted YFP—or so its original audience may well have thought. It's about gender politics too— why else does Lady Macbeth need to "unsex" herself before she can participate in murdering Duncan? Not to mention all the business about men born of women and from their mother's womb untimely ripped. The fact is, Professor OMP, that what you presume to be the universal human experience in Arnold and Shakespeare is male experience presented as if it were universal. You don't need to notice the politics of sexuality because for you patriarchy is the normal state of affairs. You can afford to ignore the sexual politics of literature, or to "transmute" them, as you put it, onto a universal plane, but that's a luxury I don't enjoy.

There are many possible ways to describe what happened here, but one of them would be to say that "theory" had broken out. What we have come to call "theory," I would suggest, is the kind of reflective discourse about practices that is generated when a consensus that was once taken for granted in a community breaks down. When this happens, assumptions that previously had gone without saying as the "normal state of affairs"—in this case OMP's assumption that literature is above sexual politics—have to be explicitly formulated and argued about.

OMP would probably complain that this trend diverts attention from literature itself. But YFP could reply that literature itself was not being ignored in their debate but discussed in a new way. It was not that she and OMP stopped talking about poetry and started talking theory. It was rather that, because their conflicting theoretical assumptions differed about how to talk about poetry, they had to talk about it in a way that highlighted those theories.

The recent prominence of theory, then, is the result of a climate of radical disagreement, and the complaint that theory is pervasive finally reduces to the complaint that literature and criticism have become too controversial. Yet the complaint only has the effect of generating more theory and more of the theoretical disagreement being deplored. Forced by the disagreement to articulate his principles, OMP, the traditional humanist, was "doing theory" just as much as was YFP, articulating assumptions that previously he could have taken as given. For this reason, the belief that the theory trend is a mere passing fad is likely to be wishful thinking.

The question is: Who and what are hurt by this situation? Who and what are damaged by conflicts like the one in the faculty lounge? The obvious answer would seem to be "Dover Beach." But just how well was "Dover Beach" doing in college (and high school) literature classes before radical teachers like YFP came along? We need only look at the complaint by OMP that triggered the lounge debate to be reminded that such classics have often inspired deep apathy in students even when taught in the most reverential fashion—perhaps especially when taught in that fashion.

Considered in this light, one might argue that "Dover Beach" has little to lose from the debate between OMP and YFP and a good deal to gain. In an odd way, YFP is doing "Dover Beach" a favor: In treating Arnold's poem as a significant instance of ideological mystification, her critique does more to make the poem *a live issue* in the culture again than does the respectful treatment of traditionalist teachers like OMP, which, as he himself complains, fails to arouse his class.

What the debate between OMP and YFP really threatens is not "Dover Beach," I think, but OMP's conception of "Dover Beach" as a repository of universal values that transcend the circumstances of its creation and reception. Whereas this decontextualized concept of culture was once axiomatic in humanistic education, it has now become one theory among others, a proposition that has to be argued for rather than taken as given. What is threatened by the canon controversy, in other words, is not the classics but their unquestioned status.

But again, when the classics enjoyed that unquestioned status there is little evidence that it made them seem more compelling to students than they seem now. In short, from an educational point of view, the classics have less to fear from newfangled ideological hostility than from old-fashioned indifference.

11   What is most unfortunate about the conflict between OMP and YFP is not *that* it is taking place but *where* it is taking place, behind the educational scenes where students cannot learn anything from it. My thought as I watched OMP and YFP go back and forth in the faculty lounge was that if OMP's students could witness this debate they would be more likely to get worked up over "Dover Beach" than they are now. They might even find it easier to gain access to the poem, for the controversy over it might give them a context for reading it that they do not now possess.

12   Then again, it might not. The controversy would have to be presented in a way that avoids pedantry, obscurity, and technicality, and this is difficult to do. And even when it is done, many students will still have as much trouble seeing why they should take an interest in critical debates over "Dover Beach" as they do seeing why they should take an interest in "Dover Beach" itself. The alienation of students from academic culture runs deep, and it may deepen further as the terms of that culture become more confusingly in dispute than in the past.

13   In such a situation, helping students gain access to academic discourse means clarifying conflicts like the one between OMP and YFP (and numerous others not so neatly polarized). If the goal is to help students become interested participants in the present cultural conversation instead of puzzled and alienated spectators, the aim should be to *organize* such conflicts of principle in the curriculum itself. They are, after all, only an extension of the real-life conflicts that students experience every day.

14   Just opening reading lists to noncanonical works—necessary as that step is—will not in itself solve the problem. Replacing "Dover Beach" with *The Color Purple* does not necessarily help the student who has difficulty with the intellectual vocabularies in which both texts are discussed in the academic environment. What makes reading and interpretation difficult for many students is not the kind of text being read, whether canonical or noncanonical, highbrow or popular, but the heavily thematic and symbolic ways in which all texts, irrespective of status, are discussed in the academic setting. (The student phrase for it is "looking for 'hidden meaning.' ") If the practice of looking for hidden meaning seems strange to you, it will seem no less strange to look for it in *The Color Purple* than in *Hamlet.*

15   This last point needs underscoring, because educational progressives have been too quick to blame student alienation from academic literacy on the elitist or conservative aspects of that literacy. But students can be as alienated from democratized forms of academic literacy as from conservative forms. What alienates these students is academic literacy *as such,* with its unavoidably abstract and analytical ways of talking and writing, regardless of whether that literacy is traditional or populist.

16   There is no question of occupying a neutral position here: In my view, the

shift from the traditionalist to the revisionist view of culture is very much a change for the better. But from the vantage point of students who feel estranged from the intellectual life as such, revisionist culture can easily seem like the same old stuff in a new guise. To such students a feminist theorist and an Allan Bloom would seem far more similar to each other than to people like themselves, their parents, and friends. In the students' eyes, the feminist and Bloom would be just a couple of intellectuals speaking a very different language from their own about problems the students have a hard time regarding as problems.

The new climate of ideological contention in the university seems to me a **17** sign of democratic vitality rather than the symptom of "disarray," relativism, and declining standards that the critics on the Right take it to be. But so far the university *has* failed to make a focused curriculum out of its contentiousness. For this reason, it is failing to tap its full potential for drawing students into its culture.

The best way to do this is to make the conflicts themselves part of the object **18** of study. There are worse things that could happen to literature than having a passionate controversy erupt over it.

DOVER BEACH
1867
Matthew Arnold (1822–1888)

The sea is calm tonight.
The tide is full, the moon lies fair
Upon the straits;—on the French coast the light
Gleams and is gone; the cliffs of England stand,
Glimmering and vast, out in the tranquil bay. 5
Come to the window, sweet is the night-air!
Only, from the long line of spray
Where the sea meets the moon-blanched land,
Listen! you hear the grating roar
Of pebbles which the waves draw back, and fling, 10
At their return, up the high strand,
Begin, and cease, and then again begin,
With tremulous cadence slow, and bring
The eternal note of sadness in.

Sophocles long ago 15
Heard it on the Aegean, and it brought
Into his mind the turbid ebb and flow
Of human misery; we
Find also in the sound a thought,
Hearing it by this distant northern sea. 20

The Sea of Faith
Was once, too, at the full, and round earth's shore
Lay like the folds of a bright girdle furled.
But now I only hear

<pre>
25   Its melancholy, long, withdrawing roar,
      Retreating, to the breath
      Of the night-wind, down the vast edges drear
      And naked shingles° of the world.   gravel beaches

      Ah, love, let us be true
30   To one another! for the world, which seems
      To lie before us like a land of dreams,
      So various, so beautiful, so new,
      Hath really neither joy, nor love, nor light,
      Nor certitude, nor peace, nor help for pain;
35   And we are here as on a darkling° plain   darkened or darkening
      Swept with confused alarms of struggle and flight,
      Where ignorant armies clash by night.
</pre>

▼ TOPICAL CONSIDERATIONS

1. OMP is described by Graff as a "traditional humanist" (paragraph 7) because of his theories regarding the teaching of "Dover Beach." In what way are his views traditional? What are some of his views? How do these views come into conflict with a nonsexist approach to teaching literature? And how do they conflict with a multicultural approach to teaching literature? Explain your answer.

2. In contrast to OMP, YFP is described as a "radical" (paragraph 8) in her approach to teaching literature. List some of YFP's radical views in relation to teaching "Dover Beach." Do her interpretations make good sense to you? Or, do they seem farfetched?

3. Do you think YFP would be a likely candidate for a multicultural approach to teaching literature? Explain your answer.

4. In paragraph 10, Graff writes, "What is threatened by the canon controversy . . . is not the classics but their unquestioned status." What does Graff mean by this statement? Do you agree with him? Why or why not? Do you think the status of "classics" of Western literature should be questioned? Explain your answer.

5. OMP cannot believe that his students are unable to understand the last stanza of Arnold's poem. Are you able to understand this stanza? What about the poem as a whole? Does it speak to you in context of today's world? Explain your answer.

▼ RHETORICAL CONSIDERATIONS

1. At the beginning of the essay, the author recreates the dispute he witnessed in the faculty lounge. How do the tone and point of view change beginning with paragraph 5?

2. In paragraph 10 Graff talks about "a repository of universal values that transcend the circumstances of its creation and reception." He also uses words like "decontextualized," "axiomatic," and "ideological hostility." Isn't this the very language he criticizes in paragraph 12? Do you think he intentionally used such language as that he criticizes? What kind of audience is he writing for? Explain your answer.

3. The stanzas of "Dover Beach" follow a pattern of point of view. The first and last stanzas are similar; so are the second and third. How are they similar in point of view?

4. How would the essay be different if the author did not make the sex and/or age distinctions between the two professors? Use specific examples. Would it be more or less effective?

5. In "Dover Beach," Matthew Arnold sets a calm tone at the beginning of stanza 1 which ends with ". . . and bring / The eternal note of sadness in." The next two stanzas reinforce the sadness with "human misery" and "melancholy." Is the last stanza different in form and tone, or is it similar? Explain how.

▼ WRITING ASSIGNMENTS

1. Write a letter to OMP in which you try to persuade him to include the teaching of a specific contemporary work in his curriculum. You may want to refer to his arguments for the teaching of "Dover Beach" so you can respond to your audience (OMP) appropriately.

2. Write a letter to YFP describing another classic literary work which you feel presents the role of women in an outdated historical context. You may want to refer to her arguments in the essay to get the tone of your audience (YFP).

3. You have been assigned to select the reading list for the curriculum in a literature course dealing with great works of poetry or fiction. List the literary works you would include in the curriculum and give a reason for including each work.

4. With the push in the 1990s to include more multicultural literature, one must consider selecting a variety of works representing many cultures. Select a work from a culture other than your own. In a well-written essay explain why this work is important to you even though it was written by someone from another culture.

5. "Dover Beach" is a poem that deals with love, commitment to overcome loneliness in a cruel and dangerous world. Write your own contemporary "Dover Beach."

▼ CAN AMERICA BE NO. 1 IN MATH? YOU BET YOUR NOOGIE

Dave Barry

Before reading this piece, recall that moment when a math problem rendered you apoplectic with humiliation and frustration. You'll be in the proper state of mind to appreciate Dave Barry's hilarious observations on mathematics—and the way it's taught in America. Dave Barry has been described as "America's most preposterous newspaper columnist," a man "incapable of not being funny." He is the author of ten books and is a Pulitzer Prize–winning humorist whose *Miami Herald* column is syndicated in more than 200 publications. Collections of his essays include *Bad Habits* (1987), *Dave Barry Turns Forty* (1990), and *Dave Barry's Only Travel Guide You'll Ever Need* (1991). This essay first appeared in his column in April 1991.

1   Last week I witnessed a chilling example of what US Secretary of Education Arthur A. Tuberman was referring to in a recent speech when he said that, in terms of basic mathematics skills, the United States has become, and I quote, "a nation of stupids."

2   This incident occurred when my son and I were standing in line at Toys "R" Us, which is what we do for father-son bonding because it involves less screaming than Little League. Our immediate goal was to purchase an item that my son really needed, called the Intruder Alert. This is a battery-operated Surveillance Device that can be placed at strategic locations around the house; it makes an irritating electronic shriek when you, the intruder, walk past. This important technological breakthrough enables the child to get on your nerves even when he is not home.

3   The woman ahead of us wanted to buy four Teenage Mutant Ninja Turtle drinks, which come in those little cardboard drink boxes that adults cannot operate without dribbling on themselves, but which small children can instinctively transform into either drinking containers or squirt guns. The Toys "R" Us price was three drinks for 99 cents, but the woman wanted to buy *four* drinks. So the mathematical problem was: How much should the cashier charge for the fourth box?

4   Talk about your brain teasers! The cashier tried staring intently at the fourth box for a while, as if maybe one of the Ninja Turtles would suddenly blurt out the answer, but *that* didn't work. Then she got on the horn and talked to somebody in Management "R" Us, but *that* person didn't know the answer, either. So the cashier made another phone call, and then another. By now, I

assumed she was talking to somebody in the highest echelon of the vast Toys "R" Us empire, some wealthy toy executive out on his giant yacht, which is powered by 176,485 "D" cell batteries (not included).

Finally, the cashier got the word: The fourth box should cost—I am not **5** making this up—29 cents.

This is, of course, ridiculous. As anyone with a basic grasp of mathematics **6** can tell you, if *three* drinks cost 99 cents, then a *fourth* drink would cost, let's see, four boxes, divided by 99 cents, carry your six over here and put it on the dividend, and your answer is . . . OK, your answer is definitely *not* 29 cents. And this is not an isolated incident of America's mathematical boneheadism. A recent study by the American Association of Recent Studies shows 74 percent of US high-school students—nearly half—were unable to solve the following problem:

"While traveling to their high-school graduation ceremony, Bill and Bob **7** decide to fill their undershorts with Cheez Whiz. If Bill wears a size 32 brief and Bob wears a 40, and Cheez Whiz comes in an 8-ounce jar, how many times do you think these boys will have to repeat their senior year?"

Here is the ironic thing: America produces "smart" bombs, while Europe **8** and Japan do not; yet our young people don't know the answers to test questions that are child's play for European and Japanese students. What should be done about this? The American Council of Mathematicians, after a lengthy study of this problem, recently proposed the following solution: "We tell Europe and Japan to give us the test answers, and if they don't, we drop the bombs on them."

Ha ha! Those mathematicians! Still bitter about not having prom dates! **9** Seriously, though, this nation is a far cry from the America of the 1950s, when I was a student and we were No. 1 in math and science, constantly astounding the world with technical innovations such as color television, crunchy peanut butter and Sputnik. What was our secret? How did we learn so much?

The answer is that, back then, math was taught by what professional **10** educators refer to as: The Noogie Method. At least this was the method used by Mr. O'Regan, a large man who taught me the times tables. Mr. O'Regan would stand directly behind you and yell: *"Nine times seven!"* And if you didn't state the answer immediately, Mr. O'Regan would give you a noogie. You can easily identify us former O'Regan students, because we have dents in our skulls large enough for chipmunks to nest in. Some of us also have facial tics: These were caused by algebra, which was taught by Mr. Schofield, using the Thrown Blackboard Eraser Method. But the point is that these systems worked: To this day, I can instantly remember that nine times seven is around 50.

It's good that I remember my math training, because I can help my son with **11** his homework. He'll be sitting at the kitchen table, slaving over one of those horrible pages full of long-division problems, having trouble, and I'll say: "You know, Robert, this may seem difficult and boring now, but you're learning a skill that you'll probably never use again." If more parents would take the time to show this kind of concern, we Americans could "stand tall" again, instead of being a lazy, sloppy nation where—prepare to be shocked—some newspaper columnists, rather than doing research, will simply make up the name of the secretary of education.

▼ TOPICAL CONSIDERATIONS

1. Even though Barry's essay is not serious and Robert A. Hazen's ("Why My Kids Hate Science") is, how does Barry's description in paragraph 11 of his son's "difficult and boring" math experience resemble the experience of Hazen's children learning science?

2. At several points in the essay the author presents statistics as if they were real. Give some examples of such made-up figures. How do these figures and Barry's calculations add to the humor? How do they illustrate the problem of declining math skills?

3. In the final paragraph, explain the logic in Barry's words of comfort to his son. Beneath the humor of it, what truth does his advice underscore about Robert's efforts? Do you agree with him? Do you think there is, nonetheless, good reason for the boy to continue in his efforts?

4. What part of this essay did you find to be most humorous? Why was it so funny to you? Did any jokes fall flat for you? If so, explain your answer.

5. Did any part of this essay make you rethink the math skills of Americans? Did it make you wonder about how we compare to other nations? Do you think there is any cause to worry about the state of math education in America? Explain your answer.

▼ RHETORICAL CONSIDERATIONS

1. At what point in the essay do you know the author is not being serious?

2. How does Barry manipulate the reader into almost believing some of his points? Give specific examples.

3. How much truth do you see behind the humor here? Find an example of exaggeration that is funny but that points to a serious problem or issue.

4. Writers employ several strategies in creating various humorous effects. Try to find humorous passages whose effects were created by allusion, surprise, irony, understatement, overstatement, a deliberate pretense to ignorance, and absurd logic. Can you find other comic devices?

5. Were you "shocked" when at the end Barry reveals that he made up the name of the Secretary of Education? What's the point of that

confession? How is this deception consistent with other "deceptions" in the piece? Do you think this confession gives the essay good closure?

▼ WRITING ASSIGNMENTS

1. Did you ever have an experience in a class which you could compare in an exaggerated, humorous way to the author's experiences with Mr. O'Regan and Mr. Schofield? If so, try your hand at capturing the experience.

2. Through satire and humor, Dave Barry is making fun of our educational system. Is there a message here? If so, what is it, and what are your feelings about the problem?

3. After stating the problems with math education in America, create satirical, humorous solutions. Draw from your years of experience and make up fictitious organizations, exaggerated statistics, interviews, quotations, examples, and so on for your report. Have fun.

4. Write a letter to a math teacher you've had explaining how a method he/she has used was or was not effective for your learning of math.

5. " 'You're learning a skill that you'll probably never use again' " (paragraph 11); ". . . and this is not an isolated incident of America's boneheadism" (paragraph 6); ". . . which is what we do for father-son bonding" (paragraph 2). Select from Barry's essay a quotation such as one of these and use it as a thesis statement for an essay. You may be serious or humorous in your treatment.

▼ A BAG OF POSSIBLES AND OTHER MATTERS OF THE MIND

Robert Fulghum

In this piece, best-selling author Robert Fulghum explores the nature of learning. He introduces us to a group of students each of whom unabashedly claims to be a musician, a poet, an actor, and an artist—all in one! What separates these young, grade-school kids from college students, aside from a dozen or so years, is simply self-image. In this inspiring essay, the author exhorts us to rediscover and celebrate our innate ability to learn and our natural bent for creativity. At the same time, he offers a challenge to educators to consider doing something about "what went wrong between kindergarten and college." Robert Fulghum is the author of the extraordinarily popular book *All I Really Needed to Know I Learned in Kindergarten* (1990) and *Uh-Oh!* (1991). This article first appeared in *Newsweek* magazine in September 1990.

1   Since my apotheosis as Captain Kindergarten, I have been a frequent guest in schools, most often invited by kindergartens and colleges. The environments differ only in scale. In the beginners' classroom and on the university campuses the same opportunities and facilities exist. Tools for reading and writing and scientific experimentation are there—books and paper, labs and workboxes—and those things necessary for the arts—paint, music, costumes, room to dance—likewise available. In kindergarten, however, the resources are in one room, with access for all. In college, the resources are in separate buildings, with limited availability. But the most radical difference is in the self-image of the students.

2   Ask kindergartners how many can draw—and all hands shoot up. Yes, of course we draw—all of us. What can you draw? Anything! How about a dog eating a firetruck in a jungle? Sure! How big you want it?

3   How many of you can sing? All hands. Of course we sing! What can you sing? Anything. What if you don't know the words? No problem, we can make them up. Let's sing! Now? Why not!

4   How many of you dance? Unanimous again. What kind of music do you like to dance to? Any kind! Let's dance! Now? Sure, why not?

5   Do you like to act in plays? Yes! Do you play musical instruments? Yes! Do you write poetry? Yes! Can you read and write and count? Soon! We're learning that stuff now.

6   Their answer is Yes! Again and again and again, Yes! The children are large, infinite and eager. Everything is possible.

Try those same questions on a college audience. Only a few of the students will raise their hands when asked if they draw or dance or sing or paint or act or play an instrument. Not infrequently, those who do raise their hands will want to qualify their responses—I only play piano, I only draw horses, I only dance to rock and roll, I only sing in the shower. **7**

College students will tell you they do not have talent, are not majoring in art or have not done any of these things since about third grade. Or worse, that they are embarrassed for others to see them sing or dance or act. **8**

What went wrong between kindergarten and college? What happened to Yes! of course I can? **9**

2 As I write I am still feeling exuberant from an encounter with the cast of Richard Wagner's opera "Die Walküre." Last night I watched a stirring performance of this classic drama. This morning I sat onstage with the cast and discussed just how the production happens. I especially wanted to know how they went about learning their parts—what strategies they used to commit all to memory. **10**

The members of the cast are students in kindergarten and first grade. They did indeed perform "Die Walküre"—words, music, dance, costumes, scenery, the works. Next year they will do "Siegfried"—already in production—as part of a run through the entire "Ring" cycle. And no, this is not a special school of the performing arts for gifted children. It's the Spruce Street School in Seattle, Wash. **11**

They are performing Wagner because they are not yet old enough to know they cannot. And they understand the opera because they make up stories and songs just like it out of their own lives. **12**

To answer the question, "How do children learn?", I did something schools never do: I asked children. Because they know. They have not been hanging in a closet somewhere for six years waiting for school to begin so they could learn. Half their mental capacity has developed before they come to the schoolhouse door. I repeat for emphasis—they know how to learn. **13**

Brünnhilde, still wearing her helmet, explains that it works best for her if she learns her lines in small sections and then pays careful attention to the first three words of a section and then learns those. In case she needs prompting, just a word or two will set off a chain reaction in her mind. She also switches around and sings the talking words and talks the singing words, doing all of this while she moves around instead of sitting still. Siegfried and Wotan have other methods of their own. All seem to know. All have different ways. **14**

The skeptical author is thinking maybe the children are just doing a trained-seal act—I mean Wagner is heavy stuff—surely they don't really get it. So I ask the young actress playing Brünnhilde to tell me how her character fits into the story. "Do you know about Little Red Riding Hood?" she asks. Yes. "Well it's kind of like that—there's trouble out there in the world for the girl and her grandmother and the wolf and everybody." And then, so I will understand better, she compared the role to that of Lady Macbeth. Yes. She knows about **15**

that, too. The school did "Macbeth" last fall. She also talks about "The Hob-
bit" and "Star Wars" and a radio play the class is writing that is a spoof on all
this—"MacDude." "Do you understand?" she asks with concern. I do. And so
does she.

16   (By the way, the only significant deviation from the script came at the very
end of "Die Walküre," where Wotan is supposed to take his sleeping daughter
in his arms and kiss her eyelids. No way. Art may have its standards, but no
7-year-old boy is going to kiss a girl on her eyelids or anywhere else. There are
limits.)

17   **3** We are sent to school to be civilized and socialized. Why? Because we
believe that knowledge is better than ignorance and that what is good for
the group and what is good for the individual are intertwined.

18   As a nation we have concluded that it is better for us all if all of us go to
school.

19   Thomas Jefferson first proposed, in 1779 to the Virginia Legislature, that all
children be educated at public expense, but it was not until well into the next
century that such a plan was put into place, and even then without enthusiasm
on the part of the public. The idea was resisted by a substantial part of the
population—sometimes with armed force. As late as the 1880s the law had to
be enforced in some towns by militia who marched children to school under
guard.

20   In an aspiring nation in the age of the Industrial Revolution, it became a
matter of political economy to have educated citizens.

21   We still believe that it is important to be sent out of the home into the world
to be initiated into society. We call that ritual ground "School." And when we
get there we are required to learn the rules and regulations of community, to
acquire certain skills and to learn something of human values and the long
history of the reaching for light and dignity.

22   Society puts its best foot forward in kindergarten and first grade.

23   **4** Want to have an exciting conversation about education? Don't ask someone what they think of the schools. Never. Ask instead that they tell you
about the best teacher they ever had. Ask instead that they tell you about
the best learning experience they ever had. Ask them if they wish they could sing
and dance and draw. Or ask what they are learning now or would like to learn
soon. And ask them how they go about learning something. And then ask them
if they were to design an educational system to support what they've just said,
what would it be like.

24   **5** There is no such thing as "the" human brain—no generic brain. What we
know, how we know it, our strategies for learning and our idiosyncratic
ways of being alive, differ significantly from person to person. The implications of this for education are almost overwhelming.

25   There are as many ways to learn something as there are learners.

26   There is no one way to be human.

We achieve community with metaphors and consensus. **27**

And this makes a teacher's task impossible. **28**

Unless the teacher sees the task not as one of conveying prescribed informa- **29** tion, but a way of empowering the student to continue doing what he came in the door doing pretty well—learning for himself. To do any less is to diminish his self-esteem.

6 As a teacher of drawing and painting and philosophy in a senior high **30** school for 20 years, I offered a course the students called "drawing for turkeys." The prerequisites for the course, as described in the school catalog: "To qualify, you must think you have no talent or skill in drawing and wish otherwise, hoping that the art fairy will look you up someday. Further, you must be able to tie your shoelaces, write your name and be able to find your way to the studio regularly." The classes were always oversubscribed.

Every student learned to draw competently. **31**

Because drawing is a matter of skill. Skills can be acquired with practice. **32**

Because drawing is a matter of looking closely at something—carefully **33** enough to translate what is seen three dimensionally into the language of two-dimensional line and shape and shadow.

To draw is to look. To look is to see. To see is to have vision. To have vision **34** is to understand. To understand is to know. To know is to become. To become is to live.

And to the student who would acknowledge that she had acquired skills but **35** still could not draw because she had no imagination, I would only say: "Tell me about your dreams at night." And she would—at length. And then I would ask, "Who is doing that inside your head?"

Now if drawing requires careful observation, the acquisition of skill, the **36** application of visionary creative imagination—and that's exactly what graduate school, business, industry, government and these times need—then there is some reason to believe that the arts . . . etc. You take it from there.

After sharing this thinking with parents, they would say they wished they **37** could do what their kids were doing in the drawing class (because they still half believed that all I had done was uncover their particular child's hidden talents). So I would say come on to class. And we had night school for parents. And all the parents (except one) learned to draw competently, taking their drawings home to put in that place of artistic honor—the refrigerator door. (As for the one failure, she taught me humility and pushed my teaching skills and her learning skills as far as possible in the process. She's a good photographer now, though. She sees very well.)

7 On the occasion of his graduation from engineering college this June (*cum* **38** *laude,* thank you very much), I gave my number-two son a gift of a "possible bag."

The frontiersmen who first entered the American West were a long way **39** from the resources of civilization for long periods of time. No matter what gear and supplies they started out with, they knew that sooner or later these would run out and they would have to rely on essentials. These essentials they called their "possibles"—with these items they could survive, even prevail, against all odds. In small leather bags strung around their necks they carried a brass case containing flint and steel and tinder to make fire. A knife on their belt, powder and shot and a gun completed their possibles.

40   But many survived when all these items were lost or stolen.

41   Because their real possibles were contained in a skin bag carried just behind their eyeballs. The lore of the wilderness won by experience, imagination, courage, dreams, self-confidence—these were what really armed them when all else failed.

42   I gave my son a replica of the frontiersmen's possibles bag to remind him of this spirit.

43   In a sheepskin sack I placed flint and steel and tinder that he might make his own fire when necessary; a Swiss Army knife—the biggest one with the most tools; a small lacquer box that contained a wishbone from a Thanksgiving turkey—my luck; a small, velvet pouch containing a tiny bronze statue of Buddha; a Cuban cigar in an aluminum tube; and a miniature bottle of Wild Turkey whisky in case he wants to bite a snake or vice versa. His engineering degree simply attests that he has come home from an adventure in the wilderness.

44   The possibles bag inside his head is what took him there, brought him back and sends him forth again and again and again.

45   **8** I kept a journal during the years I taught. And in time I boiled my experience down into some one-line statements that became a personal litany to be said when school began and when school was not going well. You will have found some of these notions already expressed at length in the sections above; for emphasis, I restate them here:

46   Learning is taking place at all times in all circumstances for every person.

47   There are as many ways to learn something as there are people.

48   There is no one way to learn anything—learn how you learn—help the student do likewise.

49   There is nothing everyone must know.

50   All I have to do is accept the consequences of what I do not know.

51   There is no one way to be human.

52   Imagination is more important than information.

53   The quality of education depends more on what's going on at home than in the school. And more on what is going on in the student than what is going on in the teacher.

54   In learning, don't ask for food; ask for farming lessons. In teaching, vice versa.

55   If nobody learns as much as the teacher, then turn students into teachers.

56   Every student has something important to teach the teacher.

57   Discontent and ferment are signs the fires of education are burning well.

58   In education, look for trouble. If you can't find any, make some.

▼ TOPICAL CONSIDERATIONS

1. What evidence does Fulghum offer to make his point that something "went wrong" between kindergarten and college? Can you recall something you were willing to try in kindergarten or first grade that you wouldn't do now? Explain your answer.

2. Why does Fulghum describe a presentation of Wagner's "Die Walküre?" What is his point here? Can you explain a learning method of your own? Is it similar to any of Brünnhilde's techniques?

3. Who first proposed public education? Was the idea favorably accepted? Do you agree or disagree with Fulghum that "society puts its best foot forward in kindergarten and first grade" (paragraph 22)? On what do you base your answer?

4. Does Fulghum advocate teacher-centered or student-centered learning? Why? Do you learn best in a teacher-centered or student-centered class? Describe a particular incident in your education that illustrates your point.

5. Fulghum explains in paragraph 30 how he taught "drawing for turkeys" in a senior high school. Explain his example and why you think he used it. Did you ever have an experience being a "turkey" before you mastered a skill? If so, describe it.

6. Summarize Fulghum's main points in this essay and tell how they relate to the title. Do you think it is a catchy title? Is it an effective one? Explain.

7. Did you learn something about education from this essay, and about the process of learning? If so, what exactly? Has Fulghum made you aware of some "trouble" in education? Has he inspired you to look for some trouble in education, or to make some? Explain.

▼ RHETORICAL CONSIDERATIONS

1. Fulghum begins with an imaginary dialogue between teacher and kindergarten class and poses two questions in paragraph 9. Does the essay answer the two questions? If so, how?

2. The author gives both general and specific information in this essay. Do you think his personal examples are effective in proving his point? Why or why not?

3. Describe the tone of Fulghum's essay. Does it help to make his point, or would the essay be more effective using a different tone? Explain your answer.

4. Did you find any of this essay humorous? If so, point to an example of Fulghum's humor. Do you think the humor helps or hinders the essay? Explain.

5. What is the purpose of the author's digression into the history of public education in paragraphs 17 to 22? Is any of the information here new to you? How does this material relate to your own experience in public or private education?
6. Describe the author's use of the metaphor "possibles bag" (paragraphs 38–44). Does it work for you or not?

▼ WRITING ASSIGNMENTS

1. At the end of his essay, Fulghum lists some one-line statements of self-advice. Select one of these as your theme and write an essay using specific examples from your own life and educational experience.
2. As a college student, describe how you would change things to provide a greater opportunity for student involvement in the arts. If you feel there are enough opportunities, or too many, explain why. Use specific examples from your own educational experience.
3. Write a letter to one of your professors telling him or her specifically how that course could be improved. In light of the importance of "empowering the student" to learn, consider the teacher's effectiveness, the presentation of material, and the amount learned in the course. You might also consider the workload; the degree of difficulty; the textbooks and readings; the syllabus, outlines, overviews; course organization; outside assignments, and so on. Is your professor the kind of person who would welcome such suggestions? Dare you send the letter signed?

14 ON DEATH AND DYING

Nobody wants to think about death. Nobody plans to die for a long time. And though it may seem morose, reading about death may make us better appreciate life while helping us come to terms with death's inevitability.

In the next hour 10,000 people will die. Some will be killed by fire, some by floods, some by famine, some by accident, some by another's hand. Whatever the circumstance, each person will have faced death in his or her own way. And each will have been one more reminder that dying is as natural as living. Such is the approach of the first essay, "On Natural Death," by physician and biologist Lewis Thomas. In as grand a context as our planet's biosphere, death does not seem so unreasonable or so cruel.

But accepting its naturalness will not eliminate one's fear of death—a fear that has long made the subject a taboo. The next piece explores the reasons why there is an increased fear of death in our society today. "On the Fear of Death" was written by Elisabeth Kübler-Ross, renowned for her work with dying patients.

By writing about the scourge of AIDS on others, George Whitmore felt he would earn immunity for himself. But, as he says in "AIDS: Bearing Witness," the disease did not keep up its end of the bargain. What Whitmore's narrative describes is how he came to terms with the brutal impact of his own killer.

The final piece is a more cheerful reflection on one's own death written by America's most famous baby doctor, Benjamin Spock. In "A Way to Say Farewell," the author spells out just the kind of funeral and memorial service he wants when he dies—and the cocktail party to follow. It's an upbeat view of one's own end. And a good note on which to bid our own farewell.

▼ ON NATURAL DEATH
Lewis Thomas

In this chapter's first selection, Dr. Lewis Thomas reflects on the subject of death from the viewpoint of a physician and biologist. When regarded in so grand a context as the natural world, dying might not seem the cruel and extraordinary phenomenon we have made of it. As he points out, dying is as "natural" as living. Thomas, who has served as chair of the Departments of Medicine and Pathology at New York University and Bellevue Medical Center and dean of Yale Medical School, has also distinguished himself as a writer. His articles have appeared in both scientific and popular journals. The following originally appeared in his column, "Notes of a Biology Watcher," for the *New England Journal of Medicine* in 1979. His many books include *The Lives of the Cell* (1974), *Late Night Thoughts on Listening to Mahler's Ninth Symphony* (1983), and his most recent work, *Fragile Species* (1992).

There are so many new books about dying that there are now special shelves set aside for them in bookshops, along with the health-diet and home-repair paperbacks and the sex manuals. Some of them are so packed with detailed information and step-by-step instructions for performing the function that you'd think this was a new sort of skill which all of us are now required to learn. The strongest impression the casual reader gets, leafing through, is that proper dying has become an extraordinary, even an exotic experience, something only the specially trained get to do. 1

Also, you could be led to believe that we are the only creatures capable of the awareness of death, that when all the rest of nature is being cycled through dying, one generation after another, it is a different kind of process, done automatically and trivially, more "natural," as we say. 2

An elm in our backyard caught the blight this summer and dropped stone dead, leafless, almost overnight. One weekend it was a normal-looking elm, maybe a little bare in spots but nothing alarming, and the next weekend it was gone, passed over, departed, taken. Taken is right, for the tree surgeon came by yesterday with his crew of young helpers and their cherry picker and took it down branch by branch and carted it off in the back of a red truck, everyone singing. 3

The dying of a field mouse, at the jaws of an amiable household cat, is a spectacle I have beheld many times. It used to make me wince. Early in life I gave up throwing sticks at the cat to make him drop the mouse, because the dropped mouse regularly went ahead and died anyway, but I always shouted unaffections at the cat to let him know the sort of animal he had become. Nature, I thought, was an abomination. 4

Recently I've done some thinking about that mouse, and I wonder if his 5 dying is necessarily all that different from the passing of our elm. The main difference, if there is one, would be in the matter of pain. I do not believe that an elm tree has pain receptors, and even so, the blight seems to me a relatively painless way to go even if there were nerve endings in a tree, which there are not. But the mouse dangling tail-down from the teeth of a gray cat is something else again, with pain beyond bearing, you'd think, all over his small body.

6   There are now some plausible reasons for thinking it is not like that at all, and you can make up an entirely different story about the mouse and his dying if you like. At the instant of being trapped and penetrated by teeth, peptide hormones are released by cells in the hypothalamus and the pituitary gland; instantly these substances, called endorphins, are attached to the surfaces of other cells responsible for pain perception; the hormones have the pharmaco-logic properties of opium; there is no pain. Thus it is that the mouse seems always to dangle so languidly from the jaws, lies there so quietly when dropped, dies of his injuries without a struggle. If a mouse could shrug, he'd shrug.

7   I do not know if this is true or not, nor do I know how to prove it if it is true. Maybe if you could get in there quickly enough and administer naloxone, a specific morphine antagonist, you could turn off the endorphins and observe the restoration of pain, but this is not something I would care to do or see. I think I will leave it there, as a good guess about the dying of a cat-chewed mouse, perhaps about dying in general.

8   Montaigne had a hunch about dying, based on his own close call in a riding accident. He was so badly injured as to be believed dead by his companions, and was carried home with lamentations, "all bloody, stained all over with the blood I had thrown up." He remembers the entire episode, despite having been "dead, for two full hours," with wonderment:

> It seemed to me that my life was hanging only by the tip of my lips. I closed my eyes in order, it seemed to me, to help push it out, and took pleasure in growing languid and letting myself go. It was an idea that was only floating on the surface of my soul, as delicate and feeble as all the rest, but in truth not only free from distress but mingled with that sweet feeling that people have who have let themselves slide into sleep. I believe that this is the same state in which people find themselves whom we see fainting in the agony of death, and I maintain that we pity them without cause. . . . In order to get used to the idea of death, I find there is nothing like coming close to it.

9   Later, in another essay, Montaigne returns to it:

> If you know not how to die, never trouble yourself; Nature will in a moment fully and sufficiently instruct you; she will exactly do that business for you; take you no care for it.

10   The worst accident I've ever seen was on Okinawa, in the early days of the invasion, when a jeep ran into a troop carrier and was crushed nearly flat. Inside were two young MPs, trapped in bent steel, both mortally hurt, with only their

heads and shoulders visible. We had a conversation while people with the right tools were prying them free. Sorry about the accident, they said. No, they said, they felt fine. Is everyone else okay, one of them said. Well, the other one said, no hurry now. And then they died.

Pain is useful for avoidance, for getting away when there's time to get away, but when it is end game, and no way back, pain is likely to be turned off, and the mechanisms for this are wonderfully precise and quick. If I had to design an ecosystem in which creatures had to live off each other and in which dying was an indispensable part of living, I could not think of a better way to manage. **11**

▼ TOPICAL CONSIDERATIONS

1. Thomas remarks on all the new literature about death and dying in the bookstores. How does he seem to regard this current fascination?
2. What exactly does Thomas mean by "natural" death (paragraph 2)? How, by implication, might death be *unnatural?*
3. What is the point of Thomas's anecdote about his elm tree dying? How does it connect to the central idea of the essay?
4. Observing the fate of the field mouse, Thomas decided that nature "was an abomination" (paragraph 4). Why might he have drawn this conclusion? Why, after reflecting upon the mouse's death, did Thomas change his view of nature?
5. What observations about dying does Montaigne make? How do they support Thomas's thesis?

▼ RHETORICAL CONSIDERATIONS

1. This essay is a fine example of building a central thesis through the use of anecdotes. Explain how each of the anecdotes Thomas chose helps develop his thesis. What purpose does each serve? How are they thematically connected to each other?
2. Evaluate the tone of this essay. In your analysis, consider the use of language, in particular his mixture of colloquial expressions (for example, "Montaigne had a hunch about dying") and scientific terminology (see paragraph 6).
3. Where exactly does Thomas offer his thesis statement in the essay? What is the strategy for placing it here?

▼ WRITING ASSIGNMENTS

1. Having read Lewis Thomas's reflections on death, have your own feelings about the subject changed any? Does death seem more

"natural" to you now? In an essay, write your own reflections on the topic incorporating your response to Dr. Thomas's essay.

2. Have you ever had an experience with death? If so, write an essay on the loss of that person. Try to capture the feelings you experienced—anger, grief, and fear. Does Thomas's essay on the *naturalness* of death help you to come to terms with the experience?

▼ ON THE FEAR OF DEATH
Elisabeth Kübler-Ross

Elisabeth Kübler-Ross, a Swiss-born American psychiatrist, is considered one of the world's foremost experts on the treatment of the terminally ill. She has conducted seminars and written widely about death and dying in order to help people better understand and cope with the process. Of her nine books on the subject her most famous is *On Death and Dying* (1969), from which this essay is taken. In 1988 she published *AIDS: The Ultimate Challenge* which describes her interaction with victims of this devastating disease.

> Let me not pray to be sheltered from
> dangers but to be fearless in facing
> them.
> Let me not beg for the stilling of
> my pain but for the heart to conquer it.
> Let me not look for allies in life's
> battlefield but to my own strength.
> Let me not crave in anxious fear to
> be saved but hope for the patience to win my freedom.
> Grant me that I may not be a
> coward, feeling your mercy in my
> success alone; but let me find the grasp
> of your hand in my failure.
> Rabindranath Tagore, *Fruit-Gathering*

1   Epidemics have taken a great toll of lives in past generations. Death in infancy and early childhood was frequent and there were few families who didn't lose a member of the family at an early age. Medicine has changed greatly in the last decades. Widespread vaccinations have practically eradicated many illnesses, at least in western Europe and the United States. The use of chemotherapy, especially the antibiotics, has contributed to an ever-decreasing num-

ber of fatalities in infectious diseases. Better child care and education has effected a low morbidity and mortality among children. The many diseases that have taken an impressive toll among the young and middle-aged have been conquered. The number of old people is on the rise, and with this fact come the number of people with malignancies and chronic diseases associated more with old age.

Pediatricians have less work with acute and life-threatening situations as they have an ever-increasing number of patients with psychosomatic disturbances and adjustment and behavior problems. Physicians have more people in their waiting rooms with emotional problems than they have ever had before, but they also have more elderly patients who not only try to live with their decreased physical abilities and limitations but who also face loneliness and isolation with all its pains and anguish. The majority of these people are not seen by a psychiatrist. Their needs have to be elicited and gratified by other professional people, for instance, chaplains and social workers. It is for them that I am trying to outline the changes that have taken place in the last few decades, changes that are ultimately responsible for the increased fear of death, the rising number of emotional problems, and the greater need for understanding of and coping with the problems of death and dying. **2**

When we look back in time and study old cultures and people, we are impressed that death has always been distasteful to man and will probably always be. From a psychiatrist's point of view this is very understandable and can perhaps best be explained by our basic knowledge that, in our unconscious, death is never possible in regard to ourselves. It is inconceivable for our unconscious to imagine an actual ending of our own life here on earth, and if this life of ours has to end, the ending is always attributed to a malicious intervention from the outside by someone else. In simple terms, in our unconscious mind we can only be killed; it is inconceivable to die of a natural cause or of old age. Therefore death in itself is associated with a bad act, a frightening happening, something that in itself calls for retribution and punishment. **3**

One is wise to remember these fundamental facts as they are essential in understanding some of the most important, otherwise unintelligible communications of our patients. **4**

The second fact that we have to comprehend is that in our unconscious mind we cannot distinguish between a wish and a deed. We are all aware of some of our illogical dreams in which two completely opposite statements can exist side by side—very acceptable in our dreams but unthinkable and illogical in our wakening state. Just as our unconscious mind cannot differentiate between the wish to kill somebody in anger and the act of having done so, the young child is unable to make this distinction. The child who angrily wishes his mother to drop dead for not having gratified his needs will be traumatized greatly by the actual death of his mother—even if this event is not linked closely in time with his destructive wishes. He will always take part of the whole blame for the loss of his mother. He will always say to himself—rarely to others—"I did it, I am responsible, I was bad, therefore Mommy left me." It is well to remember that **5** the child will react in the same manner if he loses a parent by divorce, separation, or desertion. Death is often seen by a child as an impermanent thing and has therefore little distinction from a divorce in which he may have an opportunity to see a parent again.

6   Many a parent will remember remarks of their children such as, "I will bury my doggy now and next spring when the flowers come up again, he will get up." Maybe it was the same wish that motivated the ancient Egyptians to supply their dead with food and goods to keep them happy and the old American Indians to bury their relatives with their belongings.

7   When we grow older and begin to realize that our omnipotence is really not so omnipotent, that our strongest wishes are not powerful enough to make the impossible possible, the fear that we have contributed to the death of a loved one diminishes—and with it the guilt. The fear remains diminished, however, only so long as it is not challenged too strongly. Its vestiges can be seen daily in hospital corridors and in people associated with the bereaved.

8   A husband and wife may have been fighting for years, but when the partner dies, the survivor will pull his hair, whine and cry louder and beat his chest in regret, fear, and anguish, and will hence fear his own death more than before, still believing in the law of talion—an eye for an eye, a tooth for a tooth—"I am responsible for her death, I will have to die a pitiful death in retribution."

9   Maybe this knowledge will help us understand many of the old customs and rituals which have lasted over the centuries and whose purpose is to diminish the anger of the gods or the people as the case may be, thus decreasing the anticipated punishment. I am thinking of the ashes, the torn clothes, the veil, the *Klage Weiber** of the old days—they are all means to ask you to take pity on them, the mourners, and are expressions of sorrow, grief, and shame. If someone grieves, beats his chest, tears his hair, or refuses to eat, it is an attempt at self-punishment to avoid or reduce the anticipated punishment for the blame that he takes on the death of a loved one.

10   This grief, shame, and guilt are not very far removed from feelings of anger and rage. The process of grief always includes some qualities of anger. Since none of us likes to admit anger at a deceased person, these emotions are often disguised or repressed and prolong the period of grief or show up in other ways. It is well to remember that it is not up to us to judge such feelings as bad or shameful but to understand their true meaning and origin as something very human. In order to illustrate this I will again use the example of the child—and the child in us. The five-year-old who loses his mother is both blaming himself for her disappearance and being angry at her for having deserted him and for no longer gratifying his needs. The dead person then turns into something the child loves and wants very much but also hates with equal intensity for this severe deprivation.

11   The ancient Hebrews regarded the body of a dead person as something unclean and not to be touched. The early American Indians talked about the evil

Klage Weiber: wailing wives. [Ed.]

spirits and shot arrows in the air to drive the spirits away. Many other cultures have rituals to take care of the "bad" dead person, and they all originate in this feeling of anger which still exists in all of us, though we dislike admitting it. The tradition of the tombstone may originate in the wish to keep the bad spirits deep down in the ground, and the pebbles that many mourners put on the grave are leftover symbols of the same wish. Though we call the firing of guns at military funerals a last salute, it is the same symbolic ritual as the Indian used when he shot his spears and arrows into the skies.

I give these examples to emphasize that man has not basically changed. **12** Death is still a fearful, frightening happening, and the fear of death is a universal fear even if we think we have mastered it on many levels.

What has changed is our way of coping and dealing with death and dying and **13** our dying patients.

Having been raised in a country in Europe where science is not so advanced, **14** where modern techniques have just started to find their way into medicine, and where people still live as they did in this country half a century ago, I may have had an opportunity to study a part of the evolution of mankind in a shorter period.

I remember as a child the death of a farmer. He fell from a tree and was not **15** expected to live. He asked simply to die at home, a wish that was granted without question. He called his daughters into the bedroom and spoke with each one of them alone for a few moments. He arranged his affairs quietly, though he was in great pain, and distributed his belongings and his land, none of which was to be split until his wife should follow him in death. He also asked each of his children to share in the work, duties, and tasks that he had carried on until the time of the accident. He asked his friends to visit him once more, to bid goodbye to them. Although I was a small child at the time, he did not exclude me or my siblings. We were allowed to share in the preparations of the family just as we were permitted to grieve with them until he died. When he did die, he was left at home, in his own beloved home which he had built, and among his friends and neighbors who went to take a last look at him where he lay in the midst of flowers in the place he had lived in and loved so much. In that country today there is still no make-believe slumber room, no embalming, no false makeup to pretend sleep. Only the signs of very disfiguring illnesses are covered up with bandages and only infectious cases are removed from the home prior to the burial.

Why do I describe such "old-fashioned" customs? I think they are an indica- **16** tion of our acceptance of a fatal outcome, and they help the dying patient as well as his family to accept the loss of a loved one. If a patient is allowed to terminate his life in the familiar and beloved environment, it requires less adjustment for him. His own family knows him well enough to replace a sedative with a glass of his favorite wine; or the smell of a home-cooked soup may give him the appetite to sip a few spoons of fluid which, I think, is still more enjoyable than an infusion. I will not minimize the need for sedatives and infusions and realize full well from my own experience as a country doctor that they are sometimes life-saving and often unavoidable. But I also know that patience and familiar people and foods could replace many a bottle of intravenous fluids given for the simple reason that it fulfills the physiological need without involving too many people and/or individual nursing care.

17   The fact that children are allowed to stay at home where a fatality has struck and are included in the talk, discussions, and fears gives them the feeling that they are not alone in their grief and gives them the comfort of shared responsibility and shared mourning. It prepares them gradually and helps them view death as part of life, an experience which may help them grow and mature.

18   This is in great contrast to a society in which death is viewed as taboo, discussion of it is regarded as morbid, and children are excluded with the presumption and pretext that it would be "too much" for them. They are then sent off to relatives, often accompanied by some unconvincing lies of "Mother has gone on a long trip" or other unbelievable stories. The child senses that something is wrong, and his distrust in adults will only multiply if other relatives add new variations of the story, avoid his questions or suspicions, shower him with gifts as a meager substitute for a loss he is not permitted to deal with. Sooner or later the child will become aware of the changed family situation and, depending on the age and personality of the child, will have an unresolved grief and regard this incident as a frightening, mysterious, in any case very traumatic experience with untrustworthy grownups, which he has no way to cope with.

19   It is equally unwise to tell a little child who lost her brother that God loved little boys so much that he took little Johnny to heaven. When this little girl grew up to be a woman she never solved her anger at God, which resulted in a psychotic depression when she lost her own little son three decades later.

20   We would think that our great emancipation, our knowledge of science and of man, has given us better ways and means to prepare ourselves and our families for this inevitable happening. Instead the days are gone when a man was allowed to die in peace and dignity in his own home.

21   The more we are making advancements in science, the more we seem to fear and deny the reality of death. How is this possible?

22   We use euphemisms, we make the dead look as if they were asleep, we ship the children off to protect them from the anxiety and turmoil around the house if the patient is fortunate enough to die at home, we don't allow children to visit their dying parents in the hospital, we have long and controversial discussions about whether patients should be told the truth—a question that rarely arises when the dying person is tended by the family physician who has known him from delivery to death and who knows the weaknesses and strengths of each member of the family.

23   I think there are many reasons for this flight away from facing death calmly. One of the most important facts is that dying nowadays is more gruesome in many ways, namely, more lonely, mechanical, and dehumanized; at times it is even difficult to determine technically when the time of death has occurred.

24   Dying becomes lonely and impersonal because the patient is often taken out of his familiar environment and rushed to an emergency room. Whoever has

been very sick and has required rest and comfort especially may recall his experience of being put on a stretcher and enduring the noise of the ambulance siren and hectic rush until the hospital gates open. Only those who have lived through this may appreciate the discomfort and cold necessity of such transportation which is only the beginning of a long ordeal—hard to endure when you are well, difficult to express in words when noise, light, pumps, and voices are all too much to put up with. It may well be that we might consider more the patient under the sheets and blankets and perhaps stop our well-meant efficiency and rush in order to hold the patient's hand, to smile, or to listen to a question. I include the trip to the hospital as the first episode in dying, as it is for many. I am putting it exaggeratedly in contrast to the sick man who is left at home— not to say that lives should not be saved if they can be saved by a hospitalization but to keep the focus on the patient's experience, his needs and his reactions.

When a patient is severely ill, he is often treated like a person with no right **25** to an opinion. It is often someone else who makes the decision if and when and where a patient should be hospitalized. It would take so little to remember that the sick person too has feelings, has wishes and opinions, and has—most important of all—the right to be heard.

Well, our presumed patient has now reached the emergency room. He will be **26** surrounded by busy nurses, orderlies, interns, residents, a lab technician perhaps who will take some blood, an electrocardiogram technician who takes the cardiogram. He may be moved to X-ray and he will overhear opinions of his condition and discussions and questions to members of the family. He slowly but surely is beginning to be treated like a thing. He is no longer a person. Decisions are made often without his opinion. If he tries to rebel he will be sedated and after hours of waiting and wondering whether he has the strength, he will be wheeled into the operating room or intensive treatment unit and become an object of great concern and great financial investment.

He may cry for rest, peace, and dignity, but he will get infusions, transfu- **27** sions, a heart machine, or tracheotomy if necessary. He may want one single person to stop for one single minute so that he can ask one single question—but he will get a dozen people around the clock, all busily preoccupied with his heart rate, pulse, electrocardiogram or pulmonary functions, his secretions or excretions but not with him as a human being. He may wish to fight it all but it is going to be a useless fight since all this is done in the fight for his life, and if they can save his life they can consider the person afterwards. Those who consider the person first may lose precious time to save his life! At least this seems to be the rationale or justification behind all this—or is it? Is the reason for this increasingly mechanical, depersonalized approach our own defensiveness? Is this approach our own way to cope with and repress the anxieties that a terminally or critically ill patient evokes in us? Is our concentration on equipment, on blood pressure, our desperate attempt to deny the impending death which is so frightening and discomforting to us that we displace all our knowledge onto machines, since they are less close to us than the suffering face of another human being which would remind us once more of our lack of omnipotence, our own limits and failures, and last but not least perhaps our own mortality?

28   Maybe the question has to be raised: Are we becoming less human or more human? . . . it is clear that whatever the answer may be, the patient is suffering more—not physically, perhaps, but emotionally. And his needs have not changed over the centuries, only our ability to gratify them.

▼ TOPICAL CONSIDERATIONS

1. To what does Kübler-Ross attribute the increased fear of death and related emotional problems in our society?
2. What point is Kübler-Ross illustrating in her anecdote of the farmer? How does the farmer's dying differ from the way most people die today?
3. According to the author, what are the potential dangers of excluding children from the experience of another's death?
4. What is the thrust of Kübler-Ross's argument regarding the treatment of terminally ill patients? Do you agree with her view? Do you think that there is some justification for this kind of treatment?
5. To what does the author attribute the "depersonalized approach" (paragraph 27) to a patient's dying?

▼ RHETORICAL CONSIDERATIONS

1. Where in the essay does Kübler-Ross move from explanation to argument?
2. Where does the author give the thesis statement in this piece?
3. Divide this essay into three parts. Which paragraphs constitute the beginning? Which constitute the middle? Which constitute the end? Briefly explain how each of the parts are logically connected to each other.

▼ WRITING ASSIGNMENTS

1. The author opens her essay with a quotation. Write a paper in which you discuss the appropriateness of this quotation to the essay.
2. Do you recall your fear of death as a child? If so, try to describe it and any experiences that might have contributed to it.
3. Has anyone close to you ever died? If so, in a paper try to describe how you dealt with that person's death. In the process of grief did you feel conflicting emotions of shame, guilt, and anger?

4. Kübler-Ross recalls the memory of a farmer who took charge of his own dying. What would you do if you were so critically wounded?

5. The author criticizes the impersonal treatment of emergency-room patients. Did you ever find yourself in an emergency room? Did you think the treatment you received was "lonely, mechanical, and dehumanized"? Try to recapture the experience, whether you were the patient or someone you accompanied.

6. In a paper, try to explain what it means to "die with dignity." You may choose to refer to the Kübler-Ross essay or other readings. (You might first read the essay "It's Over, Debbie" and the editorial responses.) Try to make your discussion concrete, even personal if possible.

7. Toward the end of this essay Kübler-Ross criticizes the "well-meant efficiency" of medical people. Do you think that cool efficiency of medical care is sometimes needed in order to save lives? Explore this question in a paper.

▼ AIDS: BEARING WITNESS

George Whitmore

It has been called the most devastating disease of the century. Since the first cases appeared in 1981, over 130,000 victims of acquired immune deficiency syndrome have been reported in America, and over half have resulted in death. Worldwide, 9 to 10 million men, women, and children have been infected with the AIDS-producing virus. The very name of AIDS produces responses of fear and uncertainty—and sometimes hysteria. Dozens of books have been written about the disease. One of the most gripping accounts is George Whitmore's *Someone Was Here: Profiles in the AIDS Epidemic* (1988), from which the following was adapted. Whitmore, a freelance journalist who wrote about the brutal effects of AIDS on others, describes the impact of the disease upon himself. This article first appeared in *The New York Times Magazine* in 1988. Whitmore died of the disease in April 1989 at the age of 43.

> *And we go,*
> *And we drop like the fruits of*
> *the tree,*
> > *Even we,*
> > *Even so.*
> > —George Meredith
> > "Dirge in Woods"

1   Three years ago, when I suggested an article to the editors of this magazine on "the human cost of AIDS," most reporting on the epidemic was scientific in nature and people with AIDS were often portrayed as faceless victims. By profiling a man with AIDS and his volunteer counselor from Gay Men's Health Crisis, I proposed to show the devastating impact AIDS was having on a few individual lives. It had certainly had an impact on mine. I suspected that I was carrying the virus and I was terrified.

2   Plainly, some of my reasons for wanting to write about AIDS were altruistic, others selfish. AIDS was decimating the community around me; there was a need to bear witness. AIDS had turned me and others like me into walking time bombs; there was a need to strike back, not just wait to die. What I didn't fully appreciate then, however, was the extent to which I was trying to bargain with AIDS: If I wrote about it, maybe I wouldn't get it.

3   My article ran in May 1985. But AIDS didn't keep its part of the bargain. Less than a year later, after discovering a small strawberry-colored spot on my calf, I was diagnosed with Kaposi's sarcoma, a rare skin cancer that is one of the primary indicators of acquired immune deficiency syndrome.

4   Ironically, I'd just agreed to write a book on AIDS. The prospect suddenly

seemed absurd, but "Write it," my doctor urged without hesitation. And on reflection, I had to agree. I don't believe in anything like fate. And yet clearly, along with what looked like a losing hand, I'd just been dealt the assignment of a lifetime.

That I was able to take it on isn't as remarkable as some might think. **5** Kaposi's sarcoma alone, in the absence of the severe opportunistic infections that usually accompany AIDS, can constitute a fortunate diagnosis. Many Kaposi's sarcoma patients have lived five years and beyond. Although my own disease has steadily accelerated, I'm one of the very lucky ones. Although increasingly disabled, I haven't even been hospitalized yet.

I'm also hopeful—though it gives me pause to write that, since I value realism **6** and pragmatism over the ill-defined "positive attitude" I'm often counseled to cultivate. Last summer, I began taking the antiviral drug AZT in an experiment to test how it works in people with Kaposi's sarcoma. Partly because testing has been completed on so few other drugs in this country, AZT or something like it is our best hope for an AIDS treatment and, in spite of possible severe side effects, it has already been shown to benefit other categories of people with AIDS. I have no doubt that, administered in combination with drugs that boost the immune system, antiviral drugs like AZT will eventually prolong the lives of countless people like me.

But I don't want to give the impression that I'm patiently waiting, hands **7** folded, for that day to come.

When I began taking AZT, I bought a pill box with a beeper that reminds **8** me to take the medication every four hours. The beeper has a loud and insistent tone, like the shrill pips you hear when a truck is backing up on the street. Ask anybody who carries one—these devices insidiously change your life. You're always on the alert, anticipating that chirp, scheming to turn off the timer before it can detonate. It's relentless. It's like having AIDS. At regular intervals your body fails to perform in some perhaps subtle, perhaps not new, but always alarming way. The clock is always ticking. Every walk in the park might be your last. Every rent check is a lease on another month's life. The beeper is a reminder that with chronic illness, there is no real peace and quiet and no satisfaction, not without the sure prospect of complete health. Paradoxically, this same sense of urgency and unrest enabled me to write my book.

Needless to say, reporting on the AIDS epidemic from my particular point **9** of view has had its advantages and handicaps. My book includes my original article on Jim Sharp, then 35, a New Yorker with AIDS, and Edward Dunn, 43, his counselor from Gay Men's Health Crisis, both white gay men, like myself. But it also profiles men, women and children, black and brown, in all walks of life, who have been touched profoundly by AIDS, too. We are more alike than not. If I felt a special affinity for Manuella Rocha, a Chicano woman in rural Colorado who defied her family and community to nurse her son at home until his death in 1986, it was in no small part because I recognized in her eyes the same thing I saw in my own mother's eyes the day I gave her the news about myself. If I was scared sitting for hours in an airless room in the South Bronx with a bunch of junkies with AIDS, it wasn't because I was scared of *them*. It was because their confusion and rage were precisely what I was feeling myself. The journalist's vaunted shield of objectivity was of little use at times like those. On the contrary, what often counted most wasn't my ability to function as a disinterested observer, but my ability to identify with my subjects.

10   Although some reporters might, I didn't need to be told what it feels like to wait a week for biopsy results or to be briefed on the unresponsiveness of governments and institutions. Nor did I need to go out of my way to research issues of AIDS discrimination—not after I was informed at my neighborhood dental clinic, where I'd been treated for years, that they would no longer clean my teeth.

11   So, there's much to be said for subjective truth. Nevertheless, I worried for a long time about the morality, even the feasibility, of producing a documentary-style piece of reportage like the one I'd contracted for—that is, without literally putting myself into it, in the first person. It wasn't until I found myself alone in a cabin in the woods, poised to write, that I began to confront just who that "first person" had become.

12   The Macdowell colony in Peterborough, N.H., is a collection of quaint artists' studios, each isolated from the others on 450 acres of dense woodland. Since 1907, the colony has served as a retreat and a safe haven for generations of writers, composers and other artists, and it surely did for me. But it would be a lie to say that people who go there can escape; up there, in the woods, the world is very much with you. Up there, away from my constant lover and loving friends, at a certain remove from the Catherine wheel of death and mourning that my life in New York had become, off the treadmill of interviews and deadlines, I came face to face with everything I'd successfully evaded about AIDS.

13   Having it, for instance. Before I went to New Hampshire, it was still possible, even necessary, to pretend that in some essential way I didn't have AIDS in order to keep working. As far as I know, no one I interviewed during the course of researching my book knew that I had AIDS. And the telltale marks hadn't spread to my face.

14   My body. I hadn't looked at it much.

15   Before I left for New Hampshire, at the Passover seder with my lover Michael's family, we took turns reading the Haggadah in booklets illustrated with line drawings. When we reached the page with the plagues God brought down on the Egyptians, there was a locust, there was a dead fish with X's for eyes, there was the outline of a man with dots all over him, signifying boils. I stared at the cartoon of the man with the boils. I knew Michael, sitting next to me, was thinking the same thing. My body was like that now. I'd had three lesions 12 months before. Now there were three dozen.

16   One day in New Hampshire, in the shower, I looked at my body. It was as if I'd never seen it before.

17   A transformation had taken place and it was written on my skin. When I met Jim Sharp three years ago, I have to confess, I could only see a dying man. A

chasm had separated me from him and the other men with AIDS I interviewed for The Times. Even though they were gay, even though most of them were my own age, each one of them remained safely at arm's length. But now that chasm was breached and there was no safety.

Grief, despair, terror—these feelings easily come to mind when AIDS does. **18** They threatened to engulf me when I began writing my book. But what about anger?

When you have AIDS, the fear and loathing, the black paranoia, the everlast- **19** ing, excruciating uncertainty of AIDS colors everything. When you walk down the street with AIDS, everything in your path is an aggravation, an impediment, a threat—for what in your life isn't now? A cab overshoots the crosswalk. Someone at the head of the line is arguing with the bank teller. All the petty frustrations of urban life get magnified to the limit of tolerance. Not even the infirm old man counting out his pennies at the newsstand is exempt from your fury—or perhaps especially not him, for in the prime of life aren't you becoming just that: elderly and infirm?

It wasn't until I returned to the transcripts of my original interviews with Jim **20** that I realized that he—a voluble ad man with a wicked sense of humor, a short fuse and an iron will to live—had a special gift for anger, and Jim was now speaking for me, too.

Anger, life-affirming anger was the lesson Jim, Manuella Rocha and that **21** room full of addicts taught me. Without it, I couldn't have written about the ocean of pain and loss that surrounds us without drowning in it.

My article about Jim Sharp and Edward Dunn was a portrait of two strang- **22** ers united in adversity. In 1984, after his lover died of AIDS, Edward felt compelled to volunteer at Gay Men's Health Crisis. He couldn't, he said, sit passively on the sidelines while the epidemic raged on. Jim's case was the first one assigned to Edward when he finished his training as a crisis counselor. It was Edward's job to help Jim negotiate the labyrinth of problems—medical, finan- cial, legal—that an AIDS diagnosis entails. In time, they became remarkably good friends as well.

An intensely private person, Edward was willing to expose himself in a series **23** of grueling interviews because he was, I think, desperate to make a difference. The sole stipulation he attached to our work together was that his lover be given a pseudonym. Edward wanted to spare "Robert's" family—who had never been able to acknowledge their son's homosexuality, even unto death—any possible hurt.

Soon after the article came out, Edward brought me a gift. It was a little **24** teddy bear—a nice ginger-colored bear with a gingham ribbon tied around its neck—and I didn't know quite what to make of it. But Edward explained to me that he often gave teddy bears to friends, as they represented warmth and gentleness to him. Later, he asked me what I was going to name mine.

"I hadn't thought of naming it . . ." **25**

"Oh, you have to name him," Edward said. **26**

"I don't know, what do you think?" **27**

28   "I thought you might call him Robert."

29   That summer, Jim, a transplanted Texan, moved back to Houston from New York. Then, Edward moved to Los Angeles, saying it was time to begin a new life. Perhaps grandiosely, I wondered if our interviews hadn't played a part in Edward's decision to leave the city—that perhaps they'd served as something of a catharsis or a watershed.

30   Over the next year and a half, Robert the bear sat on the bookshelf in the hall and only came down when the cat knocked him down. Every once in a while, I'd find Robert on the floor, dust him off and put him back on the shelf. I felt vaguely guilty about Robert. I was no longer in touch with Edward.

31   It has been called "the second wave" of the AIDS epidemic. Its casualties include, in ever-increasing numbers, drug abusers, their wives and lovers, and their babies. I knew one of those babies.

32   I first saw Frederico—this is not his real name—one gloomy day last March, in the pediatrics ward at Lincoln Hospital in the South Bronx. Room 219, where Frederico was kept out of the way, is down the hall from the nurses' station. Not many people pass by its safety-glass windows. I doubt that I would have known Frederico even existed had I not been told about him by Sister Fran Whelan, a Catholic chaplain at the hospital.

33   Sister Fran, a petite woman with a neat cap of salt-and-pepper hair, was instrumental in getting me permission to visit Lincoln to observe its "AIDS team." For a few months, I sat in on meetings, went on rounds with its members, interviewed patients and health-care workers, and attended the weekly support group for people with AIDS.

34   In the early years of the epidemic, when Sister Fran, a member of the Dominican Sisters of the Sick Poor, began working at Lincoln, there were no more than one or two people with AIDS in the hospital at any given time. By last winter, there were always more than two dozen, with dozens more on the outpatient rolls. Virtually all of the AIDS patients at Lincoln, a huge municipal hospital, were heterosexual, virtually all were black or Hispanic. Although blacks and Hispanics account for some 20 percent of the United States population, they now represent, nationwide, 39 percent of those with AIDS. In the Bronx, rates of AIDS infection are believed to be among the highest in the nation. Currently, one out of 43 newborn babies there carries antibodies to the HIV virus, indicating that their mothers were infected.

35   When I first saw him, Frederico was 2½ years old and had been living at Lincoln for nine months. His mother, an alcoholic and former drug addict, had apparently transmitted the AIDS virus to him in the womb. The summer before, a few weeks before Frederico's father died from AIDS, his mother had left him in the hospital. Then she died of AIDS, too. From then on, Frederico was a "boarder baby," one of about 300 children living in New York City hospitals last March because accredited foster homes couldn't be found for them. Frederico happened to be disabled—he was born with cerebral palsy in addition to his HIV, or human immunodeficiency virus, infection—but lots of other

children who were no longer ill and had no handicaps remained in hospital wards indefinitely.

Frederico's only visitor from the outside was a distant relation, a Parks **36** Department worker named Alfred Schult who came to the hospital religiously, on Tuesdays and Sundays. Frederico's mother had been, Mr. Schult later told me, "the daughter I never had." When she died, Mr. Schult sent a telegram to her widowed father in Florida. The telegram wasn't returned but it wasn't answered, either. Frederico's father's mother, who lived in the Bronx, visited him in the hospital once, I was told. She had custody of Frederico's five-year-old brother, whom she'd sent to Puerto Rico to live with relatives. But no one in Frederico's father's family was willing to take Frederico. Nor was Mr. Schult, ailing himself, able to.

At 2½, Frederico couldn't talk. He couldn't sit up or stand. He couldn't hold **37** a bottle. Since he'd never had any of the cancers or opportunistic infections that spell AIDS, his official diagnosis was AIDS-related complex, or ARC. He had not, however, escaped the stigma of AIDS. Sister Marie Barletta, his patient advocate at the hospital, had to argue long and vigorously with authorities and submit reams of paperwork to get Frederico into a rehabilitation day-care program elsewhere. Unfortunately, just when he was about to go to day care, Frederico got a temperature, so day care was postponed.

The hospital personnel and the volunteers who held and fed Frederico did the **38** best they could.

The day Sister Fran took me to see Frederico, he was sleeping. We stood side **39** by side, peering into his crib.

That day, he was wearing mitts made of stretch-knit bandage material knot- **40** ted at one end and fastened around his wrists with adhesive tape. These were to keep him from scratching himself or pulling out tubes; sometimes Frederico had to be fed formula through a nasal-gastric tube taped to his cheek and nose, and sometimes he had to be given antibiotics intravenously.

The nurses on Frederico's floor noticed that he picked up everything, every **41** little fungus, every little infection.

Stuffed animals were lined up at the head of Frederico's crib. A musical **42** mobile of circus animals in primary colors was fastened to the headboard. A heart-shaped balloon with the words "I Love You" was tethered to the rail. Frederico was propped up in an infant carrier in the crib, facing a blank wall with a bed-lamp on it and a red sign that said No Smoking/No Fumar.

I stood next to Sister Fran, looking at Frederico. I heard a ringing in my ears. **43** I almost bolted out of the room. Somehow, I kept my feet planted where they were on the floor.

I'd seen eyes unblinking from lesions. I'd spoken into deaf ears. I'd held the **44** hand of a dying man. But nothing prepared me for this.

Frederico was beautiful. In his sleep, he expelled little sighs. His eyelids **45** twitched. He was very fair, with light brown curly hair. His skin was translucent. You could see violet veins through the skin of his eyelids.

46   I wanted to snatch him out of his crib, snatch him up and run away with him. It was all at once horribly, cruelly clear that I wanted for Frederico what I wanted for myself, and I was powerless.

47   Later, walking down the hall beside Sister Fran, I struggled to retain my composure.

48   "It's good the nurses saw you with me," Sister Fran was saying. "Now you can come visit him lots, whenever you like, and there'll be no questions." Sister Fran has her ways. She knew I'd come back.

49   And I did, more than once. I held Frederico in my arms. He smelled like urine and baby powder, and he was quite a handful. He squirmed in my arms. I was a stranger. He didn't know me. He wanted to be put down.

50   The day I first saw Frederico, when Sister Fran was distracted for a moment, I took Robert the bear out of the plastic bag I was carrying and set him down among the other stuffed animals in the crib. I had felt I shouldn't come empty-handed. I knew Edward would approve. What I didn't know was that Edward had AIDS and would die before the year was out.

51   Irony of ironies, Jim outlived Edward, the counselor sent to aid him in his affliction.

52   Today, Jim lives in a modest bungalow house on a tree-lined street in Houston, where I visited him last June. He's something of a celebrity and has served on the board of the local AIDS foundation. He spends lots of time every day on the phone, dispensing comfort and advice to other people with AIDS. Among his other distinctions, Jim is probably the only man with AIDS in Texas who has lived through the mandatory two-year waiting period there to collect Medicare.

53   As we sat talking in Jim's living room, I noticed, on the mantelpiece, the stuffed piranha Edward once brought back from Brazil and gave to him, joking that, "This is what you look like when you don't get your way."

54   I remember vividly my reaction to the piranha, when I first interviewed Jim in New York three years ago—with its slimy hide and repulsive grin, it was the perfect image of AIDS to me. Now it seemed strange to see it in a living room in Texas, alongside all the ordinary things people accumulate. Still fearsome, still bristling with malevolence, the piranha had nevertheless somehow grown familiar, almost domesticated, like the gnawing terror Jim and I and thousands like us have had to learn to accommodate. Every time he has to go to the hospital, Jim told me, he takes along the piranha. It's a kind of talisman.

55   A week after I got back from Texas, Mr. Schult called to tell me Frederico was dead.

56   Things had been looking up for Frederico. Sister Barletta had finally gotten him into day care. The agency had placed him in a foster home. But on his second night outside the hospital, inexplicably, Frederico turned blue. By the time the ambulance arrived, he was dead. And for some reason, I was told, the emergency medical service didn't even try to revive him.

57   I went to the funeral parlor. The long, low, dim basement room in East Harlem seemed full to overflowing with grieving women—Sister Barletta, the

women from Frederico's day-care center, nurses and volunteers who'd taken care of Frederico in the hospital—all of them asking why.

Frederico's body lay up front in a little coffin lined with swagged white satin. He was dressed in a blue playsuit with speedboats on it. **58**

"You dressed him in a playsuit," I said to Mr. Schult, at my side. **59**

"And now he's at play," Mr. Schult sobbed. "He's romping in heaven now with Jesus like he never was able to down here." **60**

I held Mr. Schult's arm tightly until the sobbing passed. I couldn't help but notice, the coffin was too small for the top of the catafalque. You could see gouges and scrapes and scars in the wood in the parts the coffin didn't cover. I looked down into the coffin, at the body beyond help. I agreed aloud with Mr. Schult that Frederico was in heaven now, because it seemed to make him feel a little better. **61**

I don't know why, but I always thought Frederico would live. **62**

▼ TOPICAL CONSIDERATIONS

1. Whitmore says that for a while he felt that if he wrote about AIDS, maybe he wouldn't get it. What was the emotional "logic" behind this feeling?
2. How did Whitmore bear witness to AIDS discrimination?
3. When did Whitmore finally confront the fact that he had AIDS? How had he previously evaded the truth?
4. In her essay "On the Fear of Death," Elisabeth Kübler-Ross says that a universal reaction to death is anger. How does Whitmore characterize his own anger at having AIDS? How did anger help him cope?
5. How did Jim Sharp cope with his AIDS in Houston? Do you see a parallel between his life and Whitmore's own life? Why does Jim keep the stuffed piranha on his mantelpiece?
6. How has this article affected your own understanding of AIDS and AIDS victims?

▼ RHETORICAL CONSIDERATIONS

1. Consider George Whitmore's choice of titles. How appropriate is it? How does it connote the essential irony of Whitmore's plight?
2. In paragraph 8, Whitmore says his beeper is "like having AIDS." How does Whitmore specifically liken the two? How apt is the analogy?
3. How does "Robert" help link the story of Edward with that of Frederico? How else are they connected?
4. In his description of Frederico in his crib, Whitmore uses descrip-

tive details to evoke in the reader strong emotions of pity and sorrow. What are some of the specific details and how do they create their effect?

5. Whitmore says in paragraph 54 that the piranha on Jim's mantelpiece was "the perfect image of AIDS." How effective a metaphor is this?

6. At the end of the essay, Whitmore says he couldn't help but notice that Frederico's "coffin was too small for the top of the catafalque. You could see gouges and scrapes and scars in the wood in the parts the coffin didn't cover." Why would Whitmore record these seemingly insignificant details? How do they symbolically comment on the child's life and death?

7. Evaluate the impact of the last sentence of the essay. Why is it rendered in a paragraph all its own? How does it connect to a theme early on in the essay?

▼ WRITING ASSIGNMENTS

1. As some have pointed out, AIDS is really two epidemics: that of a disease and that of fear. Fear not only manifests itself in irrational behavior—needless discrimination against victims of the disease—but it stirs up already built-in prejudices against homosexuals, minorities, and drug addicts. In a paper, explore your own attitudes towards AIDS victims. How has this article affected your attitudes?

2. Do you know anybody with AIDS or an AIDS-related condition? If so, write a paper about that person and how he or she has coped.

3. Many books and articles have been written on the subject of AIDS. Using some of these materials from the library, write a paper on how concerned individuals are working to slow the course of the disease and ease the suffering of its victims. Consider the work done at home, in schools, at churches and synagogues, at the workplace, on campus, in the arts and media, and so on.

▼ A WAY TO SAY FAREWELL

Dr. Benjamin Spock

The subject of human death does not readily lend itself to upbeat reflections. However, we have found one that at least regards the matter in a positive spirit. Appropriately, it was written by America's most famous baby doctor who reflects on the end of a life—his own. "I don't want tiptoers around me. I want cheerful people who will look me in the eye." Dr. Spock, who was born in 1904 and who still actively writes on children, is the author of *Baby and Child Care,* which has sold more than 32 million copies. This article originally appeared in *Parade* magazine in 1985.

Being in good health and of sound mind, except for absentmindedness and a poor memory for names, I'm not expecting to die for a long time—not if I can help it. But, at 81, I'd like to give some guidelines to my relatives. As far as I know, and one never knows for sure until his time comes, I don't fear the dying as long as it's not very painful or lonely or lacking in dignity. **1**

I say "one never knows" because I've been surprised by the behavior of some physicians as they've died; by my own behavior when a patient died; and by the behavior of an old friend during a fatal illness. **2**

It is a fairly common occurrence for a physician, who should know better, to ignore obvious symptoms of cancer in himself until it is too late for treatment, apparently preferring to hope against hope that his suspicion is not correct. **3**

The mother of a patient of mine long ago called me in dismay at 7 A.M. to say that she had just found her infant son dead in his crib. I told her to rush him to a hospital that was close to their home, much closer than I was. If he was dead, I suggested she ask for an autopsy that would reassure her and her husband that there had been no neglect on their part. It was clear to me that they wanted me to meet with them—sooner or later—but I could not face them. I gave excuses. Years later, when I read that some staff people in hospitals tend to avoid, and thereby neglect, a patient who is dying, I understood. The fear of facing death is truly powerful. **4**

A close, wise friend and colleague of mine (not a physician) died slowly and painfully of inoperable cancer. She was the sole support of three young children and should have been making careful plans for their future and discussing this with them. But she never asked anyone about her diagnosis. And, respecting her apparent wish to remain in ignorance, nobody ever volunteered the information. Each time I visited, I expected her finally to ask, and each time I was flabbergasted that she did not. Now, years later, I realize that she might have preferred a frank discussion with her doctor but had been put off by his reluctance to raise the issue. Perhaps she only was following his cue. **5**

I'm reminded of an episode in Elisabeth Kübler-Ross's book *On Death and* **6**

Dying, in which she was asked by a physician to talk with his patient, whom he confidently believed did not know his diagnosis. She didn't want to shock the patient; on the other hand, she wanted to make it easy for him to communicate with her. So she simply asked, "How sick are you?" and he replied, "I am full of cancer."

7   This case made me realize that I would want a physician and a spouse who were, on the one hand, cheerful but who would not pretend that everything was lovely. I don't want around me solemn, whispering tiptoers. But I also don't want hearty, loud-voiced types who keep asking me, in a routine way, how I feel or whether there is anything I want. I want people, preferably attractive ones, who will look me in the eye in a friendly or even loving manner, discuss openly any of my concerns and ask only those questions that apply to my actual situation.

8   I would want my doctor to give any treatment available if it had a chance of curing me or keeping me alive and lively for a number of years. But I would not want to be kept alive with antibiotics, infusions, transfusions, anticancer drugs or radiation if they were just to postpone my death for a few months—especially if I had lost my marbles.

9   Having been brought up with a strong emphasis on the importance of appearances, I have a real dread of going visibly senile without realizing it.

10   I remember my distress when, some years ago, I happened to descend in a Plaza Hotel elevator with a famous architect. Though he was old, he still maintained a dashing appearance: a broad-brimmed but flat-topped cowboy hat such as Gary Cooper wore in *High Noon,* an expensive-looking suit and a flowing silk bow tie. His jacket, however, was dotted with food spots. He seemed carefree, but I felt deeply embarrassed for him. Since then, I've inspected my jacket carefully each morning, though I realized at that time that, if senility sets in, I will have forgotten this precaution.

11   Of course, the reason that physicians often will go to such extremes to keep a hopelessly ill patient alive is because their job, their training and their ethics direct them to do so. Besides, they can be sued by a disgruntled relative for not having done everything conceivable.

12   When I wonder what directions to leave, I realize that, in addition to my own wishes, there will be my wife's feelings and my doctor's ethics to consider. For instance, even though I've decided in advance that I want to be put out of my misery if the pain proves unbearable, will my doctor be willing to give the necessary dose of medication—or to leave it handy—and will Mary have the nerve to jab the needle?

13   The omission of artificial life-support systems is only one aspect of being allowed to die naturally. I would want to be at home, if that wasn't too burdensome, or in a hospice, rather than in a hospital. I have been a frequent patient in hospitals, and I am grateful for having had excellent doctors and nurses. But hospitals are nothing like home. They are more like factories—clean, modern factories to produce diagnoses and treatments. A stream of staffers barges in, as if from outer space: history taker, physical examiners,

temperature and pulse takers, meal servers, bath givers, stretcher pushers, X-ray technicians, bed makers, pill pushers, specimen takers. Not one of them is primarily interested in the person, of course.

In recent years, the hospice movement, which began in England, has spread over the U.S. The aim is to let the person die as pleasantly as possible in a homelike setting, surrounded by family and some familiar possessions and spared pain by regular, heavy medication—without any fussing that is not provided solely for comfort. That's the departure for me. **14**

I'd also like to have something to say about my memorial service, though I don't expect to be looking down from heaven at the time of the event. I don't like to think of myself as being unceremoniously buried or burned up without some kind of service to mark my passage from person to memory. **15**

I dislike intensely the atmosphere of the conventional funeral: the darkened room, the solemn people, silent or whispering or sniffling, the funeral director's assistants pretending to feel mournful. My ideal would be the New Orleans black funeral, in which friends snake-dance through the streets to the music of a jazz band. But a satisfactory compromise would be a church service for my friends to think of me together for an hour and say farewell. **16**

I would like the people to be normally noisy and cheerful. The music might consist of the ragtime and jazz to which I love to dance in order to liberate myself from my puritanical upbringing, lively hymns, and such tunes as "The Battle Hymn of the Republic" and "America the Beautiful," which always choke me up, not with sorrow but with exultation. I like the service for the dead delivered in the rich cadences that have come down to us through the centuries. I'd like the minister, preferably William Sloane Coffin Jr., who enjoys life and with whom I was put on trial for our opposition to the Vietnam war, to speak of our hope that the peacemakers really will prevail. And some child-development person or parent could speak of my belief in the infinite perfectibility of children and of my agreement with Jesus' words: "Suffer little children, and forbid them not, to come unto me: for of such is the kingdom of heaven." **17**

Then there could be a cheerful cocktail party somewhere nearby. **18**

▼ TOPICAL CONSIDERATIONS

1. What three examples does Spock give to show that one never knows what his own reaction to death will be?
2. Spock says in paragraph 7 that he doesn't want "solemn, whispering tiptoers" at his deathbed. What type of person does he want?
3. Why would Spock prefer hospice care to hospital care in the event of a long terminal illness?
4. What kind of memorial service does Spock say he would like for himself? What kind of service would you design for yourself? Consider your choice of place, guests, music, speakers, and readings.

▼ RHETORICAL CONSIDERATIONS

1. What single detail makes Dr. Spock's description of the aging architect poignant?
2. Find examples where Spock concludes a very serious, potentially grim series of sentences with a short, clipped, and cheerful remark. Why does he do this?
3. Why does Spock begin the piece with the phrase, "being in good health and of sound mind"? What is the effect?

▼ WRITING ASSIGNMENTS

1. Write an essay describing the way someone you know dealt with death.
2. Read Elisabeth Kübler-Ross's essay, "On the Fear of Death," in this chapter, then write an essay expressing your reaction to her ideas.
3. Write a mock will in which you lay down the guidelines for your own funeral. Design the kind of service you would like to have specifying the guests, location, music, readings, and so forth.

▼ ACKNOWLEDGMENTS

Frank Conroy, "Think About It," *Harper's Magazine,* 1989. Copyright © 1989 by *Harper's Magazine.* All rights reserved. Reprinted from the November issue by special permission.

Dick Gregory, "Shame." From *nigger: An Autobiography* by Dick Gregory, with Robert Libsyte. Copyright © 1964 by Dick Gregory Enterprises, Inc. Reprinted by permission of the publisher, Dutton, an imprint of New American Library, a division of Penguin Books USA Inc.

Maya Angelou, "Graduation." From *I Know Why the Caged Bird Sings* by Maya Angelou. Copyright © 1969 by Maya Angelou. Reprinted by permission of Random House, Inc. (The title "Graduation" is not Maya Angelou's.)

Langston Hughes, "Salvation." From *The Big Sea* by Langston Hughes. Copyright © 1940 by Langston Hughes. Copyright © renewed 1968 by Arna Bontemps and George Houston Bass. Reprinted by permission of Hill and Wang, a division of Farrar, Straus & Giroux, Inc.

Julianne Malveaux, "Angry," *Essence Magazine,* May 1989. Reprinted by permission of the author.

Linda Bird Francke, "The Ambivalence of Abortion." Copyright © 1976 by Linda Bird Francke. Reprinted by permission of the author.

Joy Harjo, "Ordinary Spirit." Reprinted from *I Tell You Now: Autobiographical Essays by Native American Writers,* edited by Brian Swann and Arnold Krupat, by permission of University of Nebraska Press. Copyright © 1987 by the University of Nebraska Press.

Rosario Ferré, "Out of the Frying Pan." From *Lives on the Line: The Testimony of Contemporary Latin American Authors,* edited by Doris Meyer (1988). Reprinted by permission.

Mary Ann Delmonico Kuharski, "A Love of Family Affairs," *Newsweek,* 1989. Every effort has been made to locate the copyright holder of this selection. A suitable fee for this use has been reserved by the publisher.

Alice Walker, "In Search of Our Mothers' Gardens." From *In Search of Our Mothers' Gardens* by Alice Walker. Reprinted by permission.

Patsy Neal, "My Grandmother, the Bag Lady."

Copyright © 1981 by Patsy Neal. Reprinted by permission. Originally appeared in *Newsweek.*

Mary Catherine Bateson, "The Aquarium and the Globe." From *With a Daughter's Eye* by Mary Catherine Bateson, 1985. Reprinted by permission of William Morrow and Company, Inc., Publishers, New York.

Michael Reese and Pamela Abramson, "Homosexuality: One Family's Affair," *Newsweek,* January 13, 1986. Copyright © 1986, Newsweek, Inc. All rights reserved. Reprinted by permission.

Randall Williams, "Daddy Tucked the Blanket," *The New York Times,* July 10, 1975. Copyright © 1975 by The New York Times Company. Reprinted by permission.

Barbara S. Cain, "Older Children and Divorce," *The New York Times Magazine,* February 18, 1990. Copyright © 1990 by The New York Times Company. Reprinted by permission.

Daniel Smith-Rowsey, "The Terrible Twenties," *Newsweek,* June 1991. Reprinted by permission.

Michael Ventura, "On Kids and Slasher Movies," *LA Weekly,* November 3, 1989. Reprinted by permission.

Robert C. Noble, "There Is No Safe Sex," *Newsweek,* April 1991. Reprinted by permission.

Alan Durning, "What Price Consumption?" *Technology Review,* May/June 1991. Reprinted by permission from *Technology Review,* copyright © 1991.

Andrew Ward, "They Also Wait Who Stand and Serve Themselves." Copyright © 1979 by Andrew Ward. Originally published in the May 1979 issue of the *Atlantic Monthly* by the Atlantic Monthly Company. Reprinted by permission of the author.

Jonathan Kozol, "The New Untouchables." Reprinted by permission.

Michele L Norris, "A Child of Crack," *The Washington Post National Weekly Edition,* September 11–17, 1989. Copyright © 1989 *The Washington Post.* Reprinted by permission.

Charles R. Larson, "The Value of Volunteering," *Newsweek,* July 15, 1991. Reprinted by permission.

Prudence Mackintosh, "Masculine/Feminine." From *Thundering Sneakers* by Prudence

Mackintosh (1981). Reprinted by permission of the Wendy-Weil Agency, Inc. Copyright © 1977 by Prudence Mackintosh.

Anna Quindlen, "Feminist," *The New York Times,* April 24, 1988. Copyright © 1988 by The New York Times Company. Reprinted by permission.

Key Ebeling, "The Failure of Feminism," *Newsweek,* November 19, 1990. Reprinted by permission.

Linda Bird Francke, "Requiem for a Soldier," *The New York Times,* April 21, 1991. Copyright © 1991 by The New York Times Company. Reprinted by permission.

Naomi Wolf, "The Beauty Myth." From *The Beauty Myth* by Naomi Wolf, 1991. Reprinted by permission of William Morrow and Company, Inc., Publishers, New York.

Warren Farrell, "Men as Success Objects," *Family Therapy Network,* November/December 1988. Reprinted by permission.

Sam Allis, "What Do Men Really Want?" *Time,* Fall 1990. Copyright © 1990 The Time Inc. Magazine Company. Reprinted by permission.

Ishmael Reed, "America: The Multinational Society." Reprinted with permission of Atheneum Publishers, an imprint of Macmillan Publishing Company, from *Writin' Is Fightin'* by Ishmael Reed. This essay originally appeared in *San Francisco Focus,* December 1983. Copyright © 1983 by Ishmael Reed.

Joan L. Morgan, "The Struggle Is Ours," *Essence Magazine,* May 1990. Reprinted by permission.

Brent Staples, "Black Men and Public Space." Copyright © 1986 by Brent Staples. Reprinted by permission. Originally appeared in *Harper's Magazine.*

Richard Rodriguez, "Your Parents Must Be Very Proud." From *Hunger of Memory* by Richard Rodriguez. Copyright © 1982 by Richard Rodriguez. Reprinted by permission of David R. Godine, Publisher.

Roberto Santiago, "Black and Latino," *Essence Magazine,* November 1989. Reprinted by permission.

Elizabeth Wong, "To Be an All-American Girl," *Los Angeles Times,* 1989. Every effort has been made to locate the copyright holder of this selection. A suitable fee for this use has been reserved by the publisher.

Shanlon Wu, "In Search of Bruce Lee's Grave," *The New York Times,* April 15, 1990. Copyright © 1990 by The New York Times Company. Reprinted by permission.

Clara Spotted Elk, "Indian Bones," *The New York Times,* March 8, 1989. Copyright © 1989 by The New York Times Company. Reprinted by permission.

Lynne Layton, "What's Madonna Teaching Us?" *The Boston Globe,* June 1990. Reprinted by permission.

Johanna McGeary, "Ode to a Tyrannical Muse (Or Why I Love and Hate Fashion)," *Time,* Fall 1990. Copyright © 1990 The Time Inc. Magazine Company. Reprinted by permission.

Sally B. Donnelley, "Work That Body!" *Time,* 1990. Copyright © 1990 The Time Inc. Magazine Company. Reprinted by permission.

Dave Barry, "The Fear Lobe Meets 'The Brainsucker'" *The Boston Globe,* May 31, 1990. Reprinted by permission.

Bill Boggs, "Finding the Fury," *The New York Times Magazine,* August 2, 1987. Copyright © 1987 by The New York Times Company. Reprinted by permission.

Patrick F. McManus, "The Backpacker." From *A Fine and Pleasant Misery* by Patrick McManus, edited by Jack Samson. Copyright © 1978 by Patrick F. McManus. Reprinted by permission of Henry Holt and Company, Inc.

Peter C. Kratcoski, "What Did Kids Do Before Television Was Invented?" Reprinted from *USA Today.* Copyright © 1981 by the Society for the Advancement of Education.

Marie Winn, "The Plug-In Drug." From *The Plug-In Drug: TV* by Marie Winn. Copyright © 1977, 1985 by Marie Winn Miller. Reprinted by permission of Viking Penguin, a division of Penguin Books USA Inc.

Ellen Goodman, "The Violence Is Fake, the Impact Is Real." Copyright © 1977, The Boston Globe/Washington Post Writers Group. Reprinted by permission.

Neil Postman, "Now . . . This." From *Amusing Ourselves to Death* by Neil Postman. Copyright © 1985 by Neil Postman. Used by permission of Viking Penguin, a division of Penguin Books USA Inc.

Jeff Greenfield, "Don't Blame TV." Reprinted with permission of the publisher and the author from *TV Guide* Magazine. Copyright © 1986 by Triangle Publications, Inc., Radnor, Pennsylvania.

P. J. O'Rourke, "Why I Quit Watching Television," *Parade* Magazine, December 8, 1985. Reprinted by permission.

Patricia Volk, "A Word from Our Sponsor," *The New York Times,* August 23, 1987. Copyright © 1987 by The New York Times Company. Reprinted by permission.

Charles A. O'Neill, "The Language of Advertising." Copyright © 1984 by Charles A. O'Neill. Used by permission.

Carol Moog, "Sin, Sex, and Suggestion." From *Are They Selling Her Lips?* by Carol Moog, 1990. Reprinted by permission of William Morrow and Company, Inc., Publishers, New York.

Jay Rosen, "Presence of the Word in TV Advertising," *Et cetera,* Vol. 44, No. 2, Summer 1987. Used by permission.

Mark Crispin Miller, "How Now Dow?" *Esquire,* September 1990. Reprinted by permission of the author.

Diane White, "Who Brews Up These Ads?" *The Boston Globe,* November 1990. Reprinted by permission.

Martin Luther King, Jr., "Pilgrimage to Nonviolence." From *Stride Toward Freedom: The Montgomery Story* by Martin Luther King, Jr. Copyright © 1958 by Martin Luther King, Jr. Copyright © renewed 1986 by Coretta Scott King, Dexter King, Martin Luther King III, Yolanda King and Bernice King. Reprinted by permission of Harper-Collins Publishers.

Martin Gansberg, "38 Who Saw Murder Didn't Call the Police," *The New York Times,* March 17, 1964. Copyright © 1964 by The New York Times Company. Reprinted by permission.

Kathi Maio, "Hooked on Hate?" *Ms.,* September/October 1990. Reprinted by permission of *Ms.* Magazine, copyright © 1990.

Aileen C. Hefferren, "An Incident in the Park," *Newsweek,* December 1990. Reprinted by permission.

Nancy Gibbs, "When Is It Rape?" *Time,* June 3, 1991. Copyright © 1991 The Time Inc. Magazine Company. Reprinted by permission.

Gail Buchalter, "Why I Bought a Gun," *Parade,* February 1988. Reprinted by permission.

Sarah Brady, "The Case Against Firearms." From ". . . and the Case Against Them," *Time,* January 29, 1990. Copyright © 1990 The Time Inc. Magazine Company. Reprinted by permission

Warren Cassidy, "The Case for Firearms." From "The Case for Firearms . . ." *Time,* January 29, 1990. Copyright © 1990 The Time Inc. Magazine Company. Reprinted by permission.

Faye Wattleton, "Which Way Black America?—Pro-Choice," *Ebony,* October 1989. Copyright © 1989 Johnson Publishing Company, Inc. Reprinted by permission of Faye Wattleton and Ebony magazine.

Pamela Carr, "Which Way Black America?—Anti-Abortion," *Ebony,* October 1989. Copyright © 1989 Johnson Publishing Company, Inc. Reprinted by permission of Pamela Carr and Ebony magazine.

Anonymous, "It's Over, Debbie," *Journal of the American Medical Association,* January 8, 1988, Vol. 259, No. 2, p. 272. Copyright © 1988, American Medical Association. Reprinted by permission.

Susan D. Wilson, Letter to the Editor, *Journal of the American Medical Association,* April 8, 1988, Vol. 259, No. 14, p. 2094. Copyright © 1988, American Medical Association. Reprinted by permission.

H. Y. Vanderpool, Letter to the Editor, *Journal of the American Medical Association,* April 8, 1988, Vol. 259, No. 14, p. 2096. Copyright © 1988, American Medical Association. Reprinted by permission.

D. C. Shaw, Letter to the Editor, *Journal of the American Medical Association,* April 8, 1988, Vol. 259, No. 14, p. 2096. Copyright © 1988, American Medical Association. Reprinted by permission.

Edward I. Koch, "Death and Justice: How Capital Punishment Affirms Life," *The New Republic,* April 15, 1985. Reprinted by permission.

David Bruck, "The Death Penalty," *The New Republic,* May 20, 1985. Reprinted by permission.

Charles R. Lawrence III, "Regulating Racist Speech on Campus," *Chronicle of Higher Education,* October 25, 1989. Reprinted by permission.

Nat Hentoff, "Free Speech on Campus," *The Progressive,* May 1989. Reprinted by permission.

Gwynne Dyer, "A Cruel Universe, But the Only One Where Humans Could Exist," *The Boston Globe,* November 12, 1985. Reprinted by permission of the author.

Edward Hoagland, "The Courage of Turtles." From *The Courage of Turtles* by Edward Hoagland (1985). Copyright © 1968, 1969, 1970 by Edward Hoagland. Reprinted by permission.

Charles Tyler, "Toward a Warmer World," *Geographical,* 1990. Every effort has been made to locate the copyright holder of this selection. A suitable fee for this use has been reserved by the publisher.

William McKibben, "A Path of More Resistance." From *The End of Nature* by William McKibben. Copyright © 1989 by William McKibben. Reprinted by permission of Random House, Inc.

Edward Abbey, "Eco-Defense." From *One Life*